P9-CRK-226

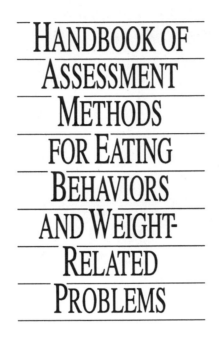

HANDBOOK OF ASSESSMENT METHODS FOR EATING BEHAVIORS AND WEIGHT-RELATED PROBLEMS

David B. Allison
EDITOR

HANDBOOK OF ASSESSMENT METHODS FOR EATING BEHAVIORS AND WEIGHT-RELATED PROBLEMS

Measures, Theory, and Research

SAGE Publications
International Educational and Professional Publisher
Thousand Oaks   London   New Delhi

Copyright © 1995 by Sage Publications, Inc.

All rights reserved. No part of this book may be reproduced or utilized in any form or by any means, electronic or mechanical, including photocopying, recording, or by any information storage and retrieval system, without permission in writing from the publisher.

For information address:

SAGE Publications, Inc.
2455 Teller Road
Thousand Oaks, California 91320

SAGE Publications Ltd.
6 Bonhill Street
London EC2A 4PU
United Kingdom

SAGE Publications India Pvt. Ltd.
M-32 Market
Greater Kailash I
New Delhi 110 048 India

Printed in the United States of America

Library of Congress Cataloging-in-Publication Data

Main entry under title:

Handbook of assessment methods for eating behaviors and weight-related
    problems: Measures, theory, and research / edited by David B. Allison.
        p. cm.
    Includes bibliographical references and indexes.
    ISBN 0-8039-4791-7 (cl.: alk. paper)
    1. Eating disorders—Diagnosis. 2. Overweight persons—
Psychological testing. 3. Eating disorders—Patients—
Psychological testing. I. Allison, David B.
    [DNLM: 1. Eating Disorders—handbooks. 2. Body Weight—handbooks.
3. Obesity—psychology. WM 34 H235 1995]
RC552.E18H357 1995
616.85′26′075—dc20
DNLM/DLC   94-33567
for Library of Congress

This book is printed on acid-free paper.

95 96 97 98 99 10 9 8 7 6 5 4 3 2 1

Production Editor: Yvonne Könneker   Typesetter: Christina Hill

Contents

Acknowledgments

This book comes to fruition only through the substantial support of many friends, colleagues, and loved ones. First and foremost, I am grateful to the authors of the chapters, all experts in their areas who devoted great efforts for the sole reward of contributing to our field. I owe a special debt to Bernard Gorman, who taught me most of what I know about tests and measures and provided substantial assistance in the preparation of the "Psychometrics Refresher" in the Introduction. Second, I would like to thank Marquita Flemming of Sage Publications for her patience and tutelage in the process of preparing this volume. Third, I wish to acknowledge the considerable encouragement and inspiration I steadily received (and continue to receive) from my colleagues here at the Obesity Research Center, particularly our director, F. Xavier Pi-Sunyer. I am especially grateful to Stan Heshka, who served as confidant, adviser, and shoulder to cry on when the going got tough, and to Steve Heymsfield for rallying behind me in all my endeavors including this one. Stephanie Nelson, Michael I. Gorun, and Myles Faith graciously helped to review early drafts of manuscripts, for which I am quite grateful. Finally, I wish to express my warmest thanks to Beth for her tolerance of the long working hours and the loving support she always offers.

Introduction

DAVID B. ALLISON

Estimates of the prevalence of obesity are as high as 25% in the U.S. adult population (National Center for Health Statistics, 1987), and recent data suggest that the prevalence is rising. The incidence of eating disorders has also increased dramatically in recent years (Agras, 1987). Not surprising, the literature on these topics is flourishing. There are at least three journals devoted to obesity (*International Journal of Obesity, Obesity Research,* and *Obesity Surgery*), at least three journals devoted to eating disorders (*International Journal of Eating Disorders, Eating Disorders: Journal of Treatment & Prevention,* and *Eating Disorders Review*), and new books on the topics emerging at frequent intervals. With all this, why is another book needed?

Another book is needed because there is no comprehensive reference guide to *measurement* in these areas. Despite the blossoming literature, there has been relatively less careful attention paid to measurement issues. This is not all that surprising. Measurement and methodology are often perceived as less glamorous than the generation and testing of theories and treatment modalities. However, it must be recognized that the ability to reliably and validly measure the constructs of interest is the essential foundation on which applied research is built.

Although *many* instruments exist to measure constructs relevant to eating and weight-related disorders, there is currently no comprehensive compendium and review of what measures are good or bad and unique or redundant. This book is intended to be such a compendium.

The impetus for this volume came from my own frustration with trying to select measures for studies in these areas. New instruments seemed to emerge so rapidly, I was often unsure if I had found all the relevant instruments or what made one different than another. It seemed that many authors appeared more intent on publishing new tests than on systematically validating or comprehensively reviewing existing tests. Thus each new research venture meant an exhausting (if not exhaustive) literature search, plodding through numerous reports describing numerous scales, and in the end not being entirely sure I had selected the best or even a good instrument.

This state of affairs does not prevail in all areas. For example, there are several general compendiums of psychological measures (e.g., Corcoran & Fischer, 1987). In the area of social and personality psychology, Robinson, Shaver, and Wrightsman (1991) in *Measures of Personality and Social Psychological Attitudes* provide an excellent source of useful measures.[1]

Who Is This Book For?

This book should be useful to researchers, graduate students, and clinicians who adhere to the scientist/practitioner model. Ultimately, this book is for anyone whose work involves measuring the thoughts, feelings, behaviors, or bodies of persons with obesity, eating disorders, or weight-related concerns and who believes in the value of rigorous measurement.

Contents of This Book

Authors of each chapter attempted to locate all available tests of the relevant constructs. Tests were then selected from this larger set on the basis of promise in the case of newer instruments or demonstrated quality in the case of more established instruments. In some cases, instruments of lesser quality but wide prominence are reviewed if only to offer readers caveats regarding their use.

Each chapter is as self-contained as possible but each also uses a similar format. With a few exceptions, each chapter reviews instruments assessing one or a few closely related constructs. Authors provide a brief introductory review of the key constructs, their history, and their current importance, followed by in-depth reviews of the "better" instruments reporting detailed information for each on its development, psychometric properties, availability, and practical issues such as cost and necessary time. Wherever possible, the scales discussed have been reprinted in their entirety. Finally, authors conclude with suggestions for future research.

Specific Contents

In Chapter 1 ("Assessment of General Personality and Psychopathology Among Persons With Eating and Weight-Related Concerns"), Leslie Morey and John Kurtz discuss general assessment instruments that are already in the armamentaria of many clinicians and researchers. The rationale for including this chapter is that people with eating and weight-related concerns are, first and foremost, people and that, like other clients, they often need to be assessed in a broad array of areas. Chapter 1 is necessarily limited in the detail it can provide but does a great deal of "routing" work, that is, referring readers to the issues and alternatives and advising them when and where to get more information. In addition, Morey and Kurtz provide an excellent review of findings using these instruments with obese and eating disordered individuals.

In Chapter 2 ("Measures of Quality of Life, Subjective Well-Being, and Satisfaction With Life"), Vincent Alfonso stresses the need to consider outcome variables beyond measures of eating and weight pathology. According to Alfonso, a major focus of research should be the accentuation of the positive (aspects of life) and not merely the elimination of the negative (aspects of life). Alfonso reviews measures of the closely related but conceptually distinct constructs of quality of life, subjective well-being, satisfaction with life, and self-esteem.

Chapter 3, written by Harold Yuker, Myles Faith, and me, reviews measures of attitudes toward, beliefs about, and knowledge of obese persons and obesity. Although obesity is generally conceptualized as a biological problem, Allon (1982) and others have shown that it can also be conceptualized as a social problem. Obese persons are often the victims of prejudice and intolerance of diversity, just as members of various ethnic and racial groups are. Moreover, it can be argued that the recent increase in the rates of anorexia and bulimia nervosa in our country is, in part, the result of negative societal attitudes toward obese persons and obesity (Agras, 1987). Finally, it has been shown that attitudes toward obese persons are strongly related to beliefs about the causes of obesity (Allison, Basile, & Yuker, 1991). Therefore it is essential that researchers study the causes and effects of attitudes toward and beliefs about obese persons. Yuker, an internationally renowned expert in the area of attitudes toward persons with disabilities, brings a unique perspective and strong expertise to this area.

Chapter 4 ("Assessment of Body Image") by Kevin Thompson introduces the two distinct components of body image: (a) the affective component (i.e., the extent to which one does or does not like one's body) and (b) the perceptual component (the extent to which one accurately or inaccurately perceives the dimensions of one's body). Thompson builds on his earlier work in this area (Thompson, 1990) to provide an excellent practical guide for the reader.

In the fifth chapter ("Measures of Restrained Eating"), Bernard Gorman and I discuss one of the most measured constructs in the field of eating disorders and obesity: dietary restraint. Three English language scales exist to measure restraint (Polivy, Herman, & Howard, 1988; Stunkard & Messick, 1985; Van Strien, Frijters, Bergers, & Defares, 1986). Despite their widespread use, there is little agreement as to which scales adequately measure restraint (Allison, Kalinsky, & Gorman, 1992; Heatherton, Herman, Polivy, King, & McGree, 1988).

In Chapter 6, "Measures of Physical Activity and Exercise," Mary Lee Shelton and Robert Klesges take on a very challenging task. The measurement of physical activity has stymied many researchers. The techniques range from self-report to mechanical transducers and direct observation, to high-tech methods such as indirect calorimetry. Moreover, as with caloric intake (see Chapter 7), physical activity is one of the few areas in which accurate measurement of the absolute value of the construct can be as important as relative position, making its measurement especially demanding.

Chapter 7 ("Measuring Food Intake: An Overview"), by Carla Wolper, Stanley Heshka, and Steven Heymsfield, discusses an issue of obvious importance in any clinical or research work in eating and weight-related areas. Nevertheless, the accurate measurement of dietary intake is one of the most difficult tasks facing the field. Among people in general and obese and eating-disordered people in particular, disclosing one's actual eating habits to others potentially brings severe social disapproval. Thus here, more than anywhere else in this book, issues in the use of self-report data are at the forefront, and Wolper et al. extensively discuss the random and systematic errors that plague the assessment of dietary intake.

Chapter 8 ("Assessment of Specific Eating Behaviors and Eating Style"), by David Schlundt, is in many ways the broadest chapter in this volume. Just as individuals' eating habits are often quite idiosyncratic, the measurement of "eating styles" has often followed the idiosyncrasies of individual investigators. Whereas many of the other chapters' authors primarily faced the task of describing measures of reasonably well-defined constructs, Schlundt traveled somewhat less charted territory and often faced the task of selecting, defining, and describing the constructs prior to describing their measures. The result is a very innovative, creative, and, I believe, ultimately useful discourse.

In Chapter 9 ("Binge Eating and Purging"), Kathleen Pike, Katharine Loeb, and Timothy Walsh describe measures of bingeing and purging behavior that are necessary for the diagnosis, differential diagnosis, and treatment monitoring of bulimics. The chapter is especially timely given the addition of "binge eating disorder" (BED) to the *DSM-IV* as a provisional diagnostic category. The assignment of this provisional status indicates that more research is necessary to fully characterize the syndrome and, in fact, determine if it is a distinct syndrome. Pike et al.'s chapter provides the measurement foundation for this essential research.

Donald Williamson, Drew Anderson, Lori Jackman, and Sheryl Jackson describe the assessment of eating disordered thoughts, feelings, and behaviors in Chapter 10. Instruments to measure eating disordered thoughts, feelings, and behaviors are proliferating. Current instruments differ widely in their quality and utility. A thorough discussion of their relative merits is clearly in order and few people could provide the expert overview that Williamson et al. offer.

Chapter 11 ("Motivational Readiness to Control Weight"), by Joseph Rossi, Susan Rossi, Wayne Velicer, and James Prochaska, discusses measurement in a burgeoning and important area. Attention has recently been focused on the *process* by which people decide to change or not to change behaviors. The extent to which people are motivated and ready to change is seen as an important construct. Additionally, individuals' reasons for changing, not changing, and discontinuing change efforts have all come under study, as have the determinants of those reasons. Rossi et al. adeptly review such measures from the vantage point of being the leaders of the *processes of change* perspective.

All too often, we develop and validate our instruments in the eating and weight fields among white, middle-class, average to higher intelligence, 18- to 22-year-old, college student females. In Chapter 12 ("Assessment of Eating and Weight-Related Problems in Children and Special Populations"), Roberta Babbitt, Lynn Edlen-Nezin, Ramasamy Manikam, Jane Summers, and Clodagh Murphy address the extent to which there are special issues in testing other populations, what methods are available, and where more development is needed. Populations considered include children, persons with intellectual impairments and mental illness, and elderly persons. Special issues in assessing ethnic minorities and gay men and lesbian women are also discussed.

Chapter 13 ("Identification of Psychological Problems of Patients With Eating and Weight-Related Disorders in General Medical Settings"), by Anne Riley, is written with the general medical practitioner in mind. Riley cogently addresses the issues of identifying patients with psychological needs regarding eating and weight-related problems who are seen in general medical settings. The majority of individuals with eating and weight-related problems are seen initially by a general medical practitioner who frequently prescribes diets and nutritional supplements. However, many of these patients can be expected to have associated emotional problems that, if addressed, may improve compliance and outcome of treatment. Moreover, medical providers are often in the difficult position of recommending mental health treatment to a patient who views his or her problem as a medical disorder. Assessment methods consistent with medical practice are reviewed.

In Chapter 14 ("Assessment of Human Body Composition"), Steven Heymsfield, Stanley Heshka, Richard Pierson Jr., and I consider both laboratory and field methods for the assessment of body composition, anthropometrics, and relative weight. Heymsfield, one of the world's leaders in body composition research, provides a very thorough overview with an emphasis on practical issues, such as availability, safety, and cost, not found in any other existing source.

Finally, Chapter 15 gives "the big picture." Stewart Agras writes from the perspective of a longtime leader in both the obesity and the eating disorders fields. A crucial decision the user of this volume will have to make prior to deciding "which scale I should use" is "which constructs I should measure." Agras suggests ways that researchers and clinicians can define their constructs of interest by careful theorizing, consideration of past research, and broad clinical interviews with patients. Finally, Agras offers some thoughts on "where we have been and where we are going" as a field.

A Psychometrics "Refresher"

In this last section of the Introduction, I provide a brief "refresher" on psychometric or measurement issues and techniques. I use the term *refresher* and not *primer* or *introduction* because any piece this short can only serve to remind readers of some key issues, terms, and techniques involved in the development and evaluation of measurement techniques. Readers who truly require an introduction to or in-depth discussion of these issues are referred to one of the major psychometric texts available (Allen & Yen, 1979; Crocker & Algina, 1986; Ghiselli, Campbell, & Zedeck, 1981; Nunnally, 1978; Nunnally & Bernstein, 1994).

When evaluating measurement techniques, one needs to consider numerous issues. Does the technique provide consistent answers (reliability)? Does it measure what it purports to measure (validity)? Does it measure equally well in all populations (validity generalization)? Can the subjects understand the questionnaire (readability)?

In the following chapters, authors comment on the following aspects of the tests reviewed (to the extent that the information is available and relevant for specific tests and constructs).

Reliability

The simplest definition of *reliability* is "consistency." A test is reliable if it measures something consistently. Of course, reliability is not an all-or-none issue. Some tests are very reliable, others are not at all reliable, and still others are "somewhat" reliable. Reliability can be quantified via reliability coefficients, the most common being correlation-based statistics such as the Pearson product-moment correlation coefficient or the intraclass correlation coefficients (Shrout & Fleiss, 1979). These coefficients typically range from 0.0 to 1.0 with higher numbers indicating greater reliability.

Classical test theory postulates that observed scores are a combination of a true score plus an error score. True variance is variation among individuals irrespective of artifacts of measurement. Error variance, however, assesses the degree to which trait-irrelevant variation contaminates an observed score. An index of reliability indicates the proportion of variance in the measure that is true variance rather than error variance. For example, a reliability coefficient of .80 indicates that 80% of the variance in the measure is true variance. Note that reliability coefficients are *not* squared to yield these estimates of true variance. Although there is no fixed rule, reliability coefficients between .70 and .80 are considered "minimally acceptable," between .80 and .90 are "adequate," and above .90 are "excellent." Given the many sources of error that could enter into observed scores, there are many kinds of reliability. One can assess whether measurements are consistent across different nontrait factors (e.g., times, raters, instrument forms, or items). Each of these nontrait factors represents a different source of error.

Internal consistency. To what degree do the items of the scale intercorrelate with each other and tap a unitary construct? In answering this question, we will typically refer to Cronbach's *alpha* coefficient (of which Kuder-Richardson 21 is a special case)—a measure of internal consistency reliability. Cronbach's α is a function of both the number of items and the intercorrelation of items. To some degree, a high α might reflect high positive correlations among the items but it can also reflect the number of items. Thus, although α is a good measure of reliability, it should not be construed as a measure of homogeneity per se.

Test-retest. Test-retest reliability addresses the question of how consistent are the answers a test gives from one time to the next. The assessment of test-retest reliability is of concern when attempting to measure a "trait" rather than a "state."

Interrater. Interrater reliability refers to the extent to which two raters or observers provide similar scores when rating the same subject at the same time. Interrater reliability is crucial when interview and observation methods are used to assess individuals.

Factor Structure

The assessment of factor structure can be seen as an early stage of validity assessment. Reliability assessment tells us whether the test is measuring *something* consistently. Assessing factor structure tells us *how many things* (underlying dimensions) the test is measuring and provides some clues as to what those things are. The questions that need to be asked of a test include the following: What are the number and nature of factors? Do they support the proposed structure and the use of the instrument; that is, do they give preliminary evidence of construct validity? Finally, is the factor structure stable across different samples, ethnic groups, genders, age groups, weight and diagnostic categories, and so on?

Validity

If reliability assessment tells us if we are measuring *something* and factor analysis tells us *how many things* (dimensions) we are measuring, then validity assessment tells us *if* (how well) we are measuring what we are trying to measure. It has been argued that all types of validity are subsumed under construct validity. Although this point is well taken, most psychometricians still find it useful to talk about the different "processes" of validation separately.

Convergent and discriminant validity. *Construct validity* refers to the network of relationships (called the nomological net) in which the scale is embedded. Two major types of construct validity are *convergent* and *divergent* or *discriminant* validity (Campbell & Fiske, 1959). *Convergent validity* refers to the relationship of the present measure with other measures that purportedly measure the same or related constructs. For example, convergent validity would demand that one measure of restrained eating correlate with other measures of restrained eating. *Discriminant validity* refers to the degree to which a measure does *not* correlate with measures of traits that it does not purport to measure. For example, discriminant validity would demand that a measure of restrained eating *not* correlate highly with a measure of reading ability—that is, we hope not. If it does, the scale may be measuring something other than restraint. Discriminant validity is obviously important but, unfortunately, infrequently assessed by test developers.

A particularly important form of discriminant validity is freedom from response sets. The problem of response sets has long plagued personality and clinical researchers. A *response set* can be defined as the tendency to endorse items for some reason other than the content of the items might suggest. Among the response sets frequently mentioned are acquiescence (the tendency to check off many positive responses, or "yea-saying," and the tendency to check many negative statements, or "nay-saying"), extreme response set (the tendency to choose extreme Likert scale values rather than use intermediate categories), and social desirability (the tendency to endorse items in terms of their perceived desirability to others rather than in terms of how the person actually feels, believes, or behaves).

Investigators are often especially concerned with social desirability. Edwards originally suggested in 1957 that many scales primarily measure the tendency to respond in a socially desirable manner, and the issue is still very much alive today (Paulhus, 1991). Alternatively, Crowne and Marlowe (1964) argued that social desirability may not be a "nuisance variable" associated with tests but a characteristic or trait of individuals. Similarly, Campbell and Fiske (1959) asserted that, when a measure of another construct (social desirability) is embedded in the nomological net of the construct of theoretical interest, then the evidence of some covariation would strengthen rather than weaken the case for construct validity. Regardless of the interpretation of social desirability, it is clear that, if measures are to have discriminant validity, their correlations with measures of social desirability must be lower than their correlations with alternative measures of the construct of interest. This is the essence of Campbell and Fiske's (1959) multitrait-multimethod matrix.

Predictive validity. Predictive validity refers to the extent to which the instrument successfully predicts prognosis, course, response to treatment, or other important endpoints.

Susceptibility to dissimulation. In testing for susceptibility to dissimulation, we are asking a question similar to but distinct from that of discriminant validity. Here the question is very simple: Can subjects "fake" their responses if they are motivated to do so?

Norms

The final psychometric issue we will consider is a characteristic less of the tests themselves than of the body of data supporting the tests. For the results of any test to be interpretable, it is necessary to have some frame of reference for the obtained scores. Two general approaches exist for establishing a frame of reference: (a) norm referencing and (b) criterion referencing.

In norm referencing, one establishes the average score for a group and then places some "range of normality" around this average. Often, the range is selected to be the 95% confidence limits, that is, the mean ± two standard deviations. People within the range are considered "normal" and people outside the range are considered "abnormal" or "unusual." This approach can be refined through the presentation of more refined categorizations such as percentiles. As Babbitt et al. (this volume) point out, it is often necessary to have separate norms for different subsections of the population. For example, the normal range of weight will obviously be very different for a 6-foot-tall, 30-year-old man than for a 3-year-old girl.

One limitation of the norm-referenced approach is that it tends to equate "average" with "normal." This is problematic when the average member of the population is not at the optimal point on the trait of interest. Relative body weight is an excellent example of this. In the United States, the average person is too heavy. If we recommended that all people be average, then we would be recommending that people be overweight. Instead, a more objective criterion is sought on which to evaluate an individual's relative weight. The most commonly chosen criterion is death. Specifically, we set as "normal" the range of body weights that are associated with minimum mortality. This use of an objective standard in determining normative values is referred to as criterion referencing.

Conclusion

I hope that this Introduction has convinced you of the necessity for rigorously evaluating your measurement instruments as well as of the merits of this book. But, as they say, "the proof of the pudding is in the eating"—so read on. Good research and clinical practice are built on a strong foundation of measurement. The authors of the following chapters took on the challenges of providing researchers and clinicians with detailed maps of our evolving and existing accomplishments in the measurement of eating behaviors and weight-related problems and are paving the way for future progress.

Note

1. In fact, readers familiar with that source should find the style of the current volume to be quite familiar as the Robinson et al. (1991) volume very much served as a "template" for this book.

References

Agras, W. S. (1987). *Eating disorders: Management of obesity, bulimia, and anorexia nervosa.* New York: Pergamon.

Allen, M. J., & Yen, W. M. (1979). *Introduction to measurement theory.* Monterey, CA: Brooks/Cole.

Allison, D. B., Basile, V. C., & Yuker, H. E. (1991). The measurement of attitudes toward and beliefs about obese persons. *International Journal of Eating Disorders, 10*(5), 599-607.

Allison, D. B., Kalinsky, L. B., & Gorman, B. S. (1992). The comparative psychometric properties of three measures of dietary restraint. *Psychological Assessment, 4,* 391-398.

Allon, N. (1982). The stigma of overweight in everyday life. In B. B. Wolman (Ed.), *Psychological aspects of obesity: A handbook* (pp. 130-174). New York: Van Nostrand Reinhold.

Campbell, D. T., & Fiske, D. W. (1959). Convergent and discriminant validation by the multitrait-multimethod matrix. *Psychological Bulletin, 56,* 81-105.

Corcoran, K., & Fischer, J. (1987). *Measures for clinical practice.* New York: Free Press.

Crocker, L., & Algina, J. (1986). *Introduction to classical and modern test theory.* New York: Harcourt Brace Jovanovich.

Crowne, D. P., & Marlowe, D. (1964). *The approval motive: Studies in evaluative dependence.* New York: Wiley.

Edwards, A. L. (1957). *The social desirability variable in personality assessment and research.* New York: Dryden.

Ghiselli, E. E., Campbell, J. P., & Zedeck, S. (1981). *Measurement theory for the behavioral sciences.* San Francisco: Freeman.

Heatherton, T. F., Herman, C. P., Polivy, J., King, G. A., & McGree, S. T. (1988). The (mis)measurement of restraint: An analysis of conceptual and psychometric issues. *Journal of Abnormal Psychology, 97,* 19-28.

National Center for Health Statistics. (1987). Anthropometric reference data and prevalence of overweight, United States, 1976-1980. In *Vital and health statistics* (Series 11, No. 238). Hyattsville, MD: Author.

Nunnally, J. C. (1978). *Psychometric theory* (2nd ed.). New York: McGraw-Hill.

Nunnally, J. C., & Bernstein, I. H. (1994). *Psychometric methods* (3rd ed.). New York: McGraw-Hill.

Paulhus, D. L. (1991). Measurement and control of response bias. In J. P. Robinson, P. R. Shaver, & L. S. Wrightsman (Eds.), *Measures of personality and social psychological attitudes* (pp. 17-59). New York: Academic Press.

Polivy, J., Herman, P. H., & Howard, K. I. (1988). Restraint Scale: Assessment of dieting. In M. Hersen & A. S. Bellack (Eds.), *Dictionary of behavioral assessment techniques* (pp. 377-380). New York: Pergamon.

Robinson, J. P., Shaver, P. R., & Wrightsman, L. S. (Eds.). (1991). *Measures of personality and social psychological attitudes.* New York: Academic Press.

Shrout, P. E., & Fleiss, J. L. (1979). Intraclass correlations: Uses in assessing rater reliability. *Psychological Bulletin, 86,* 420-428.

Stunkard, A. J., & Messick, S. (1985). The Three-Factor Eating Questionnaire to measure dietary restraint, disinhibition and hunger. *Journal of Psychosomatic Research, 29,* 71-83.

Thompson, J. K. (1990). *Body image disturbance: Assessment and treatment.* Elmsford, NY: Pergamon.

Van Strien, T., Frijters, J. E. R., Bergers, G. P. A., & Defares, P. B. (1986). The Dutch Eating Behavior Questionnaire (DEBQ) for assessment of restrained, emotional, and external eating behavior. *International Journal of Eating Disorders, 5,* 295-315.

Assessment of General Personality and Psychopathology Among Persons With Eating and Weight-Related Concerns

LESLIE C. MOREY

JOHN E. KURTZ

The assessment of personality and psychopathology in individuals with eating-related disorders is germane for several reasons. As is the case with any condition of clinical interest, personality features can have a variety of roles, including issues relevant to the etiology of the clinical condition and/or its treatment. Also, personality features may sometimes arise as a consequence of experiencing various clinical conditions, and these features themselves may become a focus of intervention. Research in this field has only begun to disentangle the causal connections between personality traits and pathological eating behavior, and this chapter does not attempt to draw conclusions in this regard. However, the chapter does describe the nature of the findings obtained when different samples of people with eating-related disorders have taken many of the more widely used clinical instruments. The pattern of these results can help to expand our view of the broader scope of the phenomenology of the various eating disorders and it may point to areas of particular promise with respect to research in the etiology, intervention, and prevention of these disorders.

Certainly, clinical lore holds that such variables often correlate with the different behavioral manifestations or subtypes of eating disorders. For example, it is often thought that anorexics typically show characteristics of obsessiveness, concerns about social approval, and high degrees of self-control. Clinical impressions maintain that bulimics tend to be more impulsive, with more interpersonal problems and emotional instability. Specific personality patterns have not been advanced as an etiological factor in obesity, although depression and low self-esteem may be frequent concomitants. Other theorists suggest more complex relationships between personality and eating pathology; Bornstein and Greenberg (1991) assert that dependency is the primary underlying factor in all eating disorders, including obesity, but that it interacts with other traits, such as perfectionism and impulsivity, to determine the specific nature of the eating behavior. In reviewing the data from personality assessment studies of persons with eating disorders, we can begin to evaluate the validity of these personality profiles.

One issue to be considered in attempts to psychologically distinguish different forms of eating disorders lies in the matter of whether some of the distinctions among these disorders are valid ones. For example, a retrospective study of anorexia nervosa patients (Rosenvinge & Mouland, 1990) found that many patients fluctuated over the course of their eating disorder between the anorexic and bulimic pattern. Similarly, Walters et al. (1993) found no differences between purging and nonpurging bulimics on a variety of weight and personality measures. Hsu (1990) reports that, in time, many restricting anorexics develop normal weight bulimia, and many bulimic patients report histories of anorexia. Extensive symptomatic overlap between anorexia and bulimia in family studies find a "pattern of familial clustering [that] suggests that these disorders may represent variable expressions of a common underlying psychopathology" (p. 8). This suggests that the anorexia/bulimia distinction may reflect different stages in the development of eating pathology, which would predict few differences between these groups in more stable personality trait variables, contrary to the clinical impressions described above. Still, one important reason to justify maintaining the distinction is that fundamental treatment goals and management issues differ for the two groups (weight gain is necessary for all anorexics, but is not necessary for all bulimics).

Another consideration in personality assessment studies of eating disorder groups (or any diagnostic group for that matter) is the difficulty in distinguishing between long-term personality traits and current mental state (e.g., psychopathology). Some objective instruments (i.e., MMPI, SCL-90-R) are probably best considered as measures of psychiatric symptomatology rather than as measures of personality traits. A study by Kennedy, McVey, and Katz (1990) of personality disorder diagnoses (which presumably reflect longstanding, problematic personality traits) at admission versus discharge found that the high rate of self-reported personality pathology found at admission dramatically decreased on remission of the eating problems. Research on the relationships between eating disorders and personality features must be cautious to assess enduring traits and interpersonal patterns that are not just reflections of a distress state.

Although the literature reviewed in the following paragraphs leaves many questions unanswered, it does provide a foundation on which to build subsequent studies. There are a host of important questions that need more data to be answered: What are the most efficacious or informative approaches to personality assessment with this population? How can the assessment data be useful in treatment planning and evaluation? Such questions should be kept in mind in reviewing the research described below.

Instruments

The Minnesota Multiphasic Personality Inventory (MMPI)

Since its introduction in the early 1940s, the MMPI (distributed by National Computer Systems, P.O. Box 1416, Minneapolis, MN 55440) has been among the most widely used self-report inventories in the mental health field. According to the most recent edition of the *Mental Measurements Yearbook,* the MMPI continues to be the most frequently referenced of all psychological tests. This popularity has led to a vast accumulation of research information on the test, and as such its strengths and weaknesses are better documented than any other test in this area. Because of this research database, the MMPI merits serious consideration for use in the assessment of any area of psychopathology.

The MMPI consists of 550 unique statements (for some forms, 16 are repeated, for a total of 566) to which the examinee is asked to respond either "true" or "false." There are a number of different forms with which to administer the test; for example, some forms present the items in a somewhat different order, and there are also numerous abbreviated versions of the MMPI including the 71-item Mini-Mult (Kincannon, 1968), the MMPI-168 (Overall & Gomez-Mont, 1974), and the 166-item FAM (Faschingbauer, 1974). These brief forms were constructed with the purpose of estimating the configuration on the 10 standardly obtained clinical scales. In general, the majority of the large body of research on the MMPI has involved the use of the complete instrument, and for most purposes it is recommended that the patient complete all items.

A comprehensive review of the wealth of research findings on the MMPI is beyond the scope of this volume. Because of the extensive research literature on the test, there are a number of excellent books that provide an indepth guide to its description, rationale, and interpretation. In addition to the encyclopedic work of Dahlstrom, Welsh, and Dahlstrom (1972, 1975), contemporary research has been incorporated into valuable works by Greene (1991) and Graham (1990), among others. The reader is referred to such additional resources for a thorough treatment of this inventory.

The MMPI was one of the earliest tests to use the *empirical* or *criterion keying* method of scale development. In this method, items for a scale are selected on the basis of their ability to discriminate between members of some criterion group (e.g., schizophrenics) and a control group of normal individuals. This method of test construction has a number of unique features. Of primary significance is that the method makes no assumptions about the honesty or insight of the person completing the items. In other words, what is being measured is not a person's beliefs about him- or herself; rather, what is obtained is a relatively structured form of self-presentation that is then compared with the self-presentation style typical of various clinical groups. Despite this empirical keying strategy, it is still the case that test results can be drastically affected by the manner in which the examinee approaches the task. As a result, various validity scales and indicators have been developed in an attempt to provide some information about potential profile distortion resulting from different test-taking attitudes.

As it has been generally used, the MMPI includes three validity scales and ten clinical scales. The scores on these scales are standardized with reference to the normative group through the use of t scores. These t scores are standard scores with a mean of 50 and a standard deviation of 10. Any t score above 70 (i.e., a score that is two standard deviations above the mean of the original reference sample) is generally considered to represent a significant deviation; however, the clinical significance of such elevations varies considerably from scale to scale. In general, the meaning of significantly low scores (e.g., t scores below 30) is less well established than the interpretation of elevated scores.

In addition to the original scales of the MMPI, literally hundreds of supplemental scales have been derived for the test, including scales based on factor analyses of items as well as scales derived from their item content. The Wiggins (1966) content scales are among the most widely used in this regard. These scales tend to yield scores that are more easily interpreted than the original MMPI scales because the item content is relatively homogeneous. For example, an elevation on the Wiggins Psychoticism scale is much more straightforward interpretively than the Sc (Schizophrenia) clinical scale. This difference arises because many constructs differentiate schizophrenics from normal controls, and elevations on the latter clinical scale could reflect any of these aspects of functioning.

Most of the original clinical scales of the MMPI were derived by comparing item responses of a specified clinical group with those of a normal control group. Items that discriminated successfully between these groups were included on the corresponding clinical scale, regardless of the content of the item. For example, if a given item was more frequently endorsed as "true" by clinically diagnosed paranoid patients than it was by the normal controls, then a "true" response to that item would be scored on the Paranoia scale. For most of the scales, the criterion psychiatric group consisted of about 50 patients who had received a consensus clinical diagnosis. The control group consisted of roughly 700 persons who were visitors at the University of Minnesota hospitals during the late 1930s, representing a reasonably wide range of individuals between the ages of 16 and 55. Given the nature of many of the test items, it is reasonable to suspect that normative performance may have changed since these data were gathered, and indeed contemporary normative data support this contention (Colligan, Osborne, Swenson, & Offord, 1983). In fact, such findings have led to revisions to the MMPI that were incorporated into the MMPI-2 (e.g., Butcher, 1990). On the MMPI-2, a majority of the items scored on the original clinical scales were kept intact, with some minor changes designed to clarify wording, eliminate sexist language, and generally update the tenor of the questions. In addition, a number of items were added that sought to address areas not well covered in the original MMPI, such as problems with alcohol and drugs, responsiveness to treatment, and other important clinical constructs. The revised inventory is also standardized against a much larger and more representative sample than was the case with the original test, and it is hoped that these changes will eliminate some of the shortcomings of the MMPI. However, to this point relatively little if any research in this area has examined the MMPI-2, and the degree of correspondence between the revision and the original has been a point of some controversy in the assessment field. As such, it should be kept in mind that the research reviewed subsequently was conducted with the MMPI and caution must be taken in extrapolating these results to the MMPI-2.

As is the case with most groups of clinical interest, there is a reasonably extensive literature using the MMPI with various eating disordered groups. We searched the journal literature since 1980 (marking the introduction of the standardized diagnostic criteria in the *DSM*) and gathered all the published data in an effort to draw conclusions about normative performance on the MMPI for anorexics, bulimics, and obese persons. In assembling these studies, we included only those where the eating disorder groups were clearly defined, the number of subjects in each group reported, and the MMPI scale scores expressed in the form of *K*-corrected *t* scores. Data were included even when scores for all major scales were not included in the report (i.e., Pendleton, Tisdale, Moll, & Marler, 1990; Shisslak, Pazda, & Crago, 1990); hence weighted composite scores were computed by scale and by group. As it turns out, the samples included were composed exclusively of women subjects. A total of 32 such studies were located, all of which used the original MMPI as there are still no published data using the MMPI-2 with eating disordered populations. Weighted composite MMPI profiles for bulimic, anorexic, and obese subjects as calculated from these studies are presented in Figure 1.1 (a complete reference list of the studies included in this composite may be obtained by request from the authors).

The bulimic profile shows mean elevations (*t* scores exceeding 70) on clinical scales 2 (Depression), 4 (Psychopathic Deviate), and 8 (Schizophrenia), with 4 being the highest score. Persons with such a profile tend to view themselves as depressed, alienated from others, and having marked difficulties with anger and impulse control. This configuration of scores appears to be a robust finding in MMPI research with bulimics; the 4-2-8 codetype seen in the composite profile in Figure 1.1 was reported in many of the individual studies as well (e.g., Norman & Herzog, 1983; Pyle, Mitchell, & Eckert, 1981; Wallach & Lowenkopf, 1984). Anorexics show no mean elevations in excess of 70T on the primary MMPI scales, and their highest score is on scale 2. As a whole, their profile suggests a person with poor self-esteem, depressed affect, and withdrawal from social contacts. Obese subjects commonly achieve scores more within the normal range on the MMPI with no marked elevations on any particular scale. Anorexics show less defensiveness (the mean of the *K* validity scale was 49) than might be expected for this group; however, they do show more social introversion than bulimics. Anorexics and bulimics are most discriminated by scale 4, suggesting more anger and impulsive acting out on the part of the bulimics. Overall, the bulimics show the greatest amount of psychopathology on the MMPI, whereas obese subjects manifest the least psychopathology of all eating disordered groups.

A comparison of these MMPI profiles points to greater differences between groups in general elevation of scores than in profile shape. Bulimics

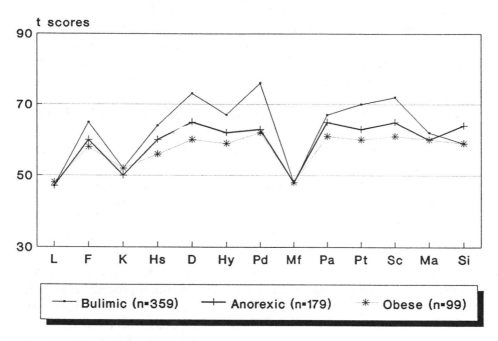

Figure 1.1. MMPI Clinical Scales

tend to have more peaked elevations on scale 4 than anorexics or obese subjects, but overall the score configurations are largely similar between the three eating disorder groups. However, this homogeneity in the configural patterns of the MMPI is not restricted to comparisons among eating disordered groups. Other MMPI studies comparing the profiles of anorexics with schizophrenics (Small et al., 1981) and with incest victims (Scott & Thoner, 1986) remark on the lack of differentiation of their mean MMPI profiles. Furthermore, the MMPI pattern of elevations on scales 2, 4, 7 (Psychasthenia, or anxiety-related conditions), and 8 that has been noted as significant for bulimic subjects (Pyle et al., 1981) has also been identified as the typical pattern for other diagnostic groups, such as alcoholics (Morey, Roberts, & Penk, 1987) and patients with borderline personality disorder (Resnick et al., 1988).

In recent years there have been a variety of efforts aimed at establishing somewhat more homogeneous subgroups of eating disorder profiles on the MMPI; these studies have generally used cluster analysis procedures to identify different profile types (e.g., Allison & Heshka, 1991; Webb, Morey, Castelnuovo-Tedesco, & Scott, 1990). Allison and Heshka (1991) identified an "android/gynoid" obesity distinction that was associated with differences in responding on the Mf scale in a gender-typed pattern. The Webb et al.

(1990) study is particularly interesting in that it identified MMPI scale 1 (Hypochondriasis) as relevant in the prediction of poor response to surgical intervention for massively obese subjects. However, these various subtyping schemes have demonstrated limited replicability, and to this point the validity evidence in support of any single subtyping scheme is unimpressive.

In sum, the MMPI has been a rich source of clinical and research information for many years, and the substantial research database that has accumulated makes the test one of the best researched tools available in the eating disorders area. Unfortunately, the test has a number of limitations. First, many of the clinical scales are based on obsolete diagnostic constructs of limited contemporary utility. Also, many of these clinical scales are of limited reliability when compared with other self-report measures (Horn, Wanberg, & Appel, 1973; Mauger, 1972), with median correlations typically in the .70 range. There are also concerns about the questionable normative sample, although improvements in this domain have been made with the MMPI-2. Finally, the test is quite lengthy in comparison with other procedures used for assessment; the SCL-90-R may provide the clinician with a comparable sense of the overall severity of psychopathology with a considerably shorter instrument (Schlundt & Johnson, 1990). Other problems with the test are numerous, and these issues have not been fully addressed in the MMPI-2 revision. In a comprehensive review of the instrument, Helmes and Redden (1993) conclude that "although the MMPI-2 is an improvement over the MMPI, both are suboptimal from the perspective of modern psychometric standards for the assessment of psychopathology" (p. 453). Thus, despite its venerable history and the considerable database that has accumulated with the instrument, there are clearly promising alternatives to the MMPI that merit consideration in clinical and research settings.

Symptom Checklist-90 (SCL-90)

Another measure of general psychopathology in common use is the revised Symptom Checklist-90 (SCL-90; Derogatis, 1977). The SCL-90-R presents respondents with a series of 90 physical and psychological complaints and asks them to rate each for the degree of distress associated with these complaints on a 5-point scale ranging from 0 (*not at all*) to 4 (*extremely*). The standard time frame that respondents use to rate the symptoms is the preceding 7 days. Three global measures of symptomatology may be obtained from the SCL-90-R: the Global Severity Index (GSI), which is the average rating on all 90 items; the Positive Symptom Total, which is the number of symptoms rated higher than zero; and the Positive Symptom Distress Index, which is the average rating of those items constituting the Positive Symptom Total. In addition, nine nonoverlapping subscales may be scored from the SCL-90-R:

Somatization, Obsessive-Compulsive, Interpersonal Sensitivity, Depression, Anxiety, Hostility, Phobic Anxiety, Paranoid Ideation, and Psychoticism. The scores for these subscales are the average of those items assigned to each subscale; the number of items in each subscale range from 6 (Paranoid Ideation) to 13 (Depression).

Extensive norms are available for males and females separately from very large samples of psychiatric outpatients, psychiatric inpatients, and nonpatient adults (Derogatis, 1977). Norms are also provided for 327 nonpatient male adolescents and 479 nonpatient female adolescents (aged 13 to 19); the latter group may provide a useful comparison group for many eating disorder patients given the early onset of many of these conditions. Estimates of internal consistency and test-retest reliability of the SCL-90-R have demonstrated satisfactory results. Validity studies are not in abundance, but pre- and post-data have generally shown the SCL-90-R to be a sensitive change measure in treatment research. However, although the global symptom measures appear reliable and valid, some research holds that the nine subscales may lack discriminant validity (Gotlib, 1984). As such, the SCL-90-R may function better as a general index of distress rather than as a diagnostic instrument.

A fair amount of research has employed the SCL-90-R with bulimic women, although we located no studies of anorexia nervosa patients that used this instrument. With respect to the Global Severity Index (GSI) scores, bulimic patients' overall level of symptomatology on the SCL-90-R shows substantial elevations but is generally comparable to the norms for psychiatric outpatients (Johnson & Connors, 1987). Garner and colleagues (1990) report that bulimics who were divided into two groups on the basis of good or poor treatment outcome did not differ in their initial GSI scores, but improvements in eating symptoms were strongly associated with a reduction in their posttreatment GSI scores. The authors conclude that the extensive psychological symptoms reported by bulimics on the SCL-90-R may be secondary to their dietary chaos, another potential discriminant validity concern.

There is considerable consistency in the SCL-90-R subscale data with bulimics. Bulimics tend to score higher on all nine subscales than controls, and their highest scores are generally seen on the Interpersonal Sensitivity and Depression subscales, with the former subscale highest in three samples (Ordman & Kirschenbaum, 1986; Weiss & Ebert, 1983; Williamson, Kelley, Davis, Ruggiero, & Blouin, 1985) and the latter highest in two (Garner et al., 1990; Johnson & Connors, 1987). Other scores that tend to show appreciable elevations with bulimics are the Anxiety and Obsessive-Compulsive subscales. One study compared 15 bulimic subjects with 15 female obese subjects and 15 female controls (Williamson et al., 1985) and found that bulimics scored significantly higher on all nine subscales than both the obese and the control groups, which did not differ from one another. This finding corroborates the MMPI research in showing greater amounts of psychopathology in bulimics than in obese persons, who do not manifest appreciable symptoms in any particular domain.

The SCL-90-R provides a broad screening of psychopathology in a brief instrument that is easy to score and has ample normative data. Given the evidence for the usefulness of the SCL-90-R in assessing changes in symptomatology over time, it may be a useful tool for clinicians to monitor treatment progress in areas unrelated to specific eating concerns. However, the scale maybe more useful as a global measure of distress than as a specific assessment of the type and nature of psychological problems experienced by the examinee.

Rorschach

The Rorschach (stimuli distributed by Western Psychological Services, 12031 Wilshire Blvd., Los Angeles, CA 90025) is the most commonly used of the *projective* methods of personality assessment. Such methods are based on the *projective hypothesis,* which assumes that, in a situation where the demands placed on the individual are very ambiguous, the individual's resulting behavior is likely to represent a projection of the person's personality onto the situation; in other words, ambiguity facilitates the process of projection. Although there are a host of projective techniques, only the Rorschach has to this point accumulated much of a research base in the area of eating disorders.

The Rorschach consists of 10 inkblots that were first introduced in a monograph named *Psychodiagnostik* published by Hermann Rorschach in 1921. In the Rorschach procedure, the subject is asked to specify what the inkblots might be (the "free association" phase) and at a later point is asked to describe what aspects of the blot led to his or her response (the "inquiry" phase). The experienced user can generally administer and score the test in approximately 90 minutes.

Although Rorschach himself died in 1922, his ideas and the 10 inkblots reproduced in his book gained great popularity as a personality assessment device. Given his premature death, Rorschach actually provided only limited information about the use of his procedure, and it remained for numerous followers to extend his initial observations. In the United States, five of these individuals had a particularly large impact on the use of the Rorschach technique: Samuel Beck, Bruno Klopfer, Marguerite Hertz, David Rapaport, and Zygmunt Pietrowski. Although each of these workers used Rorschach's work as the basis for his or her interpretive systems, the resulting approaches often diverged substantially, creating a situation where there were at least five different Rorschach tests that varied as a function of the particular system being used (Exner, 1974). This diversity served as an impediment to the establishment of a conceptually integrated research literature examining the reliability and validity of the instrument.

In recent years, Exner (1974, 1978, 1991) has attempted to integrate the more empirically supported aspect of each approach into a single system, which he calls the "comprehensive" system. Exner has emphasized interclinician reliability and clinical utility in assembling the Comprehensive system, and to a large extent it is similar to many of the more commonly used features from the different systems. Exner's system also provides a series of composite indices that combine several Rorschach variables to provide diagnostic indications of schizophrenia, depression, suicide potential, and other concepts. In recent years the Exner system has rapidly gained widespread use as the method of scoring and interpreting Rorschach data. To fully understand Rorschach administration, scoring, and interpretation through the use of Exner's approach, the reader must consult his works on the test.

The evaluation of the reliability and validity of the Rorschach procedure has long been a controversial area within psychology. Certain aspects of the test, such as the fact that different subjects give different numbers of responses and the availability of several different scoring systems, have made traditional psychometric evaluation of the test rather difficult. Furthermore, some of the properties claimed for the test, such as the ability to measure unconscious processes, would be challenging to demonstrate under any circumstances.

Early reliability studies of the Rorschach produced varied results, in part due to substantive differences in emphasis on reliability in the different scoring systems. Exner (1978) has presented data from his comprehensive system that indicate fairly good reliability. For example, the median test-retest reliability over a 7-day interval in a nonpatient adult sample was .82 for 19 major scoring categories. Impressively, these sample scoring categories had a median reliability of .80 over a 35- to 38-month interval in a nonpatient sample. These values are as high or higher than the reliability estimates noted for most of the instruments described in this chapter.

Over the years, there have been numerous studies of the association of Rorschach scores with many different behaviors; some of these results have been supportive and some have not. Exner (1974, 1978) has reported the results of a number of studies that seem to point to the validity of his procedure in the assessment of a number of diverse personological and psychopathological characteristics. Certain of these findings will be discussed in subsequent sections, but several results have been quite promising. For example, Exner identified a "suicide constellation" consisting of 11 structural summary variables, which had a 75% sensitivity for the identification of effected suicides, a 45% sensitivity for the identification of attempted suicides, a 20%

false-positive rate in depressives, and a 15% false-positive rate in schizophrenics. These validity values are quite impressive when compared with the best alternative methods for assessing suicidality. Although Exner's data need to be cross-validated, it is apparent that his application of the Rorschach technique must be considered a promising tool for personality assessment.

There is a considerable amount of research with eating disordered populations with the Rorschach, and various researchers have suggested that the test may be more sensitive than self-report inventories to subtle differences between various eating disordered patients and other psychiatric groups. Furthermore, some research has suggested that in eating disorder populations there may be a tendency for self-reported information to be distorted in a socially desirable direction (Allison & Heshka, 1993), and projective techniques are generally less vulnerable to this tendency. Smith, Hillard, Walsh, Kubacki, and Morgan (1991) used the Rorschach to investigate the hypothesis that purging bulimics would manifest greater psychopathology than bulimic patients who relied on fasting and excessive exercise to counteract binges. Although greater psychopathology was observed among the bulimics relative to a control group, the Rorschach variables did not discriminate between the two classes of bulimics. We found no published studies that compared the Rorschach protocols of bulimic, anorexic, and/or obese subjects within the same experiment; thus any comparisons made between these groups on Rorschach variables must remain tentative pending further research.

Smith et al. (1991) also found that bulimic patients showed higher scores than controls on Exner's Schizophrenia Index (although lower than those observed in schizophrenic samples); however, differences between these groups were surprisingly absent on the Depression and Egocentricity Indices. As there were only 13 subjects per group, a lack of power may be obscuring potential differences on these measures. A study of 57 outpatient females diagnosed with bulimia nervosa (Weisberg, Norman, & Herzog, 1987) compared their index scores with Exner's (1978) published norms for a matched sample of 57 depressed outpatients and 57 nonpatient controls. Significant differences were found on the Depression Index, with bulimics and depressives scoring higher than controls but comparably to each other. The depressive subjects had higher scores on the Suicide Constellation than bulimics. Contrary to the Smith et al. findings, the Schizophrenia index did not discriminate between bulimics and controls, but the depressives scored significantly higher.

A number of Rorschach variables are considered to be informative to the affective features of the respondent, and most of these variables relate to reactions to or use of color in the responses. Small, Teagno, Madero, Gross, and Ebert (1982) compared the Rorschach protocols of 27 female anorexics to those of 18 female schizophrenic patients. The anorexics showed greater use of achromatic color and shading determinants in their responses, both suggesting greater awareness of affectional needs and dysphoric affect in anorexics than in schizophrenics. However, Kaufer and Katz (1983) report no differences in use of color by a group of 20 female anorexics compared with 20 matched normal control subjects. The Weisberg et al. (1987) study of bulimic patients found both greater amounts of color-dominated form determinants (CF + C > FC) and higher affective ratios (Afr) in bulimics versus matched controls, which signify less control over emotional experience and greater attraction to emotional stimulation in bulimics. However, the matched group from the depressed outpatient normative sample were equal to the bulimics on these affect variables. The bulimics in the Smith et al. (1991) study manifest significantly more morbid responses than controls, which is suggestive of a more pessimistic attitude in the bulimics. A similar interpretation may be applied to the finding of more "morbid/damaged" response content in anorexic patients versus normals (Kaufer & Katz, 1983). As a whole, these data converge with other assessment research as well as clinical impressions of the importance of depressed affect in eating disorders.

Another set of Rorschach variables are informative to cognitive functioning and ideation. Exner has developed a set of "special scores" to apply to Rorschach responses to ascertain the degree of cognitive slippage evident in a subject's verbal protocol. Several of these special scores were shown to be more frequent in the Rorschach data of anorexic patients as compared with normal and psychiatric controls. Kaufer and Katz (1983) found a greater number of peculiar combinations of responses by anorexics, indicative of primary process thinking, whereas Sugarman, Quinlan, and Devenis (1982) found a greater number of contamination responses, which were "reflective of a breakdown in self-other boundaries" (p. 459). Although the precise meaning of such unusual verbalization during Rorschach testing may be subject to multiple interpretations and varied terminology, it is generally agreed on that they reflect cognitive distortions and reasoning problems. Other researchers (Strober & Goldenberg, 1981) have noted more excessive elaboration of Rorschach percepts by anorexic patients, which alludes to marked perfectionism and obsessional features. With regard to bulimia, Weisberg et al. (1987) found a significantly greater frequency of underincorporative style in their bulimic subjects, signifying an inefficient and hasty approach to scanning the environment and gathering information. Two studies have reported that bulimics versus controls and depressed patients (Smith et al., 1991; Weisberg et al., 1987) tend to demonstrate an "ambient" coping style, which indicates inconsistency in thinking and problem-solving strategies, leading to frequent errors in judgment and less ability to profit from experience. Thus the performance of bulimics on the Rorschach reflects the impulsivity that is so commonly ascribed to their personality. In sum, the

Rorschach data on cognitive functions suggest that greater degrees of unusual perceptions and thinking are associated with both anorexia and bulimia, which is consistent with accounts of the cognitive distortions that frequently accompany eating disorders (Johnson & Connors, 1987; Schlundt & Johnson, 1990). Note that the level of cognitive dysfunction in eating disorder patients is heightened relative to normals but still not on the order of that observed in schizophrenics.

Rorschach data are also useful for assessing self-image, interpersonal dispositions, and attitudes about others. The bulimic patients in the Weisberg et al. (1987) investigation gave more reflection responses and attained a higher score on the egocentricity index than controls. These findings, taken together, suggest a tendency for an exaggerated self-focus and self-preoccupation in bulimics. The depressed patients scored significantly lower than bulimics and controls on the egocentricity index. If this result proves valid, it demonstrates that the nature of depressive symptoms and related self-esteem problems are possibly different in nature for bulimics than for depressed outpatients.

An estimate of interest in people and interpersonal relationships can be obtained from the number of human content responses in a Rorschach protocol. Wallach and Lowenkopf (1984) note that the mean number of human content responses given by their five bulimic women fell more than one standard deviation below the mean number given in Exner's (1978) normative sample. Similarly, Parmer (1991) found that a sample of bulimic undergraduate students demonstrated more distorted or unusual human movement responses (Mu or M-) than control subjects, which is indicative of distorted or unrealistic perceptions of the self and others. However, other investigators (Weisberg et al., 1987) did not find differences in aggressive movement responses between bulimics, depressives, and controls, whereas bulimics may display difficulties in their relationships, they do not appear to show excessive expectations of aggression and hostility in their interactions with others. Collectively, these results may be interpreted as evidence for considerable emotional withdrawal and social isolation in bulimics. Two separate studies (Smith et al., 1991; Weisberg et al., 1987) report more space responses, which are putative indices of anger and negativity, in the protocols of bulimics versus controls. Weisberg and colleagues (1987) summarize their Rorschach findings in this domain with the observation that the bulimics in their study tended to be more oppositional, whereas the depressed subjects were more introspective. Food content on the Rorschach is interpreted as a sign of excessive interpersonal dependency, and Bornstein and Greenberg (1991) compared the frequency of food percepts in the Rorschachs of anorexic, bulimic, obese, and normal control subjects. Although these authors did find differences between the three eating disorder groups and controls on other indicators of "oral dependency," they did not find significant differences between patients and controls on the frequency of food content. Thus the lack of any percepts of food content in a patient's Rorschach protocol should not necessarily be taken as evidence for the absence of an eating disorder.

Further research is clearly needed on the Rorschach performances of eating disorder groups, particularly with obese samples. The data that exist look very promising and are largely consistent with the data from other modes of psychological testing as well as clinical impressions of the personality features associated with these disorders. Improvements in the methodology of this research would clarify the role of psychological conflicts or personality features in the etiology of eating disorders. Many of the studies reviewed lack power for a more conclusive test of the differences between clinical and control groups, and still others are lacking in appropriate psychiatric comparison groups to test the specificity of the findings to bulimia, anorexia, or obesity in particular (Allison, 1993).

The Rorschach has long been considered by some to be an indispensable technique for the assessment of personality. Until relatively recently, the validity evidence in support of this proposition has been rather meager, and even now the few available studies described above must be interpreted with caution. However, the more psychometrically based Exner approach to the Rorschach has injected new life into research with this procedure, and it would be premature to discard the Rorschach in light of these more recent findings.

Other Instruments

In light of clinical speculation concerning the occurrence of thought disorder in eating pathology, it is surprising that there is not more research using cognitive or neuropsychological assessment methods with this population. Small and colleagues (1982) gave the Wechsler Adult Intelligence Scale (WAIS; Wechsler, 1955) to the anorexic and schizophrenic subjects in their study and found higher verbal, performance, and full-scale IQ scores in the anorexics, with especially prominent differences in favor of the anorexics seen on the performance subtests. However, there were apparently no subtle indications on the WAIS of the cognitive anomalies obtained on the Rorschach, as described above.

The comorbidity of eating pathologies and personality disorders has been documented by several investigators using both structured diagnostic interviews (Sansone, Fine, Seuferer, & Bovenzi, 1989) and self-report instruments (Kennedy et al., 1990; Steiger, Liquornik, Chapman, & Hussain, 1991;

Yager, Landsverk, Edelstein, & Hyler, 1989). The presence of severe personality disturbances is believed to affect the length and difficulty of treatment for patients with eating disorders, hence diagnosis of these disturbances may be important for planning interventions with this population. One of the more commonly used self-report instruments for the assessment of personality disorders is the Millon Clinical Multiaxial Inventory (MCMI; Millon, 1982). Research using the MCMI (distributed by National Computer Systems, P.O. Box 1416, Minneapolis, MN 55440) with anorexics and bulimics has shown elevations on the Borderline (CC) scale in proportions of the sample ranging from 32% (Sansone et al., 1989) to 79% (Kennedy et al., 1990). The incidence of borderline personality disorder does not seem to differ between anorexic and bulimic subsamples. Dependent and avoidant personality disorders also appear to be common in these samples. However, certain psychometric aspects of the MCMI have received significant criticism. Piersma (1987) found unimpressive reliability values in an inpatient psychiatric group: .56 for Axis II and .54 for Axis I. Piersma also found that the overall agreement between MCMI personality disorder diagnosis on admission and MCMI at discharge was low: kappa = .21. The MCMI has also been criticized because of extensive item overlap among different scales (Retzlaff & Gilbertini, 1987), an item weighting scheme that renders the instrument essentially unscorable by hand (Greer, 1984; Rebillot, 1985), and questionable relationships of MCMI scale scores to the relevant diagnostic concepts (Patrick, 1988; Widiger, Williams, Spitzer, & Frances, 1985).

Another self-report measure of personality disorders that is enjoying increased usage is the revised Personality Diagnostic Questionnaire (PDQ-R; Hyler et al., 1987). Data from assessment studies that employ this instrument agree with the data from MCMI studies in showing a high incidence of personality disorder diagnoses among subjects with eating disturbances. However, Steiger et al. (1991) report no differences between anorexics, bulimics, and bulimic anorexics in the probability of specific personality disorder diagnoses or their assignment to the three putative "clusters" (dramatic, anxious, and eccentric) of personality categories. Similarly, Yager and colleagues (1989) find high percentages of PDQ-R diagnoses of borderline, dependent, avoidant, and schizotypal personality disorders in normal weight bulimics and anorexics with bulimic features, but they do not find significant associations between specific patterns of eating problems and personality disorder diagnoses or clusters.

One area of research that has been comparatively neglected in the assessment of eating disorders involves the description of normal personality variation within these groups. There have been a number of studies focused on symptomatic or maladaptive personality traits in such populations, but little investigation of more normative personality characteristics. One of the most promising techniques for the assessment of normal personality constructs is the NEO Personality Inventory (NEO-PI; Costa & McCrae, 1985). The NEO-PI (distributed by Psychological Assessment Resources, P.O. Box 998, Odessa, FL 33556) is scored for five independent personality factors that have emerged consistently from factor analytic studies of personality: Neuroticism, Extroversion, Openness to Experience, Agreeableness, and Conscientiousness. Each of these five factors is broken down into numerous facets. Internal consistency estimates range from .85 to .93 for the domain scores, with 6-month test retest reliability estimates of .86 to .91. Although there are minimal data available on the nature of these dimensions within eating disorder populations, this appears to be a promising means of assessing important personality variability *within* each of these groups.

Depression appears to be the most frequent symptom in all forms of eating disorders and thus probably represents one of the more important management issues in the treatment of such patients. Research using the Beck Depression Inventory (Beck, 1978) confirms that elevated BDI scores are seen among eating disorders, and the severity of depressive symptoms may be an important prognostic indicator (Garner et al., 1990). Hence the BDI may also be an important instrument for planning intervention strategies and monitoring patients' progress in treatment.

Personality Assessment Inventory (PAI)

The PAI (Morey, 1991) is a recently introduced multiscale inventory designed to assess constructs of significance in a wide variety of clinical settings. The development of the PAI (distributed by Psychological Assessment Resources, P.O. Box 998, Odessa, FL 33556) was based on a construct validation framework that placed a strong emphasis on a theoretically informed approach to the development and selection of items as well as on the assessment of their stability and correlates. Of paramount importance in the development of the test was the assumption that no single quantitative item parameter should be used as the sole criterion for item selection. An overreliance on a single parameter in item selection typically leads to a scale with one desirable psychometric property and numerous undesirable ones, particularly discriminant validity. The PAI was thus designed to provide reasonably specific indicators of the constructs it assesses.

The test itself contains 344 items that are answered on a four-alternative scale, with the anchors "totally false," "slightly true," "mainly true," and "very true." Each response is weighted according to the intensity of the feature that the different alternatives represent; thus a client who answers "very true" to the question "Sometimes I think I'm worthless" adds 3 points to his or her raw score on the Depression scale, whereas a client who responds "slightly true" to the same item adds only 1 point. The 344 items constitute 22 nonoverlapping full scales: 4 validity (i.e., to identify response styles), 11 clinical (e.g., for assessing depression, schizophrenia, substance abuse, or personality disorder), 5 treatment consideration (e.g., for assessing suicidal ideation or treatment motivation), and 2 interpersonal scales (assessing dominance and warmth). Ten of the full scales contain conceptually derived subscales designed to facilitate interpretation and coverage of the full breadth of complex clinical constructs.

The PAI was developed and standardized for use in the clinical assessment of individuals in the age range of 18 through adulthood. Reading-level analyses of the PAI test items indicate that reading ability at the fourth-grade level is necessary to complete the inventory, a level lower than in most comparable inventories. PAI scale and subscale raw scores are transformed to *t* scores to provide interpretation relative to a standardization sample of 1,000 community-dwelling adults. This sample was carefully selected to match 1995 U.S. census projections on the basis of gender, race, and age; the educational level of the standardization sample was selected to be representative given the required fourth-grade reading level. To facilitate other comparisons, the PAI manual also provides information about normative expectancies referenced against a representative *clinical* sample as well as a large sample of college students and various demographic subgroups of the community standardization sample.

The reliability and validity of the PAI have been examined in a number of different studies and appear to be quite promising. Median coefficient alphas for the full scales of .81, .82, and .86 for normative, college, and clinical samples, respectively, have been obtained (Morey, 1991), and examination of internal consistency estimates for the PAI full scales for groups defined by various demographic characteristics indicates that there is very little variability in internal consistency as a function of race, gender, or age. Median test-retest reliability values, over a 4-week interval, for the 11 full clinical scales was .86, leading to standard error of measurement estimates for these scales on the order of 3 to 4 *t*-score points. Validity estimates, as gauged against more than 50 different markers of related constructs (including many of the instruments described previously in this chapter), have also been consistent with theoretical expectations.

The PAI was designed to address the problems typically encountered with instruments in this area, such as limited discriminant validity, obsolete representation of clinical constructs, and reliability problems. However, because of the recency of its introduction, there is little research to date on the utility of the PAI in the eating disorders area. There is clearly a need for research directed at this population, to determine if the instrument can circumvent some of the assessment problems noted previously in this group.

Conclusion

Although some research has begun to accumulate on the performance of individuals with eating-related disorders on various indices of personality and/or psychopathology, there is clearly a great deal of fundamental research that remains to be done in this area. Much of the research performed to date has included relatively small samples and most fails to include some of the more important control groups in attempting to highlight modal performance for such subjects. However, researchers in this area should heed certain caveats that might prevent the field from repeating mistakes often made in this type of research. For example, it is likely safe to assume that there is no single "personality type" that underlies eating disorders in general or even more specific eating disorders such as bulimia or obesity. These diagnostic categories subsume a group of individuals who share certain eating-related symptomatology but can present with a wide array of other personality or even clinical features. Thus the modal findings for these groups may represent a statistical average that may provide relatively little information about the individuals in the sample. The mean MMPI profile described earlier is a case in point; similar mean profiles have been obtained for myriad different clinical groups.

Rather, a better use of such instruments is to provide a clinical database from which modifications to standard treatments can be made—a strategy that makes use of the heterogeneity of the sample rather than attempting to establish some homogeneity. The Webb et al. (1990) MMPI study, which identified correlates of a poor response to a certain type of treatment for morbid obesity *within* such a sample, is an example of this type of research. Certainly, the treatment for an eating-disordered client presenting with severe substance abuse and marked anxiety should differ in some ways from that given to a client without such additional difficulties. In identifying this heterogeneity, it is important that any instrument selected be able to discriminate between the general distress that typically accompanies eating disorders and other, independent clinical conditions (such as an anxiety disorder or a personality disorder). Thus it is critical that these instruments have satisfactory discriminant validity to perform this task, and there is clearly a need for research to determine whether any of the aforementioned procedures are suited to this task. The greatest promise of these instruments lies in establishing links between different clinical features and the planning of treatment; we would encourage future researchers to concentrate on this area in an effort to establish these links.

References

Allison, D. B. (1993). A note on the selection of control groups and control variables in comorbidity research. *Comprehensive Psychiatry, 34,* 336-339.

Allison, D. B., & Heshka, S. (1991). Toward an empirically derived typology of obese persons. *International Journal of Obesity, 15,* 741-754.

Allison, D. B., & Heshka, S. (1993). Social desirability and response bias in self-reports of "emotional eating." *Eating Disorders, 1,* 31-38.

Beck, A. T. (1978). *Beck Depression Inventory.* Philadelphia: Center for Cognitive Therapy.

Bornstein, R. F., & Greenberg, R. P. (1991). Dependency and eating disorders in female psychiatric outpatients. *Journal of Nervous and Mental Disease, 179,* 148-152.

Butcher, J. N. (1990). *MMPI-2 in psychological treatment.* New York: Oxford.

Colligan, R. C., Osborne, D., Swenson, W. M., & Offord, K. P. (1983). *The MMPI: A contemporary normative study.* New York: Praeger.

Costa, P. T., & McCrae, R. R. (1985). *The NEO Personality Inventory manual.* Odessa, FL: Psychological Assessment Resources.

Dahlstrom, W. G., Welsh, G. S., & Dahlstrom, L. E. (1972). *An MMPI handbook: Vol. I. Clinical interpretation.* Minneapolis: University of Minnesota Press.

Dahlstrom, W. G., Welsh, G. S., & Dahlstrom, L. E. (1975). *An MMPI handbook: Vol. II. Research applications.* Minneapolis: University of Minnesota Press.

Derogatis, L. R. (1977). *Symptom Checklist-90 manual.* Baltimore: Johns Hopkins University Press.

Exner, J. E. (1974). *The Rorschach: A comprehensive system.* New York: Wiley.

Exner, J. E. (1978). *The Rorschach: A comprehensive system, Vol. 2.* New York: Wiley.

Exner, J. E. (1991). *The Rorschach: A comprehensive system, Vol. 2* (2nd ed.). New York: Wiley.

Faschingbauer, T. R. (1974). A 166-item written short form of the group MMPI: The FAM. *Journal of Consulting and Clinical Psychology, 42,* 645-655.

Garner, D. M., Olmsted, M. P., Davis, R., Rockert, W., Goldbloom, D., & Eagle, M. (1990). The association between bulimic symptoms and reported psychopathology. *International Journal of Eating Disorders, 9,* 1-15.

Gotlib, I. H. (1984). Depression and general psychopathology in university students. *Journal of Abnormal Psychology, 93,* 19-30.

Graham, J. R. (1990). *The MMPI-2: Assessing personality and psychopathology.* New York: Oxford University Press.

Greene, R. L. (1991). *The MMPI-2/MMPI: An interpretive manual.* Orlando, FL: Allyn & Bacon.

Greer, S. E. (1984). A review of the Millon Clinical Multiaxial Inventory. *Journal of Counseling and Development, 63,* 262-263.

Helmes, E., & Redden, J. R. (1993). A perspective on developments in assessing psychopathology: A critical review of the MMPI and MMPI-2. *Psychological Bulletin, 113,* 453-471.

Horn, J. L., Wanberg, K., & Appel, M. (1973). Reliability of the MMPI. *Multivariate Behavioral Research, 8,* 131-142.

Hsu, L. K. G. (1990). *Eating disorders.* New York: Guilford.

Hyler, S. E., Rieder, R. O., Williams, J. B., Spitzer, R. L., Hendler, J., & Lyons, M. (1987). *Personality Diagnostic Questionnaire–Revised*. New York: New York State Psychiatric Institute.

Johnson, C., & Connors, M. E. (1987). *The etiology and treatment of bulimia nervosa: A biological perspective*. New York: Basic Books.

Kaufer, J. F., & Katz, J. L. (1983). Rorschach responses in anorectic and nonanorectic women. *International Journal of Eating Disorders, 3*(1), 65-74.

Kennedy, S. H., McVey, G., & Katz, R. (1990). Personality disorders in anorexia nervosa and bulimia nervosa. *Journal of Psychiatric Research, 24,* 259-269.

Kincannon, J. C. (1968). Prediction of the standard MMPI scale scores from 71 items: The Mini-Mult. *Journal of Consulting and Clinical Psychology, 32,* 319-325.

Mauger, P. A. (1972). *The test-retest reliability of persons: An empirical investigation utilizing the Minnesota Multiphasic Personality Inventory and the Personality Research Form*. Unpublished doctoral dissertation, University of Minnesota, MN.

Millon, T. (1982). *Millon Clinical Multiaxial Inventory manual* (2nd ed.). Minneapolis: National Computer Systems.

Morey, L. C. (1991). *Personality Assessment Inventory: Professional manual*. Odessa, FL: Psychological Assessment Resources.

Morey, L. C., Roberts, W. R., & Penk, W. (1987). MMPI alcoholic subtypes: Replicability and validity of the 2-8-7-4 subtype. *Journal of Abnormal Psychology, 96,* 164-166.

Norman, D. K., & Herzog, D. B. (1983). Bulimia, anorexia, and anorexia nervosa with bulimia: A comparative analysis of MMPI profiles. *International Journal of Eating Disorders, 2,* 43-52.

Ordman, A. M., & Kirschenbaum, D. S. (1986). Bulimia: Assessment of eating, psychological adjustment, and familial characteristics. *International Journal of Eating Disorders, 5,* 865-878.

Overall, J. E., & Gomez-Mont, F. (1974). The MMPI-168 for psychiatric screening. *Educational and Psychological Measurement, 34,* 315-319.

Parmer, J. C. (1991). Bulimia and object relations: MMPI and Rorschach variables. *Journal of Personality Assessment, 56,* 266-276.

Patrick, J. (1988). Concordance of the MCMI and the MMPI in the diagnosis of three DSM-III Axis I disorders. *Journal of Clinical Psychology, 44,* 186-190.

Pendleton, L., Tisdale, M. J., Moll, S. H., & Marler, M. R. (1990). The 4-5-6 configuration on the MMPI in bulimics versus controls. *Journal of Clinical Psychology, 46,* 811-816.

Piersma, H. L. (1987). The MCMI as a measure of DSM-III Axis II diagnoses: An empirical comparison. *Journal of Clinical Psychology, 43,* 478-483.

Pyle, R. L., Mitchell, J. E., & Eckert, E. D. (1981). Bulimia: A report of 34 cases. *Journal of Clinical Psychiatry, 42,* 60-64.

Rebillot, J. R. (1985). Scoring of the MCMI: Effects on utility. *Journal of Counseling and Development, 63,* 631.

Resnick, R. J., Goldberg, S. C., Schulz, S. C., Schulz, P. M., Hamer, R. M., & Friedel, R. O. (1988). Borderline personality disorder: Replication of MMPI profiles. *Journal of Clinical Psychology, 44,* 354-360.

Retzlaff, P., & Gilbertini, M. (1987). Factor structure of the MCMI basic personality scales and common-item artifact. *Journal of Personality Assessment, 51,* 588-594.

Rorschach, H. (1921). *Psychodiagnostics*. Bern, Switzerland: Bircher.

Rosenvinge, J. H., & Mouland, S. O. (1990). Outcome and prognosis of anorexia nervosa: A retrospective study of 41 subjects. *British Journal of Psychiatry, 156,* 92-97.

Sansone, R. A., Fine, M. A., Seuferer, S., & Bovenzi, J. (1989). The prevalence of borderline personality symptomatology among women with eating disorders. *Journal of Clinical Psychology, 45,* 603-610.

Schlundt, D. G., & Johnson, W. G. (1990). *Eating disorders: Assessment and treatment.* Boston: Allyn & Bacon.

Scott, R., & Thoner, G. (1986). Ego deficits in anorexia nervosa. *Psychological Reports, 58,* 839-846.

Shisslak, C. M., Pazda, S. L., & Crago, M. (1990). Body weight and bulimia as discriminators of psychological characteristics among anorexic, bulimic, and obese women. *Journal of Abnormal Psychology, 99,* 380-384.

Small, A. C., Madero, J., Gross, H., Teagno, L., Lieb, J., & Ebert, M. (1981). A comparative analysis of primary anorexics and schizophrenics on the MMPI. *Journal of Clinical Psychology, 37,* 733-736.

Small, A., Teagno, L., Madero, J., Gross, H., & Ebert, M. (1982). A comparison of anorexics and schizophrenics on psychodiagnostic measures. *International Journal of Eating Disorders, 1*(3), 49-56.

Smith, J. E., Hillard, M. C., Walsh, R. A., Kubacki, S. R., & Morgan, C. D. (1991). Rorschach assessment of purging and nonpurging bulimics. *Journal of Personality Assessment, 56,* 277-288.

Steiger, H., Liquornik, K., Chapman, J., & Hussain, N. (1991). Personality and family disturbances in eating-disorder patients: Comparison of "restricters" and "bingers" to normal controls. *International Journal of Eating Disorders, 10,* 501-512.

Strober, M., & Goldenberg, I. (1981). Ego boundary disturbance in juvenile anorexia nervosa. *Journal of Clinical Psychology, 37,* 433-438.

Sugarman, A., Quinlan, D. M., & Devenis, L. (1982). Ego boundary disturbance in anorexia nervosa: Preliminary findings. *Journal of Personality Assessment, 46,* 455-461.

Wallach, J. D., & Lowenkopf, E. L. (1984). Five bulimic women: MMPI, Rorschach, and TAT characteristics. *International Journal of Eating Disorders, 3*(4), 53-66.

Walters, E. E., Neale, M. C., Eaves, L. J., Heath, A. C., Kessler, R., & Kendler, K. (1993). Bulimia nervosa: A population-based study of purgers vs. non-purgers. *International Journal of Eating Disorders, 13,* 265-272.

Webb, W. W., Morey, L. C., Castelnuovo-Tedesco, P., & Scott, H. W., Jr. (1990). Heterogeneity of personality traits in massive obesity and outcome prediction of bariatric surgery. *International Journal of Obesity, 14,* 13-20.

Wechsler, D. (1955). *Manual for the Wechsler Adult Intelligence Scale.* New York: Psychological Corporation.

Weisberg, L. J., Norman, D. K., & Herzog, D. B. (1987). Personality functioning in normal weight bulimia. *International Journal of Eating Disorders, 6,* 615-631.

Weiss, S. R., & Ebert, M. H. (1983). Psychological and behavioral characteristics of normal-weight bulimics and normal-weight controls. *Psychosomatic Medicine, 45,* 293-303.

Widiger, T. A., Williams, J. B., Spitzer, R., & Frances, A. (1985). The MCMI and DSM-III: A brief rejoinder to Millon. *Journal of Personality Assessment, 49,* 366-378.

Wiggins, J. S. (1966). Substantive dimensions of self-report in the MMPI item pool. *Psychical Monographs, 80,* 22 (whole No. 630).

Williamson, D. A., Kelley, M. L., Davis, C. J., Ruggiero, L., & Blouin, D. C. (1985). Psychopathology of eating disorders: A controlled comparison of bulimic, obese, and normal subjects. *Journal of Consulting and Clinical Psychology, 53,* 161-166.

Yager, J., Landsverk, J., Edelstein, C. K., & Hyler, S. E. (1989). Screening for Axis II personality disorders in women with bulimic eating disorders. *Psychosomatics, 30,* 255-261.

2

Measures of Quality of Life, Subjective Well-Being, and Satisfaction With Life

VINCENT C. ALFONSO

The goal of this chapter is to present a review of measurement instruments in the areas of quality of life, subjective well-being, and satisfaction with life as they relate to obesity and weight-related problems. It cannot be stated that the instruments presented in this chapter will always be the *best* available under all circumstances, given that the use of any instrument is determined by many factors including theoretical framework, research/clinical purposes, and time and cost efficiency. However, a selection of the better and more use-

AUTHOR'S NOTE: I gratefully acknowledge David B. Allison for the opportunity to write this chapter and for his assistance in its preparation. In addition, Damon Rader is recognized for the extreme amount of time and energy he contributed throughout the entire process. The manuscript could not have been completed without his assistance.

ful instruments is presented that should provide most researchers and clinicians with an adequate menu from which to choose.

In this chapter, instruments assessing the cognitive component of quality of life or subjective well-being are presented. The cognitive assessment of an individual's life can take place at various levels. These levels are life in general, specific life domains (e.g., work satisfaction in general), and specific facets or aspects within a domain (e.g., satisfaction with coworkers). Therefore, when measurement of specific life domains are reviewed here, some areas contain a global or general assessment instrument of that particular domain and a facet assessment instrument within that domain. The life domains reviewed here are life in general (and global measures of life domains within one instrument), self, work, school, family, marital/relationship, sex, and social/leisure.

Criteria for Inclusion and Sources of Information

It is noted that there are dozens of instruments that have been constructed by individual researchers for a particular study and never used again, have no reported psychometric properties, or are only somewhat related to the constructs of interest. Therefore certain criteria were used in the selection of each scale.

First, the instrument had to be considered a measure of quality of life or satisfaction with life by the developers of the scale. Related scales such as client or therapist satisfaction (Tracey, 1989) were not reviewed. Second, these scales had to be used often for research or clinical purposes or be under continued development. Third, at least preliminary psychometric properties had to be established including descriptive statistics, reliability, and some type of validity. Most of the scales presented here are psychometrically sound. There was substantial variability across measures regarding the amount and types of validity data available for review. Fourth, most of the scales had to be practically useful, containing low to moderate numbers of items; fairly easily administered and scored; and applicable with a fairly wide range of samples.

Chapter Organization

In this chapter, first, a brief discussion of the constructs of quality of life, subjective well-being, and satisfaction with life will be presented. Second, the application of these constructs to the weight-related problem population will be explained. Third, reviews of available measures that have met the criteria for inclusion in this chapter will be presented as stated above. Comments and additional scales and/or related literature will follow each section. Fourth, the complete scales or sample items are presented for each scale in separate appendixes at the end of the chapter. In addition, a source table is provided that contains the names and primary authors of the scales as well as the number of items and the available sources for each scale (see Table 2.1).

Quality of Life, Subjective Well-Being, and Satisfaction With Life

Traditionally, clinicians and researchers have measured psychological and physical well-being as the absence of pathology. In more recent years, the focus of well-being has shifted to the measurement of the presence of health or to individuals' subjective evaluation of their lives in general and with respect to specific life domains such as family, relationships, work, or school (Bigelow, Brodsky, Stewart, & Olson, 1982; Diener, 1984; Hollandsworth, 1988). During the past 20 years several publications regarding quality of life, subjective well-being, and satisfaction with life have appeared (Andrews & Robinson, 1991; Andrews & Withey, 1976; Campbell, Converse, & Rogers, 1976; Strack, Argyle, & Schwarz, 1991; Veenhoven, 1984).

A problem that persists in the literature regarding quality of life, subjective well-being, and satisfaction with life is the lack of a single definition for these constructs. These constructs are sometimes used interchangeably along with others such as "life satisfaction," "psychological well-being," "happiness," and "morale" (Andrews & Robinson, 1991; Diener, 1984). As a result, a myriad of measurement instruments have been constructed and used with a wide variety of samples. All these terms, however, are concerned with subjective, positive evaluations of one's life as a whole or with respect to specific domains of life on a broad (global) or facet level.

Much of the research has broken down the broader construct of subjective well-being into cognitive and affective components (Diener & Larsen, 1993). The cognitive component usually pertains to the rational, intellectual evaluation of one's life satisfaction. The affective/emotional component usually involves the measurement of happiness in some way.

Andrews and Robinson (1991) note that existing measures of subjective well-being on the global or general life level include those that investigate cognitive and affective components separately or together within the same scale. However, there are also a number of scales designed to measure satisfaction with single life domains.

Application to Weight-Related Problems

Stunkard and Wadden (1992) reviewed the literature regarding the psychosocial effects of severe obesity. They summarized several studies and con-

TABLE 2.1 Source Table of Satisfaction Instruments

Name of Scale	Primary Author(s)	Number of Items	Availability
Satisfaction With Life Scale	Edward Diener and Associates	5	Dr. Ed Diener, Dept. of Psychology, University of Illinois, 603 East Daniel St., Champaign, IL 61820
Extended Satisfaction With Life Scale	Vincent C. Alfonso and David B Allison	50	Dr. Vincent C. Alfonso, Graduate School of Education, Fordham University, 113 West 60th St., New York, NY 10023
Quality of Life Inventory	Michael B. Frisch and Associates	48	David Roble, National Computer Systems, 5605 Green Circle Drive, Minnetonka, MN 55343; (800) 627-7271, Ext. 5129
Rosenberg Self-Esteem Scale	Morris Rosenberg	10	Florence Slade, Permissions Department, Princeton University Press, 41 William St., Princeton, NJ 08540
Self Description Questionnaire III	Herbert Marsh	136	Dr. Herbert Marsh, School of Education and Language Studies, University of Western Sidney—Macarthur, P.O. Box 555, Campbelltown, NSW 2560 Australia
Hoppock Job Satisfaction Blank	Robert Hoppock	4	Permissions Department, HarperCollins Publishers, 10 East 53rd St., New York, NY 10022
Job Descriptive Index	Patricia C. Smith and Associates	72	Dr. Patricia Smith, Department of Psychology, Bowling Green State University, Bowling Green, OH 43403
Minnesota Satisfaction Questionnaire—Short Form	David Weiss and Associates	20	Dr. David Weiss, Vocational Psychology Research, N620 Elliott Hall, University of Minnesota, 75 East River Road, Minneapolis, MN 55455
Perceived Quality of Academic Life	Morris Okun and Associates	6	Dr. Morris Okun, Department of Psychology, Arizona State University, Tempe, AZ 85287/American College Personnel Association, 1 Dupont Circle, Ste. 300, Washington, DC 20036
Kansas Family Life Satisfaction Scale	Walter Schumm and Associates	4	Dr. Walter Schumm, Dept. of Human Development and Family Studies, College of Human Ecology, Kansas State University, Manhattan, KS 66506/*Psychological Reports*, Carol H. Ammons, Ph.D., Editor, Box 9229, Missoula, MT 59807.
Family Adaptability and Cohesion Evaluation Scale II or III	David Olson and Associates	20	Dr. David Olson, Family Social Science/Family Inventory Project, 290 McNeil Hall, 1985 Buford Ave, St. Paul, MN 55108
Kansas Marital Satisfaction Scale	Walter Schumm and Associates	3	Dr. Walter Schumm, Dept. of Human Development and Family Studies, College of Human Ecology, Kansas State University, Manhattan, KS 66506/National Council on Family Relations, 3989 Central Ave. NE, Ste. 550, Minneapolis, MN 55421
Dyadic Adjustment Scale	Graham Spanier	32	Debra Green, Psychology Dept., Multi-Health Systems, Inc., 908 Niagara Falls Blvd., North Tonawanda, NY 14120; (800) 456-3003
Index of Sexual Satisfaction	Walter Hudson and Associates	25	Dr. Walter Hudson, School of Social Work, Arizona State University, Tempe, AZ 85287-1802
Leisure Satisfaction Scale	Jacob G. Beard & Mounir G. Ragheb	51	Joan Burlingame, Idyll Arbor, Inc. P.O. Box 720, Ravensdale, WA 98051; (206) 432-3231

cluded that those people exhibiting marked or severe obesity do not demonstrate higher levels of psychopathology than the general population. That is, the severely obese as a group are no more "emotionally disturbed" than average weight groups. Nevertheless, the severely obese do suffer from clinical syndromes in addition to their weight disorders. These include some types of major affective disorder (e.g., depression) and/or adjustment problems.

Problems specific to the obese include binge eating, body image disparagement, lack of confidence, sense of isolation, and humiliation (Stunkard & Wadden, 1992). Perhaps one of the greatest problems encountered by obese persons is prejudice and discrimination (Allison, Basile, & Yuker, 1991; Stunkard & Wadden, 1992; Yuker & Allison, in press). The magnitude of problems encountered by obese persons was made clear in a study by Rand and Macgregor (1991), who found that severely obese persons who had lost significant weight stated that they would prefer being deaf or diabetic to returning to their obese state.

Other weight-related groups such as bulimics and anorexics experience psychosocial and clinical problems as well (Hsu, 1990). Shisslak, Pazda, and Crago (1990) found that three different weight groups of bulimic women exhibited significantly more psychopathology, more external locus of control, lower self-esteem, and lower sense of personal effectiveness than nonbulimic women of similar weight. Lingswiler, Crowther, and Stephens (1987) reported that their sample of binge eaters experienced greater fluctuations of anxiety and depression than nonbingers while their overweight sample experienced greater fluctuations in anxiety, hostility, and depression than individuals of normal weight. Frank (1991) found that shame and guilt related to eating are experienced significantly more by eating disordered women than by normal or depressed women.

The psychosocial problems of these populations do not begin in adulthood, given that obese children's psychosocial difficulties have also been documented. Banis et al. (1988) reported that obese children evidenced significantly more behavior problems, less social competence, and poorer self-perceptions than nonobese normative samples. Similar results were reported by Wallander, Varni, Babani, Banis, and Wilcox (1988). Dieting and dietary restraint among girls as young as 9 years of age have also been reported, which is a concern because dieting behavior "may be the first step to future clinical eating problems" (Hill & Robinson, 1991, p. 267).

These additional psychosocial and clinical problems that weight disorder populations encounter can sometimes be reduced or eliminated with significant weight loss. In Stunkard and Wadden's (1992) review, they state that, after surgical treatment with weight loss, obese persons evidence increased self-esteem, positive emotions, and marital satisfaction. Results also indicate decreased body image disparagement, improved eating behavior, increased sex satisfaction, and decreased anxiety and depression.

In sum, Kral, Sjöström, and Sullivan (1992) state: "Severe obesity causes impaired quality of life above and beyond the impact of medical complications of the disease" (p. 611), and "according to the patients themselves, improved quality of life is the most important benefit of surgical treatment" (p. 614). In particular, treatment outcomes should not be limited to medical end points only (e.g., weight loss, glucose tolerance) but should also include measures of subjective well-being. Therefore the quality of life or well-being of weight-related problem populations is important to consider and measure when working with these groups (Stunkard & Wadden, 1992).

Measures of Quality of Life, Subjective Well-Being, and Satisfaction With Life

General and Specific Life Satisfaction (Global Level)

Satisfaction With Life Scale

Description. The Satisfaction With Life Scale (SWLS; Diener, Emmons, Larsen, & Griffin, 1985) is a five-item scale that "is designed around the idea that one must ask subjects for an overall judgment of their life in order to measure the concept of life satisfaction" (Diener et al., 1985, pp. 71-72). Individuals indicate their degree of agreement or disagreement on a 7-point Likert-type scale. The 5 items of the SWLS were selected from a pool of 48 items based on factor analyses. Scores range from 5 to 35 with higher scores indicating greater life satisfaction. The SWLS can be found in Appendix 2-A.

Norms. Pavot and Diener (1993) provide an extensive list of studies that have used the SWLS with corresponding normative data. The range of means for various groups of individuals (e.g., undergraduates, health workers) was 14.4 to 27.9. The range of standard deviations was 4.4 to 9.0.

Reliability. Diener et al. (1985) reported a 2-month test-retest correlation coefficient of .82 and an alpha coefficient of .87 for a sample of 176 undergraduates from the University of Illinois. In a sample of 39 elderly individuals, Pavot, Diener, Colvin, and Sandvik (1991) obtained an alpha coefficient of .83.

Validity. Validity data with two undergraduate samples have been reported by Diener et al. (1985). A principal axis factor analysis was performed for evidence of construct validity and yielded a single factor that accounted for 66% of the variance. Convergent and discriminant validity included correlational data among various subjective well-being items or scales, a social desirability scale, and personality measures of well-being. The SWLS was significantly positively correlated with other measures of subjective well-being, not correlated with a social desirability scale, and significantly negatively correlated with measures of poor adjustment or psychopathology (see Diener et al., 1985, for specific measures and correlation coefficients).

The SWLS was also correlated with trained interviewer judgments of life satisfaction and another self-report life satisfaction measure in an elderly sample of 53 individuals. Significant correlations of .43 and .46 were obtained between the SWLS and trained interviewer judgments and the life satisfaction measure, respectively (Diener et al., 1985).

Pavot et al. (1991) asked 39 elderly individuals from an Illinois community to complete at the first interview the SWLS, four subjective well-being measures, a daily rating of general satisfaction over a 5-day period, and a memory recall task (of positive versus negative events in the individual's life). In addition, three sets of peer reports regarding the participants' well-being were obtained. Participants then completed several measures at a second interview. The SWLS was significantly correlated with all subjective well-being measures with r's $\geq$ .39.

In a second study, 136 undergraduates completed the SWLS, the Fordyce scale, daily reports of affect, and a frequency affect scale. Peer and family reports of participants affect and satisfaction were also obtained. Several measures were completed at various times during the study. Results included $r = .54$ between peer and family reported life satisfaction, $r = .55$ between self- and peer-reported life satisfaction, and $r = .57$ between self- and family-reported life satisfaction (Pavot et al., 1991).

One other study is worthy of note. Arrindell, Meeuwesen, and Huyse (1991) conducted a study in the Netherlands in which the SWLS and other measures of subjective well-being were completed by adult medical outpatients. Reliability estimates, factor analysis results, and convergent and divergent validity coefficients were consistent with results reported by Diener and his colleagues, suggesting that the SWLS is reliable and valid across cultures.

Extended Satisfaction With Life Scale

Description. The Extended Satisfaction With Life Scale (ESWLS; Alfonso, Allison, & Dunn, 1992; Alfonso, Allison, & Rader, 1994; Allison, Alfonso, &

Dunn, 1991), which can be found in Appendix 2-B, is a multidimensional life satisfaction scale that taps nine domains of life, measuring them on a global level. These domains include satisfaction with one's (a) life as a whole (general life), (b) social life, (c) sex life, (d) self (self-esteem), (e) physical appearance (body image), (f) family life (immediate family), (g) school life, (h) job or work life, and (i) relationship/marriage. Each subscale consists of 5 items with the exception of the job satisfaction subscale (which consists of 10 items), yielding a total of 50 items. Individuals are asked to rate on a 7-point Likert-type scale their degree of agreement or disagreement with items in the subscales that pertain to their present lives. In essence, the ESWLS is an extension of Diener et al.'s (1985) SWLS. The global life satisfaction subscale is the SWLS, with the exception of item 5. Subscale scores range from 5 to 35 with the exception of job satisfaction, which has a range from 10 to 50, and higher scores indicate greater satisfaction.

Norms. Preliminary norms have been provided by Alfonso, Allison, and Rader (1994) for each of the subscales of the ESWLS. Corresponding means and standard deviations for two independent samples of undergraduates (*n*s = 182-302) were as follows: general life (23.9, 6.1), social life (25.1, 7.0), sex life (24.1, 7.6), relationship (23.3, 7.8), self (25.1, 5.1), physical appearance (19.6, 6.4), family life (23.8, 8.3), school life (24.8, 4.7), and job (48.2, 11.0).

Reliability. Several samples of undergraduates from local universities in the New York metropolitan area have completed the ESWLS (Alfonso & Allison, 1992; Alfonso, Allison, & Rader, 1993). Coefficient alphas for subscales ranged from .81 (school satisfaction) to .96 (relationship and sex satisfaction) for samples ranging from 182 to 302 participants. Two-week test-retest reliability coefficients for 109 participants ranged from .74 (school satisfaction) to .87 (sex satisfaction) for the subscales.

Validity. Preliminary convergent and discriminant validity have been established as well by Alfonso et al. (1993). Regarding convergent validity, statistically significant correlations were obtained between all subscales of the ESWLS (except for physical appearance with school or relationship satisfaction) and ranged from .15 (satisfaction with physical appearance and work) to .63 (satisfaction with general life and self). All correlations between the general life satisfaction subscale and other ESWLS subscales were statistically significant, ranging from .28 to .63.

Additionally, the Rosenberg Self-Esteem Scale (RSE; Rosenberg, 1965) was most strongly correlated with the self-satisfaction subscale of the ESWLS ($r = .59$). The self-deceptive positivity subscale of the Balanced Inventory of

Desirable Responding (BIDR; Paulhus, 1991), a measure of socially desirable responding, was also significantly correlated with the self-satisfaction subscale ($r = .49$). This correlation supported Taylor and Brown's (1988) research associating well-being with self-deception.

In terms of discriminant validity, all correlations between ESWLS subscales were found to be substantially lower than their respective coefficient alpha reliability correlations, indicating internal consistency or homogeneity of items within subscales. The BIDR subscales (self-deceptive positivity and impression management) were minimally correlated with the ESWLS subscales. The self-positivity subscale was most highly correlated with the RSE and self-satisfaction subscale of the ESWLS, consistent with Taylor and Brown's (1988) research. Finally, the Agreement Response Scale (ARS; Couch & Keniston, 1960), a measure of acquiescent responding, was also administered, yielding correlations no greater than $-.16$, which was not statistically significant.

Readability. Readability of the ESWLS has also been established by using four readability formulas. Estimates yielded by these formulas suggested that individuals should have a reading level of at least the seventh grade to respond competently to the ESWLS. The ESWLS has also been translated into Spanish, although no psychometric properties have been obtained as yet.

Quality of Life Inventory

Description. The Quality of Life Inventory (QOLI™; Frisch, 1993; Frisch, Cornell, Villanueva, & Retzlaff, 1992) measures satisfaction in 17 areas of life and has been designed for use with psychiatric or clinical populations. Each area/item is rated for importance (0 to 2) and satisfaction (-3 to 3), yielding a weighted satisfaction score for each area/item that ranges from (-6 to 6) with higher scores indicating greater satisfaction. The usefulness of weighting areas/items, however, has been debated for some time (e.g., Caston & Briato, 1983; Echternacht, 1976; Friedland & Michael, 1987). Areas/items that are not important to an individual are not used to compute the overall satisfaction score (Frisch, 1993). There is also a section where individuals can rate how confident they are that satisfaction can be obtained in any life area assessed. The QOLI™ can be completed in approximately 10 minutes. The QOLI™ has recently been revised. A sample item of the QOLI™ can be found in Appendix 2-C.

Norms. Norms for the QOLI™ have been provided for clinical and nonclinical adult and college-age samples by Frisch et al. (1992). Total score means for 272 nonclinical undergraduates, 127 clinical undergraduates, 54 Veterans Administration (VA) inpatients, 51 VA recovered patients, 18 private inpatients, and 19 criminal offenders were 2.63, 1.77, .08, 2.76, .97, and 1.73, respectively. Corresponding standard deviations were 1.11, 1.62, 1.88, 1.38, 2.03, and 1.94, respectively.

Reliability. Frisch et al. (1992) reported alpha coefficients of .86, .89, .77, and .83 for total satisfaction scores for samples of VA inpatients ($n = 54$), VA recovered patients ($n = 51$), general undergraduates ($n = 272$), and counseling center undergraduates ($n = 127$), respectively. Test-retest reliability coefficients (mean number of days = 33) of .91 and .80 were reported for the VA recovered and general undergraduates samples (Frisch et al., 1992).

Validity. Frisch et al. (1992) state that the QOLI™ areas were determined after reviewing the human concerns and life satisfaction literature. The areas are health, self-regard, philosophy of life, standard of living, work, recreation, learning, creativity, social service, civic action, love relationship, friendships, relationships with children, and relationships with relatives, home, neighborhood, and community.

Validity coefficients between the QOLI™, seven measures of subjective well-being (life satisfaction), and a measure of self-efficacy ranged from .17 to −.64 for the VA inpatient, counseling center undergraduate, and general undergraduate samples (Frisch et al., 1992). All but 1 of the 15 correlations were statistically significant. In addition, QOLI™ scores were significantly negatively correlated with measures of depression, anxiety, and general psychopathology. Finally, the QOLI™ was not significantly correlated with a measure of social desirability for the VA inpatient sample but was significantly correlated with this measure ($r = .22$) for the general undergraduate sample (Frisch et al., 1992).

Comments and additional information. Given the extent of "life" difficulties put forth by independent researchers (e.g., Gortmaker, Must, Perrin, Sobol, & Dietz, 1993; Kral et al., 1992; Stunkard & Wadden, 1992; Yuker & Allison, in press) regarding the severely obese, the global measurement of life satisfaction in general and in different life domains appears imperative. The SWLS is one of the best measures of general life satisfaction while the ESWLS and QOLI™ are promising measures of various life domains and quality of life, respectively.

Additional measures of quality of life that are worthy of inspection include the variety of scales titled Quality of Life Questionnaire (QLQ; Bigelow, McFarland, & Olson, 1991; Evans, Burns, Robinson, & Garrett, 1985; Keith & Schalock, 1992; Ruiz & Baca, 1993) and the Quality of Life Scale (QOL;

Blau, 1977). The reader is directed to Andrews and Robinson (1991), Larsen, Diener, and Emmons (1985), Diener (1984), George and Bearon (1980), Andrews and Withey (1976), and Spilker (1990) for excellent reviews of subjective well-being (quality of life), its component factors, and measurement instruments.

Self-Satisfaction (Self-Esteem and Self-Concept)

Rosenberg Self-Esteem Scale

Description. The Rosenberg Self-Esteem Scale (RSE; 1965) consists of 10 items that measure global self-esteem as opposed to the often considered multidimensional construct called self-concept (Rosenberg, 1979) and is the most widely used self-esteem measure. Respondents are asked to rate the 10 items on a 4-point Likert-type scale from *strongly agree* to *strongly disagree,* yielding scores between 10 and 40, although other formats have been used (Blascovich & Tomaka, 1991). Lower scores indicate greater self-esteem. The RSE can be found in Appendix 2-D.

Norms. The RSE has been in existence for many years, and norms from many samples have been produced. Wylie (1989) reported descriptive statistics for the Guttman-scale version of the RSE based on 1,583 high school students. The mean was 1.89 with a standard deviation of 1.44 (range of 1-6). Wylie (1989) also reported that other researchers have used the RSE, but did not state descriptive statistics (e.g., Byrne & Shavelson, 1986). Curbow and Somerfield (1991) produced a summary table of descriptive statistics of several studies that used the RSE.

Reliability. Coefficient alpha for the scale on a sample of more than 5,000 high school students was .77 (Rosenberg, 1965). Several additional coefficient alphas have been reported (all ranging from .82 to .87) for different samples by other researchers (Wylie, 1989). Two-week and 7-month test-retest reliability coefficients of .85 and .73 have been reported for a sample of 28 college students and a sample of 990 Canadian high school students, respectively (Wylie, 1989).

Validity. The RSE has received substantial support as a unidimensional or single-factor scale (Blascovich & Tomaka, 1991). While other researchers have cited evidence for two-factor solutions, the scale is believed to be tapping the intended unidimensional factor proposed by Rosenberg (Wylie, 1989). Convergent and discriminant validity coefficients have been reported by Byrne and Shavelson (1986) in a multitrait-multimethod matrix for a sample of 991 Canadian high school students. Additional convergent and discriminant validity data have been reported and reviewed by Byrne (1983), indicating that the RSE is one of the most valid measures of global self-esteem. Blascovich and Tomaka (1991) also reviewed the RSE and highly recommended it as a unidimensional measure of self-esteem.

Self-Description Questionnaire III

Description. The Self-Description Questionnaire III (SDQ III; Marsh & O'Neill, 1984) is based on the multifactorial theoretical models of self-concept put forth by Shavelson, Hubner, and Stanton (1976). Among the 13 factors is a general self scale that is similar to the RSE. The SDQ III is appropriate for adolescents and young adults but may not be suitable for older adults. It is composed of 136 items and respondents are asked to rate on an 8-point scale the degree to which they believe the statement is true or false about themselves (Marsh & O'Neill, 1984) with higher scores indicating greater self-esteem.

The SDQ III is closely related to the Self-Description Questionnaire (SDQ; Marsh, Relich, & Smith, 1983) for elementary school students and the Self-Description Questionnaire II (SDQ II; Marsh, 1987) for high school students. Sample items from the SDQ III can be found in Appendix 2-E.

Norms. Marsh (1991) provides *t* scores and percentile ranks for males and females as well as by age for each of the SDQ III domains. These data are based on the combined normative sample.

Reliability. Marsh and O'Neill (1984) reported alpha coefficients ranging from .75 to .95 for 12 of the subscales (median $r = .88$) for a sample of 296 girls (Sample 1) and from .74 to .95 for all 13 subscales (median $r = .90$) for a sample of 151 college/university students (Sample 2). Marsh, Richards, and Barnes (1986) reported 1-month test-retest reliability coefficients ranging from .76 to .94 (median $r = .87$) for a sample of 229 "Outward Bound" individuals.

Validity. Several factor analyses were performed to determine the final items of the SDQ III and to obtain construct validity data (Wylie, 1989). Marsh and O'Neill (1984) conducted conventional and confirmatory factor analyses on item responses from a single sample. Conventional factor analysis yielded consistently high target loadings (with 90% ≥ .50, median = .67) and consistently low nontarget loadings (with 98% ≥ .20, median = .02). Confirmatory analysis yielded large, statistically significant factor loadings. These factor analyses were also conducted on a second independent sample yielding similar results (Marsh, Barnes, & Hocevar, 1985; Marsh & O'Neill, 1984). Further factorial validity is provided by Byrne (1988a, 1988b).

Convergent validity coefficients ranged from .33 to .90 between SDQ III factor scores and summary description scores, which were one-sentence statements that thoroughly described each factor, for both samples (Marsh & O'Neill, 1984; Marsh et al., 1985). Convergent validity coefficients between self-report ratings and ratings made by persons familiar with the first sample ranged from .31 to .79 (Marsh & O'Neill, 1984; Marsh et al., 1985). Discriminant validity data were reported by Marsh and O'Neill (1984) for both samples in multitrait-multimethod matrices. The mean correlation for SDQ III scores was .08 (heterotrait-monomethod) and the mean correlation for summary ratings was .15 (heterotrait-heteromethod) for the first sample. For the second sample, most heterotrait-monomethod and all heterotrait-heteromethod correlations were smaller than the convergent validity correlations.

Comments and additional information. There are data to support the contention that, as a partial result of prejudice and discrimination, obese persons in general have lower self-esteem (e.g., Allon, 1982; Stein, 1987) and that self-esteem improves after significant weight loss (Gentry, Halverson, & Heisler, 1984). Hsu (1990) discusses the negative consequences regarding the relationship between self-concept and physical attractiveness for anorexic females, which represents the other extreme of weight-related disorders. Therefore this dimension of satisfaction is important to address.

The self-satisfaction domain produced the largest number of measurement instruments as well as a great amount of theoretical literature. Much of this literature is applied to children and their development of self-concept. There appears to be at least moderate similarity in the hierarchical or additive conceptualization of self-concept and subjective well-being, because both involve subjective judgments about oneself with respect to various aspects of one's life.

The RSE has been one of the most frequently used measures of self-esteem that can be used with many age groups from adolescents to the elderly (Wylie, 1989). It is strongly recommended as a measure of global self-esteem for research and clinical purposes. Marsh and colleagues have conducted considerable research with respect to the SDQ III's psychometric properties and clinical utility (Byrne, 1988a, 1988b; Byrne & Shavelson, 1986; Marsh & O'Neill, 1984; Marsh et al., 1985). Wylie (1989) offers a complete summary of the SDQ III. The SDQ III is perhaps the most psychometrically sound self-concept questionnaire available for adolescents and young adults and can provide a wealth of information. Reviews of theory, research, and various measures of self-esteem and self-concept are available (Blascovich & Tomaka, 1991; Byrne, 1983; Marsh, 1987; Marsh et al., 1985; Shavelson et al., 1976; Wylie, 1989).

Job Satisfaction

Hoppock Job Satisfaction Blank

Description. Hoppock's job satisfaction questionnaire (Hoppock, 1935) is a four-item measure that yields a global job satisfaction score as the sum of the ratings of these items on a 7-point response format (Hoppock, 1935). Scores range from 4 to 28 with higher scores indicating greater job satisfaction. Hoppock's measure can be found in Appendix 2-F.

Norms. McNichols, Stahl, and Manley (1978) reported descriptive statistics for four studies involving 30,000 employees. Means were 21.25, 19.31, 17.69, and 15.87 for 360 managers, 17,110 civil servants, 10,996 military personnel, and 628 other military personnel, respectively. Corresponding standard deviations were 2.73, 4.07, 4.98, and 5.08, respectively. Cook, Hepworth, Wall, and Warr (1981) provide a list of additional studies that have used Hoppock's measure.

Reliability. McNichols et al. (1978) reported alpha coefficients ranging from .76 to .89 for samples of managers ($n = 360$), Department of Defense civil service employees ($n = 17,110$), various military personnel ($n = 10,996$), and military personnel in a strategic missile wing ($n = 628$). Test-retest reliability coefficients were not reported.

Validity. McNichols et al. (1978) provided various data regarding the validity of Hoppock's measure. First, significantly higher satisfaction scores were obtained for those individuals who had higher level positions within each sample. Second, principal components analysis yielded a general factor that explained from 58% to 76% of the total variance in the four samples with factor loadings ranging from .65 to .92 across samples. Third, Hoppock's measure was significantly correlated with a multifaceted job satisfaction measure and with expressed career intent for the third sample.

Job Descriptive Index

Description. The Job Descriptive Index (JDI; Smith, Kendall, & Hulin, 1969) consists of five dimensions of the job including work, supervision, coworkers, pay, and promotion. A list of adjectives or phrases (ranging from 9 to 18; total = 72) is provided for each dimension, in which respondents are asked if the word or phrase applies to that particular aspect of the individual's job by stating yes, no, or question mark (?) (Smith et al., 1969). Scores can be calculated for each subscale as well as the total scale, with higher scores indicating greater satisfaction.

Responses of "yes" are scored with a 3, "?" with a 1, and "no" with a 0 for positive items, and vice versa for negative items. The JDI is not a direct measure of satisfaction, as it asks individuals to describe their work rather than to state how satisfied they are with their jobs (Smith et al., 1969). Development of the JDI is clearly described by Smith et al. (1969). Sample items from the JDI can be found in Appendix 2-G.

Norms. Smith et al. (1969) provides norms for 1,951 and 636 male and female employees, respectively. Means of the five subscales for men and women, respectively, were 36.57 and 35.74 (Work), 29.90 and 27.90 (Pay), 22.06 and 17.77 (Promotion), 41.10 and 41.13 (Supervision), and 43.49 and 42.09 (Coworkers). Corresponding standard deviations were 10.54 and 9.88 (Work), 14.53 and 13.65 (Pay), 15.77 and 13.38 (Promotion), 10.58 and 10.05 (Supervision), and 10.02 and 10.51 (Coworkers). The JDI has been used extensively during the past 20 years, producing additional descriptive statistics that have been summarized in tabular form by Cook et al. (1981).

Reliability. Smith et al. (1969) reported corrected split-half correlations ≥ .80 for a sample of 80 male electric plant employees. Johnson, Smith, and Tucker (1982) reported coefficient alphas ranging from .75 to .91 and from .80 to .93 for two samples of 50 psychology students. Three-week test-retest reliability coefficients ranging from .68 to .88 and from .70 to .78 were obtained for these samples, respectively.

Validity. Smith et al. (1969) describe in detail their method of validation of the JDI, which was conducted with data from over 400 subjects. Several factor analyses were performed with these data, generally supporting the structure of the JDI. Smith et al. (1969) also provide correlational convergent and discriminant validity in support of the JDI. Smith, Smith, and Rollo (1974) conducted factor analyses for samples of white and black civil service employees that resulted in similar factor structure across groups.

Gillet and Schwab (1975) used multitrait-multimethod and analysis of variance procedures with data from 273 production employees in which strong evidence of convergent and discriminant validity of the JDI was found. Correlations ranging from .49 to .70 were reported between scales common to the JDI and the Minnesota Satisfaction Questionnaire. The correlation matrix indicated that all convergent validity correlations exceeded both heterotrait-heteromethod values and heterotrait-monomethod values demonstrating discriminant validity. Johnson et al. (1982) also used multi-trait-multimethod and analysis of variance procedures to obtain convergent and discriminant validity data using a total sample of 200 students. All criteria regarding significant convergent and discriminant validity correlations were met.

Minnesota Satisfaction Questionnaire

Description. The Minnesota Satisfaction Questionnaire (MSQ; Weiss, Dawis, England, & Lofquist, 1967) is composed of 20 subscales or what have been called "job reinforcers" such as work conditions, variety, achievement, and compensation. Each job reinforcer consists of 5 items, yielding a total of 100 items for the MSQ. Individuals are asked to rate their degree of satisfaction with each item on a 5-point Likert-type scale from *very satisfied* to *very dissatisfied.* Scores are obtained by summing responses to the items of each scale.

General job satisfaction is assessed by summing those items that have the highest item-scale correlation from each subscale. This 20-item scale can be used as a short-form MSQ and yields intrinsic, extrinsic, and general satisfaction scores, which range from 12 to 60, 6 to 30, and 20 to 100, respectively. Higher scores indicate greater job satisfaction. The MSQ can be completed within 20 minutes and requires a fifth-grade reading level. The short-form MSQ can be found in Appendix 2-H.

Norms. Weiss et al. (1967) discuss the development of the MSQ and its item content and provide normative data for 25 separate occupational groups. Norms for the short form included means and standard deviations for the three satisfaction scores for 1,723 employees. They were 74.85 ($SD = 11.92$), 47.14 ($SD = 7.42$), and 19.98 ($SD = 4.78$), respectively (Weiss et al., 1967).

Reliability. Weiss et al. (1967) reported a range of coefficient alphas of .78 to .93 for 21 scales of the MSQ (the 21st scale represents the general satisfaction scale) for 25 occupational groups. The median coefficient alpha was .86. One-week test-retest reliability coefficients ranged from .66 to .91 for the 20 job reinforcer scales (a median coefficient of .83) and a coefficient of .89 for the general satisfaction scale. Rentsch and Steel (1992) reported an alpha coefficient of .88 for the short form for a sample of 60 graduate students.

Validity. Factor analysis of the 20 scales with a sample of 1,800 employees resulted in two factors labeled intrinsic and extrinsic satisfaction. Median communality was .54 with a median reliability coefficient of .88. Factor analysis of the 20-item MSQ with a sample of 1,460 employees also yielded two factors, and item intercorrelations ranged from .16 to .73 (median $r = .32$).

Significant differences among the means of the 25 occupational groups, with professional groups indicating higher satisfaction scores than unskilled workers, were obtained supporting concurrent validity (Weiss et al., 1967). Convergent and discriminant validity data were reported by Gillet and Schwab (1975) in a multitrait-multimethod matrix with the JDI (see the JDI "Validity" section). Finally, Rentsch and Steel (1992) reported correlations of .77 between the short-form MSQ and the JDI and of .70 with Andrews and Withey's (1976) job satisfaction questionnaire.

Comments and additional information. Job discrimination against obese persons in the forms of dismissals, lower wages, and lack of hirings/promotions has been recognized for years in the scientific literature as well as in personal accounts (Brink, 1988; Matusewitch, 1983; "Obesity Doesn't Mean," 1993; Rothblum, Brand, Miller, & Oetjen, 1990). Moreover, job satisfaction and the ability to keep a job increase after significant weight loss (e.g., Crisp, Kalucy, & Pilkington, 1977). Consequently, measurement of job satisfaction among obese persons, in particular, is important.

This domain of satisfaction represented an area that has been and continues to be researched extensively, especially with respect to overall quality of life and life satisfaction. Hoppock's job satisfaction questionnaire is a good, quick measure of global job satisfaction that is worthy of inspection. Despite data reported by Ferratt, Dunham, and Pierce (1981) that call into question the discriminant validity of the JDI and MSQ, and from Buckley, Carraher, and Cote (1992) that question the construct validity of the JDI, these two scales represent the most frequently used multifaceted job satisfaction instruments in industry and have received generally favorable reviews.

Discussions of the construct of job satisfaction, other measures of facet and global job satisfaction, and related topics are available (Andrews & Withey, 1976; Brayfield & Rothe, 1951; Cook et al., 1981; Dawis, 1987; Dawis & Lofquist, 1984; Hoppock, 1935; Ironson, Smith, Bronnick, Gibson, & Paul, 1989; Scarpello & Campbell, 1983; Smith et al., 1969).

School Satisfaction

Perceived Quality of Academic Life Scale

Description. The Perceived Quality of Academic Life (PQAL; Okun, Kardash, Stock, Sandler, & Baumann, 1986; Staats & Partlo, 1990) is a school satisfaction scale in which students rate six items using the 7-point *delighted* to *terrible* scale developed by Andrews and Withey (1976). The PQAL items were chosen via factor analyses (Okun et al., 1986) of the Feelings About College Scale developed by Sandler (FAC; 1981). Scores on the PQAL range from 1 to 42 with lower scores indicating greater school satisfaction. The PQAL can be found in Appendix 2-I.

Norms. Okun et al. (1986) provided descriptive statistics for four samples (*ns* ranging from 63 to 400) of undergraduates. Means and standard deviations of 15.52 (*SD* = 4.88), 17.69 (*SD* = 5.31), 16.43 (*SD* = 3.47), and 17.36 (*SD* = 5.59) were reported.

Reliability. Coefficient alphas ranged from .74 to .86 with a median estimate of .83 for four undergraduate samples from the Southwest (Okun et al., 1986). Sample 3 received the PQAL 2 weeks later and a .70 test-retest reliability coefficient was obtained. Staats and Partlo (1990) reported a 10-week test-retest reliability coefficient of .43 for a sample of mostly white college students from a midwestern university.

Validity. Okun et al. (1986) conducted two principal components analyses using varimax rotations on the FAC with samples of 195 and 400. The first factor for each sample yielded the same six items, which were then called the PQAL. The PQAL correlated –.62 with the Quality of Education subscale of the College Student Satisfaction Questionnaire (CSSQ-QE; Starr, Betz, & Menne, 1983) and –.27 with the Social Life subscale of the CSSQ (Okun et al., 1986) providing adequate convergent validity evidence.

Staats and Partlo (1990) used three samples of mostly white college students from a southwestern university to provide validity data for the PQAL. A range of correlations from –.27 to –.34 between the PQAL and a measure of intent to get a college degree were reported for the three samples. Additional ranges of correlations for these samples were –.18 to –.29 between the PQAL and the SWLS and –.33 to –.66 between the PQAL and the Satisfaction with School Scale (SWSS; Staats, 1983). All correlations were negative because low scores on the PQAL represent higher satisfaction.

Comments and additional information. The review of the school satisfaction domain yielded minimal measures and discussions of the construct, even though education is purportedly valued by most individuals in this country. It appears that level of educational attainment is the more carefully studied construct. Perhaps more research should be devoted to school satisfaction and its relationship to dependent variables, especially given that evidence exists that obese persons are discriminated against academically and financially in school (e.g., Crandall, 1991) and that overweight women complete fewer years of school than normal weight women or those with other chronic health conditions (Gortmaker et al., 1993). Staats and Partlo (1990), Okun et al. (1986), and Starr et al. (1983) are good starting points for the interested reader.

Family Satisfaction

Kansas Family Life Satisfaction Scale

Description. The Kansas Family Life Satisfaction Scale (KFLS; Schumm, McCollum, Bugaighis, Jurich, & Bollman, 1986) is a four-item family satisfaction scale in which individuals indicate their degree of satisfaction on a 7-point Likert-type scale from *extremely dissatisfied* to *extremely satisfied* (Schumm, McCollum, et al., 1986). Higher scores indicate greater satisfaction. The four items pertain to family life in general, parents' relationship, relationship of parents with children, and relationship of siblings.

Those who provided the preliminary data for the KFLS were 620 families from 12 states participating in a study of differences in perceived quality of life between rural and urban areas. All families had at least one adolescent member and the parents' marriage was of at least 13 years. The KFLS can be found in Appendix 2-J.

Norms. Schumm, McCollum, et al. (1986) provided means and standard deviations for fathers, mothers, and adolescents from 620 families. They were 24.19 ($SD = 3.46$), 24.44 ($SD = 3.16$), and 23.52 ($SD = 3.94$), respectively. Additional norms for 182 individuals were provided by McCollum, Schumm, and Russell (1988). The mean (based on a different scoring system) for these individuals was 6.68 ($SD = 2.33$). Higher scores for this sample indicated less satisfaction.

Reliability. Coefficient alpha for 12 items (4 items for each of three family members) was .85. No test-retest data were reported.

Validity. Schumm, McCollum, et al. (1986) cite correlations of the KFLS with satisfaction with a single-item measure of quality of life, a measure of perceived locus of control, and religiosity as evidence of construct validity. Significant correlations of .46, .46, and .50 were reported between the KFLS with the single quality of life item for fathers, mothers, and adolescents, respectively. Locus of control was significantly correlated with the KFLS for mothers, $r = .36$, and for fathers, $r = .36$. Negative correlations of $-.11$, $-.12$, and

−.18 were obtained for fathers, mothers, and adolescents, respectively, between the KFLS and religiosity.

Family Adaptability and Cohesion Evaluation Scales III

Description. The Family Adaptability and Cohesion Evaluation Scales III (FACES III; Olson, Portner, & Lavee, 1985) is a 20-item self-report questionnaire that conceptualizes satisfaction as the discrepancy between perceived and ideal evaluations of families with greater discrepancy indicating less family satisfaction. It represents the newest available version of scales developed by Olson and colleagues, which taps cohesion and adaptability as orthogonal factors and is part of a theoretical framework called the Circumplex Model (Olson, 1986).

Final items were selected from a pool of items used in a national survey of 1,000 "normal" families. The FACES III can be used for research and clinical purposes with many different types of families. The FACES III has two scales called "perceived" and "ideal," each consisting of 20 items that each family member completes.

The FACES II rather than the FACES III can be found in Appendix 2-K because Olson prefers that individuals use FACES II as it has certain advantages over FACES III and as FACES IV is in preparation. Although FACES II does not yield a satisfaction score, some clinicians and researchers may choose to use it. All data presented here pertain to FACES III (see Olson, Portner, & Bell, 1982, for information regarding FACES II).

Norms. Norms are available based on 2,453 adults across the life cycle, 412 adolescents, and several types of problem families. Cutoff scores are also available for the various adaptability and cohesion dimensions.

Reliability. Coefficient alphas of .77, .62, and .68 for cohesion, adaptability, and total scores, respectively, were obtained. Test-retest reliabilities were not reported. Perosa and Perosa (1990), using a sample of 183 high school and university students, reported internal consistency coefficients of .89 and .71 for the cohesion and adaptability scales, respectively.

Validity. Validity data include a small insignificant correlation between the cohesion and adaptability scales, small correlations with social desirability ($r = .00$ for cohesion and $r = .39$ for adaptability), and family member correlations of .41 and .25 for cohesion and adaptability, respectively, which represent some convergent and discriminant validity evidence.

Perosa and Perosa (1990) reported significant convergent validity coefficients ranging from .59 to .86 for cohesion and from −.17 to .53 for adaptability between the FACES III subscales and several other measures of these constructs. The FACES III subscales were found to correlate significantly but were of low magnitude ($r = .33$). The authors report that the discriminant validity of the FACES III was "upheld." Edman, Cole, and Howard (1990) also provide validity data in support of the FACES III.

Comments and additional information. Family satisfaction is an important variable to measure among families that include an individual with an eating disorder, especially those with children who are obese, anorexic, or bulimic. Research has shown that families may hold negative attitudes toward these children, and negative interaction patterns may be produced (Banis et al., 1988; Wallander et al., 1988). In addition, links between family pathology and later eating disorders have been documented (e.g., Yager, 1982).

Although the KFLS is limited because it is applicable to families of four or more unless the sibling item is deleted, there seems to be no other "pure" family satisfaction measure in existence. That is, a scale that purports and does measure global family satisfaction. While Olson's conceptualization has been criticized (Green, Harris, Forte, & Robinson, 1991), the FACES III and its predecessors have been widely used for years (Daley, Sowers-Hoag, & Thyer, 1990). Much of the supporting data for the FACES III, however, involves the subscales rather than the satisfaction index. One may want to review all of the FACES instruments so as to make a more informed decision regarding the selection of one of them.

An instrument worthy of note is the Family Environment Scale (FES; Moos & Moos, 1986), which measures the social environment of the family, even though it does not purport to measure satisfaction. Further information regarding family satisfaction and assessment can be found in Margolin and Fernandez (1983), Fredman and Sherman (1987), and Olson (1988).

Marital/Relationship Satisfaction

Kansas Marital Satisfaction Scale

Description. The Kansas Marital Satisfaction Scale (KMS; Schumm, Nichols, Shectman, & Grigsby, 1983) is a three-item global marital satisfaction scale in which individuals indicate their degree of satisfaction on a 7-point Likert-type scale from *extremely dissatisfied* to *extremely satisfied,* yielding scores between 3 and 21, with higher scores indicating greater marital satisfaction. The KMS evolved from studies of perceived quality of life in Kansas communities in 1977 and 1978 (Schumm et al., 1983). The items simply ask how satisfied one is with one's partner as a spouse, with one's marriage, and with the relationship with one's partner (Schumm et al., 1983). The KMS can be found in Appendix 2-L.

Norms. Descriptive statistics for the KMS have been provided by Schumm et al. (1983), who reported means and standard deviations of 17.97 ($SD =$ 2.74) and 17.43 ($SD = 3.15$) for 79 husbands and wives, respectively. Additional descriptive statistics for various samples are also available (e.g., Shectman, Bergen, Schumm, & Bugaighis, 1985).

Reliability. In a sample of 51 wives from Kansas, an alpha coefficient of .92 was obtained by Grover, Paff-Bergen, Russell, and Schumm (1984). Shectman et al. (1985) sampled 61 women attending childbirth classes in Kansas and obtained an alpha coefficient of .90. A 10-week test-retest reliability coefficient of .71 was reported by Mitchell, Newell, and Schumm (1983) for a sample of 106 mothers.

Validity. Schumm et al. (1983) found that, although marital satisfaction was significantly correlated with marital social desirability (i.e., being happily married is socially desirable), $r = .41$, it was not significantly correlated with individual social desirability, $r = .05$. Individual correlations ranging from .39 to .75 were obtained between the satisfaction items of the Dyadic Adjustment Scale (DAS; Spanier, 1976) and the KMS (Grover et al., 1984). Shectman et al. (1985) found marital satisfaction to be significantly correlated with two additional items involving husband support and parent behavior ($r = .50$ and $r = .46$, respectively).

Further concurrent and discriminant validity were provided by Schumm, Paff-Bergen, et al. (1986) with a sample of 61 women from Kansas. The KMS correlated significantly with the DAS, $r = .83$, and with the Quality Marriage Index (QMI; Norton, 1983), $r = .91$. Additionally, the KMS correlated significantly more with the satisfaction subscale of the DAS than with the affection or consensus subscales. The KMS (as well as the other satisfaction scales) was significantly correlated with marital social desirability, a finding similar to that of Schumm et al. (1983).

In an attempt to rule out common method variance, Schumm, Paff-Bergen, et al. (1986) asked participants to indicate their satisfaction with items believed to have no relation to marital satisfaction such as the weather and politics. Although correlations were significant, they were often low in magnitude and less than these items with the other marital satisfaction scales and Locke-Wallace Marital Adjustment Test (LMAT; Locke & Wallace, 1959).

Dyadic Adjustment Scale

Description. The Dyadic Adjustment Scale (DAS; Spanier, 1976) is a 32-item, four-facet marital satisfaction scale that can be used with married and unmarried cohabiting couples (Spanier, 1976). Higher scores indicate better adjustment. The 32 items were selected after analyses revealed that they differentiated between married and divorced individuals. Subscale scores and a total scale score that ranges from 0 to 151 can be obtained. Sample items from the DAS can be found in Appendix 2-M.

Norms. Spanier (1976) reported total score means of 114.8 ($SD = 17.8$) and 70.7 ($SD = 23.8$) for 218 married and 94 divorced couples, respectively. Sharpley and Cross (1982) obtained a mean of 108.5 with a standard deviation of 19.7 for 95 married couples.

Reliability. Coefficient alphas ranged from .73 to .94 for the subscales, and alpha for the total scale was .96 (Spanier, 1976). Two-week test-retest reliability evidence has been provided by Carey, Spector, Lantinga, and Krauss (1993), who reported coefficients ranging from .75 to .87 for all scores for 107 men and women.

Validity. Early factor analyses conducted with data from 218 white, married individuals and 94 white, divorced individuals indicated four factors that were labeled consensus, cohesion, satisfaction, and affection (Spanier, 1976). This factor structure was later supported by Spanier and Thompson (1982). Concurrent validity has been supported by correlations ranging from .86 to .88 with the LMAT, which had been the most frequently used measure of marital satisfaction before the DAS (Kazak, Jarmas, & Snitzer, 1988).

Despite the persuasive data provided by Spanier and associates (Spanier, 1976; Spanier & Thompson, 1982) in support of the factor structure of the DAS, data from other studies have not been as supportive (Norton, 1983; Sharpley & Cross, 1982). Recently Kazak et al. (1988) conducted separate factor analyses for women ($n = 219$) and men ($n = 190$) on data obtained in studies of family stress and coping. The solutions indicated that one factor accounted for approximately 75% of the variance for women and approximately 78% of the variance for men. The items constituting these factors were not identical and the authors concluded that "the results of factor analyses of the DAS indicate weak support for the presence of four subscales" (Kazak et al., 1988, p. 89).

Comments and additional information. This domain produced a large number of scales and a great amount of literature, which is probably due, in part, to evidence supporting greater physical and psychological health among happily married couples (Gove, Hughes, & Style, 1983). Marital satisfaction improves in relationships where surgical treatment for obesity has taken place, especially when the marriage was unconflicted before surgery (Rand & Macgregor, 1990). Moreover, S. W. Foster (1986) revealed that marital therapy is a valid treatment (i.e., leads to greater satisfaction) for relationships in which an eating disorder is present. Finally, there are data indicating that men and women who had been overweight as adolescents or young adults are less likely to be married as adults than their nonoverweight cohort (Gortmaker et al., 1993).

The psychometric properties of the KMS have been researched fairly well and this instrument represents a viable, short, global marital satisfaction scale. The DAS has received considerable attention in the marital and family literature and, despite some contradictory evidence regarding its factor structure, it still represents one of the most frequently used multifaceted marital satisfaction scales (Kazak et al., 1988).

Additional noteworthy scales include the LMAT by Locke and Wallace (1959), QMI (Norton, 1983), Marital Satisfaction Scale (MSS; Roach, Frazier, & Bowden, 1981), Marital Satisfaction Inventory (MSI; Snyder, 1979; Snyder, Wills, & Keiser, 1981), and ENRICH Marital Inventory (EMI; Fowers & Olson, 1989). Reviews of the marital satisfaction construct and scales are available (e.g., Burnett, 1987; Fredman & Sherman, 1987; Snyder, 1979; Spanier, 1979; Spanier & Lewis, 1980).

Sex Satisfaction

Index of Sexual Satisfaction

Description. The Index of Sexual Satisfaction (ISS; Hudson, Harrison, & Crosscup, 1981) is a 25-item questionnaire designed to measure overall sex satisfaction with one's relationship. Responses range from rarely or none of the time to most or all of the time. The items were selected based on "clinical and personal experience" (Hudson et al., 1981). There are positively and negatively worded items of which the positive items must be reverse-scored yielding a range of scores from 0 to 100. Higher scores indicate less satisfaction. Reliability and validity data regarding the ISS on three separate samples were reported by Hudson et al. (1981). These samples consisted of 378 individuals participating in a study of affective and interpersonal disorders, 689 persons participating in a study regarding person and social functioning, and 100 persons seeking counseling for relationship difficulties. The ISS can be found in Appendix 2-N.

Norms. Although Hudson et al. (1981) obtained psychometric data for three samples, they reported a means and a standard deviation for 100 persons seeking counseling. This sample was divided into problem and no-problem groups. Means for these groups were 41.5 and 15.2, respectively. A combined standard deviation of 11.28 was reported.

Reliability. Coefficient alphas ranged from .91 to .93 for the three heterogenous samples with an average alpha of .92 (Hudson et al., 1981). A one-week test-retest reliability coefficient of .93 was obtained with a sample of social work graduate students.

Validity. Hudson et al. (1981) demonstrated discriminant validity using the clinical sample of 100 persons. This sample completed the ISS, a marital satisfaction index, a sexual attitude scale, and a social background questionnaire. Significant mean differences between the "sex problem" and "no sex problem" groups were obtained for the ISS and the marital satisfaction index.

Squared point biserial correlations between these scales and the criterion variable were also reported. The difference between the squared correlations of the ISS ($r^2 = .58$) and the marital satisfaction index ($r^2 = .27$) was significant. Hudson et al. (1981) state that construct validity of the ISS is supported because the ISS correlates more highly with a criterion variable than two other variables also related to the criterion but to a significantly lesser degree. Hudson et al. (1981) report that a score of 28 to 30 can serve as a clinical cutoff score with an overall error rate of 13% to 14%, further supporting the discriminant validity of the ISS.

Factorial validity of the ISS was demonstrated by using multiple groups factor analysis by combining all three samples and examining the correlations of ISS items with total scores of several scales and demographic variables (Hudson et al., 1981). According to Hudson, all but four ISS items demonstrate good convergent and discriminant validity "since they correlate highly with the total score they are supposed to correlate with, less highly with the total scores for the other scales, and very low with the measures they should not correlate with" (Hudson et al., 1981, p. 169).

Finally, Hudson et al. (1981) reported moderately significant correlations between the ISS and the IMS ($r = .68$), a depression scale ($r = .47$), and a self-esteem scale ($r = .44$). Small correlations that were not significant were obtained between the ISS and the SAS ($r = .14$), gender ($r = .01$), age ($r = -.06$), education ($r = -.10$), and income ($r = .01$).

Comments and additional information. Hsu (1990) reported that recovering anorexic women had better psychosexual adjustment than those who did not recover and suggested that some researchers have linked fear of sexuality with the development of anorexia later in life. Stunkard and Wadden (1992) stated: "Both the frequency of sexual relations and the satisfaction that they engender are increased" (p. 529) after surgical treatment of obesity. Therefore this is another area worthy of assessment for individuals with eating disorders.

This domain yielded few pure sex satisfaction scales that have demonstrated adequate psychometric properties or extensive use. This was also noted by Alfonso et al. (1992). The ISS is certainly worthy of inspection and use depending on the nature of one's study. Sexual satisfaction scales related to specific acts are available (A. L. Foster, 1977; LoPiccolo & Lobitz, 1973; Whitley & Paulsen, 1975) as well as global sexual satisfaction scales that are included as subscales in longer measures of sexual functioning (Derogatis, 1978; LoPiccolo & Steger, 1974). Conte (1983) offers a review of measures of sexual functioning that may be useful.

Social Life/Leisure Satisfaction

Leisure Satisfaction Scale

Description. The Leisure Satisfaction Scale (LSS; Beard & Ragheb, 1980) is a 51-item scale that measures "the extent to which individuals perceive that certain personal needs are met or satisfied through leisure activities" (Beard & Ragheb, 1980, p. 22). It is rated on a 5-point Likert-type scale from *almost never true for you* to *almost always true for you* (yielding a score range of 51 to 255) and can be completed in approximately 20 minutes. Higher scores indicate less satisfaction. There is also a short version consisting of 24 items that is sometimes referred to as the Leisure Satisfaction Index (LSI). Sample items from the LSS can be found in Appendix 2-O.

Norms. Beard and Ragheb (1980) reported a mean of 137.17 and a standard deviation of 27.24 for the LSS for 347 students. Riddick (1986) reported means and standard deviations of the LSI for 400 individuals divided into 10 age groups but did not, however, report a total mean and standard deviation.

Reliability. A sample of 600 students, full-time and part-time employees, and retired workers as well as a second sample of 347 students completed the LSS. Coefficient alpha for the entire scale was .93 and alphas ranged from .76 to .86 for the six subscales for the first sample. Coefficient alpha for the total scale was .96 and alphas ranged from .85 to .92 for the subscales for the second sample (Beard & Ragheb, 1980).

Validity. Content validity consisted of item ratings by 160 experts and judges from the Society of Park and Recreation Educators. Original items were tapped from literature on leisure behavior that were relevant to the construct of leisure satisfaction. Based on the first sample mentioned above, six components of leisure satisfaction were identified through principal components factor analyses using both orthogonal and oblique rotations. These components were labeled psychological, educational, social, relaxation, physiological, and aesthetic.

After these preliminary factor analyses, 51 items remained. The scale was then administered to the second sample mentioned above. Factor analyses were also conducted with this sample using both orthogonal and oblique rotations. The factor structure was similar to that found with the first sample. Subscale intercorrelations ranged from .38 to .66 with a median correlation of .52.

Comments and additional information. Even though leisure time appears to be a very important part of American life, with considerable available literature (e.g., Beard & Ragheb, 1980; Iso-Ahola, 1979; Ragheb & Beard, 1980; Trafton & Tinsley, 1980; see the *Journal of Leisure Research*), this area produced the least amount of measurement instruments. Social life satisfaction or satisfaction with friendships yielded no relevant publications regarding measurement.

This area, in particular, may be important to measure among individuals with eating disorders given the physiological relationship between weight and activity. Indeed, Stunkard and Wadden (1992) summarized several outcome studies that indicated greater increased stamina and mobility as well as participation in previously unattempted activities after weight-loss surgery.

There is at least one scale that measures satisfaction with social support, called the Social Support Questionnaire, by Sarason, Levine, Basham, and Sarason (1983), which may be useful. Studies by Iso-Ahola and Buttimer (1982), Riddick (1986), Paul, Smith, Tisak, and Cranny (1991), and Russell (1987) provide some additional psychometric data for the LSS or LSI.

Concluding Remarks

In this chapter, measures of quality of life, subjective well-being, and life satisfaction have been reviewed. The instruments presented here are certainly worthy of examination by researchers and clinicians, but the final decision regarding their use should be made after considering additional factors. The areas presented in this chapter cover several major domains of life and represent a good "jumping off point" when attempting to quantify these complex constructs. It is hoped that this review will also facilitate more researchers and clinicians to assess these areas, as they are related to the overall quality of life of individuals with eating disorders.

References

Alfonso, V. C., & Allison, D. B. (1992, August). *Further development of the Extended Satisfaction with Life Scale.* Paper presented at the annual meeting of the American Psychological Association, Washington, DC.

Alfonso, V. C., Allison, D. B., & Rader, D. E. (1994). *The Extended Satisfaction With Life Scale: Development and psychometric properties.* Manuscript submitted for publication.

Alfonso, V. C., Allison, D. B., & Dunn, G. M. (1992). The relationship between sexual fantasy and satisfaction: A multidimensional analysis of gender differences. *Journal of Psychology and Human Sexuality, 5,* 19-37.

Alfonso, V. C., Allison, D. B., & Rader, D. E. (1993, August). *The Extended Satisfaction With Life Scale: Convergent and discriminant validity.* Paper presented at the annual meeting of the American Psychological Association, Toronto, Canada.

Allison, D. B., Alfonso, V. C., & Dunn, G. M. (1991). The Extended Satisfaction With Life Scale. *The Behavior Therapist, 14,* 15-16.

Allison, D. B., Basile, V. C., & Yuker, H. E. (1991). The measurement of attitudes toward and beliefs about obese persons. *International Journal of Eating Disorders, 10,* 599-607.

Allon, N. (1982). The stigma of overweight in everyday life. In B. B. Wolman (Ed.), *Psychological aspects of obesity: A handbook* (pp. 130-174). New York: Van Nostrand Reinhold.

Andrews, F. M., & Robinson, J. P. (1991). Measures of subjective well-being. In J. P. Robinson, P. R. Shaver, & L. W. Wrightsman (Eds.), *Measures of personality and social psychological attitudes* (pp. 61-114). New York: Academic Press.

Andrews, F. M., & Withey, S. B. (1976). *Social indicators of well-being: Americans' perceptions of life quality.* New York: Plenum.

Arrindell, W. A., Meeuwesen, L., & Huyse, F. J. (1991). The Satisfaction With Life Scale (SWLS): Psychometric properties in a non-psychiatric medical outpatients sample. *Personality and Individual Differences, 12,* 117-123.

Banis, H. T., Varni, J. W., Wallander, J. L., Korsch, B. M., Jay, S. M., Adler, R., Garcia-Temple, E., & Negrete, V. (1988). Psychological and social adjustment of obese children and their families. *Child Care, Health, and Development, 14,* 157-173.

Beard, J. G., & Ragheb, M. G. (1980). Measuring leisure satisfaction. *Journal of Leisure Research, 12,* 20-33.

Bigelow, D. A., Brodsky, G., Stewart, L., & Olson, M. (1982). The concept and measurement of quality of life as a dependent variable in evaluation of mental health services. In G. J. Stahler & W. R. Tash (Eds.), *Innovative approaches to mental health evaluation* (pp. 345-365). New York: Academic Press.

Bigelow, D. A., McFarland, B. H., & Olson, M. M. (1991). Quality of life of community mental health program clients: Validating a measure. *Community Mental Health Journal, 27,* 43-55.

Blascovich, J., & Tomaka, J. (1991). Measures of self-esteem. In J. P. Robinson, P. R. Shaver, & L. W. Wrightsman (Eds.), *Measures of personality and social psychological attitudes* (pp. 115-160). New York: Academic Press.

Blau, T. H. (1977). Quality of life, social indicators, and criteria of change. *Professional Psychology, 8,* 464-473.

Brayfield, A. H., & Rothe, H. F. (1951). An index of job satisfaction. *Journal of Applied Psychology, 35,* 307-311.

Brink, T. L. (1988). Obesity and job discrimination: Mediation via personality stereotypes. *Perceptual and Motor Skills, 66,* 494.

Buckley, M. R., Carraher, S. M., & Cote, J. A. (1992). Measurement issues concerning the use of inventories of job satisfaction. *Educational and Psychological Measurement, 52,* 529-543.

Burnett, P. (1987). Assessing marital adjustment and satisfaction: A review. *Measurement and Evaluation in Counseling and Development, 20,* 113-121.

Byrne, B. M. (1983). Investigating measures of self-concept. *Measurement and Evaluation in Guidance, 16,* 115-126.

Byrne, B. M. (1988a). Measuring adolescent self-concept: Factorial validity and equivalency of the SDQ III across gender. *Multivariate Behavioral Research, 23,* 361-375.

Byrne, B. M. (1988b). The Self Description Questionnaire III: Testing for equivalent factorial validity across ability. *Educational and Psychological Measurement, 48,* 397-406.

Byrne, B. M., & Shavelson, R. J. (1986). On the structure of adolescent self-concept. *Journal of Educational Psychology, 78,* 474-481.

Campbell, A., Converse, P. E., & Rogers, W. L. (1976). *The quality of American life: Perceptions, evaluations, and satisfactions.* New York: Russell Sage.

Carey, M. P., Spector, I. P., Lantinga, L. J., & Krauss, D. J. (1993). Reliability of the Dyadic Adjustment Scale. *Psychological Assessment, 5,* 238-240.

Caston, R. J., & Briato, R. (1983). On the use of facet importance as a weighting component of job satisfaction. *Educational and Psychological Measurement, 43,* 339-350.

Conte, H. R. (1983). Development and use of Self-Report Techniques for assessing sexual functioning: A review and critique. *Archives of Sexual Behavior, 12,* 555-576.

Cook, J. D., Hepworth, S. J., Wall, T. D., & Warr, P. B. (1981). *The experience of work.* New York: Academic Press.

Couch, A., & Keniston, K. (1960). Yeasayers and naysayers: Agreeing response set as a personality variable. *Journal of Abnormal and Social Psychology, 60,* 151-174.

Crandall, C. S. (1991). Do heavy-weight students have more difficulty paying for college? *Personality and Social Psychology Bulletin, 17,* 606-611.

Crisp, A. H., Kalucy, R. S., & Pilkington, T. R. E. (1977). Some psychological consequences of ileojejunal bypass surgery. *American Journal of Clinical Nutrition, 30,* 109-120.

Curbow, B., & Somerfield, M. (1991). Use of the Rosenberg Self-Esteem Scale with adult cancer patients. *Journal of Psychosocial Oncology, 9,* 113-131.

Daley, J. G., Sowers-Hoag, K., & Thyer, B. A. (1990). Are FACES II "family satisfaction" scores valid? *Journal of Family Therapy, 12,* 77-81.

Dawis, R. V. (1987). The Minnesota Theory of Work Adjustment. In B. Bolton (Ed.), *Handbook of measurement and evaluation in rehabilitation* (2nd ed., pp. 203-217). Baltimore: Paul Brooks.

Dawis, R. V., & Lofquist, L. H. (1984). *A psychological theory of work adjustment.* Minneapolis: University of Minnesota Press.

Derogatis, L. R. (1978). *Derogatis Sexual Functioning Inventory* (rev. ed.). Baltimore: Johns Hopkins University.

Diener, E. (1984). Subjective well-being. *Psychological Bulletin, 95,* 542-575.

Diener, E., Emmons, R. A., Larsen, R. J., & Griffin, S. (1985). The Satisfaction With Life Scale. *Journal of Personality Assessment, 49,* 71-75.

Diener, E., & Larsen, R. J. (1993). The experience of emotional well-being. In M. Lewis & J. M. Haviland (Eds.), *Handbook of emotions* (pp. 405-415). New York: Guilford.

Echternacht, G. (1976). Reliability and validity of item option weighting schemes. *Educational and Psychological Measurement, 36,* 301-309.

Edman, S. O., Cole, D. A., & Howard, G. S. (1990). Convergent and discriminant validity of FACES III: Family adaptability and cohesion. *Family Process, 29,* 95-103.

Evans, D. R., Burns, J. E., Robinson, W. E., & Garrett, O. J. (1985). The Quality of Life Questionnaire: A multidimensional measure. *American Journal of Community Psychology, 13,* 305-322.

Ferratt, T. W., Dunham, R. B., & Pierce, J. L. (1981). Self-report measures of job characteristics and affective responses: An examination of discriminant validity. *Academy of Management Journal, 24*(4), 780-794.

Foster, A. L. (1977). The Sexual Compatibility Test. *Journal of Consulting and Clinical Psychology, 45,* 332-333.

Foster, S. W. (1986). Marital treatment of eating disorders. In N. S. Jacobson & A. S. Gurman (Eds.), *Clinical handbook of marital therapy* (pp. 575-593). New York: Guilford.

Fowers, B. J., & Olson, D. H. (1989). ENRICH Marital Inventory: A discriminant validity and cross-validation assessment. *Journal of Marriage and Family Therapy, 15,* 65-79.

Frank, E. S. (1991). Shame and guilt in eating disorders. *American Journal of Orthopsychiatry, 61,* 303-306.

Fredman, N., & Sherman, R. (1987). *Handbook of measurements for marriage and family therapy.* New York: Brunner/Mazel.

Friedland, D. L., & Michael, W. B. (1987). The reliability of a promotional job knowledge examination scored by number of items right and by four confidence weighting procedures and its corresponding concurrent validity estimates relative to performance criterion ratings. *Educational and Psychological Measurement, 47,* 179-188.

Frisch, M. B. (1993). The Quality of Life Inventory: A cognitive-behavioral tool for complete problem assessment, treatment planning, and outcome evaluation. *The Behavior Therapist, 16,* 42-44.

Frisch, M. B., Cornell, J., Villanueva, M., & Retzlaff, P. J. (1992). Clinical validation of the Quality of Life Inventory: A measure of life satisfaction for use in treatment planning and outcome assessment. *Psychological Assessment, 4,* 92-101.

Gentry, K., Halverson, J. D., & Heisler, S. (1984). Psychological assessment of morbidly obese patients undergoing gastric bypass: A comparison of preoperative and postoperative adjustment. *Surgery, 95,* 215-220.

George, L. K., & Bearon, L. B. (1980). *Quality of life in older persons: Meaning and measurement.* New York: Human Science Press.

Gillet, B., & Schwab, D. P. (1975). Convergent and discriminant validities of corresponding Job Descriptive Index and Minnesota Satisfaction Questionnaire scales. *Journal of Applied Psychology, 60,* 313-317.

Gortmaker, S. I., Must, A., Perrin, J. M., Sobol, A. M., & Dietz, W. H. (1993). Social and economic consequences of overweight in adolescence and young adulthood. *New England Journal of Medicine, 329,* 1008-1012.

Gove, W. R., Hughes, M., & Style, C. B. (1983). Does marriage have positive effects on the psychological well being of the individual? *Journal of Health and Social Behavior, 24,* 122-131.

Green, R. G., Harris, R. N., Jr., Forte, J. A., & Robinson, M. (1991). Evaluating FACES III and the circumplex model: 2,440 families. *Family Process, 30,* 55-73.

Grover, K. J., Paff-Bergen, L. A., Russell, C. S., & Schumm, W. R. (1984). The Kansas Marital Satisfaction Scale: A further brief report. *Psychological Reports, 54,* 629-630.

Hill, A. J., & Robinson, A. (1991). Dieting concerns have a functional effect on the behavior of nine-year-old girls. *British Journal of Clinical Psychology, 30,* 265-267.

Hollandsworth, J. G. (1988). Evaluating the impact of medical treatment on the quality of life: A 5-year update. *Social Science and Medicine, 4,* 425-434.

Hoppock, R. (1935). *Job satisfaction.* New York: Harper.

Hsu, L. K. G. (1990). *Eating disorders.* New York: Guilford.

Hudson, W. W., Harrison, D. F., & Crosscup, P. C. (1981). A short-form scale to measure discord in dyadic relationships. *Journal of Sex Research, 17,* 157-174.

Ironson, G. H., Smith, P. C., Bronnick, M. T., Gibson, W. M., & Paul, K. B. (1989). Construction of a job in general scale: A comparison of global, composite, and specific measures. *Journal of Applied Psychology, 74,* 193-200.

Iso-Ahola, S. E. (1979). Basic dimensions of definitions of leisure. *Journal of Leisure Research, 11,* 28-39.

Iso-Ahola, S. E., & Buttimer, K. J. (1982). On the measurement of work and leisure ethics and resultant intercorrelations. *Educational and Psychological Measurement, 42,* 429-435.

Johnson, S. M., Smith, P. C., & Tucker, S. M. (1982). Response format of the Job Descriptive Index: Assessment of reliability and validity by the multitrait-multimethod matrix. *Journal of Applied Psychology, 67,* 500-505.

Kazak, A. E., Jarmas, A., & Snitzer, L. (1988). The assessment of marital satisfaction: An evaluation of the Dyadic Adjustment Scale. *Journal of Family Psychology, 2,* 82-91.

Keith, K. D., & Schalock, R. L. (1992). The Quality of Life Questionnaire. *The Behavior Therapist, 15,* 106-107.

Kral, J. G., Sjöström, L. V., & Sullivan, M. B. E. (1992). Assessment of quality of life before and after surgery for severe obesity. *American Journal of Clinical Nutrition, 55,* 611S-614S.

Larsen, R. J., Diener, E., & Emmons, R. A. (1985). An evaluation of subjective well-being measures. *Social Indicators Research, 17,* 1-17.

Lingswiler, V. M., Crowther, J. H., & Stephens, M. A. P. (1987). Emotional reactivity and eating in binge eating and obesity. *Journal of Behavioral Medicine, 10,* 287-299.

Locke, H. J., & Wallace, K. M. (1959). Short marital adjustment and prediction tests: Their reliability and validity. *Marriage and Family Living, 25,* 251-255.

LoPiccolo, J., & Lobitz, W. C. (1973). Behavior therapy of sexual dysfunction. In L. A. Hammerlynch, L. Handy, & E. Mash (Eds.), *Behavior change: Methodology, concepts, and practice.* Champaign, IL: Research Press.

LoPiccolo, J., & Steger, J. C. (1974). The Sexual Interaction Inventory: A new instrument for assessment of sexual dysfunction. *Archives of Sexual Behavior, 3,* 585-595.

Margolin, G., & Fernandez, V. (1983). Other marriage and family questionnaires. In E. E. Filsinger (Ed.), *Marriage and family assessment: A sourcebook for family therapy* (pp. 317-338). Beverly Hills, CA: Sage.

Marsh, H. W. (1987). Masculinity, femininity, and androgyny: Their relations with multiple dimensions of self-concept. *Multivariate Behavioral Research, 22,* 91-118.

Marsh, H. W. (1991). *Self-Description Questionnaire (SDQ) III: A theoretical and empirical basis for the measurement of multiple dimensions of late adolescent self-concept: An interim test manual and a research monograph.* Faculty of Education, University of Western Sydney, Macarthur.

Marsh, H. W., Barnes, J., & Hocevar, D. (1985). Self-other agreement on multidimensional self-concept ratings: Factor analysis and multitrait-multimethod analysis. *Journal of Personality and Social Psychology, 49,* 1360-1377.

Marsh, H. W., & O'Neill, R. (1984). Self-Description Questionnaire III: The construct validity of multidimensional self-concept ratings by late adolescents. *Journal of Educational Measurement, 24,* 153-174.

Marsh, H. W., Relich, J. D., & Smith, I. D. (1983). Self-concept: The construct validity of interpretations based upon the SDQ. *Journal of Personality and Social Psychology, 45,* 173-187.

Marsh, H. W., Richards, G. D., & Barnes, J. (1986). Multi-dimensional self-concepts: The effect of participation in an Outward Bound program. *Journal of Personality and Social Psychology, 50,* 195-204.

Matusewitch, E. (1983). Employment discrimination against the obese. *Personnel Journal, 62,* 446-450.

McCollum, E. E., Schumm, W. R., & Russell, C. S. (1988). Reliability and validity of the Kansas Family Life Satisfaction Scale in a predominantly middle-aged sample. *Psychological Reports, 62,* 95-98.

McNichols, C. W., Stahl, M. J., & Manley, T. R. (1978). A validation of Hoppock's job satisfaction measure. *Academy of Management Journal, 21,* 737-742.

Mitchell, S. E., Newell, G. K., & Schumm, W. R. (1983). Test-retest reliability of the Kansas Marital Satisfaction Scale. *Psychological Reports, 53,* 545-546.

Moos, R. H., & Moos, B. (1986). *Family Environment Scale manual* (2nd ed.). Palo Alto, CA: Consulting Psychologists Press.

Norton, R. (1983). Measuring marital quality: A critical look at the dependent variable. *Journal of Marriage and the Family, 45,* 141-151.

Obesity doesn't mean you can't pull your weight. (1993, October). *Newsday,* p. 32.

Okun, M. A., Kardash, C. A., Stock, W. A., Sandler, I. N., & Baumann, D. J. (1986). Measuring perceptions of the quality of academic life among college students. *Journal of College Student Personnel, 27,* 447-451.

Olson, D. H. (1986). Circumplex model VII: Validation studies and FACES III. *Family Process, 25,* 337-351.

Olson, D. H. (1988). Family types, family stress, and family satisfaction: A family development perspective. In C. J. Falicov (Ed.), *Family transitions: Continuity and change over the life cycle* (pp. 55-79). New York: Guilford.

Olson, D. H., Portner, J., & Bell, R. Q. (1982). *FACES II: Family adaptability and cohesion scales.* St. Paul: University of Minnesota, Family Social Science.

Olson, D. H., Portner, J., & Lavee, Y. (1985). *FACES III.* St. Paul: University of Minnesota, Family Social Science.

Paul, K. B., Smith, P. C., Tisak, J., & Cranny, C. J. (1991, August). *Leisure satisfaction and job satisfaction: Their interrelation and use in prediction.* Paper presented at the third annual convention of the American Psychological Society, Washington, DC.

Paulhus, D. L. (1991). Measurement and control of response bias. In J. P. Robinson, P. R. Shaver, & L. W. Wrightsman (Eds.), *Measures of personality and social psychological attitudes* (pp. 17-59). New York: Academic Press.

Pavot, W., & Diener, E. (1993). Review of the Satisfaction With Life Scale. *Psychological Assessment, 5,* 164-172.

Pavot, W., Diener, E., Colvin, R., & Sandvik, E. (1991). Further validation of the Satisfaction With Life Scale: Evidence for the cross-method convergence of well-being measures. *Journal of Personality Assessment, 57,* 149-161.

Perosa, L. M., & Perosa, S. L. (1990). Convergent and discriminatory validity for family self-report measures. *Educational and Psychological Measurement, 50,* 855-868.

Ragheb, M. G., & Beard, J. G. (1980). Leisure satisfaction: Concept, theory, and measurement. In S. E. Iso-Ahola (Ed.), *Social psychological perspectives on leisure and recreation* (pp. 329-353). Springfield, IL: Charles C Thomas.

Rand, C. S. W., & Macgregor, A. M. C. (1990). Morbidly obese patients' perceptions of social discrimination before and after surgery for obesity. *South Medical Journal, 83,* 1390-1395.

Rand, C. S. W., & Macgregor, A. M. C. (1991). Successful weight loss following obesity surgery and the perceived liability of morbid obesity. *International Journal of Obesity, 15,* 577-579.

Rentsch, J. R., & Steel, R. P. (1992). Construct and concurrent validation of the Andrews and Withey Job Satisfaction Questionnaire. *Educational and Psychological Measurement, 52,* 357-367.

Riddick, C. C. (1986). Leisure satisfaction precursors. *Journal of Leisure Research, 18,* 259-265.

Roach, A. J., Frazier, L. P., & Bowden, S. R. (1981). The Marital Satisfaction Scale: Development of a measure for intervention research. *Journal of Marriage and the Family, 43,* 537-546.

Rosenberg, M. (1965). *Society and the adolescent self-image.* Princeton, NJ: Princeton University Press.

Rosenberg, M. (1979). *Conceiving the self.* New York: Basic Books.

Rothblum, E. D., Brand, P. A., Miller, C. T., & Oetjen, H. A. (1990). The relationship between obesity, employment discrimination, and employment-related victimization. *Journal of Vocational Behavior, 37,* 251-266.

Ruiz, M. A., & Baca, E. (1993). Design and validation of the Quality of Life Questionnaire. *European Journal of Psychological Assessment, 9,* 19-32.

Russell, R. V. (1987). The importance of recreation satisfaction and activity participation to the life satisfaction of age-segregated retirees. *Journal of Leisure Research, 19,* 273-283.

Sandler, I. N. (1981, August). *On buffers and booster: Social support for negative and positive life events.* Paper presented at the annual meeting of the American Psychological Association, Los Angeles.

Sarason, I. G., Levine, H. M., Basham, R. B., & Sarason, B. R. (1983). Assessing social support: The Social Support Questionnaire. *Journal of Personality and Social Psychology, 44,* 127-139.

Scarpello, V., & Campbell, J. P. (1983). Job satisfaction: Are all the parts there? *Personnel Psychology, 36,* 577-600.

Schumm, W. R., McCollum, E. E., Bugaighis, M. A., Jurich, A. P., & Bollman, S. R. (1986). Characteristics of the Kansas Family Life Satisfaction Scale in a regional sample. *Psychological Reports, 58,* 975-980.

Schumm, W. R., Nichols, C. W., Shectman, K. L., & Grigsby, C. C. (1983). Characteristics of responses to the Kansas Marital Satisfaction Scale by a sample of 84 married mothers. *Psychological Reports, 53,* 567-572.

Schumm, W. R., Paff-Bergen, L. A., Hatch, R. C., Obiorah, F. C., Copeland, J. M., Meens, L. D., & Bugaighis, M. A. (1986). Concurrent and discriminant validity of the Kansas Marital Satisfaction Scale. *Journal of Marriage and the Family, 48,* 381-387.

Sharpley, C. F., & Cross, D. G. (1982). A psychometric evaluation of the Spanier Dyadic Adjustment Scale. *Journal of Marriage and the Family, 44,* 739-741.

Shavelson, R. J., Hubner, J. J., & Stanton, G. C. (1976). Self-concept: Validation of construct interpretations. *Review of Educational Research, 46,* 407-441.

Shectman, K. L., Bergen, M. B., Schumm, W. R., & Bugaighis, M. A. (1985). Characteristics of the Kansas Marital Satisfaction Scale among female participants in community childbirth education classes. *Psychological Reports, 56,* 537-538.

Shisslak, C. M., Pazda, S. L., & Crago, M. (1990). Body weight and bulimia as discriminators of psychological characteristics among anorexic, bulimic, and obese women. *Journal of Abnormal Psychology, 99,* 380-384.

Smith, P. C., Kendall, L. M., & Hulin, C. L. (1969). *The measurement of satisfaction in work and retirement.* Chicago: Rand McNally.

Smith, P. C., Smith, O. W., & Rollo, J. (1974). Factor structure for blacks and whites of the Job Descriptive Index and its discrimination of job satisfaction. *Journal of Applied Psychology, 59,* 99-100.

Snyder, D. K. (1979). Multidimensional assessment of marital satisfaction. *Journal of Marriage and the Family, 41,* 813-823.

Snyder, D. K., Wills, R. M., & Keiser, T. W. (1981). Empirical validation of the Marital Satisfaction Inventory: An actuarial approach. *Journal of Consulting and Clinical Psychology, 49,* 262-268.

Spanier, G. B. (1976). Measuring dyadic adjustment: New scales for assessing the quality of marriage and similar dyads. *Journal of Marital and Family Therapy, 38,* 15-38.

Spanier, G. B. (1979). The measurement of marital quality. *Journal of Sex and Marital Therapy, 5,* 288-300.

Spanier, G. B., & Lewis, R. A. (1980). Marital quality: A review of the seventies. *Journal of Marriage and the Family, 42,* 96-110.

Spanier, G. B., & Thompson, L. (1982). A confirmatory analysis of the Dyadic Adjustment Scale. *Journal of Marriage and the Family, 44,* 731-738.

Spilker, B. (1990). *Quality of life assessments in clinical trials.* New York: Raven.

Staats, S. (1983). Perceived sources of stress and happiness in married and single college students. *Psychological Reports, 52,* 179-184.

Staats, S., & Partlo, C. (1990). Predicting intent to get a college degree. *Journal of College Student Development, 31,* 245-249.

Starr, A. M., Betz, E. L., & Menne, J. W. (1983). *Manual: College Student Satisfaction Questionnaire* (rev. ed.). Ames: Central Iowa Associates.

Stein, R. F. (1987). Comparison of self concept of nonobese and obese university junior female nursing students. *Adolescence, 22,* 77-90.

Strack, F., Argyle, M., & Schwarz, N. (1991). *Subjective well-being: An interdisciplinary perspective.* New York: Pergamon.

Stunkard, A. J., & Wadden, T. A. (1992). Psychological aspects of severe obesity. *American Journal of Clinical Nutrition, 55,* 524S-532S.

Taylor, S. E., & Brown, J. D. (1988). Illusion and well-being: A social psychological perspective on mental health. *Psychological Bulletin, 103,* 193-210.

Tracey, T. J. (1989). Client and therapist session satisfaction over the course of psychotherapy. *Psychotherapy, 26,* 177-182.

Trafton, R. S., & Tinsley, H. E. A. (1980). An investigation of the construct validity of measures of job, leisure, dyadic, and general life satisfaction. *Journal of Leisure Research, 12,* 34-44.

Veenhoven, R. (1984). *Conditions of happiness.* Dordrecht, Holland: Reidel.

Wallander, J. L., Varni, J. W., Babani, L., Banis, H. T., & Wilcox, K. T. (1988). Children with chronic physical disorders: Maternal reports of their psychological adjustment. *Journal of Pediatric Psychology, 13,* 197-212.

Weiss, D. J., Dawis, R. V., England, G. W., & Lofquist, L. H. (1967). *Manual for the Minnesota Satisfaction Questionnaire.* Minneapolis: University of Minnesota, Minnesota Studies in Vocational Rehabilitation.

Whitley, M. P., & Paulsen, S. B. (1975). Assertiveness and sexual satisfaction in employed professional women. *Journal of Marriage and the Family, 37,* 573-581.

Wylie, R. C. (1989). *Measures of self-concept.* Lincoln: University of Nebraska Press.

Yager, J. (1982). Family issues in the pathogenesis of anorexia nervosa. *Psychosomatic Medicine, 44,* 43-60.

Yuker, H. E., & Allison, D. B. (in press). Obesity: Socio-cultural perspectives. In L. A. Alexander (Ed.), *Eating disorders anthology.* Washington, DC: Hemisphere.

Appendix 2-A

Satisfaction With Life Scale

1 = Strongly disagree

2 = Disagree

3 = Slightly disagree

4 = Neither agree nor disagree

5 = Slightly agree

6 = Agree

7 = Strongly agree

_____ 1. In most ways my life is close to my ideal.

_____ 2. The conditions of my life are excellent.

_____ 3. I am satisfied with my life.

_____ 4. So far I have gotten the important things I want in life.

_____ 5. If I could live my life over, I would change almost nothing.

SOURCE: From "The Satisfaction With Life Scale," by E. Diener, R. A. Emmons, R. J. Larsen, and S. Griffin, 1985, *Journal of Personality Assessment, 49,* pp. 71-75. Reprinted with permission.

Appendix 2-B

Extended Satisfaction With Life Scale

Below are some statements with which you may agree or disagree. Use the scale below to show your agreement with each item. Place the number on the line for that item. Please be open and honest in your answers.

1 = Strongly disagree

2 = Disagree

3 = Slightly disagree

4 = Neither agree nor disagree

5 = Slightly agree

6 = Agree

7 = Strongly agree

_____ 1. In most ways my life is close to my ideal.

_____ 2. The conditions of my life are excellent.

_____ 3. I am satisfied with my life.

_____ 4. So far I have gotten the important things I want from life.

_____ 5. I am generally pleased with the life I lead.

_____ 6. In most ways my social life is close to my ideal.

_____ 7. The conditions of my social life are excellent.

_____ 8. I am satisfied with my social life.

_____ 9. So far I have gotten the important things I want from my social life.

_____ 10. I am generally pleased with the social life I lead.

_____ 11. In most ways my sex life is close to my ideal.

_____ 12. The conditions of my sex life are excellent.

_____ 13. I am satisfied with my sex life.

_____ 14. So far I have gotten the important things I want from my sex life.

_____ 15. I am generally pleased with the quality of my sex life.

_____ 16. In most ways my actual self is close to my ideal self.

_____ 17. As an individual I consider myself excellent.

_____ 18. I am satisfied with my person or self as an individual.

_____ 19. So far I have gotten the important things I want from myself.

_____ 20. I am generally pleased with myself as an individual.

_____ 21. In most ways my actual physical appearance is close to my ideal physical appearance.

_____ 22. I consider my physical appearance excellent.

_____ 23. I am satisfied with my physical appearance.

_____ 24. There is nothing about my physical appearance that I would like to change.

_____ 25. I am generally pleased with my physical appearance.

The questions below pertain to your current "immediate" family, not your "extended" family.

_____ 26. In most ways my family life is close to my ideal.

_____ 27. The conditions of my family life are excellent.

_____ 28. I am satisfied with my family life.

_____ 29. So far I have gotten the important things I want from my family life.

_____ 30. I am generally pleased with the quality of my family life.

DO YOU GO TO SCHOOL?   _____ Yes   _____ No

IF NOT, SKIP THE NEXT 5 QUESTIONS.

_____ 31. The education I get at school is great.

_____ 32. I like or respect the other students at school.

_____ 33. I am satisfied with my classes.

_____ 34. So far I have learned the important things I wanted at school.

_____ 35. I am generally pleased with the quality of my teachers.

DO YOU HAVE A JOB? _____ Yes _____ No

IF NOT, SKIP THE NEXT 10 QUESTIONS.

_____ 36. The chance for advancement on my job is good.

_____ 37. I like the company policies and practices.

_____ 38. I like or respect my coworkers.

_____ 39. I am pleased with the praise I get for doing a good job.

_____ 40. I am given enough freedom to use my own judgment.

_____ 41. I like the way my job provides for steady employment.

_____ 42. My boss handles his or her employees well.

_____ 43. I am happy with the competence of my supervisor.

_____ 44. The working conditions of my job are excellent.

_____ 45. Overall, I am satisfied with my job.

ARE YOU NOW IN AN "EXCLUSIVE" RELATIONSHIP?

_____ YES	_____ NO (BUT I HAVE BEEN IN THE PAST)	_____ NO (AND I HAVE NOT BEEN IN THE PAST)
If you checked this box, please answer the questions below based on your current relationship.	If you checked this box, please answer the questions below based on your past relationship.	If you checked this box, you may stop here.

_____ 46. In most ways my relationship/marriage is close to my ideal.

_____ 47. The conditions of my relationship/marriage are excellent.

_____ 48. I am satisfied with my relationship/marriage.

_____ 49. So far I have gotten the important things I want from my relationship/marriage.

_____ 50. I am generally pleased with the quality of my relationship/marriage.

SOURCE: From *The Extended Satisfaction With Life Scale: Convergent and Discriminant Validity,* by V. C. Alfonso, D. B. Allison, and D. E. Rader, 1993, paper presented at the annual meeting of the American Psychological Association, Toronto, Canada. Reprinted with permission.

Appendix 2-C

Quality of Life Inventory
(Sample Item)

LOVE is a very close romantic relationship with another person. LOVE usually includes sexual feelings and feeling loved, cared for, and understood.

1. How important is LOVE to your happiness?

0	1	2
Not Important	Important	Extremely Important

2. How satisfied are you with the LOVE in your life? (If you are not in a LOVE relationship, say how satisfied you feel about not having a LOVE relationship.)

−3	−2	−1	+ 1	+ 2	+ 3
Very	Somewhat	A Little	A Little	Somewhat	Very
DISSATISFIED					SATISFIED

3. How sure or confident are you that you can do what it takes to get your needs met in the area of LOVE?

Not at all confident   Completely confident

0%	10%	20%	30%	40%	50%	60%	70%	80%	90%	100%

SOURCE: Copyright © 1988 Michael B. Frisch, Ph.D. All rights reserved. Published and distributed by National Computer Systems, Inc. Reproduced by permission. "QOLI" is a trademark of Michael B. Frisch, Ph.D.

Appendix 2-D

Rosenberg Self-Esteem Scale

Please record the appropriate answer per item, depending on whether you strongly agree, agree, disagree, or strongly disagree with it.

1 = Strongly agree

2 = Agree

3 = Disagree

4 = Strongly disagree

_____ 1. On the whole, I am satisfied with myself.

_____ 2. At times I think I am no good at all.

_____ 3. I feel that I have a number of good qualities.

_____ 4. I am able to do things as well as most other people.

_____ 5. I feel I do not have much to be proud of.

_____ 6. I certainly feel useless at times.

_____ 7. I feel that I'm a person of worth, at least on an equal plane with others.

_____ 8. I wish I could have more respect for myself.

_____ 9. All in all, I am inclined to feel that I am a failure.

_____10. I take a positive attitude toward myself.

SOURCE: Rosenberg, Morris; SOCIETY AND THE ADOLESCENT SELF-IMAGE. Copyright © 1965 by Princeton University Press, renewed 1993. Reprinted by permission of Princeton University Press.

Appendix 2-E

Self-Description Questionnaire III

This is a chance for you to consider how you think and feel about yourself. This is not a test—there are no right or wrong answers, and everyone will have different responses. The purpose of this study is to determine how people describe themselves and what characteristics are most important to how people feel about themselves.

On the following pages are a series of statements that are more or less true (or more or less false) descriptions of you. Please use the following 8-point response scale to indicate how true (or false) each item is as a description of you. Respond to the items as you now feel even if you felt differently at some other time in your life. In a few instances, an item may no longer be appropriate to you, though it was at an earlier period of your life (e.g., an item about your present relationship with your parents if they are no longer alive). In such cases, respond to the item as you would have when it was appropriate. Try to avoid leaving any items blank.

After completing all the items, you will be asked to select those that best describe important aspects—either positive or negative—of how you feel about yourself. Consider this as you are completing the survey.

1 = Definitely False

2 = False

3 = Mostly False

4 = More False than True

5 = More True than False

6 = Mostly True

7 = True

8 = Definitely True

_____ 1. Mathematics makes me feel inadequate.

_____ 2. Spiritual/religious beliefs make my life better and make me a happier person.

_____ 3. Overall, I don't have much respect for myself.

_____ 4. I nearly always tell the truth.

_____ 5. Most of my friends are more comfortable with members of the opposite sex than I am.

_____ 6. I am an avid reader.

_____ 7. I am anxious much of the time.

_____ 8. My parents have usually been unhappy or disappointed with what I do and have done.

_____ 9. I have trouble with most academic subjects.

_____ 10. I enjoy working out new ways of solving problems.

_____ 11. There are lots of things about the way I look that I would like to change.

_____ 12. I make friends easily with members of the same sex.

_____ 13. I hate sports and physical activities.

_____ 14. I am quite good at mathematics.

_____ 15. My spiritual/religious beliefs provide the guidelines by which I conduct my life.

_____ 16. Overall, I have a lot of self-confidence.

_____ 17. I sometimes take things that do not belong to me.

_____ 18. I am comfortable talking to members of the opposite sex.

_____ 19. I do not do well on tests that require a lot of verbal reasoning ability.

_____ 20. I hardly ever feel depressed.

_____ 21. My values are similar to those of my parents.

_____ 22. I'm good at most academic subjects.

_____ 23. I'm not much good at problem solving.

_____ 24. My body weight is about right (neither too fat nor too skinny).

_____ 25. Other members of the same sex find me boring.

_____ 26. I have a high energy level in sports and physical activities.

SOURCE: From _Self-Description Questionnaire (SDQ) III: A Theoretical and Empirical Basis for the Measurement of Multiple Dimensions of Late Adolescent Self-Concept: An Interim Test Manual and a Research Monograph,_ by H. W. Marsh, 1991, Faculty of Education, University of Western Sydney, Macarthur. Copyright © 1991 by H. W. Marsh. Reprinted with permission.
NOTE: The items here represent a sample of the complete scale. The numbers assigned to the items above correspond to item numbers 40 through 65 on the complete SDQ III.

Appendix 2-F

Hoppock Job Satisfaction Blank

A. Which one of the following shows how much of the time you feel satisfied with your job?

   1. Never.

   2. Seldom.

   3. Occasionally.

   4. About half of the time.

   5. A good deal of the time.

   6. Most of the time.

   7. All the time.

B. Choose the one of the following statements which best tells how well you like your job.

   1. I hate it.

   2. I dislike it.

   3. I don't like it.

   4. I am indifferent to it.

   5. I like it.

   6. I am enthusiastic about it.

   7. I love it.

C. Which one of the following best tells how you feel about changing your job?

   1. I would quit this job at once if I could.

   2. I would take almost any other job in which I could earn as much as I am earning now.

   3. I would like to change both my job and my occupation.

   4. I would like to exchange my present job for another one.

5. I am not eager to change my job, but I would do so if I could get a better job.

6. I cannot think of any jobs for which I would exchange.

7. I would not exchange my job for any other.

D. Which one of the following shows how you think you compare with other people?

1. No one dislikes his job more than I dislike mine.

2. I dislike my job much more than most people dislike theirs.

3. I dislike my job more than most people dislike theirs.

4. I like my job about as well as most people like theirs.

5. I like my job better than most people like theirs.

6. I like my job much better than most people like theirs.

7. No one likes his job better than I like mine.

SOURCE: CHART from JOB SATISFACTION by ROBERT HOPPOCK. Copyright © 1935 by National Occupational Conference. Copyright renewed 1962 by Mr. Robert Hoppock. Reprinted by permission of HarperCollins Publishers, Inc.

Appendix 2-G

The Job Descriptive Index
(Sample Items)

WORK ON PRESENT JOB

Think of the work you do at present. How well does each of the following words or phrases describe your work? In the blank beside each word below, write

Y for "Yes" if it describes your work

N for "No" if it does NOT describe it

? if you cannot decide

_____ Routine

_____ Satisfying

_____ Good

SUPERVISION

Think of the kind of supervision that you get on your job. How well does each of the following words or phrases describe this? In the blank beside each word below, write

Y for "Yes" if it describes the supervision you get on your job

N for "No" if it does NOT describe it

? if you cannot decide

_____ Impolite

_____ Praises good work

_____ Doesn't supervise enough

PRESENT PAY

Think of the pay you get now. How well does each of the following words or phrases describe your present pay? In the blank beside each word below, write

Y for "Yes" if it describes your pay

N for "No" if it does NOT describe it

? if you cannot decide

_____ Income adequate for normal expenses

_____ Insecure

_____ Less than I deserve

COWORKERS (PEOPLE)

Think of the majority of the people that you work with now or the people you meet in connection with your work. How well does each of the following words or phrases describe these people? In the blank beside each word below, write

Y for "Yes" if it describes the people you work with

N for "No" if it does NOT describe them

? if you cannot decide

_____ Boring

_____ Responsible

_____ Intelligent

OPPORTUNITIES FOR PROMOTION

Think of the opportunities for promotion that you have now. How well does each of the following words or phrases describe these? In the blank beside each word below, write

Y for "Yes" if it describes your opportunities for promotion

N for "No" if it does NOT describe them

? if you cannot decide

_____ Dead-end job

_____ Unfair promotion policy

_____ Regular promotions

SOURCE: The Job Descriptive Index is copyrighted by Bowling Green State University, 1975, 1985, used here by permission. The complete forms of the scales, scoring key, instructions, and norms can be obtained from Dr. Patricia C. Smith, Department of Psychology, Bowling Green State University, Bowling Green, OH 43403.
NOTE: The items here represent sample items of the JDI as provided by the author. The items here are actual items from the JDI. However, there are more descriptive phrases per area on the complete scale.

Appendix 2-H

Minnesota Satisfaction Questionnaire
(Short Form)

1 = Very dissatisfied

2 = Dissatisfied

3 = I can't decide whether I am satisfied or not

4 = Satisfied

5 = Very satisfied

On my present job, this is how I feel about:

_____ 1. Being able to keep busy all the time

_____ 2. The chance to work alone on the job

_____ 3. The chance to do different things from time to time

_____ 4. The chance to be "somebody" in the community

_____ 5. The way my boss handles his men

_____ 6. The competence of my supervisor in making decisions

_____ 7. Being able to do things that don't go against my conscience

_____ 8. The way my job provides for steady employment

_____ 9. The chance to do things for other people

_____ 10. The chance to tell people what to do

_____ 11. The chance to do something that makes use of my abilities

_____ 12. The way company policies are put into practice

_____ 13. My pay and the amount of work I do

_____ 14. The chances for advancement on this job

_____ 15. The freedom to use my own judgment

_____ 16. The chance to try my own methods of doing the job

_____ 17. The working conditions

_____ 18. The way my coworkers get along with each other

_____ 19. The praise I get for doing a good job

_____ 20. The feeling of accomplishment I get from the job

SOURCE: Copyright © 1993, Vocational Psychology Research, University of Minnesota. Reproduced by permission.

Appendix 2-I

Perceived Quality of Academic Life Scale

1 = Delighted

2 = Pleased

3 = Mostly satisfied

4 = Mixed (about equally satisfied and dissatisfied)

5 = Mostly dissatisfied

6 = Unhappy

7 = Terrible

How do you feel about . . .

1. Your education at _____?

2. The classes you are taking at _____?

3. What you are learning at _____?

4. Your instructors at _____?

5. The progress you are making toward your educational goals? _____

_____

_____

6. How well you are doing in your classes? _____

_____

_____

SOURCE: From "Measuring Perceptions of the Quality of Academic Life Among College Students," by M. A. Okun, C. A. Kardash, W. A. Stock, I. N. Sandler, and D. J. Baumann, 1986, *Journal of College Student Personnel, 27,* pp. 447-451. Copyright © 1986 by American College Personnel Association. Reprinted with permission. See also Staats and Partio (1990).

72

Appendix 2-J

Kansas Family Life Satisfaction Scale

1 = Extremely dissatisfied

2 = Very dissatisfied

3 = Somewhat dissatisfied

4 = Mixed

5 = Somewhat satisfied

6 = Very satisfied

7 = Extremely satisfied

_____ A. How satisfied are you with your family life?

_____ B. How satisfied are you with your relationship with your spouse?

_____ C. How satisfied are you with your relationship with your child(ren)?

_____ D. How satisfied are you with your children's relationship with each other? (answer only if you have more than one child)

SOURCE: Reproduced with permission of authors and publisher from:
Schumm, W. R., McCollum, E. E., Bugaighis, M. A., Jurich, A. P., and Bollman, S. R. Characteristics of the Kansas Family Life Satisfaction Scale in a regional sample. *Psychological Reports,* 1986, 58, 975-980. © *Psychological Reports* 1986

Appendix 2-K

Family Adaptability and Cohesion Evaluation Scale II: Family Version

1 = Almost Never

2 = Once in a While

3 = Sometimes

4 = Frequently

5 = Almost Always

Describe Your Family:

_____ 1. Family members are supportive of each other during difficult times.

_____ 2. In our family, it is easy for everyone to express his/her opinion.

_____ 3. It is easier to discuss problems with people outside the family than with other family members.

_____ 4. Each family member has input regarding major family decisions.

_____ 5. Our family gathers together in the same room.

_____ 6. Children have a say in their discipline.

_____ 7. Our family does things together.

_____ 8. Family members discuss problems and feel good about the solutions.

_____ 9. In our family, everyone goes his/her own way.

_____ 10. We shift household responsibilities from person to person.

_____ 11. Family members know each other's close friends.

_____ 12. It is hard to know what the rules are in our family.

_____ 13. Family members consult other family members on personal decisions.

_____ 14. Family members say what they want.

_____ 15. We have difficulty thinking of things to do as a family.

_____ 16. In solving problems, the children's suggestions are followed.

_____ 17. Family members feel very close to each other.

_____ 18. Discipline is fair in our family.

_____ 19. Family members feel closer to people outside the family than to other family members.

_____ 20. Our family tries new ways of dealing with problems.

_____ 21. Family members go along with what the family decides to do.

_____ 22. In our family, everyone shares responsibilities.

_____ 23. Family members like to spend their free time with each other.

_____ 24. It is difficult to get a rule changed in our family.

_____ 25. Family members avoid each other at home.

_____ 26. When problems arise, we compromise.

_____ 27. We approve of each other's friends.

_____ 28. Family members are afraid to say what is on their minds.

_____ 29. Family members pair up rather than do things as a total family.

_____ 30. Family members share interests and hobbies with each other.

SOURCE: For details on scoring, norms, reliability, and validity, contact David H. Olson, Ph.D., Family Social Science, University of Minnesota, St. Paul, MN 55108. Reprinted with permission.

Appendix 2-L

Kansas Marital Satisfaction Scale

1 = Extremely Dissatisfied

2 = Very Dissatisfied

3 = Somewhat Dissatisfied

4 = Mixed

5 = Somewhat Satisfied

6 = Very Satisfied

7 = Extremely Satisfied

_____ 1. How satisfied are you with your marriage?

_____ 2. How satisfied are you with your husband as a spouse?

_____ 3. How satisfied are you with your relationship with your husband?

SOURCE: From "Concurrent and Discriminant Validity of the Kansas Maarital Satisfaction Scale," by W. R. Schumm, L. A. Paff-Bergen, R. C. Hatch, F. C. Obiorah, J. M. Copeland, L. D. Meens, and M. A. Bugaighis, 1986, *Journal of Marriage and the Family, 48*, pp. 381-387. Copyright © 1986 by the National Council on Family Relations, 3989 Central Ave. NE, Suite 550, Minneapolis, MN 55421. Reprinted with permission.

Appendix 2-M

Dyadic Adjustment Scale
(Sample Items)

Most persons have disagreements in their relationships. Please indicate below the approximate extent of agreement or disagreement between you and your partner for each item on the following list.

1 = Always agree

2 = Almost always agree

3 = Occasionally disagree

4 = Frequently disagree

5 = Almost always disagree

6 = Always disagree

____ 1. Handling family finances

____ 2. Matters of recreation

____ 3. Religious matters

____ 4. Demonstrations of affection

____ 5. Friends

____ 6. Sex relations

SOURCE: Reproduced with permission of Multi-Health Systems, Inc., 908 Niagara Falls Blvd., North Tonawanda, NY 14120-2060 (800-456-3003).
NOTE: The items here represent a sample of the complete scale. They are the first six items of the DAS.

Appendix 2-N

INDEX OF SEXUAL SATISFACTION (ISS)

Name: _____ Today's Date: _____

This questionnaire is designed to measure the degree of satisfaction you have in the sexual relationship with your partner. It is not a test, so there are no right or wrong answers. Answer each item as carefully and as accurately as you can by placing a number beside each one as follows.

1 = None of the time
2 = Very rarely
3 = A little of the time
4 = Some of the time
5 = A good part of the time
6 = Most of the time
7 = All of the time

1. ____ I feel that my partner enjoys our sex life.
2. ____ Our sex life is very exciting.
3. ____ Sex is fun for my partner and me.
4. ____ Sex with my partner has become a chore for me.
5. ____ I feel that our sex is dirty and disgusting.
6. ____ Our sex life is monotonous.
7. ____ When we have sex it is too rushed and hurriedly completed.
8. ____ I feel that my sex life is lacking in quality.
9. ____ My partner is sexually very exciting.
10. ____ I enjoy the sex techniques that my partner likes or uses.
11. ____ I feel that my partner wants too much sex from me.
12. ____ I think that our sex is wonderful.
13. ____ My partner dwells on sex too much.
14. ____ I try to avoid sexual contact with my partner.
15. ____ My partner is too rough or brutal when we have sex.
16. ____ My partner is a wonderful sex mate.
17. ____ I feel that sex is a normal function of our relationship.
18. ____ My partner does not want sex when I do.
19. ____ I feel that our sex life really adds a lot to our relationship.
20. ____ My partner seems to avoid sexual contact with me.
21. ____ It is easy for me to get sexually excited by my partner.
22. ____ I feel that my partner is sexually pleased with me.
23. ____ My partner is very sensitive to my sexual needs and desires.
24. ____ My partner does not satisfy me sexually.
25. ____ I feel that my sex life is boring.

Copyright © 1993, Walter W. Hudson   Illegal to Photocopy or Otherwise Reproduce

1, 2, 3, 9, 10, 12, 16, 17, 19, 21, 22, 23.

SOURCE: Available from WALMYR Publishing Company, P.O. Box 24779, Tempe, AZ 85285-4779. Reprinted with permission.

Appendix 2-O

Leisure Satisfaction Scale
(Sample Items)

Below are listed a number of statements. Please read each statement and use the scale below to reflect how true a particular item is in your life. Place the corresponding number on the line next to that item.

> 1 = If the item is Almost Never True for you.
>
> 2 = If the item is Seldom True for you.
>
> 3 = If the item is Sometimes True for you.
>
> 4 = If the item is Often True for you.
>
> 5 = If the item is Almost Always True for you.

_____ 1. I freely choose the activities I do in my leisure time.

_____ 2. I enjoy doing my leisure activities.

_____ 3. My leisure activities give me self-confidence.

_____ 4. I use many different skills and abilities in my leisure activities.

_____ 5. When I am doing leisure activities I become fully involved in the activity.

_____ 6. I feel lonely in my free time.

_____ 7. Generally my leisure activities have a positive effect upon my life.

_____ 8. I do leisure activities which restore me spiritually.

_____ 9. My leisure activities encourage me to learn new skills.

_____ 10. My leisure activities help to satisfy my curiosity.

_____ 11. My leisure activities help me to learn about myself.

_____ 12. My leisure activities help me to learn about society in general.

_____ 13. My leisure activities help me to accept differences among individuals.

_____ 14. I have social interaction with others through leisure activities.

_____ 15. I prefer leisure activities in which I am among others in groups.

_____ 16. I associate with stimulating people in my leisure activities.

_____ 17. I first met many of my present friends through leisure activities.

_____ 18. I have a strong sense of belonging toward those with whom I do leisure activities.

_____ 19. My leisure activities help me to relax.

_____ 20. My leisure activities contribute to my emotional well-being.

_____ 21. My leisure activities are physically challenging.

_____ 22. I do leisure activities which restore me physically.

_____ 23. My leisure activities help control my weight.

_____ 24. The areas or places where I engage in my leisure activities are fresh and clean.

_____ 25. The areas or places where I engage in my leisure activities are beautiful.

_____ 26. The areas or places where I engage in my leisure activities are pleasing to me.

SOURCE: From "Measuring Leisure Satisfaction," by J. G. Beard and M. G. Ragheb, 1980, *Journal of Leisure Research, 12*, pp. 20-33. Copyright © 1980 by Idyll Arbor, Inc. Reprinted with permission.

3

Methods for Measuring Attitudes and Beliefs About Obese People

HAROLD E. YUKER

DAVID B. ALLISON

MYLES S. FAITH

Why Study Attitudes and Beliefs?

One might question why one even needs to study attitudes toward obese persons when obesity is clearly a medical problem. However, considerable research now confirms what nearly every obese person in modern Western society could tell—that obese persons face a degree of social discrimination that is every bit as terrible as the medical sequelae of their fatness. Negative attitudes toward obese persons are frequently held by laypersons and health

professionals alike (Yuker & Allison, 1994). Obese persons receive lower salaries (Frieze, Olson, & Good, 1990; Register & Williams, 1990) and less
financial support for college from their parents (Crandall, 1991). They are
less likely to be offered jobs (Klesges et al., 1990) and rented apartments
(Karris, 1977). Obese children are often described as "lazy," "stupid," "dirty,"
and "immature" (Sherman, 1981). Many physicians report that they are reluctant to perform preventive health examinations on obese patients (Adams,
Smith, Wilbur, & Grady, 1993). These are just a few of the social sequelae of
obesity.

These harsh facts necessitate that we develop methods for the measurement of attitudes toward obese persons so that we can understand their
causes and evaluate efforts to change this unpleasant picture. Furthermore,
past research has shown that beliefs about the controllability of obesity can
have strong effects on attitudes toward obese persons (Worsley, 1981). Thus it
is essential that we develop ways to index these beliefs as well.

Scope of This Chapter

Figure 3.1 graphically depicts two sets of constructs that are closely related. On the left are what might be considered attitudinal/affective components about obese persons and obesity. On the right are what might be
considered beliefs about obese persons and obesity. The upper part of the figure, separated by the hashed line, focuses primarily on the interpersonal or
social level and will be the main focus of this chapter. The lower part focuses
primarily on the intrapersonal aspects and is covered in other chapters in this
text. On the attitude side, one's attitude toward one's own obesity (or body
shape in general) is generally studied under the heading of "body image" and
is covered by Thompson (this volume). On the belief side, the primary belief
set that has been studied is the belief in the controllability of obesity. As one
descends into the *intra*personal realm to study individuals' beliefs about the
controllability of their own obesity, these beliefs are generally studied under
the closely related but conceptually different (see Peterson & Stunkard, 1992)
headings of "locus of control" and "self-efficacy." With respect to weight,
these constructs and their measurements are covered by Rossi et al. (this volume). Thus this chapter is fundamentally social in scope, dealing primarily
with individuals' attitudes toward and beliefs about other persons who are
obese.

Finally, with respect to scope, we wish to make clear that we discuss *beliefs*
rather than *knowledge*. Although an occasional investigator describes a scale
as a measure of knowledge (e.g., Dash & Brown, 1977), we believe there is
often too little consensus among obesity researchers on too many issues to

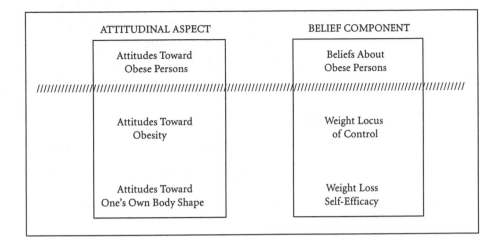

Figure 3.1. Schematic Representation of Scope of Chapter

allow unequivocal tests of knowledge to be constructed. What one person considers "knowledge" others may consider "myths" (see Rothblum, 1990). We occasionally describe a scale that the investigator described as a measure of "knowledge" but place knowledge in quotation marks to indicate our skepticism in this regard.

Measurement Techniques

Many different techniques are available for measuring attitudes and beliefs about people. Most of them have been applied to the development of measures relating to obesity or obese people. Most are self-report measures although there are a few observational studies. The measures vary along several dimensions including the type of stimulus used, the type of response recorded, and the way the responses are scored.

Stimuli. Studies have used various stimuli to evoke attitudinal responses and different words to describe obese individuals. Some studies asked direct questions about obese or overweight people (Allon, 1979); others used line drawings or pictures (Chetwynd, Stewart, & Powell, 1974; Counts, Jones, Frame, Jarvie, & Strauss, 1986; Richardson, Goodman, Hastorf, & Dornbusch, 1961; Staffieri, 1967). Some have used incomplete sentences (Canning & Mayer, 1967).

Response formats. Responses range from being highly structured, as in attitude scales, to completely unstructured, as in some questionnaires and interviews. Highly structured responses are often more reliable than unstructured ones, in which reliability depends heavily on the scoring system.

Types of Techniques

Several different techniques are available for measuring attitudes and beliefs about people who are obese. At one extreme are attitude scales, which tend to be complex, highly structured, reliable, valid, and difficult to construct. At the other are unstructured questions, which tend to be easy to formulate but are usually psychometrically weak.

Attitude Scales

Attitude scales consist of a series of statements about a topic such as obese persons. People respond by indicating the extent of their agreement or disagreement with each statement. The measure can consist of from a few to more than 100 statements. While responses to individual items are sometimes analyzed (e.g., Rand & MacGregor, 1990), this procedure can be criticized because individual responses are often quite unreliable. Moreover, conducting a separate significance test for each item greatly inflates one's Type I error rate. Instead, responses to a number of statements are summed to yield an overall score and/or several subscale scores based on factor analysis. Usually, the more statements there are in a scale or subscale, the more reliable the scores are.

The Likert-type of attitude scale (Likert, 1932) is probably used most frequently.[1] With this type of scale, the respondent indicates the degree of agreement with each statement using a series of from 2 to 11 categories, such as *strongly agree, agree, neither agree nor disagree, disagree, strongly disagree.* Scores are then assigned to each category and can be summed to yield a total score. Attitude scales frequently are factor analyzed, yielding additional content information.

Attributing Characteristics to Obese Persons

There are several slightly different techniques. In some research, people are asked to describe the characteristics of obese persons. In others, they are asked to select appropriate adjectives from a list they are given. The semantic differential technique (described below) can also be used for this purpose.

These techniques were used by Chetwynd et al. (1974) and by Harris, Harris, and Bochner (1982) among others.

Behavioral Measures

As described earlier, several investigations have used behavioral measures of how persons respond to obese and nonobese individuals. These studies were typically designed to measure discriminatory behavior. Among the variables studied have been salespersons' response time (Pauley, 1989), behavior toward persons seeking to rent an apartment (Karris, 1977), and job hiring decisions and salaries (Frieze et al., 1990; Klesges et al., 1990). To obtain reliable measures, several studies (Frieze et al., 1990; Pauley, 1989) computed the percentage of interrater agreement, which ranged from 80% to 100%. In these studies, data were typically discarded when raters could not agree on them. However, not all studies reported reliability data.

Although relatively few in number, these studies vary in terms of their design and data collection procedures. For example, some studies used experimental manipulations whereas others used ex post facto (correlational) designs. Examples of the former include research by Karris (1977), who varied the body weight (obese versus nonobese) of students interviewing with landlords for available apartments. On the other hand, Frieze et al. (1990) used a correlational design to evaluate the relationship between job salaries (both immediately following and 10 years' postgraduation) and body mass index among individuals graduating with M.B.A. degrees.

These studies also varied the nature of exposure to the obese person. That is, some studies used actual in vivo exposure, whereas other (i.e., analog) studies have relied on video recordings of obese persons. As an example of the former, Pauley (1989) measured salespersons' reaction times to actual obese and nonobese customers entering a shoe store. On the other hand, Klesges et al. (1990) had business students watch videotaped job interviews with diabetic, normal weight, or obese persons and then rate whether or not they would hire these individuals.

Body Attitudes

These are considered to be indirect measures of attitudes toward various aspects of the body including obesity. Ben-Tovim and Walker (1991) reviewed several types of instruments used for measuring women's body attitudes: self-report questionnaires, projective tests, silhouette choices, and interview assessments as well as semantic differential and self-concept measures. They emphasized the need for better measuring instruments because many current measures are technically inadequate and measure a restricted range of attitudes. A more detailed discussion of body attitudes in the context of "body image" can be found in Thompson (this volume).

Projective Techniques

Projective tests entail providing subjects with ambiguous stimuli and allowing them to make responses in a relatively unstructured format. These responses are then interpreted as "projections" of a dynamic unconscious. Projective tests have occasionally been used, particularly to measure body attitudes (Ben-Tovim & Walker, 1991). There are many problems relating to both the reliability and the validity of interpretations (Parker, Hansen, & Hunsley, 1988). Most social psychologists today do not consider projective responses to be indicative of unconscious attitudes, and therefore projective tests are rarely used in attitude research.

Questionnaires and Interviews

Questionnaires contain a set of printed items designed to elicit self-reports of attitudes. The questions can either be open ended or fixed response. The latter require an individual to choose one from among a set of possible answers, making it somewhat similar to items in an attitude scale. Open-ended questions have to be coded into categories—which could be a source of unreliability. Fixed-response answers need only be tabulated.

The analysis of questionnaire data most often involves an analysis of the responses to individual questions. While these data are interesting, as was stated earlier, individual item responses are seldom reliable. Summing the responses to a number of items, as is done in attitude scales, yields much more reliable data.

Interviews usually are based on questionnaires. The interviewer reads from the printed questionnaire and records the answers given by the interviewee. Questionnaires are usually used with people who have difficulty reading or writing such as young children or persons with certain disabilities. They can also be administered by telephone. It is important to use interviewers who are carefully selected and trained.

Interview procedures often have been used with clinical populations of obese persons (Ben-Tovim & Walker, 1991). They have been used by Allon (1979) and Cahnman (1968), while questionnaires have been used by Ashwell and Etchell (1974), Harris and Furukawa (1986), and others.

Questionnaires are usually considered to have several advantages over interviews. They are less expensive and can be distributed either through the mail or to groups of individuals. They also are more objective, because interviewers, particularly untrained ones, can bias answers by the way that they ask the questions. Questionnaires can be anonymous. Although an interviewer can give an assurance of anonymity, the interviewee may not be convinced. Moreover, the mere face-to-face presence of an interviewer may deter subjects from expressing socially undesirable responses. Finally, both questionnaires and interviews share the limitations of self-report measures, as discussed below.

Rankings

In a number of studies, subjects have been asked to rank persons with characteristics such as obesity according to a criterion such as attractiveness or likability. People may be described in "vignettes"; subjects may respond to pictures or drawings; or both. This technique has been used by Counts et al. (1986) and Richardson et al. (1961).

Ratings

Ratings involve subjective judgments about the characteristics of a person or a thing, for example, obese persons or obesity in general. Ratings can come from a variety of sources, including peers and teachers. They are similar to other techniques such as attributions, rankings, and sociometry. Rating scales also may use categories such as those used in attitude scales or the semantic differential. For example, Strauss, Smith, Frame, and Forehand (1985) compared the popularity of obese versus nonobese children using peer ratings. Specifically, elementary school students were asked to list the three classmates with whom they had the most and least desire to play. Students also rated their desire to play with every classmate on a 5-point Likert-type scale.

Unfortunately, data gleaned from rating scales are sometimes biased, unreliable, and dependent on the characteristics of the person doing the rating so that they often lack convergent validity. They also can be distorted by the halo effect in which an overall impression of a person influences responses to individual items.

Semantic Differential

Semantic differential measures, popularized by Osgood, Suci, and Tannenbaum (1957), consist of a series of bipolar adjectives (e.g., good-bad, happy-sad, competent-incompetent, intelligent-stupid, friendly-unfriendly) separated by a line marked off in about 7 to 11 intervals. A concept such as "obese person" or "obesity" is listed at the top of the page, and respondents are asked to indicate where along the line between the two extremes they would rate the concepts. In addition to yielding an overall score, semantic differential scales can be scored for the three variables of evaluation, potency, and activity. These three dimensions are not always used.

Although not referring to them as such, Harris (1983) used five semantic differential-type items (strong-weak, passive-active, energetic-lazy, attractive-unattractive, to be pitied-to be envied) with a 7-point scale to obtain ratings of "people who are overweight." The total scores for the five evaluative items yielded an alpha coefficient of .66. These techniques also have been used by Agell and Rothblum (1991), Bagley, Conklin, Isherwood, Pechiulis, and Watson (1989), and Harris et al. (1982).

Each of the techniques described above can be used to measure attitudes either directly or indirectly. Some can also be used to measure beliefs.

Measures discussed in the next section are listed by the names of the authors rather than the names of the instruments because few of them are known by specific names. Measures of attitudes and beliefs are discussed together because they were often combined in the same instrument, and it is sometimes hard to make distinctions among them.

Specific Attitude Measures

Each of the following descriptions summarizes the information provided in the article cited, including a description of the instrument, an indication of whether the items used are listed, reliability and validity data, the results of factor analysis, and an indication of the number of subjects who filled out the measure.[2] When these data are not included, it is because they were not provided in the reference. We warn the reader in advance that, despite being relatively rich in applied studies, the area of attitudes toward obese persons is extremely poor in terms of measurement instruments and detailed evaluations of their psychometric properties. Thus the remainder of our chapter will frequently read like a simple list of promising (and sometimes not so promising) measurement techniques that beg for further development and evaluation. We present the instruments alphabetically by the authors' names.

Agell and Rothblum (1991)

A total of 282 psychotherapists filled out a 28-item Person Perception Inventory (items listed by factors). This is a semantic differential-type scale with seven categories referring to personality attributes and social attractiveness. Factor analysis yielded eight factors that accounted for 38.6% of the variance. The factors were Social Attributes (6 items, 13.4% of the variance), Appearance (4 items, 7.7%), Energy (6 items, 4.6%), Dullness (4 items,

4.0%), Embarrassment (4 items, 3.1%), Softness/Kindness (2 items, 2.3%), Dependency (1 item, 1.9%), and Anger (1 item, 1.6%).

Allison, Basile, and Yuker (1991)

Allison et al. (1991) developed two companion scales: the Attitudes Toward Obese Persons Scale (ATOP) and the Beliefs About Obese Persons Scale (BAOP). Much of the theoretical underpinning for the instrument is based on the work of Yuker (1988a, 1988b) in the field of attitudes toward persons with disabilities. This model tends to focus on "discriminatory" and "stereotypical" perceptions of stigmatized individuals as exemplars of negative attitudes toward these people. In this context, *discriminate* is not (necessarily) meant in the sense of providing differential or negative treatment toward members of a stigmatized group but in the more classic sense of "to mark or perceive the distinguishing or particular features . . . to distinguish by discerning or exposing differences" (Gove, 1969, p. 238). In other words, people who focus on or exaggerate group differences and downplay or ignore within-group individual variability are seen as holding stereotypical and discriminatory attitudes.

Item development. The ATOP was modeled on Yuker and Block's (1986) Attitudes Toward Disabled Persons Scale (ATDP). Many of the ATOP items were adapted from the ATDP. Others were created by the authors or adapted from the disparaging image factor of the scale by Maiman, Wang, Becker, Finlay, and Simonson (1979). BAOP items were developed by the authors and initial testing and item analyses eliminated poor items. The final ATOP and the BAOP used 20 and 8 six-category Likert-type items and are reprinted in Appendixes 3-A and 3-B, respectively.

Scoring instructions for ATOP.

Step 1: Multiply the response to the following items by –1 (i.e., reverse the direction of scoring):
- Item 2 through Item 6, Item 10 through Item 12, Item 14 through Item 16, Item 18 through Item 20

Step 2: Add up the responses to all items.

Step 3: Add 60 to the value obtained in Step 2. This value is the ATOP score. Higher numbers indicate more positive attitudes.

TABLE 3.1 Normative Data

	ATOP			BAOP		
Sample	Mean	SD	Range	Mean	SD	Range
Undergraduates	63.9	16.7	23-96	19.4	8.7	0-41
Graduate students	64.8	14.8	32-104	20.8	7.0	6-33
NAAFAn's	67.6	18.6	0-120	31.7	10.5	1-48

Scoring instructions for BAOP.

Step 1: Multiply the response to the following items by −1 (i.e., reverse the direction of scoring):

– Item 1, Items 3 through Item 6, Item 8

Step 2: Sum the responses to all items.

Step 3: Add 24 to the value obtained in Step 2. This value is the BAOP score. Higher numbers indicate a stronger belief that obesity is *not* under the obese person's control.

Normative data. Data are available on samples consisting of 514 members of the National Association to Advance Fat Acceptance and 124 college and graduate students. ATOP and BAOP means, standard deviations, and ranges are presented in Table 3.1.

Factor structure. Factor analysis of the ATOP yielded three orthogonal factors, which accounted for 42% of the variance. The first factor (accounting for 23% of the variance) was labeled "Different Personality" and reflected the attribution of negative or different characteristics or abilities to obese persons. Factor I is probably the "purest" measure of attitudes in the ATOP. The second factor (11% of the variance) is labeled "Social Difficulties" and reflects the perception that obese people experience and/or produce social difficulties. Finally, Factor III (8% of the variance) was labeled "Self-Esteem" and contained items relating to how obese persons evaluate themselves.

Reliability. For the ATOP, coefficient alphas range from .80 to .84 in various samples. For the BAOP, the alpha range was .65 to .82. No test-retest reliability data have been collected.

Validity. At this time, the only validity data available for the ATOP and BAOP are for content validity and construct validity. The BAOP and ATOP tend to correlate between .40 and .45 with each other, which is predicted from past research and theory. There is also a small but statistically significant correlation between positive ATOP scores and percentage of friends that are obese.

Readability. Readability was assessed using the Flesch-Kincaid and Flesch Reading Indexes. The Flesch-Kincaid Index refers to the grade level at which a scale is written. The Flesch Reading Index refers to the general ease of reading, ranging from 1 to 100, where lower scores represent greater difficulty and higher scores represent greater ease of reading. The ATOP's Flesch-Kincaid Index was 7.7. This means that a student whose standardized reading score falls at the seventh month of the seventh grade should be able to understand the scale. The Flesch Reading Index was 57. Both indexes are considered acceptable. For the BAOP, the Flesch-Kincaid and Flesch Reading Indexes were 8.5 and 56.2, respectively.

Limitations of the ATOP. The primary limitation of the ATOP stems from the theoretical rationale that views perceptions of group differences as indicators of "negative" attitudes. For example, consider item 8: "Most obese people are not dissatisfied with themselves." Suppose someone strongly disagrees. Does this mean that he or she has a negative attitude or merely that he or she is aware of the considerable data indicating that obese persons do have lower self-esteem (Davis, Wheeler, & Willy, 1987; Hoover, 1984; Martin et al., 1988; O'Brien, Smith, Bush, & Peleg, 1990; Stein, 1987). Similarly, other items may inadvertently tap the perception that obese persons are discriminated against (e.g., item 5) rather than the perception that obese persons are inherently different. In addition to the theoretical limitation of the ATOP, more descriptive data are needed on its psychometric properties.

Bagley et al. (1989)

These authors developed an instrument to assess nurses' attitudes toward obese patients. Through "component analysis" and other unspecified statistical procedures (on an unspecified sample), the initial 70-item questionnaire was reduced to 28 items. This questionnaire consisted of two scales, "Nursing Management" (15 items) and "Personality and Lifestyle" (13 items). These two scales correlate .75 with each other, indicating that a negative attitude toward caring for obese patients is associated with a negative attitude toward obese persons in general. Reliability data were not provided, although correlations with other scales were described. Specifically, among a sample of 107 nurses, scores on the two scales correlated in expected directions (*r* values ranging between .54 and .64) with various semantic differential ratings of "an obese adult." The Flesch-Kincaid and Flesch Reading Indexes were 7.7 and 57.0, respectively. Appendix 3-C presents the two scales.

Bray (1972) and Sims (1979)

An early scale was developed in a doctoral thesis by Bray (1972). The author used "curricular validation" to support the 47-item instrument. That is, the preliminary 76-item scale was sent to eight obesity experts who indicated whether or not each item reflected an attitude concerning obesity. Using a 75% agreement criterion, 47 items were retained from the initial instrument. The author reported a split-half reliability of .87.

Bray's (1972) instrument was revised in Sims's (1979) doctoral thesis and used to test attitude differences between Caucasian, black, and Native American church attenders. To do so, Sims reduced the scale to 24 items. This was done by first having nine judges classify each item as reflecting either a favorable or an unfavorable attitude toward obesity. Then, Sims statistically identified the 24 items that best discriminated the high (favorable attitude) from low (unfavorable attitude) scoring subjects. The Spearman split-half reliability for these statements was .74.

Neither Bray's (1972) nor Sims's (1979) scale appears to have been used in other studies. No other data on psychometric properties have been published.

Canning and Mayer (1967)

The authors administered a questionnaire dealing with attitudes and knowledge of weight control to 225 obese and 213 nonobese subjects. It included both sentence completion items and items to which subjects responded by indicating agreement, disagreement, or undecided. As an example of the latter, the following three statements were used to measure "stereotypical views of obesity and weight control": "Thin people get sick more easily than heavier people." "Boys prefer girls who are plump rather than skinny." "The fact that a fat person can live longer without food is one real advantage to being overweight." Reliability data on these and other items were not cited.

Chetwynd et al. (1974)

Chetwynd et al. used what they referred to as a grid technique in which subjects (number not reported) were asked to describe personality characteristics of six female physiques represented by line drawings indicative of three different somatotypes: ectomorph, endomorph, and mesomorph. Although it is not clear, specific questions apparently were asked regarding each figure. Reliability data were not cited.

Counts et al. (1986)

Investigators interviewed 12 obese and 12 nonobese third- to fifth-grade children, asking each of them eight questions pertaining to a photograph of an overweight 14-year-old girl who might be visiting their school as a student teacher. Questions asked for ratings of her attractiveness, competence as a teacher, and how much contact they wanted to have with her. A 5-point Likert-type scale was used. Reliability data were not cited.

Crandall and Biernat (1990)

Antifat attitudes were conceptualized as being part of a larger constellation of politically conservative and authoritarian attitudes. To test this theoretical model, Crandall and Biernat constructed a scale designed to tap antifat attitudes. Specifically, 1,072 undergraduates returned questionnaires consisting of four 6-point Likert-type antifat attitude items plus a ranking question. The scale has a one-factor solution and a reliability coefficient of .65.

Crandall (1994)

Expanding on Crandall and Biernat's (1990) research, Crandall (1994) conceptualized antifat attitudes as being similar in structure to symbolic racism. That is, antifat attitudes stem from the belief that obese persons voluntarily behave self-defeatingly (that is, by overindulging) and lack appropriate self-discipline. According to the theory, those with antifat attitudes value the Puritan work ethic and believe in self-determination. For these persons, obesity is perceived as being anti-American. To test these hypotheses in a series of experiments, Crandall constructed a scale.

A total of 250 undergraduates answered questions reflecting antifat attitudes using a 10-point Likert-type scale. Factor analysis yielded three factors: "Dislike," measuring degree of negative feelings about fat people (seven items, alpha = .84), "Fear of Fat" (three items, alpha = .79), and "Willpower," measuring beliefs about the degree to which a fat person is perceived as responsible for being fat (three items, alpha = .66). Factor loadings are cited for 13 items. The Dislike scale correlated .38 with the Willpower scale and .05 with the Fear of Fat scale. The correlation between Willpower and Fear of Fat was .16. Each scale is scored by summing pertinent items and dividing by the number of items. Validity is indicated by correlation with other attitude measures. Flesch-Kincaid and Flesch Reading Indexes were 5.6 and 77.6, respectively. Appendix 3-D presents this instrument.

Harris (1983)

A total of 222 Australian university students filled out questionnaires. Attitudes were measured by five 7-point semantic differential-type rating scales, questions about ideal weights, and minimum and maximum weights for a 5-foot 4-inch tall woman and a 5-foot 10-inch tall man to be considered attractive. The five rating scales were summed to yield a Positive Attitude score with an alpha coefficient of .66. Eight true/false "knowledge" of obesity items (cited on p. 276) had very low reliability (alpha = .11), which Harris attributed to guessing.

Harris and Harris (1992)

A total of 310 8- to 77-year-old subjects were asked to indicate their reactions to 12 3-inch-high line drawings (6 women, 6 men) which varied in width or apparent weight. Five questions were asked including the following: "Who is the best looking?" and "Who is the healthiest?" Reliability data were not cited.

Harris et al. (1982)

A total of 146 Australian university students used 12 7-point scales to rate a person described as male or female, average weight or overweight, and wearing glasses or not. Ratings were made on the following dimensions: assertive to unassertive, active to passive, unintelligent to intelligent, hardworking to lazy, reserved to outgoing, happy to unhappy, feminine to unfeminine, unattractive to attractive, unpopular to popular, unsuccessful to successful, athletic to unathletic, masculine to unmasculine. Reliability data were not cited.

Harris and Hopwood (1983)

A sample of 200 13- to 91-year-old Australians were surveyed using a combination of open-ended questions and several 5-point scales to rate their feelings about very fat people. Some subjects were interviewed; others filled out the questionnaire. Reliability data were not cited. Subjects' responses to open-ended questions were classified into groups and the percentage of responses falling into each category was computed. For example, responses to the first question, which asked subjects to list their causal attributions for obesity, were categorized as follows: eating too much (56%), lack of exercise (37.5%), eating the wrong foods (29%), emotional reasons (17%), general bad habits and/or upbringing (13%), medical causes (12.5%), lack of concern (12%), excessive drinking (11.5%), heredity (4%), compulsive eating (3.5), appetite or liking for food (3.5%), other reasons (2.5%), and don't know (.5%). The survey is presented in Appendix 3-E.

Harris and Koehler (1991)

A total of 318 subjects filled out a questionnaire that included eight questions about weight attitudes (from Stern, Pugh, Gaskill, & Hazuda, 1982) and nine questions regarding beliefs about weight control and nutrition (from Sims, 1979). Reliability data were not cited.

Harris, Walters, and Waschull (1991)

A sample of 645 college students used a 7-point scale to rate men and women who are substantially overweight, using 18 adjectives (items listed) representing nine sets of antonyms (i.e., a semantic differential-type scale). Average scores were obtained to represent stereotypical attitudes. Alpha reliabilities for four scales ranged from .67 to .76. Subjects also filled out a 12-item "knowledge" of obesity scale developed by Price, O'Connell, and Kukulka (1985; see below).

Harris, Waschull, and Walters (1990)

A total of 47 women and 8 men who considered themselves overweight rated how men and women who are substantially overweight are viewed by most people and by the respondents themselves. They used a 7-point scale to rate 16 adjectives. Reliabilities ranged from .74 to .76. Appendix 3-F presents the scale. Subjects also indicated whether they thought being overweight was worse than 20 other handicapping conditions. Finally, they completed a 12-item "knowledge" scale (items not listed) scored T, ?, or F (Price et al., 1985). Alpha equaled .15, which, although very low, "was consistent with earlier research."

Maiman et al. (1979)

The investigators used a 22-item scale in a six-category Likert-type format (items not listed) administered to 52 professionals, mostly nutritionists, attending a continuing education conference on obesity. Reliability and validity data were not given. Although the data were not factor analyzed, the authors stated that there appear to be three dimensions: disparaging image of obese persons, causes of obesity, and ways to lose weight, each of which was scored separately.

Price, Desmond, Krol, Snyder, and O'Connell (1987)

The authors administered a 23-item questionnaire (items not listed) to 318 physicians. Many items used a seven-category Likert-type scale. No reliability information was given.

Price, Desmond, Ruppert, and Stelzer (1987)

A 50-item questionnaire (items not listed but some items cited) pertaining to perceptions and practices regarding child obesity was administered to 220 school nurses. Many items used a seven-category Likert-type scale. The alpha reliability was .80.

Price, Desmond, and Stelzer (1987)

A 34-item questionnaire (items not listed but many items cited) dealing with perceptions of obesity and the role of the schools was administered to 222 elementary school principals. Many items used a seven-category Likert-type scale. The alpha reliability was .84.

Price, O'Connell, and Kukulka (1985)

A 12-item Obesity "knowledge" Quiz was developed to measure general information, "knowledge" of etiology, weight loss techniques, and diseases related to obesity. The items were presented to 187 college students in one of four different response formats. Low to moderate reliability was obtained. The highest K-R 20 coefficient was .40 and the highest 2-day test-retest reliability was .75. The relationship between "knowledge" and attitudes was not reported. They also studied the influence of format by comparing two true/false formats with a five-category Likert-type format and a multiple choice format in a 12-item scale measuring "knowledge" of obesity. All of the reliabilities were low. As in some of the other scales described, this probably was due to the small number of items but might have resulted from random guessing by the college students. This measure was used in several studies by Harris, consistently yielding alphas below .20.

Richardson et al. (1961)

A picture-ordering task was first used by Richardson in 1961 to obtain children's reactions to children with several different stigmatizing conditions, one of which was obesity. It has subsequently been used in many studies by him and others, including Maddox, Back, and Liederman (1968). The task involves asking people to rank order six sketches of children of the same sex as the subject in terms of which stimulus person the subject would find easiest to like, the next best, and so on. The line drawings represent various stigmatizing characteristics including a child in a wheelchair, a child with crutches, and an obviously overweight child.

Robinson, Bacon, and O'Reilly (1993)

Robinson et al. (1993) presented one of the more recent and well-developed instruments, which they call the "Fat Phobia Scale" (FPS). Robinson et al. ground their instrument in a theoretical orientation in which "the term 'fat phobia' refers to a pathological fear of fatness often *manifested as negative attitude* [sic] and stereotypes about fat people" (p. 468, emphasis added).

Item development. Items for the FPS were developed by asking people (exact number not reported) who entered a motor vehicle license bureau in a Minnesota suburb to list adjectives descriptive of fat people. Combining these items and "clinical experience" produced a 50-item modified 5-point semantic differential. The FPS appears in Appendix 3-G.

Scoring instructions for the FPS.

Step 1: For items 4, 7-9, 11-12, 14, 20-22, 26, 28-30, 32-33, 35-36, and 43, score the FPS as follows:

1 2 3 4 5

Step 2: For items 1-3, 5-6, 10, 13, 15-19, 23-25, 27, 31, 34, 37-42, and 44-50, score the FPS as follows:

5 4 3 2 1

Step 3: Add up the score for each item to get the total score for the FPS. The range of scale is 50-250.

– High score = more "fat phobia"

– Low score = less "fat phobia"

TABLE 3.2 Fat Phobia Scale: Subscale Information

Factor Number and Label	Coefficient α	Mean	SD
1. Undisciplined/inactive/ unappealing	.88	3.6	.54
2. Grouchy and unfriendly	.83	2.5	.52
3. Poor hygiene	.80	3.1	.55
4. Passivity	.78	3.1	.48
5. Emotional/psychological problems	.78	3.5	.64
6. Stupid and uncreative	.70	2.8	.52

Fat phobia is defined as dislike of, hatred for, or disgust for fat people and a fear of becoming fat oneself. Three additional interpretations are made: First, people with negative stereotypes about obese or fat people are seen as being likely to have fat phobic attitudes; second, people with positive stereotypes about obese or fat people are seen as being the least likely to have fat phobic attitudes; third, people with "neutral" attitudes, who do not stereotype obese or fat people, are seen as being less likely to have fat phobic attitudes.

Factor structure. The main sample consisted of 1,135 subjects who were actually pooled from 44 separate samples. A principal components analysis was conducted. The first six components were retained and rotated to simple structure via the varimax procedure. A six-factor solution was retained based on an a priori hypothesized factor structure. The six factor labels can be found in Table 3.2.

Reliability. With respect to internal consistency, the total scale yielded a coefficient alpha of .92. As can be seen in Table 3.2, individual subscales had alphas ranging from .70 to .88. No test-retest reliability was reported.

Validity. Robinson et al. (1993) claim that their method of item development demonstrates that the scale has "content validity." No convergent or discriminant validity information is reported. Initial evidence of construct validity was provided by a quasi-experimental study that showed that a treatment designed to improve attitudes toward obese persons did demonstrate significantly improved attitudes as measured by the total FPS and each of the six subscales.

Staffieri (1967)

The investigator had 90 6- to 10-year-old boys assign adjectives from a list of 39 items (listed) representing behavior or personality traits to silhouettes representing "extreme" ectomorph, endomorph, and mesomorph body types. A sociometric measure was used to relate body types to popularity. Reliability data were not cited.

Wolfgang and Wolfgang (1971)

Subjects were 30-year-old male students and military personnel. An Interpersonal Distance Test was used in which subjects drew stick figures to represent the distance at which they would feel comfortable in relation to eight persons they presumably knew, four male, four female, who were obese, a drug user, a homosexual, or a police officer. The distances between the heads of the figures were measured and compared. No reliability data were cited.

Methodological Considerations

Many studies of attitudes, beliefs, or knowledge about obese persons suffer from one or more methodological flaws. Some authors have pointed out methodological problems with studies documenting prejudiced attitudes and behaviors. Harris and Hopwood (1983) stated that the data indicating prejudice toward obese persons is weak because much of it is anecdotal or based on ratings of drawings, photographs, or descriptions. Similarly, Feldman, Feldman, and Goodman (1988) noted that many investigations of children's attitudes toward fatness are flawed by small, unrepresentative samples, instruments with questionable reliability and validity, and poor experimental designs that can yield biased results.

Stimuli. The type of stimulus used might well influence the responses in these types of studies. As Counts et al. (1986) pointed out, negative stereotypes of obese persons may be dominant when the only cue is information about body type, whereas attitudes are influenced by other personality and social characteristics as well as obesity. The importance of standardized question wording was indicated in a study by Price, Desmond, and Hallinan (1987), who reported that the terms *heavy, obese,* and *overweight* can lead to significantly different data.

In some studies, people were asked to react to pictures, films, or vignettes describing people they do not know. Often the subjects were given minimal information, sometimes responding to a 30-second videotaped incident. While we know that impressions are formed very quickly, one could legitimately ask whether such impressions provide valid information about how attitudes toward obese people develop in the "real world."

One of the greatest overall problems in this field is a lack of information about the measures that were used. Not only did most reports neglect to describe the reliability and validity of the measures used, some even failed to mention the number of items in the questionnaire. Although the size of the samples was usually mentioned, the way the sample was selected and other characteristics of the sample were seldom described. Although this information was most often lacking in the earlier studies, it was also lacking in quite a few of those published more recently.

Failure to build cumulatively. Isaac Newton once said, "If I have seen further it is by standing on the shoulders of giants" (Newton, 1675/1676, cited in Thrower, 1990). In this quotation, Newton epitomizes the way in which scientific progress is typically made. In the context of paradigmatic science, a knowledge base is built one brick at a time on a foundation of strong methodology including strong measurement techniques. Unfortunately, this seems not to be the case in the area of attitudes toward obese persons. Too many investigators appear to rush headlong into making their own measurement instruments without justifying why such instruments are preferable to existing ones. Worse yet, by often not reprinting their own scales and publishing detailed psychometric information, they fail to leave an adequate foundation for other investigators to build on.

Sample size and representativeness. Comparatively few studies used large samples, and many used samples of less than 30, with some using only 8 or 10. Furthermore, most used convenience samples of whoever was available and willing to cooperate. In addition, problems could arise because of low response rates. People who cooperate in a specific research project may be quite different than those who refuse to participate, which can lead to nonresponse bias. These problems are often ignored because most attitude studies, other than public opinion polls, fail to use representative samples. The representativeness of the samples and the situations is rarely discussed. This brings the ecological validity of the studies into question.

Measures of low or unknown reliability and validity. Many studies used locally developed measures, often without providing psychometric data pertaining to reliability and validity, rather than standardized measures with known psychometric characteristics. When indices of reliability were obtained, they were often low. While there are no absolute standards, a reliability coefficient of .70 is often considered a minimal acceptable standard. Although several standardized instruments with demonstrated reliability and validity exist, many researchers continue to develop and use measures whose reliability and validity were either unreported or questionable.

Problems of self-report measures. The major problem with self-report measures of attitudes concerns validity. It is often difficult or impossible to determine the accuracy of the responses. Answers either may be deliberately distorted (e.g., to minimize the expression of prejudiced attitudes) or they may be inaccurate as a consequence of carelessness, faulty memory, or misinterpretation of a question.

Cameron and Evers (1990) suggested strategies for discouraging inaccurate self-report data. These strategies included retrieval cues to enhance memory recall, more anonymous data collection procedures, and better incentives to reinforce accurate data recording.

Summary and Discussion

Almost none of the measures has been used in more than one or two studies. Occasionally Harris has employed measures previously used either by others or in her own prior research. Many measures, particularly the early ones, failed to cite either reliability or validity data. When data were cited, reliabilities were often low. The measures with adequate reliability are all recent.

The few factor analytic studies of attitudes toward obese persons yielded nonconvergent results. Crandall and Biernat (1990) used only four items and obtained a one-factor solution. Maiman et al. (1979) used a 22-item scale. Although the data were not factor analyzed, they stated that there appeared to be three dimensions: Disparaging Image of Obese Persons, Causes of Obesity, and Ways to Lose Weight. Allison et al. (1991), using 20 items, found three factors: Different Personality, Social Difficulties, and Self-Esteem. Most recently, Crandall (1994) used a 10-point Likert-type scale that yielded three factors: Dislike, Fear of Fat, and Willpower. Obviously, because these results are not convergent, we do not definitively know which factors underlie attitudes toward obese persons. Clearly, the attitude scales often measure different aspects of attitudes. This is not surprising given the different theoretical orientations of the developers. Thus Crandall (1994) developed a scale that taps authoritarian/fascist attitudes toward obese persons; Allison et al. (1991) designed a measure to tap "stereotypical" attitudes; Robinson et al. (1993) approached the problem from a more psychodynamic point of view where negative attitudes represent the manifestations of pathological fears. Each measure may be best in a given situation depending on the goals and orientation of the investigator.

Even though there appear to be no instruments that have been generally accepted or widely used, we would urge researchers not to attempt to develop new instruments *unless* there is a compelling *theoretical* reason for doing so.

Instead, it would be better to try to revise existing measures to make them more reliable and valid. To date, scales by Allison et al. (1991), Bray (1972), Crandall (1994), and Robinson et al. (1993) demonstrate the best psychometric properties and should be incorporated in future research.

Notes

1. It should be noted that the Likert scale as originally conceived involved a rigorous approach to item selection and not merely a 1 to 7 response format (Dawis, 1987). Unfortunately, the former aspect seems to have been largely forgotten.

2. Data on readability were provided for four scales (Allison et al., 1991; Bagley et al., 1989; Crandall, 1994). However, these statistics were computed by the authors of this book chapter.

References

Adams, C. H., Smith, N. J., Wilbur, D. C., & Grady, K. E. (1993). The relationship of obesity to the frequency of pelvic examinations: Do physician and patient attitudes make a difference? *Women and Health, 20,* 45-57.

Agell, G., & Rothblum, E. D. (1991). Effects of clients' obesity and gender on the therapy judgments of psychologists. *Professional Psychology: Research and Practice, 22,* 223-229.

Allison, D. B., Basile, V. C., & Yuker, H. E. (1991). The measurement of attitudes toward and beliefs about obese persons. *International Journal of Eating Disorders, 10,* 599-807.

Allon, N. (1979). Self-perceptions of the stigma of overweight in relationship to weight-losing patients. *American Journal of Nutrition, 32,* 470-480.

Ashwell, M., & Etchell, L. (1974). Attitude of the individual to his own body weight. In A. Howard (Ed.), *Recent advances in obesity research* (Vol. 1, pp. 232-235). Westport, CT: Technomic.

Bagley, C. R., Conklin, D. N., Isherwood, R. T., Pechiulis, D. R., & Watson, L. A. (1989). Attitudes of nurses toward obesity and obese patients. *Perceptual and Motor Skills, 68,* 954.

Ben-Tovim, D. I., & Walker, M. K. (1991). Women's body attitudes: A review of measurement techniques. *International Journal of Eating Disorders, 10,* 155-167.

Bray, C. (1972). *The development of an instrument to measure attitudes toward obesity.* Unpublished doctoral dissertation, University of Mississippi, University, MS.

Cahnman, W. J. (1968). The stigma of obesity. *Sociological Quarterly, 9,* 283-299.

Cameron, R., & Evers, S. (1990). Self-report issues in obesity and weight management: State of the art and future directions. *Behavioral Assessment, 12,* 91-106.

Canning, H., & Mayer, J. (1967). Obesity: Analysis of attitudes and knowledge of weight control in girls. *Research Quarterly, 39,* 894-899.

Chetwynd, S. J., Stewart, R. A., & Powell, G. E. (1974). Social attitudes towards the obese physique. In A. Howard (Ed.), *Recent advances in obesity research* (Vol. 1, pp. 223-225). Westport, CT: Technomic.

Counts, C. R., Jones, C., Frame, C. L., Jarvie, G. J., & Strauss, C. C. (1986). The perception of obesity by normal-weight versus obese school-age children. *Child Psychiatry & Human Development, 17,* 113-120.

Crandall, C. S. (1991). Do heavy-weight students have more difficulty paying for college? *Personality and Social Psychology Bulletin, 17*, 606-611.

Crandall, C. S. (1994). Prejudice against fat people: Ideology and self-interest. *Journal of Personality and Social Psychology, 66*, 882-894.

Crandall, C. S., & Biernat, M. (1990). The ideology of anti-fat attitudes. *Journal of Applied Social Psychology, 20*, 227-243.

Dash, J. D., & Brown, R. A. (1977). The development of a rating scale for the prediction of success in weight reduction. *Journal of Clinical Psychology, 33*, 748-752.

Davis, J. M., Wheeler, R. W., & Willy, E. (1987). Cognitive correlates of obesity in a nonclinical population. *Psychological Reports, 67*, 879-884.

Dawis, R. V. (1987). Scale construction. *Journal of Counseling Psychology, 34*, 481-489.

Feldman, W., Feldman, E., & Goodman, J. T. (1988). Culture versus biology: Children's attitudes toward thinness and fatness. *Pediatrics, 81*, 190-194.

Frieze, I. H., Olson, J. E., & Good, D. C. (1990). Perceived and actual discrimination in the salaries of male and female managers. *Journal of Applied Social Psychology, 20*, 46-67.

Gove, P. B. (Ed.). (1969). *Webster's seventh new collegiate dictionary*. Springfield, MA: Merriam Webster.

Harris, M. B. (1983). Eating habits, restraint, knowledge, and attitudes toward obesity. *International Journal of Obesity, 7*, 271-286.

Harris, M. B., & Furukawa, C. (1986). Attitudes toward obesity in an elderly sample. *Journal of Obesity and Weight Regulation, 5*, 5-16.

Harris, M. B., & Harris, R. J. (1992). Response to pictures of varying body weight by rural south-western groups. *Journal of Nutrition Education, 24*, 37-40.

Harris, M. B., Harris, R. J., & Bochner, S. (1982). Fat, four-eyed, and female: Stereotypes of obesity, glasses, and gender. *Journal of Applied Social Psychology, 12*, 503-516.

Harris, M. B., & Hopwood, J. (1983). Attitudes toward the obese in Australia. *Journal of Obesity and Weight Regulation, 2*, 107-120.

Harris, M. B., & Koehler, K. M. (1991, June 14). *Culture and gender differences in weight, eating, and exercise behaviors and attitudes*. Poster presentation at APS, Washington, DC.

Harris, M. B., & Smith, S. D. (1982). Beliefs about obesity: Effects of age, ethnicity, sex, and weight. *Psychological Reports, 51*, 1047-1055.

Harris, M. B., Walters, L. C., & Waschull, S. (1991). Gender and ethnic differences in obesity-related behaviors and attitudes in a college sample. *Journal of Applied Social Psychology, 21*, 1545-1555.

Harris, M. B., Waschull, S., & Walters, L. (1990). Feeling fat: Motivations, knowledge, and attitudes of overweight women and men. *Psychological Reports, 67*, 1191-1202.

Hoover, M. L. (1984). The self-image of overweight adolescent females: A review of the literature. *Maternal-Child Nursing Journal, 13*, 125-137.

Karris, L. (1977). Prejudice against obese renters. *Journal of Social Psychology, 101*, 159-160.

Klesges, R. V., Klem, M. L., Hanson, C. L., Eck, L. H., Ernst, J., O'Laughlin, D., Garrott, A., & Rife, R. (1990). The effects of applicant's health status and qualifications on simulated hiring decisions. *International Journal of Obesity, 14*, 525-535.

Likert, R. (1932). A technique for the measurement of attitudes. *Archives of Psychology, 22*, 1-55.

Maddox, G. L., Back, K. W., & Liederman, W. R. (1968). Overweight as social deviance and disability. *Journal of Health and Social Behavior, 9*, 287-298.

Maiman, L. A., Wang, L. W., Becker, M. H., Finlay, J., & Simonson, M. (1979). Attitudes toward obesity and the obese among professionals. *Research, 74*, 331-336.

Martin, S., Housley, K., McCoy, H., Greenhouse, P., et al. (1988). Self-esteem of adolescent girls as related to weight. *Perceptual and Motor Skills, 67*, 879-884.

O'Brien, R. W., Smith, S. A., Bush, P. J., & Peleg, E. (1990). Obesity, self-esteem, and health locus of control in black youths during transition to adolescence. *American Journal of Health Promotion, 5,* 133-139.

Osgood, C. E., Suci, C. J., & Tannenbaum, P. H. (1957). *The measurement of meaning.* Urbana: University of Illinois Press.

Parker, K. C. H., Hansen, R. K., & Hunsley, J. (1988). MMPI, Rorschach, and WAIS: A meta-analytic comparison of reliability, stability, and validity. *Psychological Bulletin, 103,* 367-373.

Pauley, L. L. (1989). Customer weight as a variable in salespersons' response time. *Journal of Special Psychology, 129,* 713-714.

Peterson, C., & Stunkard, A. J. (1992). Cognates of personal control: Locus of control, self-efficacy, and explanatory style. *Applied and Preventive Psychology, 1,* 111-117.

Price, J. H., Desmond, S. M., & Hallinan, C. J. (1987). The importance of questionnaire wording: Assessments of weights as an example. *Health Education Quarterly, 18,* 40-43.

Price, J. H., Desmond, S. M., Krol, R. A., Snyder, F. F., & O'Connell, J. K. (1987). Family practice physicians beliefs, attitudes, and practices regarding obesity. *American Journal of Preventive Medicine, 3,* 339-345.

Price, J. H., Desmond, S. M., Ruppert, E. S., & Stelzer, C. M. (1987). School nurses' perceptions of childhood obesity. *Journal of School Health, 57,* 332-336.

Price, J. H., Desmond, S. M., & Stelzer, C. M. (1987). Elementary school principals' perceptions of childhood obesity. *Journal of School Health, 57,* 367-370.

Price, J. H., O'Connell, J. K., & Kukulka, G. (1985). Development of a short obesity knowledge scale using four different response formats. *Journal of School Health, 55,* 382-384.

Rand, C. S. W., & MacGregor, A. M. C. (1990). Morbidly obese patients' perceptions of social discrimination before and after surgery for obesity. *Southern Medical Journal, 83,* 1390-1395.

Register, C. A., & Williams, D. R. (1990). Wage effects of obesity among young workers. *Social Science Quarterly, 71,* 130-141.

Richardson, S., Goodman, N., Hastorf, A., & Dornbusch, S. (1961). Cultural uniformity and reaction to physical disability. *American Sociological Review, 26,* 241-247.

Robinson, B. E., Bacon, J. G., & O'Reilly, J. (1993). Fat phobia: Measuring, understanding and changing anti-fat attitudes. *International Journal of Eating Disorders, 14,* 467-480.

Rothblum, E. D. (1990). Women and weight: Fad and fiction. *Journal of Psychology, 124,* 5-24.

Sherman, A. A. (1981). *Obesity and sexism: Parental child preferences and attitudes toward obesity.* Unpublished master's thesis, University of Cincinnati.

Sims, H. J. (1979). *A study to identify and evaluate the attitudes toward obesity among three ethnic groups of women in Oklahoma: Black, white, and Indian.* Unpublished doctoral dissertation, University of Oklahoma.

Staffieri, J. R. (1967). A study of social stereotype of body image in children. *Journal of Personality and Social Psychology, 7,* 101-104.

Stein, R. F. (1987). Comparison of self-concept of nonobese and obese university junior female nursing students. *Adolescence, 22,* 77-90.

Stern, M. P., Pugh, J., Gaskill, S., & Hazuda, H. (1982). Knowledge, attitudes, and behavior related to obesity and dieting in Mexican Americans and Anglos: The San Antonio heart study. *American Journal of Epidemiology, 115,* 917-928.

Strauss, C. C., Smith, K., Frame, C., & Forehand, R. (1985). Personal and interpersonal characteristics associated with childhood obesity. *Journal of Pediatric Psychology, 10,* 337-343.

Thrower, N. J. W. (1990). *Standing on the shoulders of giants: A longer view of Newton and Halley.* Los Angeles: University of California Press.

Wolfgang, A., & Wolfgang, J. (1971). Exploration of attitudes via physical interpersonal distance toward the obese, drug users, homosexuals, police, and other marginal figures. *Journal of Clinical Psychology, 27,* 510-515.

Worsley, A. (1981). Teenagers' perceptions of fat and slim people. *International Journal of Obesity, 5,* 15-24.

Yuker, H. E. (Ed.). (1988a). *Attitudes toward persons with disabilities.* New York: Springer.

Yuker, H. E. (1988b). Perceptions of severely and multiply disabled persons. *Journal of the Multihandicapped Person, 1,* 5-16.

Yuker, H. E., & Allison, D. B. (1994). Obesity: Sociocultural perspectives. In L. Alexander-Mott & B. D. Lumsden (Eds.), *Understanding eating disorders* (pp. 243-270). Washington, DC: Taylor & Francis.

Yuker, H. E., & Block, J. R. (1986). *Research with the Attitudes Toward Disabled Persons Scale (ATDP) 1960-1985.* Hempstead, NY: Hofstra University, Center for the Study of Attitudes Toward Persons With Disabilities.

Appendix 3-A

Attitudes Toward Obese Persons Scale (ATOP)

Please mark each statement below in the left margin, according to how much you agree or disagree with it. Please do not leave any blank. Write a +1, +2, +3, or −1, −2, −3, according to the scale below.

+3 = I strongly agree

+2 = I moderately agree

+1 = I slightly agree

−1 = I slightly disagree

−2 = I moderately disagree

−3 = I strongly disagree

1. _____ Obese people are as happy as nonobese people.

2. _____ Most obese people feel that they are not as good as other people.

3. _____ Most obese people are more self-conscious than other people.

4. _____ Obese workers cannot be as successful as other workers.

5. _____ Most nonobese people would not want to marry anyone who is obese.

6. _____ Severely obese people are usually untidy.

7. _____ Obese people are usually sociable.

8. _____ Most obese people are not dissatisfied with themselves.

9. _____ Obese people are just as self-confident as other people.

10. _____ Most people feel uncomfortable when they associate with obese people.

11. _____ Obese people are often less aggressive than nonobese people.

12. _____ Most obese people have different personalities than nonobese people.

13. _____ Very few obese people are ashamed of their weight.

14. _____ Most obese people resent normal weight people.

15. _____ Obese people are more emotional than other people.

16. _____ Obese people should not expect to lead normal lives.

17. _____ Obese people are just as healthy as nonobese people.

18. _____ Obese people are just as sexually attractive as nonobese people.

19. _____ Obese people tend to have family problems.

20. _____ One of the worst things that could happen to a person would be for him to become obese.

SOURCE: Adapted from *Research With the Attitudes Toward Disabled Persons Scale (ATDP) 1960-1985,* by H. E. Yuker and J. R. Block, 1986, Hofstra University, Center for the Study of Attitudes Toward Persons With Disabilities, Hempstead, NY.

Appendix 3-B

Beliefs About Obese Persons Scale (BAOP)

Please mark each statement below in the left margin, according to how much you agree or disagree with it. Please do not leave any blank. Write a +1, +2, +3, or −1, −2, −3, according to the scale below.

+3 = I strongly agree

+2 = I moderately agree

+1 = I slightly agree

−1 = I slightly disagree

−2 = I moderately disagree

−3 I strongly disagree

1. _____ Obesity often occurs when eating is used as a form of compensation for lack of love or attention.

2. _____ In many cases, obesity is the result of a biological disorder.

3. _____ Obesity is usually caused by overeating.

4. _____ Most obese people cause their problem by not getting enough exercise.

5. _____ Most obese people eat more than nonobese people.

6. _____ The majority of obese people have poor eating habits that lead to their obesity.

7. _____ Obesity is rarely caused by a lack of willpower.

8. _____ People can be addicted to food, just as others are addicted to drugs, and these people usually become obese.

SOURCE: Some items adapted from "Beliefs About Obesity: Effects of Age, Ethnicity, Sex, and Weight," by M. B. Harris and S. D. Smith, 1982, *Psychological Reports, 51,* pp. 1047-1055, and "Attitudes Toward Obesity and the Obese Among Professionals," by L. A. Maiman, L. W. Wang, M. H. Becker, J. Finlay, and M. Simonson, 1979, *Research, 74,* pp. 331-336.

Appendix 3-C

Attitudes Toward Obese Adult Patients

Note: All statements (items) are scored using a 1-5 Likert-type scale:

1 = Strongly Agree

2 = Agree

3 = Unsure

4 = Disagree

5 = Strongly Disagree

1. _____ Obesity in adults can be prevented by self-control. (P&L)

2. _____ Most obese adults have poor food selection. (P&L)

3. _____ Obese adults should be put on a diet when in hospital. (NM)

4. _____ Most obese adults are pushy and aggressive. (P&L)

5. _____ Caring for an obese adult is physically exhausting. (NM)

6. _____ Nurses often feel uncomfortable when caring for obese adult patients. (NM)

7. _____ Obese adults experience less success in life. (P&L)

8. _____ It is unlikely that an adult of normal weight would want to marry an obese adult. (P&L)

9. _____ Weight loss is only a matter of changing one's lifestyle. (P&M)

10. _____ Caring for an obese patient is stressful. (NM)

11. _____ Caring for an obese adult patient usually repulses me. (NM)

12. _____ Most obese adults are more demanding than other patients. (NM)

13. _____ Caring for an obese adult patient is emotionally draining. (NM)

14. _____ I often feel impatient when caring for an obese adult patient. (NM)

15. _____ Most nurses find it difficult to obtain the cooperation of obese adult patients. (NM)

16. _____ Most obese adults lack self-confidence. (P&L)

17. _____ If given the choice, most nurses would prefer not to care for an obese adult patient. (NM)

18. _____ I'd rather not touch an obese adult. (NM)

19. _____ It is difficult to feel empathy for an obese adult. (NM)

20. _____ Most obese adults are overindulgent. (P&L)

21. _____ It does not hurt to apply "scare" tactics to obtain the compliance of the obese adult patient. (NM)

22. _____ Most obese adults are unkempt. (P&L)

23. _____ Obese adults rarely express their true feelings. (P&L)

24. _____ Obese adult patients require a firm approach. (NM)

25. _____ Most obese adults can lose weight if they change their eating habits. (P&L)

26. _____ I feel disgust when I am caring for an obese adult patient. (NM)

27. _____ Most obese adults experience unresolved anger. (P&L)

28. _____ Most obese adults are lazy. (P&L)

SOURCE: Reproduced with permission of authors and publisher from:
    Bagley, C. R., Conklin, D. N., Isherwood, R. T., Pechiulis, D. R., & Watson, L. A.
    Attitudes of nurses toward obesity and obese patients. *Perceptual and Motor Skills,*
    1989, 68, 954. © *Perceptual and Motor Skills* 1989
NOTE: P&L = Personality & Lifestyle Scale; NM = Nursing Management Scale.

Appendix 3-D

Attitudes About Weight and Dieting

For the following questions, circle a number between 0 and 9 to indicate how much you agree or disagree with each of the following statements.

Strongly Disagree	Neutral	Strongly Agree
0———1———2———3———4———5———6———7———8———9		

1. I worry about becoming fat.

   Strongly Disagree   0 1 2 3 4 5 6 7 8 9   Strongly Agree

2. I feel disgusted with myself when I gain weight.

   Strongly Disagree   0 1 2 3 4 5 6 7 8 9   Strongly Agree

3. One of the worst things that could happen to me would be if I gained 25 pounds.

   Strongly Disagree   0 1 2 3 4 5 6 7 8 9   Strongly Agree

4. Some people are fat because they have no willpower.

   Strongly Disagree   0 1 2 3 4 5 6 7 8 9   Strongly Agree

5. I have a hard time taking fat people too seriously.

   Strongly Disagree   0 1 2 3 4 5 6 7 8 9   Strongly Agree

6. I really don't like fat people much.

   Strongly Disagree   0 1 2 3 4 5 6 7 8 9   Strongly Agree

7. People who weigh too much could lose at least some part of their weight through a little exercise.

   Strongly Disagree   0 1 2 3 4 5 6 7 8 9   Strongly Agree

8. Fat people tend to be fat pretty much through their own fault.

   Strongly Disagree   0 1 2 3 4 5 6 7 8 9   Strongly Agree

9. Although some fat people are surely smart, in general, I think they tend not to be quite as bright as normal weight people.

Strongly Disagree   0 1 2 3 4 5 6 7 8 9   Strongly Agree

10. I tend to think that people who are overweight are a little untrustworthy.

Strongly Disagree   0 1 2 3 4 5 6 7 8 9   Strongly Agree

11. I don't have many friends who are fat.

Strongly Disagree   0 1 2 3 4 5 6 7 8 9   Strongly Agree

12. If I were an employer looking to hire, I might avoid hiring a fat person.

Strongly Disagree   0 1 2 3 4 5 6 7 8 9   Strongly Agree

13. Fat people make me feel somewhat uncomfortable.

Strongly Disagree   0 1 2 3 4 5 6 7 8 9   Strongly Agree

SOURCE: From "Prejudice Against Fat People: Ideology and Self-Interest," by C. S. Crandall, 1994, *Journal of Personality and Social Psychology, 66,* pp. 882-894. Reprinted with permission.

Appendix 3-E

Survey From Harris and Hopwood

1. What do you think are the major reasons why people are overweight?

2. Do you think that people who are fat are unable to control it or just unwilling to do anything about it?

3. How do you, personally, feel about people who are extremely overweight?

4. Do you think that Australians are prejudiced against people who are overweight?

   ____ yes ____ no ____ unsure

   If yes, in what ways?

5. Do you think that being overweight is more of a handicap for a man or for a woman or equally for both? Why?

   ____ man ____ woman ____ both ____ not a handicap

6. Do you know any people who are overweight?

   ____ yes ____ no

   If so, are they friends, relatives, or what?

   ____ friends ____ relative ____ both

7. Do you consider yourself overweight? ____ yes ____ no

   If yes, by approximately how many pounds? ____ pounds

   If yes, do you feel that your weight influences how other people behave toward you?

   ____ yes ____ no

   If so, how?

8. Overall, which of the following statements best describes how you feel about people who are very fat?

   ____ I really dislike them.

   ____ I dislike them.

   ____ I have no particular feelings toward them one way or another.

_____ I like them slightly.

_____ I really like them.

9. How would you feel about being very fat yourself?

    _____ I would really dislike it.

    _____ I would dislike it slightly.

    _____ I would have no particular feelings about it one way or another.

    _____ I would like it slightly.

    _____ I would really like it.

10. Do you think there are some jobs that very fat people should not be permitted to hold?

    _____ yes   _____ no

    If yes, which ones?

    _____

    _____

    _____

11. Are you: _____ male _____ female

    Your age: _____

    Occupation: _____

    Education: _____ (last year of school or degree completed)

    Were you born in Australia?   _____ yes   _____ no

12. Have you any other feelings about overweight or fatness to share with us?

    _____

    _____

    _____

SOURCE: From "Attitudes Toward the Obese in Australia," by M. B. Harris and J. Hopwood, 1983, *Journal of Obesity and Weight Regulation, 2,* pp. 107-120. Copyright © 1983 by Human Sciences Press, Inc. Reprinted with permission.

Appendix 3-F

Attitude Scales From
Harris, Waschull, and Walters

A. How are most women who are substantially overweight viewed:

a. By most people in the United States?   b. By you personally?

1 = Not at all; 7 = Extremely

		a								b				
lazy	1	2	3	4	5	6	7	1	2	3	4	5	6	7
sexless	1	2	3	4	5	6	7	1	2	3	4	5	6	7
neat	1	2	3	4	5	6	7	1	2	3	4	5	6	7
ugly	1	2	3	4	5	6	7	1	2	3	4	5	6	7
attractive	1	2	3	4	5	6	7	1	2	3	4	5	6	7
weak	1	2	3	4	5	6	7	1	2	3	4	5	6	7
happy	1	2	3	4	5	6	7	1	2	3	4	5	6	7
selfish	1	2	3	4	5	6	7	1	2	3	4	5	6	7
self-denying	1	2	3	4	5	6	7	1	2	3	4	5	6	7
energetic	1	2	3	4	5	6	7	1	2	3	4	5	6	7
sexy	1	2	3	4	5	6	7	1	2	3	4	5	6	7
generous	1	2	3	4	5	6	7	1	2	3	4	5	6	7
self-indulgent	1	2	3	4	5	6	7	1	2	3	4	5	6	7
sad	1	2	3	4	5	6	7	1	2	3	4	5	6	7
sloppy	1	2	3	4	5	6	7	1	2	3	4	5	6	7
powerful	1	2	3	4	5	6	7	1	2	3	4	5	6	7

B. How are most men who are substantially overweight viewed:

a. By most people in the United States?   b. By you personally?

1 = Not at all; 7 = Extremely

lazy	1	2	3	4	5	6	7	1	2	3	4	5	6	7
sexless	1	2	3	4	5	6	7	1	2	3	4	5	6	7
neat	1	2	3	4	5	6	7	1	2	3	4	5	6	7
ugly	1	2	3	4	5	6	7	1	2	3	4	5	6	7
attractive	1	2	3	4	5	6	7	1	2	3	4	5	6	7
weak	1	2	3	4	5	6	7	1	2	3	4	5	6	7
happy	1	2	3	4	5	6	7	1	2	3	4	5	6	7
selfish	1	2	3	4	5	6	7	1	2	3	4	5	6	7
self-denying	1	2	3	4	5	6	7	1	2	3	4	5	6	7
energetic	1	2	3	4	5	6	7	1	2	3	4	5	6	7
sexy	1	2	3	4	5	6	7	1	2	3	4	5	6	7
generous	1	2	3	4	5	6	7	1	2	3	4	5	6	7
self-indulgent	1	2	3	4	5	6	7	1	2	3	4	5	6	7
sad	1	2	3	4	5	6	7	1	2	3	4	5	6	7
sloppy	1	2	3	4	5	6	7	1	2	3	4	5	6	7
powerful	1	2	3	4	5	6	7	1	2	3	4	5	6	7

SOURCE: Reproduced with permission of authors and publisher from:
Harris, M. B., Waschull, S., & Walters, L. Feeling fat: motivations, knowledge, and attitudes of overweight women and men. *Psychological Reports*, 1990, 67, 1191-1202. © *Psychological Reports* 1990

Appendix 3-G

Fat Phobia Scale (FPS)

Listed below are adjectives sometimes used to describe *obese or fat* people. Please indicate your beliefs about what fat people are like on the following items by placing an **X** *on the line* that best describes your feelings and beliefs.

1. lazy ___ ___ ___ ___ ___ industrious
2. sloppy ___ ___ ___ ___ ___ neat
3. disgusting ___ ___ ___ ___ ___ not disgusting
4. friendly ___ ___ ___ ___ ___ unfriendly
5. nonassertive ___ ___ ___ ___ ___ assertive
6. no willpower ___ ___ ___ ___ ___ has willpower
7. artistic ___ ___ ___ ___ ___ not artistic
8. creative ___ ___ ___ ___ ___ uncreative
9. warm ___ ___ ___ ___ ___ cold
10. depressed ___ ___ ___ ___ ___ happy
11. smart ___ ___ ___ ___ ___ stupid
12. reads a lot ___ ___ ___ ___ ___ doesn't read a lot
13. unambitious ___ ___ ___ ___ ___ ambitious
14. easy to talk to ___ ___ ___ ___ ___ hard to talk to
15. unattractive ___ ___ ___ ___ ___ attractive
16. miserable ___ ___ ___ ___ ___ jolly
17. selfish ___ ___ ___ ___ ___ selfless
18. poor self-control ___ ___ ___ ___ ___ good self-control
19. inconsiderate of others ___ ___ ___ ___ ___ considerate of others
20. good ___ ___ ___ ___ ___ bad

21. popular	___	___	___	___	___	unpopular
22. important	___	___	___	___	___	insignificant
23. slow	___	___	___	___	___	fast
24. ineffective	___	___	___	___	___	effective
25. careless	___	___	___	___	___	careful
26. having endurance	___	___	___	___	___	having no endurance
27. inactive	___	___	___	___	___	active
28. nice complexion	___	___	___	___	___	bad complexion
29. tries to please people	___	___	___	___	___	doesn't try to please people
30. humorous/funny	___	___	___	___	___	humorless/not funny
31. inefficient	___	___	___	___	___	efficient
32. strong	___	___	___	___	___	weak
33. individualistic	___	___	___	___	___	not individualistic
34. pitiful	___	___	___	___	___	not pitiful
35. independent	___	___	___	___	___	dependent
36. good-natured	___	___	___	___	___	irritable
37. self-indulgent	___	___	___	___	___	self-sacrificing
38. passive	___	___	___	___	___	aggressive
39. indirect	___	___	___	___	___	direct
40. likes food	___	___	___	___	___	dislikes food
41. dirty	___	___	___	___	___	clean
42. does not attend to own appearance	___	___	___	___	___	very attentive to own appearance
43. easygoing	___	___	___	___	___	uptight
44. shapeless	___	___	___	___	___	shapely
45. overeats	___	___	___	___	___	undereats
46. smells bad	___	___	___	___	___	smells good
47. sweaty	___	___	___	___	___	not sweaty
48. moody	___	___	___	___	___	even-tempered
49. insecure	___	___	___	___	___	secure
50. low self-esteem	___	___	___	___	___	high self-esteem

SOURCE: From "Fat Phobia: Measuring, Understanding and Changing Anti-Fat Attitudes," by B. E. Robinson, J. G. Bacon, and J. O'Reilly, 1993, *International Journal of Eating Disorders, 14,* pp. 467–480. Copyright © 1993 by John Wiley & Sons, Inc. Reprinted with permission.

4

Assessment of Body Image

J. KEVIN THOMPSON

Body image has a long and storied association with eating and weight-related problems (Rosen, 1990; Thompson, 1990). Bruch (1962) articulated the integral role of body image in the development, maintenance, and treatment of anorexia nervosa. In later years, researchers also agreed that body image was a central factor in bulimia nervosa (American Psychiatric Association, 1987; Thompson, Berland, Linton, & Weinsier, 1986). Finally, although often ignored as a feature of obesity (see Thompson, 1990), Stunkard and Burt (1967) demonstrated almost 30 years ago the importance of body image to an understanding of individuals with excessive weight.

One index of the importance of body image disturbance involves its relevance to agreed-on clinical disorders. The *Diagnostic and Statistical Manual of Mental Disorders IV* (American Psychiatric Association, 1994) contains a body image criterion that is required for the diagnosis of anorexia nervosa or bulimia nervosa. In addition, one type of Somatoform Disorder—Body Dysmorphic Disorder—is a specific clinical syndrome consisting of extreme body image disparagement. It has also been suggested that, when there is psychological comorbidity with obesity, it may be strongly due to problematic body image issues (Thompson, 1992). Today, researchers and clinicians agree that including an assessment and evaluation of body image disturbance is crucial to any treatment program targeting obesity or eating disorders.

This chapter will focus on the assessment of the multiple forms of body image. A common misconception is that *body image disturbance* is synonymous with *dissatisfaction* with some aspect of physical appearance. However, appearance dissatisfaction is only one manifestation of body image disturbance, albeit a very common associate of some weight and eating problems. In fact, there are many aspects to the construct of body image. An understanding of the many types, and definitions, of this important variable is a crucial first step in the delineation of assessment methodologies. The next section will provide such an overview, to be followed by an exploration of specific measures for each component of body image disturbance. Finally, some practical guidelines for the development of a battery of methodologies for body image assessment will be offered. Information for obtaining these materials will be included in a table, and many of the measures will be reproduced in the appendixes.

Definitions of
Body Image Disturbance

Body image disturbance has been used by a wide variety of researchers and clinicians to designate a great number of phenomena with little or no overlapping characteristics (Thompson, 1992). For instance, the phrase has been used to refer to phantom limb syndrome, neuropsychological deficits (anosognosia), and the psychodynamic concept of "body boundary" (Thompson, 1990). In this chapter, I will focus exclusively on a physical appearance-related definition that is quite broad—*body image disturbance* is any form of affective, cognitive, behavioral, or perceptual disturbance that is directly concerned with an aspect of physical appearance.

Using this definition, it would seem easy to categorize and discuss the extant measures. Unfortunately, many of the widely used measures are composite indices, measuring more than one of the above components. In addition, some questionnaire measures tap into a generic type of *global dissatisfaction* as opposed to a more precise affective versus cognitive distinction. Finally, some self-report scales can be *affective* or *cognitive* depending on the specific instructional protocol used.

Therefore I will place some measures in a category that recognizes their global subjective nature. Indices that have been categorized by their developers or appear to be a relatively precise measure of affective, cognitive, behavioral, or perceptual disturbance will then be reviewed. It is impossible to offer a full exposition of the large number of available measures, which currently approaches a total of almost 100. Therefore representative and widely used scales and techniques will be discussed; specifics about many more methods are contained in Tables 4.1 and 4.2. In addition, only those measures that have been found to be psychometrically sound (generally defined as having reliabilities of at least .70 or greater) will receive extensive discussion in the text of this chapter.

Generic Measures of Size, Shape, Weight, and Appearance Satisfaction

Figural Stimuli

There are a number of different types of *figural* stimulus materials for the assessment of overall satisfaction. For example, Stunkard, Sorenson, and Schlusinger (1983) developed a widely used set of nine male and nine female schematic figures that range from underweight to overweight. Recently, M. A. Thompson and J. J. Gray (in press) developed a similar set of schematic figures with precisely graduated increments between adjacent sizes (see Appendix 4-A). Collins (1991) has also developed a series of figures for use with adolescent-age samples (see Appendix 4-B). Table 4.1 contains information regarding a number of other figural methods of assessment.

Generally, subjects are asked to rate the figures based on the following instructional protocol: (a) current size and (b) ideal size. The difference between the ratings is a *discrepancy* index and is considered to represent the individual's level of dissatisfaction. Thompson (1992) and colleagues have found that the *current size* rating may be affected by the particular way that this instruction is worded. Specifically, *affective* ratings (based on how the subject *feels*) are larger than current size ratings based on *cognitive* instructions (based on how subjects *think* they look). In fact, the discrepancy between affective and cognitive ratings is significantly related to level of eating disturbance (Altabe & Thompson, 1992). Recently, Allison, Hoy, Fournier, and Heymsfield (in press) offered a *latitude of acceptance* measure that is the discrepancy between ratings of the thinnest and heaviest figure that subjects would consider dating.

(text continued on p. 128)

TABLE 4.1 Measures Commonly Used for the Assessment of Global Subjective Affective, Cognitive, and Behavioral Components of Body Image Disorder

Name of Instrument	Author(s)	Description	Reliability 1, 2		Standardization Sample	Address of Author
A. Figures/Silhouettes						
Figure Rating Scale (FRS)	1. Stunkard et al. (1983) 2. Thompson & Altabe (1991)	Subjects select from 9 figures, which vary in size from underweight to overweight	1. IC: 2. TR:	Not applicable 2 wks: Ideal (males, .82; females, .71); Self-think (males, .92; females, .89); Self-feel (males, .81; females, .83)	1. 92 normal males and females (under-graduates)	Albert J. Stunkard, M.D. Univ. of Pennsylvania Dept. of Psychiatry 133 S. 36th Street Philadelphia, PA 19104
None given	1. Counts & Adams (1985)	Silhouettes are drawn from subjects' photos—sizes increased and decreased by specific percentages	1. IC: TR:	Not applicable None given	1. Bulimics, dieting females, formerly obese and non-dieting females	H. E. Adams, Ph.D. Dept. of Psychology Univ. of Georgia Athens, GA 30602
Body Image Silhouette Scale	1. Powers & Erickson (1986)	Subjects select from 7 figures of various sizes	1. IC: TR:	Not applicable None given	1. 164 female undergraduates	Pamela D. Powers, Ph.D. Dept. of Psychology Academic Center Virginia Commonwealth Univ. Richmond, VA 23284
Contour Drawing Rating Scale	1. M. A. Thompson & Gray (in press)	9 male and 9 female sche-matic figures, ranging from underweight to overweight	1. IC: TR:	Not applicable 1 wk: self (.79)	1. Undergraduates: 40 males and females	James J. Gray, Ph.D. American University Dept. of Psychology Asbury Building Washington, DC 20016-8062
Breast/Chest Rating Scale (BCRS)	1. Thompson & Tantleff (1992)	5 male and 5 female sche-matic figures, ranging from small to large upper torso	1. IC: TR:	Not applicable Current (.85) Ideal Breast (.81) Ideal Chest (.69)	1. 43 males and females	J. Kevin Thompson, Ph.D. Dept. of Psychology Univ. of South Florida Tampa, FL 33620-8200

(Continued)

Name of Instrument	Author(s)	Description	Reliability 1, 2	Standardization Sample	Address of Author
None given	1. Collins (1991) 2. Wood et al. (1993)	7 boy and 7 girl figures, which vary in size	1. IC: Not applicable TR: 3 days (self, .71; ideal self, .59; ideal other child, .38; ideal adult, .55; ideal other adult, .49) 2. TR: 2 wks (self, .70; ideal self, .63)	1. 1,118 preadolescent children 2. 109 males and 95 females (age 8-10)	M. E. Collins, H.S.D., M.P.H. Centers for Disease Control and Prevention 4770 Buford Highway, NE Mailstop K26 Atlanta, GA 30341-3724
Body Image Assessment (BIA)	1. Williamson, Davis, Bennett, et al. (1989)	Subjects select from 9 figures of various sizes	1. IC: Not applicable TR: Importance 8 wks (.60-.93) bulimics (ideal, .74; current, .83); obese (ideal, N.S.; current, .88); binge eaters (ideal, .65; current, .81)	1. 659 females including bulimics, binge eaters, anorexics, normals, obese subjects, and atypical eating disordered subjects	Donald A. Williamson, Ph.D. Dept. of Psychology Louisiana State Univ. Baton Rouge, LA 70803-5501

B. Global Body Satisfaction/Questionnaire Measures

Name of Instrument	Author(s)	Description	Reliability 1, 2	Standardization Sample	Address of Author
Eating Disorders Inventory— Body Dissatisfaction Scale	1. Garner et al. (1983) 2. Shore & Porter (1990) 3. Wood et al. (1993)	Subjects indicate their degree of agreement with 9 statements about body parts being too large (7 items)	1. IC: (anorexics, .90) (controls, .91) 2. IC: Adolescents (11-18) (females: .91) (males: .86) 3. IC: Children (8-10) (females: .84) (males: .72)	1. 113 female anorexics and 577 female controls 2. 196 boys 414 girls 3. 109 males and 95 females	David M. Garner, Ph.D. c/o Psychological Assessments Resources P.O. Box 998 Odessa, FL 33556
Color-a-Person Body Dissatisfaction Test	1. Wooley & Roll (1991)	Subjects use 5 colors to indicate level of satisfaction with body sites by masking on a schematic figure	1. IC: .74-.85 TR: 2 wks (.72-.84) 4 wks (.75-.89)	1. Male and female college students ($n = 102$); bulimic ($n = 103$)	Orland W. Wooley, Ph.D. Dept. of Psychiatry Univ. of Cincinnati College of Medicine Cincinnati, OH 45267

TABLE 4.1 (Continued)

Name of Instrument	Author(s)	Reliability 1, 2	Description	Standardization Sample	Address of Author
Extended Satisfaction With Life Scale—Physical Appearance Scale	1. Alfonso & Allison (1993)	1. IC: .91 TR: 2 wks (.83)	Subjects rate general satisfaction with appearance on a 7-point scale (5 items)	1. Male and female undergraduates (n = 170)	David B. Allison, Ph.D. Obesity Research Center St. Luke's/Roosevelt Hospital Columbia Univ. College of Physicians and Surgeons New York, NY 10025
Body Satisfaction Scale (BSS)	1. Slade et al. (1990)	1. IC: Range (.79-.89) TR: None given	Subjects indicate degree of satisfaction with 16 parts (3 subscales; general, head, body)	1. Females: under-graduates, nursing students, volunteers, overweight subjects, anorexics, bulimics	P. D. Slade, Ph.D. Dept. of Psychiatry and Dept. of Movement Science Liverpool Univ. Medical School P.O. Box 147 Liverpool, L69 3BX England
Body Esteem Scale	1. Franzoi & Shields (1984)	1. IC: Females (.78-.87) Males (.81-.86) TR: None given	Modification of body cathexis scale with 16 new items; factor analysis yielded 3 factors each for male and female samples	1. 366 female and 257 male under-graduates	Stephen L. Franzoi, Ph.D. Department of Psychology Marquette Univ. Milwaukee, WI 53237
Body Esteem Scale	1. Mendelson & White (1985) 2. White (personal communication, Sept. 5, 1990)	1. IC: Split-half reliability (.85) 2. TR: 2 yrs (.66)	Subjects report their degree of agreement with various statements about their bodies	1. 97 boys/girls (ages: 8.5-17.4) 48 overweight, 49 normal weight 2. 105 boys/girls (ages 8-13)	Donna Romano White, Ph.D. Dept. of Psychology Concordia University 1455 de Maisonneuve West Montreal, Quebec Canada H3G-1M8
Body Shape Questionnaire (BSQ)	1. P. J. Cooper et al. (1987)	1. IC: None given 2. TR: None given	34 items that determine concern with body shape	1. Bulimics, several control samples	Peter Cooper, Ph.D. Univ. of Cambridge Dept. of Psychiatry Addenbrooke's Hospital Hills Road Cambridge, CB2 2QQ England

Name of Instrument	Author(s)	Description	Reliability 1, 2	Standardization Sample	Address of Author
Self-Image Questionnaire for Young Adolescents—Body Image Subscale	1. Peterson et al. (1984)	Designed for 10- to 15-year-olds: 11-item body image subscale assesses positive feelings toward the body	1. IC: (Boys, .81) (Girls, .77) TR: 1 yr (.60) 2 yrs (.44)	1. 335 sixth-grade students who were followed through the eighth grade	Anne C. Peterson, Ph.D. College of Health and Human Development 101 Henderson Bldg. Pennsylvania State Univ. University Park, PA 16802
Overweight Preoccupation Scale	1. Cash et al. (1991)	4 items selected from Cash's MBSRQ (Brown et al., 1990)	1. IC: .73 TR: 2 wks (.89)	1. 79 female undergraduates	Thomas F. Cash, Ph.D. Dept. of Psychology Old Dominion Univ. Norfolk, VA 23529-0267
Goldfarb Fear of Fat Scale	1. Goldfarb et al. (1985)	10 statements ("very untrue" to "very true") that reflect overconcern with fatness and body size	1. IC: .85 TR: 1 wk (.88)	1. 98 high school females	Meg Gerrard, Ph.D. Dept. of Psychology Iowa State Univ. Ames, IA 50011

C. Cognitive Measures

Name of Instrument	Author(s)	Description	Reliability 1, 2	Standardization Sample	Address of Author
Bulimia Cognitive Distortions Scale (BCDS)—Physical Appearance Subscale	1. Schulman et al. (1986)	Subjects indicate degree of agreement with 25 statements that measure physical appearance-related cognitions	1. IC: (.97 for entire scale)	1. 55 female outpatient bulimics aged 17-45 and 55 normal females aged 18-40	Bill N. Kinder, Ph.D. Dept. of Psychology Univ. of South Florida 4202 Fowler Ave. Tampa, FL 33620-8200

(Continued)

TABLE 4.1 (Continued)

Name of Instrument	Author(s)	Description	Reliability 1, 2		Standardization Sample	Address of Author
Body Image Automatic Thoughts Question-naire (BIATQ)	1. Cash et al. (1987) 2. Cash (personal communication, April 11, 1990)	Subjects indicate frequency with which they experience 37 negative and 15 positive body image cognitions	1. IC: 2. TR:	(.90) for bulimic and normal subjects for both positive and negative subscales 2 wks (positive scales: males, .73; females, .71) (nega-tive scale: males .84; females, .90)	1. 33 female bulimic in-patients and 79 female undergraduates	Thomas F. Cash, Ph.D. Dept. of Psychology Old Dominion Univ. Norfolk, VA 23529-0267
D. Affective Measures						
Mirror Focus Procedure	1. Butters & Cash (1987) Keeton et al. (1990)	Subjects look at themselves in a 3-way mirror and then rate their level of discomfort	1. IC: TR:	Not applicable None given	1. Undergraduates	Thomas F. Cash, Ph.D. Dept. of Psychology Old Dominion Univ. Norfolk, VA 23529-0267
Physical Appearance State and Trait Anxiety Scale (PASTAS)	1. Reed et al. (1991)	Subjects rate the anxiety associated with 16 body sites (8 weight relevant, 8 non-weight relevant); trait and state versions available	1. IC: TR:	(Trait: .88-.82) (State: .82-.92) 2 wks (.87)	1. Undergraduates	J. Kevin Thompson, Ph.D. Dept. of Psychology 4202 Fowler Ave. Univ. of South Florida Tampa, FL 33620-8200
E. Behavioral Measures						
Body Image Avoidance Question-naire (BIAQ)	1. Rosen et al. (1991)	Subjects indicate the fre-quency with which they en-gage in body image-related avoidance behaviors	1. IC: TR:	(.89) 2 wks (.87)	1. 145 female undergraduates	James C. Rosen, Ph.D. Dept. of Psychology Univ. of Vermont Burlington, VT 05405

126

Name of Instrument	Author(s)	Description	Reliability 1, 2	Standardization Sample	Address of Author
Physical Appearance Behavioral Avoidance Test (PABAT)	1. Thompson, Heinberg, & Marshall (1993)	Subjects approach own image in a mirror, from a distance of 20 feet; SUDS ratings and approach distance are dependent measures	1. IC: Not applicable 2. TR: None given	1. Female undergraduates	J. Kevin Thompson, Ph.D. Dept. of Psychology Univ. of South Florida 4202 Fowler Ave. Tampa, FL 33620-8200
F. Miscellaneous Measures					
Physical Appearance Related Teasing Scale (PARTS)	1. Thompson, Fabian, et al. (1991)	18-item scale that assesses history of weight/size and general appearance-related teasing	1. IC: weight/size scale, .91; appearance scale, .71 2. TR: 2 wks (weight/size, .86; appearance scale, .87)	1. Female undergraduates	same as above
Physical Appearance Comparison Scale (PACS)	1. Thompson, Heinberg, & Tantleff (1991)	5-item scale that assesses degree subject compares own appearance with that of other individuals	1. IC: .78 2. TR: 2 wks (.72)	1. Female undergraduates	same as above
Perception of Teasing Scale (POTS)	1. Thompson, Cattarin, et al. (in press)	11 items index general weight, teasing, and competency teasing	1. IC: general weight (.94) competency (.78)	1. 227 female undergraduates	same as above
Hand Appearance Scale	1. Vamos (1990)	16-item scale to measure hand appearance concerns: 4 factors (evaluation, negative emotions, concealment, display)	1. IC: None given 2. TR: None given	1. 84 patients with rheumatoid arthritis	Marina Vamos, Ph.D. Dept. of Psychiatry and Behavioral Science School of Medicine Univ. of Auckland Auckland, New Zealand

NOTE: Internal consistency estimates are not applicable for measures that yield a single index or conceptually distinct indices (e.g., some whole-body adjustment methods and figural rating scales). This is a revision of the tables presented in Thompson (1990, 1992).
1. IC = Internal consistency.
2. TC = Test-retest reliability.

Because of the variety of possible instructional protocols, it is important to be precise and consistent in the wording used for subject ratings with all figural stimuli. As Table 4.1 notes, to date, only the ideal and self-ratings appear to meet acceptable standards of reliability. In addition, the distinction between affective and cognitive aspects of an individual's current size rating may be useful information from a clinical viewpoint. Of interest, we have recently found that this type of discrepancy may decrease with age (Altabe & Thompson, 1993). Finally, as noted by Allison et al. (in press), some figural stimuli have Caucasian features, which may make them inappropriate for use with all ethnic groups. In this case, along the lines of Allison et al. (in press), silhouette figures might be used (Williamson, Davis, Bennett, Goreczny, & Gleaves, 1989). Wood, Becker, and Thompson (1993) dealt with this problem by replacing the faces on the figures with a generic circle, instructing subjects to focus exclusively on the rest of the figure.

The great majority of figural measures are designed to document overall size satisfaction. However, Thompson and Tantleff (1992) constructed a figural stimulus that allows for the assessment of breast and chest size preference (see Appendix 4-C). Use of the same rating protocol described above for the overall figural methods allows for a determination of dissatisfaction with breast or chest size.

Questionnaire Measures

There are a large number of questionnaire measures that assess a generic aspect of body satisfaction. One of the most widely used is the Body Dissatisfaction subscale of the Eating Disorder Inventory-2 (EDI-BD; Garner, 1991; Garner, Olmsted, & Polivy, 1983; see Williamson et al., this volume). This instrument uses a 6-point scale to measure satisfaction with nine different body sites. This measure also has good reliabilities with adolescent samples (Shore & Porter, 1990; Thompson, Altabe, Johnson, & Stormer, in press). In addition, with some minor rewording of items, Wood et al. (1993) found the scale reliable in children as young as 8 years of age.

The Body Areas Satisfaction Scale of the Multidimensional Body Self Relations Questionnaire (MBSRQ-BASS; Brown, Cash, & Mikulka, 1990), like the EDI-BD, assesses satisfaction with specific body sites. Cash, Wood, Phelps, and Boyd (1991) recently developed the four-item Weight Preoccupation Scale, which measures an excessive focus on weight-related issues. There are also a number of measures of a more global appearance satisfaction, including the Body Shape Questionnaire (BSQ; P. J. Cooper, Taylor, Cooper, & Fairburn, 1987) and the Physical Appearance subscale of the Extended Satisfaction with Life Scale (ESWLS-PA; Alfonso & Allison, 1993; Alfonso, this volume). Table 4.1 contains a broader listing of measures in this category.

Measures of the Affective Component

Reed, Thompson, Brannick, and Sacco (1991) developed the Physical Appearance State and Trait Anxiety Scale (PASTAS) to tap into the anxiety component of appearance concern. There are two subscales of eight items each: Weight (W) and Nonweight (NW) factors. In addition, there are two versions: The Trait version is designed as a measure of general or characterological body image anxiety and the State version assesses current or immediate level of anxiety. The State version was created for repeated use, to index transient changes in anxiety, such as might occur immediately after a treatment session targeting body image issues. Appendix 4-D contains the PASTAS. The Physical Appearance Evaluation scale of the Multidimensional Body Self Relations Questionnaire (MBSRQ-PAE; Brown et al., 1990) is another widely used measure of the affective component of body image developed by Cash and colleagues (Cash, 1991).

The Mirror Distress Rating is a nonquestionnaire measure that involves an individual's self-evaluation while gazing at body features for 30 seconds while standing in front of a mirror (Butters & Cash, 1987). The rating is a Subjective Units of Discomfort (SUDS) index, based on a range from 0 (absolute calm) to 100 (extreme discomfort). Fisher and Thompson (1994) recently modified this measure, requiring subjects to make ratings while imagining standing in front of the mirror. Although this may prove beneficial from a logistical viewpoint (in a therapy setting where access to a mirror is limited), the equivalence between the in vivo and imaginal methods has not been established.

Measures of the Cognitive Component

Yet another subscale of the MBSRQ provides a measure of the cognitive component of body image (Brown et al., 1990). The Appearance Orientation scale is an eight-item measure that indexes a cognitive "attentional" aspect of body image. The Bulimia Cognitive Distortions Scale also contains a Physical Appearance subscale that deals specifically with cognitive distortions related to physical appearance (BCDS-PA; Schulman, Kinder, Powers, Prange, & Gleghorn, 1986).

Measurement of the Behavioral Component

There are two types of procedures for the assessment of a behavioral aspect of body image. The first method involves a self-report of avoidance of body image-related situations. Rosen, Srebnik, Saltzberg, and Wendt (1991) developed the Body Image Avoidance Questionnaire (BIAQ), which contains four scales: clothing, social activities, eating restraint, and grooming/

weighing. Importantly, the scores on this scale converge well with ratings made by observers (roommates). Another self-report measure, the Physical Appearance Comparison Scale, indexes a tendency to make behavioral social comparisons with other individuals' bodies and appearance (Thompson, Heinberg, & Tantleff, 1991).

The second type of procedure is the direct observation of body image-related behaviors. This is probably the least developed area in the assessment of body image disturbance. However, there are some interesting procedures that could prove useful as additions to an overall body image assessment protocol. For instance, as noted above, Rosen et al. (1991) found that roommates' ratings correlated well with subjects' self-report of avoidance behaviors. Weiner, Seime, and Goetsch (1989) developed an escape button that subjects can engage to terminate the video presentation of an image of their body increasing in size.

Thompson, Heinberg, and Marshall (1993) developed the Physical Appearance Behavioral Avoidance Test (PABAT), a procedure that requires subjects to approach their own image in a mirror, from a 20-foot distance, in 2-foot intervals. Subjects evaluate the image for a period of 30 seconds at each interval and also make a SUDS rating (0-100) similar to that discussed above for the Mirror Distress Rating. Subjects are informed that they can discontinue the process if a level of "extreme discomfort" is reached. Thus the behavioral measure is the point of termination. SUDS ratings can be used as an index of the affective component of body image.

Measures of the Perceptual Component: Size Overestimation

Much of the early research in body image focused on the assessment of a perceptual component. The reasons for this are most likely twofold. First, early researchers noted that one of the most dramatic symptoms of anorexia nervosa was "the distortion of body image associated with it . . . and the vigor and stubbornness with which the often gruesome appearance is defended as normal and right, *not* too thin" (Bruch, 1962, p. 189). This "distortion" of appearance among anorexics received empirical support when Slade and Russell (1973) demonstrated that patients overestimated the size of several body sites in comparison with control subjects. This "overestimation" has been considered for many years to be primarily a perceptual aspect of body image disturbance. In recent years, some researchers have begun to question this assumption. Before dealing with this issue, however, I will first provide a brief review of assessment procedures (for a detailed discussion, see Thompson, 1990, 1992).

As Table 4.2 demonstrates, there are a wealth of technologies, some quite sophisticated, for the assessment of the perceptual component. The procedures can be divided into two broad categories: single-site methods and whole-image adjustment methods. The single-site measures provide for the assessment of size perception accuracy at individual body sites. Askevold (1975) pioneered the Image Marking Procedure, which requires subjects to estimate the width of body sites by marking on white paper attached to the wall. Ruff and Barrios (1986) developed the Body Image Detection Device (BIDD), which projects a beam of light onto an adjacent wall; subjects adjust the light to a width that matches their conception of the width or a particular body site. Thompson and Thompson (1986) modified the design of the BIDD to allow for the simultaneous presentation of four light beams, reflecting the cheeks, waist, hips, and thighs. This procedure is called the Adjustable Light Beam Apparatus (ALBA).

With any of the single-site procedures, subjects' actual size measures are measured with body calipers. The degree of overestimation is arrived at by a simple formula: estimated size divided by actual size (for a specific body site). This figure can be converted to a percentage over- or underestimation of size, which is the unit most used by researchers and clinicians.

Whole-image adjustment methods are the second category for the measurement of the perceptual component of body image. With these procedures, the individual views a whole-body image, via pictorial, mirror, or video presentation. The images can be modified to represent an image smaller or larger than actual size. Subjects are generally asked to match the image to their conception of actual size. An index of over- or underestimation is computed from the matching process.

As noted above, there are several limitations to the perceptual procedures, severely limiting current belief that the methods yield a pure "perceptual" index of size perception accuracy (see Thompson, 1992). For instance, Penner, Thompson, and Coovert (1991) found that an individual's *actual* size affected level of overestimation; smaller body sites were associated with higher levels of overestimation. When anorexics and size-matched controls were tested, there were no differences in degree of overestimation (Penner et al., 1991). A second problem involves the effect of the specific instructional protocol on levels of overestimation. For instance, Thompson and Dolce (1989) found that the affective versus cognitive instructions (similar to the findings discussed earlier with figural stimuli) produced different levels of inaccuracy. Recently, Thompson and Spana (1991) found that overestimation may be associated with general visuospatial disturbance, as indexed with neuropsychological measures.

There are a number of other problematic issues associated with the methods of size perception assessment. However, many researchers continue to

(text continued on p. 135)

TABLE 4.2 Measures Commonly Used for the Assessment of the Perceptual Component of Body Image Disorder

Name of Instrument	Author(s)	Description	Reliability 1, 2	Standardization Sample	Address of Author
A. Body Site Estimation Procedures					

Adjustable Light Beam Apparatus (ALBA)	1. Thompson & Spana (1988)
	 2. Thompson, Coovert, et al. (in press)
		Adjust width of 4 light beams projected on wall to match perceived size of cheeks, waist, hips, and thighs	1. IC: (.83)
			     TR: Imm. (.83-.92)
			          1 wk (.56-.86)
			 2. IC: (.75)
				1. 159 female undergraduates
				 2. 63 female adolescents (10-15) years old
					J. Kevin Thompson, Ph.D.
					 Department of Psychology
					 University of South Florida
					 4202 Fowler Ave.
					 Tampa, FL 33620-8200

Body Image Detection Device (BIDD)	1. Ruff & Barrios (1986)
	 2. Barrios et al. (1989)
		Adjust width of light beam projected on wall to match perceived size of specific body site	1. IC: (.91, .93)
			     TR: 3 wks (bulimia, .82-.87; controls, .72-.85)
			 2. IC: (.21-.82)
			     TR: 3 wks (.34)
			          4 wks (.94)
			          7 wks (.37)
				1. 20 normal and 20 bulimic undergraduates
				 2. Female undergraduates
					Billy A. Barrios, Ph.D.
					 College of Liberal Arts
					 Department of Psychology
					 University of Mississippi
					 Oxford, MS 38677

Movable Caliper Technique (MCT): Visual Size Estimation (VSE)	1. Slade & Russell (1973)
	 2. Slade (1985)
	 3. Ben-Tovim & Crisp (1984), Ben-Tovim et al. (1990)
		Adjust distance between two lights to match perceived size	1. IC: (anorexics, .72-.93)
			          (controls, .37-.79)
			 2. IC: (anorexia, .72)
			          (controls, .63)
			 3. TR: 2 wks (.79-.95)
				1. 14 female anorexics and 20 female post-graduates and secretaries
				 2. Anorexics
				 3. Normal females
					Peter Slade, Ph.D.
					 Department of Psychiatry and Department of Movement Science
					 Liverpool University Medical School
					 Ashton Street
					 P.O. Box 147
					 Liverpool L69 3BX, England
					
					 David I. Ben-Tovim, Ph.D.
					 Department of Psychiatry
					 Repatriation General Hospital
					 Daws Road
					 Daw Park
					 South Australia, 5041

Name of Instrument	Author(s)	Description	Reliability 1, 2	Standardization Sample	Address of Author

Image Marking Procedure (IMP)	1. Askevold (1975)
	2. Barrios et al. (1989)
	3. Gleghorn et al. (1987)
	4. Bowden et al. (1989)
		Subjects indicate their perceived size by marking 2 endpoints on a life-size piece of paper	1. None given
			2. IC: (.25–.62)
			   TR: 3 wks (.17)
			   4 wks (.33)
			   7 wks (.14)
			3. TR: Imm. (.72–.92)
			4. TR: 1 day (.38–.85)
				1. Anorexics, obese patients, and other medical samples
				2. College females
				3. Bulimics, normal females
				4. 12 anorexics, 12 bulimics, 24 controls
					Finn Askevold, Ph.D.
					Psychosomatic Department
					Oslo University Hospital
					Oslo (Norway)

B. Whole-Image Adjustment Procedures

Name of Instrument	Author(s)	Description	Reliability 1, 2	Standardization Sample	Address of Author
TV-Video Method	1. Gardner et al. (1987) 2. Gardner & Moncrieff (1988)	Subjects adjust the horizontal dimensions of a TV image of themselves to match perceived size	1. IC: Not applicable TR: None given	1. 38 normal and eating disordered adults 2. Normal and anorexic females	Rick M. Gardner, Ph.D. Department of Psychology University of Southern Colorado Pueblo, CO 81001
None given	1. Allenback et al. (1976)	Subjects adjust the horizontal dimension of a video image to match perceived size	1. IC: Not applicable TR: None given	1. 69 male and female adults consisting of obese and control subjects	Peter Allenback, Ph.D. Furugatan SA 171 50 Solna, Sweden

Distorting Video Camera	1. Freeman et al. (1984)
	2. Brodie et al. (1989)
		Subjects adjust a video image varied from 60% larger to 25% thinner	1. IC: Front profile (.62).
			   TR: 7–22 days (frontal—bulimics and anorexics, .91; controls, .83)
			2. IC: (.56–.84)
			   TR: 4 days (.17–.70)
				1. 20 eating disordered females (bulimics and anorexics) and 20 normal
				2. Female controls
					Richard J. Freeman, Ph.D.
					Department of Psychology
					Simon Fraser University
					Burnaby, B.C.
					Canada V5A 1S6

(Continued)

TABLE 4.2 (Continued)

Name of Instrument	Author(s)	Description	Reliability 1, 2	Standardization Sample	Address of Author
Distorting Photograph Technique (DPT)	1. Glucksman & Hirsch (1969) 2. Garfinkel et al. (1978) 3. Garfinkel et al. (1979)	Subjects indicate size by adjusting a photograph that is distorted from 20% under to 20% over actual size	1. IC: Not applicable 2. TR: 1 wk (anorexics, .75; controls, .45) 3. 1 yr (anorexics, .70; controls, .14)	1. Obese patients 2. Anorexics and controls 3. Anorexics and controls	David M. Garner, Ph.D. c/o Psychological Assessment Resources, Inc. P.O. Box 998 Odessa, FL 33556
Distorting Video Technique	1. Touyz et al. (1985)	Subjects indicate size by adjusting photograph that is distorted by 50% under to 50% over actual size	1. IC: Not applicable TR: Imm. (.82); 1 day (.63) 8 wks (.61)	1. Anorexics and bulimics	S. W. Touyz, Ph.D. Department of Clinical Psychology Westmead Hospital Westmead 2145 New South Wales, Australia
Distorting Television Method	1. Bowden et al. (1989)	Photograph distorted by video camera to 50% over and under actual size	1. IC: Not applicable TR: 1 day (.92)	1. Anorexics, bulimics, controls	J. K. Collins, Ph.D. School of Behavioral Science Macquarie University North Ryde, NSW Australia 2113
None given	1. Huon & Brown (1986)	Concave, convex, and ordinary mirrors; adjustable TV image	1. IC: Not applicable TR: None given	1. Anorexics, bulimics, controls	G. F. Huon or L. B. Brown School of Psychology University of New South Wales Box 1, Kensington, NSW 2033 Australia
Distorting Mirror	1. Brodie et al. (1989)	Distorting mirror (thinner to fatter images)	1. IC: (.61-.92) TR: 4 days (.34-.84)	1. 29 female university students	Dr. D. A. Brodie School of Movement Science University of Liverpool P.O. Box 147 Liverpool L69 3BX England

NOTE: Internal consistency estimates are not applicable for measures that yield a single index or conceptually distinct indices (e.g., some whole-body adjustment methods). This table is a revision of the tables in Thompson (1990, 1992).
1. IC = Internal consistency.
2. TR = Test-retest reliability.

believe that this aspect of disturbance may have important clinical implications, such as being prognostic of outcome (Rosen & Srebnik, 1993). Therefore it continues to be included in most assessment batteries. Anyone using the methods, however, should become conversant with the issues that may temper their reliability and validity (Thompson, 1992).

Interview Methods

Although interview methodologies lag behind the development of questionnaire measures for the assessment of body image, these procedures offer a useful addition to any evaluative strategy. For instance, they provide for a flexibility and precision that may not be available if one relies solely on self-report questionnaire indices. As is the case with the assessment of eating disorders and obesity, an optimal approach consists of an integration of interview and traditional assessment procedures (see also Agras, this volume).

Z. Cooper and Fairburn (1987) created the multidimensional Eating Disorder Examination (EDE), which uses an interview format to index symptoms of eating disorders. The format contains two subscales—Shape Concern and Weight Concern—designed to gauge the degree of importance an individual places on shape and weight as a component of self-evaluation. This technique has good psychometric qualities (Z. Cooper & Fairburn, 1987) and may be better at differentiating clinically diagnosed eating disordered patients from at-risk individuals (i.e., restrained eaters) than questionnaire measures (Wilson & Smith, 1989). Another standardized format, the Body Dysmorphic Disorder Examination, developed by Rosen and colleagues, will be discussed shortly under a specific section devoted to Body Dysmorphic Disorder.

Miscellaneous Measures

There are a number of scales that might prove useful in the assessment of body image that don't fit clearly into one of the above categories. For instance, Vamos (1990) designed a self-report measure of concern regarding hand appearance in rheumatoid arthritic individuals. Cash (1989) developed a scale to gauge concern with hair loss. In addition, as noted above in the discussion of figural ratings, Thompson and Tantleff (1992) developed a measure of breast/chest size satisfaction.

Researchers have lately become interested in the measurement of developmental factors that may lead to body image disturbance. These measures may yield information essential for the effective treatment of body dissatisfaction. For instance, Thompson and colleagues have developed a series of measures that assess the presence of *feedback* from others regarding one's appearance (Thompson, Cattarin, Fowler, & Fisher, in press; Thompson, Fabian, Moulton, Dunn, & Altabe, 1991). For instance, the Perception of Teasing Scale (POTS), a revision of the Physical Appearance Related Teasing Scale (PARTS), has subscales that measure *teasing* about weight and non-weight-related appearance features (see Table 4.1). Rosen (1991) developed the Critical Incidents Interview to index the occurrence of a wide variety of possible experiences that may have initially fostered a concern related to physical appearance. For instance, subjects are asked to "think of any specific *things, such as events, time periods, places, people,* or *things about a person* that would have an impact, *positive* or *negative,* on how people think and feel about their body." Information obtained from the early experiences that influence body image formation may prove quite useful in the formation of an effective treatment program.

Body Dysmorphic Disorder

Body Dysmorphic Disorder is an extremely complex phenomenon that has just begun to pique the curiosity of large numbers of researchers and clinicians. It first appeared as a diagnostic entity in the *DSM-III-R* (American Psychiatric Association, 1987), contained within the Somatoform Disorders. The essential feature is an extreme disparagement of some aspect of appearance, although the belief should not be of a delusional intensity; that is, the individual can acknowledge that the disparagement is excessive. The locus of the physical appearance debasement may be any aspect of the body; however, common sites include weight-related areas (hips, thighs, waist, and so on), cheeks, eyes, hair, lips, genitals, or wrinkles. The heterogeneity of the source of concern is illustrated by Marks and Mishan (1988), who describe a case of a male's excessive concern over body odor, which they consider to be an instance of Body Dysmorphic Disorder.

The diagnostic issues in this category are currently in a state of controversy (Phillips, 1991). Because of the occurrence of strong obsessive-compulsive behaviors and social avoidance, researchers debate whether the disorder might more appropriately belong in the Anxiety Disorders categorization. Another diagnostic conundrum involves its confusion, and possible overlap, with Delusional (Paranoid) Disorder. The differential seems to be based on the *certainty* that the individual has regarding the presence of the defect. If the patient is completely unwilling to acknowledge the possibility of an *exaggeration* of the extent of the defect, Delusional Disorder receives utmost consideration. If the disparagement is more of the form of an overvalued idea, and the person acknowledges that the preoccupation may be excessive, Body Dysmorphic Disorder is considered to be the diagnosis.

Historically, the clinical interview was the primary means of assessment for the presence of body dysmorphia. Because of the idiosyncratic nature of the specific target of appearance disparagement, it has been difficult to design a standardized measure. Questionnaire measures that contain a listing of body sites (e.g., EDI-BD, MBSRQ-BASS, PASTAS) could be useful but require that the clinician pay special attention to individual item responses. Recently, Rosen and Reiter (1994) developed the Body Dysmorphic Disorder Examination (BDDE), which is a structured interview for the assessment of this disorder that provides objective criteria for diagnosis. It is appropriate for a variety of populations where physical appearance might be a concern, including those with eating disorders, obesity, victims of physical or sexual abuse, cosmetic surgery patients, orthodontia or dermatology patients, or the physically injured/disabled individual.

The Body Dysmorphic Disorder Examination has excellent psychometric qualities and should greatly facilitate the assessment of this disorder (Rosen, Reiter, & Orosan, in press). It should be used in any case of body image disturbance where the individual's dissatisfaction, anxiety, discomfort, or concern with some aspect of appearance is seemingly excessive, that is, beyond that expected for the defect that is present. The length of this structured interview prohibits its inclusion in this chapter; however, the interested reader is encouraged to write Rosen at the address contained in Table 4.1 for further information on the BDDE. The following question is an example of items included in the BDDE regarding the body dysmorphic symptom of avoidance: "Over the past four weeks have you avoided looking at your body, particularly at your (specify defect) in order to control feelings about your appearance? This includes avoiding looking at yourself clothed or unclothed either directly or in mirrors or windows."

Summary and Recommendations

Because of the large number of measures available for the assessment of body image, some investigators have begun factor analytic studies to determine if the measures actually index unique aspects of disturbance. In an early review of the relationships among various measures, Thompson, Penner, and Altabe (1990) concluded that there was a good deal of overlap among self-report questionnaire measures; however, correlations between questionnaire and perceptual methods were quite small. In addition, even the correlations between perceptual measures are often minimal (Thompson, 1992).

Recent factor analytic work with self-report questionnaires reveals a good deal of overlap among these inventories (Thompson, Altabe, et al., in press; Williamson, Barker, Bertman, & Gleaves, in press). Future research will ultimately reveal the distinctiveness of extant measures of body image, leading to an empirically driven, psychometrically sound assessment battery. However, this process will likely take many years. In the interim, the clinician may find that the following suggestions are useful in the compilation of a body image assessment armamentarium.

1. Include at least one measure from *each* of the categories noted above, that is, generic dissatisfaction, affective, cognitive, behavioral, perceptual.

2. Be sure that measures have adequate reliability (generally .70 or better), have been used widely by leading researchers, and have been validated on subject samples appropriate for your individual case (i.e., adolescents, males, and so on).

3. Use overall scale scores in comparison with the available norms. In addition, from a clinical perspective, an evaluation of individual items may yield potentially useful information.

4. Include an assessment of developmental issues. For instance, as noted earlier, teasing may lead to appearance dissatisfaction.

5. Review research on the etiology and treatment of body image disturbance (Butters & Cash, 1987; Cash, 1991; Cash & Pruzinsky, 1990; Phillips, 1991; Pruzinsky, 1990; Pruzinsky & Edgerton, 1990; Rosen, 1990, 1992; Rosen, Cado, Silberg, Srebnik, & Wendt, 1990; Rosen, Saltzberg, & Srebnik, 1989; Thompson, 1990, 1992).

6. It is difficult to recommend certain instruments over others. However, some of the measures have received widespread psychometric evaluation and use in a variety of research investigations. Some of these are included in the appendixes; however, some measures could not be reproduced herein because of copyright problems or preferences of the questionnaire developers. Information for obtaining these measures is contained in the tables (see the author addresses).

In addition, individual clinical cases will often determine the specific measure chosen. For example, if the body image issue deals with breast size/shape disparagement, the scale developed by Thompson and Tantleff (1992) might be suitable, whereas the measure would be irrelevant for a case where overall size/weight dissatisfaction was the body image concern. If repeated measurements, over a short period of time, are clinically necessary, the State version of the PASTAS (Reed et al., 1991) or the Mirror Distress Rating (Butters & Cash, 1987) might be appropriate. Therefore the clinician should closely evaluate the specific case and the available measures.

Conclusions

Body image may be manifested in many different forms, including affective, cognitive, behavioral, and perceptual aspects of disturbance. Research strongly indicates its importance in the clinical management of eating disorders and obesity. In addition, extreme disparagement of appearance may lead to the presence of Body Dysmorphic Disorder. In this chapter, a variety of body image assessment methodologies were reviewed, specific clinical guidelines were offered, and information for the procurement of specific measures noted in tables and appendixes. This chapter was necessarily brief and focused almost exclusively on assessment-related issues; however, the reader is strongly encouraged to seek a broader understanding of body image disturbance via the resources on history, theory, associated features, and treatment offered in the text.

References

Alfonso, V. C., & Allison, D. B. (1993, August). *Further development of the Extended Satisfaction with Life Scale.* Paper presented at the American Psychological Association, Toronto.

Allenback, P., Hallberg, D., & Espmark, S. (1976). Body image: An apparatus for measuring disturbances in estimation of size and shape. *Journal of Psychosomatic Research, 20,* 583-589.

Allison, D. B., Hoy, M. K., Fournier, A., & Heymsfield, S. B. (in press). Can ethnic differences in men's preferences for women's body shapes contribute to ethnic differences in female adiposity? *Obesity Research.*

Altabe, M. N., & Thompson, J. K. (1992). Size estimation vs. figural ratings of body image disturbance: Relation to body dissatisfaction and eating dysfunction. *International Journal of Eating Disorders, 11,* 397-402.

Altabe, M. N., & Thompson, J. K. (1993). Body image changes during early adulthood. *International Journal of Eating Disorders, 13,* 323-328.

American Psychiatric Association. (1987). *Diagnostic and statistical manual of mental disorders* (3rd ed. rev.). Washington, DC: Author.

American Psychiatric Association. (1994). *Diagnostic and statistical manual of mental disorders* (4th ed.). Washington, DC: Author.

Askevold, R. (1975). Measuring body image: Preliminary report on a new method. *Psychotherapy and Psychosomatics, 26,* 71-77.

Barrios, B. A., Ruff, G. A., & York, C. I. (1989). Bulimia and body image: Assessment and explication of a promising construct. In W. G. Johnson (Ed.), *Advances in eating disorders* (Vol. 2, pp. 67-89). New York: JAI.

Ben-Tovim, D. I., & Crisp, A. H. (1984). The reliability of estimates of body width and their relationship to current measured body size among anorexic and normal subJects. *Psychological Medicine, 14,* 843-846.

Ben-Tovim, D. I., Walker, M. K., Murray, H., & Chin, G. (1990). Body size estimates: Body image or body attitude measures? *International Journal of Eating Disorders, 9,* 57-68.

Bowden, P. K., Touyz, S. W., Rodriguez, P. J., Hensley, R., & Beumont, P. J. V. (1989). Distorting patient or distorting instrument? Body shape disturbance in patents with anorexia nervosa and bulimia. *British Journal of Psychiatry, 155,* 196-201.

Brodie, D. A., Slade, P. D., & Rose, H. (1989). Reliability measures in disturbing body image. *Perceptual and Motor Skills, 69,* 723-732.

Brown, T. A., Cash, T. F., & Mikulka, P. J. (1990). Attitudinal body-image assessment: Factor analysis of the Body Self Relations Questionnaire. *Journal of Personality Assessment, 55,* 135-144.

Bruch, H. (1962). Perceptual and conceptual disturbances in anorexia nervosa. *Psychosomatic Medicine, 24,* 187-194.

Butters, J. W., & Cash, T. F. (1987). Cognitive behavioral treatment of women's body-image dissatisfaction. *Journal of Consulting and Clinical Psychology, 55,* 889-897.

Cash, T. F. (1989). Psychological effects of male pattern baldness. *Patient Care, 1,* 18-23.

Cash, T. F. (1991). *Body image therapy: A program for self-directed change* [Audiocassette series including client workbook and clinician's manual]. New York: Guilford.

Cash, T. F., Lewis, R. J., & Keeton, W. P. (1987, March). *The Body Image Automatic Thoughts Questionnaire: A measure of body-related cognitions.* Paper presented at the Southeastern Psychological Association, Atlanta, GA.

Cash, T. F., & Pruzinsky, T. (1990). *Body images: Development, deviance, and change.* New York: Guilford.

Cash, T. F., Wood, K. C., Phelps, K. D., & Boyd, K. (1991). New assessments of weight-related body image derived from extant instruments. *Perceptual and Motor Skills, 73,* 235-241.

Collins, M. E. (1991). Body figure perceptions and preferences among preadolescent children. *International Journal of Eating Disorders, 10,* 199-208.

Cooper, P. J., Taylor, M. J., Cooper, Z., & Fairburn, C. G. (1987). The development and validation of the Body Shape Questionnaire. *International Journal of Eating Disorders, 6,* 485-494.

Cooper, Z., & Fairburn, C. G. (1987). The Eating Disorder Examination: A semi-structured interview for the assessment of the specific psychopathology of eating disorder. *International Journal of Eating Disorders, 6,* 1-8.

Counts, C. R., & Adams, H. E. (1985). Body image in bulimia, dieting, and normal females. *Journal of Psychopathology and Behavioral Assessment, 7,* 289-300.

Fisher, E., & Thompson, J. K. (1994). A comparative evaluation of cognitive-behavior therapy (CBT) versus exercise therapy (ET) for treatment of body image disturbance: Preliminary findings. *Behavior Modification, 18,* 171-185.

Franzoi, S. L., & Shields, S. A. (1984). The Body Esteem Scale: Multidimensional structure and sex differences in a college population. *Journal of Personality Assessment, 48,* 173-178.

Freeman, R. F., Thomas, C. D., Solyom, L., & Hunter, M. A. (1984). A modified video camera for measuring body image distortion: Technical description and reliability. *Psychological Medicine, 14,* 411-416.

Gardner, R. M., Martinez, R., & Sandoval, Y. (1987). Obesity and body image: An evaluation of sensory and non-sensory components. *Psychological Medicine, 17,* 927-932.

Gardner, R. M., & Moncrieff, C. (1988). Body image distortion in anorexics as a non-sensory phenomena: A signal detection approach. *Journal of Clinical Psychology, 44,* 101-107.

Garfinkel, P. E., Moldofsky, H., & Garner, D. M. (1979). The stability of perceptual disturbances in anorexia nervosa. *Psychological Medicine, 9,* 703-708.

Garfinkel, P. W., Moldofsky, H., Garner, D. M., Stancer, H. C., & Coscina, D. U. (1978). Body awareness in anorexia nervosa: Disturbances in "body image" and "satiety." *Psychosomatic Medicine, 40,* 487-498.

Garner, D. M. (1991). *EDI-2: Professional manual.* Odessa, FL: Psychological Assessment Resources, Inc.

Garner, D. M., Olmsted, M. A., & Polivy, J. (1983). Development and validation of a multidimensional eating disorder inventory for anorexia nervosa and bulimia. *International Journal of Eating Disorders, 2,* 15-34.

Gleghorn, A. A., Penner, L. A., Powers, P. S., & Schulman, R. (1987). The psychometric properties of several measures of body image. *Journal of Psychopathology and Behavioral Assessment, 9,* 203-218.

Glucksman, M., & Hirsch, J. (1969). The response of obese patients to weight reduction: III. The perception of body size. *Psychosomatic Medicine, 31,* 1-17.

Goldfarb, L. A., Dykens, E. M., & Gerrard, M. (1985). The Goldfarb Fear of Fat scale. *Journal of Personality Assessment, 49,* 329-332.

Huon, G. F., & Brown, L. B. (1986). Body images in anorexia nervosa and bulimia nervosa. *International Journal of Eating Disorders, 5,* 421-439.

Keeton, W. P., Cash, T. F., & Brown, T. A. (1990). Body image or body images? Comparative, multidimensional assessment among college students. *Journal of Personality Assessment, 54,* 213-230.

Marks, I., & Mishan, J. (1988). Dysmorphophobic avoidance with disturbed bodily perception: A pilot study of exposure therapy. *British Journal of Psychiatry, 152,* 674-678.

Mendelson, B. K., & White, D. R. (1985). Development of self-body-esteem in overweight youngsters. *Developmental Psychology, 21,* 90-96.

Penner, L. A., Thompson, J. K., & Coovert, D. L. (1991). Size estimation among anorexics: Much ado about very little? *Journal of Abnormal Psychology, 100,* 90-93.

Petersen, A. C., Schulenberg, J. E., Abramowitz, R. H., Offer, D., & Jarcho, H. D. (1984). A self-image questionnaire for young adolescents (SIQYA): Reliability and validity studies. *Journal of Youth and Adolescence, 13,* 93-11.

Phillips, K. A. (1991). Body dysmorphic disorder: The distress of imagined ugliness. *American Journal of Psychiatry, 148,* 1138-1149.

Powers, P. D., & Erickson, M. T. (1986). Body image in women and its relationship to self-image and body satisfaction. *Journal of Obesity and Weight Regulation, 5,* 37-50.

Pruzinsky, T. (1990). Psychopathology of body experience: Expanded perspectives. In T. F. Cash & T. Pruzinsky (Eds.), *Body images: Development, deviance, and change* (pp. 170-189). New York: Guilford.

Pruzinsky, T., & Edgerton, M. T. (1990). Body image change in cosmetic plastic surgery. In T. F. Cash & T. Pruzinsky (Eds.), *Body images: Development, deviance, and change* (pp. 217-236). New York: Guilford.

Reed, D., Thompson, J. K., Brannick, M. T., & Sacco, W. P. (1991). Development and validation of the Physical Appearance State and Trait Anxiety Scale (PASTAS). *Journal of Anxiety Disorders, 5,* 323-332.

Rosen, J. C. (1990). Body image disturbance in eating disorders. In T. F. Cash & T. Pruzinsky (Eds.), *Body images: Development, deviance, and change* (pp. 190-214). New York: Guilford.

Rosen, J. C. (1991, November). *Body image disorder and social anxiety*. Paper presented at the annual meeting of the Association for Advancement of Behavior Therapy, New York.

Rosen, J. C. (1992). Body image disorder: Definition, development and contribution to eating disorders. In J. H. Crowther, D. L. Tennenbaum, S. E. Hobfoll, & M. A. P. Stephens (Eds.), *The etiology of bulimia: The individual and familial context* (pp. 157-177). Washington, DC: Hemisphere.

Rosen, J. C., Cado, S., Silberg, N. T., Srebnik, D., & Wendt, S. (1990). Cognitive behavior therapy with and without size perception training for women with body image disturbance. *Behavior Therapy, 21*, 481-498.

Rosen, J. C., & Reiter, J. (1994). *Development of the Body Dysmorphic Disorder Examination (BDDE)*. Unpublished manuscript.

Rosen, J. C., Reiter, J., & Orosan, P. (in press). Assessment of body image in eating disorders with the Body Dysmorphic Disorder Examination. *Behavior Research and Therapy*.

Rosen, J. C., Saltzberg, E., & Srebnik, D. (1989). Cognitive behavior therapy for negative body image. *Behavior Therapy, 20*, 393-404.

Rosen, J. C., & Srebnik, D. (1993). The assessment of eating disorders. In P. McReynolds, J. C. Rosen, & E. Cheline (Eds.), *Advances in psychological assessment* (pp. 229-260). New York: Plenum.

Rosen, J. C., Srebnik, D., Saltzberg, E., & Wendt, S. (1991). Development of a body image avoidance questionnaire. *Psychological Assessment: A Journal of Consulting and Clinical Psychology, 3*, 32-37.

Ruff, G. A., & Barrios, B. A. (1986). Realistic assessment of body image. *Behavioral Assessment, 8*, 237-252.

Schulman, R. G., Kinder, B. N., Powers, P. S., Prange, M., & Gleghorn, A. A. (1986). The development of a scale to measure cognitive distortions in bulimia. *Journal of Personality Assessment, 50*, 630-639.

Shore, R. A., & Porter, J. E. (1990). Normative and reliability data for 11 to 18 year olds on the Eating Disorder Inventory. *International Journal of Eating Disorders, 9*, 201-208.

Slade, P. D. (1985). A review of body-image studies in anorexia nervosa and bulimia nervosa. *Journal of Psychiatric Research, 19*, 255-265.

Slade, P. D., Dewey, M. E., Newton, T., Brodie, D., & Kiemle, G. (1990). Development and preliminary validation of the Body Satisfaction Scale (BSS). *Psychology and Health, 4*, 213-220.

Slade, P. D., & Russell, G. F. M. (1973). Awareness of body dimensions in anorexia nervosa: Cross-sectional and longitudinal studies. *Psychological Medicine, 3*, 188-199.

Stunkard, A. J., & Burt, V. (1967). Obesity and the body game: II. Age of onset of disturbances in body image. *American Journal of Psychiatry, 123*, 1447-1447.

Stunkard, A., Sorenson, T., & Schlusinger, F. (1983). Use of the Danish Adoption Register for the study of obesity and thinness. In S. Kety, L. P. Rowland, R. L. Sidman, & S. W. Matthysse (Eds.), *The genetics of neurological and psychiatric disorders* (pp. 115-120). New York: Raven.

Thompson, J. K. (1990). *Body image disturbance: Assessment and treatment*. Elmsford, NJ: Pergamon.

Thompson, J. K. (1992). Body image: Extent of disturbance, associated features, theoretical models, assessment methodologies, intervention strategies, and a proposal for a new DSM IV diagnostic category—Body Image Disorder. In M. Hersa, R. M. Eisler, & P. M. Miller (Eds.), *Progress in behavior modification* (Vol. 28, pp. 3-54). Sycamore, IL: Sycamore.

Thompson, J. K., & Altabe, M. N. (1991). Psychometric qualities of the Figure Rating Scale. *International Journal of Eating Disorders, 10,* 615-619.

Thompson, J. K., Altabe, M. N., Johnson, S., & Stormer, S. (in press). A factor analysis of multiple measures of body image disturbance: Are we all measuring the same construct? *International Journal of Eating Disorders.*

Thompson, J. K., Berland, N. W., Linton, P. H., & Weinsier, R. (1986). Assessment of body distortion via a self-adjusting light beam in seven eating disorder groups. *International Journal of Eating Disorders, 7,* 113-120.

Thompson, J. K., Cattarin, J., Fowler, B., & Fisher, E. (in press). The Perception of Teasing Scale (POTS): A revision and extension of the Physical Appearance Related Teasing Scale. *Journal of Personality Assessment.*

Thompson, J. K., Coovert, M., Richards, K. J., Johnson, S., & Cattarin, J. (in press). Development of body image and eating disturbance in young females: Covariance structure modeling and longitudinal analyses. *International Journal of Eating Disorders.*

Thompson, J. K., & Dolce, J. J. (1989). The discrepancy between emotional vs. rational estimates of body size, actual size, and ideal body ratings: Theoretical and clinical implications. *Journal of Clinical Psychology, 45,* 473-478.

Thompson, J. K., Fabian, L. J., Moulton, D. O., Dunn, M. F., & Altabe, M. N. (1991). Development and validation of the physical appearance related testing scale. *Journal of Personality Assessment, 56,* 513-521.

Thompson, J. K., Heinberg, L., & Marshall, K. (1993). The Physical Appearance Behavior Avoidance Test (PABAT): Preliminary findings. *The Behavior Therapist, 17,* 9-10.

Thompson, J. K., Heinberg, L., & Tantleff, S. (1991). The Physical Appearance Comparison Scale (PACS). *The Behavior Therapist, 14,* 174.

Thompson, J. K., Penner, L., & Altabe, M. (1990). Procedures, problems, and progress in the assessment of body images. In T. F. Cash & T. Pruzinsky (Eds.), *Body images: Development, deviance, and change* (pp. 21-48). New York: Guilford.

Thompson, J. K., & Spana, R. E. (1988). The adjustable light beam method for the assessment of size estimation accuracy: Description, psychometrics, and normative data. *International Journal of Eating Disorders, 7,* 521-526.

Thompson, J. K., & Spana, R. E. (1991). Visuospatial ability, accuracy of size estimation, and bulimic disturbance in a noneating-disordered college sample: A neuropsychological analysis. *Perceptual and Motor Skills, 73,* 335-338.

Thompson, J. K., & Tantleff, S. (1992). Female and male ratings of upper torso: Actual, ideal, and stereotypical conceptions. *Journal of Social Behavior and Personality, 7,* 345-354.

Thompson, J. K., & Thompson, C. M. (1986). Body size distortion and self-esteem in asymptomatic, normal weight males and females. *International Journal of Eating Disorders, 5,* 1061-1068.

Thompson, M. A., & Gray, J. J. (in press). Development and validation of a new body image assessment scale. *Journal of Personality Assessment.*

Touyz, S. W., Beumont, P. J. V., Collins, J. K., & Cowie, L. (1985). Body shape perception in bulimia and anorexia nervosa. *International Journal of Eating Disorders, 4,* 261-265.

Vamos, M. (1990). Body image in rheumatoid arthritis: The relevance of hand appearance to desire for surgery. *British Journal of Medical Psychology, 63,* 267-277.

Wiener, A., Seime, R., & Goetsch, V. (1989, March). *A multimethod assessment of fear of weight gain in bulimic and low risk females.* Paper presented at the annual meeting of the Southeastern Psychological Association, Washington, DC.

Williamson, D. A., Barker, S. E., Bertman, L. J., & Gleaves, D. H. (in press). Body image, body dysphoria, and dietary restraint: Factor structure in nonclinical subjects. *Behaviour Research and Therapy.*

Williamson, D. A., Davis, C. J., Bennett, S. M., Goreczny, A. J., & Gleaves, D. H. (1989). Development of a simple procedure for assessing body image disturbances. *Behavioral Assessment, 11,* 433-446.

Williamson, D. A., Davis, C. J., Goreczny, A. J., & Blouin, D. C. (1989). Body-image disturbances in bulimia nervosa: Influences of actual body size. *Journal of Abnormal Psychology, 98,* 97-99.

Wilson, G. T., & Smith, D. (1989). Assessment of bulimia nervosa: An evaluation of the Eating Disorder Examination. *International Journal of Eating Disorders, 8,* 173-180.

Wood, K. C., Becker, J. A., & Thompson, J. K. (1993). *Reliability of body image assessment for young children (ages 8-10).* Unpublished manuscript.

Wooley, O. W., & Roll, S. (1991). The Color-a-Person Body Dissatisfaction test: Stability, internal consistency, validity, and factor structure. *Journal of Personality Assessment, 56,* 395-413.

Appendix 4-A

Contour Drawing Rating Scale

Instructions: Subjects are asked to rate their "ideal" figure and their "current" size. As noted in the text, it may be useful to consider other instructional rating protocols. The discrepancy between "ideal" and "current" size is an index of body size dissatisfaction.

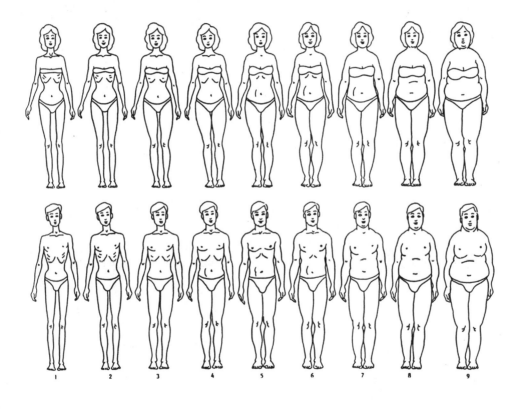

SOURCE: From "Development and Validation of a New Body Image Assessment Scale," by M. A. Thompson and J. J. Gray, in press, *Journal of Personality Assessment.* Copyright © by Lawrence Erlbaum Associates, Inc. Reprinted with permission. (Contact: James J. Gray, Ph.D., Department of Psychology, American University, Washington, DC 20016-8062)

Appendix 4-B

Schematic Figures (Child/Adolescent Version)

Instructions: Subjects are asked to rate their "ideal" figure and their "current" size. The discrepancy between "ideal" and "current" size is an index of body size dissatisfaction.

SOURCE: From "Body Figure Perceptions and Preferences Among Preadolescent Children," by M. E. Collins, 1991, *International Journal of Eating Disorders, 10*, pp. 199-208. Copyright © 1991 by John Wiley & Sons, Inc. Reprinted with permission.

Appendix 4-C

Upper Torso Rating Scale

Instructions: Subjects are asked to rate their "ideal" breast/chest and their "current" size. The discrepancy between "ideal" and "current" is an index of upper torso dissatisfaction.

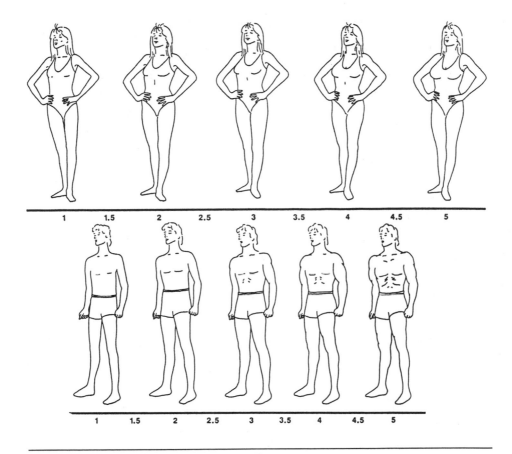

SOURCE: From "Female and Male Ratings of Upper Torso: Actual, Ideal, and Stereotypical Conceptions," by J. K. Thompson and S. Tantleff, 1992, *Journal of Social Behavior and Personality, 7*, pp. 345-354. Reprinted with permission. (Contact: J. Kevin Thompson, Ph.D., Dept. of Psychology, USF, 4202 Fowler Ave., Tampa, FL 33620-8200)

Appendix 4-D

Physical Appearance State and Trait Anxiety Scale: Trait Version

The statements listed below are used to describe how anxious, tense, or nervous you feel *in general* about your body or specific parts of your body. Use the following scale:

0	1	2	3	4	
Never	Rarely	Sometimes	Often		Almost Always

In general, I feel anxious, tense, or nervous about:

1.	The extent to which I look overweight	0	1	2	3	4
2.	My thighs	0	1	2	3	4
3.	My buttocks	0	1	2	3	4
4.	My hips	0	1	2	3	4
5.	My stomach (abdomen)	0	1	2	3	4
6.	My legs	0	1	2	3	4
7.	My waist	0	1	2	3	4
8.	My muscle tone	0	1	2	3	4
9.	My ears	0	1	2	3	4
10.	My lips	0	1	2	3	4
11.	My wrists	0	1	2	3	4
12.	My hands	0	1	2	3	4
13.	My forehead	0	1	2	3	4
14.	My neck	0	1	2	3	4
15.	My chin	0	1	2	3	4
16.	My feet	0	1	2	3	4

The State version has the same items. However, the instructions right now replace in general. In addition, the following are the response choices:

0	1	2	3	4
Not at all	Slightly	Moderately	Very Much So	Exceptionally So

NOTE: The first items constitute the *Weight* subscale and items 9-16 comprise the *Nonweight* subscale. For further information, see Table 4.1.

5

Measures of Restrained Eating

BERNARD S. GORMAN

DAVID B. ALLISON

R*estrained eating* can be defined as a person's tendency to eat less than desired. The construct of dietary restraint plays a major role in weight reduction, weight maintenance, obesity, and eating disorders. To understand the origins of this concept, consider a classic study by Schachter and colleagues (Schachter, 1971; Schachter, Goldman, & Gordon, 1968; Schachter & Rodin, 1974).

On a physiological level, it is known that, among animals, low blood glucose levels are associated with hunger and high blood glucose levels are asso-

AUTHORS' NOTE: We would like to thank C. Peter Herman, Michael R. Lowe, and Albert J. Stunkard for their insightful and cogent commentary. However, the interpretations expressed in this chapter are solely the responsibility of the present authors.

ciated with satiety. Glucose levels are monitored by the hypothalamus at, at least, two sites. The lateral hypothalamus senses low glucose levels and triggers the onset of eating. The ventromedial hypothalamus provides a check and balance of the lateral hypothalamus's activity by sensing high glucose levels and inducing satiation. In theory, hypothalamic monitoring is a relatively autonomous homeostatic process. Under this simple formulation, dietary intake should be strongly correlated with needs for glucose. Therefore weight regulation should be relatively automatic. Yet, it is obvious that humans and domestic animals show both intraindividual and interindividual differences in eating behavior and weight status. Therefore factors other than simple internal regulation of eating behavior may be operative.

Schachter (1971) postulated that obese persons may be more responsive to external food cues, including the availability, sight, and smell of food, than to internal cues (e.g., blood glucose levels). In a laboratory experiment, Schachter et al. (1968) asked obese and nonobese male subjects to participate in a "taste testing" experiment. All subjects were requested to do without the meal that preceded the experiment. When the subjects first arrived at the laboratory, they either were given a "preload" of roast beef sandwiches or were fed nothing. The subjects were then presented with five bowls of crackers and were instructed to rate each cracker in terms of flavor. Subjects were free to eat as many or as few crackers as they desired to form their taste judgments. Fifteen minutes later, the researchers collected rating sheets and counted the number of crackers that each subject consumed. If a simple hypothalamic process, alone, were operative, then subjects who ate sandwiches prior to consuming crackers should have eaten fewer crackers afterward than did subjects who had no sandwiches. In fact, this is what normal weight subjects did. However, obese subjects who were given roast beef sandwiches prior to tasting the crackers actually ate slightly more crackers than did those who had no sandwiches at all. Further experiments reported by Schachter (1971) indicated that food intake by obese people might be strongly influenced by such external cues as the sight, smell, and taste of food. According to this formulation, not only would obese persons eat more than normal weight people when external food cues are strong but they should also eat less than normal weight persons when external food cues are absent.

Nisbett (1972) reexamined Schachter's findings and proposed a "set point" model that attempted to explain the seeming inability of obese persons to regulate their eating by internal cues. According to this model, different persons have highly individual, ideal physiological points, perhaps genetically acquired, called *set points*, that regulate body weight. For some individuals, these points may be set fairly low so that the person naturally eats small to moderate amounts of food. For others, however, the person may have to ingest large amounts of food to maintain the weight dictated by the set point. According to this model, such individuals will often become heavy.

Although their set points may have been achieved, their appearance might not be at levels that their cultures would consider attractive or healthy. If individuals with high set points attempt to stay within the normal or slim weight range, they may have to fight against their natural set points and enter a state akin to chronic starvation.

Herman and colleagues (Herman & Mack, 1975; Herman & Polivy, 1975) extended Nisbett's set-point conjecture beyond the study of obese subjects. They raised the possibility that it may be incorrect to create a sharp division between obese persons and normal weight persons. It may be the case that many normal weight individuals are people who have constantly fought against their set points. They have kept their weights within socially desirable limits through constant vigilance and behavioral control. Obese persons, on the other hand, may have succumbed to the tendency to follow their set points. In a sense, one could consider some normal weight individuals to be obese individuals "in disguise." Pudel and his colleagues in Germany (Pudel, Metzdorff, & Oetting, 1975, cited in Stunkard & Messick, 1985) also noticed that, in laboratory studies, nonobese people tend to decrease their rates of eating over the course of a meal, indicating the approach of satiety. In contrast, obese subjects typically do not reduce their eating rates. However, there are also some nonobese subjects whose rates of eating do not decelerate. Pudel suggested that these subjects might be called the "latent obese"— people who generally regulate their behavior through restraint. Pudel developed a 40-item questionnaire to measure the construct of latent obesity.

Herman and Polivy devised questionnaires that asked people to rate the degree to which they showed dietary restraint by consciously monitoring their weight and appearance and by regulating their food intakes to meet self-imposed or socially imposed targeted weight ranges. Restrained eaters were defined as those who were consciously aware of constantly monitoring their food intake. Conversely, "nonrestrained" eaters are those who were not particularly concerned with monitoring their dietary intake. In a series of experiments (see Heatherton, Herman, Polivy, King, & McGree, 1988; Herman & Polivy, 1980; Ruderman, 1986, for reviews), normal weight dieters were given "preloads" of a pleasant-tasting high-calorie food such as a milk shake. Subjects were then asked to participate in a "taste test" in which they were allowed to eat as much ice cream as they wished during a 15-minute period. Earlier studies by Schachter et al. (1968) with obese and normal weight subjects had shown that normal weight subjects ate less food after a preload but obese subjects failed to compensate for the preload. Like Schachter's obese subjects, Herman's normal weight dieters also failed to compensate for the preload. However, it was also found that, under these conditions, restrained eaters actually "counterregulated" by eating more than a matched group of restrained eaters who did not get a milk shake preload. Unrestrained eaters, however, tended to eat less in the tasting phase to compensate for the preload.

The relationships of counterregulation to restrained eating behaviors, however, are not unequivocal (Lowe, 1993). For example, Ruderman and colleagues (Ruderman & Christensen, 1983; Ruderman & Wilson, 1979) suggested that obese subjects may actually eat less after a preload and that nonobese subjects may not differ by much in their eating after a preload. Although the explanation for counterregulation remains an open question (Herman & Polivy, 1988), it is evident that restrained eaters can lose their self-imposed control of eating and will counterregulate under some circumstances.

Herman and colleagues (Heatherton, Herman, & Polivy, 1991; Herman & Polivy, 1975) found that disinhibiting or counterregulatory effects in restrained eaters were likely to occur when the people were distracted, anxious, depressed, or disinhibited by alcohol (Polivy & Herman, 1976a, 1976b). One might conjecture that distraction and alcohol interfere with sanctions to stay on a diet. According to Herman and Polivy (1988), these anxious or depressed disinhibiting effects may occur because dieting no longer seems important, or because the person believes that eating will be calming, or because negative affect provides a rationalization for breaking a diet.

It can be seen that dietary restraint should bear a relationship to eating disorders. However, the relationship is neither simple nor clear-cut. For example, weight status, alone, is not directly related to dietary restraint. Polivy, Herman, and Howard (1988) do not view dietary restraint as a strong predictor of successful or unsuccessful dieting because some restrained dieters may practice consistent restraint and stay slim, whereas others will attempt restraint at times but fluctuate considerably in eating patterns, weight status, and restraining behaviors. Recently, Lowe (1993) proposed a multifaceted model of dieting behavior that examines interactions among weight status (e.g., underweight, normal weight, overweight), dieting types (e.g., frequency of dieting/overeating, current dieting, weight suppression), and potential mediating mechanisms (e.g., psychological, biological, sensory). It is possible to see many combinations of restraint and obesity, depending on the phase of the dieting cycle in which an individual might be found. Given the presence of other factors in Lowe's model, the correlation between dietary restraint and obesity is neither strong nor direct.

Lowe contends, as do Herman and Polivy, that many people are engaged in a vicious cycle in which chronic dieting causes overeating, and overeating, in turn, causes a need for dieting. Lowe further contends that it is not simply dieting but chronic dieting that causes overeating. Because Herman and Polivy's RS taps chronic rather than acute dieting, there will be a small, positive relationship between RS scores and weight status.

Many clinicians have stated that anorexic people are constantly obsessed by thoughts of food and eating but strive to maintain self-imposed unhealthy weight levels through extreme means. Anorexic subjects usually fall within the high range of the restraint continuum, despite their thin appearance. Both anorexics and bulimics can be seen as displaying variants of an extremely restrained eating style. On the one hand, anorexic persons are obsessed with food but dare not eat for fear of becoming obese. Conversely, bulimics are also obsessed by food and show disinhibited bingeing and, for some, violent purging to regulate weight.

Other researchers have followed Herman and Polivy's pioneering work and have developed measures of restrained eating to assess this construct. In the next section, we shall discuss strategies for evaluating restraint, including Herman and Polivy's Restrained Eating Scale (RS), Stunkard and Messick's (1985) Three Factor Eating Questionnaire Restraint Scale, and the Dutch Eating Behavior Questionnaire (Van Strien, Frijters, Bergers, & Defares, 1986). We will briefly touch on other measures.

Herman and Polivy's Restraint Scale

Description

Polivy et al. (1988) describe the Restraint Scale (RS) as "a 10-item self report questionnaire assessing weight fluctuations, degrees of chronic dieting, and related attitudes toward weight and eating." As such, it was developed to identify individuals who are chronically concerned about their weight and attempt to control or reduce it by dieting or curtailing intake. A five-item scale was initially developed by Herman and Mack (1975) to measure chronic dieting. The items were rationally derived and selected for face validity. Item analyses of data from 45 women produced a scale with a Cronbach's α coefficient of .65. Herman and Polivy (1975) revised the scale to an 11-item form. In that revision, six items formed a "Diet and Weight History" subscale with an α coefficient of .62. The remaining five items formed a "Concern with Dieting" subscale (α coefficient of .68). The subscales correlated .48 and the α coefficient for the whole scale was .75. The present form of the Restrained Eating Scale (RS), shown in Table 5.1, appeared in Herman and Polivy (1980) and contains 10 items.

Items 2, 3, 4, and 10 form the "Weight Fluctuation" subscale. The remaining items form the "Concern for Dieting" subscale. According to Polivy et al. (1988), the whole scale should not be considered a measure of dieting success or a measure of weight fluctuation. Rather, it reflects *patterns* of eating behaviors characteristic of dieters, who usually are unsuccessful dieters, inasmuch as they both attempt to restrain eating and periodically lose control.

TABLE 5.1 Restrained Eating Scale (RS): Items

Items and Scoring Instructions

1. How often are you dieting?

2. What is the maximum amount of weight (in pounds) that you have ever lost in one month?

3. What is your maximum weight gain within a week?

4. In a typical week, how much does your weight fluctuate?

5. Would a weight fluctuation of 5 pounds affect the way you live your life?

6. Do you eat sensibly in front of others and splurge alone?

7. Do you give too much time and thought to food?

8. Do you have feelings of guilt after overeating?

9. How conscious are you of what you are eating?

10. How many pounds over your desired weight were you at your maximum weight?

SOURCE: From "Restrained Eating," by C. P. Herman and J. Polivy, 1980, in A. J. Stunkard (Ed.), *Obesity*, pp. 208-225, Philadelphia: Saunders. Copyright © 1980 by A. J. Stunkard. Reprinted with permission.

Sample

The initial samples used to develop the RS consisted of 42 (Herman & Mack, 1975) and 45 (Herman & Polivy, 1975) female college-age subjects. Subsequent studies have employed considerably larger samples that contained both obese and nonobese men and women.

Preliminary Norms

Many studies that employed the RS have obtained correlation coefficients between the RS and other measures. Thus statements typically take the form of "Subjects with higher scores on the RS were (more) (less) likely to ____ ." In such approaches, establishing cutoff points for classifying people as "restrained" or "unrestrained eaters" is usually unnecessary because the researcher is typically interested in reporting relative statements about varying degrees of restraint. However, if one wants to know whether a given sample or subject is unusually high or low on restraint, then it becomes increasingly important to have norms on the scale.

For females, the median RS score seems to be around 16 (Drewnowski, Riskey, & Deser, 1982; Polivy et al., 1988). Polivy et al. (1988) report that the median for males seems to be around 12. Table 5.2 presents means, sample sizes, and standard deviations for the whole RS and its subscales from some recent, large-scale studies. It appears that the general suggestion of a median

TABLE 5.2 RS Distributions Reported in the Literature

Scale and Subjects	Author	n	Mean	SD
Whole scale				
American college students	Allison et al. (1992)	901	15.1	7.0
female		617	16.4	6.9
male		282	12.3	6.4
American college students	Klem, Klesges, Bene, et al. (1990)	497	12.6	5.9
female		346	13.4	5.8
male		151	10.8	5.8
British men	Wardle and Beales (1986)	45	8.5	5.8
British women	Wardle and Beales (1986)	102	13.5	5.4
Weight fluctuation scale				
American college students	Allison et al. (1992)	901	5.8	3.3
female		617	5.9	3.3
male		282	5.3	3.5
American college students	Klem, Klesges, Bene, et al. (1990)			
female		346	5.0	3.0
male		151	4.8	3.4
British women	Wardle and Beales (1986)	102	4.9	2.8
British men	Wardle and Beales (1986)	45	3.1	3.1
Concern with dieting scale				
American college students	Allison et al. (1992)	901	9.3	4.7
female		617	10.4	4.6
male		282	6.9	3.9
American college students	Klem, Klesges, Bene, et al. (1990)			
female		346	8.4	4.0
male		151	5.9	3.4
British women	Wardle and Beales (1986)	102	7.8	3.7
British men	Wardle and Beales (1986)	45	4.7	3.0

of 16 for females and 12 for males on the total RS seems reasonable. However, it also should be noted that, because RS means differ by nationality, such choices must be tentative. Given some discrepancies from sample to sample on the subscales, researchers should be especially cautious in choosing cutoff points.

Stein (1988) cautioned readers against using median splits on the RS to form subject groups for use in ANOVA designs. He showed that more predictive power could be gained when using a continuous measure of RS in regression analysis. Similarly, Maxwell and Delany (1993) showed not only that the use of median splits to form levels of factors in analyses of variance may be a less powerful strategy than the use of continuous variables in regression models but also that such strategies may produce erroneous conclusions about interactions among factors. Allison, Gorman, and Primavera (1993) discuss the disadvantages of dichotomization in general. Unless one has a strong rationale for classifying people into groups like "dieters versus non-dieters" or "restrained versus nonrestrained," there should be no reason to split samples into discrete classes. Therefore the means and medians offered here are for guidance purposes and we do not suggest dichotomizing restraint scores for statistical analyses.

Reliability

Internal Consistency

As Table 5.3 shows, most studies of the internal consistency of the RS and its subscales agree that Cronbach's α typically exceeds .75 on the whole RS. As might be predicted by the fact the subscales necessarily have fewer items than the whole scale, there are lower subscale reliabilities. For example, α's range from .66 to .71 on the WF scale and .70 to .80 on the CD scale (Allison et al., 1992; Herman & Polivy, 1975; Klem, Klesges, Bene, et al., 1990). Klem, Klesges, Bene, et al. (1990) found that α's for blacks and whites were the same for all scales, as were α's for men and women.

In general, when variance on a predictor measure, on a criterion measure, or both measures are restricted, Pearson product-moment correlations will be lower than when variance is not restricted (Crocker & Algina, 1986). Therefore Cronbach's α, which depends on both the number of items and the average correlations among items, will typically be lower in more homogeneous groups. This can clearly be seen in Table 5.3, where subgroup reliabilities frequently fall below .75. It can be concluded that, in heterogenous groups, the internal consistency of the RS and subscales is high. However, internal consistency will be predictably lower within selected subgroups.

Test-Retest Reliability

According to the data in Table 5.4, it seems that RS scores tend to be stable, supporting the notion that dietary restraint is a consistent trait rather than a transitory state.

Validity

Content Validity

Factorial composition. When the RS was initially developed by Herman and Polivy (1975), the items were partitioned into two subscales: a "Diet and Weight History" and a "Concern with Food and Eating" scale with the corre-

TABLE 5.3 Reliability of Dietary Restraint Scales: Internal Consistency

Reference	n	Coefficient	Sample Characteristics
RS			
Allison et al. (1992)	823	.83	Normal weight college students
Allison et al. (1992)	78	.72	Obese college students
Allison et al. (1992)	901	.82	Above two samples combined
Laessle et al. (1989)	60	.78	Normal weight women; 18-30 yrs old; mostly college students
Ruderman (1983)	89	.86	Normal weight female college students
Ruderman (1983)	58	.51	Obese female college students
Johnson et al. (1983)	51	.79	Normal weight
Johnson et al. (1983)	58	.50	Obese nondieters
Johnson et al. (1983)	27	.83	Obese dieters
Johnson et al. (1986)	26	.57	Bulimic women; 16-41 yrs old
Klem, Klesges, Bene, et al. (1990)	497	.78	College students (151 men; 346 women)
Klem, Klesges, Bene, et al. (1990)	124	.68	Obese college students
Klem, Klesges, Bene, et al. (1990)	373	.78	Normal weight college students
TFEQ-R			
Allison et al. (1992)	823	.91	Normal weight college students
Allison et al. (1992)	78	.88	Obese college students
Allison et al. (1992)	901	.90	Above two samples combined
Laessle et al. (1989)	60	.80	Normal weight women; 18-30 yrs old; mostly college students
Stunkard and Messick (1988)	45	.92	Unrestrained eaters
Stunkard and Messick (1988)	53	.79	Restrained eaters
Stunkard and Messick (1988)	98	.93	Above two samples combined
DEBQ-R			
Allison et al. (1992)	823	.95	Normal weight college students
Allison et al. (1992)	78	.91	Obese college students
Allison et al. (1992)	901	.95	Above two samples combined
Laessle et al. (1989)	60	.89	Normal weight women; 18-30 yrs old; mostly college students
Van Strien, Frijters, Bergers, et al. (1986)	114	.94	Obese adults (71 men, 73 women)
Van Strien, Frijters, Bergers, et al. (1986)	996	.95	Normal weight adults (427 men, 569 women)
Van Strien, Frijters, Bergers, et al. (1986)	1169[a]	.95	Above two samples combined

NOTE: RS = Herman and Polivy Revised Restraint Scale; TFEQ-R = Stunkard and Messick Three Factor Eating Inventory; DEBQ-R = Dutch Eating Behavior Questionnaire.
a. It should be noted that the sum, 1,169, as reported in their article, does not equal the total number of men and women studied.

lation between the two subscales being .48. Several factor analyses found correlated factors whose intercorrelations ranged from .17 to .62. Factor analytic studies in samples with primarily normal weight subjects typically retain two-factor solutions (Allison et al., 1992; Blanchard & Frost, 1983; Cole & Edelmann, 1987; Drewnowski et al., 1982; Heatherton et al., 1988; Lowe,

TABLE 5.4 Reliability of Dietary Restraint Scales: Test-Retest Reliability

Reference	n	Coefficient	Interval	Sample Characteristics
RS				
Allison et al. (1992)	34	.95	2 weeks	College students
Hibscher and Herman (1977)	86	.92	"a few weeks"	Male college students
Polivy et al. (1988)	514	.93	1 week	College students; 166 male, 348 female
Kickham and Gayton (1977)	44	.93	4 weeks	Normal weight college students (28 females, 16 males)
Klesges et al. (1991)	305	.74	2½ years	98 males, 207 females
TFEQ-R				
Allison et al. (1992)	34	.91	2 weeks	College students
Stunkard and Messick (1988)	17	.93	4 weeks	College students
DEBQ-R				
Allison et al. (1992)	34	.92	2 weeks	College students

NOTE: RS = Herman and Polivy Revised Restraint Scale; TFEQ-R = Stunkard and Messick Three Factor Eating Inventory; DEBQ-R = Dutch Eating Behavior Questionnaire.

1984; Polivy et al., 1988; Ruderman, 1983). Most researchers find that items 1, 5, 6, 7, 8, and 9 load on a Concern for Dieting factor (CD) and that items 2, 3, 4, and 10 load on a Weight Fluctuation (WF) factor (Blanchard & Frost, 1983; Drewnowski et al., 1982; Ruderman, 1983). It is common, however, to find that two factors account for 50% to 60% of the variance. Polivy et al. (1988), however, contend that the whole RS should be used because neither factor in isolation seems to predict as well as the whole RS.

Allison et al. (1992) performed both orthogonal and oblique confirmatory factor analyses. They found the familiar two-factor pattern of CD (39% of the total variance) and WF (15% of the total variance) with the oblique factor scale intercorrelation being .03. Correlations between the original CD and WF scales were .50.

Not all studies find two-factor solutions. For example, when oblique factor rotations are performed in samples with substantial numbers of obese subjects, items 6 ("Do you eat sensibly in front of others and splurge alone?") and 7 ("Do you give too much time and thought to food?") are often found on a third factor, possibly a binge eating factor, or on the WF factor. Additionally, item 6 sometimes is found on the CD factor. Klem, Klesges, Bene, et al. (1990) performed a series of confirmatory factor analyses of the RS in a sample of 229 college students (117 males, 112 females). Although a two-factor solution had a fair fit with the data, the solution did not correspond closely to the structure proposed by Herman and Polivy. Furthermore, simple structure was not well achieved. Lowe (1984) performed an exploratory principal components analysis and found three factors with eigenvalues > 1.0. He performed oblique rotations and found that items 1, 5, 8, 9, and 10 loaded on the first factor (29.3% of the variance), which he labeled "Dietary Concern and Weight History." Items 2-4 formed the Weight Fluctuation scale (28.3% of the variance) and item 6 (splurging) and item 7 (thoughts about food) loaded on a third factor (17.6% of the variance).

More complex factor structures consisting of three or more factors have also been reported (e.g., Williams, Spencer, & Edelmann, 1987). This has occurred when the samples contained substantial portions of obese or bulimic subjects (Johnson, Corrigan, Crusco, & Schlundt, 1986; Johnson, Lake, & Mahan, 1983; Lowe, 1984; Ruderman, 1983). For example, Ruderman (1983) found a four-factor solution among a small and homogeneous sample of obese subjects.

In general, psychometric studies of the RS suggest that its factorial composition differs in normal weight and overweight samples (Ruderman, 1986). The greater the proportion of overweight people in a sample, the more factors emerge (Ruderman, 1986). Such factor instability across populations is often taken as a sign of differential validity. However, as mentioned earlier, restriction of variance always reduces correlation coefficients. Consequently, the number of common factors that can be obtained in a factor analysis will increase.

Despite some differences in their findings, factor analytic studies agree that multiple-factor solutions provide a better psychometric description of the RS than single-factor solutions. Several researchers such as Wardle (1986) believe that the total RS score can no longer be taken as a pure measure of restraint. A frequent criticism of the RS is that, because it contains several factors, it is difficult to determine whether it is the CD, the WF, or other components of the Restraint Scale that are responsible for observed covariation between the RS and other constructs of interest. It is true that the multicomponent RS correlates with other behaviors, much in the same way that multiple regression can be used to predict a behavior from a battery of measures. However, we might ask if the components of the RS work together additively, multiplicatively, as mediators, or as moderators of the relationship of the Restraint Scale to other behaviors. Without isolation of separate factors, it would be difficult to disentangle the networks of relationships involved in restrained eating.

Factor stability. Blanchard and Frost (1983) evaluated the factor stability of the RS subfactors in two independent samples. They obtained Tucker's congruence coefficients (Tucker, 1951) above .99 for both factors, indicating excellent factor stability. Allison et al. (1992) also used Tucker's coefficient of congruence (CC) as a measure of factor stability. The CC for each of the RS factors over genders was over .95. The CC for each of the RS factors over random splits of the sample was over .99, indicating that factor structures are probably not functions of a few odd, "outlier" subjects. The CCs for a comparison of obese with nonobese subjects was .96 for the CD factor and .92 for the WF factor. In general, it can be said the factor patterns are the same in both obese and nonobese samples.

Construct Validity: Convergent and Discriminant Validity

Weight and obesity status. The RS was designed to be a measure of chronic dieting behaviors. Therefore it seems plausible that RS scale scores should be related to dieting behavior. However, these relationships are neither direct nor simple.

Several researchers have used percentage overweight as a criterion to be predicted by the RS and its subscales. Drewnowski et al. (1982) found that only the Weight Fluctuation scale correlated with percentage overweight. Among 217 students (96 male, 118 female, 3 unclassified), Lowe (1984) found that CD was related to overweight status ($r = .41$) but not WF ($r = -.01$). Lowe (1984) found that the CD, the WF, and the total RS correlated over .40 with a measure of weight suppression that he operationally defined by subtracting current percentage overweight from maximum percentage overweight. In two studies, Ruderman found correlations of .37 and .38 between RS scores and percentage overweight (Ruderman, 1983, 1985). Klem, Klesges, and Shadish (1990) found that overweight subjects were significantly higher on RS, CD, and WF than nonoverweight Ss. However, Klesges, Klem, Epkins, and Klesges (1991) did not obtain a significant correlation between weight change and dietary restraint. Allison et al. (1992) found that, when 823 nonobese subjects were compared with 78 obese Ss, the obese Ss displayed significantly higher scores on both the whole RS and the WF.

Klesges, Isbell, and Klesges (1992) performed a longitudinal study that followed restrained and unrestrained eaters over a 1-year period. Among men, restraint scores did not add significantly to a regression equation that predicted 13% of the variance in weight gain from a combination of variables that included age, weight, body mass, restraint, energy intake, and activity variables. However, among women, restraint had a significant positive relationship in an equation that predicted 21% of the variance in weight gain, in addition to the other physiological, demographic, and activity variables. Lowe (1984) found that restrained nonobese subjects may tend to be more overweight than unrestrained subjects.

Although positive and statistically significant, the relationships among RS scores, obesity, and weight change are not extremely high. It seems that obese subjects are highly concerned with restraining their eating behaviors.

However, correlations, alone, do not establish a causal relationship between dietary restraint and obesity. For example, do the correlations suggest that some obese people would like to eat less but have lost their personal "battles of the bulge"? Alternately, could it be that obese persons avow restraint because their obesity is socially stigmatized but, otherwise, do not particularly restrain their eating?

One study that seems to shed light on this question was performed by K. J. Ferguson, Brink, Wood, and Koop (1992), who studied a group of 142 dieters who had been overweight by at least 21 lbs prior to their entry into a dieting program. Based on a "success" criteria of a loss of 5% of body weight, maintenance of weight loss for a year, and a gain of no more than 5 lbs, 41 women and 41 men were considered "successful" and 32 women and 28 men were classified as "unsuccessful." Item-by-item comparisons on the RS showed that unsuccessful dieters were significantly more likely than successful dieters to endorse the items, "Do you eat sensibly in front of others and splurge alone?" and "Do you give too much time and thought to food?" Conversely, the unsuccessful dieters were less likely to endorse, "How conscious are you of what you are eating?" It would appear that some unsuccessful dieters would achieve high scores on the RS because they actually would like to eat more but wish to appear "sensible" in front of others.

Counter to most predictions, Drewnowski et al. (1982) found that, although overweight subjects obtained higher total RS scores and higher WF scores than normal weight subjects, their CD scores were lower. Because the main result lay in the WF scale, Drewnowski et al. suggested that the overweight subjects may simply be reporting that they had more difficulty in regulating their weight. Herman and Polivy (1982) countered by stating that the correlation between the RS weight fluctuation and dietary concern scale is moderate and positive ($r = .32$); therefore the relationship of the RS to weight status cannot be solely attributed to variance in the Weight Fluctuation scale. Further, they stated that two weight fluctuation items, "How often are you dieting?" and "Do you eat sensibly in front of others and splurge alone?" are both manifestations of a pattern that would lead both to unsuccessful dieting and overweight status. More recently, Laessle, Tuschl, Kotthaus, and Pirke (1989) found an $r = -.04$ between RS scale scores and mean caloric intake. Thus it appears that the RS and its subscales cannot be used as simple predictors of weight regulation and dieting behavior.

Eating disorders. It would seem reasonable to assume that eating disorders and restraint behavior should be related. For example, Ruderman and Grace (1987) studied 108 women who were given the RS and the BULIT (Smith & Thelen, 1984), a measure of bulimia. BULIT scores were significantly correlated with the RS. Moreover, the partial correlation between the BULIT and

CD subscale was still statistically significant when WF subscale scores were controlled. However, the relationship between WF and the BULIT was insignificant when the CD scores were controlled. Thus it appears that the CD and bulimic behavior bear a relationship to each other that goes beyond their relationship to weight fluctuation. Prussin and Harvey (1991) studied 174 female runners and found that 19% of the women fit the *DSM-III-R* classification of bulimia. Within their selected sample of subjects, all of whom were both in the normal weight range and, presumably, more physically active than average persons, bulimic subjects in their study ($n = 38$) scored significantly higher on the RS than nonbulimics ($n = 136$). Therefore the cognitive component of the RS rather than weight change, per se, seems to serve as an important link to eating disorders.

Age. Among college students who ranged in age from 17 to 57, there were no significant age differences on the RS, CD, or WF (Allison et al., 1992; Klem, Klesges, Bene, et al., 1990). These studies were cross-sectional studies with relatively few older adults. Therefore it is difficult to state whether the lack of age differences is due to the possibility that dietary restraint is a trait that is formed early and does not change throughout the life span or whether generational and cohort effects canceled relationships of restraint to age. In any case, more extensive developmental studies with both younger and older subjects will be needed to explore the relationship between restraint and age.

Gender. Klem, Klesges, Bene, et al. (1990) found that college women scored significantly higher than men on the CD subscale but not on the whole RS or the WF subscale. Allison et al. (1992) found that women received significantly higher RS and CD scores than men. However, men and women did not differ significantly in their WF scores. One can conclude that, although men and women do not differ significantly in terms of weight fluctuation, women are more concerned with culturally imposed mandates for dieting.

Susceptibility to response sets. Kickham and Gayton (1977) reported a correlation of .11 between the RS and Edwards Social Desirability Scale, suggesting that the RS is not unduly affected by social desirability. Likewise, Johnson et al. (1983, 1986) found small and nonsignificant correlations between the RS, the MMPI Lie Scale, and the Marlowe-Crowne Social Desirability Scale (MCSD) for bulimics, obese nondieters, and "normals." Similarly, small and nonsignificant correlations were observed between the RS and MCSD among average weight persons (Corrigan & Ekstrand, 1988; Ruderman, 1983) and obese persons (Ruderman, 1983).

Johnson et al. (1983), in a study of 27 obese dieters, obtained moderate negative correlations between the RS and the MMPI Lie Scale ($r = -.33$) and the RS and MCSD ($r = -.51$). Attempts to appear socially desirable may distort the restraint scale scores of some obese persons. However, Ruderman (1983) found a significantly stronger relation between the Eysenck Lie Scale (Eysenck & Eysenck, 1975) and the RS among nonobese subjects ($r = -.70$) than among obese subjects ($r = -.13$).

In a subset ($n = 73$) of subjects, Allison et al. (1992) found that the RS correlated $-.27$ with the Marlowe/Crowne SD scale and $-.05$ with the Edwards SD scale. As the MCSD measures the need for social approval more than it measures simple test faking, it appears that the correlation may be tapping a normative standard for less restrictive eating. That is, people may not wish to admit that they overeat and that their weights fluctuate. Allison et al. (1992) also performed an experiment in which subjects were instructed to dissimulate RS responses. Subjects who were given instructions to create a good impression displayed low RS scores (mean = 8.57). However, subjects who were instructed to create a poor impression produced extremely high scores (mean = 30.65). Allison et al. also found a correlation of .40 between the desirability ratings of individual RS scale items and their frequencies of endorsement. That is, those items that were rated as more desirable were endorsed more frequently.

It should be noted that all of the studies cited obtained *negative* correlations between restrained eating and socially desirable behavior. That is, high restraint is correlated with "bad" behavior. This is interesting because, presumably, restrained subjects wish to "look good." Perhaps the negative relationship is due to the possibility that several of the RS scale items are worded so that they suggest undesirable behaviors (e.g., "too much," "splurge alone," "feelings of guilt," and "pounds over your desired weight"). Taken as a whole, the above studies suggest that the RS is a "transparent" scale that can easily be faked when people are motivated to do so. Even under ordinary circumstances, there is some evidence that the RS is somewhat confounded by socially desirable response sets.

Unfortunately, none of the studies reported social desirability effects for the RS subscales. Further research should investigate whether the CD and WF scales differ in their relationships to social desirability.

Predictions of laboratory behavior. Herman and Polivy (1975) found that, when subjects were threatened with electric shock, unrestrained normal eaters ate significantly less food but restrained eaters ate slightly more food. However, neither anxiety nor restraint, alone, affected consumption.

Westerterp-Plantenga, Wouters, and ten Hoor (1991) presented a four-course meal to 6 obese and 18 normal weight women. The women were permitted to eat as much as they wanted to eat in the second course but the other three courses had fixed amounts of food. Eating behavior and the amount of food consumed was observed directly by means of an electronic scale that was built into the table under each subject's plate. Normal weight women who scored low on the Herman-Polivy (1980) restraint questionnaire displayed intake deceleration on the second course and later courses. However, as predicted by Herman and Polivy's restraint thesis, normal weight and obese restrained women displayed a progressive, linear cumulative food intake in the second and later courses.

Several findings support the notion that restrained eaters will disinhibit their eating behavior. Disinhibition is likely to occur when the subject is experiencing a negative affect or if food is available in a preload situation (e.g., Knight & Boland, 1989; Schotte, Cools, & McNally, 1990; see Lowe, 1993, for a current review and synthesis). Studies using manipulations of "placebo" caloric loads (e.g., Heatherton, Polivy, & Herman, 1991) have shown that this counterregulatory disinhibition phenomenon is at least as cognitively as it is physiologically driven.

Given these findings, the prediction of disinhibited or counterregulatory laboratory eating has become a benchmark against which the predictive validity of restraint scales is checked. In this regard, the RS performs well (although the moderators of the RS-disinhibition relationship can be quite complex; again, see Lowe, 1993). However, there is a conceptual difficulty here. Perhaps the label "Restraint Scale" is a misnomer because the scale contains items and factors that reflect not only restraint but disinhibition and weight fluctuation as well. The scale might be relabeled a "Dieting Scale" (C. P. Herman, personal communication, 1993) as dieting behavior may involve an intermix of all of these components. Clearly, some combinations of the items of the RS successfully predict disinhibited eating. Again, without a more detailed analysis of the components of the RS and their interrelationships with respect to eating behavior, it is difficult to specify the nature of the relationship.

Construct Validity: Concurrent Validity

Klesges et al. (1992) performed a multivariate study of 141 men (68 high restraint, 73 low restraint) and 146 women (76 high restraint, and 70 low restraint). The dependent variables in their study consisted of a battery of measures that included age, body mass, amounts of food intake, and levels of activity. The independent variables were sex and dietary restraint. No significant sex by restraint interactions were found. However, separate significant main effects were found for sex and for restraint. In general, women had higher restraint scores than did men. In terms of restraint differences, high restraint eaters were more likely to have a larger body mass index and ingested fewer carbohydrates but more fat than lower restraint subjects. Among men, restraint was a significant predictor of body mass. Thus the finding that RS scores are related to different patterns of eating behavior lends support to the concurrent validity of the scale.

Readability

The reading level of the RS has been estimated to be between the fourth and ninth grades (Allison & Franklin, 1993).

Stunkard and Messick's
TFEQ-R Restraint Scale

Description

Stunkard (1981) and, later, Stunkard and Messick (1985) built on Herman and Polivy's research on the Restraint Scale and its correlates. They were concerned with several issues. First, they stated that the RS did not predict the behavior of obese persons, per se. For example, some studies found that obese people did not necessarily overeat after they were given a preload. Therefore the RS does not establish a clear relationship between restrained eating and degree of obesity.

Second, the RS does not contain one source of variance but at least two: a concern for dieting factor and a weight fluctuation factor. Weight fluctuation may be a concomitant of obesity that has very little to do with restraint. Stunkard and Messick cited Drewnowski et al.'s (1982) work, which showed that percentage overweight was more correlated with WF than with CD. They also cited research that suggested that, at least among overweight individuals, social desirability scale values are significantly correlated with RS scores.

In response to these difficulties with the RS, Stunkard and Messick devised a new instrument. Instead of focusing on a single factor of restrained eating, Stunkard and Messick examined the literature and selected items for an instrument that would tap several facets of eating behavior. Some items for their initial eating scale were borrowed from Herman and Polivy's RS (1975) and Pudel's Latent Obesity Questionnaire (1975). In addition, they wrote 17 new items. The preliminary set of 67 items were given to a sample of 220 subjects (97 men and 123 women) including both obese and nonobese individuals.

A factor analysis of Stunkard and Messick's initial 67-item pool produced three factors. These factors emerged as Behavioral Restraint, Lability in Behavior and Weight, and Hunger. Intercorrelations among the factors ranged from .37 to .63. Further selection and rewriting of the items produced three new factors: I, Cognitive Control of Eating; II, Disinhibition; and III, Susceptibility to Hunger. The scale originally appeared in 1985 as the Three-Factor Eating Questionnaire (TFEQ; Stunkard & Messick, 1985), but, currently, the scale is published by the Psychological Corporation as the *Eating Inventory* (Stunkard & Messick, 1988). For the purposes of the present chapter, we shall confine our discussion mainly to the Restraint Factor scale and shall refer to the restraint scale of the TFEQ as the TFEQ-R.

Sample

Stunkard and Messick developed the initial scale in 1985 with a group of 300 subjects (97 men and 123 women), aged 17 to 77 (mean age = 44). The sample consisted of several subgroups. One subgroup contained 18 male and 60 female members of a weight reduction group. Each member of the group solicited the single most "free-eating" nonobese person of his or her acquaintance to form a subgroup of 62 unrestrained eaters; 57 males and 23 female neighbors of the dieting group were added to the sample and, finally, 80 unselected members of community groups were recruited for the study.

Preliminary Norms

Means, sample sizes, and standard deviations for subject groups on the TFEQ-R are presented in Table 5.5. Stunkard and Messick (1988) suggest tentative guidelines of 0-10 as "low to average," 11-13 as "high," and 14 or more as "clinical range." As can be seen, sample means seem to differ widely by gender and by nationality. Therefore researchers should be cautious when attempting to classify subjects into high- or low-restraint groups.

Reliability

Internal Consistency

As can be seen in Table 5.3, every study we were able to locate reported quite respectable internal consistency coefficients (i.e., ≥ .80). Moreover, unlike the RS, the TFEQ is not markedly less reliable among obese persons.

Test-Retest

Stunkard and Messick (1985) cited an unpublished manuscript by Ganley that reported a test-retest correlation over a 1-month interval to be .93. Allison et al. (1992) found test-retest reliability to be .91 over a 2-week span.

TABLE 5.5 TFEQ-R Distributions Reported in the Literature

Subjects	Author	N	Mean	SD
Unrestrained eaters	Stunkard and Messick (1985)	62	6.0	5.5
Swedish control group	Bjorvell et al. (1986)[a]	58	9.8	4.2
Chilean university students	Lolas (1987)[a]	88	7.7	5.1
U.S. control sample	Ganley (1986)[a]	30	11.0	5.3
Japanese high school girls	Nogami (1986)[a]	243	5.6	3.7
American college students	Allison et al. (1992)	901	9.0	5.8
Females only		617	10.2	5.6
Males only		282	6.1	5.1
Japanese nursing students	Nogami (1986)[a]	270	6.3	3.6
German women	Laessle et al. (1989)	62	6.5	4.7
German women in a weight reduction program	Westenhoffer (1991)	46,132	13.1	4.3
German men in a weight reduction program	Westenhoffer (1991)	8,393	10.6	4.7

a. Reported in Stunkard and Messick (1988).

Validity

Content Validity

Factorial composition. Stunkard and Messick (1985) performed several factor analyses of the TFEQ as they shaped the instrument to its final version. Although some variation in factor structure was found across samples, Cognitive Restraint, the first factor, was quite robust. Highly similar results were obtained by Hyland, Irvine, Thacker, Dann, and Dennis (1989) and Ganley (1988).

The previous studies found that a strong restraint factor emerged when the entire set of TFEQ items were submitted to factor analysis. In a more detailed study, Allison et al. (1992) performed a principal components factor analysis on only the 21 TFEQ restraint items to investigate whether a single restraint factor could be obtained. Two factors were found in the data provided by their sample of 901 college students. The first factor accounted for 35% of the total variation and the second factor accounted for an additional 6% of the variance. Cattell's scree test and the Guttman-Kaiser eigenvalues > 1 rule each suggested a two-factor solution. However, the Minimum Average Partial test (MAP) (Zwick & Velicer, 1986) indicated only one factor, and LISREL (Jöreskog & Sörbom, 1986) goodness-of-fit indices were fair to good for a one-factor solution. Although equivocal, a two-factor solution was retained. The first orthogonal varimax factor resembled Stunkard and Messick's Cognitive Restraint factor and the second factor resembled a "Behavioral Restraint" factor. A varimax rotation did not result in a highly simple structure. Although oblique rotation simplified the factor pattern, the two factors were highly ($r = .56$) correlated. Allison et al. (1992) noted that the TFEQ contains two highly correlated primary factors that can be considered to be nested within a broader secondary factor.

Westenhoffer (1991) explored the nature of the two highly correlated sources of variance in the TFEQ-R in a study that employed the German version of the TFEQ with 54,525 subjects (46,132 female, 8,393 male) in a weight reduction program. Using a variant of discriminant analysis, he constructed two scales that he called "Flexible" control and "Rigid" control. The Flexible control scale was associated with low disinhibition, whereas the Rigid control scale was associated with high disinhibition. These "Flexible" and "Rigid" control scales correspond roughly to Allison et al.'s (1992) cognitive and behavioral TFEQ-R subscales.

Gorman, Allison, and Primavera (1993) reexamined Allison et al.'s (1992) findings and noted several anomalies in the factor analysis. First, the high intercorrelations among the factors seemed excessive for a two-factor solution. Second, the item endorsement frequencies of the TFEQ-R varied considerably. Most items that appeared on the cognitive restraint factor were endorsed with high frequencies. However, items that appeared on the behavioral restraint factor were typically endorsed at very low rates.

Previous psychometric literature suggested that, when items that differ considerably in their endorsement rates are factored by conventional linear factor analysis techniques, they often produce more factors than their content would suggest (G. A. Ferguson, 1941; Gibson, 1967; Horst, 1965; McDonald & Ahlawat, 1974). In such cases, inherently nonlinear techniques, such as multidimensional scaling, latent profile analysis, and item response theory models, might prove to be superior to traditional factor analyses. Therefore Gorman et al. (1993) subjected the correlation matrix of TFEQ-R items to a multidimensional scaling solution and the item pattern to Rasch Model Scaling (Hambleton, Swaminathan, & Rogers, 1991). Multidimensional scaling revealed that the first dimension of multidimensional scaling solution was bipolar, with behavioral restraint items loading at one end of the dimension and cognitive restraint items at the other. Rasch Model Scaling indicated that the TFEQ-R items formed a highly ordered continuum in which cognitive restraint items could be found at one end and behavioral restraint items at the other end of the continuum. Under this formulation, a person's TFEQ restraint score can be considered a point on a single continuum that starts with common thoughts about reducing eating and ends with overt, deliberate, but relatively rare actions to reduce eating.

Factor stability. Using Tucker's coefficient of congruence (CC), Allison et al. (1992) found that the congruence coefficients across random splits of the subject sample were high (CC > .97). However, congruence coefficients across genders were low (CC < .80) and modest (CC < .90) when comparing obese with nonobese subjects. Therefore the TFEQ-R may not be measuring the same constructs in the same ways in different subgroups.

Construct Validity: Convergent and Divergent Validity

Westenhoffer (1991) found that the TFEQ-R correlated −.37 with the TFEQ disinhibition and .64 with the TFEQ hunger scale. Simmons (1991) found that the TFEQ restraint scale correlated significantly ($r = .55$) with the drive for thinness scale and the body dissatisfaction scale of the Eating Disorder Inventory (Garner, Olmsted, & Polivy, 1984). It also had significant negative correlations with appearance, atmosphere, nutrition, and religion scales of Simmons's Eating Values Survey (EVS; Simmons, 1991). It also had positive correlations with the EVS convenience, enthusiasm, inner hunger, recreation, and reward subscales of the EVS. Laessle obtained an r of .46 between restraint factor scores and mean caloric intake. That is, subjects who showed high restraint actually ate less.

Weight and obesity. Stunkard and Messick (1985) found a correlation of .20 of restraint with weight. However, Allison et al. (1992) found no significant differences between obese and nonobese Ss on the TFEQ-R. Stunkard and Wadden (1990) reported several studies that showed that restraint scores of obese persons who were in treatment were significantly higher than scores for those who were not in treatment. LaPorte and Stunkard (1990) studied the relationship of score patterns on the eating inventory to adherence, attrition, and dysphoric emotional states in 81 severely obese patients who were treated with very low calorie diets (VLCD). It was found that subjects who had scores above the mean on disinhibition and hunger and below the mean on restraint had consistently poorer outcomes. Disinhibition and hunger were significantly related to anxiety and depression, whereas restraint was not. Thus it appears that the relationship between restraint and obesity is weak. However, restraint may moderate or mediate other variables that are related to obesity.

Relationship with social desirability. Allison et al. (1992) found the TFEQ-R to correlate .05 with the Edwards (1957) and −.21 with the Marlowe/Crowne SD scale (Crowne & Marlowe, 1964). Allison et al. (1992) found that the correlation of item endorsement frequencies with scaled social desirability ratings for each item was .01. Thus it seems highly unlikely that subjects were endorsing items based on their perceived desirability. Under instructions to "fake good" and "fake bad," subjects in Allison et al.'s study (1992) did not produce significantly different mean TFEQ-RS scores. It appears that the TFEQ-R is not unduly influenced by socially desirable responding.

Predictions of laboratory behavior. According to previously cited work by Herman and Polivy, restrained eaters should be more likely to overeat following a food preload. However, when using the TFEQ-R, the relationship between restraint and disinhibited laboratory eating has been somewhat weak and inconsistent (Lowe & Maycock, 1988; Rogers & Hill, 1989; Tuschl, Laessle, Platte, & Pirke, 1990; Westerterp, Nicolson, Boots, Mordant, & Westerterp, 1988; Westerterp-Plantenga et al., 1991). As discussed earlier, whether this should be taken as an indication of validity or lack of it is open to debate. Given that Stunkard and Messick attempted to separate restraint and disinhibition into separate scales, this lack of prediction can be taken as a sign of discriminative validity.

Readability

The reading level of the TFEQ-R has been estimated to be between the sixth and ninth grades (Allison & Franklin, 1993).

Availability

The TFEQ can be purchased from the Psychological Corporation, 555 Academic Court, San Antonio, TX 78204-2498. Due to copyright regulations, we are unable to reprint the scale here.

Dutch Eating Behavior Questionnaire

Description

Van Strien, Frijters, Bergers, and Defares (1986) noted that the Herman and Polivy (1980) Restraint Scale (RS) is multifactorial because it contains both a weight fluctuation factor and a concern for dieting factor. They also

TABLE 5.6 DEBQ-R Items

1. When you have put on weight do you eat less than you usually do?

2. Do you try to eat less at mealtimes than you would like to eat?

3. How often do you refuse food or drink offered you because you are concerned about your weight?

4. Do you watch exactly what you eat?

5. Do you deliberately eat foods that are slimming?

6. When you have eaten too much, do you eat less than usual the following day?

7. Do you deliberately eat less in order not to become heavier?

8. How often do you try not to eat between meals because you are watching your weight?

9. How often in the evenings do you try not to eat because you are watching your weight?

10. Do you take your weight into account with what you eat?

SOURCE: From "The Dutch Eating Behavior Questionnaire (DEBQ) for Assessment of Restrained, Emotional, and External Eating Behavior," by T. Van Strien, J. E. R. Frijters, G. P. A. Bergers, and P. B. Defares, 1986, *International Journal of Eating Disorders, 5,* p. 304. Nederlandse Vragenlijst voor Eetgedrag (NVE). Copyright © 1986 by Swets and Zeitlinger, B. V., Lisse. Reprinted with permission.

stated that, although many theoretical and empirical works on eating behavior and dieting spoke about restrained eating, emotionally triggered eating, and eating in response to external or internal hunger cues, the measures of eating behavior did not always make clear distinctions among these constructs. As a result, they developed the Dutch Eating Behavior Questionnaire (DEBQ), a 33-item questionnaire to assess three separate factors of eating behavior: restrained eating, emotional eating, and external eating. The restrained eating scale, displayed in Table 5.6, asks subjects to endorse items concerning deliberate, planned weight control. The emotional eating scale has items that refer to increased eating when the person is bored, irritated, or angry. The external eating scale contains items that refer to eating behaviors that are triggered by the sight and odor of foods or the presence of other people who are eating.

The initial item pool for the DEBQ consisted of 100 items. Some items were derived from items that were used in previous research by Van Strien, Frijters, Bergers, and Defares (1986). Other items came from Pudel's Latent Obesity Scale (Pudel et al., 1975). It should be noted that some of Stunkard and Messick's TFEQ (1985) items also came from Pudel's questionnaire, and therefore correlations between the DEBQ and TFEQ should not be surprising. All items are presented in a Likert-type scale form with the categories: *never* (1), *seldom* (2), *sometimes* (3), *often* (4), and *very often* (5). In addition, there is a "not relevant" category.

Through a series of factor analyses and item analyses that eliminated factorially complex items and items with unusual content, they developed a final four-factor, 33-item inventory that was based on the responses of 653 female and 517 male subjects. Although the aim was to develop a three-scale solution, factor analyses reveal a small fourth factor that contained items referring to emotional eating when the subject is bored. For our purposes, all further discussion will refer to the Restraint Scale, derived from the restraint factor.

Sample

The sample reported for the final form of the DEBQ restrained eating scale consisted of 1,169 subjects. Of these, 114 were reported to be obese. Men and women constituted 44% and 56% of the sample, respectively.

Preliminary Norms

Preliminary norms for the DEBQ Restraint Scale are presented in Table 5.7. As can be seen, men generally have lower restraint scores than women and obese subjects generally have higher scores than nonobese subjects. Given the variability in means from one national sample to another, however, researchers should be careful when assigning cutoff points to classify subjects as "restrained" and "nonrestrained" eaters.

Reliability

Internal Consistency

The items of the DEBQ were derived through repeated applications of factor analysis and item analysis. Not surprising, the scale's internal consistency, as measured by Cronbach's α, is quite high (usually $\geq .90$; see Table 5.3). It appears that DEBQ items were well chosen. Given their high internal consistency, shorter forms of the DEBQ might be possible. Moreover, the DEBQ-R is not differentially reliable among obese and nonobese persons.

Test-Retest

Allison et al. (1992) found test-retest reliability to be .92 over a 2-week span. We have not been able to find other reports of test-retest reliability for the DEBQ-R.

TABLE 5.7 DEBQ Restraint Scale Distributions Reported in the Literature

Subjects	Author	N	Mean	SD
Dutch adults	Van Strien, Frijters, Bergers, and Defares (1986)	1169	2.2	0.9
Men only		498	1.8	0.8
Obese men only		71	2.3	0.8
Nonobese men only		427	1.8	0.7
Women only		642	2.5	0.9
Obese women only		73	3.0	0.8
Nonobese women only		569	2.4	0.9
American college students	Allison et al. (1992)	901	2.9	1.0
Men only		281	2.3	0.9
Obese men only[a]		7	3.1	0.8
Nonobese men only		274	2.3	0.0
Women only		607	3.1	1.0
Obese women only[a]		23	3.2	0.8
Nonobese women only		584	3.1	1.0
English men	Wardle (1986)	45	1.88	0.8
English women	Wardle (1986)	102	2.7	0.0
German women	Laessle et al. (1989)	60	2.4	0.6

a. Computed by the authors for the present chapter.

Validity

Factorial Composition

The factor structure of the DEBQ appears to have been assessed in only a few studies. Van Strien et al. (Van Strien, Frijters, Bergers, & Defares, 1986; Van Strien, Frijters, Staveren, Defares, & Deurenberg, 1986) and Wardle (1987) both reported what appears to be a stable factor solution with a highly simple structure for the total DEBQ consisting of three scales and 33 items. In each case, the existence of a restraint scale factor that was well separated from emotional eating and external eating factors was clearly confirmed. Importantly, their derived solutions also appear to be stable across gender and relative weight categories (Van Strien, Frijters, Bergers, & Defares, 1986). Unlike previous analyses that extracted DEBQ factors from a battery of items in which the 10 Restraint Scale items were embedded in all 33 items, Allison et al. (1992) performed both exploratory and confirmatory factor analyses on the 10 items of the DEBQ restraint scale in isolation. They found that 68% of the variance among the 10 items could be explained by a single factor. Based on the results of Cattell's scree test, Zwick and Velicer's MAP test, and LISREL goodness of fit indices, it was clear that, unlike the RS and the TFEQ, the DEBQ-R could be unambiguously described by a one-factor solution.

Ogden (1993), however, stated that the DEBQ restrained eating scale confounds two aspects of caloric restriction: intentions to diet and actual dieting success. She noted that 3 out of 10 DEBQ questions contained the word *try*, whereas the others ask, "Do you . . . ." In a study with 189 Ss (102 men, 87 women) that combined DEBQ items with two additional questions: "Do you *attempt* to diet in order to lose weight?" and "Do you regard yourself as a *successful dieter?*" she found that all items but item 4—"Do you watch exactly what you eat?"—loaded on a factor that contained both of the additional questions. The "attempt" item loaded on a second factor with the item, "Do you take your weight into account with what you eat?" The "successful dieter item" shared a small factor with item 4, "Do you watch exactly what you eat."

It may be, as in Gorman et al.'s (1993) study of the TFEQ restraint scale, that restrained eating varies along a single dimension that spans cognitions about eating on one end and overt restraint behavior at the other end. As in Allison et al.'s (1992) study, Ogden's two-factor solution may have tapped both ends of a single continuum.

Factor Stability

Although they did not carry out separate factor analyses on obese and nonobese subsamples of their initial subject groups, Van Strien, Frijters, Bergers, and Defares (1986) performed item analyses in which they assessed item-total scale correlations within each subsample. All items of the DEBQ restraint scale had similar patterns of correlations across samples. Allison et al. (1992) performed separate factor analyses of the DEBQ-R within obese and nonobese subjects, within men and women, and within two random splits of the subject sample. They found that the Tucker's congruence coefficients were at least .990 in each split. Based on these data, the factor stability of the DEBQ-R seems excellent.

Construct Validity: Convergent and Discriminative

Van Strien, Frijters, Staveren, et al. (1986) studied 110 women for whom dieticians made unannounced home visits. During these visits, the dieticians would assess the mean daily amounts of nutrients and calories that each subject consumed over a 3-day period. They estimated the number of calories that an average woman of a given weight would require. They then formed a caloric deviation score by subtracting each woman's required caloric intake from her reported caloric intake. Van Strien et al. obtained a correlation of −.47 between the DEBQ restraint scale score and the caloric deviation score.

This suggested that restrained eaters tended to eat less than the number of calories that typical persons of their body size require. Similarly, Van Strien, Frijters, Bergers, and Defares (1986) obtained a correlation of −.28 between the DEBQ Restraint scale and fat intake, suggesting that restrained eaters lower dietary fat. Laessle et al. (1989) also found that the DEBQ-R correlated −.49 with mean caloric intake, indicating that highly restrained subjects tend to eat less. However, these findings must be viewed cautiously, given that recent research has shown self-reports of dietary intake may be unreliable (Wolper, Heshka, & Heymsfield, this volume).

Hill, Weaver, and Blundell (1991) performed a two-phase study to investigate whether dieting causes food cravings as a result of food energy deprivation. In the first phase of their study, 206 women completed the DEBQ, the TFEQ, and a food craving scale. A correlational analysis found food craving to be only weakly related to dietary restraint but highly and significantly correlated with other eating behavior factors such as external eating, emotional eating, and susceptibility to hunger. Thus it could be said that Van Strien's goal of providing a measure of restraint that is independent of hunger and weight fluctuation was supported.

Susceptibility to Response Sets

Corrigan and Ekstrand (1988) and Van Strien, Frijters, Roosen, Knuiman-Hijl, and Defares (1985) both obtained small and insignificant correlations between the Marlowe-Crowne Social Desirability Scale and the DEBQ-R, suggesting some initial discriminant validity. Allison et al. (1992) also correlated scores on the DEBQ Restraint scales with the MCSD and Edwards social desirability scales and found small negative but statistically insignificant correlations with the Marlowe-Crowne ($r = -.08$) and the Edwards ($r = -.24$) scales.

Allison et al. (1992) investigated the relationship of perceived desirability of items to their endorsement frequencies. In this situation, the social desirability ratings for each item received were correlated with the proportions of subjects endorsing the items in the standard administration condition. The correlation of item endorsement frequencies with item desirability ratings for the DEBQ-R was .67, indicating that items that appeared to be more desirable were endorsed more frequently. Allison et al. (1992) also compared the responses of subjects on the DEBQ under three sets of instructions: the standard instructions for the scale, a set of "fake bad" instructions, and a set of "fake good" instructions. Under conditions to fake bad, DEBQ mean restraint scores were slightly higher than mean standard instruction scores. Conversely, "fake good" instructions produced slightly less restrained scores. However, an analysis of variance showed that these means were not significantly different.

Thus the DEBQ-R does not seem to be unduly influenced by the tendency to respond in a socially desirable manner or to be especially susceptible to dissimulation.

Relationship to Laboratory Behavior

With regard to laboratory behavior, few data are available for the DEBQ-R. In one laboratory study, Wardle and Beales (1987) used the DEBQ and did not find that restraint scores were related to either a counterregulation or a regulation effect. However, as with the TFEQ-R, whether this lack of prediction is an indicator of a lack of validity or whether it is an indicator of its ability to measure something different than disinhibition is open to debate.

Concurrent Validity

Ogden (1993) studied three groups of dieters that she labeled "successful," "reasonable," and "failed" dieters. Successful dieters were those who rated their dieting success as higher than their attempts to diet. Reasonable dieters rated their success at dieting as equal to their attempts, and failed dieters rated their success as less than their attempts. Among these groups, failed dieters scored the highest on the DEBQ restraint scale and the Herman and Polivy Restraint Scale. Successful dieters had the lowest scores on the restraint scales, and reasonable dieters had intermediate scale scores. Thus, with this single-factor scale, it appears that high restraint may be an indicator of failed attempts at dieting.

Readability

The reading level of the TFEQ-R has been estimated to be between the fifth and eighth grades (Allison & Franklin, 1993).

Availability

The DEBQ-R was originally printed in Van Strien, Frijters, Bergers, and Defares (1986).

Other Scales

Although we will not review them in detail here, several other scales of restraint warrant brief mention. Rand and Kuldau (1991) made a restraint "interview." Interviews are often desirable as there is some thought that, given a skilled interviewer, they may be less susceptible to dissimulation. Moreover, interviews do not require that the subject can read, and they can be conducted over the telephone. Hill et al. (Hill, Rogers, & Blundell, 1989; Hill, Weaver, & Blundell, 1990) have modified both the RS and the TFEQ for use with children. Other instruments that purport to measure restraint have been developed by Coker and Roger (1990) and Smead (1990). Finally, Fairburn developed a subscale (see Williamson et al., this volume, for a review) that measures restrained eating. However, none of these scales has enjoyed widespread use, and extensive psychometric information is not available.

Relationships Among the Restraint Scales

The TFEQ contains some items from the RS. Both the DEBQ and the TFEQ contain items that originally appeared in Pudel's Latent Obesity Scale. Given the overlap of items, there should be intercorrelations among the three scales. Laessle et al. (1989) and Allison et al. (1993) found that the RS and TFEQ were significantly correlated ($r = .35$ and $r = .74$, respectively). Laessle et al. and Allison et al. also found that the RS and DEBQ were highly correlated ($r = .59$ and $r = .80$, respectively). Additionally, Wardle and Beales (1986) found that, among women, the DEBQ correlated .72 with the whole RS, .24 with the RS WF subscale, and .75 with the RS CD subscale. Among men, Wardle and Beales (1986) found the DEBQ correlated .75 with the whole RS and .37 with both the RS and the CD subscale. Laessle et al. (1989) and Allison et al. (1992) also found that the TFEQ and DEBQ were strongly correlated ($r = .66$ and $r = .89$, respectively).

Several studies have performed factor analyses to identify the overlap among the three scales. Allison et al. (1992) performed a second-order principal components factor analysis of the factor scales obtained in separate factor analyses of each restraint scale analysis and obtained three factors. The first factor contains high loadings from the RS Concern with Dieting scale, the DEBQ, and TFEQ-R Factor I (Cognitive Restraint). Therefore this factor could be considered a cognitive restraint factor. The second factor had high loadings from both TFEQ factors and appears to be related to a general restraint factor that is specific to the TFEQ. The third factor contained a single high loading of .99 from the RS WF scale. Thus it appears that all three scales tend to share common variance, especially in the cognitive aspects of restraint. However, behavioral restraint is tapped only by the Stunkard and Messick TFEQ, and weight fluctuation is tapped only by the RS WF scale.

Laessle et al. (1989) also conducted a factor analytic investigation of the relationships among the three scales and measures of self-reported mean daily caloric intake, disordered eating, and body figure consciousness. Their analysis suggested that each restraint scale measures different components of the restraint construct. Their first factor had high loadings from the RS, the TFEQ disinhibition scale, and the Eating Disorder Inventory Bulimia, Disinhibition, Body Dissatisfaction, and Drive for Thinness scales. Their second factor had high loadings from the RS, Body Mass Index, Maximum BMI, and a BMI fluctuation index. Their third factor had high positive loadings from the TFEQ restraint scale, the DEBQ, and the EDI drive for thinness scale, and high negative loadings with self-reported daily caloric intake. Laessle et al. suggest that the three scales have a common motivational component of restrained eating, including concerns about shape and weight as well as desire for thinness. However, high scores on the RS are closely related to consequences of mostly unsuccessful dieting, such as disinhibited eating and weight fluctuations, but not to successful overall caloric restriction in everyday life. In contrast, high scores on the TFEQ-R and the DEBQ-R represented the more successful dieting behavior component of restraint.

Thus correlational and factor analytic evidence indicates that, although there is substantial overlap among the three restraint scales, there are also sources of variance that are unique to each scale. The CD subscale of the RS, the DEBQ, and the first factor of the TFEQ-R reflect concerns and beliefs about dieting. Because the RS has items pertaining to weight fluctuation, it contains a unique source of variance that is not shared with the other scales. Unfortunately, studies that use the whole RS may be confounding the effects of its two subfactors and may obscure rather than clarify the meaning of relationships of restraint to other variables.

The TFEQ can be considered to have either two highly correlated factors or, as Gorman et al. (1993) suggest, an underlying bipolar continuum. Because the two factors are highly correlated, it is possible that the meaning of many relationships between the TFEQ and other measures may be clouded by the combination of items that refer to intentions to restrain eating and overt restraint behavior.

Finally, it appears that the DEBQ restraint scale may come closest to a pure dietary restraint scale. We assert this because the DEBQ has a single-factor structure and it has high communality with other restraint scales, especially with subscales that address the cognitive aspects of restraint. Additionally, the scale was constructed so that its items reflect restraint rather than disinhibition, hunger, or weight fluctuation.

Future Research Directions

Dietary restraint plays an important role in dieting behavior and eating disorders. As is true for any instruments that are designed to assess major constructs, the process of construct validation is an ongoing venture. Norms for these measures are just starting to emerge. More ambitious studies will be needed to establish a comprehensive set of norms for children, adolescents, and adults within specific cultures. To date, it can be said that the RS, the TFEQ-R, and the DEBQ have reasonable test-retest and internal consistency reliability. Although there are substantial correlations among the three restraint scales, the scales are not interchangeable. Factor analyses suggest that each scale may tap a unique aspect of eating behavior not accounted for by other scales. It appears that, although DEBQ and TFEQ scores are unlikely to be affected by attempts to dissimulate in socially desirable or undesirable directions, RS scores can easily be distorted.

The relationship of these scales to dieting success and eating disorders is probably not as clear and direct as many researchers and practitioners would wish it to be. It should be noted that, over the years, the RS has probably shown the most correlations with other measures, and the TFEQ and the DEBQ restraint scales have shown fewer relationships to disinhibitory and counterregulatory behaviors. It is probable that restraint is just one component, albeit important, in eating behavior. Because the RS is a composite dieting behavior and belief scale that often has been used to predict other composite behaviors, some of its components are related to components of the targeted behaviors. However, without careful isolation of components, it is difficult to explore the network of relationships. On the other hand, the DEBQ and the TFEQ were designed to be more narrowly focused. As such, they may fail to correlate with behaviors that are not related to pure restraint. Further, it may be, as Lowe (1993) argues, that the TFEQ-R and DEBQ-R, unlike the RS, measure momentary restraint rather than the factor of chronic dieting behavior. Restraint, as measured by the TFEQ-R and DEBQ-R scales, may, however, be combined with other measures of aspects of eating behavior to predict the network of relationships of complex eating behaviors. It is hoped that, as the scales are refined or as future scales will supplant them, the major role of restraint in eating behavior will be clarified.

References

Allison, D. B., & Franklin, R. D. (1993). The readability of three measures of dietary restraint. *Psychotherapy in Private Practice, 12,* 53-57.

Allison, D. B., Gorman, B. S., & Primavera, L. H. (1993). Some of the most common questions asked of statistical consultants: Our favorite responses and recommended readings. *Genetic, Social, and General Psychology Monographs, 119,* 155-185.

Allison, D. B., Kalinsky, L. B., & Gorman, B. S. (1992). The comparative psychometric properties of three measures of dietary restraint. *Psychological Assessment, 4,* 391-398.

Blanchard, F. A., & Frost, R. O. (1983). Two factors of restraint: Concern for dieting and weight fluctuation. *Behaviour Research and Therapy, 21,* 259-267.

Coker, S., & Roger, D. (1990). The construction and preliminary validation of a scale for measuring eating disorders. *Journal of Psychosomatic Research, 34,* 223-231.

Cole, S. H., & Edelmann, R. J. (1987). Restraint, eating disorders and need to achieve in state and public school subjects. *Personality and Individual Differences, 8,* 475-482.

Corrigan, S. A., & Ekstrand, M. L. (1988). An investigation of the construct validity of the Dutch Restrained Eating Scale. *Addictive Behaviors, 13*(3), 303-306.

Crocker, L., & Algina, J. (1986). *Introduction to classical and modern test theory.* New York: Holt, Rinehart & Winston.

Crowne, D. P., & Marlowe, D. (1964). *The approval motive: Studies in evaluative dependence.* New York: Wiley.

Drewnowski, A., Riskey, D., & Deser, J. A. (1982). Feeling fat yet unconcerned: Self-reported overweight and the restraint scale. *Appetite, 3,* 273-279.

Edwards, A. L. (1957). *The social desirability variable in personality assessment and research.* New York: Dryden.

Eysenck, H. J., & Eysenck, S. B. G. (1975). *The Eysenck Personality Questionnaire Manual.* London: University of London.

Ferguson, G. A. (1941). The factorial interpretation of test difficulty. *Psychometrika, 6,* 323-329.

Ferguson, K. J., Brink, P. J., Wood, M., & Koop, P. M. (1992). Characteristics of successful dieters as measured by guided interview responses and Restraint Scale scores. *Journal of the American Dietetic Association, 92,* 1119-1121.

Ganley, R. M. (1988). Emotional eating and how it relates to dietary restraint, disinhibition, and perceived hunger. *International Journal of Eating Disorders, 7,* 635-647.

Garner, D. M., Olmsted, M. P., & Polivy, J. (1984). *The Eating Disorder Inventory manual.* Odessa, FL: Psychological Assessment Resources.

Gibson, W. A. (1967). A latent structure for the simplex. *Psychometrika, 32,* 33-46.

Gorman, B. S., Allison, D. B., & Primavera, L. H. (1993, April). *The scalability of items of the Three-Factor Eating Questionnaire Restraint Scale: When is a personality scale a "scale"?* Arlington, VA: Eastern Psychological Association Convention.

Hambleton, R. K., Swaminathan, H., & Rogers, J. (1991). *Fundamentals of item response theory.* Newbury Park, CA: Sage.

Heatherton, T. F., Herman, C. P., & Polivy, J. (1991). Effects of physical threat and ego threat on eating behavior. *Journal of Personality & Social Psychology, 60,* 138-143.

Heatherton, T. F., Herman, C. P., Polivy, J., King, G. A., & McGree, S. T. (1988). The (mis)measurement of restraint: An analysis of conceptual and psychometric issues. *Journal of Abnormal Psychology, 97,* 19-28.

Heatherton, T. F., Polivy, J., & Herman, C. P. (1991). Restraint and internal responsiveness: Effects of placebo manipulations of hunger state on eating. *Journal of Abnormal Psychology, 98,* 89-92.

Herman, C. P., & Mack, D. (1975). Restrained and unrestrained eating. *Journal of Personality, 143,* 647-660.

Herman, C. P., & Polivy, J. (1975). Anxiety, restraint, & eating behavior. *Journal of Abnormal Psychology, 84,* 666-672.

Herman, C. P., & Polivy, J. (1980). Restrained eating. In A. J. Stunkard (Ed.), *Obesity* (pp. 208-225). Philadelphia: Saunders.

Herman, C. P., & Polivy, J. (1982). Weight change and dietary concern: Are they really independent? *Appetite, 3,* 280-281.

Herman, C. P., & Polivy, J. (1988). Studies of eating in normal dieters. In B. T. Walsh (Ed.), *Eating behavior in eating disorders.* Washington, DC: American Psychiatric Association Press.

Hibscher, J. A., & Herman, C. P. (1977). Obesity, dieting, and the expression of "obese" characteristics. *Journal of Comparative and Physiological Psychology, 91,* 374-380.

Hill, A. J., Rogers, P. J., & Blundell, J. E. (1989). Dietary restraint in young adolescent girls: A functional analysis. *British Journal of Clinical Psychology, 28,* 165-176.

Hill, A. J., Weaver, C. F., & Blundell, J. E. (1990). Dieting concerns of 10-year-old girls and their mothers. *British Journal of Clinical Psychology, 29,* 346-348.

Hill, A. J., Weaver, C. F., & Blundell, J. E. (1991). Food craving, dietary restraint and mood. *Appetite, 17,* 187-197.

Horst, P. (1965). *Factor analysis of data matrices.* New York: Holt, Rinehart & Winston.

Hyland, M. E., Irvine, S. H., Thacker, C., Dann, P. L., & Dennis, I. (1989). Psychometric analysis of the Stunkard-Messick Eating Questionnaire (SMEQ) and comparison with the Dutch Eating Behavior Questionnaire (DEBQ). *Current Psychology Research and Reviews, 8,* 228-233.

Johnson, W. G., Corrigan, S. A., Crusco, A. H., & Schlundt, D. G. (1986). Restraint among bulimic women. *Addictive Behaviors, 11,* 351-354.

Johnson, W. G., Lake, L., & Mahan, J. M. (1983). Restrained eating: Measuring an elusive construct. *Addictive Behaviors, 8,* 413-418.

Jöreskog, K. G., & Sörbom, D. (1986). *LISREL VI: Analysis of linear structural relationships by the method of maximum likelihood.* Mooresville, IN: Scientific Software.

Kickham, K., & Gayton, W. F. (1977). Social desirability and the Restraint Scale. *Psychological Reports, 40,* 550.

Klem, M. L., Klesges, R. C., Bene, C. R., & Mellon, M. W. (1990). A psychometric study of restraint: The impact of race, gender, weight and marital status. *Addictive Behaviors, 15,* 147-152.

Klem, M. L., Klesges, R. C., & Shadish, W. (1990, November). *Application of confirmatory factor analysis to the dietary restraint scale.* Paper presented to the Association for the Advancement of Behavior Therapy, San Francisco.

Klesges, R. C., Isbell, T. R., & Klesges, L. M. (1992). Relationship between dietary restraint, energy intake, physical activity, and body weight: A prospective analysis. *Journal of Abnormal Psychology, 101,* 668-674.

Klesges, R. C., Klem, M. L., Epkins, C., & Klesges, L. M. (1991). A longitudinal evaluation of dietary restraint and its relationship to changes in body weight. *Addictive Behaviors, 16,* 363-368.

Knight, L. J., & Boland, F. J. (1989). Restrained eating: An experimental disentanglement of the disinhibiting variables of perceived calories and food type. *Journal of Abnormal Psychology, 98,* 412-420.

Laessle, R. G., Tuschl, R. J., Kotthaus, B. C., & Pirke, K. M. (1989). A comparison of the validity of three scales for the assessment of dietary restraint. *Journal of Abnormal Psychology, 98,* 304-307.

LaPorte, D. J., & Stunkard, A. J. (1990). Predicting attrition and adherence to a very low calorie diet: A prospective investigation of the eating inventory. *International Journal of Obesity, 14,* 97-206.

Lowe, M. R. (1984). Dietary concern, weight fluctuation and weight status: Further explorations of the Restraint Scale. *Behaviour Research and Therapy, 22*, 243-248.

Lowe, M. R. (1993). The effects of dieting on eating behavior: A three-factor model. *Psychological Bulletin, 114*, 100-121.

Lowe, M. R., & Maycock, B. (1988). Restraint, disinhibition, hunger and negative affect eating. *Addictive Behaviors, 3*, 369-377.

Maxwell, S. E., & Delany, H. D. (1993). Bivariate median splits and spurious statistical significance. *Psychological Bulletin, 113*, 181-190.

McDonald, R. P., & Ahlawat, K. S. (1974). Difficulty factors in binary data. *British Journal of Mathematical and Statistical Psychology, 27*, 82-99.

Nisbett, R. (1972). Hunger, obesity, and the ventromedial hypothalamus. *Psychological Review, 79*, 433-453.

Ogden, J. (1993). The measurement of restraint: Confounding success and failure? *International Journal of Eating Disorders, 13*, 69-76.

Polivy, J., & Herman, C. P. (1976a). Clinical depression and weight change: A complex relation. *Journal of Abnormal and Social Psychology, 85*, 338-340.

Polivy, J., & Herman, C. P. (1976b). Effects of alcohol on weight change: Influences of mood and perceived intoxication. *Journal of Abnormal and Social Psychology, 85*, 601-606.

Polivy, J., Herman, P. H., & Howard, K. I. (1988). Restraint Scale: Assessment of dieting. In M. Hersen & A. S. Bellack (Eds.), *Dictionary of behavioral assessment techniques* (pp. 377-380). New York: Pergamon.

Pudel, V., Metzdorff, M., & Oetting, M. (1975). Zur Persönlichkeit Adiposer in psychologischen Tests unter Berücksichtigung latent Fettsüchtiger. *Zeitschrift für Psychosomatische Medizin und Psychoanalyse, 21*, 345-361.

Prussin, R. A., & Harvey, P. D. (1991). Depression, dietary restraint, and binge eating in female runners. *Addictive Behaviors, 16*, 295-301.

Rand, C. S. W., & Kuldau, J. M. (1991). Restrained eating (weight concerns) in the general population and among students. *International Journal of Eating Disorders, 10*, 699-708.

Rogers, P. J., & Hill, A. J. (1989). Breakdown of dietary restraint following mere exposure to food stimuli: Interrelationships between restraint, hunger, salivation, and food intake. *Addictive Behaviors, 14*, 387-397.

Ruderman, A. J. (1983). The Restraint Scale: A psychometric investigation. *Behaviour Research and Therapy, 21*, 258-283.

Ruderman, A. J. (1985). Restraint, obesity, and bulimia. *Behaviour Research and Therapy, 23*, 151-156.

Ruderman, A. J. (1986). Dietary restraint: A theoretical and empirical review. *Psychological Bulletin, 99*, 247-262.

Ruderman, A. J., & Christensen, H. C. (1983). Restraint theory and its applicability to overweight individuals. *Journal of Abnormal Psychology, 92*, 210-215.

Ruderman, A. J., & Grace, P. S. (1987). Restraint, bulimia, and psychopathology. *Addictive Behaviors, 12*, 249-255.

Ruderman, A. J., & Wilson, G. T. (1979). Weight, restraint, cognitions, and counterregulation. *Behavior Research and Therapy, 17*, 581-590.

Schachter, S. (1971). Some extraordinary facts about obese humans and rats. *American Psychologist, 26*, 129-145.

Schachter, S., Goldman, R., & Gordon, A. (1968). Effects of fear, food deprivation, and obesity on eating. *Journal of Personality and Social Psychology, 10*, 91-97.

Schachter, S., & Rodin, J. (1974). *Obese humans and rats.* Potomac, MD: Lawrence Erlbaum.

Schotte, D. E., Cools, J., & McNally, R. J. (1990). Film-induced negative affect triggers overeating in restrained eaters. *Journal of Abnormal Psychology, 99*, 317-320.

Simmons, D. D. (1991). Dietary restraint as value-related motivation: A psychometric clarification. *Journal of Psychology, 125*, 189-194.

Smead, V. S. (1990). A psychometric investigation of the Rigorous Eating Scale. *Psychological Reports, 67*, 555-561.

Smith, M. C., & Thelen, M. H. (1984). Development and validation of a test for bulimia. *Journal of Consulting and Clinical Psychology, 52*, 863-872.

Stein, D. M. (1988). The scaling of restraint and the prediction of eating. *International Journal of Eating Disorders, 7*, 713-717.

Stunkard, A. J. (1981). "Restrained eating": What it is and a new scale to measure it. In L. A. Cioffi, W. P. T. James, & T. B. Van Itallie (Eds.), *The body weight regulatory system: Normal and disturbed mechanisms* (pp. 243-251). New York: Raven.

Stunkard, A. J., & Messick, S. (1985). The three factor eating questionnaire to measure dietary restraint, disinhibition, and hunger. *Journal of Psychosomatic Research, 29*, 71-81.

Stunkard, A. J., & Messick, S. (1988). *The Eating Inventory.* San Antonio, TX: Psychological Corporation.

Stunkard, A. J., & Wadden, T. A. (1990). Restrained eating and human obesity. *Nutrition Reviews, 48*, 78-86.

Tucker, L. R. (1951). A method for synthesis of factor analysis studies. In *Personnel research report* (No. 984, Contract DA-49-083, Department of the Army). Princeton, NJ: ETS.

Tuschl, R. J., Laessle, R. G., Platte, P., & Pirke, K. M. (1990). Differences in food-choice frequencies between restrained and unrestrained eaters. *Appetite, 14*, 9-13.

Van Strien, T., Frijters, J. E. R., Bergers, G. P. A., & Defares, P. B. (1986). The Dutch Eating Behavior Questionnaire (DEBQ) for assessment of restrained, emotional, and external eating behavior. *International Journal of Eating Disorders, 5*, 295-315.

Van Strien, T., Frijters, J. E. R., Roosen, R. G. F. M., Knuiman-Hijl, W. J. H., & Defares, P. B. (1985). Eating behavior, personality traits and body mass in women. *Addictive Behaviors, 10*, 333-343.

Van Strien, T., Frijters, J. E. R., Staveren, W. A., Defares, P. B., & Deurenberg, P. (1986). The predictive validity of the Dutch restrained eating questionnaire. *International Journal of Eating Disorders, 5*, 747-755.

Wardle, J. (1986). The assessment of restrained eating. *Behaviour Research and Therapy, 24*, 213-215.

Wardle, J. (1987). Eating style: A validation study of the Dutch Eating Behavior Questionnaire in normal subjects and women with eating disorders. *Journal of Personality Assessment, 31*, 161-169.

Wardle, J., & Beales, S. (1986). The assessment of restrained eating. *Behaviour Research and Therapy, 24*, 213-215.

Wardle, J., & Beales, S. (1987). Restraint and food intake: An experimental study of eating behavior patterns in the laboratory and real life. *Behaviour Research and Therapy, 25*, 179-185.

Westenhoffer, J. (1991). Dietary restraint and disinhibition: Is restraint a homogeneous construct? *Appetite, 15*, 45-55.

Westerterp, K. R., Nicolson, N. A., Boots, J. M., Mordant, A., & Westerterp, M. S. (1988). Obesity, restrained eating and the cumulative intake curve. *Appetite, 11*, 119-128.

Westerterp-Plantenga, M. S., Wouters, L., & ten Hoor, F. (1991). Restrained eating, obesity, and cumulative food intake curves during four-course meals. *Appetite, 16*, 149-158.

Williams, A., Spencer, C. P., & Edelmann, R. J. (1987). Restraint theory, locus of control and the situational analysis of binge eating. *Personality and Individual Differences, 8,* 67-74.

Zwick, W. R., & Velicer, W. F. (1986). Comparison of five rules for determining the number of components to retain. *Psychological Bulletin, 99,* 432-442.

Measures of
Physical Activity
and Exercise

MARY LEE SHELTON

ROBERT C. KLESGES

Physical activity is defined as "any bodily movement produced by skeletal muscles that results in energy expenditure" (Caspersen, Powell, & Christenson, 1985, p. 126). Of all the components of energy expenditure (resting energy expenditure, thermic effect of food, and thermic effect of activity), the effect of physical activity is the most variable and can account for as much as 30% of total daily energy expenditure (Poehlman, 1989). Physical activity can be characterized by work, sports, leisure, or minute muscular activities (i.e., fidgeting) and is usually measured with the same metric (kilocalories) as dietary intake. The term *exercise* is often used interchangeably with *physical activity*; however, the two are not synonymous (Caspersen et al., 1985). Exercise

is a subcomponent of physical activity; it is defined as structured and repeated and has as its goal the improvement or maintenance of physical fitness
(Caspersen et al., 1985).

Over the past 30 years, a great deal of behavioral research has been directed at the cardiovascular benefits of physical activity (Klesges, Eck, Isbell,
Fulliton, & Hanson, 1991; Paffenbarger, Brand, Scholtz, & Jung, 1978; Paffenbarger, Wing, & Hyde, 1978; Sallis, Patterson, Buono, & Nader, 1988; Siscovick, LaPorte, & Newman, 1985) as well as its implications for the
reduction of morbidity and mortality (Paffenbarger, Hyde, Wing, & Hsieh,
1986). The purpose of this chapter is to summarize the background of physical activity assessment, to describe the physical activity measures that would
be most relevant to the area of eating disorders and obesity, and to highlight
the strengths and the limitations of these methods.

Empirical studies dealing with the assessment of physical activity can be
split into two general categories. First, many researchers have been interested
in physical activity as a health-related behavior. Increased physical activity
and increased exercise have been linked to increased life expectancy, lower
body weight, reduced resting heart rate, reduced resting blood pressure, increased high density lipoprotein cholesterol, and increased skeletal muscle
strength (Klesges et al., 1991; Paffenbarger, Wing, Hyde, & Jung, 1983; Saris,
1986; Paffenbarger et al., 1986; Siconolfi, Lasater, Snow, & Carleton, 1985;
Siscovick et al., 1985). Although physical activity levels vary among individuals, just about everyone performs some level of physical activity each day.
When they do, people experience not only a number of physiological adjustments (Siconolfi et al., 1985) but also some psychological adjustments
(Wardlaw & Insel, 1990). As a result, physical activity is rarely performed in
the absence of other beneficial or possibly detrimental health-related behaviors, as in the case of anorexia (Blair, Jacobs, & Powell, 1985).

Although much research has been directed toward understanding the relationship between physical activity and overall health, other researchers have
been interested in studying how physical activity relates to specific chronic
diseases. For example, numerous studies have examined the relationship between physical activity and coronary heart disease. The construct of physical
activity has also been used in studies of diseases such as obesity, anorexia nervosa, bulimia, hypertension, hypercholesteremia, diabetes, and cancer
(Brownell & Kaye, 1982; Chirico & Stunkard, 1960; Paffenbarger et al., 1983;
Sallis et al., 1988; Siscovick et al., 1985). This research emphasizes the need to
better understand how physical activity affects various health and disease
outcomes and the need to determine what independent contribution physical
activity might have on such outcomes (Caspersen, 1989; Chirico & Stunkard,
1960; Kriska et al., 1990; LaPorte, Montoye, & Caspersen, 1985; Sallis et al.,
1988; Saris, 1986; Wilson, Paffenbarger, Morris, & Havlik, 1986).

In the course of these two general lines of research, several direct and indirect measures have been developed to assess physical activity in both active and inactive individuals (for reviews, see Baranowski, 1988; Blair, 1984; Jacobs, Ainsworth, Hartman, & Leon, 1993; LaPorte et al., 1985; Montoye & Taylor, 1984; Tyron, 1991; Washburn & Montoye, 1986). Direct methods of physical activity assessment are those that are designed to measure physical activity or constructs related to physical activity. Examples of direct methods include questionnaires, diaries, electronic monitors, direct observation, and calorimetry (i.e., measurement of metabolic rate). Indirect methods are those methods thought to highly correlate to physical activity but that don't directly measure physical activity per se. These include job classifications, dietary assessment, and body composition assessment. Despite the numerous attempts that have been made to develop and test methods of physical activity assessment, no single instrument fulfills the multiple criteria of being valid, reliable, and practical while at the same time not affecting behavior (i.e., being reactive; Caspersen, 1989; LaPorte et al., 1985). Therefore it is often advocated that a multimethod approach to the measurement of physical activity is needed to assess the true relationship between physical activity and health.

Current interest in physical activity among exercise physiologists, psychologists, physicians, and other health-related professionals can be traced not only to the importance of understanding the impact physical activity can have on our lifestyles but also to the need for improving methods of assessment. It is not surprising that, because physical activity is so complexly enmeshed in our lifestyles, its measurement and assessment are also highly complicated. In a recent report by Paffenbarger, Blair, Lee, and Hyde (1993), the authors concluded that the demand for better knowledge about physical activity, dietary habits, and health has far outstripped our success in producing it.

Measures Reviewed Here

Although physical activity, exercise, obesity, and eating disorders are thought to be closely interrelated, the correlations among them are not as high as one might expect (Klesges et al., 1991; LaPorte et al., 1985). People may exercise excessively with few obvious indications of their inner distress or appear lazy and inactive even though they are not overweight. Eating disorders are sometimes related to observable behavior, but there is no necessary relationship between eating disorders and levels of physical activity (Eppling, Pierce, & Stefan, 1983; Klesges & Hanson, 1988; Klesges et al., 1991; Waxman & Stunkard, 1980).

The operational definitions and methods of measuring components of physical activity vary with the interests and needs of investigators and evaluators (LaPorte et al., 1985). Therefore the distinction noted above is an important one because the physical activity measures discussed in this chapter differ in the degree to which they can be used as methods for assessing obesity and other eating disorders.

As a complete review of physical activity and exercise assessment methods is beyond the scope of this chapter (for reviews, see Blair, 1984; Caspersen, 1989; LaPorte et al., 1985; Montoye & Taylor, 1984; Saris, 1986; Tyron, 1991; Washburn & Montoye, 1986), only those scales that are most applicable for assessing weight-related behaviors will be included. The measures reviewed in this chapter are all considered to be direct methods of physical activity assessment. Only the most widely used and validated measures were included. These instruments can be grouped into five categories and are presented below. More detailed information regarding the psychometric qualities of each scale are presented in Appendix Table 6-A.

1. Questionnaire Assessments (self- or interviewer administered)
   a. Baecke (Baecke, Burema, & Frijters, 1982)
   b. Harvard Alumni Activity Survey or Paffenbarger (Paffenbarger, Wing, & Hyde, 1978)
   c. Lipid Research Clinics Prevalence Study Questionnaire (Haskell, Taylor, Wood, Schrott, & Heiss, 1980)
   d. Minnesota Leisure Time Physical Activity Questionnaire (Taylor et al., 1978)
   e. Stanford Seven-Day Physical Activity Recall Questionnaire (PAR; Blair, 1984; Blair, Haskell, et al., 1985)
2. Diary Annotation (self- or observer recorded)
3. Direct Observation (subjective ratings of intensity)
   a. Behaviors of Eating and Activity for Children's Health Evaluation System (BEACHES; McKenzie et al., 1991)
   b. Studies of Children's Activity and Nutrition/Children's Activity Time-sampling Survey (SCAN CATS; Klesges, Eck, Hanson, Haddock, & Klesges, 1990)
4. Mechanical or Electronic Monitoring (self- or remote recorded)
   a. Electronic Motion Sensors
      – Caltrac Accelerometer (Hemokinetics, Madison, WI)
      – Large-Scale Integrated Motor Activity Monitor (LSI; GMM Electronics, Verona, PA)
   b. Heart Rate Monitors

5. Calorimetry
   a. Direct
   b. Indirect

Measurement Overview

Questionnaire Assessments

There have been many attempts at estimating energy expenditure associated with physical activity via questionnaires (Montoye, 1971). This method focuses on the ability to classify one's level of activity and/or recall activities over various time periods (e.g., 24 hours, 7 days, or 1 year). In general, if one is interested in studying a large group of individuals, then the questionnaire method is the only viable instrument of choice. The first five measures listed above are among the most widely used questionnaires for assessing physical activity. However, they differ in important ways. Differences exist in method of administration, time frame over which the activity is assessed, type of activity assessed, and the measurement scale used.

Baecke

The Baecke is a general survey for assessing habitual levels of physical activity over a 1-year period of time (Baecke et al., 1982). It consists of only 16 self-report items, yet it is well written and carefully analyzes typical types of activity (Jacobs et al., 1993). The Baecke asks questions pertaining to the amount of physical activity an individual participates in while at work, while playing sports, and during leisure time. The Baecke is a commonly used self-report measure for annual assessments of physical activity.

Lipid Research Clinics Questionnaire

The Lipid Research Clinics Questionnaire provides a very simple method for assessing physical activity. It consists of two questions regarding the regularity and perceived intensity of strenuous work or leisure activity (Haskell et al., 1980). During an interview, the subjects are asked to respond to the question, "Do you regularly engage in strenuous exercise or hard physical labor?" If the response is yes, the subject is asked, "Do you exercise or labor at least three times per week?" According to the responses given, subjects can be categorized as highly active, moderately active, or inactive. Despite the simplicity of this questionnaire, it appears to be related to measures of fitness as well as disease risk factors (Washburn & Montoye, 1986). If one is interested in merely indexing persons at the lower end versus the higher end of the physical activity spectrum, this is the survey one would probably use (LaPorte et al., 1985).

Minnesota Leisure-Time Physical Activity Questionnaire

The Minnesota Leisure-Time Physical Activity Questionnaire is an interviewer-administered questionnaire that requires recall of all activities over the past year (Taylor et al., 1978). This scale differs from the others in this section in both its advantages and its disadvantages. First, in terms of advantages, the Minnesota has been well researched and is the most validated physical activity instrument. Washburn and Montoye (1986) point out that the Minnesota has been validated by comparing results with physical fitness, caloric intake, and objective measures of physical activity. Second, the Minnesota survey was used in an extensive Multiple Risk Factor Intervention Trial (MRFIT), and the results of the trial indicated that a consistent gradient of benefit against coronary heart disease was demonstrated along the categories of increasing leisure-time physical activity measured in kilocalories per day (Paffenbarger et al., 1993). Third, the Minnesota has been used with a wide variety of groups and appears to be the most appropriate tool for assessing the relationship between intensity of activity and disease (Washburn & Montoye, 1986). Despite its advantages, it also possesses some potential disadvantages. The Minnesota is often not selected as the method of choice in large studies for four reasons: (a) Compared with other questionnaire methods, the Minnesota is much longer; (b) the Minnesota is time consuming to administer; (c) the Minnesota is difficult to score; and (d) individuals completing the Minnesota often have a hard time recalling all the activities they have performed over the last year.

Paffenbarger

The Paffenbarger, another recall questionnaire, is a one-page form that asks general questions about the amount of activity performed on an average day and during a typical week (Paffenbarger, Wing, & Hyde, 1978). Specifically, the Paffenbarger probes for distance walked, stairs climbed, and sports or recreational activities undertaken during the previous week. This scale has high face validity and, like the Physical Activity Recall (see below), was designed to have a relatively short recall period for increased accuracy, to be simple and easy to administer and score, and to be applicable to both sexes across a wide age spectrum (Washburn & Montoye, 1986).

In addition, several studies have shown a relationship between answers on the Paffenbarger and various chronic disease and risk factors (Washburn

& Montoye, 1986). Overall, the Paffenbarger appears to be a useful question-naire for the assessment of physical activity changes of a large population over time. Its use in small-scale studies, however, could be problematic, given its global nature.

Stanford Seven-Day Physical Activity Recall

The final questionnaire to be discussed is the Stanford Seven-Day Physi-cal Activity Recall (PAR). The PAR assesses occupational and leisure activities over the previous 7 days and categorizes activity according to sleep and light, moderate, heavy, or very heavy intensities (Blair, 1984; Blair, Haskell, et al., 1985; Sallis et al., 1985; Taylor et al., 1984). Two versions of the PAR exist: the original interviewer-administered version (Blair, 1984; Sallis et al., 1985) and the simplified, self-administered version (Blair, 1984). The PAR protocol has also been modified slightly, and the modified version has been used with chil-dren and adolescents (Sallis, Buono, Roby, Micale, & Nelson, 1993; Sallis et al., 1988). The PAR is appropriate in assessing physical activity for indi-viduals, evaluating changes in physical activity habits, characterizing activity patterns of a given group, and estimating metabolic rate (Sallis et al., 1985). For example, the PAR would be recommended if one wanted to assess weekly changes in physical activity during a 12-week weight-loss intervention. Al-though the PAR is appropriate in studies where one would expect to see changes in activity over a short period of time (e.g., a weight-loss study), it is not appropriate as a measure of long-term levels of physical activity.

Diary Annotation

Diary annotation is a direct method of assessment in which one notes physical activity performed on a given day. Notes should be made on week-days as well as weekends, and sampling should include various seasons of the year (Montoye & Taylor, 1984). In general, diaries are beneficial because a variety of variables are available from one source. For example, diaries can provide information on the duration of the activity, the intensity, the fre-quency over some time interval, the physical location, the social environ-ment, and self-generated reasons for activity-inactivity, among a variety of other variables (Baranowski, 1988). Diaries are usually self-administered, but they can be observer administered or interviewer administered (Paffenbarger et al., 1993). Because physical activity diaries require a great deal of coopera-tion and time of the subjects, they have limited use in large epidemiological studies (Montoye & Taylor, 1984). Modified diary techniques for population studies have been established, and a review of some of these techniques can be found in LaPorte et al. (1985). In smaller scale energy balance studies, however, detailed physical activity diaries have proven to be quite useful, and the recording of dietary intake and energy expenditure has been an integral component of treatment in most obesity studies to date (Linscheid, Tarnowski, & Richmond, 1988). As with assessment of dietary intake, parent and child recording methods are often used and consist of filling out a structured activity diary. For example, Aragona, Cassady, and Drabman (1975) had parents monitor their children's exercise compliance with use of a point chart, whereas Minderaa and Witt (1983) had children complete a self-observation record. Overall, diaries are an excellent method for obtaining detailed information regarding the activity patterns of individuals. However, problems with diaries include high response burden by the participant and problems with missing or incomplete data.

Direct Observation

Recently, direct observation recordings of activity by nonparticipant observers in home and school settings have been employed (Baranowski et al., 1984; Epstein, Woodall, Goreczny, Wing, & Robertson, 1984; O'Hara, Baranowski, Simons-Morton, Wilson, & Parcel, 1989; Puhl, Greaves, Hoyt, & Baranowski, 1990). These methods use time-sampling procedures and subjective ratings of intensity. The intensity ratings are most important because it is the intensity of activity that is clearly related to significant energy expenditure (Thompson, Jarvie, Lahey, & Cureton, 1982). Advantages of the observation method of assessment include the following: (a) It can provide information on the specific type of activity that occurs; (b) it is not limited by recall ability or self-reporting biases of individuals; and (c) it is particularly useful with younger children, from whom accurate and detailed self-report data are more difficult to obtain (Baranowski et al., 1984; Puhl et al., 1990). Disadvantages of the direct observation method are that it can be reactive, time consuming, and require extreme diligence on the part of the observer. Also, because observation time is typically short, one does not always know if the activity observed is representative of a person's typical behavior.

Behaviors of Eating and Activity for Children's Health Evaluation System

Compared with other methods of physical activity assessment, there are several direct observation systems that have been designed specifically for children (Klesges et al., 1983; Klesges et al., 1990; McKenzie et al., 1991; Puhl et al., 1990). One of these, the Behaviors of Eating and Activity for Children's Health Evaluation System (BEACHES), is a comprehensive direct observation system designed to simultaneously code children's physical activity and eating behaviors and related environmental events (McKenzie et al., 1991). The system was developed within a framework of behavior analysis and includes coding for 10 separate dimensions (McKenzie et al., 1991). The 10 dimensions of BEACHES are environment, physical location, activity level, eating behavior, interactor, antecedents, prompted event, child response to prompt, consequences, and events receiving consequences (McKenzie et al., 1991). BEACHES is one of several SCAN (Studies of Children's Activity and Nutrition) methods for assessing physical activity in children, which were used as part of a multisite, prospective study of the determinants of activity and eating in children funded by the National Heart, Blood, and Lung Institute. In general, the SCAN methods are recommended for assessing physical activity in children because they encompass a wide range of factors that contribute to children's levels of physical activity. Although using BEACHES as a method of physical activity assessment can be time consuming, the system is quite advantageous in that it can be used in nearly all settings in which a targeted child might be found.

Children's Activity Timesampling Survey

SCAN CATS (Children's Activity Timesampling Survey) is another SCAN method of direct observation designed specifically for children. SCAN CATS was designed to assess discriminable body movements and the physical and social environmental variables related to those body movements (Klesges et al., 1990). Like BEACHES, SCAN CATS is a system that quantifies directly observed physical activity in the natural environment. Specifically, observers record (a) the physical environment in which the activity occurs, (b) the activity level of the child, (c) the persons who are present during the activity, and (d) the type of interaction (if any) between the child and the persons present in the environment (Klesges et al., 1990). Thus one can analyze the sets of behaviors that contribute to children's activity levels rather than examining only the overall index of physical activity. As a result, one can identify precise targets for change should the results be used for clinical practice. For example, it might be observed that parental participation in the child's activity actually increased the amount of time the child engaged in physical activity. Treatment could then focus on increasing the kind and number of activities that parents and children can participate in together.

Mechanical or Electronic Monitors

Another approach for monitoring physical activity in epidemiological and other studies is the use of mechanical or electronic monitors for detecting movement, particularly in children (Ellison et al., 1992; Klesges & Klesges, 1987; Maliszewski, Freedson, Ebbeling, Crussemeyer, & Kastango, 1991; Mukeshi, Gutin, Anderson, Zybert, & Basch, 1990; Sallis, Buono, Roby, Carlson, & Nelson, 1990; Tyron, 1991). Although these methods have numerous advantages, some investigators have questioned their usefulness because studies that have investigated the reliability and validity of some of these measures have reported variable accuracy and reproducibility (Klesges, Klesges, Swenson, & Pheley, 1985; Williams, Klesges, Hanson, & Eck, 1989). Overall, however, there appears to be enough evidence to support the usefulness of mechanical or electronic monitors for assessing physical activity, at least when strict standardization procedures are used.

Heart rate monitors, movement sensors, and accelerometers are all objective and are generally more practical and less time consuming than direct observation (Ellison et al., 1992; Glagov, Rowley, Cramer, & Page, 1970; Horton, 1984; Mukeshi et al., 1990). These procedures have also proven to be useful in helping to describe the activity status of persons assigned to an exercise training program (Haskell, Yee, Evans, & Irby, 1993). However, each method has limitations in its ability to accurately characterize the intensity, duration, and frequency of a wide range of activities typically performed on the job and during leisure time by many persons (Haskell et al., 1993). Moreover, these sensors typically are expensive; monitors can easily break in field settings; and subject compliance can be problematic.

A great deal of research over recent years has been directed at electronic motion sensors (Ellison et al., 1992; Freedson, 1989; Klesges & Klesges, 1987; Klesges et al., 1985; Maliszewski et al., 1991; Mukeshi et al., 1990; Sallis et al., 1990). Motion sensors can be classified into instruments that only assess the quantity of movement (Large-Scale Integrated Activity Monitor) and instruments that assess both the quantity and the intensity of movement (Caltrac accelerometers; LaPorte et al., 1985). Information on the availability and cost of these motion sensors is presented in Appendix Table 6-B.

Large-Scale Integrated Activity Monitor

The Large-Scale Integrated Activity Monitor (LSI) is a small instrument that measures body movements and can be placed on various parts of the body (i.e., hip and ankle; McGowan, Bulik, Epstein, Kupfer, & Robertson, 1984). This method of physical activity assessment is useful for reliably estimating energy expenditure and for discriminating between various groups (LaPorte et al., 1985; McGowan et al., 1984). However, the LSI is expensive and, if broken, can potentially expose the subject to mercury.

Caltrac Accelerometer

Compared with the LSI, the Caltrac accelerometer has received increased investigation because of its ability to assess both the quantity and the quality of movement (Klesges & Klesges, 1987). This instrument has been shown to accurately reflect activity levels and energy expenditure and appears to be feasible and relatively inexpensive for monitoring physical activity in epidemiological studies (Ellison et al., 1992; Klesges & Klesges, 1987).

Heart Rate Monitors

Heart rate monitoring is an easy and commonly employed physiological measurement of activity (Saris, 1985, 1986). Heart rate monitors have been found to be attractive measures of physical activity because they directly measure physiological parameters related to physical activity and because they provide continuous records that may reflect both intensity and duration of daily activities (LaPorte et al., 1985). Direct heart rate measurements appear to be strong indicators of quality of physical activity and energy expenditure in the natural environment (Freedson, Evenson, Hamill, & Washburn, 1988; Glagov et al., 1970). In addition, this method has been validated by simultaneous indirect calorimetry measurements and has the advantage of being applicable to field studies (Horton, 1984). Heart rate monitors, however, are not highly correlated with low levels of activity (Horton, 1984), are sensitive to such things as anxiety or change in posture (Horton, 1984), and can be expensive, therefore limiting their usefulness in large epidemiological studies.

Calorimetry

Direct Calorimetry

Of all the methods for assessing physical activity, by and large the most accurate measure is direct calorimetry (measuring maximum energy release), with estimates of less than 1% error (LaPorte et al., 1985). However, direct calorimetry is not suitable for many situations because of the confined space, limits on the types of exercise that can be performed, slow response time, high cost, and lack of availability (Horton, 1984).

Indirect Calorimetry

Indirect calorimetry (measuring oxygen uptake) is nearly as accurate as direct calorimetry and the various techniques for measuring oxygen consumption and carbon dioxide production during physical activity allow for a wide range of applications (Horton, 1984). Although indirect calorimetry techniques are accurate and useful for validating other measures of physical activity, LaPorte et al. (1985) concluded that they are not useful in epidemiological studies because they alter or inhibit normal physical activity patterns and are too costly for use with large populations.

All of the assessment methods reviewed in this chapter have demonstrated reliability and validity as measures of physical activity and related constructs. However, they are by no means interchangeable, and researchers should exercise care to select appropriate instruments for their particular research purposes.

Suggestions for Future Research and Development of Instruments Assessing These Criteria

As is evident above, researchers and practitioners are unlikely to find *a* or *the* measure of physical activity to use in eating disorders or obesity research. The best instrument varies with the type of research or clinical question. Further, a better understanding of the interrelationships of diet, body size, fitness, and exercise is needed (Paffenbarger et al., 1993) to accurately assess physical activity in epidemiological research on eating disorders.

Future studies are also needed to clarify the role of physical activity assessment in the area of eating disorders. The importance of assessing physical activity has been continuously reported in the obesity literature, but the need for assessing physical activity in the area of anorexia and bulimia is much less clear. Whereas physical activity is often assessed before, during, and after treatment with the obese individual, physical activity is often assessed only initially with the anorexic person or sometimes not at all. This distinction is important because it highlights the need for a better understanding of the different roles of physical activity in eating disorders. For example, is it necessary to assess physical activity to determine whether or not excess exercise contributed to an individual's anorexia but unnecessary to assess physical activity after the diagnosis has been made?

In the absence of an accurate, complete, inexpensive measure of physical activity designed especially for eating disorders, it is recommended that a combination of physical activity assessment methods be used to assess eating disorders. This approach may be superior if precise constructs have been defined and if measurement error is not duplicated in the various assessment methods (Montoye & Taylor, 1984). In addition, using several types of instruments may reflect different activity patterns, which, in turn, may be differentially related to eating disorders.

Additional basic research on reliability, validity, and stability of physical activity assessment techniques is also needed. As noted in Appendix Table 6-A, several methods appear promising for assessing physical activity in eating disordered individuals, but normative data are lacking for the general population, let alone in the area of eating disorders. Studies that actually assess physical activity as a viable measure to be used in eating disorders are lacking. Methodological studies that permit analysis of the accuracy of the various measures of physical activity in individuals with weight-related problems will most likely contribute to our understanding of the complex relationship between physical activity and eating disorders.

Future research should focus on investigating the long-term effects of physical activity in the area of eating disorders. For example, it has been recently reported that physical activity and, more important, *changes* in physical activity predict changes in adiposity in both men and women (Klesges, Klesges, Haddock, & Eck, 1992). Does such a pattern replicate in children? Does physical activity predict changes in childhood obesity, or is lowered physical activity merely a *consequence* of childhood obesity? More prospective research is needed in this area.

In conclusion, assessing physical activity habits in individuals with eating disorders is a difficult but not impossible task. The physical activity methods presented in this chapter can provide meaningful data for researchers and practitioners interested in weight-related behaviors. These methods can be applied to large populations or to small clinical groups depending on the need of the investigator.

References

Aragona, J., Cassady, J., & Drabman, R. S. (1975). Treating overweight children through parental training and contingency contracting. *Journal of Applied Behavior Analysis, 8,* 269-278.

Baecke, J. A. H., Burema, J., & Frijters, J. E. R. (1982). A short questionnaire for the measurement of habitual physical activity in epidemiological studies. *American Journal of Clinical Nutrition, 36,* 936-942.

Baranowski, T. (1988). Validity and reliability of self-report measures of physical activity: An information-processing perspective. *Research Quarterly for Exercise and Sport, 59*(4), 314-327.

Baranowski, T., Dworkin, R., Cieslik, C. J., Hooks, P., Rains, D., Ray, L., Dunn, J. K., & Nader, P. R. (1984). Reliability and validity of children's self-report of aerobic activity: Family health project. *Research Quarterly for Exercise and Sport, 55,* 309-317.

Blair, S. N. (1984). How to assess exercise habits and physical fitness. In J. D. Matarazzo, S. M. Weiss, J. A. Herd, N. E. Miller, & W. M. Weiss (Eds.), *Behavioral health: A handbook of health enhancement and disease prevention* (pp. 424-446). New York: Wiley.

Blair, S. N., Haskell, W. B., Ho, P., Paffenbarger, R. S., Vranizan, K. M., Farquhar, J. W., & Wood, P. D. (1985). Assessment of physical activity by a seven-day recall in a community survey and controlled experiments. *American Journal of Epidemiology, 122,* 794-804.

Blair, S. N., Jacobs, D. R., & Powell, K. E. (1985). Relationships between exercise or physical activity and other health behaviors. *Public Health Reports, 100,* 172-180.

Brownell, K. D., & Kaye, F. S. (1982). A school-based behavior modification, nutrition education, and physical activity program for obese children. *American Journal of Clinical Nutrition, 35,* 277-283.

Caspersen, C. J. (1989). Physical activity epidemiology: Concepts, methods, and applications to exercise science. In K. B. Pandolf (Ed.), *Exercise and sports science reviews* (pp. 423-473). Baltimore: Williams & Wilkins.

Caspersen, C. J., Powell, K. E., & Christenson, G. M. (1985). Physical activity, exercise, and physical fitness: Definitions and distinctions for health-related research. *Public Health Reports, 100*(2), 126-131.

Chirico, A. M., & Stunkard, A. J. (1960). Physical activity and human obesity. *New England Journal of Medicine, 263*(19), 935-940.

Ellison, R. C., Freedson, P. S., Zevallos, J. C., White, M. J., Marmor, J. K., Garrahie, E. J., & Moore, L. L. (1992). Feasibility and costs of monitoring physical activity in young children using the Caltrac accelerometer. *Pediatric Exercise Science, 4,* 136-141.

Eppling, W. F., Pierce, W. D., & Stefan, L. (1983). A theory of activity-based anorexia. *International Journal of Eating Disorders, 3,* 27-45.

Epstein, L. H., Woodall, K., Goreczny, A. J., Wing, R. R., & Robertson, R. J. (1984). The modification of activity patterns and energy expenditure in obese young girls. *Behavior Therapy, 15,* 101-108.

Freedson, P. S. (1989). Field monitoring of physical activity in children. *Pediatric Exercise Science, 1,* 8-18.

Freedson, P. S., Evenson, S. K., Hamill, J., & Washburn, R. (1988). Heart rate modalities to quantify physical activity. *Medicine and Science in Sports and Exercise, 20*(Suppl.), S2.

Glagov, S., Rowley, D., Cramer, B., & Page, R. (1970). Heart rates during 24 hours of usual activity for 100 normal men. *Journal of Applied Physiology, 29,* 799-805.

Godin, G., & Shephard, R. J. (1985). A simple method to assess exercise behavior in the community. *Canadian Journal of Applied Sport Science, 10,* 141 146.

Haskell, W. L., Taylor, H. L., Wood, P. D., Schrott, H., & Heiss, G. (1980). Strenuous physical activity, treadmill exercise test performance and plasma high-density lipoprotein cholesterol. *Circulation, 62*(Suppl. 4), 53-61.

Haskell, W. L., Yee, M. C., Evans, A., & Irby, P. J. (1993). Simultaneous measurement of heart rate and body motion to quantitate physical activity. *Medicine and Science in Sports and Exercise, 25*(1), 109-115.

Horton, E. S. (1984). Appropriate methodology for assessing physical activity under laboratory conditions in studies of energy balance in adults. In E. Pollitt & P. Amante (Eds.), *Energy intake and activity* (pp. 115-129). New York: Alan R. Liss.

Jacobs, D. R., Ainsworth, B. E., Hartman, T. J., & Leon, A. S. (1993). A simultaneous evaluation of 10 commonly used physical activity questionnaires. *Medicine and Science in Sports and Exercise, 25*(1), 81-91.

Jacobs, D. R., Luepker, R. V., Mittelmark, M. B., et al. (1986). Community-wide prevention strategies: Evaluation design of the Minnesota Heart Health Program. *Journal of Chronic Diseases, 39,* 775-788.

Kannel, W. B., & Sorlie, P. (1979). Some health benefits of physical activity: The Framingham Study. *Archives of Internal Medicine, 139,* 857-861.

Klesges, R. C., Coates, T. J., Moldenhauer-Klesges, L. M., Holzer, B., Gustavson, J., & Barnes, J. (1983). The FATS: An observational system for assessing physical activity in children and associated parent behavior. *Behavioral Assessment, 6,* 333-345.

Klesges, R. C., Eck, L. H., Hanson, C. L., Haddock, C. K., & Klesges, L. M. (1990). Effects of obesity, social interactions, and physical environment on physical activity in preschoolers. *Health Psychology, 9*(4), 435-449.

Klesges, R. C., Eck, L. H., Isbell, T. R., Fulliton, W., & Hanson, C. L. (1991). Physical activity, body composition, and blood pressure: A multimethod approach. *Medicine and Science in Sports and Exercise, 23*(6), 759-765.

Klesges, R. C., & Hanson, C. L. (1988). Determining the environmental precursors and correlates of childhood obesity: Methodological issues and future research directions. In N. A. Krasnegor, G. D. Grave, & N. Kretchmer (Eds.), *Childhood obesity: A biobehavioral perspective* (pp. 89-118). Caldwell, NJ: Telford.

Klesges, L. M., & Klesges, R. C. (1987). The assessment of children's physical activity: A comparison of methods. *Medicine and Science in Sports and Exercise, 19*(5), 511-517.

Klesges, R. C., Klesges, L. M., Haddock, C. K., & Eck, L. H. (1992). A longitudinal analysis of the impact of dietary intake and physical activity on weight change in adults. *American Journal of Clinical Nutrition, 54,* 818-822.

Klesges, R. C., Klesges, L. M., Swenson, A. M., & Pheley, A. M. (1985). A validation of two motion sensors in the prediction of child and adult physical activity levels. *American Journal of Epidemiology, 122*(8), 400-410.

Kriska, A. M., Knowler, W. C., LaPorte, R. E., Drash, A. L., Wing, R. R., Blair, S. N., Bennett, P. H., & Kuller, L. H. (1990). Development of questionnaire to examine relationship of physical activity and diabetes in Pima Indians. *Diabetes Care, 13*(4), 401-411.

LaPorte, R. E., Montoye, H. J., & Caspersen, C. J. (1985). Assessment of physical activity in epidemiologic research: Problems and prospects. *Public Health Reports, 100*(2), 131-146.

Linscheid, T. R., Tarnowski, K. J., & Richmond, D. A. (1988). Behavioral approaches to anorexia nervosa, bulimia, and obesity. In D. K. Routh (Ed.), *Handbook of pediatric psychology* (pp. 332-362). New York: Guilford.

Maliszewski, A. F., Freedson, P. S., Ebbeling, C. J., Crussemeyer, J., & Kastango, K. B. (1991). Validity of the Caltrac accelerometer in estimating energy expenditure and activity in children and adults. *Pediatric Exercise Science, 3,* 141-151.

McGowan, C. R., Bulik, C. M., Epstein, L. H., Kupfer, D. J., & Robertson, R. J. (1984). The use of the large-scale integrated sensor (LSI) to estimate energy expenditure. *Journal of Behavioral Assessment, 6*(1), 51-57.

McKenzie, T. L., Sallis, J. F., Nader, P. R., Patterson, T. L., Elder, J. P., Berry, C. C., Rupp, J. W., Atkins, C. J., Buono, M. J., & Nelson, J. A. (1991). BEACHES: An observational system for assessing children's eating and physical activity behaviors and associated events. *Journal of Applied Behavior Analysis, 24,* 141-151.

Minderaa, R. B., & Witt, J. M. (1983). Behavior therapy of obese children and results in 21 months after treatment. *International Journal of Obesity, 7,* 143-152.

Montoye, H. J. (1971). Estimation of habitual physical activity by questionnaire and interviews. *American Journal of Clinical Nutrition, 24,* 1113-1118.

Montoye, H. J., & Taylor, H. L. (1984). Measurement of physical activity in population studies: A review. *Human Biology, 56*(2), 195-216.

Mukeshi, M., Gutin, B., Anderson, W., Zybert, P., & Basch, C. (1990). Validation of the Caltrac movement sensor using direct observation in young children. *Pediatric Exercise Science, 2,* 249-254.

O'Hara, N. M., Baranowski, T., Simons-Morton, B. G., Wilson, B. S., & Parcel, G. S. (1989). Validity of the observation of children's physical activity. *Research Quarterly Exercise Sport, 60,* 42-47.

Paffenbarger, R. S., Blair, S. N., Lee, I. M., & Hyde, R. T. (1993). Measurement of physical activity to assess health effects in free-living populations. *Medicine and Science in Sports and Exercise, 25*(1), 60-70.

Paffenbarger, R. S., Brand, R. J., Scholtz, R. I., & Jung, D. L. (1978). Energy expenditure, cigarette smoking, and blood pressure level as related to death from specific diseases. *American Journal of Epidemiology, 108*, 12-18.

Paffenbarger, R. S., Hyde, R. T., Wing, A. L., & Hsieh, C. C. (1986). Physical activity, all-cause mortality, and longevity of college alumni. *New England Journal of Medicine, 314*, 605-613.

Paffenbarger, R. S., Wing, A. L., & Hyde, R. T. (1978). Physical activity as an index of heart attack risk in college alumni. *American Journal of Epidemiology, 108*, 161-175.

Paffenbarger, R. S., Wing, A. L., Hyde, R. T., & Jung, D. L. (1983). Physical activity and incidence of hypertension in college alumni. *American Journal of Epidemiology, 117*, 245-257.

Poehlman, E. T. (1989). A review: Exercise and its influence on resting energy metabolism in man. *Medicine and Science in Sports and Exercise, 21*(5), 515-525.

Puhl, J., Greaves, K., Hoyt, M., & Baranowski, T. (1990). Children's activity rating scale (CARS): Description and calibration. *Research Quarterly, 61*(1), 26-36.

Reiff, G. G., Montoye, H. J., Remington, R. D., Napier, J. A., Metzner, H. L., & Epstein, F. H. (1967). Assessment of physical activity by questionnaire and interview. *Journal of Sports Medicine and Physical Fitness, 7*, 135-142.

Sallis, J. F., Buono, M. J., Roby, J. J., Carlson, D., & Nelson, J. A. (1990). The Caltrac accelerometer as a physical activity monitor for school-age children. *Medicine and Science in Sports and Exercise, 22*(5), 698-703.

Sallis, J. F., Buono, M. J., Roby, J. J., Micale, F. G., & Nelson, J. A. (1993). Seven-day recall and other physical activity self-reports in children and adolescents. *Medicine and Science in Sports and Exercise, 25*(1), 99-108.

Sallis, J. F., Haskell, W. L., Wood, P. D., et al. (1985). Physical activity assessment methodology in the Five-City Project. *American Journal of Epidemiology, 121*, 91-106.

Sallis, J. F., Patterson, T. L., Buono, M. J., & Nader, P. R. (1988). Relationship of physical fitness and physical activity to cardiovascular risk factors in children and adults. *American Journal of Epidemiology, 127*, 933-941.

Saris, W. H. M. (1985). The assessment and evaluation of daily physical activity in children. A review. *Acta Paediatric Scandinavian, 318*(Suppl.), 37-48.

Saris, W. H. M. (1986). Habitual physical activity in children: Methodology and findings in health and disease. *Medicine and Science in Sports and Exercise, 18*(3), 253-263.

Shapiro, S., Weinblatt, E., Frank, C. H., & Sager, R. V. (1965). The H.I.P. study of incidence of myocardial infraction and angina. *Journal of Chronic Diseases, 18*, 527-558.

Siconolfi, S. F., Lasater, T. M., Snow, R. C. K., & Carleton, R. A. (1985). Self-reported physical activity compared with maximal oxygen uptake. *American Journal of Epidemiology, 122*, 101-105.

Sidney, S., Jacobs, D. R., Haskell, W. L., et al. (1990). Comparison of two methods of assessing physical activity in the CARDIA study. *American Journal of Epidemiology, 133*, 1231-1245.

Siscovick, D. S., LaPorte, R. E., & Newman, J. M. (1985). The disease-specific benefits and risks of physical activity and exercise. *Public Health Reports, 100*, 180-188.

Taylor, C. B., Coffey, T., Berra, K., Iaffaldano, R., Casey, K., & Haskill, W. L. (1984). Seven-day activity and self-report compared to a direct measure of physical activity. *American Journal of Epidemiology, 120*, 818-824.

Taylor, H. L., Jacobs, D. R., Schucker, B., Knudsen, J., Leon, A. S., & DeBacker, G. (1978). A questionnaire for the assessment of leisure time physical activities. *Journal of Chronic Disease, 31*, 741-755.

Thompson, J. K., Jarvie, G. J., Lahey, B. B., & Cureton, K. J. (1982). Exercise and obesity: Etiology, physiology, and intervention. *Psychological Bulletin, 91*, 55-79.

Tyron, W. W. (1991). *Activity measurement in psychology and medicine.* New York: Plenum.

Wardlaw, G. M., & Insel, P. M. (1990). *Perspective in nutrition.* St. Louis: Times Mirror.

Washburn, R. A., & Montoye, H. J. (1986). The assessment of physical activity by questionnaire. *American Journal of Epidemiology, 123*, 563-576.

Waxman, M., & Stunkard, A. J. (1980). Calorie intake and expenditure of obese boys. *Journal of Pediatrics, 96*, 187-193.

Williams, E., Klesges, R. C., Hanson, C. L., & Eck, L. H. (1989). A prospective study of the reliability and convergent validity of three physical activity measures in a field research trial. *Journal of Clinical Epidemiology, 42*(12), 1161-1170.

Wilson, P. W. F., Paffenbarger, R. S., Morris, J. N., & Havlik, R. J. (1986). Assessment methods for physical activity and physical fitness in populations studies: Report of a NHLBI workshop. *American Heart Journal, 111*, 1177-1192.

Yasin, S., Alderson, M. R., Marr, J. W., Pattison, D. C., & Morris, J. N. (1967). Assessment of habitual physical activity apart from occupation. *British Journal of Preventive Social Medicine, 21*, 163-169.

APPENDIX TABLE 6-A Summary Evaluations of Physical Activity Measures

Reliability	Factor Structure	Validity	Readability	Norms	Practicality

BAECKE, BUREMA, & FRIJTERS (1982):

Reliability	Factor Structure	Validity	Readability	Norms	Practicality

Test-Retest (1 month)
total $r = .93$
work $r = .78$
sport $r = .90$
leisure $r = .86$
 	
Test-Retest (3 months)
work $r = .88$
sport $r = .81$
leisure $r = .74$
	Number and Nature of Factors
	16 items assess habitual physical activity over the past year
	
	3 factors were distinguished:
	—physical activity at work
	—sport during leisure time
	—physical activity during leisure time excluding sport
	
	Stability of Factor Structure
	—Age was related to the work index only in females (higher in older females)
	—Level of education was inversely related to the work index and positively related to the sport index in both sexes
	—subjective experience of work was inversely related to the sport and leisure indices in both sexes
		Convergent/Discriminant
		with
		—VO$_2$ max $r = .54$
		—4-week history $r = .50$
		—Paffenbarger
		  work $r = .06$
		  sport $r = .48$
		  leisure $r = .19$
		—caloric intake
		  work $r = -.31$
		  sport $r = .08$
		  leisure $r = .15$
		
		Related to
		—lean body mass in males
		—subjective experience of work
			Information on the level of reading ability necessary to complete the questionnaire is not available
			
			The measure can be used for the various socioeconomic classes in the general population
				Normative data were obtained on a number of subjects (males: $n = 139$; females: $n = 167$) in three age groups (20-22, 25-27, 30-32) and three levels of education (low, medium, high)
				
				Scale scores range from 16 (sedentary person) to 70 (person with considerable work, sport, and leisure activity)
				
				The mean scores of the work and leisure time indices were significantly higher in females than in males; the mean score of the sport index was significantly higher in males
					Availability
					Based on Baecke et al. (1982), one is to contact the third author[a]
					
					Administration
					—easy to complete
					—self-report
					
					Scoring
					—moderate difficulty
					—5-point scales factor analyzed
					—index for each category based on energy expenditure

LIPID RESEARCH CLINICS PREVALENCE STUDY QUESTIONNAIRE;
HASKELL, TAYLOR, WOOD, SCHROTT, & HEISS (1980):

Reliability	Factor Structure	Validity	Readability	Norms	Practicality
Test-Retest (1 month)	*Number and Nature of Factors*	*Convergent/Discriminant* with	Not applicable	This measure was initially used with 2,319 white men and 2,067 white women aged 20 to 69	*Availability*
$r = .93$	2 questions assess usual activity over a 1-week period	—VO$_2$ max $r = .49$			Two simple questions: "Do you regularly engage in strenuous exercise or hard physical labor?" "Do you exercise or labor at least 3 times per week?"
	A yes response to the second question classifies a subject as highly active; a no response to the first question classifies a subject as inactive; a yes response to the first and a no response to the second question classifies a subject as moderately active	—4-week history $r = .24$ —workload 160 $r = .52$		The reliability and validity of the measure have recently been evaluated in 78 men and women, aged 20-59, with varying levels of activity	
		Related to —physical fitness —disease risk factors			
					Administration —simple to administer
	Stability of Factor Structure At all ages men and women who reported performing strenuous exercise on a daily basis had —higher levels of HDL cholesterol —lower heart rates at rest and during treadmill exercise —longer exercise test durations				*Scoring* —low difficulty of scoring —classified as active, moderately active, inactive

(Continued)

APPENDIX TABLE 6-A (Continued)

MINNESOTA LEISURE TIME PHYSICAL ACTIVITY QUESTIONNAIRE;
TAYLOR, JACOBS, SCHUCKER, KNUDSEN, LEON, & DEBACKER (1978):

Reliability	Factor Structure	Validity	Readability	Norms	Practicality
Test-Retest (1 month) total $r = .92$ light $r = .73$ moderate $r = .80$ heavy $r = .95$ household $r = .88$ *Test-Retest (1 year)* total $r = .69$ light $r = .60$ moderate $r = .32$ heavy $r = .71$ household $r = .71$	*Number and Nature of Factors* 62 items evaluate leisure activity over the past year Examples of activities include —walking —conditioning exercises —water activities —sports —garden work —home repair —fishing —hunting *Stability of Factor Structure* The Minnesota has been used in many studies with various populations and has been found to be useful in assessing physical activity when the concern is the relationship between intensity of activity and disease Found to be useful in weight control clinics	*Convergent/Discriminant* with —physical fitness $r = .45$ —4-week history $r = .74$ —workload 160 $r = .45$ —VO_2 max $r = .43$ —caloric intake $r = -.24$ —hydrostatic weighing $r = -.24$ Related to —HDL cholesterol —Type A behavior —CHD death —sudden death —heart attack —all cause mortality	Specific information is not available; however, the measure has been used with a wide variety of socioeconomic populations	Normative data have been obtained in many studies. In the Multiple Risk Factor Intervention Trial, intensity of leisure activity was assessed in 9,000 men The reliability and validity of the measure have recently been evaluated in 78 men and women aged 20-59 with varying levels of physical activity	*Availability* Printed in the article by Taylor et al. (1978) *Administration* —difficult and time consuming to administer —subjects fill out part of the form alone then the interviewer spends 20 minutes or so filling in the details *Scoring* —difficult and time consuming to score —results are expressed as a total metabolic index calculated by means of intensity codes based on literature values for oxygen consumption —light/moderate/heavy activity metabolic indices can be calculated

204

Reliability	Factor Structure	Validity	Readability	Norms	Practicality
	PAFFENBARGER OR HARVARD ALUMNI SURVEY; PAFFENBARGER, WING, & HYDE (1978)				
Test-Retest (1 month) index $r = .72$ stairs $r = .78$ blocks $r = .63$ sports $r = .75$ *Test-Retest (8 months)* index $r = .50$ stairs $r = .30$ blocks $r = .39$ sports $r = .63$	*Number and Nature of Factors* 7 items assess the types and duration of activities engaged in over the past week Also assesses —flights of stairs climbed/day —city blocks walked/day —sports in hrs/wk *Stability of Factor Structure* The relationship between the Paffenbarger and chronic disease and risk factors has been fairly well established in epidemiological investigations	*Convergent/Discriminant* with —LSI $r = .33$ —VO_2 max $r = .52$ —4-week history $r = .31$ —workload 160 $r = .52$ —hydrostatic weighing $r = -.30$ —sweat episodes $r = -.46$ Related to —risk of first heart attack —risk of hypertension —HDL cholesterol	Specific information is not available; but the measure has been used successfully in numerous large populations	Original sample included 16,936 male Harvard alumni (35-74) Norms also exist for women (42-77) Recent normative data exist for 78 men and women (20-59)	*Availability* Based on Paffenbarger et Al. (1978), one is to contact the senior author[b] *Scoring* —easy to score —PAI physical activity index calculated —PAI based on time and intensity of activity —responses are weighted to yield kilocalories burned/day

(Continued)

205

APPENDIX TABLE 6-A (Continued)

Reliability	Factor Structure	Validity	Readability	Norms	Practicality
— STANFORD SEVEN-DAY PHYSICAL ACTIVITY RECALL QUESTIONNAIRE; BLAIR, HASKELL, HO, PAFFENBARGER, VRANIZAN, FARQUHAR, & WOOD (1985)					

STANFORD SEVEN-DAY PHYSICAL ACTIVITY RECALL QUESTIONNAIRE; BLAIR, HASKELL, HO, PAFFENBARGER, VRANIZAN, FARQUHAR, & WOOD (1985)

Reliability	Factor Structure	Validity	Readability	Norms	Practicality

Test-Retest (2 weeks)
sleep $r = .74$
light $r = .65$
moderate $r = .08$
hard $r = .31$
very hard $r = .61$
kcal/day $r = .67$
 	
Test-Retest (1 month)
sleep $r = .76$
light $r = .56$
moderate $r = .12$
hard $r = .31$
very hard $r = .33$
heavy $r = .37$
work $r = .42$
nonwork $r = .41$
total $r = .34$
 	
Reliability data in children are also good $r = .77$
	Number and Nature of Factors
	9 items assess occupational, leisure, and home activities over past 7 days
	
	A series of closed-ended questions were used to estimate the level of participation in sleep, moderate, hard, and very hard activities
	
	Light activity is calculated as the number of hours out of 24 hours not included in sleep or in moderate, hard, or very hard activity
	
	Stability of Factor Structure
	—Found to be useful in both sexes and across many ages
	—Correlations have been shown to be higher in males and in overweight individuals
		Convergent/Discriminant with
		—daily logs
		  moderate $r = .75$
		  hard $r = .42$
		  very hard $r = .55$
		  hard + vh $r = .39$
		  kcal $r = .81$
		—4-week history $r = .36$
		—VO$_2$ max $r = .33$
		—body mass $r = .50$
		—heart rate monitoring in children $r = .53$
			Specific data are not available
			
			The measure has been used successfully in numerous studies with adults and children
				Values based on random samples of more than 2,000 men and women (aged 20-74)
				
				Normative data for children have also been reported in several studies
				
				Reliability and validity of the measure were recently assessed in 102 male and female children (grades 5, 8, 11) and in 78 men and women (aged 20-59)
					Availability
					Based on Sallis et al. (1993), a detailed interviewer manual plus testing tapes are available from first author[c]
					
					Administration
					—self- or interviewer administered
					—easy to give
					—for adults and children
					—10-20 minutes to complete
					
					Scoring
					—moderate level of difficulty for scoring energy expenditure in kcal and kcal/kg/day

Reliability	Factor Structure	Validity	Readability	Norms	Practicality
DIARY ANNOTATION:					
Test-Retest (weekly) High with correlations ranging from 0.77 to 0.91	Requires monitoring of specific tasks and activities performed throughout the day Monitoring usually includes —time of activity —duration of activity —the intensity of the activity (examples are generally provided) Due to the flexibility of this measure, it has been found to be useful across many different populations It has been found that men report performing more leisure time activity than women but that women report expending more energy during leisure activities	*Convergent* with Stanford —1st week $r = .68$ —2nd week $r = .84$ —3rd week $r = .82$ This method is commonly used as a "gold standard"	Not applicable	While used extensively, no normative database is available	*Availability* —Readily available —Constructed based on need —Blair (1984) offers some guidelines *Administration* —self-, observer, or interviewer administered —easy to administer —time consuming and tedious for individual to complete *Scoring* —easy unless individual has kept poor records —often scored according to total minutes in sleep and light, moderate, hard, and very hard activity

(Continued)

APPENDIX TABLE 6-A (Continued)

BEACHES—BEHAVIORS OF EATING AND ACTIVITY FOR CHILDREN'S HEALTH EVALUATION SYSTEM;
MCKENZIE, SALLIS, NADER, PATTERSON, ELDER, BERRY, RUPP, ATKINS, BUONO, & NELSON (1991)

Reliability	Factor Structure	Validity	Readability	Norms	Practicality
Interrater —Home observa- tions' median kappas ranged from 0.71 to 1.0 —Videotaped tests' median kappas ranged from 0.72 to 0.92	*Number and Nature of Factors* 10 separate dimensions with 51 coding items for assessing children's physical activity and eating behaviors and related environmental events Factors coded —physical activity —dietary behaviors —physical location —antecedents —consequences Child physical activity was coded into 5 mutually exclu- sive categories: —lying down —sitting —standing —walking —very active *Stability of Factor Structure* It can be used at home, at schools, and in most other settings in which a targeted child might be found	Validated by heart rate monitoring, and evidence of validity for the measure is suggested (McKenzie et al., 1991)	Not applicable	42 children (4-8 years old) were observed for 8 consecu- tive weeks at hom and at school in the original study Normative data are lacking	*Availability* Based on McKenzie et al. (1991), one is to contact the senior author[d] *Administration* —time consuming —60-minute obser- vations —requires 40 hours of training *Scoring* —difficult to score —complex coding system

Reliability	Factor Structure	Validity	Readability	Norms	Practicality

SCAN CATS—STUDIES OF CHILDREN'S ACTIVITY AND NUTRITION/CHILDREN'S TIMESAMPLING SURVEY; KLESGES, ECK, HANSON, HADDOCK, & KLESGES (1990):

Reliability	Factor Structure	Validity	Readability	Norms	Practicality
Interrater —Kappas ranged from 0.83 for interaction to 1.00 for environment with 0.91 as the average across the four categories	*Number and Nature of Factors* System quantifies directly observed physical activity in the natural environment Factors coded —the environment the activity occurs in —activity level —persons present during activity —interactions between persons present and child *Stability of Factor Structure* —parental obesity was associated with lower levels of physical activity —childhood relative weight was related to slightly higher levels of physical activity —more outdoor activity was associated with higher activity levels	Construct and discriminative validity reportedly high (Klesges et al., 1990)	Not applicable	Original sample consisted of 219 male and female preschoolers (aged 3-6 years) Subjects were both overweight and normal weight, and all subjects were Caucasian	*Availability* See Klesges et al. (1990) *Administration* —time consuming —usually 1 hour —observe 10 seconds; record 10 seconds *Scoring* —quantifies directly observed physical activity

(Continued)

209

APPENDIX TABLE 6-A (Continued)

Reliability	Factor Structure	Validity	Readability	Norms	Practicality
CALTRAC ACCELEROMETER:					
	Designed to assess both the quantity and the intensity of movement	*Convergent/Discriminant* with (Adults)	Not applicable	Normative data are lacking although the Caltrac has been tested and used with both adults and children of various ages, ethnic groups, and socioeconomic groups	*Availability* Mukeshi et al. (1990) report the manufacturer is Hemokinetics in Madison, WI[e]
Interinstrument		—daily log			
Children		—1st wk $r = .11$			
—field $r = .96$		—2nd wk $r = .37$			
—lab $r = .89$	Due to the nature of this device, it has been found to be useful in both children and adults with varying levels of physical activity	—3rd wk $r = .34$			*Administration* The Caltrac is usually worn on the hip and is attached to a belt
Adults		—Stanford			
—lab $r = .70$		—1st wk $r = .14$			
$r = .94$		—2nd wk $r = .12$			Subjects can engage in their typical physical activity while wearing the accelerometer
		—3rd wk $r = .37$			
		—observed physical activity $r = .69$			
		—LSI $r = .83$			
		with (Children)			
		—observed physical activity $r = .35$			
		—LSI $r = .42$			*Scoring* The counts that accumulate reflect total vertical acceleration of the body
Test-Retest	*Stability of Factor Structure*	—activity heart rates			
Modest in adults with correlations ranging from 0.35 to 0.54	It has been found to record indoor activity (mainly walking) more accurately than playground movements	—day 1 $r = .54$			
		—day 2 $r = .42$			These counts are used with age, sex, height, and weight to compute an estimate of the energy expenditure

LARGE-SCALE INTEGRATED ACTIVITY MONITOR (LSI):

Reliability	Factor Structure	Validity	Readability	Norms	Practicality
Interinstrument LSI day and evening counts per hour —controls $r = .51$ —walkers $r = .52$	Measures body movements and can be placed on various body locations (ankle, hip)	*Convergent/Discriminant* with (Adults) —observed physical activity —Caltrac $r = .65$ —treadmill $r = .83$	Not applicable	Normative data are lacking for both adults and children Studies on the reliability and validity of the monitor have been conducted in both adults and children	*Availability* Klesges et al. (1985) report the manufacturer is GMM Electronics Inc. in Verona, PA
Relatively high correlations have been reported between ankle movements and trunk movements $r = .72$	Within the monitor is a cylinder with a ball of mercury A 3% inclination or declination causes the closing of a mercury switch that registers in an internal counter	—trunk $r = .98$ —ankle $r = .92$ with (Children) —observed physical activity $r = .40$ Correlates highly with laboratory measures of physical activity			*Administration* Easy to instruct subjects on how and when to wear the monitor
Test-Retest With subjects walking and running, coefficients were 0.76 to 0.99	*Stability of Factor Structure* Has been shown to index individual activity as well as changes in activity over 1 year				*Scoring* LSI activity is expressed in counts per hour for the day's activity

(Continued)

APPENDIX TABLE 6-A (Continued)

Reliability	Factor Structure	Validity	Readability	Norms	Practicality
HEART RATE MONITORS:					
Interinstrument $r = .98$	Directly measures a physiological parameter known to be related to physical activity Provides a continuous record that may reflect both intensity and duration of daily activity Direct heart rate measurements appear to be strong indicators of quality of physical activity and energy expenditure in the natural environment for both children and adults *Stability of Factor Structure* Heart rate is influenced by other factors: —emotional status —body posture —environmental conditions —amount of muscle mass involved in the activity	Within-person correlation between heart rate and oxygen uptake during increasing exercise intensity on a motor-driven treadmil' or cycle ergometer frequently exceeds 0.95 Various types of heart rate monitors have been validated in the laboratory with adults and children and in the field with children	Not applicable	Normative data are lacking	*Availability* Numerous manufacturers exist and monitors are available at a variety of retail stores[f] *Administration* —easy and commonly employed —a wireless, portable monitor is easiest on subjects —monitors are worn during all daily activities *Scoring* —Intensity, duration, and average heart rates are evaluated —baseline heart rates and a heart rate activity index are determined

212

Reliability	Factor Structure	Validity	Readability	Norms	Practicality
DIRECT AND INDIRECT CALORIMETRY:					
Direct calorimetry is the most reliable method of assessing energy expenditure in the laboratory	Measures energy expenditure through the production of heat	Highly valid; errors of measuring physical activity as low as 1%	Not applicable	Normative data are unavailable	Direct calorimetry is best suited for long-term measurements of energy expenditure
	Physical activity is defined in relation to overall energy expenditure	Valuable resource for obtaining standardized data on energy expenditure			Direct calorimetry requires that individuals be sequestered in special chambers, making it expensive, limited to special tasks, and impractical for studying usual daily activity
Indirect calorimetry is nearly as reliable as direct calorimetry	Measures oxygen consumption and carbon dioxide production during physical activity, allowing for applications in the laboratory and in the field	Measurement error is 2% to 3% Significantly correlated with intensity of exercise $r = .42$			Measurement of physical activity by indirect calorimetry requires that the participant wear a face mask, a mouthpiece with a nose clip, or a canopy, and a container for the collection of expired air

SOURCES: a. Department of Human Nutrition, Agricultural University, De Dreijen 12, 6703 BC Wageningen, The Netherlands.

 b. Stanford University School of Medicine, Stanford, CA 94305.

 c. Department of Psychology, San Diego State University, San Diego, CA 92182; questionnaire can be obtained by contacting Dr. Steven N. Blair, Cooper Institute for Aerobics Research, 12300 Preston Road, Dallas, TX 75230.

 d. Child and Family Health Studies, University of California at San Diego, La Jolla, CA 92093-0927.

 e. Hemokinetics, Inc., 5930 Seminole Center Court, Madison, WI 53711; prices for Caltracs range from approximately $300 to $500 apiece, depending on the quantity purchased.

 f. Heart rate monitors can be ordered from Polar CIC, Inc., 99 Seaview Blvd., Port Washington, NY 11050; prices for heart rate monitors range from approximately $100 to $500 apiece.

NOTE: CHD = coronary heart disease; HDL = high density lipoprotein; kcal = kilocalories; kg = kilograms; LSI = Large-Scale Integrated Activity Monitor; VO_2 = volume of oxygen consumption.

Appendix 6-B

List of Instruments Located but Not Selected for Review

I. Questionnaires
1. British Civil Servants Walking Questionnaire (Yasin et al., 1967)
2. CARDIA Physical Activity History (Sidney et al., 1990)
3. Framingham Questionnaire (Kannel & Sorlie, 1979)
4. Godin-Shephard Physical Activity Survey (Godin & Shephard, 1985)
5. Health Insurance Plan of New York Questionnaire (HIP; Shapiro et al., 1965)
6. Minnesota Heart Health Program Questionnaire (Jacobs et al., 1986)
7. Stanford Usual Activity Questionnaire (Sallis et al., 1985)
8. The Tecumseh Questionnaire (Reiff et al., 1967)

II. Direct Observation
1. Children's Activity Rating Scale (CARS; Puhl et al., 1990)
2. The Fargo Activity Timesampling Survey (FATS; Klesges et al., 1983)
3. Time and Motion Studies (Horton, 1984)

III. Mechanical, Electronic, and Physiological Monitors
1. Combination of Heart Rate and Body Motion (Haskell et al., 1993)
2. Pedometers (Montoye & Taylor, 1984)
3. Vitalog Monitor (Haskell et al., 1993)

IV. Other Indirect Methods
1. Caloric Intake (see Heymsfield et al., this volume)
2. Doubly Labeled Water Method (See Heymsfield et al., this volume)
3. Job Classification (LaPorte et al., 1985)
4. Radar Motion Recorders (Horton, 1984)

7

Measuring Food Intake

An Overview

CARLA WOLPER

STANLEY HESHKA

STEVEN B. HEYMSFIELD

Accurate assessment of dietary intake in free-living humans remains one of the most basic and fundamental unsolved problems in the study of nutrition. The solution to this problem would have a revolutionary impact on our understanding of the connections linking nutrition to body functioning and disease states.

In the absence of accurate measurement methods, the researcher must choose among existing techniques with careful attention to the balance of desirable and undesirable qualities as they relate to specific study goals. The choice of an appropriate method is critical in designing a nutritional study, and the large variety of available strategies can be bewildering. For instance, investigators need to bear clearly in mind what aspect of intake is being evaluated (e.g., energy, macro- or micronutrients, patterns of intake), as well as any special characteristics of the respondent, to determine how measurements can best be made.

When selecting a food intake measurement method, it is important to realize that the answer to the question, "How good a measure of intake is _____ (e.g., food diaries)?" is always, "It depends." The answer depends on no single factor. *For whom is intake being measured?* Schoeller (1990b) has shown that self-reports of total caloric intake are far more accurate for nonobese than obese adolescent girls. Lichtman et al. (1992) clearly demonstrated that certain people present especially formidable obstacles (i.e., severe misreporting) to attempts to measure their caloric consumption. *What aspect of intake is being measured?* Under some circumstances, total caloric intake may be easier to measure than micronutrient composition, as shown by Nelson, Black, Morris, and Cole (1989). *How will the resulting data be used?* As Heymsfield et al. (this volume) discuss with self-reported height and weight, the extent to which systematic versus random reporting biases are problematic depends on whether the measurements will be used in analyses requiring accurate values in an absolute sense or only on the relative ranking yielded by the measurements. *What sort of generalizations does the investigator wish to make from the data?* For example, if one wants to determine habitual food intake, laboratory test meals probably lack the necessary external validity (Meiselman, 1992). However, if one is not necessarily interested in what people usually do but what people *can* do, then the controlled conditions of laboratory test meals may be just the ticket (see Mook, 1983, for discussion of psychological aspects in general and Kissileff, 1992, for discussion specific to studies of ingestive behavior).

It is obvious that the chosen method must be determined by the specific circumstances of the investigation, the subjects being studied, and the questions under consideration. There is no "all-purpose" assessment method and so the burden of choice requires that the investigator have a clear vision of what kind of information is needed.

Dwyer (1994) proposes a list of factors to consider when selecting a method, including reliability, validity, respondent burden, cost, and the characteristics unique to the investigation. This chapter will review some of these details on the available methods so as to facilitate selection of methodology.

A few remarks about reliability and validity of intake measures are in order. Free-living humans almost never eat exactly the same meal twice, therefore attempts to measure the reliability of a measurement method may confound measurement error with variety in diet. This problem is especially acute in measures of single meals or 24-hour intakes in which large amounts of within-subject variability may be seen. If, however, as is often the case, the study requires the measurement of average or typical intakes over periods of weeks, months, or years, then within-subject variation in intake will be a smaller portion of the total test-retest variation (assuming weight, lifestyle, and seasonal stability). A second dimension to this problem is precisely the issue of stability over long periods of time. Some of the test-retest reliability studies correlate intake measures separated by years. Again, it is unclear how much of the variability in the result is attributable to dietary changes and how much to measurement error. For the purpose of describing the reliability of measures reviewed here, studies in which the same person was measured more than once using the same instrument will be mentioned. The original articles should always be consulted as they usually contain much more information than can be discussed here. As for validity, it is often assumed that high correlations with other instruments designed to measure the same variable indicate a valid instrument (convergent validity). However, in the case of good agreement among different methods, all of which involve self-report (e.g., recall, diaries, checklists, interviews), social desirability and other self-serving motivations may be a source of distortion and error shared by all methods, producing inflated estimates of validity. Freedman, Carroll, and Wax (1991) discuss some of the problems in estimating the relation between self-reports of dietary intake and true average intake. Many of the validation studies discussed here correlate measures from two or more self-report instruments. The results of recent doubly labeled water studies and other techniques that do not rely on self-report are casting serious doubts on previous validation studies (Schoeller, 1990a).

Broadly speaking, methods for the assessment of dietary intake can be divided into seven categories: (a) short-term recall methods, (b) diaries and food records, (c) diet histories, (d) food frequency questionnaires, (e) food weighing, (f) direct observations, and (g) inferences from measurements of energy expenditure. Each category will be reviewed in turn.

Short-Term Recall Methods

Twenty-Four-Hour Recall

History. Burke (1947) pioneered the development of methodology for assessing dietary intake. Early on, she recognized that assessment of *long-term* intake was key to accurate nutritional evaluation. In the 1930s and 1940s, Burke used 24-hour recalls to cross-check mothers' 24-hour intake records of their children's consumption. Since then, the 24-hour recall method has been used in many large-scale studies, including the National Health and Nutrition Examination Surveys (NHANES; Abraham, Carroll, Dresser, & Johnson, 1979) and the Multiple Risk Factor Intervention Trial (MRFIT; Tillotson, Gorder, & Kassim, 1981).

Procedure. Typically, 24-hour recalls are administered by trained interviewers. Training of interviewers may include practice using food models to quantify portion sizes, experience in probing for information without suggesting responses, and development of objective, standardized skills in recording data (Madden, Goodman, & Guthrie, 1976). Subjects are asked to recall *all* foods eaten in a particular time period, commonly the prior 24 hours. Interviewers may use food models (available from Nasco Nutrition Teaching Aids, 1524 Princeton Avenue, Modesto, CA 95352, 1-800-558-9595) or drawings and photos of foods to help in recall of portion sizes. (The National Dairy Council, Rosemont, IL 60018-4233, publishes an excellent set of life-size food model photographs of commonly eaten foods. The complete set of "Food Models" can be ordered at a cost of approximately $20.00.) In addition, interviews can often elicit more accurate reports by probing for forgotten foods or reports of socially undesirable food consumption.

Advantages. The main advantage of this technique is its expedience, requiring only approximately 20 minutes to complete. Economy results from its speed and ease of administration, and it places a relatively small burden on the respondent. Additionally, this type of interview can be conducted via telephone if respondents are not physically present. It is simpler and less demanding than a diary as no record keeping is required by the subject, and it may be more representative of actual consumption than food frequency instruments if foods that the respondent commonly eats are not listed on the food frequency instrument (Garn, Larkin, & Cole, 1976). Due to its ease and rapidity of administration, 24-hour recall is often used as a validation tool for other methods. Finally, reactivity need not be a problem (i.e., it does not cause subjects to alter their intake) as it is conducted a posteriori.

Disadvantages. This method relies on the memory of subjects, which can be inaccurate. For this reason, it is especially unsuitable for people with cognitive deficits. Additionally, respondents need adequate communication skills to report accurately and in sufficient detail the contents and quantities of their meals and snacks. Furthermore, reports are vulnerable to intentional or unintentional distortion in accordance with respondents' desire to create a particular impression. Another problem results from the fact that the particular 24 hours chosen may not be typical of that individual's normal diet. That is, the day selected may be the respondent's birthday or a holiday associated with an eating event. There are also systematic variations according to day of the week and season (Beaton et al., 1979; Tarasuk & Beaton, 1992). Transient fluctuations in one's state of health may affect consumption, particularly for children, and may render 24-hour recalls unrepresentative of habitual consumption (Garn et al., 1976). Interviewers may influence the response by verbal or physical cues and by personal biases. Dwyer (1994) notes that certain foods tend to be incorrectly recalled, such as liquids, snacks, alcohol, fats, and sweets. Willett (1990) observed that the practical effect of using only a few days' reporting of individual intake increases the apparent between-subject variability, as those people with the highest and lowest intake have days when intake is above or below their average, producing extreme values at either end of the distribution. It is difficult to separate differences in intake from errors in assessment when looking at short-term methods. Another problem occurs when repeated interviews in close proximity influence how subjects respond (i.e., testing effects). It is also extremely difficult to conduct two interviews identically.

Best application. Twenty-four-hour recalls are most suitable when one wishes to determine the typical intake of *large groups* of subjects. The unstructured format also makes it useful in culturally diverse groups. Validation of other methods of assessing intake is sometimes carried out by comparison with 24-hour recalls.

Reliability and validity. Stunkard and Waxman (1981) found a strong linear relationship ($r = .96$) between 24-hour recalled food intake and independently observed food intake in three obese and three nonobese boys aged 4 to 13. Schoeller (1990a) noted a possible underreporting discrepancy when comparing 24-hour recall with average food purchases. NHANES 24-hour recall data per capita were 1,900 calories/day whereas per capita available energy estimated from product sales averaged 2,600 kcal/day (after correction of available energy for food waste in both the household and the food marketing system). Madden et al. (1976) made direct observations on 76 elderly subjects who took cafeteria-style meals and then carried out 24-hour recalls a day later. They found that, except for total calories, 24-hour intake did not differ significantly from the direct observation results, although most nutrients were underestimated. Regression analysis, however, suggested a "flat slope syndrome," that is, overreporting of small quantities and underreporting of large quantities ingested. The slopes of several of the regression lines were significantly different than 1.0. Eck, Klesges, Hanson, Slawson, and Lavasque (1991) correlated 1-day recalls with a 7-day food frequency method and found a correlation of .66 for total energy and correlations ranging from .43 to .88 for various nutrients. Brown et al. (1990) videotaped cafeteria trays of 37 elderly women and conducted 24-hour recalls a day later. Correlations of recall with videotaped estimates ranged from .09 to .82, depending on the nutrient. The videotape method tended to give higher estimates for most nutrients.

Thus, overall, we can see that the validity of 24-hour food recalls must be suspect. Systematic biases are clear and the correlation with alternative methods or criteria is often weak.

Four- or Seven-Day Recall

These recalls are conducted identically to 24-hour recalls but obviously are more time consuming. The primary disadvantage is the common inability of subjects to remember in detail what they ate more than 24 hours in the past. For this reason, when recall is the preferred method, it is generally only a 24-hour period that is of interest.

Diet Diary or Food Records

History. As mentioned earlier, Burke and Stuart first used 24-hour food diaries in 1938 when mothers kept food records for their children. To validate these records, the mothers were interviewed regarding the same time frame.

Procedure. With diaries, the idea is to record all ingestion immediately after it occurs. Meals, snacks, and drinks consumed over a designated time period are recorded, along with portion size and contents of mixed dishes. The typical time period is 3 or 7 days and generally includes at least one weekend day because eating patterns on weekdays frequently differ from those on weekends. Printed forms, blank paper, or pocket-sized notebooks can be used for convenience. Frequently, more stylized forms contain various prompts requiring entries for each time slot, location, and so on. In addition, depending on the purpose of data collection, other aspects may be recorded such as where food was consumed (e.g., at home, in a restaurant, in which room, at the table, in bed, watching TV); why the food was eaten; what thoughts and feelings preceded, accompanied, and followed consumption; and whether the meal was eaten alone or in company. Depending on the degree of detail required and training offered, the forms may be completed quite well by subjects who will take the time to do so, or may require extensive probing for additional detail by the interviewer. An example of a detailed form is shown in Figure 7.1.

Date	Time	Describe Food Eaten	Portion Size	Where Eaten (i.e., at home, in restaurant, work, etc.)	Estimated Number of Calories

Figure 7.1. Detailed Diary Form

Advantages. Food diaries can provide a richly detailed history of what a subject ate during the designated time frame. Errors can be reduced by providing meticulous instructions to subjects prior to the recording of data. Additionally, food diaries do not rely on memory for accuracy, as intake is recorded at the time food is consumed.

Disadvantages. Extensive food diaries can be quite demanding of subjects. Typically, initial records are complete and thorough, but a rapid deterioration in record quality occurs. Moreover, subjects must have adequate literacy to comply. Inaccurate recording, especially of portion sizes, is common, although inexpensive scales can be provided to assist in estimating portions. Lack of adequate detail may require extensive, time-consuming probing. In particular, meals eaten away from home may be more difficult for the respondent to evaluate and describe, in terms of both content and portion size.

Another major concern with food record keeping is reactivity. Changes in eating behavior may be induced by the very act of record keeping (Willett, 1990). Thus food records, even if accurate for the time they were collected, may not be reflective of habitual food intake. Intake of foods seen as "socially desirable" may be exaggerated, whereas consumption of those seen as undesirable may be minimized. Recording may not be immediate because of inconvenience so that time may affect memory and recall. Emotions attached to events may also affect accuracy.

Willett (1990) points out that how many and which days to record are not clear. Although a full week of recording intake might appear to provide a relatively complete picture of foods consumed, investigators are often reluctant to place such demands on subjects. If compliance with the demands of 7 days of recording is problematic, it is generally considered acceptable to request 3 weekdays and at least 1 weekend day for a representative sample of intake (Willett, 1990). Nelson et al. (1989) discuss how many days of records are necessary to rank dietary intake with a desired precision.

Reliability and validity. Willett et al. (1985) compared 7-day diet records separated by a 1-year interval from 173 nurses. Intraclass correlations ranged from .41 for total vitamin A to .79 for vitamin B6. Rimm et al. (1992) analyzed 7-day diet records separated by a 6-month interval from 127 male health professionals. They report intraclass correlations of .77 for calories and .75 for fat. Many additional correlations are reported in these articles.

Pietinen et al. (1988a, 1988b) correlated 2-day food records with other measures of intake. In one report, twelve 2-day food records from 158 men correlated in the range of .40 to .80 with assessments of nutrients made by a diet history questionnaire, and total energy intake correlated .57 to .59. In the other report, twelve 2-day food records from 190 men were found to correlate in the range of .33 (selenium) to .85 (polyunsaturated fat) with assessments made using food frequency instruments. Lansky and Brownell (1982), using this method in a laboratory situation, reported a 63.9% error rate in subjects' ability to estimate the actual amounts of measured quantities of a selection of premeasured foods and a 53.4% error in subjects' ability to estimate the caloric content of the same foods. They question the utility of food records based on subjects' inability to estimate energy intake. Note that conversion of food portions to calories need not be done by the respondent.

Recently, validations of 7-day diaries have been carried out using the doubly labeled water method (Livingstone et al., 1990; Schoeller, 1990b). More than half of the food records were found to have errors in caloric intake in excess of 20%. Based on the estimation of total energy expenditure achieved with this technology, stable weights dictate that energy consumed equals energy expended. Subjects' reported caloric consumption (in diaries) would necessitate weight loss. On the average, subjects' food records reported 20% fewer calories than were actually consumed.

Best application. This method is best used for smaller numbers of subjects who are highly motivated to provide the type of detail required for accuracy.

Willett (1990) suggests that using this method is practical in intervention studies to monitor group compliance to study protocols. Written records provide a rich description of total energy content and can highlight the consumption of particular macro- and micronutrients. Entries in diaries can be converted to quantitative descriptions of intake with computerized dietary analysis programs. Diaries are especially useful when consumption of a particular food or ingredient needs to be monitored. If patterns of intake relative to emotional state and daily activity are of concern, diaries can provide detailed information. Food records may also be useful in validating dietary histories, food frequency instruments, and other less intensive measurements, although, in view of the results of recent doubly labeled water studies, they are likely to underestimate intake.

Diet History

History. This method was advanced by Burke (1947) in the 1930s and 1940s at Harvard. Burke promoted the use of validating questions (questions that ask the same thing in a different way) to check the accuracy of responses given in a detailed dietary history. Diet histories have been used in many large-scale studies such as the Framingham study (Dawber et al., 1962).

Procedure. The interviewer questions the respondent about usual eating patterns at meals and snacks. Daily patterns as well as variations (e.g., holidays or sick days) are noted until the level of detail is sufficient to understand normative as well as divergent eating behaviors. The types of foods, the frequency of consumption, and the portion sizes recorded in common household measurements (e.g., half a cup, 2 tablespoons, one slice) are recorded. Condiments are noted and methods of preparation are determined (e.g., broiling, frying, baking, boiling, or steaming). Alterations to intake based on state of health, scheduling and timing of meals, holidays, celebrations, and season of the year are clarified. The interviewer needs to uncover whether altered intake on holidays is restricted to 1 day only or whether such holiday eating behaviors extend into succeeding days or weeks. Similarly, examination of changes in intake due to sickness or a new work schedule needs to be in sufficient detail to determine the total time period during which intake was altered. Detailed forms providing prompts for the interviewer can help structure the interview. After completion of this history, the interviewer validates the information by asking "cross-checking" questions. For example, if the subject has reported eating broccoli every day, the subject might be asked if he or she likes broccoli or how many green vegetables are consumed during a normal week. In this way, inconsistencies can be discovered. Using this technique, food groups are discussed relative to the subjects' preferences to compare this information with information already gathered. Smucker, Block, Coyle, Harvin, and Kessler (1989) have developed an interviewer-administered version, a self-administered version, and a computer-assisted version of a diet history assessment. A shorter, food frequency version has also been developed by Block, Hartman, and Naughton (1990). Byers, Marshall, Fiedler, Zielezny, and Graham (1985) have claimed that an abbreviated dietary history could provide useful information while covering as few as 15 to 20 food items.

The purpose of the study should be considered when determining how many foods are absolutely required for the interview. If, as Byers et al. (1985) point out, the investigator merely needs to describe variability among respondents with regard to consumption of a particular nutrient, the number of foods necessary will be smaller.

Advantages. This method provides an elaborate picture of the quantity and quality of food consumed. Dwyer (1994) considers it to be more complete and detailed than food records, 24-hour recalls, or food frequency questionnaires. Because this is a retrospective method, it does not alter intake and provides historical information that occurred prior to commencement of the retrospective study. Seasonal variation in patterns of consumption can be clarified and other sources of deviation can be characterized.

Disadvantages. Careful interviewing is necessary for successful completion of the diet history, and, in the absence of a standard interview format, different interviewers can obtain considerably different results. This method can be extremely time consuming and is dependent on the respondent's memory. It is also costly, in terms of both the nutritionist's time and the cost of evaluation, coding, and entering of data. Dwyer (1994) reports that it is not uncommon for portion sizes to be underestimated when diet histories are compared with food records gathered during the same period. This may be compounded by poor memory causing failure to account for meals that were missed or days when consumption was reduced due to illness or other alterations in intake. It is also difficult to verify the time frames reported by the subjects. Subjects may be describing what they think they eat or what they wish the interviewer to believe rather than what is being eaten.

Reliability and validity. McKeown-Eyssen, Yeung, and Bright-See (1986) conducted dietary interviews with 44 men aged 32-65, then, a year later, conducted another interview asking about diet a year ago. Correlation coefficients for different nutrients ranged from .46 to .78 for those men who reported no dietary changes during the elapsed interval. Quantities tended to underestimate intake a year ago. Bloemberg, Kromhout, Oberman-De Boer, and Van Kamper-Donker (1989) conducted repeated dietary surveys with elderly men as part of the Zutphen study in the Netherlands. Differences between interviews made after 3-month ($n = 115$) and 12-month ($n = 145$) intervals tended to be small and nonsignificant. Spearman correlation coefficients were relatively high ($> .70$) for consumption of bread, milk, and alcoholic beverages and lower ($< .52$) for meats and vegetables. Pietinen et al. (1988a) gave a self-administered diet history questionnaire to 121 men on two occasions separated by 3 months. Intraclass correlation coefficients for nutrients ranged between .60 and .70.

Several studies have been conducted by Block and associates in the course of developing a diet history questionnaire. One study found correlations between the diet history questionnaire and other more detailed methods for various nutrients to be above .70 (Block et al., 1986). NHANES II data were used to determine the nutrient composition and the frequency of consumption of various foods. Determination of portion size in NHANES included the use of three-dimensional food models (Block et al., 1986). In another study (Block, Woods, Potosky, & Clifford, 1990), three 4-day food records were kept by subjects over the course of a year, then a self-administered diet history questionnaire was administered. Mean intake amounts showed good agreement and the correlation for kilocalories was .51. Correlations for various nutrients ranged between .43 and .74. Sobell, Block, Koslowe, Tobin, and Andres (1989) report a study comparing personal interview administration of this questionnaire with a mailed self-administered version. They found that the personal interview elicited information on past diet that is as valid as many studies of current diet, but that a mailed questionnaire was not as effective. Correlations of .5 for energy consumption were found when the questionnaires were personally administered.

Dawber et al. (1962) provide some data on dietary interviews separated by 2 years. They repeated interviews on 30 subjects from the Framingham study and found close agreement: sample means within 20 kcal, correlations of .92 for kcal, and others ranging from .52 for animal protein to .88 for fat. Correlations remained high even when the second interview was conducted by a different interviewer. Jain, Howe, Johnson, and Miller (1980) readministered dietary history interviews to a sample of 45 males and 49 females, mean age 61 years, who were originally interviewed 7 years earlier. Correlations were higher for subjects claiming no dietary change during the interval. For macronutrients, r's ranged between .76 and .63 for men and between .45 and .64 for women. Correlations for micronutrients tended to be lower. Dwyer (1994) states that histories seem to describe higher intake than do food records kept for the same periods. Byers et al. (1985) showed that a large fraction of the variance of six selected nutrients could be explained by a very small number of foods.

Availability. An excellent example of a dietary history format was developed by Dr. Gladys Block. For reprints of the Block Health Habits and History Questionnaire, write to Dr. Gladys Block, 419 Warren Hall, School of Public Health, University of California, Berkeley, CA 94720. Dr. Block offers software for analysis of results.

Food Frequency Questionnaires

History. The predecessor of food frequency questionnaires was Burke's (1947) checklist of foods consumed the prior month. Burke used it in conjunction with a 24-hour recall interview and a 3-day food record in the 1940s. In 1989 Sobell et al. used a retrospective questionnaire to assess usual diet of 10-15 years in the past.

Procedure. Food frequency questionnaires typically consist of precoded forms that incorporate a selected list of essential foods arranged in food groups of comparable nutrient content. Groups might also be included that incorporate similar additives, contaminants, or other ingredients of interest. Questions are posed relating to portion sizes and frequency of consumption. Amounts are generally described in common household measurements, such as a slice of bread or a cup of rice. Questionnaires that focus only on the type of food consumed may not contain questions relating to quantity. Semiquantitative instruments provide limited choices, and subjects may be asked to indicate how often they ate each food during the specified period of time, such as the past year or 6 months, as well as questions about daily consumption such as "never consumed" or "5 plus times each day." Quantitative questionnaires allow the subject to indicate *precisely* how often he or she consumes a particular food.

Advantages. Food frequency questionnaires are inexpensive, quick, and easy to standardize (if a nonstandard assessment is to be done). They often can be self-administered and do not require trained interviewers. They are useful when studying associations between particular foods and disease, such as high fat diet and breast cancer, or eggs and heart disease, as they allow investigators to rank people according to their intake of a particular nutrient. They do not cause alterations in consumption because they are completed after the fact. Frequency questionnaires can be used to quickly estimate intake of single nutrients or food groups and to determine how often foods are eaten. Dwyer (1994) found frequency instruments useful to describe intake patterns for diet and meal planning. Frequency questionnaires are an inexpensive method of assessing large numbers of subjects when ordinal rankings constitute an adequate scale.

Disadvantages. If many items are included, questionnaires are time consuming and may not be properly completed. They may not be designed with special populations (such as particular ethnic groups or vegetarians) in mind. Not all foods can be included in these instruments and so a particular item, which might constitute a major portion of a subject's intake, could be missing. It may be easier, according to Dwyer (1994), for subjects to estimate intake of staple foods and foods consumed in large quantities than foods eaten infrequently or in small quantities. Memory will naturally affect accuracy. Validity must be established for nonstandard questionnaires, and the appropriate software must be available to translate frequency data into nutrient intake estimations. Qualitative questionnaires do not permit estimation of nutrient content of diet as amounts consumed are not available. Purely quantitative questionnaires often require an interview or food models to help subjects evaluate portion size.

Best application. Food frequency questionnaires are appropriate when average long-term diet is of interest but are not effective in achieving a precise measurement of short-term consumption. They are useful for diet and meal planning, when time and money are in short supply, or when trained interviewers are unavailable. They are excellent for ranking intake of particular foods or food groups. If subjects cannot be interviewed personally because of distance, or when there are large numbers of subjects to evaluate, frequency instruments provide a practical solution. Sempos (1992) points out that semiquantitative instruments are more efficient as no interview or food models are needed to aid subjects in evaluating portion sizes, and they can be optically scanned because they are precoded. Sobell et al. (1989) and Willett et al. (1988) reported using frequency instruments to assess past intake, looking as far back as 10 to 15 years. Sobell found that, when questionnaires are used to assess past intake, correlations are better though still weak when questionnaires are personally administered (correlations for energy of .5) than when mailed to respondents (correlations of .14 for total energy consumption).

Validity and reliability. Eck et al. (1991) gave 7-day food frequency instruments to 17 students, then asked them to repeat the assessment again after a 3-hour delay. As might be expected, correlations were high (for total energy = .91; for other nutrients, in the range of .81 to .96). When asked to repeat the assessment after 1 week, correlations dropped to .63 for energy, and others ranged from .25 to .75. Memory and striving for consistency are likely to play a large role in repeat assessment separated by a short interval. Rimm et al. (1992) correlated results from food frequency instruments given on two occasions separated by 1 year to 127 male health professionals. Intraclass correlations were .65 for calories and .66 for fat. (Many other correlations are given in the article.) Salvini et al. (1989) gave food frequency instruments to 173 nurses with a 1-year interval between administrations. Mean correlation for frequency of intake of 55 foods was .57 with a range of .24 to .93. Sobell et al. (1989) found mean nutrient intake was plus or minus 10% of nutrient values found on food records for intake 10 to 15 years ago using a 98-item semiquantitative questionnaire. Block, Woods, et al. (1990) compared three 4-day food records with a semiquantitative instrument and found that the questionnaire produced group mean nutrient estimates very similar to the 4-day records, with most correlations in the .5 to .6 range. In the Block comparison, correlations for percentage of calories from fat were .67 and .65 in the two groups in the study. Willett (1990) referred to his 1988 study, which assessed past diet of 150 women with a self-administered food frequency instrument, looking at diet 4 years in the past. He found correlations with food records made 3 to 4 years previously in the range of .44 (total carbohydrate) to .62 (vitamin C). In another study of 173 nurses measured after a 1-year interval (Willett et al., 1985), intraclass correlations using a food frequency instrument on both occasions ranged from .52 for vitamin A to .71 for sucrose. Pietinen et al. (1988b) report a study of 107 men measured at different times separated by 3 months with a food frequency questionnaire. Intraclass correlations ranged from .52 (vitamin A) to .85 (polyunsaturated fat).

Availability. Rimm et al. (1992) have developed an expanded (131-item) semiquantitative questionnaire for use when time is available. Block, Woods, et al. (1990) devised a reduced (60-item) instrument for studies when time is not available for lengthy procedures.

For reprints of the Willett questionnaires, write to Dr. Walter C. Willett, Department of Nutrition, Harvard School of Public Health, 677 Huntington Avenue, Boston, MA 01225.

For reprints of the Block questionnaires, write to Dr. Gladys Block, 419 Warren Hall, School of Public Health, University of California, Berkeley, CA 94720.

Weighing Methods

History. These methods can be extremely accurate but, because of the high degree of interference with normal eating patterns, and the expense of collecting such data, they are not useful for large-scale studies. In the 1930s Widdowson and McCance (1936) performed weighed inventories on individual food intake. In the 1950s, 1960s, and 1970s, Passmore, Thomson, and Warnock (1952), Flores and Garcia (1960), and Pekkarinen (1970) used weighed inventory and aliquot samples to calculate composition of raw foods.

Procedure. There are two types of weighing methods: precise weighing and weighed inventory. Precise weighing involves weighing all food involved in meal preparation including raw food, ingredients, cooked food, consumed food, leftovers, and plate wastes. Aliquot samples of ingredients and of the prepared dish can be taken for precise nutrient analysis. The weighed inventory method is slightly different in that only the prepared, composite dish is weighed. Food is weighed just prior to consumption and plate wastes are weighed at the end of the meal (Fehily, 1983; Marr, 1971). To analyze contents, either aliquot samples or food composition tables may be used (Adelson, 1960; Widdowson, 1936). If the study requires measurement of food ingested in an institutional or research setting, the preparation and weighing can be carried out by research staff (e.g., Porikos, Hesser, & Van Itallie, 1982).

Advantages. Precise weighing can provide the most exact data regarding what was prepared and what was consumed and is sometimes considered to be the "gold standard" (Fehily, 1983). Weighed inventory methods are somewhat easier for subjects to conduct unassisted than are precise weighing methods, provided that subjects are given scales and other equipment needed to carry out the procedures.

Disadvantages. Precise weighing is expensive, requiring scales and measuring devices and possibly close supervision and training of subjects. It cannot be conducted in a large sample as it requires enormous cooperation. Fewer people are likely to volunteer due to the intrusive and onerous nature of the procedures, and therefore the method has limited applicability for epidemiological studies. If carried out for a long enough period of time to assess typical diet, perhaps a week, it can become a considerable burden to subjects. It cannot be easily used for meals eaten away from home. The actual weighing is best done by the investigators because precision might be lost otherwise. Pekkarinen (1970) points out that the work involved in measuring many different foods prepared and eaten in a meal may cause subjects to alter their usual intake by simplifying and reducing the variety and preparation of foods eaten. The weighed inventory procedure is somewhat simpler to carry out, but it too cannot be easily used for meals not eaten at home. As noted by Fehily (1983), response rates for the weighed inventory method are lower than for interviews or questionnaires. Coupled with the additional costs, these procedures are not suitable for epidemiological research.

Best application. Because the success of this method depends on a high level of cooperation from respondents, subjects need to be carefully screened. When it is critical to know the precise amounts of a particular nutrient, this is presumably the most accurate method. It is most easily used for measuring intake during meals taken in an institutional or research setting when weighing can be done, covertly if necessary, by institutional staff.

Validity. Bias may be introduced if a period of time is selected when most of the meals are eaten at home. The time period chosen may not be reflective of the subjects' true eating patterns, which might include more meals in restaurants. Adelson (1960) described just such a situation where a couple chose a week with no social engagements to make it easier to comply with the study.

Direct Observation

History. This method is most often used to measure discrete, countable events related to food ingestion such as number of meals, snacks, mouthfuls, or time spent eating, but it is only occasionally used to measure energy or nutrient intake. Stunkard and Waxman (1981) used direct observation to determine intake of three obese and three nonobese adolescents. More recently, studies have been reported by Madden et al. (1976) and Brown et al. (1990).

Procedure. Subjects are observed or videotaped (sometimes covertly) in cafeteria lines or other dining locations. Researchers then make estimates of portion sizes of each of the foods on a subject's tray or plate. The procedure is facilitated if portion sizes are standardized, as in certain types of food trays or by cafeteria staff. Subsequently, subjects must be observed to determine whether all food is consumed, and, if not, unconsumed portion sizes must be estimated. Energy and nutrient values may then be estimated from food composition data or by aliquot samples from the same source. Interobserver agreement should always be calculated and reported.

 An alternative version of direct observation is the use of food or snack dispensing machines that can be modified to record the time and the item dispensed. This method is sometimes used in metabolic wards and other in-patient or institutional settings (Wurtman, 1990).

Advantages. The greatest advantage is that the method does not rely on self-report and is therefore less prone to self-serving biases and lapses of memory. The risk of biases is still present, however, in that observers may have their own hypothesis about food intake and may unintentionally adjust their records accordingly.

Disadvantages. The method can be obtrusive if videotape cameras or observers are obviously interested in and recording eating behavior. If done in the subject's home, 24-hour surveillance would be required. If done in an institutional setting and the observation is carried out covertly, then some of these problems are alleviated; however, the subject's choices are usually somewhat limited in such settings.

Best application. As mentioned above, the method is most easily applied to variables that can be counted or timed, as, for example, in comparing mouthfuls per minute or snacking patterns of different groups of persons. It is most easily carried out in institutional settings where subjects are likely to eat all their meals in an area accessible to the observer.

Validity and reliability. The method has been compared with 24-hour recalls by Madden et al. (1976) and by Brown et al. (1990). In the latter, interobserver variability in estimates of various nutrients on subjects' trays was acceptably high with correlations ranging from .84 to .98. The average difference in estimates of a nutrient by different observers was 3.7%.

Inferences From
Measures of Energy Expenditure

Doubly Labeled Water ($^2H_2{}^{18}O$)

History. Discovery of the method is credited to Professor Nathan Lifson at the University of Minnesota. Lifson, working in the 1940s and 1950s, made the key observation that oxygen in respiratory carbon dioxide is in isotopic equilibrium with oxygen in the body. At about the same time, the development of mass spectrometers made possible the accurate measurement of isotopes, which is essential to the method. The preparation of isotopes was costly and difficult so that initial applications were to the measurement of metabolic functioning in rodents and birds, which required only small quantities of isotopes. Subsequent refinements by Schoeller (1990b) made practical the application of the method to free-living humans.

Principles of the method. The method determines the amount of energy expended over a period of 10 to 14 days. If body weight and body composition remain stable over that time, then intake must have been equal to expenditure. Alternatively, adjustments can be made based on measurements of changes in body composition.

The subject ingests a quantity of water that is enriched with ^{18}O and ^{2}H, both stable isotopes found naturally in water in concentrations of approximately 2,000 ppm and 150 ppm, respectively. The enrichment raises the concentration of each by about 100 to 200 ppm. An initial measure of concentration in body fluid is taken. During the following days, as body water is lost and replaced with ordinary water, the concentration of these two isotopes in the body declines exponentially toward natural abundance levels.

The concentration of ^{2}H, nearly all of which remains associated with water molecules, decreases as the result of loss of labeled water through evaporation, excretion and secretion, and dilution that occurs with the ingestion of additional, unlabeled water. The slope of the logarithm of ^{2}H enrichment over time indicates the rate of water movement through the subject.

The ^{18}O is also lost as water, but, in addition, some is lost as CO_2. Thus the slope of the line representing ^{18}O elimination is steeper than the line for ^{2}H elimination, and the difference between the two slopes is the result of oxygen lost in CO_2 production.

Having established the amount of CO_2 produced, it may be converted into units of heat by using records or estimates of the composition of food being oxidized, which affects the heat equivalent of each liter of CO_2 produced. The method is described more fully in Prentice (1990) and other publications.

Procedure. The subject's weight and, if possible, body composition (fat and fat-free mass) are measured. The purpose of these measurements is to permit adjustments to be made for changes in energy stores if the subject does not remain weight stable during the measurement period. A measure of total body water is also useful in that it will help in estimating the amount of ^{18}O that must be administered to increase the concentration by a desired amount.

On several days preceding the beginning of the measurement period, the subject provides baseline urine or blood samples to establish naturally occurring levels of ^{2}H and ^{18}O; then, on the day beginning the measurement period, he or she ingests a small amount of water (approximately 100 ml) containing the required quantity of each isotope. After about 3 hours, the labeled water will have adequately dispersed and equilibrated throughout the body water pool and another sample of urine or blood is taken to determine the isotope concentration at the start of the study.

Additional samples of body fluid are then taken at intervals throughout the study period, or, alternatively, several samples are taken at the beginning and several at the end. The samples are analyzed in a mass spectrometer to determine the amount of isotope in each sample and a regression line is fitted to the ^2H and ^{18}O enrichment data.

To convert CO_2 production to heat, food records may be kept to determine the food quotient, or an average value (.85, the ratio of oxygen consumed to carbon dioxide produced to metabolize food) may be assumed. The caloric expenditure is then calculated using the Weir equation (Weir, 1949). The energy balance equation is then used to calculate intake from expenditure and changes in storage.

Validity. The method requires several assumptions, none of which is critical; even with violations, the error is generally less than 10% (Prentice, 1990). Among these are that total body water remain constant during the study period, that loss of $^2H^{18}O$ occurs only via water and carbon dioxide, and that storage of $^2H^{18}O$ is negligible. Changes in background levels of ^2H and ^{18}O as a consequence of changing food and water sources during the study can also introduce error. Validation studies that compared energy expenditure measured by doubly labeled water with traditional direct CO_2 measures on small mammals and birds have found an average error within $\pm6\%$. Human models proposed by Schoeller (1990a) and Coward (1988) are accurate to 1%-3% in assessing energy expenditure.

Calculation of intake requires either that energy stores have not changed or a measurement of the amount of change in the fat and fat-free compartments. Changes in storage are converted to energy at the rate of 9 calories per gram of fat and 1 calorie per gram of carbohydrate, respectively. Thus the validity of the measurement of intake is also dependent on the validity of the body composition measurement technique used. If hydrostatic weighing or dual-energy X-ray absorptiometry (DEXA) are used to determine body composition changes, measurement error is on the order of $\pm2\%$.

Technical issues aside, perhaps the greatest threat to validity is the subject's reaction to being measured, which may result in atypical intakes and activity levels during the study period.

Reliability. The precision of the method for assessment of energy expenditure is in the range of 2%-8%. The method that uses repeated samples of body fluid collected throughout the entire measurement period yields 2%-3% better precision than the method that uses only samples taken at the beginning and end of the measurement period (Prentice, 1990).

Advantages. No other method allows for such an accurate measurement of total energy expenditure (and hence energy intake) in free-living persons. Because the isotopes are stable, no radiation or danger is involved. Results are not vulnerable to distortion or misrepresentation by the subject except insofar as the subject changes activities or intake during the period of the study.

Disadvantages. The principal disadvantage is the cost of the isotopes (over $300 per subject in 1993) and the necessity for sophisticated mass spectrometry to measure the isotopes. Also, the subject must cooperate in the collection of periodic samples of body fluid. If weight is not stable, measures of body composition must be made to calculate intake.

Labeled Bicarbonate Method

Another technique for calculating energy expenditure using isotopic dilution is the labeled bicarbonate method. This approach, like doubly labeled water, permits measurement of energy expenditure over 1- to 2-day periods in free-living subjects. As with doubly labeled water, total energy expenditure is equivalent to energy intake in weight stable subjects. Caloric values as estimated by food records kept during the infusion period can be compared with actual energy expenditure as measured by this technique.

Principles of the method. Carbon dioxide labeled with [14]carbon is infused intravenously as bicarbonate. The labeled bicarbonate is "diluted" in the body by metabolically produced CO_2. The labeled CO_2 can then be recovered from expired air and from urine (Elia, 1991). Recovered CO_2 is used to calculate total CO_2 production by comparison with the amount of labeled bicarbonate administered. In practice, the only required measurement is of labeled urea appearing in urine. This is used to correct the total counts administered for CO_2 metabolism other than that for energy expenditure, that is, carbon and oxygen used by the body for functions other than energy production.

This estimate of CO_2 produced can be used to estimate energy expenditure as described in the doubly labeled water section. Assessment of CO_2 production and the energy equivalent of carbon dioxide is required (Elia, 1991). Depending on the substrate being oxidized, there can be variation in the energy equivalent of CO_2. The oxidation of fat, for example, expends more energy per unit of CO_2 than occurs with carbohydrate oxidation.

Procedure. Resting metabolic rate is measured and the dose of bicarbonate is administered. The procedure uses a 24- to 48-hour continuous, subcutaneous infusion using a minipump, similar to an insulin infusion pump. This is generally placed at the suprailiac skinfold. One urine sample is collected postinfusion at 24 to 48 hours. The specific activity of urinary urea is then measured, that is, how much of the isotope is found in the urinary area.

Advantages and disadvantages. This technique enjoys several advantages over the doubly labeled water method in that it is far less expensive and can be accomplished in a shorter time frame. Tests as short as 1 hour can be performed, and longer-term measurements up to 5 days are also possible. It does not require tedious collection and freezing of urine by subjects. However, the infusion of bicarbonate necessitates the use of a continuous infusion pump, which could be uncomfortable for the subject.

It is important to point out that there are two forms of the isotope carbon 14: the stable form and the radioactive isotope. The stable isotope requires a very large dose for effective use, and this in turn is quite expensive. Alternatively, the radioactive isotope requires a minuscule dose of 3 cc over a 48-hour period but results in some exposure, although minimal, of 12.5 microcuries. Use of the radioactive isotope, due to the minute requisite dose, is extremely inexpensive.

There has been very little work using this technique in the United States. For more detailed descriptions of the bicarbonate method, see Elia (1991; Elia, Fuller, & Murgatroyd, 1988, 1992).

Problems Related to Data Entry and Computation of Nutrient Values

Many of the methods discussed in this chapter require the entry of data for computer analysis. This step increases the opportunity for error. Encoding errors may occur when intake is encoded for entry into a database, and transcription errors when data are put into machine readable form. Once data are entered, analysis of nutrient content is performed using a microcomputer analysis program (such as Nutritionist IV from N-Squared Computing, Salem, OR; the Minnesota Nutrition Data System from Univ. of Minn. Nutrition Coordinating Ctr., Minneapolis, MN; DINE for Windows from DINE System, Amherst, NY; the Food Processor 5.0 from WSHA Research, Salem, OR; and many others. Prices range from several hundred to several thousands of dollars). The best systems require little or no conversion of measurement units. They also have the most current analysis of the nutrient contents of foods and include fast foods as well as foods specific to particular ethnic groups and unusual food items. Because there is no uniform agreement on nutrient composition of foods, databases may provide somewhat different analyses of the same intake data.

An alternative to food composition calculations is the direct chemical analysis of aliquot samples of food. This is prohibitively expensive in all but the smallest studies. Whiting and Leverton (1960) present the results of a literature review of 300 cases where concurrent lab analysis and calculated values are reported. The two methods disagreed by more than 10% in 42% of the cases for kilocalories and in 75% of the cases for fat.

Concluding Remarks

Often, the investigator's choice of a food intake measure will be determined by some major consideration such as the amount of time and money available, whether the instrument must be self-administered, or other factors mentioned at the beginning of this chapter. For those fortunate enough to have a choice between two or more instruments, the existing literature provides only rough guidelines. The results of existing studies of suitability for a given application and population, reliability, and validity have not been systematic enough to permit the development of an adequate science of food intake measurement. The broad outlines of such a science are visible—considerations of cognitive functioning (e.g., errors of memory), social desirability (underreporting of socially disapproved foods), self-serving distortions (underreporting of intake by the obese), and so on—but the degree to which these and other factors will introduce error into a planned study cannot be adequately anticipated. At present, the reporting of such data, whether total energy, macro- or micronutrients, specific foods or food groups are presented and whether they are compared in terms of group mean differences, product-moment correlations, rank correlations, or percentage of subjects differing by more than an arbitrarily chosen percentage is at the discretion and choice of the investigator. It is important that future validation studies, especially comparing self-report methods with results of direct observation or stable isotope measures, present results in a manner that permits an adequate evaluation of group mean differences, constant bias, how differences change with initial values, and how differences might be related to characteristics of the sample under investigation. This might be done by presenting regressions of one intake measure on another and giving slopes, intercepts, and confidence intervals (see, for example, Bland & Altman, 1986).

Perhaps the future will provide economical methods for the measurement of direct biochemical markers of macro- and micronutrient status and even of specific foods, in a manner similar to the doubly labeled water technique now available for total energy intake. For the present, however, we must make a more concerted effort to identify the sources and types of error that contaminate our self-report intake measures. Because they are so easily employed and have such apparent face validity, they will probably remain with us for a long time.

References

Abraham, D., Carroll, M. D., Dresser, C. M., & Johnson, C. L. (1979). *Dietary intake source data: United States, 1971-74* (National Center for Health Statistics, DHEW Pub. No. [PHS] 79-1221). Hyattsville, MD: Public Health Service.

Adelson, S. (1960). Some problems in collecting dietary data from individuals. *Journal of the American Dietetic Association, 36*, 453-461.

Beaton, G. H., Milner, J., Corey, P., McGuire, V., Cousins, M., Stewart, E., de Ramos, M., Hewitt, D., Grambsch, P. V., Kassim, N., & Little, J. A. (1979). Sources of variance in 24-hour dietary recall data: Implications for nutrition study design and interpretation. *American Journal of Clinical Nutrition, 32*, 2456-2559.

Bland, J. M., & Altman, D. G. (1986). Statistical methods for assessing agreement between two methods of clinical measurement. *The Lancet, I*, 307-310.

Block, G., Hartman, A. M., Dresser, C. M., Carroll, M. D., Gannon, J., & Gardner, L. (1986). A data-based approach to diet questionnaire design and testing. *American Journal of Epidemiology, 124*, 453-469.

Block, G., Hartman, A., & Naughton, D. (1990). A reduced dietary questionnaire: Development and validation. *Epidemiology, 1*, 58-64.

Block, G., Woods, M., Potosky, A., & Clifford, C. (1990). Validation of a self-administered diet history questionnaire using multiple diet records. *Journal of Clinical Epidemiology, 43*, 1327-1335.

Bloemberg, B. P. M., Kromhout, D., Oberman-De Boer, G. L., & Van Kamper-Donker, M. (1989). The reproducibility of dietary intake data assessed with the cross-check dietary history method. *American Journal of Epidemiology, 130*, 1047-1056.

Brown, J. E., Tharp, T. M., Dahlberg-Luby, E. M., et al. (1990). Videotape dietary assessment: Validity, reliability, and comparison of results with 24-hour dietary recalls from elderly women in a retirement home. *Journal of the American Dietetic Association, 90*, 1675-1679.

Burke, B. S. (1947). The dietary history as a tool in research. *Journal of the American Dietetic Association, 23*, 1041-1046.

Burke, B. S., & Stuart, H. C. (1938). A method of diet analysis: Application in research and pediatric practice. *Journal of Pediatrics, 12*, 493-495.

Byers, T., Marshall, J., Fiedler, R., Zielezny, M., & Graham, S. (1985). Assessing nutrient intake with an abbreviated dietary interview. *American Journal of Epidemiology, 122*, 41-50.

Coward, W. A. (1988). The doubly-labelled water ($^2H_2$ ^{18}O) method: Principles and practice. *Proceedings of the Nutrition Society, 47*, 209-218.

Dawber, T. R., Pearson, G., Anderson, P., Mann, G. V., Kannel, W. B., Shurtleff, D., & McNamara, P. (1962). Dietary assessment in the epidemiologic study of coronary heart disease: The Framingham Study. *American Journal of Clinical Nutrition, 11*, 226-234.

Dwyer, J. T. (1994). Assessment of dietary intake. In M. E. Shils, J. A. Olson, & M. Shike (Eds.), *Modern nutrition in health and disease* (pp. 842-860). Philadelphia: Lea & Feibiger.

Eck, L. H., Klesges, R. C., Hanson, C. L., Slawson, D., & Lavasque, M. E. (1991). Measuring short-term dietary intake: Development and testing of a 1-week food frequency question-naire. *Journal of the American Dietetic Association, 91*, 940-945.

Elia, M. (1991). Energy equivalents of CO_2 and their importance in assessing energy expenditure when using tracer techniques. *American Journal of Physiology, 260*, E75-E88.

Elia, M., Fuller, N., & Murgatroyd, P. (1988). The potential use of the labelled bicarbonate method for estimating energy expenditure in man. *Proceedings of the Nutrition Society, 47*, 247-258.

Elia, M., Fuller, N. J., & Murgatroyd, P. R. (1992). Measurement of bicarbonate turnover in humans: Applicability to estimation of energy expenditure. *American Journal of Physiology, 261*, E676-E687.

Fehily, A. M. (1983). Epidemiology for nutritionists: 4 survey methods. *Human Nutrition: Applied Nutrition, 37A*, 419-425.

Flores, M., & Garcia, B. (1960). The nutritional status of children of pre-school age in the Guatemalan community of Amatitlan: 1. Comparison of family and child diets. *British Journal of Nutrition, 14*, 207-215.

Freedman, L. S., Carroll, R. J., & Wax, Y. (1991). Estimating the relation between dietary intake obtained from a food frequency questionnaire and true average intake. *American Journal of Epidemiology, 134*, 310-320.

Garn, S. M., Larkin, F. A., & Cole, P. R. (1976). The problem with one-day dietary intakes. *Ecology of Food and Nutrition, 5*, 245-247.

Jain, M., Howe, G. R., Johnson, K. C., & Miller, A. B. (1980). Evaluation of a diet history questionnaire for epidemiologic studies. *American Journal of Epidemiology, 111*, 212-219.

Kissileff, H. R. (1992). Where should human eating be studied and what should be measured? *Appetite, 19*, 61-68.

Lansky, D., & Brownell, K. D. (1982). Estimates of food quantity and calories: Errors in self-report among obese patients. *American Journal of Clinical Nutrition, 35*, 727-732.

Lichtman, S., Pisarska, K., Berman, E. R., Pestone, M., Dowling, H., Offenbacher, E., Weisel, H., Heshka, S., Matthews, D., & Heymsfield, S. B. (1992). Discrepancy between self reported and actual caloric intake and exercise in obese subjects. *New England Journal of Medicine, 327*(27), 1839-1848.

Livingstone, M. B. E., Prentice, A. M., Strain, J. J., et al. (1990). Accuracy of weighed dietary records in studies of diet and health. *British Medical Journal, 300*, 708-712.

Madden, J. P., Goodman, S. J., & Guthrie, H. A. (1976). Validity of the 24-hour recall. *Journal of the American Dietetic Association, 68*, 143-147.

Marr, J. W. (1971). Individual dietary surveys: Purposes and methods. *World Review of Nutrition and Dietetics, 23*, 105-164. (Karger: Basel)

McKeown-Eyssen, G. E., Yeung, K. S., & Bright-See, E. (1986). Assessment of past diet in epidemiologic studies. *American Journal of Epidemiology, 124*, 94-103.

Meiselman, H. L. (1992). Methodology and theory in human eating research. *Appetite, 19*, 49-55.

Mook, D. G. (1983). In defense of external invalidity. *American Psychologist, 38*, 379-387.

Nelson, M., Black, A. E., Morris, J. A., & Cole, T. J. (1989). Between- and within-subject variation in nutrient intake from infancy to old age: Estimating the number of days required to rank dietary intakes with desired precision. *American Journal of Clinical Nutrition, 50*, 155-167.

Passmore, R., Thomson, J. G., & Warnock, G. M. (1952). A balance sheet of the estimation of energy intake and energy expenditure as measured by indirect calorimetry, using the Kofranyi-Michaelis calorimeter. *British Journal of Nutrition, 6*, 253-264.

Pekkarinen, M. (1970). Methodology in the collection of food consumption data. *World Review of Nutrition and Dietetics, 12*, 145-171. (Karger: Basel)

Pietinen, P., Hartman, A. M., Haapa, E., Rasanen, L., Haapakoski, J., Palmgren, J., Albanes, D., Virtamo, J., & Huttunen, J. K. (1988a). Reproducibility and validity of dietary assessment instruments I. *American Journal of Epidemiology, 128*, 655-666.

Pietinen, P., Hartman, A. M., Haapa, E., Rasanen, L., Haapakoski, J., Palmgren, J., Albanes, D., Virtamo, J., & Huttunen, J. K. (1988b). Reproducibility and validity of dietary assessment instruments II. *American Journal of Epidemiology, 128*, 666-676.

Porikos, K., Hesser, M. F., & Van Itallie, T. B. (1982). Caloric regulation in normal-weight men maintained on a palatable diet of conventional foods. *Physiology and Behavior, 29*, 293-300.

Prentice, A. M. (Ed.). (1990, September 17). *The doubly-labeled water method for measuring energy expenditure.* NAHRES-4, International Atomic Energy Commission, Vienna.

Rimm, E. B., Giovannucci, E. L., Stampfer, M. J., Colditz, G. A., Litin, L. B., & Willett, W. C. (1992). Reproducibility and validity of an expanded self-administered semiquantitative food frequency questionnaire among male health professionals. *American Journal of Epidemiology, 135*, 1114-1126.

Salvini, A., Hunter, D. J., Sampson, L., Stampfer, M. J., Colditz, G., Rosner, B., & Willett, W. C. (1989). Food-based validation of a dietary questionnaire: The effects of week-to-week variation in food consumption. *International Journal of Epidemiology, 18*, 858-867.

Schoeller, D. A. (1990a). How accurate is self-reported dietary energy intake? *Nutrition Reviews, 48*, 373-378.

Schoeller, D. A. (1990b, September 17). Mass spectrometric analysis. In A. M. Prentice (Ed.), *The doubly-labeled water method for measuring energy expenditure.* NAHRES-4, International Atomic Energy Commission, Vienna.

Sempos, C. T. (1992). Invited commentary: Some limitations of semiquantitative food frequency questionnaires. *American Journal of Epidemiology, 135*(10), 1127-1132.

Smucker, R., Block, G., Coyle, L., Harvin, A., & Kessler, L. (1989). A dietary and risk factor questionnaire and analysis system for personal computers. *American Journal of Epidemiology, 129*, 445-449.

Sobell, J., Block, G., Koslowe, P., Tobin, J., & Andres, R. (1989). Validation of retrospective questionnaire assessing diet 10-15 years ago. *American Journal of Epidemiology, 130*, 173-187.

Stunkard, A., & Waxman, M. (1981). Accuracy of self-reports of food intake. *Journal of the American Dietetic Association, 79*, 547-551.

Tarasuk, V., & Beaton, G. (1992). Statistical estimation of dietary parameters: Implications of patterns in within-subject variation—A case study of sampling strategies. *American Journal of Clinical Nutrition, 55*, 22-27.

Tillotson, J. L., Gorder, D. D., & Kassim, N. (1981). Nutrition data collection in the Multiple Risk Factor Intervention Trial (MRFIT): Baseline nutrient intake of a randomized population. *Journal of the American Dietetic Association, 78*, 235-240.

Weir, J. B. de V. (1949). New methods for calculating metabolic rate with special reference to protein metabolism. *Journal of Physiology, 109*, 1-9.

Whiting, M. G., & Leverton, N. M. (1960). Reliability of dietary appraisal: Comparisons between laboratory analysis and calculation from tables of food values. *American Journal of Public Health, 50*, 813-823.

Widdowson, E. M. (1936). A study of English diets by the individual method: Part I. Men. *Journal of Hygiene, 36*, 269-292.

Widdowson, E. M., & McCance, R. A. (1936). A study of English diets by the individual method: Part II. Women. *Journal of Hygiene, 36*, 293-309.

Willett, W. (1990). *Nutritional epidemiology.* New York: Oxford University Press.

Willett, W., Sampson, L., Browne, M., Stampfer, M. J., Rosner, B., Hennekens, C. H., & Speizer, F. E. (1988). The use of a self-administered questionnaire to assess diet four years in the past. *American Journal of Epidemiology, 127,* 188-199.

Willett, W. C., Sampson, L., Stampfer, M. J., Rosner, B., Bain, C., Witschi, J., Hennekens, C. H., & Speizer, F. E. (1985). Reproducibility and validity of a semiquantitative food frequency questionnaire. *American Journal of Epidemiology, 122,* 51-65.

Wurtman, J. J. (1990). Carbohydrate craving: Relationship between carbohydrate intake and disorders of mood. *Drugs, 39*(Suppl.), 49-52.

8

Assessment of Specific Eating Behaviors and Eating Style

DAVID G. SCHLUNDT

There are many questions about human food intake for which we have little scientific data. How often do people eat? Are three meals a day typical, or are there other patterns of eating that are common? How much day-to-day variation is there in eating behaviors? Are some people more variable than others? For each person, is there a typical meal pattern? When and under what circumstances do people deviate from their usual eating pattern? How can we describe these deviations? How common are behaviors such as overeating, snacking, meal skipping, and binge eating? Are there certain times, places, or situations that are associated with typical and atypical eating behaviors? Is there such a thing as an eating style? If so, what are the various styles and how common are they? Are there a basic set of parameters that can be used to describe a person's eating style? Is there a relationship between eating style and obesity, diabetes, anorexia, bulimia, or other important medical and psychological conditions? Is eating responsive to internal cues, external cues, or both? Is there a way to characterize the antecedents that influence a particular eating behavior? How important are biological, behavioral, and cultural variables in food intake regulation?

In this chapter, I will review the assessment of specific eating behaviors and eating style and will review and evaluate specific measures. I hope also to illustrate that there are many aspects of eating for which there are no currently accepted methods of assessment.

Microanalysis of Eating

All animals, being incapable of photosynthesis, must take in energy to sustain life. Any individual or species that does not successfully feed will perish. Specialized feeding structures emerged early in the evolutionary record, and species evolved to fill different feeding niches. Across animal species, there is tremendous variation in feeding behavior.

Although the biology of human feeding has deep evolutionary roots, human eating behavior is also characterized by tremendous adaptability and plasticity. The human organism can survive and prosper on diets that vary tremendously in the foods eaten and in macronutrient composition. Eating is not just something people do to survive. For people, eating has personal, and cultural, meanings. Human eating is a complex behavior influenced by cognitive, environmental, biological, and emotional variables (see Schlundt, Hill, Sbrocco, Pope-Cordle, & Kasser, 1990).

How can we characterize important individual differences in people's food intake? There are two steps involved in the assessment of food intake: (a) gathering information on food-related behaviors and (b) processing this information to extract qualitative or quantitative measures that characterize individual differences.

Several methods are commonly used to gather data on people's eating behavior, including the following:

1. 24-hour recalls (Rush & Kristal, 1982)
2. Diet histories (Block, 1982; Underwood, 1986)
3. Food frequency questionnaires (Sampson, 1985)
4. Questionnaires that ask subjects to rate eating behaviors such as binge eating (Hawkins & Clement, 1980) or weight regulation (Schlundt & Zimering, 1988; Stunkard & Messick, 1985)
5. Eating diaries (Block, 1982; Schlundt, 1989; Underwood, 1986)

Several methods can be used to characterize individual differences in eating behavior, including the following:

1. Nutrient density analysis (Block, 1982; Hoover, 1983; Sorenson, Calkins, Connolly, & Diamond, 1985)
2. Food group analysis (Axelson, 1986; Brewer et al., 1987; Suitor & Crowley, 1984)
3. Hypothetical constructs such as dietary restraint (Stunkard & Messick, 1985) or severity of binge eating (Hawkins & Clement, 1980)

Traditionally, food intake has been characterized using measures of central tendency. The question addressed is this: "What is this person's typical or usual eating behavior like?"

Many aspects of human eating behavior are not easily captured by an average. Traditional approaches cannot characterize the variability in food intake over time. This problem is not quite solved by computing a within-person standard deviation or standard error. Repeated observations using diaries or recalls can be used to measure the variability of an individual's behavior (Sempos, Johnson, Smith, & Gilligan, 1985). However, some temporal patterns and qualitative aspects of eating behavior are not captured by simple measures of variability.

Detailed study of the variation in eating behavior over time is called the "microanalysis of food intake" (Blundell & Hill, 1986; Schlundt, 1985, 1989). The basic unit of analysis is the eating episode and a variety of constructs and measures can be used to differentiate one eating episode from another. For example, eating episodes can be classified into discrete meals (breakfast, lunch, supper, snacks). Meals can also be characterized using temporal parameters such as meal duration, meal frequency, or intermeal interval. Schlundt (1985) suggested that a functional analysis of behavior, involving the study of how eating behaviors are influenced by antecedents and consequences, can be applied to the microanalysis of eating. Antecedents and consequences can be environmental, behavioral, physiological, or emotional events. The goals of functional analysis are to describe how qualities of eating behavior vary with the internal and environmental context (see Schlundt & Johnson, 1990).

Using Behavioral Diaries to Assess Eating Style

Next, we will examine the use of behavioral diaries to assess eating. This overview will establish a basic set of measures or parameters for the microanalysis of food intake and serve as a standard against which questionnaire measures of eating can be evaluated.

Self-monitoring has been used for many years as a behavioral assessment strategy. Basically, the subject keeps a record of one or more target behaviors as they occur. Typically, self-monitoring is used to collect information on the base rate of problem behaviors and to evaluate the impact of treatment on the behavior problem (see Lindsley, 1968). Self-monitoring has been used with many behaviors including eating (Schlundt, Johnson, & Jarrell, 1985), smoking (Glasgow, Klesges, Godding, & Gegelman, 1983), bruxism (Rosen, 1981), blood pressure (Beiman, Graham, & Ciminero, 1978), alcohol intake (Miller, 1981), and sleep patterns (Bootzin & Engle-Friedman, 1981). Self-monitoring can also be combined with the collection of physiological data such as in ambulatory blood pressure monitoring (Weber & Drayer, 1984). According to Haynes (1984), it is one of the most cost-efficient and clinically useful behavioral assessment techniques.

Three major problems with self-monitoring are as follows:

1. It is difficult to verify the accuracy of self-monitored data.
2. Some subjects will not comply with self-monitoring procedures.
3. The act of self-monitoring may affect the behavior being observed.

Although these are potentially serious problems, there are no assessment approaches without drawbacks. When using self-monitoring, efforts should be made to minimize these problems. If the forms are designed carefully, and if subjects are properly trained and motivated, accurate self-monitoring can be achieved. The reactivity can be either minimized or enhanced depending on whether the self-monitoring is intended for data collection or behavior change. In addition, self-monitoring data should be supplemented by data collected through the use of other methods such as direct observation or questionnaires.

Microanalysis of Eating Behavior
Using the Self-Monitoring Analysis System

In this section, assessment of eating behavior using the Self-Monitoring Analysis System (SMAS) will be described in detail. The detailed description will fulfill two purposes: (a) to present the program and its capabilities and (b) to describe a set of behavioral parameters useful for evaluating questionnaire measures of eating behavior and eating style.

Time _____ Date _____ Day (Mo Tu We Th Fr Sa Su)

Meal (Break Lunch Supper Snack) Place (Home Work Restaurant Social-Event Car Other)

People (Family Friend Alone Other)

Feelings (check all that apply)

___ Depressed	___ Afraid	___ Bored
___ Worried	___ Stressed	___ Angry
___ Irritable	___ Upset	___ Happy
___ Nervous	___ Excited	___ Tired
___ Challenged	___ In Pain	___ Sick
___ Hungry	___ Weak	___ Intoxicated

Craving Sweets   (Yes _____ No _____)   Tempted to overeat (Yes _____ No _____)

Forbidden foods available   (Yes _____ No _____)   Impulsive eating (Yes _____ No _____)

Did you overeat? (Yes _____ No _____)

Food Description	Prepared	Amount
_____	_____	_____
_____	_____	_____
_____	_____	_____
_____	_____	_____
_____	_____	_____
_____	_____	_____
_____	_____	_____
_____	_____	_____
_____	_____	_____
_____	_____	_____
_____	_____	_____

Carbohydrate _____   Protein _____   Fat _____

Figure 8.1. Vanderbilt Food Diary

Weight management diary. Figure 8.1 presents a behavioral eating diary that we have used in several weight-loss studies (J. O. Hill et al., 1989; Schlundt, Hill, Sbrocco, Pope-Cordle, & Sharp, 1992; Schlundt, Hill, et al., 1993). This form is used to create a booklet containing 30-40 pages. Each meal or snack is recorded on a separate page of the diary. The diary then provides a sequential record of food intake over a period of time.

When using this diary, subjects were given a food counter and a booklet containing hundreds of common foods and their nutritional content, and were taught to use this counter to record the nutrient content of each food consumed. Alternatively, subjects can code foods using food groups or the investigator can analyze subjects' food descriptions using nutritional analysis software (see Wolper, Heshka, & Heymsfield, this volume).

The diaries are then entered into a computer database using the Self-Monitoring Analysis System (SMAS), which is software developed specifically for the management and analysis of self-monitoring data (see Schlundt, 1989; Schlundt & Bell, 1987; Schlundt & Johnson, 1990). The data for each subject are placed in order of occurrence in a separate file. Each record in the file represents a single meal or snack. The result is a sequential record of all reported meals along with information on the context of each meal.

The SMAS consists of three related programs written in Borland's Turbo Pascal version 3.0 (Borland International, 1985). SETUP is a program that can be used to design databases and data entry screens. ENTER is then used to input and edit data. SUMMARY is then used to access, analyze, and summarize the data. SUMMARY takes a file of instructions or commands that are executed on one or more data files. SUMMARY creates printed results or can be used to create additional data files for further statistical analysis. Table 8.1 summarizes the commands that are available in version 4.0 of SUMMARY.

Compliance with record keeping. In our weight loss studies, all subjects completed a 2-week baseline diary to qualify for participation. Using these recruitment procedures, complete records were obtained from all subjects at baseline. Between 20% and 30% of subjects receiving baseline diaries at a first orientation meeting did not return. However, it is impossible to tell why these people did not enroll in the study. No doubt, some did not return because they could not or would not complete the diaries. There are many other reasons for not wanting to participate in research involving random assignment to treatments along with demanding time commitments.

Of the 96 subjects randomized into two clinical studies, 77 subjects (80%) completed all follow-up data collection (J. O. Hill et al., 1989; Schlundt et al., 1992). Schlundt, Langford, and McDonel (1985) reviewed 36 weight loss studies and reported a mean dropout rate of 25%. For subjects completing our studies, 94% of the expected diaries (1/week for 11 weeks) were turned in. Only 30% of the expected diaries were received from dropouts. Overall, 82% of the total number of expected diaries were completed when all subjects are combined.

If people are screened for a research program by requiring completion of a diary, then compliance with diary keeping is excellent for those who complete the program. Even when data from dropouts are included, the diaries provide data for about 80% of all days during the study period.

TABLE 8.1 Commands for SUMMARY Version 4.0

Command	Description
CATPLOT	Calculates the probability of each category of a categorical variable and generates a plot
INTCAT	Calculates the mean value of a numerical variable for each category of a categorical variable and generates a plot
CROSSTAB	Calculates the joint frequency distribution of two categorical variables, computes probabilities and conditional probabilities, performs chi-square test, and prints table
EXCLUDE	Used to select a subset of records for analysis
LIST	Lists the data as stored in the database file
QSCORE	Creates new variables that are linear combinations of existing variables
REVERSE	Reverses rating scales
PLOTVARS	Generates a plot of a variable separately for each record in a file
MULTICON	Multivariate log-linear contingency table analysis used to fit models to categorical data
LAG	Creates new variables that are time-lagged for use in sequential analysis
BREAK	For sequential analysis, can be used to detect breaks in temporal sequences
CORREL	Calculates and prints the Pearson correlation between two numerical variables
DISPLAY	Writes selected variable from memory to printer or to an ASCII file. Can be used to export data sets to other software
UPDATE	Writes a new definition file and creates a new data file that includes created or modified variables
OUTFILE	Calculates statistics and outputs to an ASCII data file. Writes an SPSS-PC program with DATA LIST and VARIABLE LABELS commands
M	Outputs a conditional mean
P	Outputs a conditional probability
V	Outputs conditional standard deviation
X	Outputs an unconditional mean
S	Outputs a standard deviation
N	Outputs the total number of observations in a file
F	Outputs a probability
C	Conducts a coefficient of variation analysis and outputs results
A	Computes an autocorrelation coefficient
LUMP	Collapses the categories of a categorical variable
RATIO	Creates a new variable that is the ratio of two variables
STATDEV	Creates a new variable and codes each record according to its z-score
RECODE	Uses ranges on a numerical variable to create a categorical variable
PATTERN	Compares a set of variables to a prescribed pattern and computes a compliance coefficient
CLEAR	Removes all previous exclusions
VARLIST	Outputs a complete list of all variables currently loaded into memory
INTERACT	Takes SMAS commands interactively
DAYTOTAL	Uses a date variable to create a new variable that represents the daily total of a numerical variable
EVENT	Uses a list of variables to define the occurrence of an event and creates a new variable reflecting the presence or absence of that event
INTERVAL	Creates a variable that contains the interevent intervals

NOTE: Information concerning the availability of SMAS can be obtained from David Schlundt, Ph.D., Department of Psychology, 301 Wilson Hall, Vanderbilt University, Nashville, TN 37240; tel. (615) 322-7800, FAX (615) 343-8449.

Accuracy of self-recorded nutrient intake. We have asked subjects to use food counters to quantify their food intake in terms of calories, macronutrient grams, or food groups. How accurate are these people in looking up and calculating these values?

Diary entries for 34 subjects were selected for computer nutrient analysis (J. O. Hill et al., 1989). One-day diary entries were selected from baseline, as well as the final week of the program, for all subjects. Complete food intake for each selected day was entered into the Food Processor II nutrient analysis program (ESHA Research, 1987). Daily nutrient values were also estimated from subjects' reports of the number of servings from each of six food groups plus alcohol. Nutrient results for 124 days were obtained using these methods.

Mean daily intake was computed using subjects' food group coding and computer nutrient analysis for grams of protein, carbohydrates, and fats; total calorie intake; and percentage of kcal from protein, carbohydrates, and fats. Table 8.2 presents the means and standard deviations of these variables along with the mean difference scores. The mean values obtained from the two methods were very similar. The variability of nutrient estimates is greater using the food group method than using the computer nutrient analysis. Although group means were very similar using the two methods, the standard deviations of the discrepancy scores suggest that the two methods can yield very different estimates for a single subject on a single day. Table 8.2 also shows moderate to strong correlations between nutrient estimates obtained using the two methods.

Objective measures of eating: Nutritional composition and dietary compliance. In this section, we examine objective measures that can be derived from subjects' reports of foods consumed. Two data sets will be used to illustrate these measures. The obese sample consists of 2-week pretreatment diaries from 80 obese women described by Schlundt, Virts, et al. (1993). The diabetes sample consists of 4 weeks of diaries from 29 patients with insulin dependent diabetes mellitus (IDDM) who earned a small honorarium for keeping the diaries (see Schlundt, 1988).

First, each meal or snack can be described in terms of its nutritional composition. Table 8.3 presents means, standard deviations, and test-retest reliabilities for both the obese and the diabetic data samples. Test-retest reliabilities were computed by comparing Monday, Wednesday, Friday, and Sunday with Tuesday, Thursday, and Saturday.

Food intake for the two samples was similar, with the obese subjects eating slightly larger meals with higher percentages of calories from fat and lower amounts from carbohydrates. The reliability coefficients were higher for the diabetic subjects than the obese subjects. The greater reliability in estimating nutritional intake may reflect the fact that 4 weeks of data were col-

TABLE 8.2 Comparison of Computer Nutrient Analysis and Food Group Methods for Estimating Macronutrients

Variable	Mean	SD	r
Cho gm Nutrient Analysis	151.01	63.90	
Cho gm Food Group	150.99	73.08	
Cho discrepancy	0.02	45.32	.789
Pro gm Nutrient Analysis	67.90	21.27	
Pro gm Food Group	65.03	23.80	
Pro discrepancy	2.87	16.96	.722
Fat gm Nutrient Analysis	45.55	36.80	
Fat gm Food Group	44.52	37.50	
Fat discrepancy	1.03	18.95	.870
Total Kcal Nutrient Analysis	1263.39	578.06	
Total Kcal Food Group	1272.81	651.09	
Kcal discrepancy	−9.42	255.78	.920
% Kcal Cho Nutrient Analysis	48.17	11.00	
% Cho Food Group	48.99	10.88	
% Kcal discrepancy	−0.82	9.01	.661
% Kcal Pro Nutrient Analysis	23.05	7.42	
% Kcal Pro Food Group	22.08	5.53	
% Kcal Pro discrepancy	0.97	4.84	.744
% Kcal Fat Nutrient Analysis	28.53	12.17	
% Kcal Fat Food Group	28.58	10.42	
% Kcal Fat discrepancy	−0.05	8.90	.699

lected from the diabetic subjects compared with 2 weeks for the obese women. It may also reflect greater day-to-day consistency in the behavior of diabetic subjects.

If patients have been given a meal plan or diet to follow, it is possible to use the SMAS command PATTERN to compute an index that summarizes the match between prescribed and actual intake. The SMAS also has a procedure (STATDEV) that allows the user to mark certain meals as deviant or unusual. For example, it is possible to identify all suppers that are more than one standard deviation higher or lower in calories than the individual's usual supper intake. These deviation measures can be based on any quantitative variable that describes food intake.

Table 8.4 presents the compliance index and calorie deviance measure for the diabetes sample. Clearly, compliance was worse at lunch and supper. Meals that are more than one standard deviation above the person's usual intake were identified as overeating 30% of the time compared with only 7% of meals that were more than one standard deviation below the subject's usual intake. Statistically deviant meals were characterized as highly noncom-

TABLE 8.3 Nutrient Values for Obese and Diabetic Subjects

Nutrient	Obese (n = 80)			Diabetic (n = 28)		
	Mean	SD	Test-Retest	Mean	SD	Test-Retest
Calories	595	143	.85	472	111	.92
Carbohydrate Grams	57	16	.85	46	10	.87
Protein Grams	23	6	.79	20	5	.92
Fat Grams	27	9	.84	21	7	.90
% Kcal Carb	43	7	.69	45	6	.83
% Kcal Protein	16	3	.80	17	3	.85
% Kcal Fat	39	6	.72	37	6	.84
Breakfast Kcal	414	138	.65	397	140	.89
Breakfast % carb	51	13	.66	52	13	.87
Breakfast % pro	14	4	.63	16	4	.86
Breakfast % fat	32	13	.65	32	11	.86
Lunch Kcal	719	181	.51	590	147	.82
Lunch % carb	38	8	.50	39	7	.59
Lunch % pro	19	4	.57	20	4	.53
Lunch % fat	43	7	.29	42	7	.27
Supper Kcal	811	218	.64	716	221	.94
Supper % carb	35	7	.57	37	6	.77
Supper % pro	20	3	.44	21	4	.78
Supper % fat	44	6	.49	41	6	.71
Snack Kcal	394	150	.35	273	93	.69
Snack % carb	49	12	.49	50	12	.39
Snack % pro	11	4	.32	14	4	.74
Snack % fat	37	11	.36	34	10	.58

pliant, whereas those in the middle or lower part of the distribution did not differ on compliance.

Variables that reflect self-perception of eating. Caloric intake and the comparison of food groups consumed with food groups prescribed are objective in the sense that one could theoretically observe these behaviors and confirm the measures. Other eating behaviors are more subjective. Even if we could see what a person ate, we could not tell whether the individual would consider the episode an eating binge. We have defined several variables that capture how a person perceives or feels about his or her food intake. Some variables, such as overeating and impulsive eating, describe perceptions of eating behavior. Other variables, such as craving sweets or being tempted to overeat, describe the subject's perception of the eating context. Table 8.5 presents data on several subjective variables.

TABLE 8.4 Compliance Index and Calorically Deviant Meals

Compliance/Eating		Mean	SD	Test-Retest
Compliance at				
	Breakfast	11.7	11.6	.79
	Morning snack	10.3	9.3	.06
	Lunch	25.0	24.1	.37
	Afternoon snack	13.1	10.2	.46
	Supper	31.7	18.8	.71
	Evening snack	11.9	8.7	.46
Overeating at				
	Low	.07	.11	.47
	Medium	.12	.10	.74
	High	.30	.19	.49
Compliance at				
	Low	10.9	10.0	.60
	Medium	12.9	6.6	.87
	High	57.2	46.9	.70

In the diabetic sample, only 14% of meals were identified as overeating compared with 30% in the obese sample. A similar trend is observed for impulsive eating. Of interest, the obese subjects report frequent feelings of hunger and craving sweets. They are tempted to overeat more often than they actually overeat and they see themselves as constantly exposed to forbidden foods.

Measurement of meal frequency and timing. In this section, we describe the quantification of various aspects of meal frequency and timing. Meals are described as breakfast, lunch, supper, and snacks. For diabetics, snacks are often prescribed so we differentiated between morning, afternoon, and evening snacks. To describe meal frequency, the proportion of meals falling into each of the meal type categories was computed. Table 8.6 presents data on meal frequency for both the obese and the diabetic subjects. On average, the obese subjects ate 3.8 meals per day and the diabetic subjects consumed 4.5 per day.

Because the SMAS data files preserve information about the order in which meals occur, meal patterns can be examined using sequential analysis (see Schlundt, 1989). The LAG command is used to create a variable that measures the type of eating episode at the previous meal. CROSSTAB creates a table of transitions from the previous meal to the current meal. The conditional probability of column given row (current meal given previous meal) is used to estimate Markov transitional probabilities (see Kemeny & Snell, 1962). Certain transitional probabilities (e.g., the probability that breakfast is

TABLE 8.5 Variables That Reflect Self-Perception of Eating

Sample	Variable	Mean	SD
IDDM			
	Overeat	.14	.11
	Undereat	.13	.14
	Hassle—Low	.82	.13
	Hassle—Med	.15	.10
	Hassle—High	.02	.05
	Impulsive	.10	.08
	Very hungry	.16	.16
	Hungry	.29	.19
	Not hungry	.52	.27
	Full	.05	.06
	Very full	.01	.03
Obese			
	Overeat	.30	.17
	Tempted to overeat	.41	.21
	Impulsive	.29	.17
	Craving sweets	.29	.12
	Hungry	.49	.25
	Forbidden foods available	.72	.25

followed by lunch) represent normal meal patterns whereas others (e.g., supper followed by lunch) represent meal skipping.

Table 8.7 presents these meal transition probabilities for both the diabetic and the obese subjects. Meal skipping in both samples is fairly rare. However, it appears that meal skipping is slightly more common in the obese sample than in the diabetic sample. For example, 8% of the time, supper was followed by lunch in the obese sample, suggesting that breakfast was sometimes skipped. The IDDM sample skipped breakfast only 1% of the time.

Measures of variability. Tarasuk and Beaton (1992), using data from the Beltsville 1-year dietary intake study (Mertz & Kelsay, 1984), showed that the degree of variability in energy intake and micronutrient intake is a stable individual difference. Thus people not only have a usual daily caloric intake, but their variation from day to day systematically differs from that of other people.

There are two ways to characterize individual differences in variability. First, one can simply compute the standard deviation and use it as a way to characterize an individual. For food intake, several investigators have shown that the mean and standard deviation are positively correlated (Hunt, Leonard, Garry, & Goodwin, 1983; Tarasuk & Beaton, 1992). People who typically consume more calories on the average have greater day-to-day vari-

TABLE 8.6 Meal Frequency

Sample		Mean Proportion	SD
IDDM			
	Breakfast	.22	.04
	Morning snack	.07	.05
	Lunch	.22	.05
	Afternoon snack	.11	.05
	Supper	.22	.04
	Evening snack	.15	.06
Obese			
	Breakfast	.24	.06
	Lunch	.26	.06
	Supper	.26	.06
	Snack	.24	.11

ability in caloric intake. Another way to characterize individual variability is to compute the coefficient of variation (see Shea, Stein, Basch, Contento, & Zybert, 1992; Tarasuk & Beaton, 1992), which is the standard deviation divided by the mean. It is calculated as an attempt to remove the association between the mean and standard deviation. Tarasuk and Beaton (1992) showed that there were very stable individual differences in coefficients of variation for many measures of macronutrient and micronutrient intake.

Shea et al. (1992) argued that the coefficient of variation, when applied to total energy intake, may represent energy self-regulation. People with small coefficients of variation tend to regulate intake very tightly day to day whereas people with large coefficients of variation could be considered poor self-regulators. In a small sample of free-living children, the coefficient of variation for total daily energy intake was significantly smaller than the coefficients for separate meals. The authors interpret this finding as showing that children self-regulate total calorie intake more closely than they regulate the energy content of individual meals.

When food intake is self-regulated, people should compensate for eating a large meal by reducing the size of or omitting a later meal. If a small meal is eaten, total daily intake is self-regulated by eating a larger meal later. This pattern of compensatory increases and decreases in meal size should lead to a negative autocorrelation coefficient. In addition to meal-by-meal compensations, when someone overeats on one day, undereating should occur the next day to maintain long-term energy balance. This would result in a negative autocorrelation in total energy intake from one day to the next.

The SMAS program allows the user to extract variability for a variable, or the variability given the level of another variable. For example, the meal-to-

TABLE 8.7 Meal Pattern Analysis Using Transitional Probabilities

Previous Meal	Subsequent Meal					
	Breakfast	Morning Snack	Lunch	Afternoon Snack	Supper	Evening Snack
IDDM						
Break	.01	.30	.59	.04	.06	.00
Morning snack	.01	.05	.85	.05	.05	.00
Lunch	.01	.00	.01	.51	.46	.00
Afternoon snack	.00	.00	.00	.09	.87	.04
Supper	.29	.02	.01	.00	.01	.67
Evening snack	.79	.01	.03	.00	.00	.17

Previous Meal	Subsequent Meal			
	Breakfast	Lunch	Supper	Snack
Obese				
Break	.02	.70	.08	.19
Lunch	.04	.03	.60	.34
Supper	.53	.08	.02	.36
Snack	.30	.20	.33	.16

meal standard deviation of caloric intake can be computed. In addition, it is possible to compute the standard deviation separately for breakfast, lunch, supper, and snacks. Also, the coefficient of variation can be computed overall or on a meal-by-meal basis. Standard deviations or coefficients of variation conditional on location, mood, or social context can be computed to study how specific conditions are related to variation in food intake. Autocorrelation coefficients can also be computed for adjacent meals or for the same meal on adjacent days. Table 8.8 presents means and standard deviations of these variables for the diabetic and the obese data sets. For the diabetic sample as a whole, there is evidence of a small negative autocorrelation (−.16). The obese subjects also showed an autocorrelation that was slightly negative on average but less than half the magnitude of the diabetics (−.07). In both cases the standard deviations suggest that many subjects had positive autocorrelations. These data suggest that the meal-to-meal autocorrelation coefficient deserves further study as a way to describe individual differences in self-regulation.

Naturalistic functional analysis. Schlundt (1985) proposed a methodology for examining the antecedents and consequences of behaviors using continuous self-monitoring records (also see Schlundt, 1989). Essentially, analysis of con-

TABLE 8.8 Description of Variability and Autocorrelation in Two Samples

Variable	Diabetic		Obese	
	Mean	SD	Mean	SD
Monday Kcal	1,988	540	1,891	666
Tuesday Kcal	1,960	605	1,962	622
Wednesday Kcal	1,950	456	1,919	641
Thursday Kcal	2,005	523	1,876	660
Friday Kcal	2,096	545	2,040	676
Saturday Kcal	2,110	711	2,056	651
Sunday Kcal	2,037	592	2,031	577
Kcal SD break	265	75	191	89
Kcal SD lunch	285	115	331	132
Kcal SD supper	590	147	811	218
CV Daily total Kcal	.34	.13	.40	.11
CV Breakfast Kcal	.42	.14	.46	.17
CV Lunch Kcal	.41	.13	.43	.14
CV Supper Kcal	.40	.11	.41	.12
Auto Cor—all meals	−.16	.15	−.07	.13
Auto Cor—breakfast	.04	.25	.04	.31
Auto Cor—lunch	−.03	.19	.00	.32
Auto Cor—supper	.00	.21	−.05	.29

ditional probabilities or conditional means allows one to identify potential antecedent-behavior and behavior-consequence relationships. The SMAS was designed to accomplish these goals at the individual level or for groups of subjects. At the individual level, we have used the SMAS to generate functional analysis data that we give to subjects as feedback during weight loss (A. J. Hill, et al., 1989; Schlundt, Hill, et al., 1993).

At the group level, naturalistic functional analysis has been used to study binge eating in bulimic and obese subjects (Schlundt, Johnson, & Jarrell, 1986). Schlundt, Sbrocco, and Bell (1990) used the methodology to study dietary slips in obese subjects attempting to lose weight. Schlundt, Virts, et al. (1993) used the methodology to examine craving sweets in obese women.

An important question that can be addressed by naturalistic functional analysis is this: To what extent do people overeat in response to negative emotions? To examine this question, the unconditional probability of overeating is compared with the conditional probability of overeating given a negative mood. Each study cited above provided evidence that overeating occurs in response to both negative and positive emotions. Table 8.9 shows the relationship between negative moods and overeating for both the diabetic and the obese samples. These data show significant associations between moods

TABLE 8.9 Naturalistic Functional Analysis of Negative Emotional Overeating

Mood	N	P(Overeat)	N	P(Impulsive)
IDDM:				
Depressed				
Very negative	6	.51*	9	.43**
Negative	12	.30*	12	.26**
Neutral	29	.13	25	.11
Positive	19	.17	14	.12
Very positive	9	.33	7	.29
Upset				
Very negative	10	.26	7	.28**
Negative	17	.28**	17	.26**
Neutral	29	.15	26	.11
Positive	17	.17	14	.14
Very positive	6	.31	5	.16
Obese:				
Depressed	32	.52**	32	.55**
Afraid	7	.76*	7	.88**
Bored	42	.53**	52	.70**
Worried	39	.45**	39	.53**
Stressed	60	.40**	58	.39**
Angry	24	.68**	26	.70**
Irritable	38	.52**	46	.57**
Upset	29	.46**	28	.51**
Nervous	42	.51**	39	.53**

*Conditional probability differs from unconditional probability based on paired t test, $p < .05$.
**Conditional probability differs from unconditional probability based on paired t test, $p < .01$.

and overeating for both samples. Showing a correlation between negative moods and overeating does not prove that moods cause people to overeat. However, the failure to find such a relationship in observational data sets can cast doubt on the existence of a phenomenon. For example, Schlundt, Virts, et al. (1993) showed that craving sweets was not associated with high carbohydrate-low protein meals as predicted by serotonergic theories of carbohydrate craving.

Cluster analysis of eating situations and eating styles. Using a behavioral diary like the one in Figure 8.1, hundreds of variables that describe different aspects of food intake in different situations can be extracted. Although each variable contains a unique piece of information from a subject's diary, the information extracted may or may not add anything to the description of eating behavior. Are there a few measures that capture important individual differences in daily food intake? Schlundt et al. (1991) extracted 170 variables from the eating diaries of 236 obese women. Cluster analysis was used to reduce these 170 variables to 20 different major categories with 27 minor categories of food intake variables. The results of this cluster analysis represent an empirically derived taxonomy of situation-specific eating behaviors. This typology offers a detailed description of ways in which people characteristically differ in their eating behavior (see Table 8.10). The clusters represent the occurrence of specific target behaviors such as overeating, impulsive eating, snacking, high caloric intake, and macronutrient intake. In addition, they reflect differential occurrence of these behaviors in response to environmental and emotional antecedents such as high calorie-high fat meals at home, restaurants, or social events and depression- or boredom-induced eating.

These findings challenge us to begin thinking of food intake as much more than simply an individual's average intake of calories or nutrients. Food intake varied considerably as a function of meal, place, social setting, and emotional state in this large sample of obese women. We expect that food intake varies consistently as a function of time of day, situation, and physical and emotional state in men and in normal weight individuals also. Microanalysis of eating provides new ways of looking at people and their eating habits.

Problems With Self-Reported Food Intake

There are serious shortcomings involved in relying on self-reported food intake as assessed from eating diaries. Random errors in recording, estimation of portion size, or calculation of nutrient content introduce unreliability and will attenuate potential correlations with other variables. Random sources of unreliability can be compensated for by increasing the number of observations. However, systematic biases in reporting, estimation of portion size, or calculation of nutrient composition are serious problems. There are many sources of potential systematic bias. Subjects could fail to record eating episodes; they could fail to record some foods; and they could be inaccurate in reporting portion sizes.

Although it is not possible to identify the exact source of bias, self-report methods usually underestimate actual energy intake. For example, Lichtman et al. (1992) showed that a small sample of obese subjects underreported energy expenditure by an average of 47%. Schoeller (1990) reviewed studies on the accuracy of self-reported intake and concluded that self-report methods usually underestimate total daily energy intake and that the degree of inaccuracy increases as actual energy expenditure increases. Bandini, Schoeller, Cyr, and Dietz (1990) also reported similar results showing that self-reported intake systematically underestimates actual intake with the degree of underreporting greater for obese than lean adolescents. Fricker, Baelde, Apfelbaum, Huet, and Apfelbaum (1992) showed that differences in accuracy occur among subgroups of obese individuals.

TABLE 8.10 Variable Clusters Based on 236 Female Subjects

Cluster	Name-Major	Name-Minor	Variables	Mean	SD
Ia	Social Meals	Friends	Fat with friends	27	17
			Kcal with friends	606	340
			CHO with friends	56	30
Ib		Social Lunches	Pro at lunch	29	19
			Pro with friends	24	24
			Pro at restaurants	29	28
			Kcal at lunch	674	253
			Fat at lunch	31	14
			Kcal from protein	95	32
			Pro when tempted	26	13
Ic		Restaurants	Fat at restaurants	32	22
			Kcal at restaurants	665	433
			CHO at restaurants	55	39
			P(restaurants)	.11	.10
II	Social Events		Fat at social events	22	22
			Kcal at social events	480	434
			Pro at social events	17	18
			CHO at social events	44	40
			P(social events)	.04	.06
IIIa	Impulsive snacks	Snack size	Kcal at snacks	382	170
			Fat at snacks	16	10
			CHO at snacks	43	19
			Pro at snacks	10	6
IIIb		Craving sweets	Fat when craving	25	14
			Kcal when craving	546	255
			Pro when craving	18	10
			CHO when craving	55	26
IIIc		Impulsive	Fat when impulsive	23	15
			Kcal when impulsive	508	278
			CHO when impulsive	51	26
			Pro when impulsive	17	12
IVa	Carbohydrate	Typical CHO	Kcal from CHO	228	71
			CHO at home	54	18
			CHO at supper	68	23
			CHO at lunch	62	24
			CHO alone	50	21
IVb		Breakfast	Kcal at breakfast	389	149
			Fat at breakfast	14	8
			Pro at breakfast	13	6
			CHO at breakfast	48	18
Va	Large meals	Family meals	Fat with family	26	13
			Kcal with family	574	249
			Pro with family	24	10
			CHO with family	55	25
Vb		Meals overeaten	Fat when overeating	35	17
			Kcal when overeating	750	343
			Pro when overeating	30	17
			CHO when overeating	69	37
VIa	Meal size	Alone	Fat when alone	19	11
			Kcal when alone	453	193

TABLE 8.10 (Continued)

Cluster	Name-Major	Name-Minor	Variables	Mean	SD
			Pro when alone	16	8
VIb		Tempted	Fat when tempted	31	15
			Kcal when tempted	677	277
			CHO when tempted	63	26
VIc		Supper	Kcal at supper	769	237
			Fat at supper	35	14
			Pro at supper	35	10
VId		Fat intake	Kcal	559	163
			Fat Kcal	230	86
			Fat at home	22	10
			Kcal at home	526	176
			Pro at home	21	8
VIIa	Overeating	Snacks	Overeat given craving	.41	.29
			Overeat given impulsive	.49	.32
			Overeat given snack	.30	.26
			Overeat given hungry	.29	.21
			Overeat given tempted	.55	.26
VIIb		Breakfast	Overeat given breakfast	.15	.18
			Overeat given alone	.23	.23
VIIc		Supper	Overeat given home	.27	.20
			P(Overeat)	.27	.18
			Overeat given available	.34	.22
			Overeat given supper	.36	.24
			Overeat given family	.28	.24
			Overeat given tired	.28	.24
			P(Tempted)	.36	.22
VIId		Restaurants	Overeat given lunch	.25	.21
			Overeat given friend	.29	.28
			Overeat given happy	.29	.26
			Overeat given restaurant	.30	.32
VIIIa	Impulsive	Unplanned social	Impulsive given family	.21	.21
			Impulse given happy	.19	.21
			Impulse given restaurant	.16	.26
			Impulse given friend	.24	.29
VIIIb		Binges	Impulse given tempted	.44	.27
			Impulse given overeat	.46	.31
			Impulse given hungry	.21	.20
VIIIc		Snacks	Impulse at home	.24	.18
			P(Impulsive)	.25	.17
			Impulse given available	.33	.21
			Impulse given alone	.31	.24
			Impulse given tired	.26	.22
			Impulse given snack	.55	.31
			Impulse given craving	.54	.31
IX	In the Car		Overeat given car	.17	.32
			Impulse given car	.31	.39
			Fat in car	17	18
			Kcal in car	363	342

(Continued)

TABLE 8.10 (Continued)

Cluster	Name-Major	Name-Minor	Variables	Mean	SD
			CHO in car	37	37
			Pro in car	12	13
			P(Car)	.04	.06
X	At Work		Fat at work	16	14
			Kcal at work	376	266
			Pro at work	14	10
			CHO at work	40	30
			Overeat given work	.17	.24
			Impulse given work	.21	.26
			P(Friend)	.19	.16
			P(Work)	.17	.14
XI	Negative emotional		Overeat given angry	.20	.35
			Impulse given angry	.18	.34
			Overeat given nervous	.21	.29
			Impulse given nervous	.24	.32
			Overeat given stress	.26	.27
			Impulse given stress	.25	.25
			Overeat given irritable	.26	.33
			Impulse given irritable	.30	.35
			Overeat given worried	.19	.30
			Impulse given worried	.22	.32
			Overeat given upset	.26	.33
			Impulse given upset	.21	.33
XII	Positive emotional		Overeat given excited	.22	.30
			Impulse given excited	.19	.23
			Overeat given challenge	.15	.28
			Impulse given challenge	.17	.30
XIII	Illness		Overeat given sick	.08	.23
			Impulse given sick	.11	.28
XIV	Stimulus exposure		P(Craving)	.26	.19
			P(Available)	.68	.26
			P(Hungry)	.47	.28
XV	Depression		Overeat given depress	.19	.30
			Impulse given depress	.21	.31
			P(Alone)	.33	.20
XVI	Boredom		P(Snack)	.24	.12
			Meals per day	3.7	.74
			Overeat given bored	.25	.33
			Impulse given bored	.36	.38
			P(Bored)	.07	.08
XVII	Somatic		Overeat given weak	.12	.29
			Impulse given weak	.09	.26
			Overeat given pain	.10	.26
			Impulse given pain	.10	.26
			P(Sick)	.03	.06
			P(Weak)	.02	.05
			P(Tired)	.29	.19
			P(Pain)	.03	.07
XVIII	Negative Moods		Overeat given afraid	.06	.21
			Impulse given afraid	.08	.24

TABLE 8.10 (Continued)

Cluster	Name-Major	Name-Minor	Variables	Mean	SD
			P(Worried)	.06	.09
			P(Upset)	.04	.06
			P(Afraid)	.01	.03
			P(Depressed)	.06	.09
			P(Angry)	.02	.04
			P(Irritable)	.07	.09
XVIX	Alcohol		P(Drunk)	.01	.01
			Kcal from alcohol	6	14
			Overeat given drunk	.08	.25
			Impulse given drunk	.06	.23
XXa	Social Adjustment	Home	P(Family)	.37	.23
			P(Home)	.52	.18
XXb		Social	Overeat given social	.26	.36
			Impulse given social	.18	.31
XXc		Breakfast	P(Breakfast)	.24	.06
XXd		Meals	P(Lunch)	.26	.06
XXe		Stress	P(Stress)	.17	.14
			P(Challenge)	.06	.09
			P(Nervous)	.07	.10
XXf		Feeling good	P(Happy)	.25	.21
			P(Excited)	.08	.10

NOTE: Unless otherwise indicated, fat, protein, and carbohydrates are measured in grams while calories are measured in Kcal. Overeating and impulsive eating are expressed as probabilities or conditional probabilities. The base rates of occurrence of events are expressed as probabilities.

If one is interested in estimating a person's average energy intake over an extended period, then a method such as doubly labeled water or indirect whole room calorimetry should be used (Schoeller & Fjeld, 1991; Webb, 1991). As long as the person is not losing or gaining weight, energy expenditure will approximate typical energy intake. However, there are no biological tests available that can substitute for self-recorded data in the microanalysis of eating. If the question involves identifying situations associated with overeating, investigating emotional eating, or relating food intake to social context, it would appear that there is no alternative to relying on self-report.

Using Questionnaires to Assess Eating Style

Questionnaires, although still relying on self-report, are an alternative to self-monitoring methods as a way to assess specific eating behaviors. In this section of the chapter, specific questionnaires that measure different aspects of eating will be reviewed in detail. We will first examine situational inventories, followed by questionnaires that measure psychological constructs related to eating. As it is covered in other chapters, we will not be focusing on the assessment of dietary restraint or binge eating.

Situational Inventories

Situation-specific behavioral inventories are derived from theories of behavioral assessment (see Goldfried & D'Zurilla, 1969; Schlundt & McFall, 1985). Several situation-specific eating inventories have been developed and are reviewed in this section.

Dieter's Inventory of Eating Temptations (DIET)

Schlundt and Zimering (1988) presented the Dieter's Inventory of Eating Temptations as a situation-specific measure of weight control competence. The DIET consists of 30 descriptions of problem situations that include a description of an effective solution. The respondent is instructed to rate the percentage of time he or she would respond as described.

Fifty descriptions of problem situations faced by people trying to lose weight were generated by four psychologists with experience leading weight reduction programs. A competent response that "promotes weight loss or weight maintenance by minimizing caloric intake and/or maximizing caloric expenditure" was generated for each item. Forty items were pretested on 21 overweight and 23 normal weight subjects. The items were grouped into six categories: (a) overeating, (b) resisting temptation, (c) food choice, (d) positive social eating, (e) negative emotional eating, and (f) exercise. Items that best discriminated between overweight and normal subjects were retained and 6 new items were written to make the final 30-item version of the DIET that included 5 items from each of the six types of problem situations.

Reliability. Schlundt and Zimering (1988) administered the DIET to 20 subjects on two occasions 1 week apart and reported test-retest correlations of overeating, resisting temptation, food choice, positive social, negative emotional, exercise, and total score of .915, .908, .809, .814, .920, and .956. They also reported coefficient alphas of .79, .733, .769, .780, .860, .684, and .926. Tucker and Schlundt (1993) empirically derived a set of five subscales for the DIET using factor analysis. Coefficient alpha reliabilities for negative emotional eating, exercise, craving sweets, overeating, and food preparation were .87, .77, .81, .80, and .73, respectively.

Factor structure. The original six subscales were based on the groupings of expert judges. Tucker and Schlundt conducted a factor analysis of the DIET using a clinical sample of 289 obese subjects who enrolled in a weight-loss clinic and a community sample of 1,657 men and woman who participated in a follow-up evaluation of a community weight-loss program. Five factors were derived from both analyses and were named emotional eating, exercise, craving sweets, overeating, and food preparation. Factor analyses conducted separately on males and females showed that these five factors are stable across gender.

Validity. Schlundt and Zimering correlated DIET questionnaire scores with data derived from eating diaries in 40 obese subjects. A multiple regression analysis predicting DIET scores from meal pattern, caloric intake, and positive and negative emotional eating accounted for between 16% and 54% of the variance in DIET questionnaire scores. Individual correlations also indicated the construct validity of the DIET scores.

Tucker and Schlundt (1993) correlated the factor analytically derived DIET subscales with measures of dietary adherence in the obese and community samples. Correlations between the DIET scores and measures derived from eating diaries in Table 8.11 provided evidence of construct validity in the clinical sample. The DIET scales correlated moderately with simple ratings of how much difficulty the community subjects had adhering to a weight-loss plan. Discriminant validity was demonstrated by showing that the Exercise scale did not correlate significantly with any of the eating diary measures or with adherence ratings.

Schlundt and Zimering (1988) showed that the DIET questionnaire scales when used in a discriminant function analysis could correctly classify 73% of overweight subjects and 73% of normal weight subjects. Tucker and Schlundt showed that the clinical sample reported more difficulty than the community sample on all of the DIET subscales except exercise. Tucker and Schlundt also reported that there was a significant correlation between body-mass index and all five of the factor analytically derived subscales in the community sample. In the community sample, small but significant correlations were found between DIET scores, and subjects reported success at losing weight and keeping it off. Multiple regressions showed that age, gender, and body-mass index accounted for 19% of the variance in initial weight loss. Adding the DIET scales as predictors increased the percentage of variance accounted for to 23%. For weight loss at a 1-year follow-up, age, gender, and body-mass index accounted for 9.6% of the variance. Addition of the DIET subscales to the regression model increased the variance accounted for to 17.6%.

The DIET questionnaire also has a moderate degree of content validity. The items were generated by psychologists who had experience with weight-

TABLE 8.11 Validity of the DIET Questionnaire Scales

Situation	Negative Emotion	Exercise	Crave Sweet	Overeat	Food Preparation	Total
Clinical (n = 200)						
Social meals	−.07	−.11	−.04	−.18*	−.10	−.11
Social event	.11	.03	.10	−.10	−.01	.03
Imp snack	−.16*	−.06	−.17*	−.20*	−.12	−.19*
Eat carbo	−.13	−.08	−.25**	−.19*	−.09	−.20*
Large meal	−.19*	−.15	−.18*	−.29**	−.16*	−.26**
Meal size	−.13	−.13	−.19*	−.30**	−.14	−.24**
Overeating	−.24**	−.08	−.17*	−.31**	−.08	−.24**
Impulsive	−.23**	−.11	−.19*	−.17*	−.04	−.20*
Eat in car	−.08	−.01	−.16*	−.14	.02	−.11
Eat at work	−.05	−.01	−.04	−.11	−.04	−.07
Neg emotion	−.19*	−.09	−.11	−.22**	−.12	−.20*
Pos emotion	−.09	−.09	−.12	−.10	.01	−.11
Illness	−.12	−.04	−.10	−.19*	.00	−.13
Stimulus exp	−.11	−.03	−.10	−.01	.05	−.06
Depressed	−.24**	.06	.01	−.09	−.05	−.10
Boredom	−.31**	−.00	−.16*	−.16*	−.05	−.19*
Somatic	−.03	−.10	−.02	−.07	−.08	−.08
Neg mood	−.05	−.08	.05	.02	.04	−.00
Alcohol	.02	−.08	−.02	−.07	.07	−.02
Soc adjst	.14	−.09	−.02	.00	.02	.01
Prob overeat	−.21**	−.08	−.16*	−.30**	−.09	−.23**
Prob impulsive	−.23**	−.12	−.20*	−.20*	−.08	−.23**
Community (n = 1,470)						
Exercise now	.21**	.50**	.19**	.22**	.20**	.33**
No. rotations	.14**	.10**	.14**	.15**	.16**	.17**
Depressed	−.49**	−.09**	−.23**	−.27**	−.22**	−.35**
Stressed	−.49**	−.11**	−.26**	−.29**	−.26**	−.38**
Social sit	−.11**	−.13**	−.23**	−.27**	−.13**	−.22**
Restaurant	−.09**	−.13**	−.23**	−.28**	−.16**	−.23**
Portion sizes	−.20**	−.12**	−.17**	−.30**	−.23**	−.26**
Hungry and tired	−.20**	−.12**	−.16**	−.20**	−.15**	−.22**

*$p < .01$; **$p < .001$.

loss therapy. This method resulted in a good sample of situations from the domain of weight-related problem situations.

Norms. Table 8.12 presents means and standard deviations for the six original DIET subscales and the five factor analytically derived scales. The item numbers that make up each scale are also presented.

Availability. The DIET questionnaire is published as an appendix in Schlundt and Johnson (1990) and is reprinted in Appendix 8-A.

TABLE 8.12 Norms for the DIET Subscales

	Original Scales						
	RT	PS	FC	EX	OE	NE	Total
Normal Weight (*n* = 193)							
Mean	56	46	49	58	61	67	56
SD	22	21	23	21	21	21	16
Overweight (*n* = 168)							
Mean	56	43	48	50	54	57	52
SD	23	23	21	20	22	25	18

	Factor Analytic Scales					
	Neg	Exer	Crave	Over	Prep	Total
Clinical (*n* = 289)						
Mean	41	50	44	46	56	47
SD	20	20	20	16	19	14
Community (*n* = 1,796)						
Mean	52	52	51	55	64	55
SD	24	22	22	19	20	17

NOTE: Norms are for averaging the items within a scale to obtain a number that represents the average percentage of the time the subject would handle each category of situations competently.

RT	Resisting temptation, items 3, 15, 16, 20, 26
PS	Positive social, items, 1, 18, 21, 22, 27
FC	Food choice, items 4, 5, 7, 8, 23
EX	Exercise, items 2, 11, 13, 17, 19
OE	Overeat, items, 6, 9, 10, 12, 14
NE	Negative emotional eating, items 24, 25, 28, 29, 30
Neg	Negative emotional eating, items 24, 25, 26, 28, 29, 30
Exer	Exercise, items 11, 13, 17, 19
Crave	Craving Sweets, items 15, 18, 20, 21, 23, 27
Over	Overeating, items 1, 4, 6, 9, 12, 14
Prep	Food preparation, 5, 7, 8, 10, 16
Total	Average of all 30 items

Situation-Based Dieting Self-Efficacy Scale (SDS)

Stotland, Zuroff, and Roy (1991) developed an inventory to measure the self-efficacy of dieters across a range of eating situations. *Self-efficacy* (see Bandura, 1986) refers to an individual's belief that he or she can solve a problem. Details on the development of the SDS are presented in an unpublished dissertation (Stotland, 1989). The scale consists of 25 eating situations that were identified in "a survey of eating behavior." For each item, the subject rates on a 100-point scale how confident she is that she could adhere to her diet in that situation, if she were to face it in the coming week. The scale was administered to 65 female college students identified as dieters. No data were presented on these subjects' weight status or whether any had an eating disorder. The scale is scored by summing the self-efficacy ratings across the 25 items. Higher scores represent greater degrees of dieting self-efficacy.

Reliability. The scale has a coefficient alpha of .95 and a short-term test-retest reliability of .80.

Validity. The total score has a moderate correlation with social desirability ($r = .25$), suggesting that subjects to some degree were trying to make themselves look good. Stotland et al. (1991) grouped 44 subjects into high and low self-efficacy groups using SDS scores. The groups did not differ on restraint, body-mass index, or preexperimental ratings of mood and hunger. Half the subjects in each group were randomly assigned to receive a preload of a large helping of cake. The subjects were then left to perform a taste rating task and the dependent variable was the number of cookies eaten. There was a main effect for SDS group with subjects having high self-efficacy scores eating fewer cookies during the taste test. The low self-efficacy subjects receiving a preload ate significantly more cookies than subjects in any of the other conditions. SDS scores were not correlated with subjects' ratings of their cognitions during the experiment, whereas restraint scores were. Subjects high in restraint were more prone to feel anxious, out of control, and upset during the cookie tasting task. The SDS was readministered after the taste testing task and reductions in self-efficacy were correlated with eating more cookies. This study suggests that dieting self-efficacy may be related to the disinhibition effect and that it is measuring something different than measures of dietary restraint.

The data suggest that the SDS has predictive validity in an experimental preload-taste testing situation. There are no other data on construct validity. Without more specific information, it would appear that generating the items from a survey gives the scale good content validity.

Norms. Norms for the SDS were not presented by Stotland et al. (1991). The cutoff scores for the low self-efficacy group (bottom third of the distribution) was a total score of 1,415, and the cutoff score for forming the high self-efficacy group (upper third of the distribution) was 1,820.

Availability. The SDS items and instructions are published in Stotland et al. (1991). The scale is also reproduced in Appendix 8-B.

Situational Appetite Measure (SAM)

Stanton, Garcia, and Green (1990) developed the Situational Appetite Measure (SAM) to assess how well dieters handle high-risk situations. Two versions of the SAM were developed. The SAM-U presents problem situations and asks subjects to rate the strength of their urges to eat. The second version, the SAM-E, has subjects rate the degree to which they believe they could control themselves in each high-risk situation, a measure of self-efficacy. The items were developed to sample high-risk situations based on Marlatt's (1985) taxonomy of high-risk situations for addiction relapse. Seventy items were administered to 246 college students who reported a history of dieting. The final version of the SAM consisted of 30 items, with 6 from each of the following domains: relaxation, food present, hunger, reward, and negative feelings.

Factor analysis. The original 70 items were factor analyzed, resulting in five factors. Thirty items (six from each factor) were selected for the final version. It was administered to 184 female undergraduates and the results show that five factors adequately describe the scale. The factor analytic studies are limited to male and female college students.

Reliability. Coefficient alphas range from .75 to .92. Test-retest reliability estimated from a sample of 50 females ranged from .70 to .79.

Validity. The SAM scales were strongly related to the Negative Affect scale of the Eating Self-Efficacy Scale (ESES; Glynn & Ruderman, 1986). Using multiple regression, the SAM scales accounted for 88% of the variance in ESES negative affect scores for males and 74% of the variance for females. The Socially Acceptable Circumstances scale of the ESES was predicted from the SAM scales using multiple regression, accounting for 53% of the variance for males and 50% of the variance for females. Positive correlations were also found between the SAM scales and the BULIT and the Restraint scale. The Negative Feelings subscale of the SAM-U was significantly correlated with depression scores. The main exception to these patterns was the SAM Hunger scale. It showed few correlations with any of the other eating measures.

The two versions of the SAM were administered to 30 undergraduate women with a history of dieting. The correlations between the two forms of the test (rating urges versus rating self-efficacy) were all negative and large, suggesting that those who experience the strongest urges to overeat have the lowest self-efficacy.

The SAM-E and SAM-U were administered to 66 women participating in a commercial weight-loss program (mean BMI of 30.3). Subjects also completed the ESES and a weight history questionnaire. The dependent variables were weight loss, program attendance, and attrition. This study further demonstrated the construct validity of the SAM and showed that the two forms were highly correlated in the clinical sample. Subjects with lower self-efficacy scores had a history of more weight loss attempts and greater weight variability. The Negative Feelings scales of the SAM were moderately correlated ($r = .28$) with weight loss as measured by the weight reduction index (Wilson, 1978). The SAM was uncorrelated with attendance and attrition.

Norms. Stanton et al. (1990) present norms for male and female college students. Although the scale was administered to a clinical sample, normative data from this sample are not available.

Availability. The items and the rating scales are published in Stanton et al. (1990). The scale is also reproduced in Appendix 8-C.

Eating Self-Efficacy Scale (ESES)

Glynn and Ruderman (1986) developed a situationally based self-efficacy measure with two subscales: negative affect and socially acceptable circumstances. These two domains of items were considered important situations for weight loss and weight maintenance. This measure is reviewed in detail by Rossi et al. (this volume).

Summary of Situational Measures

In the past few years, several groups of investigators have developed situationally based approaches to the assessment of eating behavior. These questionnaires provide an important alternative to the more time-consuming diaries as a way to perform a microanalysis of eating. There is not yet an extensive body of research using these measures. Because of the way they were developed, the measures have good content validity. Each provides a good sample of the kinds of situations people attempting to lose weight or follow a therapeutic diet face in everyday life. All scales have data suggesting moderate to good reliability. In addition, construct and predictive validity data have been presented. Of great interest is the potential ability to use these assessment approaches to predict success in weight-loss programs. The SDS, the SAM, and the ESES are all correlated with other questionnaire assessments of eating behavior. The DIET is also correlated with patterns of eating behavior measured using behavioral diaries.

Researchers and clinicians should consider including one of these measures in any comprehensive battery of tests to assess eating behavior. The promise of these assessment techniques, as yet untested, is to provide a differential diagnosis of eating problems. People who have difficulty with certain kinds of situations—emotional eating, for example—might be provided with focused treatment. If this approach proves useful, dietary therapy might someday match treatments to problems rather than providing a single treat-ment package to all patients as is the current norm.

Construct and Behavior Measures

In this section, measures that assess eating behaviors without reference to specific situations will be reviewed. Measures of dietary restraint, however, will not be covered as coverage of these is provided Gorman and Allison (this volume).

Food Craving

Weingarten and Elston (1991) argued that, in spite of its frequent appear-ance in discussions of eating pathology, there were very few good data on the phenomenon of food cravings. Most available information comes either from females or from special populations such as women with PMS or eating dis-orders. To further describe the phenomenology of food craving, Weingarten and Elston (1991) developed the Craving Questionnaire. The questionnaire was administered to 380 male and 758 female college undergraduates at a Canadian university. Significantly more women (97%) than men (68%) re-ported having experienced food cravings. For women, 32% of the sample reported that craving was linked to their menstrual cycle. There was no dif-ference in frequency of craving between women who reported being on a diet to lose weight and those who were not. No data on reliability or validity of the questionnaire were presented. The full questionnaire is reproduced in Weingarten and Elston (1991) and appears in Appendix 8-D.

A. J. Hill et al. (1991) also developed a food craving questionnaire and investigated its relationship with dietary restraint and emotional eating. The questionnaire involved making visual analog ratings to the following items (A. J. Hill et al., 1991, pp. 188-189):

1. How often do you experience strong urges to eat particular types of foods (Never/All of the time)?
2. On the average, how often do you experience a strong urge to eat a particular type of food (Several times a day/Once a month)?
3. How strong are the urges you experience to eat particular types of food (Extremely weak/Extremely strong)?
4. Are the urges to eat a particular food always of the same strength (Never/Always)?
5. How easy is it for you to ignore this strong urge to eat a particular food (Very easy/Impossible)?

Items 1 and 2 were averaged to form a Frequency of Craving scale, and items 3 to 5 were averaged to form a Strength of Craving scale.

A sample of 206 women from a variety of settings were asked to complete the Craving Questionnaire, the Three-Factor Eating Questionnaire (Stunkard & Messick, 1985), and the Dutch Eating Behavior Questionnaire (Van Strien, Frijters, Bergers, & Defares, 1986). Craving frequency was only weakly associated with dietary restraint, whereas craving intensity was not. Both craving measures were significantly associated with the Hunger scale of the Three-Factor Eating Questionnaire and with the External Eating and Emotional Eating scales of the Dutch Eating Behavior Questionnaire. There was a moderately strong correlation ($r = .62$) between frequency and intensity of craving.

In a second study reported by A. J. Hill et al. (1991), 10 women who frequently reported craving were compared with 10 who rarely experienced food cravings. Both groups of subjects kept a 5-day eating diary and monitored their moods throughout the day. The 10 high-craving subjects also kept track of the antecedents, behaviors, and consequences for every episode of food craving during a 7-day period. There was no significant difference between the two groups in total daily energy intake. The high-craving group did consume significantly more alcohol than the low-craving group. The high cravers experienced more negative affect during the 5-day period than the low cravers. A functional analysis of food craving showed that both hunger and negative moods could precipitate food cravings. Some subjects reported relief of negative affect after consuming a craved food, whereas others reported worsening of negative affect. No reliability data for this measure were reported.

Summary of food craving measures. Two very short scales are available to assess the experience of food craving. Of the two, the A. J. Hill et al. (1991) scale was presented with more evidence of validity. The results of the Hill et al. study were similar to results reported by Schlundt, Virts, et al. (1993), who made a detailed comparison of eating diaries between two groups of obese women high and low in craving sweets. Food craving does not appear to reflect a simple biological process such as energy deprivation or serotonin depletion. Rather, it is intimately associated with affective experiences and cognitions about food and eating. The role of food craving in food intake control deserves additional research attention.

Forbidden Food Survey

The Forbidden Food Survey (FFS) was developed to measure the construct of food phobia. The impetus for this scale came from the anxiety model of bulimia (see Rosen & Leitenberg, 1982; Schlundt & Johnson, 1990). According to this model, people with eating disorders experience a high degree of anxiety about weight gain after eating certain forbidden foods. This anxiety can be relieved by purging, which is hypothesized to be a major reinforcement mechanism in the maintenance of bulimic behavior.

The scale consists of a sample of 45 food items selected from three calorie levels (low, medium, and high) of five food groups (milk, meat, grains, fruits/vegetables, and beverages). The subject rates how she would feel about herself after eating each food. The ratings range from "I would feel very good about myself after eating this food" to "I would feel very bad about myself after eating this food." Ruggiero, Williamson, Davis, Schlundt, and Carey (1988) administered the scale to 193 women. Of these women, 42 were diagnosed with bulimia by *DSM-III* criteria. Of the bulimics, 21 binged and purged and 21 binged but did not purge. A second sample of 15 patients with bulimia nervosa, 15 obese women, and 15 non-eating disordered women matched for age and height were studied.

Reliability. Schlundt and Johnson (1990) reported complete reliability data using the Ruggiero et al. (1988) data set. Coefficient alpha was above .80 for all scales except those for milk, low-calorie foods, and beverages. The test-retest reliabilities (computed from 78 subjects) results were similar, ranging from .63 for milk to .90 for meat.

Validity. The validity of the Forbidden Food Survey was evaluated by comparing known groups of subjects. In general, the grains, meats, medium-, and high-calorie scales discriminated between groups. Binge-purge subjects showed the highest levels of food phobia, with nonpurging bulimics and obese having intermediate levels, and non-eating disordered subjects with the lowest levels. Schlundt and Johnson (1990) reported construct validity data from a sample of 51 undergraduate females. Scores on the High-Calorie Food scale were significantly correlated with the Body Cathexis scale, a measure of body-image disturbance. Fear of medium-calorie foods was significantly correlated with the BULIT and the Disinhibition scale of the Three-Factor Eating Questionnaire. Scores on the milk food group were correlated with disinhibition scores. The meat and grain food groups were significantly correlated with body cathexis, the BULIT, and the Restraint and Disinhibition scales of the Three-Factor Eating Questionnaire. The scales have relatively high intercorrelations and a total score could also be used as a summary measure of fear of forbidden foods. The scale appears to be valid for differentiating clinical from nonclinical groups and is associated with varying degrees of eating disturbances within a nonclinical population.

Availability. The food items are presented in Ruggiero et al. (1988, table 1) and the full inventory is reproduced in Schlundt and Johnson (1990) as well as in Appendix 8-E.

Eating-Related Characteristics Questionnaire (ECQ)

Mehrabian (1987) described a lengthy program of research designed to study eating characteristics in normal populations. He argued that most of the previous research on eating had been conducted in clinical populations of obese and eating disordered persons. In addition, his goal was to relate these measures of eating to gender, obesity, and temperament. Temperament was conceptualized as having three independent dimensions of pleasure-displeasure, arousal-nonarousal, and dominance-submissiveness (see Mehrabian, 1987, for a thorough review of the three-dimensional model of temperament).

The Eating-Related Characteristics questionnaire is a revised and expanded version of a preliminary eating questionnaire (Mehrabian, Nahum, & Duke, 1986). It consists of 179 items intended to assess behaviors thought to be related to obesity (e.g., dieting and overeating) and anorexia (e.g., food phobia, undereating, purging). Items consisted of sentences like "I crave sweets when I am bored or depressed." Subjects respond by rating their agreement on a 9-point scale (−4 very strong disagreement to +4 very strong agreement). The questionnaire was administered to 109 male and 151 female college students.

Factor analysis. Factor analysis was conducted in two stages. First, 12 factors were extracted from the raw data. The factors were named (a) dieting, (b) preoccupation with, and fear of, gaining weight, (c) obesity, (d) eating momentum beyond control, (e) food as a panacea and constant temptation, (f) secret bingeing, (g) voracious eating, (h) insufficient eating obvious to others, (i) food phobia, (j) inability to eat, (k) vomiting after meals, and (l) lack of appetite. Three of the scales (3, 7, and 12) were eliminated because of low internal consistency. Total scores were computed for each of the remaining nine scales and these scale scores were analyzed in a secondary factor analysis. Three secondary factors emerged and were named (a) predisposition to obesity, (b) uncontrollable urges to eat, and (c) predisposition to anorexia. Scores on each of the nine subscales were standardized, then summed within dimensions to form three additional scores.

Reliability. Except for obesity, voracious eating, and lack of appetite, the internal consistencies of the nine remaining scales were all greater than .80 and considered adequate. No test-retest reliability data were reported. The three combined scales were intercorrelated. Predisposition to obesity had a correlation of .47 with uncontrollable urges to eat and .19 with predisposition to anorexia. The internal consistencies of the three combined scales were not reported because they were formed after standardizing the nine primary scales rather than being composed of a summing of individual items.

Validity. All of the scales (primary and combined) except lack of appetite were significantly correlated with gender. Females had more eating problems than males on all of the scales. Dieting, preoccupation with weight, obesity, eating momentum beyond control, secret bingeing, and voracious eating were negatively correlated with ponderal index (height divided by the cubed root of weight—a measure of elongated versus round body shape). These findings suggested that round, overweight individuals had more problems with these aspects of eating behavior. Insufficient eating obvious to others was positively correlated with ponderal index, suggesting that thin, long-shaped individuals were more likely to report this pattern of behavior.

The measures of eating characteristics were also correlated with measures of arousability, pleasantness, and dominance. In general, the correlations were weak (all but one below .20) but were consistent with the interpretation that people scoring high on the measures of eating characteristics tended to have arousable, unpleasant, and submissive temperaments. Mehrabian describes this constellation of temperaments as anxious, neurotic individuals.

Mehrabian (1987) described a study of the relationship between emotions and eating that is relevant to the validity of the ECQ. Subjects were presented with descriptions of situations that involved either unpleasant-aroused (pained, humiliated, puzzled, unsafe, embarrassed) or unpleasant-unaroused (lonely, unhappy, bored, sad, depressed) emotions. Subjects imagined themselves in each of these situations and rated how this would influence their eating behavior. He reported that unpleasant-aroused emotions resulted in a decrease in eating, whereas unpleasant-unaroused emotions were associated with increases in eating. An interaction effect was found with the uncontrollable urges to eat measure. Subjects high on this factor showed a more pronounced response to situations involving unpleasant-unaroused emotions. The correlation between uncontrollable urges to eat and behavior ratings in the boredom-depression situations were only moderate ($r = .32$).

No other measures of eating behaviors were collected. The validity data are limited to the relationships between gender and actual weight status and a weak correlation with personality measures. It is not known how these measures would correlate with other assessments such as the Three-Factor Eating Questionnaire or measures of binge eating.

Norms. Mehrabian (1987) presents detailed data on norms for each scale and the interested reader is referred to his book.

Availability. The complete 179-item Eating-Related Characteristics Questionnaire along with information on its scoring is included as an appendix in Mehrabian (1987).

Supplementary Eating Characteristics Questionnaire (SECQ)

Mehrabian (1987) also described the development and validation of a second measure of eating-related characteristics. The ECQ was intended to investigate behaviors relevant to anorexia and obesity. The SECQ was developed to measure patterns or styles of eating in general. The goal was to better characterize the range and variability in the eating patterns of normal people. The SECQ consists of 196 items describing various eating behaviors such as "I hardly ever eat out of cans, cartons, or food containers" and "I like to try new flavors."

Factor analysis. The strategy used in the factor analysis of the SECQ was similar to that in the ECQ. The scale was administered to 148 male and 237 female college students. A factor analysis of the raw data resulted in 24 factors. These were scored and the scores were factor analyzed to yield eight basic dimensions of eating. The results of the two factor analyses are presented in Table 8.13. Of the 196 items, only 135 were included in one of the 24 factor analytically derived scales.

Reliability. The reliabilities of 24 factor analytically derived scales were evaluated by computing coefficient alpha. Although many scales had adequate internal consistencies above .80, several consisting of only a few items were lower (e.g., "prefers starches to protein" had four items and a coefficient alpha of .63).

Validity. The scores on the SECQ were correlated with gender, ponderal index, triceps skinfolds, and temperament measures of arousability, pleasantness, and dominance. In addition, measures of achievement and social desirability were included in the validity study. The correlations between the SECQ and the temperament measures, when significant, were weak (all less than .30 and most less than .20). In general, they confirmed the findings with the ECQ that people who could be characterized as anxious or neurotic report greater difficulties with their eating behavior. Dominant people and high achievers showed a significant positive correlation with the aesthetic approach to eating factor. Predisposition to obesity was moderately correlated with skinfolds thickness ($r = .47$) and ponderal index ($r = -.46$). A mechani-

TABLE 8.13 The Factor Analytically Derived Scales of Mehrabian's (1987) Supplementary Eating Characteristics Questionnaire

I.   Mechanical joyless eating

    1.   Continuing to eat when full
    2.   Eats rapidly without attending to food
    3.   Eats when it is unsuitable or undesirable
    4.   Eats alone and sloppily
    5.   Loses appetite when upset or tense (–)

II. Predisposition to obesity

    6.   Dieting
    7.   Eats starches with meals (–)
    8.   Full feeling inhibits work and sex
    9.   Fasts occasionally
    10. Eats before sleep or napping (–)

III. Aesthetic approach to eating

    11. Tries new, unfamiliar foods
    12. Prefers variety of courses
    13. Prefers spicy and hot foods
    14. Appreciates aesthetics of meals
    15. Savors food that takes time to eat

IV. Reduced eating when overstimulated or feeling submissive

    16. Eats less when overstimulated or hot
    17. Eats less when feeling submissive

V.   Preference for regularly scheduled meals in unarousing settings

    18. Prefers arousing settings for meals (–)
    19. Plans and eats three meals a day

VI. Some eating and drinking ancillary to other routines, work

    20. Reads during meals
    21. Sips beverages outside meal times

VII. Frequent snacks and desserts relieve boredom, provide extra stimulation

    22. Likes and eats desserts
    23. Snacks frequently, especially when bored

VIII. Prefers protein to starches

    24. Prefers proteins to starches

NOTE: Negative factor loadings are indicated by (–).

cal, joyless approach to eating was positively associated with the male gender ($r = .23$), whereas predisposition to obesity was correlated with being female ($r = -.41$).

Norms. Detailed normative data are presented in Mehrabian (1987). The norms are for college students from the University of California and may not be applicable to other geographic regions, older persons, and nonstudent populations.

Availability. All 196 items are reproduced as an appendix to Mehrabian (1987). However, the instructions for computing the 24 factor scores are not given.

Three-Factor Eating Questionnaire (TFEQ)

Stunkard and Messick's (1985) TFEQ is reviewed by Gorman and Allison (this volume). In this section, we will focus briefly on the Disinhibition and Hunger subscales. The TFEQ is a 51-item inventory that contains a mixture of true/false and multiple choice items.

Factor analysis. The investigators started with an initial item inventory. A factor analysis of data from 200 subjects resulted in three factors labeled restraint, weight and diet lability, and hunger. The factor structure replicated very well across groups of dieters and their normal weight neighbors. The analysis did not replicate so well across gender, suggesting that the second factor was somewhat unstable. A second scale consisting of 93 items was administered to 98 subjects. Factor analysis and item analysis were used to reduce the questionnaire to 51 items with three relatively stable factors labeled cognitive restraint, disinhibition, and hunger. Other factor analytic studies have suggested that the factor structure of this inventory may not be completely stable (Ganley, 1988; Westenhoefer, 1991). Due to the widespread use of these scales, further factor analytic investigations may be warranted.

Reliability. The Disinhibition scale has a coefficient alpha of .91 and the Hunger scale an alpha of .85 (Stunkard & Messick, 1985).

Validity. The correlation between hunger and disinhibition was .40 and the correlation with restraint was .43. There was a $-.04$ correlation between hunger and restraint. However, when the sample was divided into dieters and free eaters, the correlation between restraint and disinhibition disappeared for the free eaters ($r = .19$), whereas the relationship between disinhibition and hunger increased ($r = .73$). In addition, the relationship between restraint and disinhibition changed direction when examined separately in the group of dieters ($r = .45$). The dieters and free eaters differed significantly in the restraint and disinhibition scores.

Westenhoefer (1991) formed two separate restraint scales using a sample of 54,525 subjects who completed a German version of the TFEQ. The "flexible restraint" items were associated with low levels of disinhibition, whereas the "rigid restraint" items were associated with high levels of disinhibition.

Huon and Wootton (1991) and Huon, Wootton, and Brown (1991) examined the behavior of high- and low-disinhibition subjects in an experimental investigation of carbohydrate intake. They failed to find any relationship between disinhibition scores and the amount of carbohydrate consumed.

Rossiter, Wilson, and Goldstein (1989) compared bulimic patients with highly restrained nonbulimic subjects and found that the bulimics scored significantly higher on the Restraint subscale of the TFEQ. No differences were reported on the Hunger subscale.

Lowe and Caputo (1991) developed regression models to predict binge eating in a group of 122 males and 314 females participating in a modified fasting weight-loss program. All three subscales of the TFEQ contributed to the prediction of binge eating.

Schlundt and Bell (1993) examined the relationship between body image disturbance, assessed using the Body Image Testing System (BITS), and measures of eating behavior. The BITS scores accounted for 58% of the variance in restraint, 51% of the variance in disinhibition, and 57% of the variance in hunger in a sample of 144 college females.

These studies suggest that the Disinhibition and Hunger subscales of the TFEQ are measuring important constructs that are related to binge eating and body image disturbance. More research is still needed to clarify exactly what these scales measure and to define more clearly the role of these constructs in the regulation and disregulation of eating behavior.

Availability. The TFEQ is published in Stunkard and Messick (1985) and can be purchased from the Psychological Corporation. Stunkard and Messick (1985) present normative data on their derivation samples. The TFEQ has been used in many studies; therefore many normative data sets exist.

Dutch Eating Behavior Questionnaire (DEBQ)

Van Strien et al. (1986) endeavored to develop a scale to assess dietary restraint, external eating, and emotional eating. They began with an initial pool of 100 items. These items were administered to 120 subjects and a factor analysis was conducted on 72 of the items showing sufficient response variability. Three factors emerged: emotional eating, restrained eating, and external eating and perceived hunger. The items relating to hunger were dropped and a 51-item version of the scale was administered to 264 subjects. Factor analytic studies were again used to revise the scale. The third version of the scale was administered to 1,170 subjects. Factor analysis was again used to reduce the number of items to obtain pure measures of restraint, emotional eating, and external eating. The final item pool consisted of 33 items describing specific eating behaviors on which subjects make a frequency rating. A four-factor solution appeared to be stable and interpretable. The four factors were restraint, emotional eating in response to diffuse feelings, emotional eating in response to specific emotions, and external eating. This factor structure was stable for obese and nonobese subjects and for males and females. The questionnaire may be scored with three or four subscales. The three-subscale scoring involves combining the two emotional eating subscales into a single emotional eating measure.

Wardle (1987) performed a factor analysis of the DEBQ using data from 188 students and confirmed the presence of restraint, externality, and emotional eating factors.

Reliability. Van Strien et al. (1986) reported coefficient alphas of .95, .94, .93, .86, and .80 for restraint, combined emotional eating, diffuse emotions, specific emotions, and external eating, respectively.

Validity. Van Strien et al. (1986) reported no validity data in their original report of the DEBQ. Wardle (1987) administered the scale to 188 students, 107 women attending Weight Watchers, 61 women diagnosed with bulimia, and 33 anorexic patients. There were no differences among the clinical groups on restraint, whereas all three groups showed higher restraint than the normals. The bulimic patients scored higher on external eating than the anorexic and obese groups. The anorexic patients had significantly lower external eating scores than the normal women. Emotional eating was higher in the bulimics than the obese groups and the obese subjects scored higher on emotional eating than the anorexic group. Anorexic patients scored significantly lower than normal women on emotional eating and were similar to the normal men. These differences remained after controlling for age differences between the groups.

Blair, Lewis, and Booth (1990) followed 187 adults prospectively for 1 year to determine their success in losing weight. Ten of the emotional eating items from the DEBQ were administered at baseline. Emotional eating scores were correlated with BMI ($r = .35$) at baseline. Blair et al. (1990) found that emotional eating scores were significantly associated with weight-loss success. Subjects initially high on emotional eating who reduced their scores and those initially low who remained low were more successful at weight control efforts than those who were initially high who remained high or those who were initially low and whose emotional eating scores increased.

A. J. Hill et al. (1991) administered the DEBQ and a measure of craving sweets to 206 women. Sweet craving was significantly associated with external eating and emotional eating. In addition, the External Eating and Emotional Eating scales of the DEBQ showed high correlations with the Disinhibition and Hunger scales of the TFEQ.

Wardle et al. (1992) administered the DEBQ to 486 adolescents along with an assessment of food intake and attitudes toward food. Older adolescents and girls reported higher rates of emotional eating. Emotional eating was associated with perceived body size. Subjects who saw themselves as larger had more problems with emotional eating. External eating did not differ between boys and girls although it was more pronounced among the older adolescents. External eating was associated with a lower BMI. Subjects who perceived themselves as overweight engaged in less external eating. Subjects high on emotional eating reported that dietary violations made them feel fatter, and more upset, and that they had more difficulty stopping once they started eating. Subjects high in emotional eating also reported more difficulty with binge eating. Restrained eaters consumed less energy than unrestrained eaters. There was no relationship between emotional eating and energy intake, whereas there was a tendency for external eaters to consume more calories.

Allison and Heshka (1993) administered the DEBQ and two social desirability scales to 78 subjects. There was no correlation between the Marlowe-Crowne Social Desirability scale and emotional eating, but there was a correlation of .5 between emotional eating and the Edwards's Social Desirability scale. Allison and Heshka (1993) also reported that subjects could easily "fake good" and "fake bad" on the Emotional Eating scale.

In summary, the DEBQ appears to have a stable factor structure, high internal consistency, and varied evidence for its validity. The external eating and emotional eating variables are associated with disinhibition and hunger on the TFEQ. Additional research is needed to explore the relationship between emotional eating and social desirability. Studies looking at the relationship between DEBQ scores and a microanalysis of eating using behavioral diaries would also further clarify the validity of the scales.

Norms. There have been several studies conducted using the DEBQ in different populations. Many of these studies have reported means and standard deviations.

Availability. The items of the DEBQ are published in Van Strien et al. (1986) and in Wardle (1987).

Yale Eating Pattern Questionnaire

Kristeller and Rodin (1989) were interested in investigating patterns of eating in normal individuals. They developed a 139-item inventory that sampled a broad range of behaviors and attitudes toward eating and body weight. The scale was administered to 116 female and 70 male college students.

Factor analysis. After first removing items with skewed distributions, the remaining items were factor analyzed in stages. Habit items, satiation items, and weight attribution items were analyzed separately. Items with factor loading greater than .35 were retained. This method was used to form nine subscales: (a) uninhibited; (b) oversnacking; (c) bingeing; (d) dieting; (e) satiation, full; (f) satiation, nausea; (g) satiation, guilt; (h) attribute overweight to physical causes; and (i) attribute overweight to emotional causes. The details of the factor analysis were not reported.

Reliability. Coefficient alpha was computed for each subscale and all alpha levels were greater than .69.

Validity. Men and women differed significantly on uninhibited; bingeing; dieting; satiation, guilt; and attribution of weight problems to physical causes. The subjects were divided into six groups using cluster analysis. The groups were labeled uninhibited eaters, uninterested eaters, bingers, guilty dieters, high self-monitors, and low self-monitors. Women were more likely than men to be in the binger and guilty dieter groups. Bingers, and guilty dieters, had significantly higher scores on the Restraint scale than the uninhibited eaters and the uninterested eaters.

Norms. Kristeller and Rodin (1989) present means and standard deviations separately for men and woman on all nine subscales of the inventory.

Availability. The items constituting the nine subscales of the Yale Eating Pattern Questionnaire are presented in Kristeller and Rodin (1989) and are reproduced in Appendix 8-F.

Summary and Conclusions

The measurement of eating behavior need no longer be limited to simple estimates of typical caloric intake. In this chapter, we have examined a variety of measurement approaches that have been developed in the last 10 years to assess eating behaviors, eating patterns, and constructs thought to play an important role in the regulation of feeding in humans. Many patterns of eating identified using microanalysis of behavioral diaries now have counterparts in the array of questionnaires reviewed. Craving sweets, overeating, food restriction, emotional eating, and the responsivity of eating to specific environmental situations can now be assessed by scales that have at least moderate internal consistency and preliminary evidence for their validity.

The cluster analysis results in Table 8.10 suggest a few additional areas for questionnaire development. Specifically, the role of social situations and positive emotions in the regulation of food intake has received little attention. Most investigators, when they have even bothered to think about dietary composition, have assumed that eating carbohydrates is a major problem for obese and eating disordered individuals. Scales need to be constructed to assess people's preferences for high-fat meals and snacks. We have seen that people differ not only in their typical caloric consumption but also in the degree to which they vary from day to day and meal to meal. So far, none of the questionnaires available adequately measures intraindividual variability.

A few general findings about eating behavior can be drawn from this review of the literature. First, it appears that there may be a psychological component to body weight regulation. In many of the studies cited, there were small but significant correlations between measures of uncontrolled eating behaviors and body-mass index. Another general observation is that there are consistent gender differences across measures and studies. In our culture, the eating patterns of men and women appear to be consistently different. Given that much of this research was inspired by an interest in eating disorders, there is a bias toward studying women to the exclusion of men. Future research should attempt to learn more about patterns of eating in men. There is also a glaring lack of information about the eating patterns of different minority groups. Most of the research has been done on white, middle- to upper-middle-class, female college students in the United States and Western Europe. When college students were not used, patients being treated for eating disorders or obesity were studied instead.

Wardle et al.'s (1992) findings of age and age by sex interactions in emotional eating in adolescents also suggest that much more work needs to be done on how eating patterns, especially pathological dieting and binge eating patterns, develop from childhood to adulthood (see A. J. Hill, Oliver, & Rogers, 1992).

There is much more yet to be learned about how humans regulate their food intake. In all likelihood, some findings we accept as facts today will change as we refine our techniques of assessment and study more diverse populations. This chapter demonstrates that a variety of measures are currently available. At the risk of overloading participants in our studies, anyone who is working with the assessment of food intake should include multiple measures that tap the range of behaviors and constructs that can now be assessed. Just as total calorie intake doesn't tell the whole story, a single measure of dietary restraint can no longer be considered an adequate assessment of eating style.

References

Allison, D. B., & Heshka, S. (1993). Social desirability and response bias in self-reports of "emotional eating." *Eating Disorders, 1,* 31-38.

Axelson, M. L. (1986). The impact of culture on food-related behavior. *Annual Review of Nutrition, 6,* 345-363.

Bandini, L. G., Schoeller, D. A., Cyr, H. N., & Dietz, W. H. (1990). Validity of reported energy intake in obese and nonobese adolescents. *American Journal of Clinical Nutrition, 52,* 421-425.

Bandura, A. (1986). *Social foundations of thought and action.* Englewood Cliffs, NJ: Prentice-Hall.

Beiman, J., Graham, L. E., & Ciminero, A. R. (1978). Self-controlled progressive relaxation training as an alternative nonpharmacological treatment for essential hypertension: Therapeutic effects in the natural environment. *Behavior Research and Therapy, 16,* 371-375.

Blair, A. J., Lewis, V. J., & Booth, D. A. (1990). Does emotional eating interfere with success in attempts at weight control? *Appetite, 15,* 151-157.

Block, G. A. (1982). A review of dietary assessment methods. *American Journal of Epidemiology, 115,* 492-505.

Blundell, J. E., & Hill, A. J. (1986). Behavioural pharmacology of feeding: Relevance of animal experiments for studies in man. In M. O. Carruba & J. E. Blundell (Eds.), *Pharmacology of eating disorders: Theoretical and clinical developments* (pp. 51-70). New York: Raven.

Bootzin, R. R., & Engle-Friedman, M. (1981). The assessment of insomnia. *Behavioral Assessment, 3,* 107-126.

Borland International. (1985). *Turbo Pascal version 3.0.* Scotts Valley, CA: Author.

Brewer, E. R., Kassim, N., Cronin, F. J., Dennis, B. H., Kuczmarski, R. J., Haynes, S., & Graves, K. (1987). Food group system of analysis with special attention to amount and type of fat: Methodology. *Journal of the American Dietetic Association, 87,* 584-592.

ESHA Research. (1987). *The Food Processor.* Salem, OR: Author.

Fricker, J., Baelde, D., Apfelbaum, L. I., Huet, J. M., & Apfelbaum, M. (1992). Underreporting of food intake in obese "small eaters." *Appetite, 19,* 273-283.

Ganley, R. (1988). Emotional eating and how it relates to dietary restraint, disinhibition, and perceived hunger. *International Journal of Eating Disorders, 7,* 635-647.

Glasgow, R. E., Klesges, R. C., Godding, P. R., & Gegelman, R. (1983). Controlled smoking with or without carbon monoxide feedback as an alternative for chronic smokers. *Behavior Therapy, 14,* 386-397.

Glynn, S. M., & Ruderman, A. J. (1986). The development and validation of an eating self-efficacy scale. *Cognitive Therapy and Research, 10,* 403-420.

Goldfried, M. R., & D'Zurilla, T. J. (1969). A behavioral-analytic model for assessing competence. In C. D. Speilberger (Ed.), *Current topics in clinical and community psychology* (Vol. 1, pp. 151-196). New York: Academic Press.

Hawkins, R. C., & Clement, P. F. (1980). Development and construct validation of a self-report measure of binge eating tendencies. *Addictive Behaviors, 5,* 219-226.

Haynes, S. N. (1984). Behavioral assessment of adults. In G. Goldstein & M. Hersen (Eds.), *Handbook of psychological assessment* (pp. 369-401). New York: Pergamon.

Hill, A. J., Oliver, S., & Rogers, P. J. (1992). Eating in the adult world: The rise of dieting in childhood and adolescence. *British Journal of Clinical Psychology, 31,* 95-105.

Hill, A. J., Weaver, C. L., & Blundell, J. E. (1991). Food craving, dietary restraint and mood. *Appetite, 17,* 187-197.

Hill, J. O., Schlundt, D. G., Sbrocco, T., Sharp, T., Pope-Cordle, J., Stetson, B., Kaler, M., & Heim, C. (1989). Evaluation of an alternating calorie diet with and without exercise in the treatment of obesity. *American Journal of Clinical Nutrition, 50,* 248-254.

Hoover, W. (1983). Computerized nutrient data bases: I. Comparison of nutrient analysis systems. *Journal of the American Dietetic Association, 82,* 501.

Hunt, W. C., Leonard, A. G., Garry, P. J., & Goodwin, J. S. (1983). Components of variance in dietary data for an elderly population. *Nutrition Research, 3,* 433-444.

Huon, G. F., & Wootton, M. (1991). The role of dietary carbohydrate and of knowledge of having eaten it in the urge to eat more. *International Journal of Eating Disorders, 10,* 31-42.

Huon, G. F., Wootton, M., & Brown, L. B. (1991). The role of restraint and disinhibition in appetite control. *Journal of Psychosomatic Research, 35,* 49-58.

Kemeny, J. G., & Snell, J. L. (1962). *Mathematical models in the social sciences.* New York: Blaisdell.

Kristeller, J. L., & Rodin, J. (1989). Identifying eating patterns in male and female undergraduates using cluster analysis. *Addictive Behaviors, 14,* 631-642.

Lichtman, S. W., Pisarska, K., Berman, E. R., Pestone, M., Dowling, H., Offenbacher, E., Weisel, H., Heshka, S., Matthews, D. E., & Heymsfield, S. B. (1992). Discrepancy between self-reported and actual caloric intake and exercise in obese subjects. *New England Journal of Medicine, 327,* 1893-1898.

Lindsley, O. R. (1968). A reliable wrist counter for recording behavior rates. *Journal of Applied Behavior Analysis, 1,* 77-78.

Lowe, M. R., & Caputo, G. C. (1991). Binge eating in obesity: Toward the specification of predictors. *International Journal of Eating Disorders, 10,* 49-55.

Marlatt, G. A. (1985). Situational determinants of relapse and skill-training interventions. In G. A. Marlatt & J. R. Gordon (Eds.), *Relapse prevention* (pp. 71-127). New York: Guilford.

Mehrabian, A. (1987). *Eating characteristics and temperament: General measures and interrelationships.* New York: Springer-Verlag.

Mehrabian, A., Nahum, I. V., & Duke, V. (1986). Individual difference correlates and measures of predisposition to obesity and anorexia. *Imagination, Cognition, and Personality, 5,* 339-355.

Mertz, W., & Kelsay, J. L. (1984). Rationale and design of the Beltsville one-year dietary intake study. *American Journal of Clinical Nutrition, 40*(Suppl.), 1323-1326.

Miller, P. M. (1981). Assessment of alcohol abuse. In D. H. Barlow (Ed.), *Behavioral assessment of adult disorders* (pp. 271-299). New York: Guilford.

Rosen, J. C. (1981). Self-monitoring in the treatment of diurnal bruxism. *Journal of Behavior Therapy and Experimental Psychiatry, 12,* 347-350.

Rosen, J. C., & Leitenberg, H. (1982). Bulimia nervosa: Treatment with exposure and response prevention. *Behavior Therapy, 13,* 117-124.

Rossiter, E. M., Wilson, G. T., & Goldstein, L. (1989). Bulimia nervosa and dietary restraint. *Behavior Research and Therapy, 27,* 465-468.

Ruggiero, L., Williamson, D. A., Davis, C. J., Schlundt, D. G., & Carey, M. P. (1988). Forbidden Food Survey: Measure of bulimics' anticipated emotional reactions to specific foods. *Addictive Behaviors, 13,* 267-274.

Rush, D., & Kristal, A. R. (1982). Methodologic studies during pregnancy: The reliability of the 24-hour dietary recall. *American Journal of Clinical Nutrition, 35,* 1259-1268.

Sampson, L. (1985). Food frequency questionnaires as a research instrument. *Clinical Nutrition, 4,* 171-178.

Schlundt, D. G. (1985). An observational method for functional analysis. *Bulletin of the Society for Psychologists in Addictive Behaviors, 4,* 234-249.

Schlundt, D. G. (1988). Computerized behavioral assessment of dietary compliance in IDDM patients. *Diabetes Educator, 14,* 567-570.

Schlundt, D. G. (1989). Computerized behavioral assessment of eating behavior in bulimia: The self-monitoring analysis system. In W. G. Johnson (Ed.), *Advances in eating disorders: Vol. 2. Bulimia* (pp. 1-32). New York: JAI.

Schlundt, D. G., & Bell, C. (1987). Behavioral assessment of eating patterns and blood glucose in diabetes using the self-monitoring analysis system. *Behavior Research, Methods, Instruments, and Computers, 19,* 215-223.

Schlundt, D. G., & Bell, C. D. (1993). The body image testing system: A microcomputer program for the assessment of body image. *Journal of Behavioral Assessment and Psychopathology, 15,* 267-285.

Schlundt, D. G., Hill, J. O., Pope-Cordle, J., Arnold, D., Virts, K. L., & Katahn, M. R. (1993). Randomized evaluation of a low-fat ad lib carbohydrate diet for weight reduction. *International Journal of Obesity, 17,* 623-629.

Schlundt, D. G., Hill, J. O., Sbrocco, T., Pope-Cordle, J., & Kasser, T. (1990). Obesity: A biogenetic or biobehavioral problem. *International Journal of Obesity, 14,* 515-828.

Schlundt, D. G., Hill, J. O., Sbrocco, T., Pope-Cordle, J., & Sharp, T. (1992). The role of breakfast in the treatment of obesity: A randomized clinical trial. *American Journal of Clinical Nutrition, 55,* 645-651.

Schlundt, D. G., & Johnson, W. G. (1990). *Eating disorders: Assessment and treatment.* Boston: Allyn & Bacon.

Schlundt, D. G., Johnson, W. G., & Jarrell, M. P. (1985). A naturalistic functional analysis of eating in bulimia and obesity. *Advances in Behavior Research and Therapy, 7,* 149-162.

Schlundt, D. G., Johnson, W. G., & Jarrell, M. P. (1986). A sequential analysis of environmental, affective, and behavioral variables predictive of vomiting in bulimia nervosa. *Behavioral Assessment, 8,* 253-269.

Schlundt, D. G., Langford, H. G., & McDonel, E. (1985). Compliance in dietary management of hypertension. *Comprehensive Therapy, 11,* 59-66.

Schlundt, D. G., & McFall, R. M. (1985). New directions in the assessment of social competence and social skills. In M. A. Milan & L. L. L'Abate (Eds.), *Handbook of social skills training and research* (pp. 22-49). New York: Pergamon.

Schlundt, D. G., Sbrocco, T., & Bell, C. (1989). Identification of high risk situations in behavioral weight loss programs: Application of the relapse prevention model. *International Journal of Obesity, 13,* 223-234.

Schlundt, D. G., Taylor, D., Hill, J. O., Sbrocco, T., Pope-Cordle, J., Kasser, T., & Arnold, D. (1991). A behavioral taxonomy of obese female participants in a weight loss program. *American Journal of Clinical Nutrition, 53,* 1151-1158.

Schlundt, D. G., Virts, K. L., Hill, J. O., Sbrocco, T., Pope-Cordle, J., & Arnold, D. A. (1993). Sequential behavioral analysis of craving sweets in obese women. *Addictive Behaviors, 18,* 67-80.

Schlundt, D. G., & Zimering, R. T. (1988). The Dieter's Inventory of Eating Temptations: A measure of weight control competence. *Addictive Behaviors, 13,* 151-164.

Schoeller, D. A. (1990). How accurate is self-reported dietary energy intake? *Nutrition Reviews, 10,* 373-379.

Schoeller, D. A., & Fjeld, C. R. (1991). Human energy metabolism: What have we learned from the doubly labeled water method? *Annual Review of Nutrition, 11,* 355-373.

Sempos, C. T., Johnson, N. E., Smith, E. L., & Gilligan, C. (1985). Effects of intraindividual and interindividual variation in repeated dietary records. *American Journal of Epidemiology, 121,* 120-130.

Shea, S., Stein, A. D., Basch, C. E., Contento, I. R., & Zybert, P. (1992). Variability and self-regulation of energy intake in young children in their everyday environment. *Pediatrics, 90,* 542-546.

Sorenson, A. W., Calkins, B. M., Connolly, M. A., & Diamond, E. (1985). Comparison of nutrient intake determined by four dietary intake instruments. *Journal of Nutrition Education, 17,* 92-99.

Stanton, A. L., Garcia, M. E., & Green, S. B. (1990). Development and validation of the situational appetite measures. *Addictive Behaviors, 15,* 461-467.

Stotland, S. (1989). *Dieting self-efficacy: Its relation to situational and long-term dieting success.* Unpublished doctoral dissertation, McGill University, Montreal, Canada.

Stotland, S., Zuroff, D. C., & Roy, M. (1991). Situational dieting self-efficacy and short-term regulation of eating. *Appetite, 17,* 81-90.

Stunkard, A. J., & Messick, S. (1985). The Three-Factor Eating Questionnaire to measure dietary restraint, disinhibition, and hunger. *Journal of Psychosomatic Research, 29,* 71-83.

Suitor, C. J. W., & Crowley, M. F. (1984). *Nutrition principles and applications in health promotion.* Philadelphia: Lippincott.

Tarasuk, V., & Beaton, G. H. (1992). Day-to-day variation in energy and nutrient intake: Evidence of individuality in eating behavior? *Appetite, 18,* 43-54.

Tucker, D., & Schlundt, D. G. (1993). *Factor structure of the DIET questionnaire and its validity in a community and clinical sample.* Manuscript under review.

Underwood, B. A. (1986). Evaluating the nutritional status of individuals: A critique of approaches. *Nutrition Reviews/Supplement, 46,* 213-224.

Van Strien, T., Frijters, J. E. R., Bergers, G. P. A., & Defares, P. B. (1986). The Dutch Eating Behavior Questionnaire (DEBQ) for assessment of restrained, emotional, and external eating behavior. *International Journal of Eating Disorders, 5,* 295-315.

Wardle, J. (1987). Eating style: A validation study of the Dutch Eating Behavior Questionnaire in normal subjects and women with eating disorders. *Journal of Psychosomatic Research, 31,* 161-169.

Wardle, J., Marsland, L., Sheikh, Y., Quinn, M., Fedoroff, I., & Ogden, J. (1992). Eating style and eating behavior in adolescents. *Appetite, 18,* 167-183.

Webb, P. (1991). The measurement of energy expenditure. *Journal of Nutrition, 121,* 1897-1901.

Weber, M. A., & Drayer, J. I. M. (1984). *Ambulatory blood pressure monitoring.* Darmstadt, Germany: Steinkopff.

Weingarten, H. P., & Elston, D. (1991). Food cravings in a college population. *Appetite, 17,* 167-175.

Westenhoefer, J. (1991). Dietary restraint and disinhibition: Is restraint a homogeneous construct? *Appetite, 16,* 45-55.

Wilson, G. T. (1978). Methodological considerations in treatment outcome research on obesity. *Journal of Consulting and Clinical Psychology, 46,* 684-702.

Appendix 8-A

Dieter's Inventory of Eating Temptations (DIET)

Each item in this questionnaire describes a situation and a behavior that promotes weight loss or weight control. Imagine that you are in the situation described and rate the percent of the time you would behave in the way described. If you would always act in the way described then give a rating of 100%. If you would never act that way give a rating of 0%. If you would sometimes act that way then mark an "X" at the point on the scale that shows how often you would act as described. If you feel that you never get into a situation like the one described (it does not apply to you), then rate how often you engage in the kind of behavior described in general.

1. You're having dinner with your family and your favorite meal has been prepared. You finish the first helping and someone says, "Why don't you have some more?" What percent of the time would you turn down a second helping?

       0   10   20   30   40   50   60   70   80   90   100

2. You would like to exercise every day but it is hard to find the time because of your family and work obligations. What percent of the time would you set aside a daily time for exercise?

       0   10   20   30   40   50   60   70   80   90   100

3. You like to eat high calorie snack foods (e.g., cookies, potato chips, crackers, cokes, beer, cake) while watching television. What percent of the time would you watch TV without eating a high calorie snack?

       0   10   20   30   40   50   60   70   80   90   100

4. When you eat in a good restaurant, you love to order high calorie foods. What percent of the time would you order a low calorie meal?

       0   10   20   30   40   50   60   70   80   90   100

5. When planning meals, you tend to choose high calorie foods. What percent of the time would you plan low calorie meals?

       0   10   20   30   40   50   60   70   80   90   100

6. You are at a party and there is a lot of fattening food. You already have eaten more than you should and you are tempted to continue eating. What percent of the time would you stop with what you have already eaten?

       0   10   20   30   40   50   60   70   80   90   100

7. You like to flavor your vegetables with butter, margarine, ham, or bacon fat. What percent of the time would you choose a low calorie method of seasoning?

0   10   20   30   40   50   60   70   80   90   100

8. You often prepare many of your foods by frying. What percent of the time would you prepare your food in a way that is less fattening?

0   10   20   30   40   50   60   70   80   90   100

9. You allow yourself a snack in the evening but you find yourself eating more than your diet allows. What percent of the time would you reduce the size of your snack?

0   10   20   30   40   50   60   70   80   90   100

10. Instead of putting foods away after finishing a meal, you find yourself eating the leftovers. What percent of the time would you put the food away without eating any?

0   10   20   30   40   50   60   70   80   90   100

11. You are asked by another person to go for a walk but you feel tired and kind of low. What percent of the time would you overcome these feelings and say "yes" to the walk?

0   10   20   30   40   50   60   70   80   90   100

12. You often overeat at supper because you are tired and hungry when you get home. What percent of the time would you not overeat at supper?

0   10   20   30   40   50   60   70   80   90   100

13. When you have errands to run that are only a couple of blocks away you usually drive the car. What percent of the time would you walk on an errand when it only involves a couple of blocks?

0   10   20   30   40   50   60   70   80   90   100

14. You are invited to someone's house for dinner and your host is an excellent cook. You often overeat because the food tastes so good. What percent of the time would you not overeat as a dinner guest?

0   10   20   30   40   50   60   70   80   90   100

15. You like to have something sweet to eat on your coffee break. What percent of the time would you only have coffee?

0   10   20   30   40   50   60   70   80   90   100

16. When you cook a meal you snack on the food. What percent of the time would you wait until the meal is prepared to eat?

0   10   20   30   40   50   60   70   80   90   100

17. You planned to exercise after work today but you feel tired and hungry when the time arrives. What percent of the time would you exercise anyway?

0   10   20   30   40   50   60   70   80   90   100

18. There is a party at work for a co-worker and someone offers you a piece of cake. What percent of the time would you turn it down?

   0   10   20   30   40   50   60   70   80   90   100

19. You would like to climb the stairs instead of taking the elevator. What percent of the time would you take the stairs to go one or two flights?

   0   10   20   30   40   50   60   70   80   90   100

20. You are happy and feeling good today. You are tempted to treat yourself by stopping for ice cream. What percent of the time would you find some other way to be nice to yourself?

   0   10   20   30   40   50   60   70   80   90   100

21. You are at a friend's house and your friend offers you a delicious looking pastry. What percent of the time would you refuse this offer?

   0   10   20   30   40   50   60   70   80   90   100

22. You feel like celebrating. You are going out with friends to a good restaurant. What percent of the time would you celebrate without overeating?

   0   10   20   30   40   50   60   70   80   90   100

23. You finished your meal and you still feel hungry. There is cake and fruit available. What percent of the time would you choose the fruit?

   0   10   20   30   40   50   60   70   80   90   100

24. You are at home feeling lonely, blue, and bored. You are craving something to eat. What percent of the time would you find another way of coping with these feelings besides eating?

   0   10   20   30   40   50   60   70   80   90   100

25. Today you did something to hurt your ankle. You want to get something to eat to make yourself feel better. What percent of the time would you find some other way to take your mind off your mishap?

   0   10   20   30   40   50   60   70   80   90   100

26. When you spend time alone at home you are tempted to snack. You are spending an evening alone. What percent of the time would you resist the urge to snack?

   0   10   20   30   40   50   60   70   80   90   100

27. You are out with a friend at lunch time and your friend suggests that you stop and get some ice cream. What percent of the time would you resist the temptation?

   0   10   20   30   40   50   60   70   80   90   100

28. You just had an upsetting argument with a family member. You are standing in front of the refrigerator and you feel like eating everything in sight. What percent of the time would you find some other way to make yourself feel better?

   0   10   20   30   40   50   60   70   80   90   100

29. You are having a hard day at work and you are anxious and upset. You feel like getting a candy bar. What percent of the time would you find a more constructive way to calm down and cope with your feelings?

0   10   20   30   40   50   60   70   80   90   100

30. You just had an argument with your (husband, wife, boyfriend, girlfriend). You are upset and angry, and you feel like eating something. What percentage of time would you talk the situation over with someone or go for a walk instead of eating?

0   10   20   30   40   50   60   70   80   90   100

SOURCE: From *Eating Disorders: Assessment and Treatment,* by D. G. Schlundt and W. G. Johnson, 1990, Boston: Allyn & Bacon. Copyright © 1990 by Allyn & Bacon. Reprinted with permission.

Appendix 8-B

Situation-Based Dieting Self-Efficacy Scale (SDS)

Instructions: Please respond to the following statements by indicating how confident you are that you could stick to your diet in each of the situations described. Place a number from 0 to 100 in the space next to each statement, where 0 indicates that you are *not at all* confident, and 100 indicates that you are *completely* confident that you could stick to your diet in that situation. Please respond to the statements according to the way you think you could behave in them *if they were to occur in the COMING WEEK!*

$$0 \text{———————————} 100$$

Not at all confident   Completely confident

Confidence

1. Talking with several friends. You're not hungry. Your friend serves a delicious dessert. ____

2. Dinner with family. Tired and very hungry. ____

3. Out for coffee and dessert with friends. You are happy and quite hungry. ____

4. You're cooking supper. You feel calm and quite hungry. ____

5. It's early evening. You have a snack while talking to a friend (or spouse) and listening to music. You are happy and quite hungry. ____

6. You feel relaxed and very hungry while having supper with your family. ____

7. You are working at home and decide to have a late night snack. You are calm and slightly hungry. ____

8. You have an afternoon snack while working. You are relaxed and extremely hungry. ____

9. Dinner at home, feeling happy and quite hungry. ____

10. Breakfast with your family, feeling calm and slightly hungry. ____

11. Family dinner, feeling anxious and very hungry. ____

12. Dinner at home with your family, feeling angry and very hungry. ____

13. Breakfast with your family. You feel rushed and very hungry.   ____

14. Afternoon snack after shopping. You are nervous and slightly hungry.   ____

15. You have a snack while watching a movie. Your mood is neutral and you are quite hungry.   ____

16. Supper at home with a friend. You are happy and slightly hungry.   ____

17. You have a snack at home with some friends. You are calm and quite hungry.   ____

18. Snack over drinks with friends, after a movie. You are happy and slightly hungry.   ____

19. At a family supper you are quite hungry and anxious about something you have to do.   ____

20. Lunch with a friend at a restaurant. You are very hungry. You are feeling annoyed.   ____

21. Mid-morning snack (or coffee break), feeling relaxed and very hungry.   ____

22. You have lunch, feeling very hungry because you skipped breakfast.   ____

23. You have dinner with a friend (family) who heaps loads of food on your plate. You are slightly hungry.   ____

24. You attend a dinner party.   ____

25. At a party where there's good food.   ____

SOURCE: From "Situational Dieting Self-Efficacy and Short-Term Regulation of Eating," by S. Stotland, D. C. Zuroff, and M. Roy, 1991, *Appetite, 17*, pp. 81-90. Copyright © 1991 by Academic Press London. Reprinted with permission.

Appendix 8-C

Situational Appetite Measure (SAM) Scales

Factor loadings greater than .30 for Situational Appetite Measure: Urges items for female dieters ($n = 184$)

Abbreviated Items	Factors				
	I	II	III	IV	V
Factor I: *Relaxation*					
1. When I am watching television.	.60				
6. When I get home from school/work.	.36				
11. When it's late at night.	.38				
16. When I am relaxed at home.	.51				
21. When I am lying around at home.	.80				
26. When I am unwinding at home.	.59				
Factor II: *Food Present*					
2. When I pass a restaurant, store, or vending machine where food is available.		.51			
7. When I am around food or food is easily available.		.46			
12. When I try to eat just a little of some good food.					
17. When I am cooking for others.		.56			
22. When I am in a restaurant and I'm asked for my order, even when I was not planning to eat.		.66			
27. When I see others eat.	.35	.52			
Factor III: *Hunger*					
3. When my stomach growls.			.42	.45	
8. When I have stomach pangs.			.39	.41	

Abbreviated Items	Factors				
	I	II	III	IV	V
13. When I feel hungry.			.56		
18. When I am "dying" of hunger.			.84		
23. When I have not eaten for a long time and I am craving something to eat.			.82		
28. When I am "starving."			.83		

Factor IV: *Reward*

4. When I want to reward myself for something good I've done.				.68	
9. When something good has happened.				.85	
14. When I've succeeded at something.				.92	
19. When I have done well at work or on a test.				.87	
24. When I have learned some good news.				.85	
29. When I feel good about having done something well.				.90	

Factor V: *Negative Feelings*

5. When I just had an argument with someone.					.58
10. When I feel upset.					.90
15. When I am frustrated.					.90
20. When I am worried.					.89
25. When I feel nervous.					.67
30. When I feel angry with myself.					.75

SOURCE: Reprinted from *Addictive Behaviors, 15,* pp. 461-472, A. L. Stanton, M. E. Garcia, and S. B. Green, "Development and Validation of the Situational Appetite Measures," copyright © 1990, with kind permission from Elsevier Science Ltd., The Boulevard, Langford Lane, Kidlington OX5 1GB, U.K.

Appendix 8-D

The Craving Questionnaire

Name: _____   Estimated Height: _____ ft. _____ inches

Age: _____   Estimated Weight: _____ lbs.

Male _____   Female _____

Are you currently on a diet?

Yes _____   No _____

Please answer the following questions to the best of your ability.

1. Have you ever experienced food cravings (i.e., an intense desire to eat a specific food)?

Yes _____   No _____

2. If you have experienced food cravings, we would like to know what it is that you crave.

_____

_____

_____

List below foods which you crave, starting with your strongest craving. Beside each, estimate how often you experienced that craving.

	CRAVED FOOD	FREQUENCY
strongest craving	_____	_____ times/month
next strongest	_____	_____ times/month
etc.	_____	_____ times/month

3. The following questions refer only to the food which you indicated as your strongest craving (the food at the top of your craving list in Question 2).

a) Describe in as much detail as you can the food you crave the most.

_____

_____

_____

b) When you are experiencing a craving for the food you crave the most, is there any other food which would satisfy that craving?

_____

_____

_____

c) When you are experiencing a craving for the food you crave the most, how often do you follow through and eat that food?

_____% of the time

d) How do you feel when you've eaten the food you crave the most?

_____

_____

_____

e) (For women only) Do you feel that your cravings are related to your menstrual cycle?

No _____

Yes _____

If yes, then how? _____

_____

_____

Is there anything about your cravings you would like to tell us that we forgot to ask?

_____

_____

_____

SOURCE: From "Food Cravings in a College Population," by H. P. Weingarten and D. Elston, 1991, *Appetite, 17,* pp. 167-175. Copyright © 1991 by Academic Press London. Reprinted with permission.

Appendix 8-E

Forbidden Food Survey

Food Survey

Rate how you would feel about yourself after eating each food.

     1 = I would feel very good about myself

     2 = I would feel good about myself

     3 = I would feel neither good nor bad about myself

     4 = I would feel bad about myself

     5 = I would feel very bad about myself

1. English muffin	1 2 3 4 5	15. Spare ribs 1 2 3 4 5
2. Jello	1 2 3 4 5	16. Cantaloupe 1 2 3 4 5
3. Apple	1 2 3 4 5	17. Fried chicken 1 2 3 4 5
4. Corn	1 2 3 4 5	18. White bread 1 2 3 4 5
5. Hot fudge sundae	1 2 3 4 5	19. Orange juice 1 2 3 4 5
6. Pork Chops	1 2 3 4 5	20. Doughnuts 1 2 3 4 5
7. Carrots	1 2 3 4 5	21. Potato 1 2 3 4 5
8. Cheddar cheese	1 2 3 4 5	22. Milk shake 1 2 3 4 5
9. Beer	1 2 3 4 5	23. Banana 1 2 3 4 5
10. Corn bread	1 2 3 4 5	24. Shrimp 1 2 3 4 5
11. Skim milk	1 2 3 4 5	25. Wine 1 2 3 4 5
12. Sweet potato	1 2 3 4 5	26. Popcorn 1 2 3 4 5
13. Boiled ham	1 2 3 4 5	27. Spinach 1 2 3 4 5
14. Pizza	1 2 3 4 5	28. Porterhouse steak 1 2 3 4 5

29. Lima beans	1 2 3 4 5	38. Veal cutlet	1 2 3 4 5
30. Diet soda	1 2 3 4 5	39. Ice cream	1 2 3 4 5
31. Waffles with syrup	1 2 3 4 5	40. Liquor	1 2 3 4 5
32. Swiss cheese	1 2 3 4 5	41. Biscuits	1 2 3 4 5
33. Hot dog	1 2 3 4 5	42. Plain yogurt	1 2 3 4 5
34. Peanut butter	1 2 3 4 5	43. Tomato juice	1 2 3 4 5
35. Coke	1 2 3 4 5	44. Cottage cheese	1 2 3 4 5
36. Saltines	1 2 3 4 5	44. Apple juice	1 2 3 4 5
37. Sour cream	1 2 3 4 5		

Food Survey Profile Chart

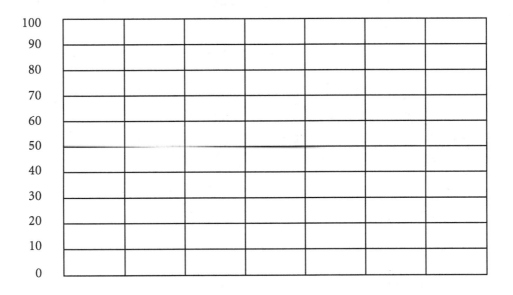

		Meat	Milk	Fruits & Vegetables	Grain	Beverage	Low	Medium	High
Items	L	13	11	7		8	19		
Items	O W	24	42	16	26	30			
Items		33	44	27	36	43			
Items	M	6	8	3	1	2			
Items	E D	17	32	21	10	25			
Items		38	39	23	41	45			
Items	H	15	22	4	14	9			
Items	I G	28	25	12	20	35	2.32	2.78	3.42
Items	H	34	37	29	31	40	0.49	0.38	0.65
Total									
Average									
M		3.10	2.92	2.16	3.12	2.79			
S		0.52	.041	0.69	0.55	0.45			
T									

Instructions for Scoring the Food Survey

1. The item numbers are listed in the boxes under each of the foods on the left side of the workspace. Write the rating given for each item in the appropriate box.

2. Add the items down each column to get a total score for each food. Divide this score by 9 to get the average rating.

3. Using M and S from each column, apply the following formula to the average in each column.

$$\left[\frac{(\text{Average} - M)}{S} \times 10 \right] + 50 = T$$

4. Plot the value of t on the profile chart.

SOURCE: From *Eating Disorders: Assessment and Treatment,* by D. G. Schlundt and W. G. Johnson, 1990, Boston: Allyn & Bacon. Copyright © 1990 by Allyn & Bacon. Reprinted with permission.

Appendix 8-F

Yale Eating Pattern Questionnaire Scale Items

Scale 1: Uninhibited

1. I have late night snacks.
2. Eating keeps me feeling better emotionally.
3. I consciously restrain my eating. (−)
4. I'm willing to make a special trip to the store or bake something to satisfy my cravings.
5. When small meals are put in front of me, I am satisfied without second helpings. (−)
6. When the afternoon comes, my stomach growls.
7. When I don't eat (or if dieting) I become nervous and anxious.
8. I feel dizzy and faint when I go without food.
9. I buy refreshments at movies, ball games, etc.

Scale 2: Oversnacking

1. I snack or nibble when watching TV.
2. I open the refrigerator door to look even though I do not take out any food.
3. I have late night snacks.
4. I eat more on weekends than on weekdays.
5. Watching other people eat makes me hungry.
6. I crave sweets more than other foods.
7. I am more likely to overeat between lunch and dinner.
8. I am more likely to overeat after dinner.
9. When I am bored I eat for something to do.
10. Snacking is a big problem for me.
11. I'm likely to eat too much if I'm doing something else at the same time (watching TV, reading).
12. I eat more when I'm alone.

Scale 3: Bingeing

1.   I snack and nibble when preparing meals.
2.   I eat more on holidays and vacations than usual.
3.   I have an uncontrollable urge to eat even to the point of making myself sick.
4.   I eat food even when it doesn't taste very good.
5.   I think about and look forward to each meal.
6.   I am more likely to overeat at dinner.
7.   I eat when I'm not really hungry, just because food is available.
8.   I just seem to crave food.
9.   I finish whatever is put in front of me.
10. I think about food when I am not actually eating or preparing it.
11. I like to celebrate important events by going out to eat.
12. I find eating is the most pleasurable activity of the day.
13. I overeat when I'm angry or depressed.

Scale 4: Dieting

1.   I have never attempted to follow a regular dietary program. (–)
2.   I have dieted successfully in the past but I seem to gain back what I lose.
3.   I can picture what I will look like when I am thinner than I am now.
4.   I am familiar with the caloric values of most foods.
5.   I often eat most when I have already eaten a lot.

Scale 5: Satiate: Full

1.   Dinner: My stomach is stuffed.
2.   Afternoon: My stomach is comfortably full.
3.   Afternoon: I have a satiated feeling.
4.   Evening: My stomach is stuffed.
5.   Evening: My stomach is comfortably full.

Scale 6: Satiate: Nausea

1.   Dinner: There is no more food in the serving bowls.
2.   Dinner: One more bite would make me feel nauseous.
3.   Dinner: There is no more food at all.
4.   Dinner: I feel nauseous.

5. Dinner: If I eat more, I'll feel bad physically (gas, indigestion, etc.).

6. Evening: There is no more food.

7. Evening: I feel nauseous.

8. Evening: If I eat more I'll feel bad physically (gas, indigestion, etc.).

Scale 7: Satiate: Guilty

1. Dinner: I've eaten enough calories.

2. Dinner: I feel guilty.

3. Dinner: There is no more food on the plate.

4. Evening: I feel guilty.

5. Evening: People will think I'm a pig if I eat more.

6. Evening: I'll feel bloated in the morning.

Scale 8: Attribute: Physical

How important are the following factors in weight problems?

1. Hereditary factors.

2. Physiological factors (metabolism, thyroid, etc.).

3. Lack of knowledge about which foods I should and should not eat.

4. Lack of knowledge about specific techniques to use in controlling my eating.

5. Lack of encouragement from family and/or friends.

6. Insufficient time to shop and/or prepare food correctly.

7. Large body frame.

8. Too little exercise.

9. Poor eating habits.

10. Lack of motivation.

Scale 9: Attribute: Emotion

How important are the following factors in weight problems?

1. Anxiety or stress.

2. Depression.

SOURCE: Reprinted from *Addictive Behaviors, 14,* pp. 631-642, J. L. Kristeller and J. Rodin, "Identifying Eating Patterns in Male and Female Undergraduates Using Cluster Analysis," copyright © 1989, with kind permission from Elsevier Science Ltd., The Boulevard, Langford Lane, Kidlington OX5 1GB, U.K.

9

Binge Eating and Purging

KATHLEEN M. PIKE

KATHARINE LOEB

B. TIMOTHY WALSH

Binge eating and purging are two of the most pervasive behavioral distur-bances among individuals with eating disorders and weight-related prob-lems. Among the eating disorders, binge eating and purging constitute hallmark features of bulimia nervosa and are common among individuals with anorexia nervosa as well. In addition, the *Diagnostic and Statistical Man-ual of Mental Disorders* (*DSM-IV*; American Psychiatric Association, 1994) included binge eating disorder in the "Appendix for Criteria Sets and Axes Provided for Further Study" in response to suggestive data that there may be a group of predominantly obese individuals for whom binge eating, in the absence of purging, is a significant problem (Marcus, Wing, & Hopkins, 1988; Marcus, Wing, & Lamparski, 1985; Marcus et al., 1990; Spitzer, Devlin, et al., 1992; Spitzer, Yanovski, Wadden, et al., 1993).

The assessment of binge eating and purging raises three issues. First, these behavioral disturbances constitute diagnostic criteria and therefore, in contrast to the assessment of associated psychopathology, greater uniformity is required in the definition of these phenomena, and adherence to the established parameters is essential for diagnostic integrity. The second issue that complicates the first is that these behaviors are usually not directly observable. Binge eating and purging typically occur in private; in addition, there are no physical manifestations of these behaviors that reliably serve as a measure of their severity. Finally, there is tremendous shame commonly associated with binge eating and purging that may result in the tendency to underreport the behavior or minimize the level of disturbance.

In this chapter, we first clarify the parameters that must be assessed to reliably measure binge eating and purging. Next, we review the range of methods for gathering these data, and the advantages and disadvantages of each. Finally, we discuss specific instruments, reviewing their psychometric properties, issues of administration, and overall utility with regard to research and treatment.

Definition of Binge Eating

For the purpose of clinical diagnosis, the most widely accepted definition of binge eating is provided by the *DSM-IV*. In the criteria for bulimia nervosa and binge eating disorder, an episode of binge eating is characterized by

1. eating, in a discrete period of time (e.g., within any 2-hour period), an amount of food that is definitely larger than most people would eat during a similar period of time and under similar circumstances, and,
2. a sense of lack of control over eating during the episode (e.g., a feeling that one cannot stop eating or control what or how much one is eating).

The criteria for a binge in the diagnosis of anorexia nervosa, binge eating/purging type, are not specified in *DSM-IV*.

Parameters of Binge Eating

Quantifying the size of the binge. The amount of food consumed during a binge varies widely. Subjectively defined, a binge may be composed of a few cookies, at one end of the continuum, to many thousands of calories, at the other end. In fact, subjective reports of binge eating are frequently characterized by high loss of control coupled with low caloric consumption (Beglin

& Fairburn, 1992; Ortega, Warranch, Maldonado, & Hubbard, 1987; Rossiter & Agras, 1990). For the purpose of clinical treatment and research, however, it is important to establish guidelines that correspond to the diagnostic criteria for binge eating.

The reliability of the assessment of binge eating would be increased by using a cutoff of a minimum number of calories per binge. Fairburn (1987) recommended an average of 1,000 kilocalories for the diagnosis of bulimia nervosa. However, he and others have since argued that, although this cutoff would certainly reduce the risk of false positives, it may be too high, and therefore result in an excessively high rate of false negatives. Thus, as the *DSM-IV* criteria for binge eating imply, the clinician or researcher must consider the context in which an episode occurred to determine if an objectively large amount of food was consumed.

Loss of control. In both bulimia nervosa and binge eating disorder, lack of control is defined as a sense that one cannot stop eating or control what or how much one is eating. In addition to the subjective experience of being out of control, binge eating disorder requires that at least three of the following indicators of impaired control be present: (a) eating much more rapidly than normal, (b) eating until feeling uncomfortably full, (c) eating large amounts of food when not feeling physically hungry, (d) eating alone because of being embarrassed by how much one is eating, and (e) feeling disgusted with oneself, depressed, or very guilty after overeating.

It should be noted that, for some individuals whose eating disorder is chronic, the feelings of "loss of control" have dissipated. The binge eating may occur automatically or on a regular schedule. In fact, some individuals report planning their binges. In these cases, loss of control should be assessed based on the individual's inability to alter or interrupt the behavior once the decision to binge has been made.

Frequency of binge eating. To meet *DSM-IV* diagnostic criteria for bulimia nervosa, an individual must binge eat a minimum average of twice per week. In contrast, to meet the diagnostic criteria for binge eating disorder, an individual must binge eat on a minimum of 2 *days* per week. In other words, in the case of bulimia nervosa, binge frequency is counted by episodes, and more than one episode can occur on any given day; in the case of binge eating disorder, frequency is counted by "binge days" and an individual must binge eat on at least 2 days per week even if several discrete episodes occur per day. To meet diagnostic criteria for anorexia nervosa, binge eating/purging type, the frequency of binge eating is not specified.

The rationale for counting binge frequency in days versus episodes for binge eating disorder is that, given the absence of compensatory behaviors, in many cases it is not possible to parse the overeating into discrete episodes within a single day. In a study of nonpurging bulimic women (Rossiter, Agras, Telch, & Bruce, 1992), the correlation between self-monitoring diaries and retrospective recall was higher for the number of days that an individual reported binge eating than for the specific number of episodes. These data suggest that recording the number of binge days rather than episodes is the level of specificity that can be measured most reliably for individuals who do not engage in compensatory behaviors after binge eating.

In the case of bulimia nervosa, usually an individual can identify the beginning and end of what he or she identifies as a binge; however, there are circumstances that make this difficult as well. In particular, discrepancies in what punctuates a binge are common. For example, if an individual purges several times throughout a protracted episode of eating, has he or she had more than one binge and more than one episode of purging? And if the individual's consumption is divided into a number of binges, must each one contain a large amount of food? Given that there are no official guidelines for answering these questions, the following recommendations are proposed. When ambiguity exists about whether the binge eating constitutes one or more episodes, the interviewer should assess the extent to which the individual describes any pauses or punctuations, such as purging, in his or her eating. If there is a significant pause in the eating, regardless of purging, each segment of eating should be counted as a distinct episode and assessed in terms of size and associated characteristics. If, for instance, an individual induces vomiting in the middle of a binge because he or she wants to continue eating, but is painfully full, the entire episode of eating should be counted as one binge, and each episode of purging should be counted separately.

Duration of binge eating. To meet diagnostic criteria for bulimia nervosa, an individual must meet the requisite criteria for a minimum of 3 months. In the case of binge eating disorder, the minimum duration is 6 months, and, in the case of anorexia nervosa, this parameter is not defined.

Macronutrient content. It is not necessary to specify the macronutrient content of food consumed to determine whether criteria are met for a binge. However, studies indicate that patterns of food selection differ slightly for binge and nonbinge episodes in that a slightly higher proportion of calories are derived from fat, and a slightly lower proportion of calories are derived from protein, during binge than nonbinge episodes (Hadigan, Kissileff, & Walsh, 1989; Rosen, Leitenberg, Fisher, & Khazam, 1986).

Whether the data are drawn from self-report diaries, interviews, or laboratory experiments, several standardized computer programs exist to provide detailed reports of caloric consumption and macronutrient distribution. However, unless self-report data are carefully reviewed, it is likely that the food descriptions will not be sufficiently detailed to allow for accurate data analysis (see Wolper, Heshka, & Heymsfield, this volume). Although most programs provide guidelines for "standard amounts" of any given food, it is likely that such standards would not accurately reflect eating that occurs in the context of a binge. Therefore it is preferable that studies of caloric content and macronutrient distribution be based on interview or directly observed data in the laboratory.

Definition of Purging

Compensatory mechanisms described in the *DSM-IV* are divided into two categories: purging and nonpurging types. All compensatory behaviors consist of inappropriate efforts aimed at counteracting the effect of binge eating; however, those that fall into the subset of compensatory behavior described as purging constitute efforts to rid oneself of calories by expelling them from the body.

Specifying various compensatory behaviors is central to diagnosing eating disorders. The presence, absence, frequency, and/or type of these behaviors draws the distinction between different disorders and the subtypes within a single syndrome. For example, the *DSM-IV* distinguishes between two categories of bulimia nervosa: "purging type" and "nonpurging type." Anorexia nervosa is divided into two types: (a) "binge-eating/purging type," which includes individuals who binge eat and/or purge, and (b) "restricting type," which includes individuals who do not engage in binge eating or purging. Individuals who meet diagnostic criteria for binge eating disorder may frequently diet or make other attempts at weight loss but do not regularly employ the inappropriate compensatory mechanisms observed in bulimia nervosa.

Parameters of Purging

According to the *DSM-IV*, purging techniques include self-induced vomiting and misuse of laxatives, diuretics, enemas, or other medications in an effort to compensate for caloric consumption and avoid weight gain. Fasting (refusing caloric intake for a day or more) and excessive exercise are not considered purging mechanisms although they are considered compensatory behaviors in the case of "nonpurging" bulimia nervosa.

When assessing the presence of compensatory behaviors, the clinician should measure not only their frequency but also the intent of the subject at the time of the episode. Compensatory mechanisms can be used to counteract a specific binge (as in bulimia nervosa) or as a means of general weight control. For instance, individuals with binge eating disorder may occasionally use laxatives or diuretics to avoid weight gain or to promote weight loss but they do not regularly employ such methods to compensate for specific binge episodes.

Range of Assessment Methods

Self-report. Self-report instruments are the most common assessment tools for binge eating and purging. There are three basic types: (a) diaries, (b) open-ended questionnaires, and (c) standardized scales.

Diaries can be detailed and lengthy or brief depending on whether the data are being collected for clinical or for research purposes. For clinical purposes, self-monitoring of binge eating and purging episodes will typically require patients not only to indicate frequencies of occurrence but also to describe the events in more detail. Using a diary format, when an individual binges or purges, he or she may be asked to record the social context, emotional state before and after, and associated thoughts. Although initially this information will be recorded by patients after the binge eating and/or purging episode has occurred, during the course of certain treatments, patients are encouraged to use these self-monitoring techniques to avert such episodes. In particular, detailed self-monitoring of binge eating and purging is used extensively in cognitive-behavioral treatment for eating disorders.

The more specific the diary, the easier it is for the clinician to assess the frequency of binge eating as defined by the *DSM-IV.* However, once patients have been educated about the formal definition of what constitutes a binge, we have found that there is a high correlation between frequencies recorded by patients and information obtained by an interviewer trained in the *DSM-IV* criteria for eating disorders (Loeb, Pike, Walsh, & Wilson, in press). These findings suggest that, once a shared definition is established, a "simple" diary will often suffice in tracking an individual's behavior during treatment. Furthermore, 7-day diaries appear to be as effective as longer (28-day) diaries for measuring changes in binge eating and purging (Loeb et al., in press).

Open-ended self-report questionnaires may ask a patient to describe, in short answers or in paragraph form, summaries of the kind of data recorded in a diary format. Questions (e.g., "How many times a week do you purge after a normal meal?") might appear on these measures. Trained raters can subsequently code or categorize the subject's answers. Although such questionnaires may have clinical utility, the lack of standardization severely limits the research applications of such instruments.

Standardized scales often have questions similar to those on open-ended instruments but provide a more structured response format, such as Likert scaling, multiple choice, true-false, or agree-disagree selections. When these measures meet appropriate standards of reliability and validity, they offer more power in the assessment of binge eating and purging.

Self-report instruments are usually inexpensive and less time-consuming compared with other assessment procedures. In addition, subjects can remain anonymous when filling out self-report questionnaires, which may promote greater honesty in their responses. However, there are inherent drawbacks to this method of assessment. One disadvantage is the risk of differential interpretations of the items in a questionnaire. For example, because many individuals with eating disorders display a distorted perspective on what is considered a small, normal, or large amount of food, relying on self-report for assessing aspects of binge eating is subject to significant subjectivity. Another concern is that the information obtained may not represent the true rating of a subject who identifies with something in between the choices presented. Some patients will choose the "best fit"; others may circle two multiple choice answers or intentionally leave questions blank. This leads to the third problem with paper-and-pencil measures: the difficulty in retrieving missing or unclear data.

Interview. Cooper and Fairburn (1987) have strongly advocated an interview format to assess binge eating so as to minimize the subjectivity inherent in self-report. They argue that this is of particular importance in treatment studies because self-report questionnaires that simply inquire about the frequency of binge eating will not detect more subtle changes in the bulimic episodes that can occur in response to treatment. For example, a patient may continue to label episodes of overeating as "binges" even though the amount of food consumed decreases and the sense of loss of control has abated.

To ensure as much accuracy as possible, Fairburn and Cooper (1993) recommend using an "investigator-based" interview as opposed to a "respondent-based" one. In the latter, the respondent is called on to make all final judgments for scoring and ratings on the instrument. In contrast, in an investigator-based interview, interviewers are trained to probe, challenge answers, explain questions, and make consistent judgments in scoring the instrument based on the information provided by the respondent.

Despite the precision to be gained by using an interview measure, this type of instrument has disadvantages as well. Interviews generally require extensive training for administration; they are also labor intensive and therefore costly to conduct. In addition, it is important to keep in mind that even an interview measure relies to a large degree on self-report.

Laboratory observation. Given the private and/or secretive nature of binge eating and purging, these behaviors are not typically directly observable. Laboratory studies that monitor eating behavior provide a more objective means of assessment given that data obtained by direct observation are not dependent on a person's self-reported eating behavior. Laboratory studies are especially useful to assess food preferences, macronutrient distribution, and behavioral aspects such as speed of consumption during a binge.

There are three particular measurement problems associated with laboratory studies. First, the issue of generalizability is paramount. To what extent do the laboratory results reflect what happens in the "real world"? Second, laboratory methods require significant resources in terms of personnel, time, and equipment. Third, there are practical and ethical issues associated with asking a patient with an eating disorder to "eat normally" or "binge" in the lab. As described below, several established research groups have developed procedures that minimize the problems inherent in this means of assessment.

Review of Specific Instruments

Self-Report Format: Early Standardized Measures

Two of the first measures that were developed for the purpose of assessing binge eating and purging are the Bingeing-Purging Questionnaire (BPQ; Coffman, 1984) and the Binge Eating Questionnaire (BEQ; Halmi, Falk, & Schwartz, 1981).

The BPQ is an example of an open-ended self-report instrument that can also be used as an unstructured interview to aid in the assessment of eating disturbance. It is not sufficiently detailed for diagnosing eating disorders, nor is it scored in any standardized way.

The Binge Eating Questionnaire (BEQ; Halmi et al., 1981) yields six subscale scores and was originally developed for use in a college sample. The BEQ inquires about frequencies of vomiting and abuse of laxatives and diuretics but only indirectly measures frequency of binge eating ("What is the average number of days between your episodes of binge eating?"). The Bingeing subscale is compromised by the heterogeneity of the items such that item-factor correlations ranged from .29 to .72. With regard to the assessment of purging, the BEQ includes a vomiting subscale and a separate subscale measuring diuretic abuse. The item-factor correlations for the vomiting subscale ranged from .67 to .80. The Diuretic subscale is composed only of one item (frequency of diuretic use), which did not load significantly on any other subscale.

Early measures such as these were important first steps in research in the field of eating disorders and provided a base from which subsequent assessment measures developed. However, given the changes that have occurred in the diagnostic criteria for the eating disorders based on revisions of the *DSM*, and given the limitations of these instruments due to their psychometric properties, their current utility is limited.

The Binge Scale Questionnaire

The Binge Scale Questionnaire (Hawkins & Clement, 1980) is a nine-item multiple choice questionnaire that assesses the behavioral and attitudinal parameters of binge eating and vomiting. Scores on these nine items are summed to provide a total score, and therefore the instrument provides a measure of global severity of bulimic symptomatology but does not address particular diagnostic criteria. The Binge Scale has demonstrated utility as a brief screening instrument that provides a severity score across the entire spectrum of binge eating. However, it does not provide a specific binge frequency. Instead, it requires respondents to choose one of four options that best describes their frequency of binge eating. Also, it does not explicitly define the term *binge*, which increases the subjectivity inherent in the instrument. Similar to assessing binge frequency, the instrument does not provide specific frequencies of purging efforts. It assesses the occurrence of vomiting from never to always but does not measure specific frequency, nor does it measure other forms of purging.

Reliability: Internal consistency. Hawkins and Clement (1980) report a Cronbach's alpha of .68 for the nine items that constitute the total score.

Test-retest reliability. One month test-retest reliability of the Binge Scale total score was .88 (Hawkins & Clement, 1980).

Factor structure. The Binge Scale yields one total score; however, Hawkins and Clement (1980) did conduct a principal components factor analysis with varimax rotation that revealed two main factors. The first factor represented feelings of guilt and concern about binge eating and accounted for 69% of the variance in item loadings. The second factor, accounting for an additional 16% of the variance, comprised items measuring the behavioral aspects of binge eating such as duration and satiety feelings associated with the eating episode.

Concurrent validity. The Binge Scale correlates .93 with the BULIT (see Smith & Thelin, 1984, and Chapter 10 in this volume for review of the BULIT).

Discriminant validity. No studies are available.

Predictive validity. Several studies indicate that the Binge Scale is particularly useful as a screening instrument to identify subclinical cases, situational binge eaters, and individuals with bulimia nervosa (Katzman & Wolchik, 1984; Ordman & Kirschenbaum, 1985; Yates & Sambrailo, 1984).

Readability. The Binge Scale Questionnaire is easy to read and very quick to administer.

Norms. The measure was initially established based on two studies conducted with college undergraduates. The initial sample was composed of 182 females and 65 males, and the replication group contained 73 females and 45 males. However, this measure has also been used successfully with clinical samples, either as a screening device (Katzman & Wolchik, 1984; Ordman & Kirschenbaum, 1985; Smith & Thelin, 1984; Williamson, Kelley, Davis, Ruggiero, & Blouin, 1985; Yates & Sambrailo, 1984) or as an assessment measure of response to treatment (Ordman & Kirschenbaum, 1985). Based on these studies, Hawkins (personal communication) suggests that a score of 10 or less on the Binge Scale reflects a "normal group" whereas a score of 15 or greater suggests true cases of eating disorders.

Practicality. The administration and scoring of the instrument are straightforward and its brevity makes it a good screening device. For the Binge Scale reference, see Hawkins and Clement (1980). The scale is reprinted in Appendix 9-A.

The Binge Eating Scale

The Binge Eating Scale (BES; Gormally, Black, Daston, & Rardin, 1982) was originally designed to assess the experience of binge eating in obese individuals, but it has been applied to other populations. The BES measures the behavioral aspects of binge eating episodes as well as the feelings and thoughts associated with such behavior. The scale provides one total score and therefore cannot be used to discern a specific measure of binge frequency, per se. Instead, the BES provides a global score of eating disturbance based on the sum of the weights for the 16 items. This provides a general measure of severity but precludes generating sufficiently specific data for diagnostic purposes.

This measure has been used successfully in several clinical research studies for the purpose of categorizing patient samples according to severity of binge eating (LaPorte, 1992; Marcus et al., 1985; Marcus et al., 1988).

Reliability: Internal consistency. Gormally et al. (1982) demonstrated the internal consistency of the BES by comparing total scale scores with scores on each item. Based on responses from 65 subjects, a Kruskall-Wallis analysis of variance of ranked data was conducted, and all χ^2 tests of significance were 9.1 or greater ($p < .01$). Results indicated that individual ratings for each item were consistent with the overall ranked total score.

Test-retest reliability. No studies are available.

Factor structure. The BES yields a total score.

Concurrent validity. In the development of this instrument, Gormally and colleagues (1982) compared scores on the BES with severity of binge eating ratings made by trained interviewers. A one-way analysis of variance showed that BES scores were significantly different across interviewer-rated severity levels (no binge eating, moderate binge eating, and severe binge eating) for two different samples of obese individuals (sample 1: $F = 13.48$, $p < .001$; sample 2: $F = 25.13$, $p < .001$).

Discriminant validity. No studies are available.

Predictive validity. No studies are available.

Readability. The BES is written in the form of "I . . ." statements, and the subject is asked to choose the statement in each item with which she or he most identifies. The measure is free of clinical jargon.

Norms. Table 9.1 reports the norms for the BES based on two samples of obese individuals. Separate norms are provided for males and females based on the second sample (Gormally et al., 1982). The cutoffs were established by comparing interview data for severity of binge eating with the BES scores.

Practicality. At the authors' request, the BES is not reprinted in this chapter. For the Binge Eating Scale reference, see Gormally et al. (1982). This scale can be easily administered, although scorers must keep in mind the uneven distribution of weights for each item (these weights are published in the article above).

TABLE 9.1 Binge Eating Scale (BES) Scores for the Three Severity Levels (as rated by a structured interview)

	Level of Severity		
Sample	None Mean (SD)	Moderate Mean (SD)	Severe Mean (SD)
1 ($N = 65$)	14.9 (8.2) ($n = 11$)	19.6 (6.7) ($n = 40$)	28.9 (7.5) ($n = 14$)
2 Total ($N = 47$)	13.4 (5.2) ($n = 14$)	21.1 (7.0) ($n = 21$)	31.3 (6.6) ($n = 12$)
males ($n = 15$)	14.4 (4.9) ($n = 7$)	17.5 (4.1) ($n = 4$)	26.0 (8.0) ($n = 4$)
females ($n = 32$)	12.4 (5.6) ($n = 7$)	22.0 (7.4) ($n = 17$)	34.0 (3.9) ($n = 8$)

SOURCE: Data from Gormally, Black, Daston, and Rardin (1982).

The Questionnaire on Eating and Weight Patterns–Revised

The Questionnaire on Eating and Weight Patterns–Revised (QEWP-R; Spitzer, Yanovski, & Marcus, 1993, cited in Yanovski, 1993) is a 28-item questionnaire that assesses binge eating and purging. The measure was designed originally to identify individuals meeting criteria for binge eating disorder. The strength of the QEWP-R is that it is a criterion-based instrument that assesses the essential diagnostic criteria for purging and nonpurging bulimia as well as binge eating disorder (BED). Thus, based on the *DSM-IV* criteria of these syndromes, the QEWP-R provides decision rules for diagnosing BED and purging and nonpurging bulimia nervosa. The instrument also assesses age, gender, ethnic background, education, height, and weight.

Reliability: Internal consistency. The binge eating syndrome represents the summation of scores on eight items: loss of control, episodic overeating, and six binge eating-associated symptoms. The Cronbach's alpha of this scale was .75 and .79 in the weight control and community samples, respectively. The individual items correlate with the total from .50 to .66 in the weight control samples and from .55 to .71 in the community samples.

Test-retest reliability. No studies are available.

Factor structure. Other than the binge eating syndrome described above, the instrument does not include empirically derived factors.

Concurrent validity. No studies are available.

Discriminant validity. No studies are available.

Predictive validity. The questionnaire is designed to diagnose binge eating disorder and purging and nonpurging bulimia nervosa. Statistical data regarding its ability to discriminate among these disorders are not available. However, there are some data regarding the predictive ability of the measure for binge eating disorder based on a comparison of results from the self-report format and a clinical interview format of the QEWP-R. A kappa of .60 was obtained for the agreement between the clinical evaluation and the self-report questionnaire based on a sample of 44 obese subjects in a weight control study (Spitzer, Yanovski, Wadden, et al., 1993). This kappa is comparable to test-retest correlations typically reported for the major psychiatric disorders (Williams et al., 1992). Furthermore, the validity of this instrument for predicting disordered eating in a laboratory setting has been established (Yanovski et al., 1992).

Readability. The questionnaire is well organized and provides clear directions for the respondent regarding the time frame of reference. The questionnaire directs respondents regarding skip patterns within the instrument, which avoids the problem of requiring individuals to respond to questions that are not applicable.

Norms. This is not applicable.

Practicality. The QEWP-R is available from Dr. Robert Spitzer, New York State Psychiatric Institute, 722 West 168th Street, New York, NY 10032, and is reprinted in Appendix 9-B.

The Eating Symptoms Inventory

The Eating Symptoms Inventory (ESI; Whitaker et al., 1989) is a self-report questionnaire designed to assess the key features of bulimia nervosa and anorexia nervosa as well as associated symptomatology (see Appendix 9-C). The measure was first developed for use as part of a survey of eating disorders in a nonreferred adolescent population. Although the ESI was designed to assess *DSM-III* diagnostic criteria, the instrument can be adapted to approximate most *DSM-IV* criteria for eating disorders. The ESI also provides a continuous measure of severity, the ESI Symptom Count, which is derived from selected items.

As can be seen in the sample questions in Appendix 9-C, the ESI's major strength in assessing binge eating is that it operationalizes the word *binge*, providing the subject with examples of various binge sizes. The time parameter specified by the ESI is that the food must be consumed in less than 2 hours. After selecting the option that most closely approximates the largest amount of food consumed within a 2-hour period, the subject then indicates the frequency of consumption. One of the limitations of this instrument is that it asks only about a lifetime total of these eating episodes and when the last one occurred. It is therefore impossible to determine a precise current frequency of binge eating that would allow one to make the diagnosis of bulimia nervosa or to measure change in a clinical trial. Additionally, the ESI does not inquire about the frequency of eating episodes that contained *less* food than the largest example the subject chose, many of which could have met diagnostic criteria for a binge (e.g., "four doughnuts and a pint of ice cream [and] 5 cookies in less than 2 hours"). This measure also does not take into account the context in which the binge occurred or the presence or absence of impaired control.

The ESI evaluates most purging techniques as well as the subject's intent when engaging in these behaviors. However, similar problems with assessing accurate frequencies exist.

Reliability: Internal consistency. Whitaker et al. (1989) report a Cronbach's alpha of .76 in girls and .54 in boys for the 17 items that constitute the ESI Symptom Count.

Test-retest reliability. No studies are available.

Factor structure. The ESI yields a continuous measure of symptomatology, the ESI Symptom Count, which consists of items from each of the three nonempirically derived "domains": concerns about weight and eating, weight control behaviors, and binge eating.

Concurrent validity. Scores on the ESI symptom count correlate with scores on the Eating Attitudes Test (Garner, Olmsted, Bohr, & Garfinkel, 1982) of .56 for girls and .36 in boys.

Discriminant validity. No studies are available.

Predictive validity. The study by Whitaker et al. (1989) indicates that the ESI is a useful screening instrument in surveys of eating disorders; the measure yielded a sensitivity of .71 and a specificity of .81.

Readability. The ESI is easy both to understand and to administer.

Norms. In the original study of the ESI, data were available from 2,544 girls and 2,564 boys in a nonreferred high school population. The mean total ESI count was 5.4 (*SD* = 2.9) in girls and 3.4 (*SD* = 2.0) in boys.

Practicality. The administration and scoring of the instrument are clearly explained in its reference; see Whitaker et al. (1989).

Related Self-Report Measures

As described in Chapter 10 in this volume, the Eating Disorder Inventory (EDI) is a 64-item self-report measure, which includes eight subscales that measure specific eating disorder symptomatology and associated psychopathology (Garner, Olmsted, & Polivy, 1983). The EDI has been revised recently by Garner (1991). Of particular interest to the assessment of binge eating and purging is the bulimia subscale, which includes items assessing both binge eating and purging behavior. However, the subscale does not provide separate scores for these two phenomena nor is it designed to provide specific frequencies of behavior. Also discussed in more detail in Chapter 10, the Bulimia Test was originally developed by Smith and Thelen (1984) and has been revised to meet *DSM-III-R* criteria (Thelen, Farmer, Wonderlich, & Smith, 1991). This questionnaire assesses eating behavior and purging but, again, does not provide sufficient detail for diagnostic purposes.

Interview Format

Although several interviews have been developed for the assessment of eating disorders, including questions pertaining to binge eating and purging, most of these instruments have not been widely employed, and very limited information is available on their psychometric properties. For example, the Clinical Eating Disorder Rating Instrument (CEDRI; Palmer, Christie, Cordle, Davies, & Kendrick, 1987), the Structured Interview for Anorexia and Bulimia (SIAB; Fichter et al., 1989), and the Interview for Diagnosis of Eating Disorders (IDED; Williamson, 1990) are three interviews, each of which has provided primary data for a research investigation in the field; however, these instruments have not been rigorously evaluated in terms of their psychometric properties. In contrast, we review in depth below the Eating Disorder Examination (EDE; Fairburn & Cooper, 1993) and the Structured Clinical Interview for Diagnosis (SCID; Spitzer, Williams, & Gibbon, 1987)—two structured clinical interviews that provide detailed information regarding their psychometric properties. These two interviews are widely used in the field.

The Eating Disorder Examination

The Eating Disorder Examination (EDE; Fairburn & Cooper, 1993) is a semistructured interview consisting of four subscales (Shape Concern, Weight Concern, Dietary Restraint, and Eating Concern) plus several individual items that assess the frequency of binge eating and various compensatory behaviors. The EDE is designed to be administered by interviewers trained in the assessment of eating disorders. The EDE questions are constructed to distinguish between three different types of overeating: objective bulimic episodes, objective overeating, and subjective bulimic episodes.

The distinctions between these three categories of overeating are based on the presence or absence of the two basic criteria for a binge episode: loss of control and the consumption of what most people would regard as a large amount of food. An *objective bulimic episode* is one that includes both of these characteristics and would thus be counted when determining the diagnosis of bulimia nervosa. *Objective overeating* is defined as the consumption of an objectively large amount of food *without* the associated loss of control. A *subjective bulimic episode* is characterized by the presence of loss of control but the absence of an objectively large amount of food.

The EDE measures the frequency of these three types of overeating and of various methods of purging in the 28 days prior to the administration of the interview. For *DSM-IV* diagnostic purposes, the previous 2 months are assessed as well. Frequencies of both the number of binge days and the number of binge episodes are obtained; this information can be averaged to calculate weekly frequencies. To facilitate the EDE, it is recommended that the patient fill out a diary for the last 4 weeks, ending with the day before the interview (a blank monthly calendar can be adapted for individual time frames). Pertinent information for this diary includes vacations or particularly stressful days during which the patient's eating habits may have changed.

In this chapter, we have reproduced selected items from the EDE that pertain only to binge eating and purging. However, it is essential to use the instrument in its original form and only after proper completion of training in its administration. Items administered out of context may not yield the same results as would be obtained if the entire EDE were given; introductory questions in the EDE set a tone of precision to the interview. Furthermore, a response to one question can influence a subject's answer to a later item and provide the interviewer with information that can be used to challenge the patient.

When using the twelfth edition of the EDE for diagnostic purposes, it is important to note the items that diverge from *DSM-IV* criteria. The EDE rates laxative or diuretic abuse as present only when the individual takes at least twice the recommended dosage of these medications; *DSM-IV* does not use this standard.

Additionally, the EDE rates excessive exercise as present when "the subject engaged in *intense* exercise that was *predominantly* intended to use calories to change shape, weight, or body composition." *DSM-IV* does not have these specific criteria but offers the following guidelines for determining when exercise is excessive: "when . . . it significantly interferes with important activities, when it occurs at inappropriate times or settings, or when the individual continues to exercise despite injury or other medical complications."

Reliability: Internal consistency. Z. Cooper, Cooper, and Fairburn (1989) demonstrated a significant degree of internal consistency in each of the five EDE subscales, with Cronbach's alpha coefficients ranging from .67 to .90. These findings support the content-based grouping of individual items of the EDE into subscales. In a recent study of 116 eating disorder patients, Beumont, Kopec-Schrader, Talbot, and Touyz (1992) reported alpha coefficients ranging from .68 to .78 for the five subscales.

Test-retest reliability. No studies are available.

Interrater reliability. Z. Cooper and Fairburn (1987) assessed the interrater reliability of the EDE with three trained raters and twelve subjects (nine women with bulimia nervosa and three normal controls); each rater administered four interviews and rated two taped interviews. Agreement on the EDE items was calculated using Pearson product-moment coefficients and was found to be consistently high. For 27 of the 62 items, there was a perfect correlation between raters, and the coefficients of the other items ranged from 0.69 to 1.00, with only three items below 0.9.

Wilson and Smith (1989) examined the interrater reliability between subscale scores on the EDE also using Pearson product-moment coefficients. Correlations ranged from .965 to .998. Rosen, Vara, Wendt, and Leitenberg (1990) found interrater reliability correlations ranging from .83 (on the Overeating scale, which has since been deleted from the EDE) to .99. Similarly, Beglin (1990, cited in Fairburn & Cooper, 1993) reported kappa values of .70 and above for all items currently included in the EDE and Pearson product-moment coefficients of above .95 for all subscales.

Factor structure. The EDE has four subscales that were theoretically derived first and then empirically tested.

Concurrent validity. Rosen et al. (1990) assessed the concurrent validity of the Overeating subscale, a scale that appeared in previous versions of the EDE, which included the frequencies of objective bulimic episodes, objective overeating, and subjective bulimic episodes. Rosen et al. correlated this subscale with information from a detailed eating diary that subjects kept for 1 week prior to the administration of the EDE. The study showed that higher overeating scale scores were associated with higher daily caloric intake ($r = .38$, $p < .0001$), a higher frequency of binge eating episodes ($r = .56$, $p < .0001$), and larger binges ($r = .54$, $p < .0001$) as reported in the diaries. In addition, vomiting frequencies obtained in the EDE were significantly correlated with vomiting frequencies recorded in the eating records ($r = .90$, $p < .0001$).

This study also found modest, but significant, correlations between the EDE Restraint subscale and information on the subjects' eating diaries that reflected dietary restraint: the higher the EDE Restraint score, the less food was consumed. Furthermore, the EDE Shape Concern and Weight Concern subscales were significantly correlated with self-report measures addressing similar variables and with the subjects' degree of overestimation of body size.

Discriminant validity. No studies are available.

Predictive validity. Z. Cooper et al. (1989) administered the EDE to 100 patients with either anorexia nervosa or bulimia nervosa (according to *DSM-III-R* criteria) and to 42 controls. All individual items of the EDE, as well as its five subscales, significantly discriminated between the two groups. Wilson and Smith (1989) added to Z. Cooper et al.'s (1989) findings, demonstrating that the EDE also discriminates between individuals with bulimia nervosa and restrained eaters (non-eating disordered controls who scored 20 or higher on the Revised Restraint Scale; Herman & Polivy, 1980). Moreover, whereas the EDE distinguished these groups effectively, the Eating Disorder Inventory (Garner et al., 1983), a self-report measure, did not. Rosen et al. found that the Weight Concern and Shape Concern subscales successfully discriminated between a sample of 20 women with bulimia nervosa and a sample of 29 dietary-restrained subjects (normal controls who were at least one standard deviation above the normative mean on the EDE Restraint scale). However, the two EDE body image subscales did not add incremental discriminant validity to the Body Shape Questionnaire (P. J. Cooper, Taylor, Cooper, & Fairburn, 1987), a paper-and-pencil scale, in distinguishing between these two groups.

Fairburn, Jones, Peveler, Hope, and O'Conner (1993) report that the EDE is sensitive to measuring change in binge eating and purging symptomatology as reflected in substantially decreased subscale scores on the EDE for women who no longer meet diagnostic criteria for bulimia nervosa.

Susceptibility to dissimulation. The EDE is administered in an interview format, and thus may be less susceptible to false information than self-report measures. The EDE interviewer is trained to point out discrepancies in the subject's responses and refer to the preinterview diary when appropriate. However, an uncooperative or disorganized patient might not provide accurate answers; in these cases, the interviewer is advised to probe as much as possible while preserving a good rapport with the subject.

Readability. This is not applicable: When necessary, the interviewer may rephrase a question in simpler language. The twelfth edition of the EDE has been designed to accommodate a wider range of educational backgrounds.

Norms. See Tables 9.2 and 9.3.

Practicality. For the EDE reference, see Fairburn and Cooper (1993). Appendix 9-D contains a comprehensive discussion of the instrument, including instructions for administration and scoring. However, training and supervision are strongly recommended, especially when the instrument is used in research. If the clinician deviates from the interview in any way, validity of the results may be jeopardized. For additional information, contact the authors of the EDE.

The Structured Clinical Interview for the DSM-III-R

The Structured Clinical Interview for the *DSM-III-R* (SCID; Spitzer et al., 1987) is an important diagnostic tool, being the only measure to correspond exactly to the criteria established by the *DSM* (see Appendix 9-E). The SCID I covers all of Axis I disorders; we will focus on the section for diagnosing bulimia nervosa, as this is the only part containing questions on binge eating and purging. Future editions of the SCID based on *DSM-IV* will most likely assess binge eating and purging in anorexia nervosa, binge eating disorder, and the subtypes of bulimia nervosa (purging type and nonpurging type).

The SCID provides questions based on each criterion as well as definitions of each criterion. The interviewer is instructed to proceed to the next item only if the patient has some degree of the symptom on the present item (a rating of subthreshold or threshold). This flowchart format affords fairly simple diagnosis.

TABLE 9.2 EDE Norms for Bulimia Nervosa

	Cooper et al. (1989) N = 53 Mean (SD)	Wilson and Smith (1989) N = 15 Mean (SD)	Beumont et al. (1992) N = 28 Mean (SD)	Fairburn et al. (1993) N = 125 Mean (SD)
Restraint	3.14 (1.22)	3.27 (0.26)	3.7 (1.7)	3.45 (1.18)
Bulimia	3.42 (0.79)	2.61 (0.22)	3.4 (0.9)	2.17 (0.86)
Eating Concern	2.43 (1.30)	2.40 (0.34)	3.5 (1.4)	2.63 (1.42)
Weight Concern	3.14 (1.44)	3.96 (0.34)	3.8 (1.7)	3.73 (0.39)
Shape Concern	3.55 (1.35)	3.82 (0.31)	4.1 (1.1)	3.90 (1.28)

TABLE 9.3 EDE Norms for Other Groups

	Normal Controls[a] N = 42 Mean (SD)	Restrained Controls[b] N = 15 Mean (SD)	Normal Controls[c] N = 337 Mean (SD)	Dieters[c] N = 57 Mean (SD)	Overweight Subjects[d] N = 15 Mean (SD)
Restraint	0.91 (0.91)	3.15 (0.33)	0.79 (0.79)	1.66 (1.07)	1.69 (1.35)
Bulimia	0.41 (0.87)	0.14 (0.10)			
Eating Concern	0.22 (0.33)	1.25 (0.23)	0.20 (0.51)	0.50 (0.84)	0.64 (0.86)
Weight Concern	0.52 (0.62)	2.12 (0.19)	1.00 (0.87)	1.79 (0.92)	1.92 (1.24)
Shape Concern	0.64 (0.75)	2.55 (0.20)	1.14 (0.98)	1.99 (1.13)	1.97 (1.33)

NOTE: *Overweight* defined as a body mass index of 30 or above. It should be noted that different studies have used different versions of the Bulimia subscale, and the study by Fairburn and colleagues (1993) used EDE 12.0D.
a. Cooper et al. (1989).
b. Wilson and Smith (1989).
c. Fairburn et al. (1993).
d. Fairburn et al. (1993).

Reliability: Internal consistency. No studies are available.

Test-retest reliability. A multisite study was conducted to assess test-retest reliability of the SCID interview (Williams et al., 1992). The results from this study indicate that, depending on the site, agreement on the bulimia nervosa section ranged from .82 to .90.

Interrater reliability. A study by Skre, Onstad, Torgersen, and Kringlen (1991) found the general interrater reliability of the SCID to be high, although eating disorders were not included in the analyses.

Factor structure. This is not applicable.

Validity. As the criterion-based interview for the *Diagnostic and Statistical Manual,* the SCID is used widely to diagnose individuals and establish patient groups. Studies comparing groups based on SCID diagnoses consistently indicate that the SCID provides valid assessment of binge eating and purging relevant to the diagnosis of the eating disorders. The SCID is designed to discriminate among all the identified mental disorders and provides the essential information for discriminating among the eating disorders, in particular.

Susceptibility to dissimulation. No studies are available. As an interview measure designed to be administered by trained clinicians, the SCID should be relatively less susceptible to false information.

Readability. There are both patient and nonpatient versions of the SCID, so that questions are phrased appropriately to the subject. The interviewer may modify the language of the SCID to accommodate various educational levels. In addition, the interviewer may add or restructure items when the subject's responses are equivocal. Information on the SCID can also be obtained from family or staff members or from written information about the patient.

Norms. This is not applicable.

Practicality. Training, supervision, clinical experience, and familiarity with the *DSM-III-R* are imperative to conducting the interview accurately. For more information, contact the authors at the Biometrics Research Department of New York State Psychiatric Institute, 722 W. 168th Street, New York, NY 10032. Spitzer, Williams, Gibbon, and First (1992) provide a comprehensive description of the history, rationale, and development of the SCID. Training sessions and videotapes are available, and a user's manual is published by American Psychiatric Press (Spitzer, Williams, Gibbon, & First, 1990).

Laboratory Observation

Several investigators have established laboratory settings to conduct studies examining eating behaviors among individuals with eating disorders. In all laboratory studies that require subjects to engage in a particular behavior, there is an adaptation period that is designed to increase the subject's familiarity with the surroundings and thereby increase the likelihood that the eating behavior to be measured is a reasonable representation of what occurs outside the lab.

Mitchell and Laine (1985) reported the first laboratory study of binge eating in patients with bulimia nervosa. Their laboratory was located in an inpatient unit where subjects were admitted to a private room and encouraged to engage in their usual eating behavior. Kaye et al. (Kaye, Gwirtsman, George, Weiss, & Jimerson, 1986; Kaye et al., 1992) have conducted several similar studies using what they call the human-feeding-laboratory design (HFL). The HFL comprises a large private room with an adjacent private bathroom that subjects can use for vomiting. Subjects are provided free access to a variety of food via two computer controlled vending machines that are in the room. An infrared television camera is used to observe subjects at approximately 15-minute intervals.

A third series of laboratory studies examining eating behavior among individuals with bulimia nervosa and binge eating disorder have been headed by Kissileff, Walsh, and colleagues (Goldfein, Walsh, LaChaussee, Kissileff, & Devlin, 1993; Hadigan et al., 1989; Kissileff, Walsh, Kral, & Cassidy, 1986; LaChaussee, Kissileff, Walsh, & Hadigan, 1992; Walsh, Hadigan, Kissileff, & LaChaussee, 1992; Walsh, Kissileff, Cassidy, & Dantzie, 1989). In contrast to the procedures of Mitchell's and Kaye's labs, subjects participating in studies conducted by this team of investigators are not admitted to the unit as inpatients, and therefore the adaptation procedures are slightly different. Typically, subjects go to the lab on two or three nonconsecutive days for several hours each day, and the first day is considered the adaptation phase. A private bathroom for purging is available outside of the observation room. Single-item meals as well as multiple-item meals have been conducted by this group. In the multi-item meals, subjects select their own foods from an identical array of foods that includes both foods believed to be typical of a binge and other foods typical of a dinner meal.

These three teams of investigators have used the laboratory procedures to study specific aspects of food consumption and behavioral patterns in patients with bulimia nervosa. The primary goal of these laboratory studies is not to diagnose binge eating or purging but to descriptively expand our knowledge of these behaviors by providing directly observed data. Despite differences in laboratory procedures, they have supplied the field with important converging data regarding the macronutrient and behavioral components of binge eating.

The macronutrient analysis of food consumed during binge eating is best accomplished in the laboratory because of the advantage of being able to directly measure the food. There are several computer programs designed to facilitate these analyses. The most commonly used programs include (a) Nutrichec (Thurman, 1981); (b) Nutripractor or Nutriplanner (Practorcare, Inc., 1992); (c) KALI 2.1.4 (Pfannendorfer & Arab, 1984); and (d) the Food Processor Software Package (Geltz & Geltz, 1984).

Summary and Recommendations

Binge eating and purging can be assessed by self-monitoring, self-report questionnaires, interview, and laboratory observation. The method and particular instrument employed should be selected based on careful consideration of the specific aim of the assessment.

Given the wide range in the definition of a *binge,* the assessment of binge eating can most reliably be measured by interview procedures. And although vomiting can be assessed with self-report measures more reliably than can binge eating, what constitutes other forms of purging can also require informed judgment, which is best provided in an interview format. The most comprehensive and rigorously investigated instrument for the assessment of binge eating and purging is the EDE. It provides the necessary data for diagnostic purposes as well as continuous data for assessment of severity and the measurement of change. In addition, the SCID is an excellent measure for the determination of diagnostic criteria for the eating disorders, including binge eating and purging; however, it is criterion based and therefore does not provide measures of severity.

Despite the precision to be gained by using interview measures, self-report instruments are most commonly employed in the assessment of binge eating and purging. The major advantage of this method of assessment is that large numbers of individuals can be evaluated without requiring vast resources in terms of time and personnel. A second advantage is that individuals can remain anonymous and therefore may be more likely to honestly answer questions pertaining to binge eating and purging. To increase the validity of self-report measures, we strongly encourage clinicians and researchers alike to make explicit the specific criteria necessary for defining an episode of binge eating and purging. Once such definitions are established, it is our experience that, at least within a clinical sample, individuals are able to provide highly reliable information regarding their binge eating and purging frequencies.

Laboratory methods offer the unique opportunity for extensive descriptive study of the behavioral, biological, and physiological processes associated with binge eating and purging. However, given the drawbacks of this method of assessment, such procedures should be employed when critical questions require directly observable or measurable data, and not for the purpose of diagnosis.

It is clear that, in addition to general issues of measurement, the assessment of binge eating or purging carries with it specific considerations. Given the secretive nature of these behaviors, their evaluation, with the exception of laboratory studies, inevitably relies on some degree of self-report. However, because studies have demonstrated that the colloquial usage of the term *binge eating* is not consistent or reliable, some kind of clinical guidance, whether in explicit written instructions in a paper-and-pencil measure or as part of an interviewer-based instrument like the EDE, is essential for the purpose of diagnosis and is strongly recommended in all clinical and research efforts.

References

American Psychiatric Association. (1994). *Diagnostic and statistical manual of mental disorders (DSM-IV)*. Washington, DC: Author.

Beglin, S. J. (1990). *Eating disorders in young adult women*. Unpublished doctoral dissertation, Oxford University, Oxford.

Beglin, S. J., & Fairburn, C. G. (1992). What is meant by the term "binge"? *American Journal of Psychiatry, 149*(1), 123-124.

Beumont, P. V. J., Kopec-Schrader, E. M., Talbot, P., & Touyz, S. W. (1992). *Measuring the specific psychopathology of eating disorder patients*. Unpublished manuscript.

Coffman, D. A. (1984). A clinically derived treatment model for the binge-purge syndrome. In R. C. Hawkins, W. J. Fremouw, & P. F. Clement (Eds.), *The binge-purge syndrome: Diagnosis, treatment, and research* (pp. 211-224). New York: Springer.

Cooper, P. J., Taylor, M. J., Cooper, Z., & Fairburn, C. G. (1987). The development and validation of the Body Shape Questionnaire. *International Journal of Eating Disorders, 6*(4), 485-494.

Cooper, Z., Cooper, P., & Fairburn, C. (1989). The validity of the Eating Disorder Examination and its subscales. *British Journal of Psychiatry, 154*, 807-812.

Cooper, Z., & Fairburn, C. (1987). The Eating Disorder Examination: A semi-structured interview for the assessment of the specific psychopathology of eating disorders. *International Journal of Eating Disorders, 6*(1), 1-8.

Fairburn, C. (1987). The definition of bulimia nervosa: Guidelines for clinicians and research workers. *Annals of Behavioral Medicine, 9*, 307.

Fairburn, C. G., & Cooper, Z. (1993). The Eating Disorder Examination (12th ed.). In C. G. Fairburn & G. T. Wilson (Eds.), *Binge eating: Nature, assessment, and treatment* (pp. 317-332). New York: Guilford.

Fairburn, C. G., Jones, R., Peveler, R. C., Hope, R. A., & O'Conner, M. (1993). Psychotherapy and bulimia nervosa: The longer-term effects of interpersonal psychotherapy, behaviour therapy, and cognitive behaviour therapy. *Archives of General Psychiatry, 50*, 419-428.

Fairburn, C. G., & Wilson, G. T. (Eds.). (1993). *Binge eating: Nature, assessment, and treatment*. New York: Guilford.

Fichter, M. M., Elton, M., Engel, K., Meyer, A., Poustka, F., Mall, H., & von der Heydte, S. (1989). The Structured Interview for Anorexia and Bulimia Nervosa (SIAB): Development and characteristics of a (semi-) standardized instrument. In M. M. Fichter (Ed.), *Bulimia nervosa: Basic research, diagnosis, and therapy* (pp. 57-70). New York: Wiley.

Garner, D. M. (1991). *The Eating Disorder Inventory-2 professional manual*. Odessa, FL: Psychological Assessment Resources.

Garner, D. M., Olmsted, M. P., Bohr, Y., & Garfinkel, P. E. (1982). The Eating Attitudes Test: Psychometric features and clinical correlates. *Psychological Medicine, 12*, 871-878.

Garner, D., Olmsted, M., & Polivy, H. (1983). Development and validation of a multidimensional eating disorder inventory for anorexia nervosa and bulimia. *International Journal of Eating Disorders, 2*, 15-34.

Geltz, B., & Geltz, B. (1984). *The Food Processor*. Salem, OR: ESHA Corporation.

Goldfein, J. A., Walsh, B. T., LaChaussee, J. L., Kissileff, H. R., & Devlin, M. J. (1993). Eating behavior in binge eating disorder. *International Journal of Eating Disorders, 14*, 427-431.

Gormally, J., Black, S., Daston, S., & Rardin, D. (1982). The assessment of binge eating severity among obese persons. *Addictive Behaviors, 7*, 47-55.

Hadigan, C. M., Kissileff, H. R., & Walsh, B. T. (1989). Patterns of food selection during meals in women with bulimia. *American Journal of Clinical Nutrition, 50*, 759-766.

Halmi, K., Falk, J. R., & Schwartz, E. (1981). Binge eating and vomiting: A survey of a college population. *Psychological Medicine, 11*, 697-706.

Hawkins, R. C., & Clement, P. F. (1980). Development and construct validation of a self-report measure of binge eating tendencies. *Addictive Behaviors, 5*, 219-226.

Herman, C. P., & Polivy, J. (1980). Restrained eating. In A. J. Stunkard (Ed.), *Obesity* (pp. 208-225). Philadelphia: Saunders.

Katzman, M. A., & Wolchik, S. A. (1984). Bulimia and binge eating in college women: A comparison of personality and behavioral characteristics. *Journal of Consulting and Clinical Psychology, 52*, 423-428.

Kaye, W. H., Gwirtsman, H. E., George, D. T., Weiss, S. R., & Jimerson, D. C. (1986). Relationship of mood alterations to bingeing behavior in bulimia. *British Journal of Psychiatry, 149*, 479-485.

Kaye, W. H., Weltzin, T. E., McKee, M., McConaha, C., Hansen, D., & Hsu, L. K. G. (1992). Laboratory assessment of feeding behavior in bulimia nervosa and healthy women: Methods for developing a human-feeding laboratory. *American Journal of Clinical Nutrition, 55*, 372-380.

Kissileff, H. R., Walsh, B. T., Kral, J. G., & Cassidy, S. M. (1986). Laboratory studies of eating behavior in women with bulimia. *Physiological Behavior, 38*, 563-570.

LaChaussee, J., Kissileff, H. R., Walsh, B. T., & Hadigan, C. M. (1992). The single item meal as a measure of binge eating behavior in patients with bulimia nervosa. *Physiological Behavior, 51*, 593-600.

LaPorte, D. J. (1992). Treatment response in obese binge eaters: Preliminary results using a very low calorie diet (VLCD) and behavior therapy. *Addictive Behaviors, 17*, 247-257.

Loeb, K. L., Pike, K. M., Walsh, B. T., & Wilson, G. T. (1994). The assessment of diagnostic features of bulimia nervosa: Interview versus self-report format. *International Journal of Eating Disorders, 16*(1), 75-81.

Marcus, M. D., Wing, R. R., Ewing, L., Kern, E., Gooding, W., & McDermott, M. (1990). Psychiatric disorders among obese binge eaters. *International Journal of Eating Disorders, 9*, 69-77.

Marcus, M. D., Wing, R. R., & Hopkins, J. (1988). Obese binge eaters: Affect, cognitions, and response to behavioral weight control. *Journal of Consulting and Clinical Psychology, 3*, 433-439.

Marcus, M. D., Wing, R. R., & Lamparski, D. M. (1985). Binge eating and dietary restraint in obese patients. *Addictive Behaviors, 10*, 163-168.

Mitchell, J. E., & Laine, D. C. (1985). Monitored binge-eating behavior in patients with bulimia. *International Journal of Eating Disorders, 4*, 177-183.

Ordman, A. M., & Kirschenbaum, D. S. (1985). Cognitive-behavioral therapy for bulimia: An initial outcome study. *Journal of Consulting and Clinical Psychology, 53*, 305-313.

Ortega, D. F., Warranch, H. R., Maldonado, A. J., & Hubbard, F. A. (1987). A comparative analysis of self-report measures of bulimia. *International Journal of Eating Disorders, 6*(2), 301-311.

Palmer, R., Christie, M., Cordle, C., Davies, D., & Kendrick, J. (1987). The clinical eating disorder rating instrument (CEDRI): A preliminary description. *International Journal of Eating Disorders, 6*, 9-16.

Pfannendorfer, H., & Arab, L. (1984). KALI-Kodierungs- und Auswertungsprogramm für Lebensmittel-Inhaltsstoffe. In Bundesforschungsanstalt für Ernährung (Ed.), *Entwicklung und Benutzung von Nahrstoff-Datenbanken in der BRD* (pp. 137-147). Karlsruhe: Berichte der Bundesforschungsanstalt für Ernährung.

Practorcare, Inc. (1992). (Product available from Practorcare, Inc., 10951 Sorrento Valley Road, San Diego, CA 92121, 800-421-9073)

Rosen, J. C., Leitenberg, H., Fisher, C., & Khazam, C. (1986). Binge eating episodes in bulimia nervosa: The amount and type of food consumed. *International Journal of Eating Disorders, 5*, 255-267.

Rosen, J. C., Vara, L., Wendt, S., & Leitenberg, H. (1990). Validity studies of the Eating Disorder Examination. *International Journal of Eating Disorders, 9*(5), 519-528.

Rossiter, E. M., & Agras, W. S. (1990). An empirical test of the DSM-III-R definition of binge. *International Journal of Eating Disorders, 9*, 513-519.

Rossiter, E. M., Agras, W. S., Telch, C. F., & Bruce, B. (1992). The eating patterns of non-purging bulimic subjects. *International Journal of Eating Disorders, 11*, 111-120.

Skre, I., Onstad, S., Torgersen, S., & Kringlen, E. (1991). High interrater reliability for the Structured Clinical Interview for the DSM-III-R Axis I (SCID-I). *Acta Psychiatrica Scandinavica, 84*, 167-173.

Smith, M. C., & Thelen, M. H. (1984). Development and validation of a test for bulimia. *Journal of Consulting and Clinical Psychology, 52*, 863-872.

Spitzer, R. L., Devlin, M., Walsh, B. T., et al. (1992). Binge eating disorder: A multisite field trial of the diagnostic criteria. *International Journal of Eating Disorders, 11*, 191-203.

Spitzer, R. L., Yanovski, S., Wadden, T., Wing, R., Marcus, M., Stunkard, A., Devlin, M., Mitchell, J., Hasin, D., & Horne, R. L. (1993). Binge eating disorder: Its further validation in a multisite study. *International Journal of Eating Disorders, 13*, 137-153.

Spitzer, R. L., Williams, J. B. W., & Gibbon, M. (1987). *Structured clinical interview for the DSM-III-R (SCID).* New York: New York State Psychiatric Institute, Biometrics Research.

Spitzer, R. L., Williams, J. B. W., Gibbon, M., & First, M. (1990). *User's Guide for the Structured Clinical Interview for the DSM-III-R.* Washington, DC: American Psychiatric Press.

Spitzer, R. L., Williams, J. B. W., Gibbon, M., & First, M. (1992). The structured clinical interview for the DSM-III-R (SCID). I: History, rationale and description. *Archives of General Psychiatry, 49*, 624-629.

Spitzer, R. L., Yanovski, S. Z., & Marcus, M. D. (1993). *The Questionnaire on Eating and Weight Patterns-Revised (QEWP-R, 1993).* (Available from the New York State Psychiatric Institute, 722 West 168th Street, New York, NY 10032)

Stunkard, A. J., Sorensen, T., & Schulsinger, F. (1983). Use of the Danish Adoption Register for the Study of Obesity and Thinness. In S. S. Kety, L. P. Roland, R. L. Sidman, & S. W. Matthysse (Eds.), *The genetics of neurological and psychiatric disorders.* New York: Raven.

Thelen, M. H., Farmer, J., Wonderlich, S., & Smith, M. (1991). A revision of the Bulimia Test: The BULIT-R. *Psychological Assessment, 3*, 119-124.

Thurman, L. D. (1981). *Nutrichec: Diet and physical activity analysis* (Version 2.0.1.D). Tulsa, OK: Oral Roberts University.

Walsh, B. T., Hadigan, C. M., Kissileff, H. R., & LaChaussee, J. L. (1992). Bulimia nervosa: A syndrome of feast and famine. In G. H. Anderson & S. H. Kennedy (Eds.), *The biology of feast and famine* (pp. 3-20). San Diego, CA: Academic Press.

Walsh, B. T., Kissileff, H. R., Cassidy, S. M., & Dantzie, S. (1989). Eating behavior of women with bulimia. *Archives of General Psychiatry, 46*, 54-58.

Whitaker, A., Davies, M., Shaffer, D., Johnson, J., Abrams, S., Walsh, B. T., & Kalikow, K. (1989). The struggle to be thin: A survey of anorexic and bulimic symptoms in a non-referred adolescent population. *Psychological Medicine, 19*, 143-163.

Williams, J. B. W., Gibbon, M., First, M. B., Spitzer, R. L., Davies, M., Borus, J., Howes, M. J., Kane, J., Pope, H. G., Jr., Roonsaville, B., & Wittchen, H. (1992). The Structured Clinical

Interview for DSM-III-R (SCID). II: Multi-site test-retest reliability. *Archives of General Psychiatry, 49,* 630-636.

Williamson, D. A. (1990). *Assessment of eating disorders.* New York: Pergamon.

Williamson, D. A., Kelley, M. L., Davis, C. J., Ruggiero, L., & Blouin, D. C. (1985). Psychopathology of eating disorders: A controlled comparison of bulimic, obese, and normal subjects. *Journal of Consulting and Clinical Psychology, 53,* 161-166.

Wilson, G. T., & Smith, D. (1989). Assessing of bulimia nervosa: An evaluation of the Eating Disorder Examination. *International Journal of Eating Disorders, 8*(2), 173-179.

Yanovski, S. Z. (1993). Binge eating disorder: Current knowledge and future directions. *Obesity Research, 1,* 308-324.

Yanovski, S. Z., Leet, M., Yanovski, J. A., et al. (1992). Food intake and selection of obese women with binge eating disorder. *American Journal of Clinical Nutrition, 56,* 975-980.

Yates, A. J., & Sambrailo, F. (1984). Bulimia nervosa: A descriptive and therapeutic study. *Behavior Research and Therapy, 22,* 503-517.

Appendix 9-A

Binge Scale Questionnaire

1. How often do you binge eat?

   a. seldom (0)

   b. once or twice a month (1)

   c. once a week (2)

   d. almost every day (3)

2. What is the average length of a binge eating episode?

   a. Less than 15 minutes (0)

   b. 15 minutes to one hour (1)

   c. One hour to four hours (2)

   d. More than four hours (3)

3. Which of the following statements best applies to your binge eating?

   a. I eat until I have had enough to satisfy me (0)

   b. I eat until my stomach feels full (1)

   c. I eat until my stomach is painfully full (2)

   d. I eat until I can't eat any more (3)

4. Do you ever vomit after a binge?

   a. Never (0)

   b. Sometimes (1)

   c. Usually (2)

   d. Always (3)

5. Which of the following best applies to your eating behavior when binge eating?

    a. I eat more slowly than usual (0)

    b. I eat about the same as I usually do (0)

    c. I eat very rapidly (1)

6. How much are you concerned about your binge eating?

    a. Not bothered at all (0)

    b. Bothers me a little (1)

    c. Moderately concerned (2)

    d. A major concern (3)

7. Which best describes your feeling during a binge?

    a. I feel that I could control the eating if I chose (0)

    b. I feel that I have at least some control (1)

    c. I feel completely out of control (2)

8. Which of the following describes your feelings after a binge?

    a. I feel fairly neutral, not too concerned (0)

    b. I am moderately upset (1)

    c. I hate myself (2)

9. Which most accurately describes your feelings after a binge?

    a. Not depressed at all (0)

    b. Mildly depressed (1)

    c. Moderately depressed (2)

    d. Very depressed (3)

SOURCE: Reprinted from *Addictive Behaviors, 5*, Hawkins, R. C., & Clement, P. F., "Development and Construct Validation of a Self-Report Measure of Binge Eating Tendencies," pp. 219-226, copyright © 1980, with kind permission from Elsevier Science Ltd., The Boulevard, Langford Lane, Kidlington 0X5 1GB, UK.

Appendix 9-B

Questionnaire on Eating and Weight Patterns– Revised (QEWP-R)[a, b, c]

Last name _____ First name _____ M.I. _____

Date _____ I.D. Number _____

Thank you for completing this questionnaire. Please circle the appropriate number or response, or write in information where asked. You may skip any question you do not understand or do not wish to answer.

1. Age: _____ years

2. Sex: 1 Male   2 Female

3. What is you ethnic/racial background?

    1 Black (not Hispanic)

    2 Hispanic

    3 White (not Hispanic)

    4 Asian

    5 Other (please specify) _____

4. How far did you get in school?

    1 Grammar school, junior high school or less

    2 Some high school

    3 High school graduate or equivalency (GED)

    4 Some college or associate degree

    5 Completed college

5. How tall are you?

    _____ feet _____ in

6. How much do you weigh now?

    _____ lbs

7. What has been your highest weight ever (when not pregnant)?

    _____ lbs

8. Have you ever been overweight by at least 10 lbs as a child or 15 lbs as an adult (when not pregnant)?

    1 Yes   2 No or not sure

    IF YES: How old were you when you were first overweight (at least 10 lbs as a child or 15 lbs as an adult)? If you are not sure, what is your best guess?

    _____ years

9. How many times (approximately) have you lost 20 lbs or more—when you weren't sick—and then gained it back?

    1 Never

    2 Once or twice

    3 Three or four times

    4 Five times or more

10. During the past *six* months, did you often eat within any two hour period what most people would regard as an unusually large amount of food?

    1 Yes   2 No

    IF NO: SKIP TO QUESTION 15

11. During the times when you ate this way, did you often feel you couldn't stop eating or control what or how much you were eating?

    1 Yes   2 No

    IF NO: SKIP TO QUESTION 15

12. During the past *six* months, how often, on average, did you have times when you ate this way—that is, large amounts of food *plus* the feeling that your

eating was out of control? (There may have been some weeks when it was not present—just average those in.)

1 Less than one day a week

2 One day a week

3 Two or three days a week

4 Four or five days a week

5 Nearly every day

13. Did you *usually* have any of the following experiences during these occasions?

    a Eating much more rapidly than usual?   Yes _____   No _____

    b Eating until you felt uncomfortably full?   Yes _____   No _____

    c Eating large amounts of food when you didn't feel physically hungry?   Yes _____   No _____

    d Eating alone because you were embarrassed by how much you were eating?   Yes _____   No _____

    e Feeling disgusted with yourself, depressed, or feeling very guilty after overeating?   Yes _____   No _____

14. Think about a typical time when you ate this way—that is, large amounts of food *plus* the feeling that your eating was out of control.

    a What time of day did the episode start?

        1 Morning (8 a.m. to 12 noon)

        2 Early afternoon (12 noon to 4 p.m.)

        3 Late afternoon (4 p.m. to 7 p.m.)

        4 Evening (7 p.m.-10 p.m.)

        5 Night (after 10 p.m.)

    b Approximately how long did this episode of eating last, from the time you started to eat to when you stopped and didn't eat again for at least two hours?

       _____ hours   _____ minutes

    c As best you can remember, please list everything you might have eaten or drunk during that episode. If you ate for more than two hours, describe the foods eaten and liquids drunk during the two hours that you ate the most. Be specific—include brand names where possible, and amounts as best you can estimate. (For example: 7 ounces Ruffles potato chips; 1 cup Breyer's chocolate ice cream with 2 teaspoons hot fudge; 2 8-ounce glasses of Coca-Cola, $1\frac{1}{2}$ ham and cheese sandwiches with mustard.)

d At the time this episode started, how long had it been since you had previously finished eating a meal or snack?

_____ hours   _____ minutes

15. In general, during the past *six* months, how upset were you by overeating (eating more than you think is best for you)?

1 Not at all

2 Slightly

3 Moderately

4 Greatly

5 Extremely

16. In general, during the past *six* months, how upset were you by the feeling that you couldn't stop eating or control what or how much you were eating?

1 Not at all

2 Slightly

3 Moderately

4 Greatly

5 Extremely

17. During the past *six* months, how important has your weight or shape been in how you feel about or evaluate yourself as a person—as compared to other aspects of your life, such as how you do at work, as a parent, or how you get along with other people?

1 Weight and shape were *not very important*

2 Weight and shape *played a part* in how you felt about yourself

3 Weight and shape *were among the main things* that affected how you felt about yourself

4 Weight and shape *were the most important things* that affected how you felt about yourself

18. During the past *three* months, did you ever make yourself vomit in order to avoid gaining weight after binge eating?

    1 Yes   2 No

    IF YES: How often, *on average*, was that?

    1 Less than once a week

    2 Once a week

    3 Two or three times a week

    4 Four or five times a week

    5 More than five times a week

19. During the past *three* months, did you ever take more than twice the recommended dose of laxatives in order to avoid gaining weight after binge eating?

    1 Yes   2 No

    IF YES: How often, *on average*, was that?

    1 Less than once a week

    2 Once a week

    3 Two or three times a week

    4 Four or five times a week

    5 More than five times a week

20. During the past *three* months, did you ever take more than twice the recommended dose of diuretics (water pills) in order to avoid gaining weight after binge eating?

    1 Yes   2 No

    IF YES: How often, *on average*, was that?

    1 Less than once a week

    2 Once a week

    3 Two or three times a week

    4 Four or five times a week

    5 More than five times a week

21. During the past *three* months, did you ever fast—not eat anything at all for at least 24 hours—in order to avoid gaining weight after binge eating?

   1 Yes   2 No

   IF YES: How often, *on average*, was that?

   1 Less than one day a week

   2 One day a week

   3 Two or three days a week

   4 Four or five days a week

   5 Nearly every day

22. During the past *three* months, did you ever exercise for more than an hour specifically in order to avoid gaining weight after binge eating?

   1 Yes   2 No

   IF YES: How often, *on average*, was that?

   1 Less than once a week

   2 Once a week

   3 Two or three times a week

   4 Four or five times a week

   5 More than five times a week

23. During the past *three* months, did you ever take more than twice the recommended dose of a diet pill in order to avoid gaining weight after binge eating?

   1 Yes   2 No

   IF YES: How often, *on average*, was that?

   1 Less than once a week

   2 Once a week

   3 Two or three times a week

   4 Four or five times a week

   5 More than five times a week

24. During the past *six* months, did you go to any meetings of an organized weight control program? (e.g., Weight Watchers, Optifast, Jenny Craig) or a self-help group (e.g., TOPS, Overeaters Anonymous)?

1 Yes   2 No

IF YES: Name of program _____

25. Since you have been an adult—18 years old—how much of the time have you been on a diet, been trying to follow a diet, or in some way been limiting how much you were eating in order to lose weight or keep from regaining weight you had lost? Would you say . . . ?

1 None or hardly any of the time

2 About a quarter of the time

3 About half of the time

4 About three-quarters of the time

5 Nearly all of the time

26. SKIP THIS QUESTION IF YOU NEVER LOST AT LEAST 10 LBS BY DIETING:

How old were you the first time you lost at least 10 lbs by dieting, or in some way limiting how much you ate? If you are not sure, what is your best guess?

_____ years

27. SKIP THIS QUESTION IF YOU'VE NEVER HAD EPISODES OF EATING UNUSUALLY LARGE AMOUNTS OF FOOD ALONG WITH THE SENSE OF LOSS OF CONTROL:

How old were you when you first had times when you ate large amounts of food and felt that your eating was out of control? If you are not sure, what is your best guess?

_____ years

28. Please take a look at the following silhouettes. Put a circle around the silhouettes that most resemble the body build of your natural father and mother *at their heaviest.* If you have no knowledge of your biological father and/or mother, don't circle anything for that parent.

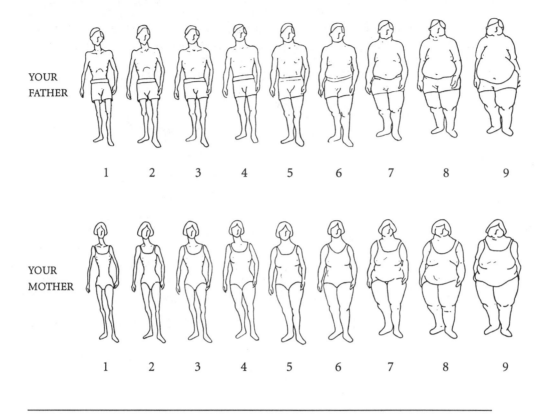

YOUR
FATHER

1   2   3   4   5   6   7   8   9

YOUR
MOTHER

1   2   3   4   5   6   7   8   9

DECISION RULES FOR DIAGNOSING BINGE EATING DISORDER USING THE
QUESTIONNAIRE ON EATING AND WEIGHT PATTERNS, Revised[a, b, c]

(FOR EXAMINER'S USE ONLY)

DIAGNOSIS OF BED

QUESTION NUMBER	RESPONSE
10 **AND** 11	1 (BINGE EATING)
12	3, 4, OR 5 (AT LEAST 2 DAYS PER WEEK FOR SIX MONTHS)
13 a through e	3 OR MORE ITEMS MARKED "YES" (AT LEAST 3 ASSOCIATED SYMPTOMS DURING BINGE EATING EPISODES)
15 **OR** 16	4 OR 5 (MARKED DISTRESS REGARDING BINGE EATING)

DIAGNOSIS OF BED REQUIRES ALL OF THE ABOVE ALONG WITH THE ABSENCE OF PURGING OR NON-PURGING BULIMIA NERVOSA, AS DEFINED BELOW.

DIAGNOSIS OF PURGING BULIMIA NERVOSA

10 **AND** 11	1 (SAME AS BED)
12	3, 4, OR 5 (AT LEAST 2 DAYS PER WEEK FOR SIX MONTHS)
	Note: This is an approximation of the *DSM-IV* criterion of at least 2 episodes/week for three months.
17	3 OR 4 (OVEREVALUATION OF WEIGHT/SHAPE)
18, 19, **OR** 20	*ANY* RESPONSE 3, 4, OR 5 (PURGING AT LEAST 2 TIMES PER WEEK FOR THREE MONTHS)

DIAGNOSIS OF NON-PURGING BULIMIA NERVOSA

10, 11, 12, 17	SAME AS PURGING BULIMIA NERVOSA
18, 19, **AND** 20	**NO** RESPONSE 3, 4, OR 5 (NO FREQUENT COMPENSATORY PURGING)
21, 22, **OR** 23	**ANY** RESPONSE 3, 4, OR 5 (COMPENSATORY NON-PURGING BEHAVIOR AT LEAST TWO TIMES PER WEEK FOR 3 MONTHS)

QUESTION FOR RESEARCH PURPOSES ONLY
(NOT TO BE USED FOR DIAGNOSIS OF BED OR BULIMIA NERVOSA, PURGING OR NON-PURGING TYPE)

14 a through d	EXAMINER'S JUDGMENT THAT AMOUNT OF FOOD DESCRIBED IS UNUSUALLY LARGE GIVEN CIRCUM-STANCES (i.e., TIME OF DAY, HOURS SINCE PREVIOUS MEAL)
	YES _____ NO _____ UNSURE _____

SOURCE: Spitzer, R. L., Yanovski, S. Z., & Marcus, M. D. (1993). *The Questionnaire on Eating and Weight Patterns-Revised (QEWP-R, 1993).* (Available from the New York State Psychiatric Institute, 722 West 168th Street, New York, NY 10032). Used by permission.
NOTES: a. Robert L. Spitzer, Susan Z. Yanovski, Marsha D. Marcus.
   b. The following individuals contributed to the development of previous versions of the QEWP: Stewart Agras, Michael Devlin, Deborah Hasin, James Mitchell, Cathy Nonas, Albert Stunkard, Thomas Wadden, B. Timothy Walsh, Rena Wing.
   c. Silhouettes from Stunkard A. J., Sorensen T., Schulsinger F. Use of the Danish Adoption Register for the Study of Obesity and Thinness. In Kety S. S., Roland L. P., Sidman R. L., Matthysse S. W., eds. *The Genetics of Neurological and Psychiatric Disorders.* Raven Press: New York. 1983:119. Used by permission.

Appendix 9-C

Sample Questions From the ESI

Below are some examples of AMOUNTS of food that people have eaten *in less than 2 hours.*

Example (1) two doughnuts and a cup of ice cream and 2 cookies in less than two hours.

Example (2) four doughnuts and a pint of ice cream [and] 5 cookies in less than 2 hours.

Example (3) six doughnuts and a quart of ice cream and 10 cookies in less than 2 hours.

Example (4) eight doughnuts and a half gallon of ice cream and 15 cookies in less than 2 hours.

9. Look at the examples . . . above. Which amount of food do you think is closest to the *largest* AMOUNT you have ever eaten in less than 2 hours (even if you did not exactly eat the same food)? (0) less than Example 1 in the box above; (1) Example 1 in the box above; (2) Example 2 in the box above; (3) Example 3 in the box above; (4) Example 4 in the box above; (5) more than Example 4 in the box above.

In questions 10 through 18, "*lots of food in less than 2 hours*" means the *largest* amount of food you have ever eaten in less than two hours (your answer to 9).

10. How many times have you eaten *lots of food in less than 2 hours?* (5) more than fifty times; (4) twenty-five to fifty times; (3) thirteen to twenty-four times; (2) three to twelve times; (1) once or twice only.

11. When was the last time you ate *lots of food in less than 2 hours?* (5) within the last two weeks; (4) within the last month; (3) within the last six months; (2) within the last year; (1) more than one year ago.

21. Have you ever made yourself throw up? (yes/no). If *no*, go on to question 22. If *yes*:

A. Describe in a few words the reason(s) you made yourself throw up:

B. How often have you ever made yourself throw up? (5) sixty or more times; (4) forty to fifty-nine times; (3) ten to thirty-nine times; (2) three to nine times; (1) one or two times.

C. When was the last time you made yourself throw up? (5) within the last two weeks; (4) within the last month; (3) within the last six months; (2) within the last year; (1) more than one year ago.

SOURCE: From "The Struggle to Be Thin: A Survey of Anorexic and Bulimic Symptoms in a Non-Referred Adolescent Population," by A. Whitaker, M. Davies, D. Shaffer, J. Johnson, S. Abrams, B. T. Walsh, and K. Kalikow, 1989, *Psychological Medicine, 19,* pp. 143-163. Copyright © 1989 by Cambridge University Press. Reprinted with the permission of Cambridge University Press.

Appendix 9-D

Sample Questions From the EDE,
Taken From the Section on the Different Types of Overeating

[THE ASTERISKED QUESTIONS MUST BE ASKED IN EVERY CASE.]

Main probe questions

 *I would like to ask you about any episodes of overeating that you may have had over the past four weeks.

 *Different people mean different things by overeating. I would like you to describe any times when you have *felt* that you have eaten too much in one go.

 *Have there been any times when you have felt that you have eaten too much, but others would not agree?

[N.B. FOR SUBJECTIVE BULIMIC EPISODES TO BE ELIGIBLE, THEY MUST HAVE BEEN VIEWED AS HAVING INVOLVED EATING AN EXCESSIVE AMOUNT OF FOOD.]

Subsidiary probe questions

To assess the amount of food eaten:

 Typically what have you eaten at these times?

 What were others eating at the time?

To assess "loss of control":

 Did you have a sense of loss of control at the time?

For chronic cases only:

 Could you have stopped eating once you had started?

 Could you have prevented the episode from occurring?

SELF-INDUCED VOMITING (Diagnostic item):

Over the past four weeks have you made yourself sick as a means of controlling your shape and weight?

[Rate the number of days on which there has been one or more episodes of self-induced vomiting as a means of controlling shape, weight, or body composition. Rate 00 if no vomiting.]

[Rate the number of discrete episodes of self-induced vomiting. Accept the subject's definition of an episode. Rate 777 if the number is so great that it cannot be calculated. Rate 000 if no vomiting.]

SOURCE: From *Binge Eating: Nature, Assessment, and Treatment,* by C. G. Fairburn and G. T. Wilson (Eds.), 1993, New York: Guilford Press. Copyright © 1993 by Guilford Press. Reprinted with permission.

Appendix 9-E

Selected Questions From the
SCID Assessing Bulimia Nervosa

? = inadequate information

1 = absent or false

2 = subthreshold

3 = threshold or true

Have you ever had an eating binge during which you ate a lot of food in a short period of time?

    A. Recurrent episodes of binge eating (rapid consumption of a large amount of food in a discrete period of time).

      ?   1   2   3

During these binges, did you feel that your eating was out of control?

    B. A feeling of lack of control over the eating behavior during the eating binges.

      ?   1   2   3

Did you do anything to counteract the effects of the binges? (Like making yourself vomit, taking laxatives, strict dieting, fasting, or exercising a lot?)

    C. The person regularly engages in either self-induced vomiting, use of laxatives or diuretics, strict dieting or fasting, or vigorous exercise in order to prevent weight gain.

      ?   1   2   3

During this time, did you have eating binges as often as twice a week for three months?

D. A minimum average of two binge eating episodes a week for at least three months.

?   1   2   3

Were you a lot more concerned about your weight and body shape than most people (your age)?

E. Persistent overconcern with body shape and weight.

?   1   2   3

CRITERIA A, B, C, D, AND E ARE CODED "3": BULIMIA NERVOSA

SOURCE: From *Structured Clinical Interview for the DSM-III-R (SCID)*, by R. L. Spitzer, J. B. W. Williams, and M. Gibbon, 1987, New York: New York State Psychiatric Institute, Biometrics Research. Reprinted with permission.

10

Assessment of Eating Disordered Thoughts, Feelings, and Behaviors

DONALD A. WILLIAMSON

DREW A. ANDERSON

LORI P. JACKMAN

SHERYL R. JACKSON

The development of objective assessment procedures for measuring eating disorder symptoms began in 1979 with publication of the first study describing the Eating Attitudes Test (Garner & Garfinkel, 1979). Over the 1980s and 1990s, there has been increased interest in the assessment of eating disorders (Williamson, 1990). This chapter reviews eight assessment procedures that were developed as (a) general measures of eating disorder symptoms, (b) measures specific to the symptoms of anorexia nervosa, (c) measures specific

to the symptoms of bulimia nervosa, and (d) measures of cognitive or emotional disturbances associated with the eating disorders. These eight assessment procedures were selected for review because of their psychometric
development. Copies of some of the questionnaires are included. Reading
level for tests that were available for review was evaluated using the Right-
Writer (RightSoft, Inc., 1989) program. The assessment methods are organized into four categories: (a) general eating disorder assessment, (b)
assessment of anorexia nervosa, (c) assessment of bulimia nervosa, and (d)
assessment of cognitive and emotional disturbances.

General Eating Disorder Assessment

Eating Disorder Inventory
and Eating Disorder Inventory-2

Description of Assessment Measure

The Eating Disorder Inventory (EDI; Garner, Olmsted, & Polivy, 1983)
was designed to assess psychological characteristics and symptoms common
to anorexia and bulimia nervosa. The original EDI has 64 items that form
eight subscales. Three of the subscales were designed to assess attitudes and
behaviors toward weight, body shape, and eating (Drive for Thinness, Bulimia, and Body Dissatisfaction). The remaining five subscales measure more
general psychological characteristics of persons with an eating disorder.
These scales are Ineffectiveness, Perfection, Interpersonal Distrust, Interoceptive Awareness, and Maturity Fears. The EDI has been translated into
Swedish, Dutch, German, French, Spanish, and Chinese. A revised edition of
the EDI, the Eating Disorder Inventory-2 (EDI-2; Garner, 1991), retained the
original 64 items and eight subscales, and added 27 items that form three additional scales (Asceticism, Impulse Regulation, and Social Insecurity). Most
of the published research pertaining to the psychometric properties of the
EDI has been conducted using the original version of the EDI.

Items on the original EDI and EDI-2 are presented in a 6-point, forced
choice format. Respondents rate whether each item applies "always," "usually," "often," "sometimes," "rarely," or "never." The most extreme eating dis-
orderlike response earns a score of 3, the immediately adjacent response
earns a score of 2, and the next response earns a 1. The three choices opposite
to the most pathological response receive no score. Scale scores are the sum-

mation of all item scores for that scale. Psychometric data pertaining to the EDI are summarized in Table 10.1.

Factor analyses of the EDI (using the original eight subscales) have been conducted for both eating disorder patient and nonpatient (female college student) samples. An eight-factor solution corresponding to the original eight subscales was found in the eating disordered patient sample that was reported by Welch, Hall, and Norring (1990). Head and Williamson (1990) found a three-factor solution in a bulimic sample ($n = 58$). The Drive for Thinness, Bulimia, Ineffectiveness, and Interoceptive Awareness subscales formed the first factor. The second factor was formed by the Interpersonal Distrust and Maturity Fears subscales. The Perfectionism subscale formed a third factor. Using a sample of college women, Welch, Hall, and Walkey (1988) also reported a three-factor solution. The perfectionism subscale formed one factor; the Drive for Thinness, Bulimia, and Body Dissatisfaction subscales formed another factor. The third factor was formed by the Ineffectiveness and Interpersonal Distrust subscales. A six-factor solution (Klemchuk, Hutchinson, & Frank, 1990) and an eight-factor solution similar to the original eight subscales (Williams, Schaefer, Shisslak, Gronwaldt, & Comerci, 1986) have also been reported using nonpatient samples. In sum, there appear to be two fairly stable factors: (a) a perfectionism factor (Perfectionism subscale) and (b) a factor that measures eating disorder behaviors and cognitions (Drive for Thinness, Bulimia, and Body Dissatisfaction). Other factors appear to be dependent on subject characteristics, such as clinical versus nonclinical samples.

Norms. Norms are available for eating disorder patients and nonpatient college females and males (Garner, 1991). Adolescent norms are also available (Rosen, Silberg, & Gross, 1988; Shore & Porter, 1990). Normative data for the three new subscales are also available for eating disorder patients and nonpatient male and female college samples.

Reliability: Internal consistency. Coefficient alphas for the original EDI scales range from .69 to .93, with the exception of maturity fears subscale (.65) in a group of 11- to 18-year-olds (Garner, 1991). Internal consistency for the three new subscales ranges from .70 to .80 except for the Asceticism subscale (.40) in a group of nonclinical subjects (Garner, 1991).

Test-retest reliability. The 1-year test-retest correlations on a sample of 282 nonpatients ranged from .41 to .75 (Crowther, Lilly, Crawford, Shepherd, & Oliver, 1990). The test-retest correlations for the Drive for Thinness and Body Dissatisfaction subscales were above .70. Test-retest reliabilities after 3

TABLE 10.1 Eating Disorder Inventory and Eating Disorder Inventory-2:
Summary of Psychometric Data

A. Norms

			Means and (Standard Deviations) for EDI Subscales					
	DT	B	BD	I	P	ID	IA	MF
ED	14.5	10.5	16.6	11.3	8.9	5.8	11.0	4.5
N = 899	(5.6)	(5.5)	(8.3)	(7.8)	(4.9)	(4.7)	(6.9)	(4.7)
CF	5.5	1.2	12.2	2.3	6.2	2.0	3.0	2.7
N = 205	(5.5)	(1.9)	(8.3)	(3.6)	(3.9)	(3.1)	(3.9)	(2.9)
14-18 F	7.1	2.2	12.1	4.2	5.0	3.4	5.5	3.8
N = 231	(5.9)	(2.8)	(8.7)	(4.9)	(4.1)	(3.6)	(5.4)	(3.1)
11-13 F	6.6	1.9	8.4	3.9	4.8	4.7	5.0	4.3
N = 183	(5.7)	(3.3)	(7.8)	(4.9)	(4.0)	(3.8)	(5.2)	(3.5)
CM	2.2	1.0	4.9	1.8	7.1	2.4	2.0	2.8
N = 101	(4.0)	(1.7)	(5.6)	(3.0)	(4.7)	(2.5)	(3.0)	(3.4)
14-18 M	2.1	2.0	3.9	2.7	5.9	4.6	3.5	3.9
N = 63	(2.6)	(3.2)	(3.8)	(3.6)	(4.3)	(3.8)	(3.5)	(3.3)
11-13 M	3.0	1.6	4.7	3.2	5.4	4.2	3.7	3.9
N = 133	(3.6)	(2.5)	(5.8)	(5.1)	(3.7)	(3.6)	(4.5)	(2.9)

	Means and (Standard Deviations) for EDI-2 Additional Subscales		
	A	IR	SI
Eating disorder	8.3	6.0	8.6
N = 107	(4.7)	(5.3)	(4.9)
Female college	3.4	2.3	3.3
N = 205	(2.2)	(3.6)	(3.3)
Male college	3.8	2.8	3.3
N = 101	(2.9)	(3.8)	(3.2)

B. Reliability

Internal Consistency

Coefficient alphas for the EDI and EDI-2 subscales were >.65 with the exception of asceticism in non-clinical samples.

Factor Structure: Three Factors

Test-Retest Reliability

Time Interval	Sample Size	Correlations
1 week	70	.67-.95
3 weeks	70	.65-.92
1 year	282	.41-.75

TABLE 10.1 (Continued)

C. Validity

Concurrent Validity

    AN > CF

    DT subscale
        r with EAT total score = .71
        r with Restraint Scale = .61

    B subscale
        r with Bulimia and Food Preoccupation subscale of EAT = .68

    BD subscale
        r with Body Shape Questionnaire = .78

    I subscale
        r with Feelings of Inadequacy Scale = .67

    SI subscale
        r with Borderline Syndrome Index = .70

NOTE: DT = Drive for Thinness, B = Bulimia, BD = Body Dissatisfaction, I = Ineffectiveness, P = Perfectionism, ID = Interpersonal Distrust, IA = Interoceptive Awareness, MF = Maturity Fears, A = Asceticism, IR = Impulse Regulation, SI = Social Insecurity. Groups: ED = Eating Disorder, CF = College Females, F = Females, CM = College Males, M = Males.

weeks for 70 nonpatients were above .81 with the exception of the Maturity Fears subscale (Wear & Pratz, 1987). Welch (1988) reported test-retest reliability of all subscales over a 1-week period to be above .80 with the exception of the Interoceptive Awareness subscale ($r = .67$).

Concurrent validity. In an early validity study of the EDI (Garner et al., 1983), agreement between clinician ratings of subscale traits and patient self-report subscales on the EDI ranged from .43 to .68. In addition, the anorexic-bulimic subgroup scored higher than the anorexic-restrictor subgroup on the Bulimia scale. Using discriminant analysis, Garner et al. (1983) found that each of the eight subscales differentiated anorexia nervosa from a female comparison group; 88% to 93% of the subjects were correctly classified using the EDI. They also found that the EDI subscales correctly classified 85% of subjects into bulimic and restrictor subtypes of anorexia nervosa.

    Scores on the original eight subscales of the EDI have been found to be positively correlated ($r = .26$ to .71) with scores on the Eating Attitudes Test (EAT; Garner, Olmsted, Bohr, & Garfinkel, 1982). The eating and weight-related subscales of the EDI were correlated ($r = .44$ to .61) with the Restraint Scale (Herman & Polivy, 1975), which measures dieting behavior. Correlations of EDI subscales and other measures of eating disorder behaviors and attitudes are summarized in Table 10.1.

Predictive validity. The Bulimia scale of the EDI has been shown to be a stable predictor of the presence of binge eating at 1-year and 2-year follow-ups (Norring, 1990).

Discriminant validity. The EDI subscales that assess attitudes and behaviors toward eating, weight, and shape (Drive for Thinness, Bulimia, and Body Dissatisfaction) have been found to be more highly correlated with other measures that assessed eating and diet behaviors, and less correlated with measures that assess more general psychopathology (Garner et al., 1983), whereas the subscales that assessed more general psychological characteristics (Ineffectiveness, Perfection, Interpersonal Distrust, Interoceptive Awareness, and Maturity Fears) were more highly correlated with general measures of psychopathology, and less correlated with the measures that assessed eating and dieting behaviors.

Susceptibility to dissimulation. One problem with self-report inventories is the risk that subjects can magnify or minimize symptom reports. The EDI is susceptible to this type of biased report.

Readability. The items on the EDI are brief. The EDI is written at a fifth-grade reading level.

Practicality. The EDI and the EDI-2 are widely used questionnaires that are easy to administer and score. The EDI can be administered in about 20 minutes. The EDI can be used as a screening instrument to detect at-risk populations, and it can be used for diagnosis. It also appears to be useful for differentiating levels of severity and/or subtypes of anorexia or bulimia nervosa, and it can be used as a treatment outcome measure. The EDI can be obtained from Psychological Assessment Resources, Inc., P.O. Box 998, Odessa, FL 33556.

Eating Disorder Examination

Description of Assessment Measure

The Eating Disorder Examination (EDE; Z. Cooper & Fairburn, 1987) is a semistructured interview for the assessment of eating disorders. It was devised to correct for some of the problems inherent in using self-report measures, such as lack of an accepted definition for the term *binge*. The authors felt that a semistructured interview format would provide more accurate and more detailed information on the psychopathology of the eating disorders than a self-report questionnaire. The EDE contains 62 questions that are divided into five subscales: dietary restraint, bulimia, eating concern, weight concern, and shape concern (Z. Cooper, Cooper, & Fairburn, 1989). All questions refer to functioning over the previous 4 weeks. Each question is scored on a 7-point rating scale. Subscale scores can be computed from these ratings. For each item, there is at least one mandatory probe question and several optional questions. The EDE was revised 10 times before being published, and an eleventh edition is now available. Psychometric data pertaining to the EDE are summarized in Table 10.2.

Norms. The EDE was developed by interviewing patients with anorexia and bulimia nervosa. Since the development of the EDE, several studies of its reliability and validity have been conducted (Z. Cooper et al., 1989; Rosen, Vara, Wendt, & Leitenberg, 1990; Wilson & Smith, 1989). Wilson and Smith (1989) provided norms, which are summarized in Table 10.2 (section A).

Reliability: Internal consistency. Internal consistency of the EDE has been shown to be good. Z. Cooper et al. (1989) found the Cronbach's alpha of the five subscales to range from .67 to .90 and found generally good item-subscale correlations. These data are summarized in Table 10.2 (section B).

Test-retest reliability. No test-retest information has been provided for the EDE. Interrater reliability is more relevant for an interview procedure, however.

Interrater reliability. Interrater reliability for the EDE has been reported to be very good in several studies, which are summarized in Table 10.2 (section B).

Concurrent validity. Rosen et al. (1990) found that all five of the subscales of the EDE were very highly correlated with subject eating records. In addition, the weight control and shape control subscales were significantly correlated with the Body Shape Questionnaire (P. J. Cooper, Taylor, Cooper, & Fairburn, 1987) and modestly correlated with a measure of body image distortion.

Z. Cooper et al. (1989) found that individual EDE items differentiated subjects with a diagnosis of anorexia or bulimia nervosa and controls. Wilson and Smith (1989) found that the EDE differentiated bulimic patients from nonbulimic restrained eaters on four of the five subscales, the exception being the restraint subscale.

Predictive validity. No information on predictive validity has been provided for the EDE.

TABLE 10.2 Eating Disorder Examination: Summary of Psychometric Data

A. Norms

Subscale	Bulimics		Restrained	
	M	SD	M	SD
Dietary Restraint	3.27	0.26	3.15	0.33
Bulimia	2.61	0.22	0.14	0.10
Eating Concern	2.40	0.34	1.25	0.23
Weight Concern	3.96	0.34	2.12	0.19
Shape Concern	3.82	0.31	2.55	0.20

B. Reliability

Internal Consistency

Subscale	Coefficient Alpha
Dietary Restraint	.75
Bulimia	.90
Eating Concern	.78
Weight Concern	.68
Shape Concern	.82

Interrater Reliability

Cooper and Fairburn (1987): $r = .69$ to 1.00 (individual items)
Wilson and Smith (1989): $r = .965$ to $.998$ (5 subscales)
Rosen et al. (1990): $r = .83$ to $.99$ (5 subscales)

C. Validity

Concurrent Validity

Dietary Restraint subscale with Eating Record: $r = -.39$
Overeating subscale[a] with Eating Record:
  r with total calories consumed per day $= .38$
  r with frequency of binge eating $= .56$
  r with average calorie content of binges $= .54$
Eating Concern subscale with Eating Record:
  r with frequency of binge eating $= .50$
  r with average calorie content of binges $= .52$
Vomiting item with Eating Record
  $r = .90$
Weight Concern subscale:
  r with BSQ $= .78$
Shape Concern subscale
  r with BSQ $= .82$

Discriminant Validity

BN > Controls, Restrained eaters
AN > Controls

NOTE: BSQ = Body Shape Questionnaire.
a. This subscale is found in the 11th version of the EDE.

Discriminant validity. No information on discriminant validity of the EDE has been published.

Susceptibility to dissimulation. As a semistructured interview with probe questions, the EDE is less susceptible to faking than many self-report measures. However, it is possible that some subjects could minimize symptom reports in an interview such as the EDE.

Readability. The EDE is very easily administered by a trained clinician. The examiner can clear up any questions or confusion on the part of the subject being interviewed.

Practicality. The main drawback to the practicality of the EDE is the fact that a trained interviewer is necessary to administer the EDE, which takes from 30 minutes to 1 hour to complete. However, because of its high reliability and validity, the use of the EDE is encouraged for use in research and for evaluating treatment outcome.

Anorexia Nervosa

Eating Attitudes Test

Description of Assessment Measure

The Eating Attitudes Test (EAT; Garner & Garfinkel, 1979) is a 40-item self-report measure designed to evaluate a range of attitudes and behaviors associated with anorexia nervosa. Each item is answered on a 6-point Likert scale (1 = *never,* 6 = *always*). Items are scored 3 points for extreme "anorexic" responses, 2 points for the adjacent alternative, 1 point for the next alternative, and no points for any of the three remaining alternatives. High total scores are indicative of symptoms, but not necessarily the diagnosis, of anorexia nervosa.

Factor analysis of the EAT yielded a 26-item version (EAT-26; Garner et al., 1982), which was highly correlated with total scores on the original EAT ($r = .98$). Children's and alternative language versions have also been created and used for clinical and research purposes (Maloney, McGuire, & Daniels, 1988; Vacc & Rhyne, 1987). Psychometric data pertaining to the EAT are summarized in Table 10.3.

TABLE 10.3 Eating Attitudes Test: Summary of Psychometric Data

A. Norms

	Mean	SD	Sample Size
Anorexia nervosa	58.9	13.3	33
Bulimia nervosa[a]	41.3	16.8	79
Binge eating disorder[a]	32.3	12.1	39
Obese	16.5	9.6	16
Recovered anorexics	11.4	5.1	9
Female controls	15.6	9.3	59
Male controls	8.6	5.3	49

B. Reliability

Internal Consistency

Coefficient alpha = .79 for AN
Coefficient alpha = .94 for combined AN and NC
EAT factor structure: seven factors
EAT-26 factor structure: three factors

Test-Retest Reliability

Time interval = 2-3 weeks
Sample size: $N = 56$
Total score: $r = .84$

C. Validity

Concurrent Validity

r with EDI scales:
Drive for Thinness = .81
Body Dissatisfaction = .50
Bulimia = .42
r with BULIT = .67
r with EQ-R = .59
r with MAC = .64
r with BITE = .70
r with GAAS scales:
r with fear of fat = .49
r with hypothermia = .45
r with poor self-care = .52

Discriminant Validity

r with EDI scales:
Ineffectiveness = .35
Perfectionism = .40
Interpersonal Distrust = .28
Interoceptive Awareness = .59
Maturity Fears = .12

NOTE: AN = anorexia nervosa, NC = nonclinical controls.
a. Unpublished data.

Norms. Garner and Garfinkel (1979) collected normative data for individuals diagnosed with anorexia nervosa (AN), female controls (FC), male controls (MC), obese subjects (Ob), and clinically recovered anorexics (RAN). Unpublished normative data have also been collected on individuals diagnosed with binge eating disorder (BED) and bulimia nervosa (BN) by Williamson. Table 10.3 (section A) summarizes the means and standard deviations for each subgroup. Garner and his colleagues suggested cutoff scores of 30 (EAT) and 20 (EAT-26) to identify disordered eating attitudes and behaviors.

Reliability: Internal consistency. The EAT has seven factors: food preoccupation, body image for thinness, vomiting and laxative abuse, dieting, slow eating, clandestine eating, and perceived social pressure to gain weight. The alpha coefficient for the total score of the EAT was found to be high. Three factors were extracted from the EAT-26 to account for 40.2% of the variance in the original correlation matrix (Garner et al., 1982). These factors were dieting, bulimia and food preoccupation, and oral control. All 26 items were found to be moderately correlated with the total score ($r > .44$).

Test-retest reliability. Carter and Moss (1984) reported the test-retest reliability over a 2- to 3-week time period for 56 subjects to be .84.

Concurrent validity. As presented in Table 10.3 (section C), Gross, Rosen, Leitenberg, and Willmuth (1986) found total scores of the EAT to be moderately correlated with the three eating disorder "symptom" scales. Williamson (1990) reported unpublished data from a sample of clinical and subclinical subjects and found the EAT to be moderately correlated with the Bulimia Test ($r = .67$; Smith & Thelen, 1984) and the Eating Questionnaire–Revised ($r = .59$; Williamson, Davis, Goreczny, Bennett, & Watkins, 1989). The Mizes Anorectic Cognitions Questionnaire (MAC; Mizes, 1988) and Bulimic Investigatory Test, Edinburgh (BITE; Henderson & Freeman, 1987), have been found to be moderately correlated with the EAT: $r = .64$ and $r = .70$, respectively.

The EAT has been found to differentiate eating disorder groups (AN, BN, and BED) and nonclinical controls (Garner & Garfinkel, 1979; Gross et al., 1986; Prather & Williamson, 1988; Williamson, Cubic, & Gleaves, 1993). The EAT has also been found to differentiate binge eaters from AN and BN (Prather & Williamson, 1988) but has not been found to differentiate samples of AN and BN (Williamson et al., 1993).

Predictive validity. On a sample of 49 bulimic patients, Williamson, Prather, et al. (1989) evaluated cognitive-behavioral treatment outcome and found the EAT to be sensitive to therapeutic changes. The EAT has also been found to reflect changes in symptomatology for recovered anorexic patients (Garner & Garfinkel, 1979).

Discriminant validity. Gross et al. (1986) found nonsignificant correlations between total EAT scores and the Ineffectiveness, Interpersonal Distrust, and Maturity Fears subscales of the EDI. Also, Garner et al. (1982) found nonsignificant correlations between total EAT scores and measures of anxiety, interpersonal sensitivity, and obsessionality.

Susceptibility to dissimulation. The questions of the EAT are face valid items that can easily be manipulated to minimize or maximize symptomatology. The motives of the test taker should be taken into account when interpreting the total score of the EAT.

Readability. The reading level of the EAT is fifth grade. Vacc and Rhyne (1987) created an adapted language version of the EAT (A-EAT) with a third-grade reading level. Vacc and Rhyne (1987) reported adequate correlations between the original and the adapted versions ($r = .75$, $p > .05$). Maloney et al. (1988) have also designed an adapted language version of the EAT for children (ChEAT) with adequate reliability and validity.

Practicality. A copy of the EAT can be found in Garner and Garfinkel's (1979) article. Administration time of this paper-and-pencil test takes less than 10 minutes.

Setting Conditions for Anorexia Nervosa Scale

Description of Assessment Measure

The Setting Conditions for Anorexia Nervosa Scale (SCANS; Slade & Dewey, 1986) was designated to identify individuals at risk of developing anorexia nervosa or bulimia nervosa (Slade, 1982). The SCANS is divided into five scales including (a) dissatisfaction and loss of control (D), (b) social and personal anxiety (S), (c) perfectionism (P), (d) adolescent problems (A), and (e) need for weight control (WC). The questionnaire contains 40 items answered on a 5-point Likert scale. Item answers are anchored by different responses depending on the nature of the question (1 = *very often,* 5 = *never,*

TABLE 10.4 Setting Conditions for Anorexia Nervosa Scale: Summary of Psychometric Data

A. Norms

	D	S	P	A	WC	N
Schoolgirls	36.01	23.97	23.04	3.11	7.85	227
	(7.41)	(5.37)	(3.97)	(2.52)	(2.06)	
College students	37.74	23.86	23.55	3.32	7.80	141
	(7.13)	(5.13)	(3.93)	(2.73)	(2.02)	
Nursing students	34.48	22.90	24.46	2.75	7.76	354
	(6.67)	(5.07)	(3.83)	(2.35)	(2.10)	
Anorexia nervosa	50.05	31.90	28.05	5.30	9.40	20
	(12.72)	(7.27)	(5.33)	(3.08)	(0.94)	
Bulimia nervosa	52.55	31.65	27.65	5.20	9.80	20
	(6.45)	(6.19)	(3.98)	(2.97)	(0.62)	

B. Reliability

Internal Consistency

Coefficient alpha	Sample 1	Sample 2
D	.84	.89
S	.76	.81
P	.66	.66
A	.81	.83
WC	.81	.90

C. Validity

Predictive Validity
    BN = AN > NC

NOTE: D = dissatisfaction and loss of control, S = social and personal anxiety, P = perfectionism, A = adolescent problems, WC = weight control, BN = bulimia nervosa, AN = anorexia nervosa, NC = nonclinical controls. Standard deviations are in parentheses.

1 = *very satisfied,* 5 = *very dissatisfied*). Some items are scored in a reverse format to allow higher scores to represent greater risk of developing AN or BN. Psychometric data pertaining to the SCANS are summarized in Table 10.4. A computerized version of the SCANS has been developed by Butler, Newton, and Slade (1988).

Norms. Slade and Dewey (1986) collected normative data on 722 nonclinical controls including schoolgirls (11th and 12th grade), college students, and nursing students. Normative data were also collected for 40 clinical subjects including anorexic and bulimic patients. The means and standard deviations for each subgroup are provided in Table 10.4 (section A). For each of the five scales, the three nonclinical groups scored significantly lower than the two clinical groups. The nonclinical subgroups did not differ and the two clinical subgroups did not differ.

Reliability: Internal consistency. Using data from a nonclinical sample, Slade and Dewey (1986) calculated Cronbach's alpha for each scale (D = .84, S = .76, P = .66, A = .81, WC = .81). These analyses were repeated on a second nonclinical sample and similar alpha coefficients were found. These results are presented in Table 10.4 (section B).

Test-retest reliability. No test-retest studies could be found for the SCANS.

Concurrent validity. SCANS scores were compared with EAT scores for 722 subjects (Slade & Dewey, 1986). Results suggested that individuals falling above the combined cutoff scores (D > 42, P > 22) scored significantly higher on both the EAT and the EAT-26 in comparison with individuals scoring below the SCANS cutoff scores.

Predictive validity. Slade and Dewey (1986) reported that the SCANS adequately discriminated nonclinical controls and clinical eating disorder subjects. The SCANS did not differentiate between anorexia nervosa and bulimia nervosa subjects. A combination of cutoff scores from the D and P scales was found to yield the greatest discriminatory power. In particular, scores above 42 on D and above 22 on P predicted individuals at risk for the development of an eating disorder.

Discriminant validity. No discriminant validity studies have been reported for the SCANS.

Susceptibility to dissimulation. The focus of the SCANS remains somewhat transparent until the final items of the questionnaire. Thus the SCANS is susceptible to motivation to either minimize or maximize symptoms of an eating disorder.

Readability. The SCANS has an 11th-grade reading level.

Practicality. A copy of the SCANS can be found in Slade and Dewey's (1986) article. Administration of the paper-and-pencil measure takes approximately 10 to 20 minutes and can be manually scored in less than 10 minutes.

Bulimia Nervosa

Bulimia Test–Revised

Description of Assessment Measure

The Bulimia Test–Revised (BULIT-R; Thelen, Farmer, Wonderlich, & Smith, 1991) was developed to measure the symptoms of bulimia nervosa (American Psychiatric Association, 1980/1987). An earlier version, the Bulimia Test (BULIT; Smith & Thelen, 1984), had been developed based on the 1980 *DSM-III* diagnostic criteria for bulimia. The BULIT-R has 28 items that are scored and 8 items pertaining to weight control behavior that are unscored. A copy of the BULIT-R is provided in Appendix 10-A. As can be seen, questions are answered using a five-choice multiple choice format. Items 6, 11, 19, 20, 27, 29, 31, and 36 are unscored. Ten items—1, 3, 4, 9, 18, 22, 24, 25, 33, and 34—are scored in a forward scoring format, where choice 1 = 1 and choice 5 = 5. The remaining 18 scored items are reverse scored, where choice 1 = 5 and choice 5 = 1. Psychometric data pertaining to the BULIT-R are summarized in Table 10.5.

Norms. Thelen et al. (1991) reported normative data for two samples of bulimia nervosa and nonclinical subjects. Means for these samples are provided in Table 10.5; standard deviations were not available for review. Bulimic subjects scored higher than nonclinical subjects in both samples.

Reliability: Internal consistency. Internal consistency for the BULIT-R is very high ($r = .97$). Thelen et al. (1991) found the BULIT-R to have five factors, though the factor structure was somewhat unstable across two samples that included both bulimic and nonclinical subjects. Future research should study the unique factor structure of the BULIT-R in bulimic and nonclinical samples.

Test-retest reliability. The BULIT-R has been found to be very stable over a 2-month test-retest interval ($r = .95$).

Concurrent validity. The BULIT-R was found to be highly correlated with the original BULIT ($r = .99$), therefore earlier concurrent validity studies pertaining to the BULIT can be interpreted as supportive of the validity of the revised version. The BULIT-R was highly correlated with the Binge Scale (Hawkins & Clement, 1980). Studies of the BULIT have found it to be correlated with frequency of binge eating and purging (Williamson, Prather, et al.,

TABLE 10.5 Bulimia Test–Revised: Summary of Psychometric Data

A. Norms

		Mean	SD	n
Bulimia nervosa	Sample 1	117.95	NA	21
	Sample 2	118.08	NA	23
Nonclinical	Sample 1	57.50	NA	100
	Sample 2	59.62	NA	157

B. Reliability

Internal Consistency
    Coefficient alpha = .97
    Factor analysis: five factors

Test-Retest Reliability
    Time interval = 2 months
    n = 98 subjects
    r = .95

C. Validity

Concurrent Validity
    r with Binge Scale = .85
    r with BULIT = .99
    r with self-reported binge eating = .59
    r with self-reported purging = .62

Discriminant Validity
    r with BDI = .48
    r with Body Weight = .24

Predictive Validity
    r with diagnosed bulimia nervosa = .74
    sensitivity index = .62 – .83
    false-negative rate = .17 – .38
    false-positive rate = .04
    specificity = .96

NOTE: NA = not available, BULIT = Bulimia Test, BDI = Beck Depression Inventory.

1987), the Eating Questionnairre–Revised (Williamson, Davis, Goreczny, et al., 1989), and body image disturbances (Williamson, Davis, Bennett, Goreczny, & Gleaves, 1989).

Predictive validity. Thelen et al. (1991) found the BULIT-R to discriminate bulimic and nonclinical samples. Williamson, Prather, McKenzie, and Blouin (1990) found the BULIT to be one of six behavioral assessment procedures to significantly discriminate bulimia nervosa, binge eating disorder, obesity, and nonclinical subjects. Thelen et al. (1991) found the BULIT-R to be highly correlated with a diagnosis of bulimia nervosa ($r = .74$). Discriminant analysis found the BULIT-R to be highly sensitive for identifying bulimics in a sample of college women. They also found that, relative to the BULIT, the BULIT-R had a lower false-positive rate and a higher false-negative rate for identifying bulimia nervosa in college women.

Discriminant validity. Unpublished data collected by Williamson using the original BULIT indicate that it is only moderately correlated with depression and body weight.

Susceptibility to dissimulation. The questions of the BULIT-R are face valid and therefore the test is susceptible to minimization or magnification of bulimic symptoms.

Readability. The BULIT-R is very easy to read and the instructions are clear. Reading level was found to be at the 11th-grade level.

Practicality. The BULIT-R can be administered in about 10 minutes. It has been found to be useful for diagnosis of bulimia nervosa, measuring the severity of bulimic symptoms, and measuring treatment outcome (Williamson, 1990; Williamson, Prather, et al., 1989).

Eating Questionnaire–Revised

Description of Assessment Measure

The Eating Questionnaire–Revised (EQ-R; Williamson, Davis, Goreczny, et al., 1989) was developed as a symptom checklist for bulimia as defined by the *DSM-III* (American Psychiatric Association, 1980/1987). The EQ-R may be used to document the symptoms of bulimia, such as binge eating, purgative habits, and loss of control over eating, and it can be scored to yield a total score that measures the overall severity of bulimic symptoms (Williamson, Davis, Goreczny, et al., 1989). The original 16-item EQ (Williamson, Kelley, Cavell, & Prather, 1987) was revised to the 15-item EQ-R by eliminating one question that was uncorrelated with the total score (Williamson, Davis, Goreczny, et al., 1989). A copy of the EQ-R is provided in Appendix 10-B. The 15 questions of the EQ-R are answered by responding to a five-alternative multiple choice format. All items except questions 7 and 10 are scored in a forward scoring format, where a = 1 and e = 5. Questions 7 and 10 are scored

TABLE 10.6 Eating Questionnaire–Revised: Summary of Psychometric Data

A. Norms

	Mean	SD	Sample Size
Bulimia nervosa	52.1	8.46	105
Anorexia nervosa	50.9	15.9	25
Binge eating disorder	49.9	7.46	45
Obese	42.4	9.20	37
Nonclinical	36.1	7.34	376

B. Reliability

Internal Consistency

　　Coefficient alpha = .87
　　Item to total correlations: all items > .30
　　Factor structure: single factor with 15 items

Test-Retest Reliability

　　Time interval = 2
　　Sample size: $N = 39$
　　Total score: $r = .90$
　　Single items: all items $r > .50$

C. Validity

Concurrent Validity

　　r with EAT = .59
　　r with BULIT = .80

Predictive Validity

　　BN = AN = BED > Ob > NC

Discriminant Validity

　　r with BDI = .33
　　r with Body Weight = .22

NOTE: EAT = Eating Attitudes Test, BULIT = Bulimia Test, BDI = Beck Depression Inventory, BN = bulimia nervosa, AN = anorexia nervosa, BED = Binge Eating Disorder, Ob = obese, NC = nonclinical.

in a reverse scoring format, where a = 5 and e = 1. Psychometric data pertaining to the EQ-R are summarized in Table 10.6.

Norms. Normative data for the EQ-R have been collected on a sample of 588 subjects including clinical and nonclinical subgroups. These normative data have not been previously published. Table 10.6 summarizes the means and standard deviations for each subgroup (section A). Comparisons of group means showed no differences between anorexia nervosa (AN), bulimia nervosa (BN), and binge eaters (BED) on EQ-R scores. All three eating disorder groups scored higher than obese and nonclinical subjects.

Reliability: Internal consistency. Williamson, Davis, Goreczny, et al. (1989) found the EQ-R to be a single-factor test with high internal consistency (coefficient alpha = .87). All 15 items of the EQ-R were found to be at least moderately ($r > .30$) correlated with the EQ-R total score.

Test-retest reliability. Williamson, Davis, Goreczny, et al. (1989) reported test-retest reliability over a 2-week period to be .90. The median test-retest reliability of single items averaged .74, and all 15 items had test-retest correlations above .50.

Concurrent validity. On a sample of 561 subjects, Williamson, Davis, Goreczny, et al. (1989) found the EQ-R to be highly correlated with the BULIT ($r = .80$) and moderately correlated with the EAT ($r = .59$), which suggests that the EQ-R is primarily measuring bulimic symptoms. Subsequent unpublished research on 156 eating disorder subjects found responses to EQ-R question 1 (How often do you binge eat?) to be correlated with frequency of binge eating ($r = .45$) as measured by 1 week of self-monitoring. In this same study, EQ-R question 4 (Do you ever vomit after a binge?) was correlated ($r = .61$) with frequency of self-reported purging.

Predictive validity. As shown in Table 10.6 (section C), the EQ-R total score differentiated clinical eating disorders (BN, AN, and BED) from obese and nonclinical groups but did not discriminate among the three eating disorder groups. Obese subjects scored higher than nonclinical subjects (Williamson, Davis, Goreczny, et al., 1989).

Discriminant validity. Unpublished data collected by Williamson, and summarized in Table 10.6 (section C), indicates that the EQ-R is not highly correlated with measures of depression or with body weight.

Susceptibility to dissimulation. The EQ-R asks face valid questions pertaining to bulimic habits. Subjects could easily minimize or maximize symptom reports if they were motivated to do so.

Readability. The questions of the EQ-R are very brief and specific to binge eating and purgative habits. The questions are written at a seventh-grade reading level.

Practicality. The EQ-R can be administered in less than 5 minutes. It has been validated as a measure of bulimic symptoms. It is reliable over time and internally consistent. Problems in the use of the EQ-R sometimes arise when the subject reports *never* bingeing, such as in the case of restricting anorexics who never overeat or binge. The EQ-R can be used to measure specific symptoms of bulimia nervosa or it can be scored to yield a total score that measures general bulimic behaviors.

Bulimic Investigatory Test, Edinburgh

Description of Assessment Measure

The Bulimic Investigatory Test, Edinburgh (BITE; Henderson & Freeman, 1987) was designed to measure binge eating and the cognitive and behavioral features of bulimia. The BITE was conceptualized both as an epidemiological tool for clinical and subclinical bulimia and as a measure for symptom severity for use in measuring treatment outcome. This 33-item questionnaire is composed of yes/no questions as well as 5-, 6-, and 7-point Likert rating scales. The measure is divided into two subscales, the Symptom Subscale and the Severity Subscale, which combine for the total score. Psychometric data pertaining to the BITE are summarized in Table 10.7.

Norms. The maximum score for the Symptom Subscale is 30, with 20 being the criterion score for clinical significance. The maximum score for the Severity subscale is 39, with 5 being the criterion score for clinical significance. A total score of 25 indicates a severely disordered eating pattern. Waller (1992) reported that the suggested criterion scores do not adequately detect anorexics with bulimic symptoms. Normative data reported by Henderson and Freeman (1987) and Waller (1992) are summarized in Table 10.7.

Reliability: Internal consistency. Henderson and Freeman (1987) reported the alpha coefficient for a sample of bulimic and nonclinical subjects to be .96 for the Symptom subscale and .62 for the Severity subscale.

Test-retest reliability. Waller (1992) reported the test-retest correlation over 1 week to be .86. The test-retest correlation for 10 bulimic subjects tested 15 weeks apart was found to be .68.

Concurrent validity. To determine concurrent validity, Henderson and Freeman (1987) correlated total BITE scores of 57 subjects with subscales of the EDI and with the EAT. Significant correlations are presented in Table 10.7 (section C). Waller (1992) found the BITE to be a useful tool for discriminating between nonclinical subjects, anorexics with or without bulimic symp-

TABLE 10.7 Bulimic Investigatory Test, Edinburgh: Summary of Psychometric Data

A. Norms

	Symptom	Severity	Total	Sample Size
Bulimia	26.03	10.16	36.19	32
	(2.25)	(3.63)	(4.47)	
Controls	2.94	.44	NA	32
	(2.94)	(.29)		

B. Reliability

Internal Consistency

    Coefficient alpha = .96 for Symptom Subscale
    Coefficient alpha = .62 for Severity Subscale

Test-Retest Reliability

    Controls: Time interval = at least 1 week
        Sample size: N = 30
        Total score: r = .86

    Bulimics: Time interval = 15 weeks
        Sample size: N = 10
        Total score: r = .68

C. Validity

Concurrent Validity

    r with EAT = .70
    r with EDI scales:
        r with drive for thinness = .59
        r with bulimia subscale = .69
    Symptom subscale: BS = BN > AN+ > AN– > NC
    Severity subscale: BS > BN > AN+ > AN– > NC
    Total score: BS = BN > AN+ > AN– = NC

Discriminant Validity

    r with EDI scales:
        Perfectionism = .14
        Interpersonal Distrust = .23

NOTE: NC = nonclinical controls, AN+ = anorexic with bulimic symptoms, AN– = anorexic without bulimic symptoms, BS = bulimic without history of anorexia, BN = bulimic with history of anorexia. Standard deviations for norms are in parentheses.

toms, and bulimics with and without a history of anorexia. The relationship between these groups is described in Table 10.7 (section C).

Predictive validity. No predictive validity studies have been reported for the BITE.

Discriminant validity. Henderson and Freeman (1987) found nonsignificant correlations between total BITE scores and the perfectionism ($r = .14$) and interpersonal distrust ($r = .23$) subscales of the EDI. Total BITE scores were also found to have a nonsignificant correlation with the Oral Control subscale of the EAT.

Susceptibility to dissimulation. The questions of the BITE are face valid and could be minimized or maximized. Because of the denial and/or embarrassment often seen with bulimia, Henderson and Freeman (1987) suggested cautious interpretation of the BITE.

Readability. The reading level of the BITE is fourth grade.

Practicality. A copy of the BITE can be found in Henderson and Freeman's (1987) article. Administration usually requires less than 10 minutes and the measure is easily scored. An optional data sheet can be added to the measure to obtain demographic information.

Cognitive/Emotional Disturbances

Mizes Anorectic Cognitions Scale

Description of Assessment Measure

The Mizes Anorectic Cognitions Scale (MACS; Mizes & Klesges, 1989) was designed to measure cognitions associated with anorexia and bulimia nervosa. The initial version of the MAC had 45 items. After eliminating items that were not highly correlated with the total score, a 33-item questionnaire was developed. Subjects were asked to rate their reaction to a statement about eating and weight on a 5-point Likert-type (1 to 5) scale ranging from "strongly disagree" to "strongly agree." Scores on the MAC range from 33 to 165. A copy of the MAC is provided in Appendix 10-C.

Factor analysis of the MAC using nonclinical males and females found a three-factor solution: (a) rigid weight and eating regulation, (b) weight and eating behavior as the basis of approval from others, and (c) self-esteem based on excessive self-control (Mizes & Klesges, 1989). Mizes (1991) replicated this three-factor solution in a sample of 100 nonclinical college women. Psychometric data are summarized in Table 10.8.

Norms. Norms for college males, college females, anorexics, bulimics, and psychiatric controls are presented in Table 10.8. Comparisons of group

TABLE 10.8 Mizes Anorectic Cognitions Scale: Summary of Psychometric Data

A. Norms

	Mean	SD	Sample Size
Bulimia nervosa (BN)	119.5	20.5	15
Anorexia nervosa (AN)	115.6	14.7	8
Psychiatric controls (PC)	65.1	12.3	11
College females (CF)	107.91	23.48	100
College males (CM)	94.59	18.13	105

B. Reliability

Internal Consistency

    Coefficient alpha > .75

    Factor structure: three factors

Test-Retest Reliability

    Time interval = 2 months

    Sample size: $N = 86$

    Total score: $r = .78$

C. Validity

Concurrent Validity

    r with BULIT = .69

    r with EAT = .64

    r with COGEAT = .78

    r with EDI total score = .80

    r with BINGE = .87

    BN > CF

    BN = AN > PC

Discriminant Validity

    r with MCSD = −.12

    r with WRAT-S = .01

    r with WRAT-A = .00

    r with Type A = .08

NOTE: BULIT = Bulimia Test, EAT = Eating Attitudes Test, COGEAT = Gormally Cognitive Factors Related Binge Eating Scale, EDI = Eating Disorder Inventory, BINGE = Gormally Binge Eating Questionnaire, MCSD = Marlow-Crowne Social Desirability Scale, WRAT-S = Spelling subscale of Wide Range Achievement Test, WRAT-A = Arithmetic subscale of Wide Range Achievement Test, Type A = Jenkins Type A Scale. Groups: BN = bulimia nervosa, AN = anorexia nervosa, PC = psychiatric controls, CF = college females, CM = college males.

means showed no difference between anorexia nervosa and bulimia nervosa patients on the MAC total score and subscale scores, but both groups scored significantly higher than a psychiatric control group.

Reliability: Internal consistency. The reliability coefficients of the MAC subscales ranged from .75 to .89. Coefficient alpha for the full scale was .91. Similar correlations were found in a replication study (Mizes, 1991).

Test-retest reliability. Test-retest reliability was found to be .78 over a 2-month interval (Mizes, 1991).

Concurrent validity. The MAC was correlated ($r = .48$ to .77) with cognitions assessed by an in vivo thought-sampling procedure that consists of food and eating, body image and weight, and self-efficacy and need for approval self-statements (Bonifazi, Baker, Crowther, & Mizes, 1992). As shown in Table 10.8, scores on the MAC were correlated with the BULIT and with the EAT. The MAC was also correlated with the Gormally Cognitive Factors Related Binge Eating Scale (COGEAT; Gormally, Black, Daston, & Rardin, 1982), which assesses rigid dieting and low self-efficacy regarding control of eating. It was also correlated with the total score of the EDI and the Gormally Binge Eating Questionnaire (BINGE; Gormally et al., 1982).

The MAC has been found to discriminate bulimics from controls (Mizes, 1988). Mizes (1992) found that both bulimics and anorexics scored significantly higher than psychiatric controls, though the clinical groups did not differ. The MAC has also been found to discriminate between bulimics, restrained eaters, and normal college females (Bonifazi & Mizes, 1992).

Discriminant validity. The MAC was not significantly correlated (see Table 10.8) with the Marlow-Crowne Social Desirability Scale (MCSD; Crowne & Marlow, 1964), the Spelling or Arithmetic subscales of the Wide Range Achievement Test (Jastak & Jastak, 1976), or the Jenkins Type A Scale (Jenkins, Zyzanski, & Rosenman, 1979), which assesses type A characteristics.

Predictive validity. Subjects who scored above the mean on the MAC were more likely than those who scored below the mean to show pathological eating attitudes and behavior in four areas: (a) They placed greater emphasis on weight regulation; (b) they had more specific benefits of losing or maintaining weight; (c) they were more likely to be involved in caloric restriction strategies; and (d) they engaged in more exercise or other calorie burning strategies (Mizes & Arbitell, in press).

Readability. Questions on the MAC are specific to anorexic and bulimic cognitions. The questions are written at the sixth-grade reading level.

Practicality. The MAC is relatively short, easily administered, and easy to score. Concurrent and discriminant validity have also been established. The MAC appears to be a promising screening tool for the assessment of anorexia and bulimia nervosa. It has also been used as a treatment outcome measure (Kettlewell, Mizes, & Wasylyshyn, 1992).

Future Research Directions

Over the past 15 years, considerable progress has been made in the development of assessment methods for eating disordered thoughts, feelings, and behaviors. At present, most of the assessment methods focus on the symptoms of a particular eating disorder or on cognitive, emotional, or behavioral features of eating disorders. There are two areas of research that need further focus: (a) evaluation of treatment outcome and (b) assessment procedures specifically designed for differential diagnosis of eating disorders.

No single assessment method has been developed for evaluating the efficacy of treatment procedures for the eating disorders. One result of this deficiency is that treatment outcome studies seldom use the same outcome measures. This diversity of outcome measurement makes comparisons of treatment studies difficult and meta-analysis of treatment research all but impossible. We recommend the development of a relatively brief self-report inventory that evaluates the specific and general psychopathology associated with the eating disorders (Williamson, 1990). The development of a single assessment instrument of this type would greatly facilitate the progress of treatment studies of psychological and pharmacological therapies for the eating disorders.

A second research need is the development of an assessment procedure specifically designed for differential diagnosis of anorexia nervosa, bulimia nervosa, binge eating disorder, and the various atypical eating disorders. We believe that an assessment instrument of this type might be developed as either a structured interview or a self-report inventory. A psychometrically developed assessment method for differential diagnosis of eating disorders would facilitate the selection of similar samples across investigations and would strengthen clinical treatment programs.

Other Assessment Methods: Not Reviewed

Bulimia Cognitive Distortions Scale. Schulman, R. G., Kinder, B. N., Powers, P. S., Prange, M., & Gleghorn, A. (1986). The development of a scale to measure cognitive distortions in bulimia. *Journal of Personality Assessment, 50,* 630-639.

Eating Behavior Inventory. O'Neil, P. M., Curry, H. S., Hirsh, A. A., Malcolm, R. J., Sexauer, J. D., Riddle, F. E., & Taylor, L. I. (1979). Development and validation of the Eating Behavior Inventory. *Journal of Behavioral Assessment, 1,* 123-132.

Goldberg Anorectic Attitude Scale. Goldberg, S. C., Halmi, K. A., Eckert, E. D., Casper, R. C., Davis, J. M., & Roper, M. (1980). Attitudinal dimensions in anorexia nervosa. *Journal of Psychiatric Research, 15,* 239-251.

Interview for Diagnosis of Eating Disorders. Williamson, D. A. (1990). *Assessment of eating disorders: Obesity, anorexia, and bulimia nervosa.* New York: Pergamon.

References

American Psychiatric Association. (1980). *Diagnostic and statistical manual of mental disorders* (3rd ed., rev. 1987). Washington, DC: Author.

Bonifazi, D. Z., Baker, L., Crowther, J. H., & Mizes, J. S. (1992, November). *Do questionnaires adequately assess cognitions in bulimia nervosa.* Paper presented at the 26th annual meeting of the Association for the Advancement of Behavior Therapy, Boston.

Bonifazi, D. Z., & Mizes, J. S. (1992, March). *Bulimic, restrained eater, and non-eating disordered women on the Anorectic Cognitions Questionnaire.* Poster presented at the annual convention of the Society of Behavioral Medicine, New York.

Butler, N., Newton, T., & Slade, P. D. (1988). Validation of a computerized version of the SCANS questionnaire. *International Journal of Eating Disorders, 8,* 239-241.

Carter, P. I., & Moss, R. A. (1984). Screening for anorexia and bulimia nervosa in a college population: Problems and limitations. *Addictive Behaviors, 9,* 417-419.

Cooper, P. J., Taylor, M. J., Cooper, Z., & Fairburn, C. G. (1987). The development and validation of the Body Shape Questionnaire. *International Journal of Eating Disorders, 6,* 485-494.

Cooper, Z., Cooper, P. J., & Fairburn, C. G. (1989). The validity of the eating disorder examination and its subscales. *British Journal of Psychiatry, 154,* 807-812.

Cooper, Z., & Fairburn, C. (1987). The eating disorder examination: A semi-structured interview for the assessment of the specific psychopathology of eating disorders. *International Journal of Eating Disorders, 6,* 1-8.

Crowne, D. P., & Marlow, D. (1964). *The approval motive: Studies in evaluative dependence.* Westport, CT: Greenwood.

Crowther, J. H., Lilly, R. S., Crawford, P. A., Shepherd, K. L., & Oliver, L. L. (1990, August). *The stability of the Eating Disorder Inventory.* Paper presented at the annual meeting of the American Psychological Association, Boston.

Garner, D. M. (1991). *Eating Disorder Inventory-2 manual.* Odessa, FL: Psychological Assessment Resources, Inc.

Garner, D. M., & Garfinkel, P. E. (1979). The Eating Attitudes Test: An index of the symptoms of anorexia nervosa. *Psychological Medicine, 9,* 273-279.

Garner, D. M., Olmsted, M. P., Bohr, Y., & Garfinkel, P. E. (1982). The Eating Attitudes Test: Psychometric features and clinical correlates. *Psychological Medicine, 12,* 871-878.

Garner, D. M., Olmsted, M. P., & Polivy, J. (1983). Development and validation of a multidimensional Eating Disorder Inventory for anorexia nervosa and bulimia. *International Journal of Eating Disorders, 2,* 15-34.

Gormally, J., Black, S., Daston, S., & Rardin, D. (1982). The assessment of binge eating severity among obese persons. *Addictive Behaviors, 7,* 47-55.

Gross, J., Rosen, J. C., Leitenberg, H., & Willmuth, M. (1986). Validity of Eating Attitudes Test and the Eating Disorder Inventory in bulimia nervosa. *Journal of Consulting and Clinical Psychology, 54*, 875-876.

Hawkins, R. C., & Clement, P. F. (1980). Development and construct validation of a self-report measure of binge eating tendencies. *Addictive Behaviors, 5*, 219-226.

Head, S. B., & Williamson, D. A. (1990). Association of family environment and personality disturbances in bulimia nervosa. *International Journal of Eating Disorders, 9*, 667-674.

Henderson, M., & Freeman, C. P. L. (1987). A self-rating scale for bulimia: The "BITE." *British Journal of Psychiatry, 150*, 18-24.

Herman, C. P., & Polivy, J. (1975). Anxiety, restraint and eating behavior. *Journal of Abnormal Psychology, 84*, 666-672.

Jastak, J. F., & Jastak, S. R. (1976). *Manual for the Wide Range Achievement Test.* Wilmington: Guidance Association of Delaware, Inc.

Jenkins, D. C., Zyzanski, S. J., & Rosenman, R. H. (1979). *Jenkins Activity Survey Manual.* New York: Psychological Corporation.

Kettlewell, P. W., Mizes, J. S., & Wasylyshyn, N. A. (1992). A cognitive-behavioral group treatment of bulimia. *Behavior Therapy, 23*, 657-670.

Klemchuk, H. P., Hutchinson, C. B., & Frank, R. I. (1990). Body dissatisfaction and eating-related problems on the college campus: Usefulness of the Eating Disorder Inventory with a nonclinical population. *Journal of Counseling Psychology, 37*, 297-305.

Maloney, M. J., McGuire, J. B., & Daniels, S. R. (1988). Reliability testing of a children's version of the Eating Attitudes Test. *Journal of the American Academy of Child and Adolescent Psychiatry, 27*, 541-543.

Mizes, J. S. (1988). Personality characteristics of bulimic and non-eating disordered female controls: A cognitive behavioral perspective. *International Journal of Eating Disorders, 7*, 541-550.

Mizes, J. S. (1991). Construct validity and factor stability of the Anorectic Cognitions Questionnaire. *Addictive Behaviors, 16*, 89-93.

Mizes, J. S. (1992). Validity of the Mizes Anorectic Cognitions Scale: A comparison between anorectics, bulimics, and psychiatric controls. *Addictive Behaviors, 17*, 283-289.

Mizes, J. S., & Arbitell, M. (in press). Predictive validity of the Anorectic Cognitions Questionnaire.

Mizes, J. S., & Klesges, R. C. (1989). Validity, reliability, and factor structure of the Anorectic Cognitions Questionnaire. *Addictive Behaviors, 14*, 589-594.

Norring, C. E. (1990). The Eating Disorder Inventory: Its relation to diagnostic dimensions and follow-up status. *International Journal of Eating Disorders, 9*, 685-694.

Prather, R. C., & Williamson, D. A. (1988). Psychopathology associated with bulimia, binge eating, and obesity. *International Journal of Eating Disorders, 7*, 177-184.

Rosen, J. C., Silberg, N. T., & Gross, J. (1988). Eating Attitudes Test and Eating Disorder Inventory: Norms for adolescent girls and boys. *Journal of Consulting and Clinical Psychology, 56*, 305-308.

Rosen, J. C., Vara, L., Wendt, S., & Leitenberg, H. (1990). Validity studies of the eating disorder examination. *International Journal of Eating Disorders, 9*, 519-528.

RightSoft, Inc. (1989). *RightWriter (Version 3.1).* Sarasota, FL: Author.

Shore, R. A., & Porter, J. E. (1990). Normative and reliability data for 11 to 18 year olds on the Eating Disorder Inventory. *International Journal of Eating Disorders, 9*, 201-107.

Slade, P. D. (1982). Towards a functional analysis of anorexia nervosa and bulimia nervosa. *British Journal of Clinical Psychology, 21*, 67-79.

Slade, P. D., & Dewey, M. E. (1986). Development and preliminary validation of SCANS: A screening instrument for identifying individuals at risk of developing anorexia and bulimia nervosa. *International Journal of Eating Disorders, 5,* 517-538.

Smith, M. C., & Thelen, M. H. (1984). Development and validation of a test for bulimia. *Journal of Consulting and Clinical Psychology, 52,* 863-872.

Thelen, M. H., Farmer, J., Wonderlich, S., & Smith, M. (1991). A revision of the Bulimia Test: The BULIT-R. *Psychological Assessment, 3,* 119-124.

Vacc, N. A., & Rhyne, M. (1987). The Eating Attitudes Test: Development of an adapted language form for children. *Perceptual and Motor Skills, 65,* 335-336.

Waller, G. (1992). Bulimic attitudes in different eating disorders: Clinical utility of the BITE. *International Journal of Eating Disorders, 11,* 73-78.

Wear, R. W., & Pratz, O. (1987). Test-retest reliability for the Eating Disorder Inventory. *International Journal of Eating Disorders, 6,* 767-769.

Welch, G. (1988). *Selected multivariate statistical techniques and eating disorders.* Unpublished doctoral dissertation, University of Otago, New Zealand.

Welch, G., Hall, A., & Norring, C. (1990). The factor structure of the Eating Disorder Inventory in a patient setting. *International Journal of Eating Disorders, 9,* 79-85.

Welch, G. W., Hall, A., & Walkey, F. H. (1988). The factor structure of the Eating Disorder Inventory. *Journal of Clinical Psychology, 44,* 51-56.

Williams, R. L., Schaefer, C. A., Shisslak, C. M., Gronwaldt, V. H., & Comerci, G. D. (1986). Eating attitudes and behaviors in adolescent women: Discrimination of normals, dieters, and suspected bulimics using the Eating Attitudes Test and Eating Disorder Inventory. *International Journal of Eating Disorders, 5,* 879-894.

Williamson, D. A. (1990). *Assessment of eating disorders: Obesity, anorexia, and bulimia nervosa.* Elmsford, NY: Pergamon.

Williamson, D. A., Cubic, B. A., & Gleaves, D. H. (1993). Equivalence of body image disturbances in anorexia and bulimia nervosa. *Journal of Abnormal Psychology, 102,* 1-4.

Williamson, D. A., Davis, C. J., Bennett, S. M., Goreczny, A. J., & Gleaves, D. H. (1989). Development of a simple procedure for assessing body image disturbances. *Behavioral Assessment, 11,* 433-446.

Williamson, D. A., Davis, C. J., Goreczny, A. J., Bennett, S. M., & Watkins, P. C. (1989). The Eating Questionnaire-Revised: A new symptom checklist for bulimia. In P. A. Keller & L. G. Ritt (Eds.), *Innovations in clinical practice: A sourcebook* (pp. 321-326). Sarasota, FL: Professional Resource Exchange, Inc.

Williamson, D. A., Kelley, M. L., Cavell, T. A., & Prather, R. C. (1987). Eating and eliminating disorders. In C. L. Frame & J. L. Matson (Eds.), *Handbook of assessment in childhood psychology: Applied issues in differential diagnosis and treatment evaluation* (pp. 461-487). New York: Plenum.

Williamson, D. A., Prather, R. C., Bennett, S. M., Davis, C. J., Watkins, P. C., & Grenier, C. E. (1989). An uncontrolled evaluation of inpatient and outpatient cognitive-behavior therapy for bulimia nervosa. *Behavior Modification, 13,* 340-360.

Williamson, D. A., Prather, R. C., McKenzie, S. J., & Blouin, D. C. (1990). Behavioral assessment procedures can differentiate bulimia nervosa, compulsive overeater, obese, and normal subjects. *Behavioral Assessment, 12,* 239-252.

Williamson, D. A., Prather, R. C., Upton, L., Davis, C. J., Ruggiero, L., & Van Buren, D. (1987). Severity of bulimia: Relationship with depression and other psychopathology. *International Journal of Eating Disorders, 6,* 39-47.

Wilson, G. T., & Smith, D. (1989). Assessment of bulimia nervosa: An evaluation of the Eating Disorder Examination. *International Journal of Eating Disorders, 8,* 173-179.

Appendix 10-A

BULIT-R

Answer each question by filling in the appropriate circle on the computer answer sheet. Please respond to each item as honestly as possible; remember all of the information you provide will be kept strictly confidential.

1. I am satisfied with my eating patterns.

    1. agree
    2. neutral
    3. disagree a little
    4. disagree
    5. disagree strongly

2. Would you presently call yourself a "binge eater"?

    1. yes, absolutely
    2. yes
    3. yes, probably
    4. yes, possibly
    5. no, probably not

3. Do you feel you have control over the amount of food you consume?

    1. most or all of the time
    2. a lot of the time
    3. occasionally
    4. rarely
    5. never

4. I am satisfied with the shape and size of my body.

    1. frequently or always
    2. sometimes
    3. occasionally
    4. rarely
    5. seldom or never

5. When I feel that my eating behavior is out of control, I try to take rather extreme measures to get back on course (strict dieting, fasting, laxatives, diuretics, self-induced vomiting, or vigorous exercise).

    1. always
    2. almost always
    3. frequently
    4. sometimes
    5. never or my eating behavior is never out of control

6. I use laxatives or suppositories to help control my weight.

    1. once a day or more
    2. 3-6 times a week
    3. once or twice a week
    4. 2-3 times a month
    5. once a month or less (or never)

7. I am obsessed about the size and shape of my body.

    1. always
    2. almost always
    3. frequently
    4. sometimes
    5. seldom or never

8. There are times when I rapidly eat a very large amount of food.

    1. more than twice a week
    2. twice a week
    3. once a week
    4. 2-3 times a month
    5. once a month or less (or never)

9. How long have you been binge eating (eating uncontrollably to the point of stuffing yourself)?

    1. not applicable; I don't binge eat
    2. less than 3 months
    3. 3 months-1 year
    4. 1-3 years
    5. 3 or more years

10. Most people I know would be amazed if they knew how much food I can consume at one sitting.

    1. without a doubt
    2. very probably
    3. probably
    4. possibly
    5. no

11. I exercise in order to burn calories.

   1. more than 2 hours per day
   2. about 2 hours per day
   3. more than 1 but less than 2 hours per day
   4. one hour or less per day
   5. I exercise but not to burn calories or I don't exercise

12. Compared with women your age, how preoccupied are you about your weight and body shape?

   1. a great deal more than average
   2. much more than average
   3. more than average
   4. a little more than average
   5. average or less than average

13. I am afraid to eat anything for fear that I won't be able to stop.

   1. always
   2. almost always
   3. frequently
   4. sometimes
   5. seldom or never

14. I feel tormented by the idea that I am fat or might gain weight.

   1. always
   2. almost always
   3. frequently
   4. sometimes
   5. seldom or never

15. How often do you intentionally vomit after eating?

   1. 2 or more times a week
   2. once a week
   3. 2-3 times a month
   4. once a month
   5. less than once a month or never

16. I eat a lot of food when I'm not even hungry.

   1. very frequently
   2. frequently
   3. occasionally
   4. sometimes
   5. seldom or never

17.   My eating patterns are different from the eating patterns of most people.

    1. always
    2. almost always
    3. frequently
    4. sometimes
    5. seldom or never

18.   After I binge eat I turn to one of several strict methods to try to keep from gaining weight (vigorous exercise, strict dieting, fasting, self-induced vomiting, laxatives, or diuretics).

    1. never or I don't binge eat
    2. rarely
    3. occasionally
    4. a lot of the time
    5. most or all of the time

19.   I have tried to lose weight by fasting or going on strict diets.

    1. not in the past year
    2. once in the past year
    3. 2-3 times in the past year
    4. 4-5 times in the past year
    5. more than 5 times in the past year

20.   I exercise vigorously and for long periods of time in order to burn calories.

    1. average or less than average
    2. a little more than average
    3. more than average
    4. much more than average
    5. a great deal more than average

21.   When engaged in an eating binge, I tend to eat foods that are high in carbo-hydrates (sweets and starches).

    1. always
    2. almost always
    3. frequently
    4. sometimes
    5. seldom, or I don't binge

22.   Compared to most people, my ability to control my eating behavior seems to be:

    1. greater than others' ability
    2. about the same
    3. less
    4. much less
    5. I have absolutely no control

23. I would presently label myself a "compulsive eater" (one who engages in episodes of uncontrolled eating).

    1. absolutely
    2. yes
    3. yes, probably
    4. yes, possibly
    5. no, probably not

24. I hate the way my body looks after I eat too much.

    1. seldom or never
    2. sometimes
    3. frequently
    4. almost always
    5. always

25. When I am trying to keep from gaining weight, I feel that I have to resort to vigorous exercise, strict dieting, fasting, self-induced vomiting, laxatives, or diuretics.

    1. never
    2. rarely
    3. occasionally
    4. a lot of the time
    5. most or all of the time

26. Do you believe that it is easier for you to vomit than it is for most people?

    1. yes, it's no problem at all for me
    2. yes, it's easier
    3. yes, it's a little easier
    4. about the same
    5. no, it's less easy

27. I use diuretics (water pills) to help control my weight.

    1. never
    2. seldom
    3. sometimes
    4. frequently
    5. very frequently

28. I feel that food controls my life.

    1. always
    2. almost always
    3. frequently
    4. sometimes
    5. seldom or never

29.   I try to control my weight by eating little or no food for a day or longer.

       1. never
       2. seldom
       3. sometimes
       4. frequently
       5. very frequently

30.   When consuming a large quantity of food, at what rate of speed do you usually eat?

       1. more rapidly than most people have ever eaten in their lives
       2. a lot more rapidly than most people
       3. a little more rapidly than most people
       4. about the same rate as most people
       5. more slowly than most people (or not applicable)

31.   I use laxatives or suppositories to help control my weight.

       1. never
       2. seldom
       3. sometimes
       4. frequently
       5. very frequently

32.   Right after I binge eat I feel:

       1. so fat and bloated I can't stand it
       2. extremely fat
       3. fat
       4. a little fat
       5. OK about how my body looks or I never binge eat

33.   Compared to other people of my sex, my ability to always feel in control of how much I eat is:

       1. about the same or greater
       2. a little less
       3. less
       4. much less
       5. a great deal less

34.   In the last 3 months, on the average how often did you binge eat (eat uncontrollably to the point of stuffing yourself)?

       1. once a month or less (or never)
       2. 2-3 times a month
       3. once a week
       4. twice a week
       5. more than twice a week

35.   Most people I know would be surprised at how fat I look after I eat a lot of food.

1. yes, definitely
2. yes
3. yes, probably
4. yes, possibly
5. no, probably not or I never eat a lot of food

36.   I use diuretics (water pills) to help control my weight.

1. 3 times a week or more
2. once or twice a week
3. 2-3 times a month
4. once a month
5. never

SOURCE: As described in the study reported in "A Revision of the Bulimia Test: The BULIT-R" by M. H. Thelen, J. Farmer, S. Wonderlich, & M. Smith, 1991, *Psychological Assessment, 3*, pp. 119-124. Used by permission.

Appendix 10-B

Eating Questionnaire–Revised

Name: _____ Date: _____

Directions: In the space provided, indicate the letter of the answer that best describes your eating behavior.

_____ 1. How often do you binge eat? (a) seldom; (b) once or twice a month; (c) once a week; (d) almost every day; (e) every day.

_____ 2. What is the average length of a binging episode? (a) less than 15 minutes: (b) 15-30 minutes; (c) 30 minutes to 1 hour; (d) 1 hour to 2 hours; (e) more than 2 hours (if e, please indicate length of episode: _____).

_____ 3. Which of the following statements best applies to your binge eating? (a) I don't eat enough to satisfy me; (b) I eat until I've had enough to satisfy me; (c) I eat until my stomach feels full; (d) I eat until my stomach is painfully full; (e) I eat until I can't eat anymore.

_____ 4. Do you ever vomit after a binge? (a) never; (b) about 25% of the time; (c) about 50% of the time; (d) about 75% of the time; (e) about 100% of the time.

_____ 5. Which of the following best applies to your eating behavior when binge eating? (a) I eat much more slowly than usual; (b) I eat somewhat more slowly than usual; (c) I eat at about the same speed as I usually do; (d) I eat somewhat faster than usual; (e) I eat very rapidly.

_____ 6. How much are you concerned about your binge eating? (a) not bothered at all; (b) bothers me a little; (c) moderately concerned; (d) a major concern; (e) the most important concern in my life.

_____ 7. Which best describes the control you feel over your eating during a binge? (a) never in control; (b) in control about 25% of the time; (c) in control about 50% of the time; (d) in control about 75% of the time; (e) always in control.

_____ 8. Which of the following describes your feelings immediately after a binge? (a) I feel very good; (b) I feel good; (c) I feel fairly neutral, not too nervous or uncomfortable; (d) I am moderately nervous and/or uncomfortable; (e) I am very nervous and/or uncomfortable.

_____ 9. Which most accurately describes your mood immediately after a binge? (a) very happy; (b) moderately happy; (c) neutral; (d) moderately depressed; (e) very depressed.

_____ 10. Which of the following best describes the situation in which you typically binge? (a) always completely alone; (b) alone but around unknown others (e.g., restaurant); (c) only around others who know about my binging; (d) only around friends and family; (e) in any situation.

_____ 11. Which of the following best describes any weight changes you have experienced in the last year? (a) 0-5 lbs; (b) 5-10 lbs; (c) 10-20 lbs; (d) 20-30 lbs; (e) more than 30 lbs.

_____ 12. On a day that you binge, how many binge episodes typically occur during that day? (a) 0; (b) 1; (c) 2; (d) 3; (e) 4 or more.

_____ 13. How often do you use restrictive diets/fasts? (a) never; (b) one time per month; (c) two times per month; (d) one time per week; (e) almost always.

_____ 14. How often do you use laxatives to lose weight? (a) never; (b) 1-3 times per month; (c) one time per week; (d) one time per day; (e) more than one time per day (if e, please indicate frequency: _____).

_____ 15. How often do you use diuretics to lose weight? (a) never; (b) 1-3 times per month; (c) one time per week; (d) one time per day; (e) more than one time per day (if e, please indicate frequency: _____).

SOURCE: From "The Eating Questionnaire–Revised: A New Symptom Checklist for Bulimia," by D. A. Williamson, C. J. Davis, A. J. Goreczny, S. M. Bennett, and P. C. Watkins, 1989, in *Innovations in Clinical Practice: A Sourcebook* (P. A. Keller & L. G. Ritt, Eds.), Sarasota, FL: Professional Resource Exchange, Inc. Copyright © 1989 by Professional Resource Exchange, Inc. Reprinted with permission.

Appendix 10-C

MAC Questionnaire

This is an inventory of beliefs and attitudes about eating and weight. There are a number of statements with which you may tend to agree or disagree. On your answer sheet there is one of five possible answers for each item. For each statement, you should circle one of the numbers, according to your own reaction to the item:

Circle over #1 if you STRONGLY DISAGREE (for example ① 2 3 4 5)

Circle over #2 if you MODERATELY DISAGREE

Circle over #3 if you NEITHER AGREE NOR DISAGREE

Circle over #4 if you MODERATELY AGREE

Circle over #5 if you STRONGLY AGREE

It is not necessary to think over any item very long. Mark your answer quickly and go on to the next statement.

Be sure to mark how you actually feel about the statement, *not* how you think you *should* feel.

Try to avoid the neutral or "3" response as much as possible. Select this answer only if you really cannot decide whether you tend to agree or disagree with a statement.

		SD	MD	N	MA	SA
1.	If I don't have a specific routine for my daily eating, I'll lose all control and I'll gain weight.	1	2	3	4	5
2.	If others comment on my weight gain, I won't be able to stand it.	1	2	3	4	5
3.	I feel superior to fat people when they are eating and I am not.	1	2	3	4	5
4.	I feel victorious over my hunger when I am able to refuse sweets.	1	2	3	4	5
5.	When I feel very hungry, I can't give in to that hunger. If I do I'll never stop eating and I'll soon be fat.	1	2	3	4	5

		SD	MD	N	MA	SA
6.	If my weight goes up a couple pounds, I don't worry about it. It's probably just temporary (due to water retention, for example), and eventually my weight will return to normal.	1	2	3	4	5
7.	No matter how much I weigh, fats, sweets, breads, and cereals are bad food because they always turn into fat.	1	2	3	4	5
8.	When I eat desserts, I get fat. Therefore, I must never eat desserts so I won't be fat.	1	2	3	4	5
9.	When people whisper and laugh so that I cannot hear what they are saying, they are probably saying that I look unattractive. Their laughing and whispering indicates that I have gained weight.	1	2	3	4	5
10.	I am proud of myself when I control my urge to eat.	1	2	3	4	5
11.	No one likes fat people; therefore, I must remain thin to be liked by others.	1	2	3	4	5
12.	When I am overweight, I am not happy with my appearance. Gaining weight will take away the happiness I have with myself.	1	2	3	4	5
13.	If I've gained 2 pounds, I can't wear shorts anymore.	1	2	3	4	5
14.	If I don't establish a daily routine, everything will be chaotic and I won't accomplish anything.	1	2	3	4	5
15.	How much I weigh has little effect on how happy I am generally.	1	2	3	4	5
16.	If I eat a sweet, it will be converted instantly into stomach fat.	1	2	3	4	5
17.	I can't enjoy anything because it will be taken away.	1	2	3	4	5
18.	It's entirely normal and OK for my weight to go up and down a few pounds.	1	2	3	4	5
19.	If I can just control my eating, I can control my life.	1	2	3	4	5

		SD	MD	N	MA	SA
20.	If I can cut out all carbohydrates, I will never be fat.	1	2	3	4	5
21.	I feel guilty when I have eaten foods that I shouldn't, and exercising makes the guilt go away.	1	2	3	4	5
22.	My ability to deny myself food demonstrates that I am better than other people.	1	2	3	4	5
23.	When I eat something fattening, it doesn't bother me that I have temporarily let myself eat something I'm not supposed to.	1	2	3	4	5
24.	I am embarrassed when other people see me eat.	1	2	3	4	5
25.	Just because I can diet and control my hunger, it doesn't make me a better person than those who can't.	1	2	3	4	5
26.	Gaining 5 pounds would push me over the brink.	1	2	3	4	5
27.	How much I weigh has little to do with how popular I am.	1	2	3	4	5
28.	My friends will like me regardless of how much I weigh.	1	2	3	4	5
29.	When I am hungry, I know that I will eventually stop eating because I'll eventually get full and feel satisfied.	1	2	3	4	5
30.	If I'm not in complete control, I lose all control.	1	2	3	4	5
31.	People like you because of your personality, not whether you are overweight or not.	1	2	3	4	5
32.	When I see someone who is overweight, I worry that I will be like him/her.	1	2	3	4	5
33.	If I gain one pound, I'll go on and gain a hundred pounds, so I must keep precise control of my weight, food, and exercise.	1	2	3	4	5

SOURCE: From "Validity of the Mizes Anorectic Cognitions Scale: A Comparison Between Anorectics, Bulimics, and Psychiatric Controls," by J. S. Mizes, 1992, *Addictive Behaviors, 17*, 283-289. Copyright © 1986 by J. S. Mizes. Reprinted with permission.

11

Motivational Readiness to Control Weight

JOSEPH S. ROSSI

SUSAN R. ROSSI

WAYNE F. VELICER

JAMES O. PROCHASKA

F or individuals faced with the task of losing weight, there are two main issues: losing the weight in the first place and then maintaining the loss. In this respect, the problem of weight control is not very different than many other health problems that are refractory to change, such as smoking cessation or exercise adoption. The challenge for researchers is to develop models

AUTHORS' NOTE: The research reported in this chapter was partially supported by grants CA27821 and CA50087 from the National Cancer Institute. We thank Colleen Redding for helpful comments on the manuscript.

of health behavior that can encompass the wide range of attitudes, cognitions, affect, and activities that characterize individuals throughout the process of change, from initial motivation, through relapse, and to eventual success. An organizing principle that has been especially successful and popular in this regard, particularly in the field of the addictions, is the notion of *motivational readiness*. Several models incorporating this theme have been developed in recent years, including relapse prevention (Marlatt & Gordon, 1985) and motivational interviewing (Miller & Rollnick, 1991).

One model of motivational readiness that has received considerable empirical support is the *transtheoretical model* of behavior change (Baranowski, 1989-1990; Prochaska, DiClemente, & Norcross, 1992; Shaffer, 1992). Readiness to change is embodied in the levels of the model's core construct, the *stages of change*. Transitions between the stages of change are effected by a set of independent variables known as the *processes of change*. The model also incorporates a series of intervening or outcome variables. These include *decisional balance* (the pros and cons of change), *self-efficacy* (confidence in the ability to change across problem situations), and *situational temptations* to engage in the problem behavior. Also included among these intermediate or dependent variables would be any other psychological, environmental, cultural, socioeconomic, physiological, biochemical, or even genetic variables or behaviors specific to the problem being studied. For weight control, these might include percentage overweight, proportion of body fat, goal or ideal weight, weight loss targets, body-mass index, caloric intake, or energy expenditure.

The idea of discrete stages of change reflecting varying degrees of readiness to modify a problem behavior is not unique to the transtheoretical model. Similar concepts have been discussed by others (Brownell, Marlatt, Lichtenstein, & Wilson, 1986; Horn, 1976; Horn & Waingrow, 1966). What is distinctive about the transtheoretical model is the explicit acknowledgment of *all* stages of readiness as important components of the change process, and the emphasis placed on examining the transitions between stages as a function of other important dimensions of health behavior change, such as decision making and self-efficacy. In particular, the model stresses the importance of the early stages of change, which are undifferentiated in most other models of behavior change and health promotion. An advantage of this model is that it shows when, how, and where different theories are most applicable to the change process. For example, consciousness-raising, a process of change that is most likely to move precontemplators into the contemplation stage, is related to the health belief model (Becker, 1974) and similar concepts from educational theory (e.g., values clarification). Skills-oriented approaches advocated by social learning theory (Bandura, 1977, 1982) and based on the principles of behavior modification have been incorporated into the behavioral processes of change, which are most applicable to individuals in the action or maintenance stages of change. The emphasis on behavioral intentions in bridging the transition from contemplation to action reflects the theory of reasoned action (Ajzen & Fishbein, 1980; Fishbein & Ajzen, 1975). The pros and cons of behavior change are based, in part, on the decision-making model of Janis and Mann (1968, 1977) but also incorporate the concepts of barriers and facilitators from the health beliefs model as well as the concept of social and behavioral (subjective) norms from the theory of reasoned action. The self-efficacy construct employed in the transtheoretical model represents an integration of the model of self-efficacy proposed by Bandura (1977, 1982) and the coping models of relapse and maintenance described by Shiffman (1982, 1986). The transtheoretical model thus attempts to provide an integrated, multidimensional view of how people change a problem behavior that is applicable to individuals throughout the range of readiness to change behavior. The model has proved generalizable to a wide variety of problem areas, including both addictive (e.g., smoking, alcohol use, cocaine use, heroin use, obesity) and nonaddictive (e.g., dietary fat reduction and fiber increase, exercise adoption, sun exposure and sunscreen use, radon gas exposure, mammography screening, stress management, adolescent delinquency, HIV risk reduction and condom use, psychotherapy) behaviors (Marcus, Rossi, Selby, Niaura, & Abrams, 1992; Prochaska, 1979, 1993; Prochaska, DiClemente, & Norcross, 1992; Prochaska et al., 1994; Rakowski et al., 1992; Redding & Rossi, 1993; J. S. Rossi, 1990, 1992; J. S. Rossi et al., 1993; S. R. Rossi, Rossi, Prochaska, & Velicer, 1992; Snow, Prochaska, & Rossi, in press).

A more complete review of the transtheoretical model is beyond the scope of this chapter. For more detailed discussions, the reader may consult the existing literature (e.g., DiClemente, 1993; Prochaska, 1993; Prochaska & DiClemente, 1983, 1992; Prochaska, DiClemente, & Norcross, 1992; Prochaska, DiClemente, Velicer, & Rossi, 1992; J. S. Rossi, in press). In this chapter, we describe the instruments that have been developed to assess the various dimensions of the transtheoretical model as applied to the problem of weight control, including stages of change, processes of change, decisional balance, and self-efficacy. Also described are instruments developed by other investigators that measure aspects of motivational readiness, including the Dieting Readiness Test (Brownell, 1990), the Motivation Scale from the Master Questionnaire (Straw et al., 1984), and the Eating Self-Efficacy Scale (Glynn & Ruderman, 1986).

Overview of Measures

General Approach to Instrument Development

Construction of measures for weight control based on the transtheoretical model of change has typically employed the sequential methods of scale development described by Jackson (1970, 1971) and Comrey (1988). Initial item pools are generated based on theoretical construct definitions. Many of the items are adapted and revised from existing transtheoretical model instruments (e.g., smoking cessation), but item content is typically modified to more closely reflect the nature of the problem or population being studied. Content validity is established by having three to five raters experienced with the transtheoretical model classify items according to the conceptual definitions of the constructs. Items not receiving unanimous agreement as to which construct is being measured are typically deleted or revised to eliminate ambiguities. Race and gender bias are also reduced (insofar as possible) and reading levels improved at this point. Initial psychometric analyses are then conducted, including examination of item distributions, internal consistency analyses, dimensional exploration and reduction, and social desirability assessments (Jackson, 1967). Poorly functioning items are eliminated. The goal of these initial analyses is to develop an instrument that reflects the hypothesized theoretical model and is as short as possible while still retaining adequate psychometric properties. However, the results of these analyses sometimes require that theoretical constructs be reevaluated and merged with other constructs, enhanced through the addition of more items, or deleted altogether. When sample sizes are large enough to permit split-half cross-validation, or when additional samples are available, structural equation modeling (Jöreskog & Sörbom, 1989) is used to conduct confirmatory factor analysis. To avoid confirmation bias, and as a further test of the adequacy of the theoretically preferred model, several plausible alternative models are developed and compete with the hypothesized model to best represent the data. Additional information and examples of our approach to model-based instrument development are reported in Clark, Abrams, Niaura, Eaton, and Rossi (1991), Marcus, Rossi, et al. (1992), Prochaska, Velicer, DiClemente, and Fava (1988), S. R. Rossi et al. (1994), and Velicer, DiClemente, Rossi, and Prochaska (1990).

Stages of Change Algorithm

Description. The central organizing concept of the transtheoretical model is the notion of stages of change. Five ordered categories of readiness to change have been defined, providing a temporal or developmental dimension that represents when particular changes occur: *precontemplation, contemplation, preparation, action,* and *maintenance* (DiClemente et al., 1991; Prochaska, DiClemente, & Norcross, 1992). A sixth stage, *termination,* is also sometimes included. To date, neither the preparation stage nor the termination stage has been operationalized for weight control.

The Stages of Change Algorithm consists of a brief series of self-report questions assessing weight loss intentions and current activities. Individuals are classified into one of four discrete stage categories. Precontemplation includes those who have no intention of losing or controlling weight in the next 6 months. Contemplation includes those who are not actively trying to lose or control weight but are seriously considering doing so in the next 6 months. The action stage includes those who are actively trying to lose or control weight or who have successfully done so but for less than 6 months. In classifying individuals into the action stage, a minimum weight loss criterion is typically established as a goal. For example, O'Connell and Velicer (1988) set a weight loss criterion of at least 10 pounds for their college student sample. Others have used 10% of ideal body weight (Norcross, Prochaska, & DiClemente, 1992; S. R. Rossi, Rossi, & Prochaska, 1991). Alternatively, body-mass index or percentage overweight, as defined by an accepted standard (e.g., Metropolitan Life Insurance Company, 1983), could be employed. The maintenance stage includes those who have successfully maintained their weight loss for at least 6 months.

Samples. The Stages of Change Algorithm has been used with samples of 123 college students (O'Connell & Velicer, 1988) and 420 participants in a self-change smoking cessation study (Norcross et al., 1992; S. R. Rossi et al., 1991). Distribution across the precontemplation, contemplation, action, and maintenance stages was 15%, 53%, 18%, and 15%, respectively, for the college students, and 2%, 19%, 51%, and 27%, respectively, for the smoking cessation study participants.

Reliability. No reliability data for the Stages of Change Algorithm for weight control are available. However, the stages construct has been found reliable across a wide range of other problem behaviors (Marcus, Selby, Niaura, & Rossi, 1992; Prochaska, DiClemente, & Norcross, 1992; Prochaska et al., 1994).

Construct validity. Individuals in the four stages of change differ on several dimensions of the transtheoretical model in accordance with the predictions of the model, including decisional balance (O'Connell & Velicer, 1988) and the processes of change (Norcross et al., 1992; S. R. Rossi et al., 1991).

Practicality and location. The Stages of Change Algorithm is easy to administer and score. The weight control version of the stages algorithm is presented here, in Appendix 11-A, for the first time.

University of Rhode Island Change Assessment Scale (URICA)

Description. The University of Rhode Island Change Assessment Scale (URICA) consists of 32 items designed to measure four stages of change: *precontemplation, contemplation, action,* and *maintenance.* There are eight items per scale, scored using a 5-point Likert-type format. Higher scores indicate greater agreement with statements reflecting attitudes, cognitions, and affect associated with each stage of change. The range of possible total (summed) scores on each scale is 8 to 40. Standardized (*T*) scores (*M* = 50, *SD* = 10), based on the development of local norms, are also frequently used to report URICA scale scores, especially when the instrument is used to develop typologies.

The URICA was originally developed for use with clients in psychotherapy reporting on their problems (McConnaughy, DiClemente, Prochaska, & Velicer, 1989; McConnaughy, Prochaska, & Velicer, 1983). However, the instrument is general in format, insofar as clients are asked to complete the questionnaire with respect to their presenting problem for treatment. Thus the URICA has been used without adaptation (i.e., without modifying item content or scale administration and scoring procedures) for measuring readiness to change across a wide variety of problem behaviors, especially the addictions, including smoking cessation (Velicer, Hughes, Fava, & Prochaska, 1992), alcohol use (DiClemente & Hughes, 1990), and cocaine use (J. S. Rossi et al., 1993). However, it is preferable, when appropriate, to modify the item content of the scale if this will more accurately reflect the problem behavior being studied. The URICA has been successfully modified for use with other problem behaviors, including exposure to ultraviolet light, exercise adoption, and weight control (Blais & Rossi, 1991; Prochaska, Norcross, Fowler, Follick, & Abrams, 1992; Reed, Velicer, Rossi, & Marcus, 1993).

There has been some confusion as to the relationship and intended purposes of the Stages of Change Algorithm and the URICA (sometimes referred to, colloquially, as the stages of change "long form"; Davidson, 1992; Prochaska, DiClemente, Velicer, & Rossi, 1992). The URICA extends the conceptualization of the stages construct that underlies the Stages of Change Algorithm. The purpose of the algorithm is to classify an individual into one of the stages of change. Although the algorithm has been well validated across a diverse set of problem behaviors, the attempt to capture in only a few discrete categories the wide range of attitudes, cognitions, feelings, and behaviors of individuals engaged in problem behavior change is likely to result in some misclassification. In contrast, the URICA results in a score on each of the four stage scales. The profile patterns that emerge reflect the possibility that individuals are likely to be engaged in attitudes and behaviors character-istic of more than one stage of change at a time. The correlation between the four scale scores of the URICA suggests a simplex pattern, in which adjacent stages are more highly correlated than nonadjacent stages (McConnaughy et al., 1983, 1989). Thus the transition between stages of change is seen as a gradual progression rather than as abrupt or discontinuous.

The URICA has occasionally been used to place individuals into one of the discrete stages of change, for example, by identifying the scale on which an individual scores highest (e.g., Prochaska, Norcross, et al., 1992). The mo-tivation to do this is understandable, but the practice is not well justified from a measurement point of view and should be discouraged. The primary purpose of the URICA is to identify specific stage profiles (typologies) char-acteristic of transitions between the four basic stages of change or to identify subtypes of individuals within a stage of change. Approximately 8-10 consis-tent stage profiles have emerged across problem areas (Blais & Rossi, 1992). The URICA may also be used to evaluate progress in treatment (e.g., Prochaska, Rossi, & Wilcox, 1991) and it is primarily for this purpose that the instru-ment has been used for weight control (Prochaska, Norcross, et al., 1992).

Samples. The URICA has been used with a sample of 184 hospital staff mem-bers enrolled in a 10-week work site behavioral treatment program for weight control (Prochaska, Norcross, et al., 1992).

Factor structure. The theoretical four-factor structure of the URICA has been consistently supported using both principal components analyses (Di-Clemente & Hughes, 1990; McConnaughy et al., 1983, 1989) and structural equation modeling (Blais & Rossi, 1991; Reed et al., 1993; J. S. Rossi et al., 1993). The structure of the URICA has not yet been examined with data from a weight control sample.

Reliability: Internal consistency. Internal consistency for the URICA has not been reported for a weight control sample. However, the internal consistency of the instrument has proved adequate when used for other problem behav-iors. For 155 clients in therapy, McConnaughy et al. (1983) reported internal consistency (Cronbach's alpha) coefficients of .88, .88, .89, and .88, respec-tively, for the precontemplation, contemplation, action, and maintenance scales. A follow-up study of 293 clients in therapy resulted in coefficients of .79, .84, .84, and .82, respectively (McConnaughy et al., 1989). For 224 adults entering outpatient alcoholism treatment, alphas of .69, .75, .82, and .80, respectively, were obtained for the four URICA scales (DiClemente & Hughes, 1990).

Construct validity. Prochaska, Norcross, et al. (1992) administered the URICA to participants in a work site weight control program. Contemplation scores decreased and action scores increased significantly between weeks 1 and 5 of the program. These gains were maintained at week 10. The precontemplation and maintenance scales showed no significant differences over the course of treatment.

Predictive validity. Prochaska, Norcross, et al. (1992) also used the URICA to predict attendance and weight loss. Attendance was predicted by higher action scale scores. Weight loss was predicted by higher action scores and by lower precontemplation and maintenance scores.

Practicality and location. The URICA is easy to administer and score. Determination of scale scores involves simple unit weighting of the items to produce either a total or a mean scale score. Use of the URICA for identifying stage-specific typologies is less straightforward and generally requires the use of cluster analysis with fairly large sample sizes (e.g., 150-250) and the use of standardized scoring. With small sample sizes, pattern matching could be employed. Researchers attempting to use the URICA for this purpose should carefully examine the description of the various stage profiles given by McConnaughy et al. (1983, 1989), DiClemente and Hughes (1990), and Blais and Rossi (1992). The general version of the URICA may be found in McConnaughy et al. (1989). The weight control version of the instrument is presented here, in Appendix 11-B, for the first time.

Dieting Readiness Test (DRT)

Description. The Dieting Readiness Test (DRT) consists of 23 items designed to measure three board categories of readiness: motivation, commitment, and life circumstances (Brownell, 1990). Six subscales measuring specific aspects of motivational readiness to lose weight are included in the test: *goals and attitudes, hunger and eating cues, control over eating, binge eating and purging, emotional eating,* and *exercise patterns and attitudes.* The number of items per scale ranges from three to six. Most items are scored using a 5-point Likert-type scale, although dichotomous scoring and 6-point frequency ratings are also employed for some items.

Although no explicit theoretical model or orientation is espoused by Brownell (1990), it is reasonable to suppose, from the content of the scales and from the author's other writings, that the major influences include relapse prevention (Brownell et al., 1986; Marlatt & Gordon, 1985), social learning theory (Bandura, 1977, 1982), and the transtheoretical model (Prochaska & DiClemente, 1982, 1983, 1986). The DRT was developed based on the author's experience with hundreds of dieters at the University of Pennsylvania School of Medicine Obesity Research Clinic. No specific data on the DRT are available at this time, although psychometric analyses are currently being conducted (K. D. Brownell, personal communication, July 7, 1993).

Practicality and location. The DRT is easy to administer and score. Determination of scale scores involves simple unit weighting of the items to produce a total score for each scale. Higher scale scores indicate greater readiness to lose weight. In addition, an interpretational scoring guide is provided for each scale by arbitrarily trichotomizing scale scores. Although this procedure lacks a sound measurement basis, it is clearly intended as a general guide for individuals who self-administer the test. (See Appendix 11-C.)

Motivation Scale (MS) of the Master Questionnaire

Description. The Master Questionnaire is a 56-item true/false instrument designed to measure five dimensions of change related to the authors' cognitive-behavioral orientation to obesity treatment, including *hopelessness, physical attributions, motivation, stimulus control,* and *energy balance knowledge.* The authors describe no theoretical basis for the design of the questionnaire, selection of relevant scales, or inclusion of specific item content other than cognitive-behavioral. Of primary relevance to the topic of this chapter is the questionnaire's 12-item Motivation Scale (MS) (see Appendix 11-D), which measures "ability to maintain motivation for weight loss and self-efficacy expectations" (Straw et al., 1984, p. 7).

Samples. Straw et al. (1984) administered the MS to a sample of 216 clinically obese individuals who applied for admission into two research-oriented, weight-loss treatment programs. All of the data reported here are based on this sample or subsets of this sample.

Factor structure. Initial structural analysis, item selection, and scale development on the original 265-item version of the Master Questionnaire was accomplished through the use of hierarchical cluster analysis (Straw et al., 1984). Cluster analysis is not frequently recommended for use as a dimensional reduction technique in scale development (e.g., Nunnally, 1978). However, under certain conditions and with appropriate technical procedures, this approach may be justifiable (Revelle, 1979). Straw et al. (1984) employed Revelle's (1979) cluster-analytic techniques, which resulted in a 56-item, five-cluster solution, including a 12-item motivation cluster. The 56 items were then subjected to a conventional principal components analysis with varimax rotation in an attempt to replicate the cluster analysis solution. A four-component solution, in which the motivation and hopelessness scales merged, was found. Examination of the item content of these two scales clearly reveals a common theme of discouragement and low efficacy to lose weight. Taken together, the lack of conceptual clarity, the use of dichotomous item format, which is known to affect instrument structure (Velicer & Stevenson, 1978), and the use of a novel and relatively unproven analytical technique for scale construction suggest that the MS lacks a clearly defined and replicable factor structure.

Test-retest reliability. A sample of 42 clients in treatment was used to establish 2-week test-retest reliability of .789 for the MS.

Reliability: Internal consistency. Coefficient alpha for the MS, based on the total sample of 216 subjects, was .77.

Construct validity. MS scores increased significantly from pretest to a 1-year follow-up assessment for 42 clients in a weight-loss treatment program.

Practicality and location. No explicit administrative or scoring instructions are provided by Straw et al. (1984). However, the MS appears to be simple and easy to administer and score. We provide here an arbitrary scoring procedure that seems consistent with the discussion of the scale provided by Straw et al. (1984), in which higher scores indicate greater motivation. Determination of scale scores involves simple unit weighting of the items to produce a total scale score.

Processes of Change Questionnaire for Weight Control (PCQ)

Description. The Processes of Change Questionnaire (PCQ) for weight control consists of 48 items that measure the strategies that individuals use in their attempts to lose weight. The conceptual basis for the PCQ is the transtheoretical model. Specifically, an individual's progress from one stage of change to the next is assumed to be the result of using the processes of change. Twelve process dimensions have been hypothesized: *consciousness raising, counterconditioning, dramatic relief, environmental reevaluation, helping relationships, interpersonal systems control, reinforcement (contingency)*

TABLE 11.1 The Processes of Change: Definitions and Representative Interventions

Processes of Change	Definition/Interventions
Consciousness Raising	Efforts by the individual to seek new information and to gain understanding and feedback about the problem behavior/ observations, confrontations, interpretations, bibliotherapy
Counterconditioning	Substitution of alternatives for the problem behavior/relaxation, desensitization, assertion, positive self-statements
Dramatic Relief	Experiencing and expressing feelings about the problem behavior and potential solutions/psychodrama, grieving losses, role playing
Environmental Reevaluation	Consideration and assessment of how the problem behavior affects the physical and social environment/empathy training, documentaries
Helping Relationships	Trusting, accepting, and using the support of caring others during attempts to change the problem behavior/therapeutic alliance, social support, self-help groups
Interpersonal Systems Control	Avoiding people or social situations that encourage the problem behavior/seeking people or situations that encourage healthier behavior, restructuring social relationships
Reinforcement Management	Rewarding oneself or being rewarded by others for making changes/contingency contracts, overt and covert reinforcement, self-reward
Self-Liberation	Choice and commitment to change the problem behavior, including belief in the ability to change/decision-making therapy, New Year's resolutions, logotherapy techniques, commitment enhancing techniques
Self-Reevaluation	Emotional and cognitive reappraisal of values by the individual with respect to the problem behavior/value clarification, imagery, corrective emotional experience
Social Liberation	Awareness, availability, and acceptance by the individual of alternative, problem-free lifestyles in society/empowering, policy interventions
Stimulus Control	Control of situations and other causes that trigger the problem behavior/adding stimuli that encourage alternative behaviors, restructuring the environment, avoiding high-risk cues, fading techniques
Substance Use	Use of prescribed or nonprescribed medications or other substances directed at appetite, metabolism, or emotions/suppressants, nicotine, alcohol

SOURCE: Adapted from table 1 in *Addictive Behaviors*, Vol. 17, Prochaska, J. O., Norcross, J. C., Fowler, J. L., Follick, M. J., and Abrams, D. B., "Attendance and Outcome in a Work Site Weight Control Program: Processes and Stages of Change as Process and Predictor Variables," pp. 35-45, copyright © 1992, with kind permission from Elsevier Science Ltd., The Boulevard, Langford Lane, Kidlington OX5 1GB, UK.

management, self-liberation, self-reevaluation, social liberation, stimulus control, and *substance use (medication).* Brief definitions of the processes and interventions representative of their use for weight control are given in Table 11.1. There are 4 items per scale, scored using a 5-point Likert-type format. Respondents are asked to rate the frequency of use of each process strategy, with higher scores indicating more frequent use. The range of possible total (summed) scores on each scale is 4 to 20. Standardized (T) scores ($M = 50$, $SD = 10$), based on the development of local norms, are also frequently used to report PCQ scale scores.

Samples. An initial, 60-item version of the PCQ was used with 420 participants in a study of the weight-loss habits of smokers and ex-smokers (Norcross et al., 1992; Prochaska & DiClemente, 1985; S. R. Rossi et al., 1991) and with 104 hospital staff members enrolled in a work site behavioral weight control program (Norcross et al., 1992). A shortened, 48-item version of the PCQ was used with 184 hospital staff members enrolled in a 10-week work site behavioral treatment program for weight control (Prochaska, Norcross, et al., 1992). An abbreviated, 32-item version of the PCQ was administered to a sample of 285 participants enrolled in three community-based weight-loss programs (S. R. Rossi et al., 1994).

Factor structure. Prochaska and DiClemente (1985) conducted a principal components analysis of the 60-item version of the PCQ. Their results supported the proposed 12-factor structure of the PCQ with the exception that two processes—self-liberation and self-reevaluation—merged. The 11 components accounted for approximately 70% of the total item variance. The theoretical structure of the PCQ was confirmed using structural equation modeling in a study conducted by S. R. Rossi et al. (1994). The theoretical model outperformed several alternative, theoretically plausible models. Because data were collected by telephone in this study, only an abbreviated, 32-item (eight-process) version of the PCQ was administered. However, the self-liberation and self-reevaluation processes did emerge separately in this study. S. R. Rossi et al. (1994) also explored the hierarchical structure of the PCQ, confirming the existence of two higher order factors: the experiential and behavioral processes of change. These results are consistent with the findings for eight other problem behaviors (J. S. Rossi, 1992).

Reliability: Internal consistency. Internal consistency (alpha) coefficients for the PCQ are available for three samples (Norcross et al., 1992; S. R. Rossi et al., 1991, 1994). Median alphas across samples were .78 for consciousness raising, .77 for counterconditioning, .88 for dramatic relief, .80 for environmental reevaluation, .82 for helping relationships, .71 for reinforcement management, .67 for self-liberation, .79 for self-reevaluation, .62 for social liberation, .78 for stimulus control, and .88 for substance use. No internal consistency coefficients have been reported for interpersonal systems control.

Construct validity. S. R. Rossi et al. (1991) examined the relationship between the stages and processes of change. Differential use of the processes of change across the stages of change was found for nine scales: consciousness raising, counterconditioning, dramatic relief, helping relationships, reinforcement management, the combined self-liberation and self-reevaluation scales, social liberation, stimulus control, and substance use. Interpersonal systems control was not included in this study.

Prochaska, Norcross, et al. (1992) examined process use over the course of a 10-week behavioral treatment program for weight control. Use of counterconditioning, interpersonal systems control, reinforcement management, social liberation, and stimulus control increased significantly over the course of treatment, whereas substance use decreased.

Predictive validity. Predictive validity for the PCQ was obtained in a study of 184 employees enrolled in a 10-week weight-loss program (Prochaska, Norcross, et al., 1992). Consciousness raising, counterconditioning, social liberation, and stimulus control predicted the number of treatment sessions attended. Consciousness raising, counterconditioning, reinforcement management, self-liberation, self-reevaluation, and social liberation predicted weight loss.

Practicality and location. The PCQ is easy to administer and score. Determination of scale scores involves simple unit weighting of the items to produce either a total or a mean scale score. The abbreviated, 32-item version of the PCQ is given in S. R. Rossi et al. (1994). The full 48-item version of the PCQ is presented here for the first time. (See Appendix 11-E.)

Decisional Balance Inventory (DBI)

Description. The Decisional Balance Inventory (DBI) consists of 20 items designed to measure two hypothesized dimensions of decision making for weight control, the *pros* and *cons* of losing weight. The conceptual bases for the DBI are the decision-making model of Janis and Mann (1968, 1977) and the transtheoretical model (Velicer, DiClemente, Prochaska, & Brandenburg, 1985). It is assumed that an individual's evaluation of the pros and cons of changing behavior depends on motivational readiness to change (Velicer et al., 1985). Evidence supporting the relationship between the pros and cons and the stages of change has been obtained across a wide range of problem behaviors (Prochaska et al., 1994).

Although factor analytic studies have supported only the two pros and cons factors of the DBI, all eight of the original Janis and Mann (1977) categories were included in the content development of the questionnaire. Each of the two scales contains 10 items scored using a 5-point Likert-type format. Respondents are asked to rate the importance of each statement in influencing their decision on whether or not to lose weight. Higher scores indicate assignment of greater importance. The range of possible total (summed) scores on each scale is 10 to 50. Standardized (T) scores ($M = 50$, $SD = 10$), based on the development of local norms, are frequently used to report DBI scale scores.

Samples. O'Connell and Velicer (1988) used the DBI with a sample of 264 college students.

Factor structure. Consistent with the results of previous studies for other problem behaviors (Prochaska et al., 1994), principal components analysis of the DBI for weight control yielded two clear components reflecting the pros and cons of losing weight. The two components accounted for 50% of the total item variance.

Reliability: Internal consistency. Coefficient alpha was .91 for the pros scale and .84 for the cons scales.

Construct validity. Construct validity for the DBI was also established by O'Connell and Velicer (1988). They obtained the characteristic pattern of relationships between the pros and cons of weight loss and the stages of change predicted by the transtheoretical model and replicated across 11 other health behavior problems (Prochaska et al., 1994). The cons of weight loss were significantly greater than the pros for individuals in the precontemplation stage of change. This pattern was reversed for those in the contemplation stage. Individuals in the action stage showed the greatest difference in the pros of weight loss over the cons.

Practicality and location. The DBI is easy to administer and score. Determination of scale scores involves simple unit weighting of the items to produce either a total or a mean scale score. The DBI is presented in O'Connell and Velicer (1988). (See Appendix 11-F.)

Weight Efficacy Life-Style Questionnaire (WEL)

Description. The Weight Efficacy Life-Style Questionnaire (WEL) consists of 20 items designed to measure five hypothesized dimensions of efficacy for weight management: *availability, negative emotions, physical discomfort, positive activities,* and *social pressure.* There are four items per scale, scored using a 10-point Likert-type format. Respondents are asked to rate their confidence in resisting overeating in 20 tempting situations. Higher scores indicate greater confidence. The range of possible total (summed) scores on each scale is 10 to 40.

The conceptual basis of the WEL includes the coping models of relapse and maintenance proposed by Shiffman (1982, 1986), Bandura's (1977, 1982) self-efficacy model, and the transtheoretical model (Velicer et al., 1990). In this integrated model, efficacy is assumed to be related to motivational readiness to change, increasing linearly from precontemplation to maintenance (DiClemente, 1986; DiClemente, Prochaska, & Gibertini, 1985; Prochaska, DiClemente, Velicer, Ginpil, & Norcross, 1985; Prochaska, Velicer, Guadagnoli, Rossi, & DiClemente, 1991).

Samples. An initial, 40-item version of the WEL has been used with 162 obese patients enrolled in a 14-session structured behavioral weight loss program for the work site (Clark et al., 1991) and with 184 hospital staff members enrolled in a 10-week work site behavioral treatment program for weight control (Prochaska, Norcross, et al., 1992). The shortened, 20-item version of the WEL has been used with samples of 220 clients at a hospital-based outpatient weight-management service, with 38 obese diabetic clients enrolled in a 19-week weight-management program, and with 21 participants in a 26-week weight-management program combining behavior therapy and a very low calorie diet (Clark et al., 1991).

Factor structure. Structural analysis of the WEL has been conducted by Clark et al. (1991). The original 40-item version was administered to a sample of 162 obese patients and subjected to principal components analysis, which resulted in a five-factor solution reflecting the five hypothesized dimensions of efficacy. Based on these results, a shortened, 20-item version of the questionnaire was developed and administered to a sample of 220 weight-management patients. The theoretical structure of the WEL was confirmed in this sample through the use of structural equation modeling (Jöreskog & Sörbom, 1989). The five-factor model outperformed several alternative, theoretically plausible models. Factor loadings for the 20 items ranged from .62 to .92 (mean = .76).

Reliability: Internal consistency. Internal consistency (alpha) coefficients for the WEL are available for two samples (Clark et al., 1991). Alphas were .76 and .83 for the availability scale, .87 and .88 for the negative emotions scale, .82 and .84 for the physical discomfort scale, .70 and .79 for the positive activities scale, and .90 and .89 for the social pressure scale.

Construct validity. Total scores on the 40-item version of the WEL increased significantly from week 1 to week 5, and were maintained at week 10, for 184 participants in a behavioral treatment program for weight control (Prochaska, Norcross, et al., 1992). Construct validity is also available for the shortened version of the WEL based on samples of 38 and 21 participants in two weight-management programs (Clark et al., 1991). Over the 19 weeks of treatment for the first sample, efficacy scores significantly increased for the negative emotions and positive activities scales and for the total WEL score. For the second sample, over 26 weeks of treatment, there were significant increases for the availability, negative emotions, and social pressure scales as well as for the total WEL score.

Convergent validity. Concurrent validity information is available for the WEL and two of its subscales, based on the 21 participants in the 26-week treatment program. The WEL total score correlated .67 with total score on the Eating Self-Efficacy Scale (ESES; Glynn & Ruderman, 1986). The availability subscale of the WEL correlated with the socially acceptable circumstances subscale of the ESES .75 at pretreatment and .51 at posttreatment. The negative emotion subscale of the WEL correlated with the negative affect subscale of the ESES .80 at pretreatment and .50 at posttreatment.

Predictive validity. Higher total WEL scores on the 40-item version of the WEL predicted weight loss for 184 employees enrolled in a 10-week weight-loss program (Prochaska, Norcross, et al., 1992). Total WEL scores did not predict attendance in the program.

Practicality and location. The WEL is easy to administer and score. Determination of scale scores involves simple unit weighting of the items to produce either a total or a mean scale score. (See Appendix 11-G.)

Eating Self-Efficacy Scale (ESES)

Description. The Eating Self-Efficacy Scale (ESES) consists of 25 items designed to measure two hypothesized dimensions of efficacy in controlling overeating: *negative affect* (15 items) and *socially acceptable circumstances* (10 items). A 7-point Likert-type format is employed. Respondents are asked to rate the difficulty of controlling overeating in 25 challenging situations. Lower scores indicate greater eating self-efficacy. The range of possible total (summed) scores is 15 to 105 for the negative affect scale and 10 to 70 for the socially acceptable circumstances scale. The ESES is conceptually based on Bandura's (1977) model of self-efficacy.

Samples. The ESES has been used with five samples of undergraduate students in introductory psychology courses (*N*s = 328, 362, 484, 618, and 79) and with a sample of 32 participants from three behaviorally oriented weight-loss programs ranging in duration from 6 to 13 weeks (Glynn & Ruderman, 1986). The ESES has also been administered to a sample of 21 participants in a 26-week weight-management program combining behavior therapy and a very low calorie diet (Clark et al., 1991).

Factor structure. A 79-item version of the ESES was administered to a sample of 328 undergraduates and subjected to principal components analysis with orthogonal rotation. The resulting five-factor, 59-item version of the ESES was administered to a second sample of 362 undergraduates and analyzed using the same procedure. A five-factor solution again resulted, but only two factors were consistent across the two analyses. These two factors accounted for 27% of the total item variance and were labeled *negative affect* and *socially acceptable circumstances*. The 25 items measuring these two factors were retained for the final version of the ESES and administered to a sample of 484 female undergraduates. Three factors were obtained, accounting for 33% of the total item variance. The negative affect scale emerged intact, but the socially acceptable circumstances scale split into two factors consisting of seven and three items (Glynn & Ruderman, 1986). The same pattern of results was obtained on a sample of 618 undergraduates, except that the three-factor solution accounted for 54% of the total item variance. The same pattern of results was also obtained for separate analyses of male and female subjects (Glynn & Ruderman, 1986). Although the authors consider the structure of the ESES to be stable, some caution, especially for the socially acceptable circumstances scale, is probably warranted.

Reliability: Internal consistency. Internal consistency (alpha) coefficients for the two ESES scales are reported for a sample of 484 female undergraduates (Glynn & Ruderman, 1986). Alpha was .92 for the entire ESES scale, .94 for the negative affect scale, and .85 for the socially acceptable circumstances scale. Alphas for the entire scale and for the two subscales were reported as greater than .88 for a sample of 618 undergraduates (Glynn & Ruderman, 1986).

Test-retest reliability. Test-retest reliability of the ESES is based on a subsample of 85 female undergraduates who returned for testing 7 weeks after an initial administration. The test-retest reliability of .70 reported by Glynn and Ruderman (1986) presumably refers to the entire ESES.

Construct validity. Total ESES scale scores revealed significant increases in self-efficacy for 32 participants over the course of treatment in three behaviorally oriented weight-loss programs (Glynn & Ruderman, 1986).

Convergent validity. Concurrent validity is available both for the total ESES scale and for its two subscales. Glynn and Ruderman (1986) reported that total ESES score correlated .47 with the restraint scale (Ruderman, 1982), a measure of concern with dieting and weight fluctuation, and .51 with the Tennessee Self-Concept Scale (Fitts, 1965), a global measure of self-esteem, based on a sample of 484 female undergraduates. Clark et al. (1991) reported that total ESES score correlated .67 with total score on the Weight Efficacy Life-Style Questionnaire (WEL) for 21 participants in a 26-week weight treatment program. Clark et al. (1991) also reported that the negative affect subscale of the ESES correlated with the negative emotion subscale of the WEL .80 at pretreatment and .50 at posttreatment. The socially acceptable circumstances subscale of the ESES correlated with the availability subscale of the WEL .75 at pretreatment and .51 at posttreatment.

Predictive validity. Higher efficacy on the ESES predicted weight loss ($r = .35$) for 32 participants in three behaviorally oriented weight-loss programs (Glynn & Ruderman, 1986).

Practicality and location. The ESES is easy to administer and score. Determination of scale scores involves simple unit weighting of the items to produce either a total or a mean scale score. (See Appendix 11-H.)

Future Research Directions

Over the past 15 years, motivational readiness has proved a useful construct for understanding how people change addictive behaviors, such as alcohol and tobacco use, and for the development of interventions to help people change (DiClemente, 1991, 1993; Miller & Rollnick, 1991; Prochaska, DiClemente, & Norcross, et al., 1992). The research reported in this chapter supports the utility of the construct for weight control as well and further suggests that the transtheoretical model may provide a useful organizing framework for understanding the relationship between motivational readiness and how people change. Continued progress will depend, at least in part, on the resolution of outstanding measurement problems and additional psychometric research on the instruments reviewed here.

Perhaps the most critical measurement issues involve the stages of change, particularly with respect to increasing precision of measurement of the Stages of Change Algorithm. At least three of the six hypothesized stages are in need of refinement, including the action, preparation, and termination stages. These issues take on added importance because the Stages of Change Algorithm has become the instrument of choice for assessing motivational readiness to change, not only for weight control but for most other problem behaviors as well (Prochaska, DiClemente, & Norcross, 1992; Prochaska, DiClemente, Velicer, & Rossi, 1992; Velicer, Prochaska, Rossi, & Snow, 1992).

Most important is the development of a strict criterion for defining the action stage. In smoking cessation, for example, it is not sufficient to reduce smoking by 50% or to switch to low tar and nicotine brands. Although such changes in smoking probably reduce some health risks, health professionals have agreed that complete abstinence is necessary for sustained health benefits. Therefore action is defined as abstinence from smoking (Velicer, Prochaska, et al., 1992). Unfortunately, no consensus has yet developed in the field of weight control over what constitutes an ideal, a healthy, or even a reasonable standard for weight. The difficulty is understandable, as an acceptable criterion must take height, age, sex, and perhaps even changing cultural norms into account. The problem is further complicated in that weight control is not a specific behavior, like smoking a cigarette or using a condom, but a goal to be reached. In addition, not all strategies employed to control weight are healthy or low-risk behaviors (e.g., smoking cigarettes, purging). Successful, healthy, low-risk weight control is likely to be dependent on multiple behavior changes, including maintenance of a low fat diet, regular exercise, and abstinence from binge eating (Prochaska, 1993). Whether such whole scale lifestyle change is likely to be acceptable to individuals or even effective as a means of weight control, and how to design and implement health promotion programs to change multiple behaviors, are important challenges for researchers.

A preparation stage for weight control has not yet been defined. The preparation stage has been found very useful for other problem behaviors, such as smoking cessation and exercise adoption (DiClemente et al., 1991; Marcus, Rossi, et al., 1992). At the present time, preparation is defined both by the intention to take action in the immediate future (e.g., quit smoking cigarettes in the next 30 days) and by a recent action episode (e.g., quit smoking for at least 24 hours once in the past year). Whether both components of the definition are necessary is an issue that has not yet been completely resolved even for the problem of smoking cessation (Tsoh, Rossi, & Prochaska,

1992). Creation of a preparation stage for weight control is likely to depend on the adoption of an adequate definition of action for weight control.

Is a termination stage possible for weight control, or is a lifetime of maintenance required? The issue is likely to be controversial insofar as abstinence for the central behavior (eating) is obviously not possible. An operational definition for termination that has been useful for both smoking (J. S. Rossi et al., 1989) and alcohol use (Snow et al., in press) is complete confidence (efficacy) that one will not relapse in previously tempting situations and the absence of temptations to relapse in problematic situations. Based on these definitions, 16% of former smokers and 17% of former alcoholics had reached the termination stage. Other definitions of termination should also be explored. Most models of health behavior change do not address the question of termination, and even in the transtheoretical model this stage is not particularly well articulated. Establishing the existence of a termination stage for weight control is more than of theoretical interest, however. Discovering predictors of termination would clearly have important implications for the design of treatment programs as well as for the development of models of problem behavior change.

Investigators should give serious consideration to using the URICA instead of (or in combination with) the stages algorithm whenever possible, but especially when assessment of progress in treatment is important. The measurement properties of the URICA are, in general, superior to those of the algorithm, although additional work on the factor structure and reliability of the weight control version of the URICA is needed. The chief disadvantage of the URICA is that it is much longer than the algorithm. However, with the use of structural modeling techniques, it should be relatively easy to develop a 12- to 16-item version of the URICA with adequate measurement properties (see J. S. Rossi et al., 1993). The relationship of the URICA to other transtheoretical model constructs also needs to be investigated.

The DRT has potential for contributing to an understanding of readiness to change in several areas of concern for weight control not measured by other instruments reviewed in this chapter. Insofar as no psychometric data are currently available for this instrument, basic measurement work is the top priority for the DRT at this time. Several scales appear to measure efficacy as well as motivation. Relationship of the DRT to the stages of change and to measures of self-efficacy would be especially valuable in providing conceptual clarity for the subscales.

Additional work on the conceptual basis and measurement structure of the Motivation Scale would enhance its utility. In particular, it is not clear if the MS is measuring motivational readiness or self-efficacy. Additional structural analysis and the relationship of the instrument to other measures of readiness (e.g., the URICA and DRT) and efficacy (e.g., the WEL and ESES) are needed.

Decision making is a critical component of motivational readiness, yet it is the least well studied of all the constructs reviewed in this chapter. The DBI has been administered to only a single sample of subjects. This is unfortunate, because the relationship between readiness to change and decision making has recently been demonstrated to be remarkably consistent across a wide variety of problem behaviors (Prochaska et al., 1994), leading to the formulation of two general principles of behavior change (Prochaska, 1994). Validation of the DBI with clinical samples is thus important not only for a greater understanding of weight control but also as a further test of a general model of behavior change.

Two measures of self-efficacy for weight control are currently available, the WEL and the ESES. The WEL is probably the most psychometrically sound instrument of all those reviewed in this chapter. The WEL is shorter than the ESES while measuring more dimensions, including those assessed by the ESES. The ESES was primarily developed on a college population and has been validated on only a very small clinical sample. The factor structure of the ESES is also not clear, as several analyses indicated three factors rather than two. Neither instrument has been integrated with other constructs of motivational readiness. The transtheoretical model hypothesizes a linear relationship between self-efficacy and the stages of change. A test of this hypothesis using either the WEL or the ESES would be very valuable, insofar as the integration of these two constructs has proved very useful for other problem behaviors (e.g., Prochaska, DiClemente, & Norcross, 1992; Prochaska, Velicer, et al., 1991; Velicer et al., 1990).

References

Ajzen, I., & Fishbein, M. (1980). *Understanding attitudes and predicting social behavior.* Englewood Cliffs, NJ: Prentice-Hall.

Bandura, A. (1977). Self-efficacy: Toward a unifying theory of behavior change. *Psychological Review, 84,* 191-215.

Bandura, A. (1982). Self-efficacy mechanism in human agency. *American Psychologist, 37,* 122-147.

Baranowski, T. (1989-1990). Reciprocal determinism at the stages of behavior change: An integration of community, personal and behavioral perspectives. *International Quarterly of Community Health Education, 10,* 297-327.

Becker, M. H. (Ed.). (1974). The health belief model and personal health behavior. *Health Education Monographs, 2,* 324-508.

Blais, L. M., & Rossi, J. S. (1991, March). *The stages of change of sun exposure.* Paper presented at the 12th annual meeting of the Society of Behavioral Medicine, Washington, DC.

Blais, L. M., & Rossi, J. S. (1992, August). *Stages of change: Comparing clusters across four health behaviors.* Paper presented at the 100th annual convention of the American Psychological Association, Washington, DC.

Brownell, K. D. (1990). Dieting readiness. *Weight Control Digest, 1*(1), 1, 5-9.

Brownell, K. D., Marlatt, G. A., Lichtenstein, E., & Wilson, G. T. (1986). Understanding and preventing relapse. *American Psychologist, 41,* 765-782.

Clark, M. M., Abrams, D. B., Niaura, R. S., Eaton, C. A., & Rossi, J. S. (1991). Self-efficacy in weight management. *Journal of Consulting and Clinical Psychology, 59,* 739-744.

Comrey, A. L. (1988). Factor-analytic methods of scale development in personality and clinical psychology. *Journal of Consulting and Clinical Psychology, 56,* 754-761.

Davidson, R. (1992). Prochaska and DiClemente's model of change: A case study? *British Journal of Addiction, 87,* 821-822.

DiClemente, C. C. (1986). Self-efficacy and the addictive behaviors. *Journal of Social and Clinical Psychology, 4,* 302-315.

DiClemente, C. C. (1991). Motivational interviewing and the stages of change. In W. R. Miller & S. Rollnick (Eds.), *Motivational interviewing: Preparing people to change addictive behaviors* (pp. 191-202). New York: Guilford.

DiClemente, C. C. (1993). Changing addictive behaviors: A process perspective. *Current Directions in Psychological Science, 2,* 101-106.

DiClemente, C. C., & Hughes, S. O. (1990). Stages of change profiles in outpatient alcoholism treatment. *Journal of Substance Abuse, 2,* 217-235.

DiClemente, C. C., Prochaska, J. O., Fairhurst, S. K., Velicer, W. F., Velasquez, M. M., & Rossi, J. S. (1991). The process of smoking cessation: An analysis of precontemplation, contemplation and preparation stages of change. *Journal of Consulting and Clinical Psychology, 59,* 295-304.

DiClemente, C. C., Prochaska, J. O., & Gibertini, M. (1985). Self-efficacy and the stages of self-change of smoking. *Cognitive Therapy and Research, 9,* 181-200.

Fishbein, M., & Ajzen, I. (1975). *Belief, attitude, intention, and behavior: An introduction to theory and research.* Reading, MA: Addison-Wesley.

Fitts, W. H. (1965). *Tennessee Self-Concept Scale.* Nashville, TN: Counselor Recordings and Tests.

Glynn, S. M., & Ruderman, A. J. (1986). The development and validation of an Eating Self-Efficacy Scale. *Cognitive Therapy and Research, 10,* 403-420.

Horn, D. A. (1976). A model for the study of personal choice health behavior. *International Journal of Health Education, 19,* 89-98.

Horn, D. A., & Waingrow, S. (1966). Some dimensions of a model for smoking behavior change. *American Journal of Public Health, 56,* 21.

Jackson, D. (1967). *Personality research form.* Port Huron, MI: Research Psychologists Press.

Jackson, D. (1970). A sequential system for personality scale development. In C. D. Spielberger (Ed.), *Current topics in clinical and community psychology* (Vol. 2, pp. 61-96). New York: Academic Press.

Jackson, D. (1971). The dynamics of structured personality tests. *Psychological Review, 78,* 229-248.

Janis, I. L., & Mann, L. (1968). A conflict theory approach to attitude and decision making. In A. Greenwald, T. Brook, & T. Ostrom (Eds.), *Psychological foundations of attitudes* (pp. 327-360). New York: Academic Press.

Janis, I. L., & Mann, L. (1977). *Decision making: A psychological analysis of conflict, choice, and commitment.* New York: Free Press.

Jöreskog, K. G., & Sörbom, D. (1989). *LISREL 7: A guide to the program and applications* (2nd ed.). Chicago: SPSS, Inc.

Marcus, B. H., Rossi, J. S., Selby, V. C., Niaura, R. S., & Abrams, D. B. (1992). The stages and processes of exercise adoption and maintenance in a worksite sample. *Health Psychology, 11,* 386-395.

Marcus, B. H., Selby, V. C., Niaura, R. S., & Rossi, J. S. (1992). Self-efficacy and the stages of exercise behavior change. *Research Quarterly for Exercise and Sport, 63,* 60-66.

Marlatt, G. A., & Gordon, J. R. (Eds.). (1985). *Relapse prevention: Maintenance strategies in addictive behavior change.* New York: Guilford.

McConnaughy, E. A., DiClemente, C. C., Prochaska, J. O., & Velicer, W. F. (1989). Stages of change in psychotherapy: A follow-up report. *Psychotherapy, 26,* 494-503.

McConnaughy, E. A., Prochaska, J. O., & Velicer, W. F. (1983). Stages of change in psychotherapy: Measurement and sample profiles. *Psychotherapy: Theory, Research and Practice, 20,* 368-375.

Metropolitan Life Insurance Company. (1983). *Revised standards for overweight.* New York: Author.

Miller, W. R., & Rollnick, S. (1991). *Motivational interviewing: Preparing people to change addictive behavior.* New York: Guilford.

Norcross, J. C., Prochaska, J. O., & DiClemente, C. C. (1992, August). *Stages and processes of change: Two replications with weight control.* Paper presented at the 100th annual meeting of the American Psychological Association, Washington, DC.

Nunnally, J. C. (1978). *Psychometric theory.* New York: McGraw-Hill.

O'Connell, D., & Velicer, W. F. (1988). A decisional balance measure and the stages of change model for weight loss. *International Journal of the Addictions, 23,* 729-750.

Prochaska, J. O. (1979). *Systems of psychotherapy: A transtheoretical analysis.* Homewood, IL: Dorsey.

Prochaska, J. O. (1993). Working in harmony with how people change naturally. *Weight Control Digest, 3,* 249, 252-255.

Prochaska, J. O. (1994). Strong and weak principles for progressing from precontemplation to action based on twelve problem behaviors. *Health Psychology, 13,* 47-51.

Prochaska, J. O., & DiClemente, C. C. (1982). Transtheoretical therapy: Toward a more integrative model of change. *Psychotherapy: Theory, Research and Practice, 19,* 276-288.

Prochaska, J. O., & DiClemente, C. C. (1983). Stages and processes of self-change of smoking: Toward an integrative model of change. *Journal of Consulting and Clinical Psychology, 51,* 390-395.

Prochaska, J. O., & DiClemente, C. C. (1985). Common processes of self-change in smoking, weight control, and psychological distress. In S. Shiffman & T. A. Wills (Eds.), *Coping and substance use* (pp. 345-363). New York: Academic Press.

Prochaska, J. O., & DiClemente, C. C. (1986). Toward a comprehensive model of change. In W. R. Miller & N. Heather (Eds.), *Treating addictive behaviors* (pp. 3-27). New York: Plenum.

Prochaska, J. O., & DiClemente, C. C. (1992). Stages of change in the modification of problem behaviors. In M. Hersen, R. M. Eisler, & P. M. Miller (Eds.), *Progress in behavior modification* (pp. 184-214). Sycamore, IL: Sycamore.

Prochaska, J. O., DiClemente, C. C., & Norcross, J. C. (1992). In search of how people change: Applications to addictive behaviors. *American Psychologist, 47,* 1102-1114.

Prochaska, J. O., DiClemente, C. C., Velicer, W. F., Ginpil, S., & Norcross, J. C. (1985). Predicting change in smoking status for self-changers. *Addictive Behaviors, 10,* 395-406.

Prochaska, J. O., DiClemente, C. C., Velicer, W. F., & Rossi, J. S. (1992). Criticisms and concerns of the transtheoretical model in light of recent research. *British Journal of Addiction, 87,* 825-828.

Prochaska, J. O., Norcross, J. C., Fowler, J. L., Follick, M. J., & Abrams, D. B. (1992). Attendance and outcome in a work site weight control program: Processes and stages of change as process and predictor variables. *Addictive Behaviors, 17,* 35-45.

Prochaska, J. O., Rossi, J. S., & Wilcox, N. S. (1991). Change processes and psychotherapy outcome in integrative case research. *Journal of Psychotherapy Integration, 1,* 103-120.

Prochaska, J. O., Velicer, W. F., DiClemente, C. C., & Fava, J. (1988). Measuring processes of change: Applications to the cessation of smoking. *Journal of Consulting and Clinical Psychology, 56,* 520-528.

Prochaska, J. O., Velicer, W. F., Guadagnoli, E., Rossi, J. S., & DiClemente, C. C. (1991). Patterns of change: Dynamic typology applied to smoking cessation. *Multivariate Behavioral Research, 26,* 83-107.

Prochaska, J. O., Velicer, W. F., Rossi, J. S., Goldstein, M. G., Marcus, B. H., Rakowski, W., Fiore, C., Harlow, L., Redding, C. A., Rosenbloom, D., & Rossi, S. R. (1994). Stages of change and decisional balance for twelve problem behaviors. *Health Psychology, 13,* 39-46.

Rakowski, W., Dube, C. E., Marcus, B. H., Prochaska, J. O., Velicer, W. F., & Abrams, D. B. (1992). Assessing elements of women's decisions about mammography. *Health Psychology, 11,* 111-118.

Redding, C. A., & Rossi, J. S. (1993, March). *The processes of safer sex adoption.* Paper presented at the 14th annual convention of the Society of Behavioral Medicine, San Francisco.

Reed, G. R., Velicer, W. F., Rossi, J. S., & Marcus, B. H. (1993, August). *The URICA-E: A continuous measure of the stages of change for exercise.* Paper presented at the 101st annual convention of the American Psychological Association, Toronto, Ontario, Canada.

Revelle, W. (1979). Hierarchical cluster analysis and the internal structure of tests. *Multivariate Behavioral Research, 14,* 57-74.

Rossi, J. S. (1990, August). Radon and ultraviolet light exposure: Emerging cancer risk factors. In J. O. Prochaska (Chair), *The stages of change: Extensions to new areas of behavior change.* Symposium presented at the 98th annual conference of the American Psychological Association, Boston.

Rossi, J. S. (1992, August). *Common processes of change across nine problem behaviors.* Paper presented at the 100th annual convention of the American Psychological Association, Washington, DC.

Rossi, J. S. (in press). Why do people fail to maintain weight loss? In D. B. Allison & F. X. Pi-Sunyer (Eds.), *Obesity treatment: Establishing goals, improving outcomes, and reassessing the research agenda.* New York: Plenum.

Rossi, J. S., Redding, C. A., Snow, M. G., Fava, J., Rossi, S. R., Velicer, W. F., Prochaska, J. O., & DiClemente, C. C. (1989, August). *Smoking habit strength during maintenance: A termination stage for smoking cessation?* Paper presented at the 97th annual meeting of the American Psychological Association, New Orleans, LA.

Rossi, J. S., Rosenbloom, D., Monti, P. M., Rohsenow, D. J., Prochaska, J. O., & Martin, R. A. (1993, August). *Transtheoretical model of behavior change for cocaine use.* Paper accepted for presentation at the 101st annual convention of the American Psychological Association, Toronto, Ontario, Canada.

Rossi, S. R., Rossi, J. S., & Prochaska, J. O. (1991, August). *Processes of change for weight control: A follow-up study.* Paper presented at the 99th annual meeting of the American Psychological Association, San Francisco.

Rossi, S. R., Rossi, J. S., Prochaska, J. O., & Velicer, W. F. (1992). Application of the transtheoretical model of behavior change to dietary fat reduction. *International Journal of Psychology, 27*, 628.

Rossi, S. R., Rossi, J. S., Rossi-DelPrete, L. M., Prochaska, J. O., Banspach, S. W., & Carleton, R. A. (1994). A processes of change model for weight control for participants in a community-based weight loss program. *International Journal of the Addictions, 29*, 161-177.

Ruderman, A. (1982). The restraint scale: A psychometric investigation. *Behaviour Research and Therapy, 21*, 253-258.

Shaffer, H. J. (1992). The psychology of stage change: The transition from addiction to recovery. In J. H. Lowinson, P. Ruiz, R. B. Millman, & J. G. Langrod (Eds.), *Substance abuse: A comprehensive textbook* (2nd ed., pp. 100-105). Baltimore, MD: Williams & Wilkins.

Shiffman, S. (1982). Relapse following smoking cessation: A situational analysis. *Journal of Consulting and Clinical Psychology, 50*, 71-86.

Shiffman, S. (1986). A cluster-analytic classification of smoking relapse episodes. *Addictive Behaviors, 11*, 295-307.

Snow, M. G., Prochaska, J. O., & Rossi, J. S. (in press). Processes of change in Alcoholics Anonymous: Maintenance factors in long-term sobriety. *Journal of Studies on Alcohol.*

Straw, M. K., Straw, R. B., Mahoney, M. J., Rogers, T., Mahoney, B. K., Craighead, L. W., & Stunkard, A. J. (1984). The Master Questionnaire: Preliminary report on an obesity assessment device. *Addictive Behaviors, 9*, 1-10.

Tsoh, J. Y., Rossi, J. S., & Prochaska, J. O. (1992, August). *Effects of intention and behavior on contemplating smoking cessation.* Paper presented at the 100th annual convention of the American Psychological Association, Washington, DC.

Velicer, W. F., DiClemente, C. C., Prochaska, J. O., & Brandenburg, N. (1985). Decisional balance measure for assessing and predicting smoking status. *Journal of Personality and Social Psychology, 48*, 1279-1289.

Velicer, W. F., DiClemente, C. C., Rossi, J. S., & Prochaska, J. O. (1990). Relapse situations and self-efficacy: An integrative model. *Addictive Behaviors, 15*, 271-283.

Velicer, W. F., Hughes, S. L., Fava, J. L., & Prochaska, J. O. (1992). An empirical typology of subjects within stages of change [Abstract]. *International Journal of Psychology, 27*, 623.

Velicer, W. F., Prochaska, J. O., Rossi, J. S., & Snow, M. G. (1992). Assessing outcome in smoking cessation studies. *Psychological Bulletin, 111*, 23-41.

Velicer, W. F., & Stevenson, J. F. (1978). The relation between item format and the structure of the Eysenck Personality Inventory. *Applied Psychological Measurement, 2*, 293-304.

Appendix 11-A

Stages of Change Algorithm

1. In the past month, have you been actively trying to lose weight?   YES   NO

2. In the past month, have you been actively trying to keep from gaining weight?   YES   NO

3. Are you seriously considering trying to lose weight to reach your goal weight in the next 6 months?   YES   NO

4. Have you maintained your desired weight for more than 6 months?   YES   NO

Scoring:

Stage	Q1	Q2	Q3	Q4
Precontemplation	N	N	N	
Contemplation	N	N	Y	
Action	Y on Q1 or Q2			N
Maintenance	Y on Q1 or Q2			Y

Appendix 11-B

University of Rhode Island
Change Assessment Scale (URICA)

Each statement describes how a person might feel about controlling his or her weight. Please indicate the extent to which you tend to AGREE or DISAGREE with each statement. In each case, make your choice in terms of how you feel *right now*, not what you have felt in the past or would like to feel. There are FIVE possible responses to each of the questionnaire items. Please circle the number that best describes how much you agree or disagree with each statement.

1 = strongly disagree
2 = disagree
3 = undecided
4 = agree
5 = strongly agree

1. As far as I am concerned, I do not have any weight problems that need changing.

2. I think I might be ready for some self-improvements in my weight.

3. I am doing something about my weight that has been bothering me.

4. It might be worthwhile for me to work on my weight.

5. I am not the problem one. It doesn't makes much sense for me to be here.

6. It worries me that I might slip back on a weight problem I have already changed, so I am ready to work on my problem.

7. I am finally doing some work on my weight problem.

8. I have been thinking that I might want to change my weight.

9. I have been successful in working on my weight but I am not sure I can keep up the effort on my own.

10. At times my weight is a difficult problem, but I am working on it.

11. Working on my weight is pretty much a waste of time for me because it does not have anything to do with me.

12. I am working on my weight in order to better understand myself.

13. I guess I have weight difficulties, but there is nothing that I really need to change.

14. I am really working hard to change my weight.

15. I have a weight problem and I really think I should work on it.

16. I am not following through with the changes I have already made as well as I had hoped, and I am working to prevent a relapse of my weight problem.

17. Even though I am not always successful in changing, I am at least working on my weight.

18. I thought once I had resolved my weight problem, I would be free of it, but sometimes I still find myself struggling with it.

19. I wish I had more ideas on how to solve my weight problem.

20. I have started working on my weight but I would like some help.

21. Maybe someone will be able to help me with my weight.

22. I may need a boost right now to help me maintain the changes I have already made in my weight.

23. I may be a part of my weight problem, but I do not really think I am.

24. I hope that someone will have some good advice for me about weight control.

25. Anyone can talk about changing their weight; I am actually doing something about it.

26. All this talk about psychology is boring. Why can't people just forget about their weight?

27. I am working to prevent myself from having a relapse of my weight problem.

28. It is frustrating, but I feel I might be having a recurrence of the weight problem I thought I had resolved.

29. I have worries about my weight, but so does the next person. Why spend time thinking about it?

30. I am actively working on my weight problem.

31. I would rather cope with my weight than try to change it.

32. After all I have done to try to change my weight, every now and then it comes back to haunt me.

Scoring:

Precontemplation	= 1 + 5 + 11 + 13 + 23 + 26 + 29 + 31
Contemplation	= 2 + 4 + 8 + 12 + 15 + 19 + 21 + 24
Action	= 3 + 7 + 10 + 14 + 17 + 20 + 25 + 30
Maintenance	= 6 + 9 + 16 + 18 + 22 + 27 + 28 + 32

SOURCE: From "Stages of Change in Psychotherapy: A Follow-Up Report," by E. A. McConnaughy, C. C. DiClemente, J. O. Prochaska, and W. F. Velicer, 1989, *Psychotherapy, 26,* pp. 494-503. Copyright © 1989 by the American Psychological Association. Reprinted with permission.

Appendix 11-C

Dieting Readiness Test (DRT)

Answer the questions below to see how well your attitudes equip you for a weight-loss program. For each question, circle the answer that best describes your attitude. As you complete each of the six sections, add the numbers of your answers and compare them with the scoring guide at the end of each section.

Section 1: Goals and Attitudes

1. Compared to previous attempts, how motivated to lose weight are you this time?

1	2	3	4	5
Not at All Motivated	Slightly Motivated	Somewhat Motivated	Quite Motivated	Extremely Motivated

2. How certain are you that you will stay committed to a weight loss program for the time it will take to reach your goal?

1	2	3	4	5
Not at All Certain	Slightly Certain	Somewhat Certain	Quite Certain	Extremely Certain

3. Consider all outside factors at this time in your life (the stress you're feeling at work, your family obligations, etc.). To what extent can you tolerate the effort required to stick to a diet?

1	2	3	4	5
Cannot Tolerate	Can Tolerate Somewhat	Uncertain	Can Tolerate Well	Can Tolerate Easily

4. Think honestly about how much weight you hope to lose and how quickly you hope to lose it. Figuring a weight loss of 1 to 2 pounds per week, how realistic is your expectation?

1	2	3	4	5
Very Unrealistic	Somewhat Unrealistic	Moderately Unrealistic	Somewhat Realistic	Very Realistic

415

5. While dieting, do you fantasize about eating a lot of your favorite foods?

1	2	3	4	5
Always	Frequently	Occasionally	Rarely	Never

6. While dieting, do you feel deprived, angry, and/or upset?

1	2	3	4	5
Always	Frequently	Occasionally	Rarely	Never

Section 1—TOTAL Score _____

If you scored:

6 to 16:   This may not be a good time for you to start a weight loss program. Inadequate motivation and commitment together with unrealistic goals could block your progress. Think about those things that contribute to this, and consider changing them before undertaking a diet program.

17 to 23: You may be close to being ready to begin a program but should think about ways to boost your preparedness before you begin.

24 to 30: The path is clear with respect to goals and attitudes.

Section 2: Hunger and Eating Cues

7. When food comes up in conversation or in something you read, do you want to eat even if you are not hungry?

1	2	3	4	5
Never	Rarely	Occasionally	Frequently	Always

8. How often do you eat because of **physical hunger**?

1	2	3	4	5
Always	Frequently	Occasionally	Rarely	Never

9. Do you have trouble controlling your eating when your favorite foods are around the house?

1	2	3	4	5
Never	Rarely	Occasionally	Frequently	Always

Section 2—TOTAL Score _____

If you scored:

3 to 6:   You might occasionally eat more than you would like, but it does not appear to be a result of high responsiveness to environmental cues. Controlling the attitudes that make you eat may be especially helpful.

7 to 9:   You may have a moderate tendency to eat just because food is available. Dieting may be easier for you if you try to resist external cues and eat only when you are physically hungry.

10 to 15: Some or most of your eating may be in response to thinking about food or exposing yourself to temptations to eat. Think of ways to minimize your exposure to temptations, so that you eat only in response to physical hunger.

Section 3: Control Over Eating

If the following situations occurred while you were on a diet, would you be likely to eat **more** or **less** immediately afterward and for the rest of the day?

1	2	3	4	5
Would Eat Much Less	Would Eat Somewhat Less	Would Make No Difference	Would Eat Somewhat More	Would Eat Much More

10. Although you planned on skipping lunch, a friend talks you into going out for a midday meal.

11. You "break" your diet by eating a fattening, "forbidden" food.

12. You have been following your diet faithfully and decide to test yourself by eating something you consider a treat.

Section 3—TOTAL Score _____

If you scored:

3 to 7:   You recover rapidly from mistakes. However, if you frequently alternate between eating out of control and dieting very strictly, you may have a serious eating problem and should get professional help.

8 to 11:   You do not seem to let unplanned eating disrupt your program. This is a flexible, balanced approach.

12 to 15: You may be prone to overeat after an event breaks your control or throws you off track. Your reaction to these problem-causing eating events can be improved.

Section 4: Binge Eating and Purging

13. Aside from holiday feasts, have you ever eaten a large amount of food rapidly and felt afterward that this eating incident was excessive and out of control?

2	0
Yes	No

14.   If you answered yes to #13 above, how often have you engaged in this behavior during the last year?

1	2	3	4	5	6
Less Than Once a Month	About Once a Month	A Few Times a Month	About Once a Week	About Three Times a Week	Daily

15.   Have you ever purged (used laxatives or diuretics or induced vomiting) to control your weight?

5	0
Yes	No

16.   If you answered yes to #15 above, how often have you engaged in this behavior during the last year?

1	2	3	4	5	6
Less Than Once a Month	About Once a Month	A Few Times a Month	About Once a Week	About Three Times a Week	Daily

Section 4—TOTAL Score _____

If you scored:

0 to 1:   It appears that binge eating and purging is not a problem for you.

2 to 11:   Pay attention to these eating patterns. Should they arise more frequently, get professional help.

12 to 19:   You show signs of having a potentially serious eating problem. See a counselor experienced in evaluating eating disorders right away.

Section 5: Emotional Eating

17.   Do you eat more than you would like to when you have negative feelings such as anxiety, depression, anger, or loneliness?

1	2	3	4	5
Never	Rarely	Occasionally	Frequently	Always

18.   Do you have trouble controlling your eating when you have positive feelings— do you celebrate feeling good by eating?

1	2	3	4	5
Never	Rarely	Occasionally	Frequently	Always

19. When you have unpleasant interactions with others in your life, or after a diffi-
     cult day at work, do you eat more than you'd like?

1	2	3	4	5
Never	Rarely	Occasionally	Frequently	Always

Section 5—TOTAL Score _____

If you scored:

3 to 8:   You do not appear to let your emotions affect your eating.

9 to 11:   You sometimes eat in response to emotional highs and lows. Monitor this
            behavior to learn when and why it occurs and be prepared to find alter-
            nate activities.

12 to 15:   Emotional ups and downs can stimulate your eating. Try to deal with the
            feelings that trigger the eating and find other ways to express them.

Section 6: Exercise Patterns and Attitudes

20. How often do you exercise?

1	2	3	4	5
Never	Rarely	Occasionally	Somewhat	Frequently

21. How confident are you that you can exercise regularly?

1	2	3	4	5
Not at All Confident	Slightly Confident	Somewhat Confident	Highly Confident	Completely Confident

22. When you think about exercise, do you develop a positive or negative picture
     in your mind?

1	2	3	4	5
Completely Negative	Somewhat Negative	Neutral	Somewhat Positive	Completely Positive

23. How certain are you that you can work regular exercise into your daily
     schedule?

1	2	3	4	5
Not at All Certain	Slightly Certain	Somewhat Certain	Quite Certain	Extremely Certain

Section 6—TOTAL Score _____

If you scored:

4 to 10:   You're probably not exercising as regularly as you should. Determine whether your attitudes about exercise are blocking your way, then change what you must and put on those walking shoes.

11 to 16:   You need to feel more positive about exercise so you can do it more often. Think of ways to be more active that are fun and fit your lifestyle.

17 to 20:   It looks like the path is clear for you to be active. Now think of ways to get motivated.

After scoring yourself in each section of this questionnaire, you should be able to better judge your dieting strengths and weaknesses. Remember that the first step in changing eating behavior is to understand the conditions that influence your eating habits.

SOURCE: Reproduced with permission of American Health Publishing Company, Dallas, Texas. Brownell KD. The Dieting Readiness Test. *The Weight Control Digest,* 1990; 1:6-8. All rights reserved. For ordering information call 1-800-736-7323.

Appendix 11-D

Motivation Scale (MS)

	0	1
	True	False

1. I often wonder if I am not just kidding myself when I go on a new reducing plan.

2. There was a time when I think I could have stayed thin, but now it may be too late.

3. When I am dieting, I don't feel like I am making progress unless I feel hungry.

4. My enthusiasm for reducing has decreased a lot.

5. I would probably be disappointed if I didn't lose at least 10 pounds per month.

6. I often doubt whether I have what it takes to succeed at weight control.

7. I doubt that I would ever stick to an exercise program long enough for it to do me much good.

8. I have trouble focusing on the long range benefits of reducing.

9. My motivation is seldom very lasting.

10. I would classify myself as a weak-willed person.

11. If I couldn't lose more than a pound a week, I would probably give up.

12. If exercise were the only way to reduce, I would be in trouble.

Scoring:

MS $= 1 + 2 + 3 + 4 + 5 + 6 + 7 + 8 + 9 + 10 + 11 + 12$

SOURCE: Reprinted from *Addictive Behaviors*, Vol. 9, Straw, M. K., Straw, R. B., Mahoney, M. J., Rogers, T., Mahoney, B. K., Craighead, L. W., & Stunkard, A. J., "The Master Questionnaire: Preliminary Report on an Obesity Assessment Device," pp. 1-10, copyright © 1984, with kind permission from Elsevier Science Ltd., The Boulevard, Langford Lane, Kidlington OX5 1GB, UK.

Appendix 11-E

Processes of Change Questionnaire (PCQ)

The following experiences can affect the weight of some people. Think of any similar experiences you may have had in trying to lose weight or keep from gaining weight. Please rate how FREQUENTLY you used each of these during the past month. There are FIVE possible responses to each of the questionnaire items. Please circle the number that best describes your experience.

> 1 = Never
>
> 2 = Seldom
>
> 3 = Occasionally
>
> 4 = Often
>
> 5 = Repeatedly (always)

1. I read about people who have successfully lost weight.

2. Instead of eating I engage in some physical activity.

3. Warnings about the health hazards of being overweight move me emotionally.

4. I consider the belief that people who lose weight will help to improve the world.

5. I can be open with at least one special person about my experience with over-eating behavior.

6. I leave places where people are eating a lot.

7. I am rewarded by others when I lose weight.

8. I tell myself I can choose to overeat or not.

9. My dependency on food makes me feel disappointed in myself.

10. I am the object of discrimination because of my being overweight.

11. I remove things from my place of work that remind me of eating.

12. I take some type of medication to help me control my weight.

13. I think about information from articles or ads concerning the benefits of losing weight.

14. I find that doing other things with my hands is a good substitute for eating.

15. Dramatic portrayals of the problems of overweight people affect me emotionally.

16. I stop to think that overeating is taking more than my share of the world's food supply.

17. I have someone who listens when I need to talk about my losing weight.

18. I change personal relationships which contribute to my overeating.

19. I expect to be rewarded by others when I don't overeat.

20. I tell myself that I am able to lose weight if I want to.

21. I get upset when I think about my overeating.

22. I notice that overweight people have a hard time buying attractive clothes.

23. I keep things around my place of work that remind me not to eat.

24. I use diet aids to help me lose weight.

25. I think about information from articles and advertisements on how to lose weight.

26. When I am tempted to eat, I think about something else.

27. I react emotionally to warnings about gaining too much weight.

28. I consider the view that overeating can be harmful to the environment.

29. I have someone whom I can count on when I am having problems with over-eating.

30. I relate less often to people who contribute to my overeating.

31. I reward myself when I do not overeat.

32. I tell myself that if I try hard enough I can keep from overeating.

33. I reassess the fact that being content with myself includes changing my over-eating.

34. I find society more supportive of thin people.

35. I put things around my home that remind me not to overeat.

36. I take drugs to help me control my weight.

37. I recall information people have personally given me on how to lose weight.

38. I do something else instead of eating when I need to relax or deal with tension.

39. Remembering studies about illnesses caused by being overweight upsets me.

40. I consider the idea that overeating could be harmful to world food supplies.

41. I have someone who understands my problems with eating.

42. I ask people not to overeat in my presence.

43. Other people in my daily life try to make me feel good when I do not overeat.

44. I make commitments to lose weight.

45. I struggle to alter my view of myself as an overweight person.

46. I notice the world's poor are asserting their rights to a greater share of the food supplies.

47. I remove things from my home that remind me of eating.

48. I take diet pills to help me lose weight.

Scoring:

Consciousness Raising	= 1 + 13 + 25 + 37
Counterconditioning	= 2 + 14 + 26 + 38
Dramatic Relief	= 3 + 15 + 27 + 39
Environmental Reevaluation	= 4 + 16 + 28 + 40
Helping Relationships	= 5 + 17 + 29 + 41
Interpersonal Systems Control	= 6 + 18 + 30 + 42
Reinforcement Management	= 7 + 19 + 31 + 43
Self Liberation	= 8 + 20 + 32 + 44
Self Reevaluation	= 9 + 21 + 33 + 45
Social Liberation	= 10 + 22 + 34 + 46
Stimulus Control	= 11 + 23 + 35 + 47
Substance Use	= 12 + 24 + 36 + 48

SOURCE: From "A Processes of Change Model for Weight Control for Participants in a Community-Based Weight Loss Program," by S. R. Rossi, J. S. Rossi, L. M. Rossi-DelPrete, J. O. Prochaska, S. W. Banspach, and R. A. Carleton, 1994, *International Journal of the Addictions, 29,* 161-177. Copyright © 1994 by Marcel Dekker, Inc., NY. Reprinted by courtesy of Marcel Dekker, Inc.

Appendix 11-F

Decisional Balance Inventory

Each statement represents a thought that might occur to a person who is deciding whether or not to lose weight. Please indicate how IMPORTANT each of these statements might be to you if you were considering a decision to lose weight. There are FIVE possible responses to each of the items that reflect your answer to the question "How important would this be to you?" Please circle the number that best describes how important each statement would be to you if you were deciding whether or not to lose weight.

1 = not important at all

2 = slightly important

3 = moderately important

4 = very important

5 = extremely important

---

1. The exercises needed for me to lose weight would be a drudgery.

2. I would feel more optimistic if I lost weight.

3. I would be less productive in other areas if I was trying to lose weight.

4. I would feel sexier if I lost weight.

5. In order to lose weight I would be forced to eat less appetizing foods.

6. My self-respect would be greater if I lost weight.

7. My dieting could make meal planning more difficult for my family or housemates.

8. My family would be proud of me if I lost weight.

9. I would not be able to eat some of my favorite foods if I were trying to lose weight.

10. I would be less self-conscious if I lost weight.

425

11. Dieting would take the pleasure out of meals.

12. Others would have more respect for me if I lost weight.

13. I would have to cut down on some of my favorite activities if I try to lose weight.

14. I could wear more attractive clothing if I lost weight.

15. I would have to avoid some of my favorite places if I were trying to lose weight.

16. My health would improve if I lost weight.

17. Trying to lose weight could end up being expensive when everything is taken into account.

18. I would feel more energetic if I lost weight.

19. I would have to cut down on my favorite snacks while I was dieting.

20. I would be able to accomplish more if I carried fewer pounds.

Scoring:

Pros   = 2 + 4 + 6 + 8 + 10 + 12 + 14 + 16 + 18 + 20

Cons   = 1 + 3 + 5 + 7 + 9 + 11 + 13 + 15 + 17 + 19

SOURCE: From "A Decisional Balance Measure and the Stages of Change Model for Weight Loss," by D. O'Connell and W. F. Velicer, 1988, *International Journal of the Addictions, 23,* pp. 729-750. Copyright © 1988 by Marcel Dekker, Inc., NY. Reprinted by courtesy of Marcel Dekker, Inc.

Appendix 11-G

Weight Efficacy Life-Style Questionnaire (WEL)

This form describes some typical eating situations. Everyone has situations which make it very hard for them to keep their weight down. The following are a number of situations relating to eating patterns and attitudes. This form will help you to identify the eating situations which you find the hardest to manage.

Read each situation listed below and decide how confident (or certain) you are that you will be able to resist eating in each of the difficult situations. In other words, pretend that you are in the eating situation right now. On a scale from 0 (not confident) to 9 (very confident), choose ONE number that reflects how confident you feel now about being able to *successfully resist* the desire to eat. Write this number down next to each item.

Not confident at all that you can
resist the desire to eat

Very confident that you can
resist the desire to eat

| 0 | 1 | 2 | 3 | 4 | 5 | 6 | 7 | 8 | 9 |

EXAMPLES

I AM CONFIDENT THAT: CONFIDENCE NUMBER

1. I can control my eating on weekends.   8

2. I can say "no" to snacks.   6

I AM CONFIDENT THAT:

1. I can resist eating when I am anxious (nervous).   ____

2. I can control my eating on the weekends.   ____

3. I can resist eating even when I have to say "no" to others. ____

4. I can resist eating when I feel physically run down.   ____

5. I can resist eating when I am watching TV.   ____

6. I can resist eating when I am depressed (or down).   ____

7. I can resist eating when there are many different kinds
    of food available.   ____

8. I can resist eating even when I feel it is impolite to refuse a
    second helping.   ____

9. I can resist eating even when I have a headache.   ____

10. I can resist eating when I am reading.   ____

11. I can resist eating when I am angry (or irritable).   ____

12. I can resist eating even when I am at a party.   ____

13. I can resist eating even when others are pressuring me to eat. ____

14. I can resist eating when I am in pain.   ____

15. I can resist eating just before going to bed.   ____

16. I can resist eating when I have experienced failure.   ____

17. I can resist eating even when high-calorie foods are available. ____

18. I can resist eating even when I think others will be upset if I
    don't eat.   ____

19. I can resist eating when I feel uncomfortable.   ____

20. I can resist eating when I am happy.   ____

Scoring:

Negative Emotions	= 1 + 6 + 11 + 16
Availability	= 2 + 7 + 12 + 17
Social Pressure	= 3 + 8 + 13 + 18
Physical Discomfort	= 4 + 9 + 14 + 19
Positive Activities	= 5 + 10 + 15 + 20

SOURCE: From "Self-Efficacy in Weight Management," by M. M. Clark, D. B. Abrams, R. S. Niaura, C. A. Eaton, and J. S. Rossi, 1991, *Journal of Consulting and Clinical Psychology, 59,* pp. 739-744. Copyright © 1991 by the American Psychological Association. Reprinted with permission.

Appendix 11-H

Eating Self-Efficacy Scale (ESES)

For numbers 1-25 you should rate the likelihood that you would have difficulty controlling your overeating in each of the situations listed on the next pages, using this scale:

1	2	3	4	5	6	7
No difficulty controlling eating			Moderate difficulty controlling eating		Most difficulty controlling eating	

For example, if you thought you had great difficulty controlling your eating when you are at parties, you might complete an item specifying parties this way:

Overeating at parties   1   2   3   4   5   (6)   7

Please complete every item.

How difficult is it to control your . . .

1. Overeating after work or school
2. Overeating when you feel restless
3. Overeating around holiday time
4. Overeating when you feel upset
5. Overeating when tense
6. Overeating with friends
7. Overeating when preparing food
8. Overeating when irritable
9. Overeating as part of a social occasion with food—like at a restaurant or dinner party
10. Overeating with family members
11. Overeating when annoyed
12. Overeating when angry

13. Overeating when you are angry at yourself

14. Overeating when depressed

15. Overeating when you feel impatient

16. Overeating when you want to sit back and enjoy some food

17. Overeating after an argument

18. Overeating when you feel frustrated

19. Overeating when tempting food is in front of you

20. Overeating when you want to cheer up

21. Overeating when there is a lot of food available to you (refrigerator is full)

22. Overeating when you are overly sensitive

23. Overeating when nervous

24. Overeating when hungry

25. Overeating when anxious or worried

Scoring:

Socially Acceptable Circumstances   = 1 +   3 +   6 +   7 +   9 + 10 + 16
                                      + 19 + 21 + 24

Negative Affect   = 2 +   4 +   5 +   8 + 11 + 12 + 13
                                      + 14 + 15 + 16 + 17 + 18 + 20
                                      + 22 + 23 + 25

SOURCE: From "The Development and Validation of an Eating Self-Efficacy Scale," by S. M. Glynn and A. J. Ruderman, 1986, *Cognitive Therapy and Research, 10,* pp. 403-420. Copyright © 1986 by Plenum Publishing Corp. Reprinted with permission.

12

Assessment of Eating and Weight-Related Problems in Children and Special Populations

ROBERTA L. BABBITT

LYNN EDLEN-NEZIN

RAMASAMY MANIKAM

JANE A. SUMMERS

CLODAGH M. MURPHY

Recent eating disorders research has called into question the traditional focus on young, white, middle-class females. Eating disorders can and do occur across ages, races, cultures, and genders. In addition, mental, physical, and developmental disabilities can affect eating and feeding practices. Instrumentation has not kept pace with research.

It could be argued that current research among these special groups has placed the cart before the horse. Specifically, there have been relatively few psychometrically sound instruments developed for any of these unique populations. Additionally, studies have used assessment instruments and procedures lacking appropriate normative values. If valid research among these groups is to continue, it is imperative that (a) instruments be psychometrically evaluated in these groups, (b) group-specific normative data be generated for existing instruments, and (c) new instruments and/or techniques be developed as needed.

This chapter will review literature pertinent to issues of age, gender, race, culture, disability, and sexual orientation. The exclusive focus on these populations, and not on other possible diverse groups, merely reflects the limited amount of information and not a willful neglect of any excluded group. The limited number of available appropriate instruments for assessing disorders of eating and/or feeding will be described. Assessment methods for anthropometry, body composition, exercise, and activity will be discussed. In addition to providing specific information on the assessment of specific groups, we hope this chapter encourages researchers to consider the unique assessment issues involved in the measurement of special populations. Perhaps this chapter will even serve as an impetus for the development of stronger batteries of assessment instruments for these diverse populations.

Children and Individuals With Developmental Disabilities

The goal of this section is to outline and discuss some of the issues that may arise when assessing eating behavior and weight-related problems in children and special populations. Current theoretical approaches and instrumentation have been developed and validated primarily on a relatively homogeneous group of individuals—that is, college-age, white, middle-class females. As a consequence, their applicability to a large sector of the population is limited. Moreover, the impact of potentially important factors—such as the effects of physical impairment, cognitive limitation, and/or disease process—is often overlooked.

Assessment of eating and weight-related disorders has relied primarily on medical assessment, direct observation of behavior, semistructured interviews, and food recalls rather than on standardized self- or parent-report instruments. These issues will be discussed in greater detail in the following subsections, along with a review of assessment instruments (where available) and suggestions for future research.

Assessment Issues With Young Children

One of the major issues that arises when assessing eating and weight-related problems in young children (around 6 years of age and younger) is that they are often unable to provide reliable data regarding their food consumption (Saris, 1986) or to respond to questions that are presented within a questionnaire-type format. In these cases, the parent is the most important source of information about the child's food intake.

Individuals With Physical Impairments

Physical impairments may have deleterious effects on both nutrient uptake and energy expenditure, altering the balance that is necessary to maintain body weight within appropriate limits. On the one hand, impairments may affect the development and control of musculature that is involved in feeding, mastication, and digestion (Thommessen, Kase, Riis, & Heiberg, 1991). Impairment may arise from neurological insult (e.g., stroke, anoxia at birth), neuromuscular disorders (e.g., muscular dystrophy or multiple sclerosis), congenital anomalies (e.g., cleft palate, spina bifida), disease (e.g., arthritis), and so on. Other physical conditions may indirectly affect feeding, such as congenital heart failure, which is associated with poor growth, reduced appetite, and inadequate nutrient intake (Thommessen, Heiberg, & Kase, 1992), or spastic or athetoid movements in individuals with cerebral palsy, which give rise to increased energy requirements and undernutrition (Kalisz & Ekvall, 1984). Many of these factors are also responsible for reduced motility and lowered levels of activity (Chad, Jobling, & Frail, 1990), which in turn affect energy expenditure and caloric regulation. Overweight and obesity may be a common occurrence among individuals with physical impairments, further exacerbating their health-related concerns and contributing to problems with self-image (e.g., Mita et al., 1993). In some cases, reduced activity may be associated with inadequate nutrition and underweight as appetite is not stimulated sufficiently.

Assessment Issues

Modifications in procedures that are used to gather anthropometric data are often necessary when assessing individuals with physical disabilities or impairments. For instance, braces or prosthetic devices should be removed before weighing the individual, whereas the weight of casts must be estimated when calculating body weight. For individuals who are unable to stand, height and weight measurements may be made while they are in a reclining position (Cloud, 1987) or in a chair with an attached weight (Kalisz & Ekvall, 1984). Assessing body composition may be difficult in nonambulatory individuals in cases where body fat may be classified erroneously as muscle mass (Kalisz & Ekvall, 1984).

Individuals With Developmental Disabilities

Individuals with developmental disabilities present special challenges to the assessment and treatment of eating behavior and weight-related problems. Problems with overweight and obesity are sometimes reported to be more prevalent among individuals with mental retardation (Rimmer, Braddock, & Fujiura, 1993) and may help perpetuate negative attitudes toward them (McCarran & Andrasik, 1990). Physical and sensory impairments are often present and may influence the frequency, range, and rate of food consumption (Sisson & Van Hasselt, 1989) as well as contribute to reduced activity due to problems with mobility and ambulation (Suzuki et al., 1991).

Environmental variables have a strong impact on eating behavior. For instance, parents may inadvertently contribute to their children's eating problems. The parent may use food rewards to assuage their feelings of guilt or inadequacy toward the disabled child (Kalisz & Ekvall, 1984). The child's disability may result in lowered expectations for developing independent self-feeding and ambulation. Maladaptive behaviors such as aggression and tantrums may preclude imposing dietary restrictions and enforcing exercise regimens, both of which may contribute to overweight and obesity. Physical living arrangements also affect food intake and weight. For example, the incidence of obesity in the developmentally disabled population may be related in part to institutional diets, which are often high in fats, as well as to a reduced emphasis on physical activity that may occur in some institutional settings (Burkhart, Fox, & Rotatori, 1988). By contrast, food may be more accessible in the home, mealtime may be less structured, and parents may find it difficult to provide opportunities for regular exercise (Rimmer et al., 1993). In addition, eating and weight-related problems may be associated with the use of psychotropic medication. Some medications act to suppress or stimulate appetite, affecting food consumption (Sovner & Hurley, 1988), whereas other medications produce states of lethargy and drowsiness, which in turn result in lowered levels of activity, contributing to weight gain (Sovner & Hurley, 1986).

Assessment Issues

In addition to the modifications that are necessitated by the presence of a physical impairment, other factors must come into consideration when assessing eating behavior and weight-related problems in the developmentally

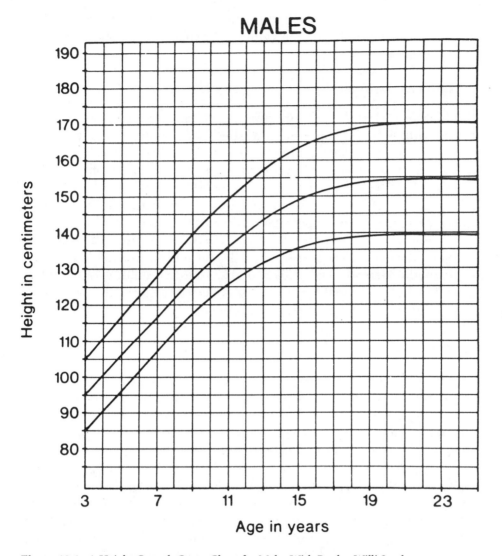

Figure 12.1. A Height Growth Curve Chart for Males With Prader-Willi Syndrome
SOURCE: From *Management of Prader-Willi Syndrome*, by L. R. Greenswag and R. C. Alexander (Eds.), 1988, p. 239, New York: Springer-Verlag. Copyright © 1988 by Springer-Verlag. Reprinted with permission.

disabled population. First, standard height-weight charts may not be appropriate in the assessment of body weight as certain conditions (e.g., Down syndrome) may be associated with reduced linear growth (Chumlea & Cronk, 1981; Cloud, 1987) and decreased metabolic rate (Chad et al., 1990). Growth charts have been prepared for specialized populations, such as Prader-Willi syndrome (Greenswag & Alexander, 1988), and should be used when interpreting anthropometric data (see Figure 12.1). Second, communication deficits and cognitive limitations often preclude using self-report measures of eating and activity levels. In these cases, direct observation, data reported by the parent or caregiver, and data gathered by mechanical means (e.g., actometer) should be used.

Assessment Instruments

Standardized instruments for assessing eating and weight-related issues that arise within the developmentally disabled population are rare (an exception is the Children's Eating Behavior Inventory, which will be presented later). By contrast, general approaches to assessment have been outlined. For instance, Ekvall (1993), Kalisz and Ekvall (1984), and Torisky, Torisky, Kaplan, and Speicher (1992) outline models for evaluating the nutritional status of persons with developmental disabilities (see Figure 12.2).

Data are gathered through clinical interviews, direct observation, and reviewing written records. Details are elicited regarding the individual's feeding history, food preferences and dislikes, and self-feeding skills. Anthropometric, biochemical, and dietary measures are collected to thoroughly assess eating behavior and formulate a treatment approach.

Genetic Disorders

Certain developmental disability syndromes are associated with obesity. Perhaps the most well-known example is Prader-Willi syndrome (PWS), which is associated with a deletion on the long arm of chromosome 15 (Ledbetter et al., 1981). PWS is characterized by hypotonia and feeding problems (poor suck, problems with swallowing, failure to thrive) in neonates and infants. This pattern gives way to increased appetite, hyperphagia, and obesity in early childhood (Holm et al., 1993), which remain significant concerns throughout the lives of these individuals (M. G. Butler, 1990; Greenswag, 1987). Exemplary approaches to the prevention and treatment of obesity in individuals with PWS are multidimensional and usually involve the following components: (a) modifying the physical environment, so as to strictly control caloric intake and reduce external cues that may trigger excessive eating (e.g., locking food away), (b) daily exercise, (c) using behavior modification approaches to decrease food stealing and scavenging, (d) education to promote the selection of healthy foods, and (e) social skills training to improve adaptation to the disability and enhance interactions with family and peers (e.g., Mullins & Vogl-Maier, 1987).

Medical Assessment

A medical team, usually including a pediatric gastroenterologist and developmental pediatrician, evaluates the child's health and growth status, using anthropometric measurements, such as weight, height, and weight-for-height percentiles. If caregivers report problems with feeding, or the child's growth indicates a problem with development, then the team tries to rule out and medically treat any physiological causes for the feeding and/or growth problem, such as gastroesophageal reflux, esophagitis, metabolic disorder, or food allergy. The medical evaluation may include a physical examination, an upper endoscopy, a barium swallow/videofluoroscopy, a PH probe, and metabolic or genetic screens (Babbitt, Hoch, Coe, Cataldo, et al., 1994).

The team also evaluates the necessity of enteral nutritional supplementation, via a gastrostomy tube, nasogastric tube, or other enteral access device (Monturo, 1990). Unfortunately, although such medical management is essential, it also carries with it great potential for disrupting or even preventing development of oral feeding as well as disrupting family routines and exacerbating family stressors (Babbitt, Hoch, & Coe, 1994; Vogel, 1986).

Nutritional Assessment

Krantzler and colleagues compiled a comprehensive annotated bibliography of food intake assessment methods (Krantzler et al., 1982). Food records, recalls, and nutritional interviews are diagnostic tools used to evaluate the dietary intake and nutritional status of the child during a specified time interval. These reports rely heavily on parents and school personnel as sources of information. The structure of food records and recalls vary by practitioner, but most evaluate the same variables. Food records require that an individual keep concurrent or nearly immediate data on the types and amounts of foods and beverages consumed, specific brands and preparation methods, time of meals, and other important variables such as setting and people present (see Wolper, Heshka, & Heymsfield, this volume, for more details). An example is presented in Figure 12.3.

Keeping an accurate food record requires skills many children do not possess—namely, reading, writing, and measurement skills, the ability to decipher food labels, compliance, and the motivation to keep the food record.

Food recalls are semistructured interviews that require the child to remember what and how much was eaten during a specific time period, usually 1 to 3 days. Accurately responding to a food recall requires abstract thinking and good memory skills.

Problems abound with these types of assessments (see Wolper et al., this volume, for more details). The day of recall can affect the results (Todd, Hudes, & Calloway, 1983). Children between the ages of 10 and 12 have been found to be more reliable respondents (Frank, Berenson, Schilling, & Moore, 1977) than adolescents, who are capable but less motivated than their younger peers (Frank, 1991). Observer variation increases the error in a

(text continued on p. 441)

NAME: _____   ADDRESS: _____
BIRTHDATE: _____   _____
AGE: _____ SEX: _____ RACE: _____   TELEPHONE: _____
BIRTH WEIGHT: _____   INFORMANT: _____
DATE SEEN: _____   EVAL. COORDINATOR: _____
_____   Interviewer: _____

BACKGROUND INFORMATION: Press. Nutr. Prob. _____

	Mother	Father	Siblings
Height:			
Weight:			
Age:			
Parents:			

Med. Diagnosis: _____
_____
IQ. _____ A.B. _____

ANTHROPOMETRIC MEASUREMENTS:

Ht. cm. _____ %ile _____   Upper Arm Segment cm. _____ MAMC cm. _____
Wt. kg. _____ %ile _____   Upper Arm Circum. cm. _____ Bone Ag/Den. _____
Wt/Ht. Index ___/___ %ile ___   Fatfold Tricep mm. _____ Blood Pressure _____
Avg. _____   Head Circumference cm. _____

CHEMISTRY:

Hb. _____ Serum Fe _____
Hct. _____ Other _____
Vit/Mineral Supp. (Doctor's orders Y/N)
(frequency/type) _____
Meds: _____
Nutrient/Drug Interaction Discussed:
Yes _____ No _____ NA _____
Caretaker knowledge demonstrated Y/N

INTERDISCIPLINARY FINDINGS:

Gross Motor: _____
Speech: _____

DENTAL CARE:

Daily Source of Fluoride? Y/N
Brushes teeth regularly? Y/N
Sees dentist regularly? Y/N
Caries-causing foods named _____

SOCIO-ECONOMIC:

Income: $ _____
Food: $ _____ Weekly/Monthly
No. of family members: _____
Using Food Stamp Program or Supplemental
Food Program Yes _____ No _____ NA _____

PRENATAL DIETARY CARE:

MEDICAL:

Hx. of hospitalizations _____
_____
Hx. Infections: _____
_____
_____

NEONATAL FEEDING HISTORY:

Period Breast Fed _____
Period Formula Fed _____
Type Tolerated _____
Feeding Problems: Sucking, Swallowing,
Colic, Vomiting, Diarrhea,
Constipation, Weight Gain Abnormal

ORDER OF INFANT FOOD ADDED:

	Age	Amts	How Taken

(Solid food should not be given before four months of age)

### SUPPLEMENTS:	### AGE BEGAN:	### TIME CONTINUED:

AGE: Weaned from bottle _____ Liquid from cup _____   Unassisted _____
Age: Finger Fed _____ Used Spoon _____   Unassisted _____
Bottle night feeding (other than water) Yes _____ No _____

Figure 12.2. A Nutrition Assessment Record for Individuals With Developmental Disabilities

SOURCE: From *Pediatric Nutrition in Chronic Diseases and Developmental Disorders*, by S. Ekvall Wahlberg (Ed.), 1993, New York: Oxford University Press p. 453. Copyright © 1993 by Oxford University Press. Used with permission.

PRESENT FEEDING ABILITIES:

Table Foods _____ Chopped Foods _____ Jr. Foods _____ Strained _____
Normal Feeding Period: _____ Behavioral Problems _____ Reward System _____
(Circle): Choking, Swallowing, Chewing, Tongue Thrust, Constipation, Anorexia, Pica,
(Clay, Starch, Plaster, Ashes, Bugs, Crayons) — How much? _____

DIETARY EVALUATION

Name: _____

FOOD INTAKE (24 Hr. Recall)*

Patterns:		Breakfast	Amt.
Time	Fruit	_____	_____
	Meat	_____	_____
_____	Egg	_____	_____
Where	Bread	_____	_____
_____	Fat	_____	_____
With Whom	Cereal	_____	_____
	Beverage	_____	_____
Who Pre-pared	Other	_____	_____

		Lunch	
Time	Meat	_____	_____
_____	Veg.	_____	_____
Where	Bread	_____	_____
_____	Fruit	_____	_____
With Whom	Beverage	_____	_____
	Other	_____	_____
Who Pre-pared			

		Dinner	
Time	Soup	_____	
_____	Meat or subst.	_____	_____
Where	Potato		
_____	Vegetable: Cooked	_____	_____
With Whom	Raw	_____	_____
Who Pre-pared	Salad	_____	_____
_____	Bread	_____	_____
	Fat	_____	_____
	Desert	_____	_____
	Beverage	_____	_____
	Other	_____	_____

Time:		Between Meals	
_____	_____	_____	
_____	_____	_____	
_____	_____	_____	
_____	_____	_____	
_____	_____	_____	
_____	_____	_____	

FOOD SUMMARY

GROUP	Amt. per day	Amt. per week	Possible points or daily serv.	**Actual Points
Dairy Products:			3	
Milk	_____	_____	_____	_____
Cheese	_____	_____	_____	_____
Cottage Cheese	_____	_____	_____	_____
Yogurt	_____	_____	_____	_____
Other	_____	_____	_____	_____
Meat or Alternatives: ***Fat & Chol.			2	
***Meat, Eggs Fish, Poultry	_____	_____	_____	_____
Dr. Beans/ peas	_____	_____	_____	_____
Peanut Butter	_____	_____	_____	_____
Vegetables: (No Vit. A/C-1/2 cr)			3	
Vit A Veg.	_____	_____	_____	_____
Vit C Veg.	_____	_____	_____	_____
Other	_____	_____	_____	_____
Fruits:			2	
Vit C Fruit	_____	_____	_____	_____
Other Fruits	_____	_____	_____	_____
Whole Grains/Starches: (No w/grains-1/2 cr)			6	
Cereal	_____	_____	_____	_____
Bread	_____	_____	_____	_____
Pasta, Rice	_____	_____	_____	_____
Other	_____	_____	_____	_____
TOTAL			16	_____
Others:				
Candy/Sugar	_____	_____	If daily-1	_____
Chips/t. salt	_____	_____	If daily-1	_____
Soft Drinks	_____	_____	If daily-1	_____
Desserts	_____	_____	If daily-1	_____
Water	_____	_____	None daily-1	_____
***Fats & Chol.	_____	_____	3 ser. d.-1	_____
Fiber	_____	_____	None daily-1	_____
TOTAL				_____

Frequency/wk. of eating outside the home: _____
Food allergies: _____
Foods regularly omitted: _____
_____ Why: _____
Favorite Foods: _____
Impression of diet: _____
Validity of record: _____
Activity Score: _____

Are you using iodized salt? _____ Cooking: _____ Table: _____ Using vitamin D fortified mix? Yes/No
Caretaker knowledge/fiber & fluid Yes/No   Can plan Basic 4 diet Yes/No

---

*If dietary recall, anthropometric measures, or clinical assessment abnormal, obtain 3 day food intake record and 3 day physical activity record for evaluation.

**When the number of servings eaten exceeds the number possible, those servings are not counted. Score below 10 requires follow-up visit, score 10–12 is borderline nutritionally.

***Group with possible high fat and cholesterol is shown.

Expanded Food Diary (Sample)

Meal	Food and Amount	Time	Feelings	Activity	Calories
Breakfast					
	Coffee, 6 oz	7:30	Tired	Reading paper	0
	Poached Egg, 1 med				79
	Bagel, 1/2 med				92
	Orange Juice, 1 cup				111
	Total Calories from This Meal				282
Lunch					
	Roast Beef Sandwich, 2 oz, with 2T mayonnaise	12:30	Hurried	Working at desk	442
	Water, 1 glass				0
	Raspberry Yogurt, 8 oz				90
	Total Calories from This Meal				532
Dinner					
	Chicken Breast - Grilled, 3.5 oz	7:30	Relaxed	Watching TV	193
	Green Beans, 1cup				44
	Carrots, 1 cup cooked				70
	Wheat Bread, 1 slice, dry				61
	Skim Milk, 1 cup				86
	Total Calories from This Meal				454
Snacks					
	Celery, 4 stalks	10:00	Tense	Working at desk	24
	Apple, 1 medium	3:00	Frustrated	On break	81
	Total Calories from Snacks				105
	Total Calories for the Day				1373

Today's Date_____, 19___.

Figure 12.3. A Sample Expanded Food Diary

SOURCE: From *The LEARN program for weight control* (p. 34) by K. D. Brownell, 1994, Dallas: American Health Publishing Company. Copyright © 1994 by American Health Publishing Company. Reprinted with permission. All rights reserved. For ordering information call 1-800-736-7323.

child's record or recall. These biases can be minimized through the use of criterion-based training (Frank, Hollatz, & Webber, 1984) and standardization of these approaches (Stone, Perry, & Luepker, 1989). Ethnicity and sex have also been reported to influence accuracy (Baranowski et al., 1986; Frank et al., 1977).

Reliability

One investigation did not find any significant differences between multiple recalls for 10-year-old children (Frank, 1985).

Validity

Validity of the food record and recall is typically tested by comparing results with direct observation and/or biochemical measures (Frank, 1991). Estimates of validity have varied widely, but one study reported an 83% agreement between a child's daily self-report and an adult's 12-hour observation (Baranowski et al., 1986; Carter, Sharbaug, & Stapell, 1981). Some investigators measure validity indirectly by comparing two different methods of dietary monitoring, such as a food record and a recall. Studies using adult respondents typically report poor agreement among methods (Karvetti & Knuts, 1981), whereas the agreement has been higher between child self-report and parental written records (Eck, Klesges, & Hanson, 1989; Van Horn et al., 1990).

Direct Observation

One of the most comprehensive ways to assess a child's eating, as well as the parent-child interaction surrounding this activity, is through observational assessment. Direct observation resolves the problem of poor correlation between self-report and actual eating behavior. In addition, direct observations, unlike most self-report measures, are sometimes able to document the environmental variables and interaction patterns that influence a child's eating behavior (Klesges, Klesges, & Coates, 1988).

Behavioral Eating Test

The Behavioral Eating Test is an assessment tool that measures food and beverage consumption (Jeffrey et al., 1980). See Hersen and Bellack (1988, pp. 64-66) for a detailed description of the procedure, psychometric properties, and clinical uses.

Bob and Tom's Method of Assessing Nutrition (BATMAN)

The BATMAN uses time-sampling data collection to measure a child's behavior during mealtime as well as environmental and social variables that may influence the child's behavior. A description of this measurement system may be found in Hersen and Bellack (1988, pp. 317-318) and in Table 12.1.

The Kennedy Krieger Institute Behavioral Feeding Assessment Procedure

The Department of Behavioral Psychology at the Kennedy Krieger Institute/Johns Hopkins Medical Institutions houses a specialized pediatric inpatient and outpatient program for the assessment and treatment of pediatric feeding disorders. The assessment process entails consideration of the child's feeding history as well as direct observation of the child and caregiver under a variety of conditions. Multidisciplinary evaluation includes assessment of the child's medical status, behavioral skills, and caregiver's management skills (Babbitt, Hoch, & Coe, 1994). Behavioral assessment begins with a semistructured interview in which caregivers detail the child's behavioral and medical history. The goal of the interview is to provide basic information to guide subsequent direct observation and data collection. Information is assembled on the natural course of the feeding problems, their current status, previous and current strategies that may or may not have helped the child, food types and textures that have been and are now consumed or rejected regularly, meal duration, amounts of food consumed, family routines and home structure, and caregivers' reports of environment-behavior relations surrounding eating (Babbitt & Hoch, 1992; Luiselli, 1989).

Repeated, objective measures of the targeted eating behaviors are necessary to determine stability and trend, as any one observation could potentially yield aberrant data (Iwata, Riordan, Wohl, & Finney, 1982; Palmer & Horn, 1978). Initially, target behaviors are operationally defined in terms of their quantifiable physical characteristics, such as topography, frequency, duration, latency, and intensity.

Once target behaviors have been defined, direct observations can be made under a series of pretreatment baseline conditions. Under the home conditions, the caregiver is given general instructions to feed as she or he would at home. The standard baseline assessment is individually adapted for each child, dependent primarily on whether the child feeds him- or herself

TABLE 12.1 Bob and Tom's Method of Assessing Nutrition (BATMAN) Response Categories

After every 10-second observation period, the following are always coded:

Child's environment	Child's behavior
1) Bedroom	1) Bites, sucks, places food in mouth
2) Living Room	2) Playing with food, utensils, or nonfood items
3) Kitchen	3) Crying
4) Bathroom	4) Talking/Babbling/Whining
5) Dining Room	5) Away from table
6) Activity Room/Basement	6) Engaged in other activity
	7) Food requests
	8) Refusing food
	9) Spitting up

If during a 10-second observation someone encourages or discourages child activity, the following are coded:

Who interacted	Child behavior that is being encouraged/discouraged
1) Mother	1) Physical encouragement
2) Father	2) Physical discouragement
3) Sister	3) Verbal encouragement
4) Brother	4) Verbal discouragement
5) Grandmother	5) Presents food
6) Grandfather	6) Offers food
7) Other relative	7) Modeling eating
8) Babysitter/Caretaker	
	1) Bites, sucks, places food in mouth
	2) Playing with food, utensils, or nonfood items
	3) Crying
	4) Talking/Babbling/Whining
	5) Away from table
	6) Engage in other activity
	7) Food requests
	8) Refusing food
	9) Spitting up

Child's response to interaction

1) Bites, sucks, places food in mouth
2) Playing with food, utensils, or nonfood items
3) Crying
4) Talking/Babbling/Whining
5) Away from table
6) Engage in other activity
7) Food requests
8) Refusing food
9) Spitting up

(Continued)

TABLE 12.1 (Continued)

Operational Definitions of BATMAN Categories

PARENT BEHAVIOR

1. *Physical encouragement*
   Pats, hugs, kisses, pushes, or moves, directs physically, holds and points, models

2. *Physical discouragement*
   Hits, restrains from action, removes child or object, redirects or moves in another direction, pushes, spanks

3. *Verbal encouragement*
   Suggests, commands, directs, makes positive statements about

4. *Verbal discouragement*
   Forbids, scolds, refuses, makes negative statements about, yells

5. *Presents food*
   Feeds, places food in child's direction without physically encouraging food intake

6. *Offers food*
   A verbal food offer; e.g., "Do you want more food?" This differs from verbal encouragements in that a desired behavior is not explicit (e.g., "Eat more food.")

7. *Modeling eating*
   Parent demonstrates desired eating behavior and tells child to eat like himself or herself

CHILD BEHAVIOR

1. *Bites, sucks, or places food in mouth*
   Child sucks milk from bottle or breast, bites or chews on object, places food in mouth or solid food is placed in mouth by parent

2. *Playing with food, utensils, or nonfood items*
   Child messes, stirs, throws, crumbles, or otherwise treats food as a toy; child plays with toy, utensil, person, clothes, or parts of body

3. *Crying*
   Audible crying; not scored when cry is for a specific food object

4. *Talking, babbling, whining*
   Child babbles, talks or whines to self, sibling, parent, or other; not scored if vocalizations are for food

5. *Away from table*
   Child gets up from table or is taken away from table by parent, sibling, or other person

6. *Engaged in other activity*
   Child is at table, but is sitting quietly, staring, and not otherwise engaged in any behavior rated as 1 to 9

7. *Food requests*
   Child points to food so as to request it, asks for food, begins to whine or cry for food

8. *Refusing food*
   Child closes mouth, turns head away, pushes food away when presented by parent, sibling, or other person

9. *Spitting up*
   Child spits up or vomits

SOURCE: From "Parent Influences on Children's Eating Behavior and Relative Weight," by R. C. Klesges, T. J. Coates, G. Brown, J. Sturgeon-Tillisch, L. M. Moldenhauer-Klesges, B. Holzer, J. Woolfrey, and J. Vollmer, 1983, *Journal of Applied Behavior Analysis, 16,* pp. 373-374. Copyright © 1983 by *Journal of Applied Behavior Analysis.* Reprinted with permission.

(self-feeder) or is fed by a caregiver (non-self-feeder). For a non-self-feeding child, a bite of food or drink is presented approximately once every 30 seconds, simultaneous with an instruction to take a bite. There are no differential consequences for any behavior. Each meal consists of 50 bites, rotating through all food groups and drinks present. For a self-feeding child, a premeasured, age-appropriate-portion sized meal is served to the child, with a verbal prompt about every 30 seconds to take a bite or drink. Once again, no differential consequences follow any behavior. A baseline meal is terminated either after the child consumes the whole meal or after 20 minutes have elapsed (Babbitt, Hoch, Coe, Cataldo, et al., 1994). Detailed information on the target behaviors used in these baseline assessments can be found elsewhere (Babbitt, Hoch, & Coe, 1994).

Data are collected on percentage of bites accepted (non-self-feeders) or frequency counts of bites/drinks per minute by food type (self-feeders) as these are relatively discrete events with clear onset and offset points. Data for inappropriate behaviors, such as negative vocalizations, are recorded using interval data collection (Kazdin, 1982) because their onset and offset are less clear. The observer only records whether or not a behavior occurred during each interval. Finally, pre- and postmeal weights (in grams) of foods and liquids, as well as spillage on napkins and bibs, are calculated for calorie counts.

Concurrent with baseline assessment, a functional analysis (Babbitt, Hoch, Coe, Cataldo, et al., 1994) of the interaction between caregiver's feeding and a child's eating behaviors provides information on interpersonal variables that may contribute to the feeding problems. Specifically, data are collected on the caregiver's correct use of antecedent stimuli (e.g., verbal instructions to eat), prompts (e.g., following a verbal spoken-gestural-physical prompt sequence), and consequences (e.g., providing positive reinforcement for consuming food).

Behavioral assessment of a child's feeding problem is conducted from a functional perspective. Once these problems are operationally defined, in terms of their functions, then particular treatment strategies can be chosen to address those functions (Babbitt, Hoch, & Coe, 1994).

Currently, little to no data exist on normative eating patterns and feeding practices. Future research should delineate these norms and provide standardized treatment objectives and goals.

Assessment Instruments

Several assessment instruments have been developed for use with the pediatric population, which will now be reviewed.

Children's Eating Behavior Inventory (CEBI)

Description of measure. The Children's Eating Behavior Inventory (CEBI; Archer, 1991; Archer, Rosenbaum, & Streiner, 1991) was designed to assess eating and mealtime behavior. The 40-item questionnaire contains yes/no questions and a 5-point, Likert-type rating scale and is divided into two areas: child and parent domains. In the former case, 28 items are used to gather information about the child's food preferences and dislikes, self-feeding-skills, and compliance during mealtimes. In the latter case, the parents' interactions with family members are surveyed, along with their perceived stresses about mealtime events. The measure yields two scores—(a) a total eating problem score and (b) the total number of items perceived to be a problem—by adding together all the "yes" responses (Archer et al., 1991).

Norms. The standardization sample is composed of two groups. The clinical group, children ranging in age from 2 to 12 years, was referred for assessment/treatment of eating problems or had developmental or medical disorders that placed them at risk for eating problems (e.g., autistic, developmentally and/or physically disabled). The nonclinical group was made up of normally developing children whose mothers were recruited from physicians' offices.

Reliability: Internal consistency. With only one exception, alpha coefficients exceeded .70.

Test-retest reliability. The authors report correlation coefficients of .87 for the total eating problem score and .84 for the percentage of items that were perceived to be a problem when reliability was assessed during retesting 4-6 weeks later.

Construct validity. Total eating problem scores are significantly higher in a clinical sample than a nonclinical sample.

Readability. The items are easy to read, with clear instructions for completing the questionnaire.

Practicality. The questionnaire can be reproduced from the Archer and associates (1991) article. The authors report that the CEBI can be completed in about 15 minutes.

Comments. This is one of the few questionnaires that was designed in part to be used to assess eating behaviors in children with developmental and physical disabilities. Moreover, specific problems can be identified by inspecting specific items. The authors point out possible selection bias when recruiting mothers, and it is important to bear in mind that fathers or other caregivers did not respond to the questionnaire. A revised, briefer version of the CEBI, currently under development, is reproduced in Appendix 12-A.

Children's Eating Attitude Test (ChEAT)

Description of measure. The Children's Eating Attitude Test (ChEAT; Maloney, McGuire, & Daniels, 1988; see Appendix 12-B) was designed to assess children's attitudes toward their eating and dieting behavior. The authors modified the Eating Attitudes Test (Garner, Olmsted, Bohr, & Garfinkel, 1982), which was developed and tested on adolescents and adults. The ChEAT is a 26-item questionnaire that contains a 6-point, Likert-type rating scale on which respondents are required to mark their response to questions about perceived body image, obsessions/preoccupations with food, and dieting practices.

Norms. The standardization sample comprises 318 elementary school-aged children (range from 8 to 13 years; $M = 9.7$ years) from middle to upper socioeconomic backgrounds. The group of children was predominantly white (92%), with males and females being represented approximately equally.

Internal reliability. The authors report alpha coefficients of .76 for the total population, and .68-.80 when the population is stratified by grade level.

Test-retest reliability. The 3-week test-retest correlation coefficient was .81.

Validity. No validity data are reported by the authors.

Readability. The authors modified the wording of items on the EAT-26 to make them more easily understood by children in the third or fourth grade. Directions for completing the questionnaire were presented orally to all children, and actual items were read to the younger children (third grade).

Practicality. The questionnaire is appended in the Maloney et al. (1988) article. The time for completion (with directions) is about 30 minutes.

Comments. A strength of this assessment measure is that it can be presented orally, which may make it appropriate for use with children with reading problems. The findings may not be applicable to children from diverse ethnic backgrounds or cultures, however, because the measure was tested on predominantly white, middle- to upper-class children.

Behaviors of Eating and Activity for Children's Health Evaluation System (BEACHES)

Description of measure. The Behaviors of Eating and Activity for Children's Health Evaluation (BEACHES; McKenzie et al., 1991; see Appendix 12-C) is a coding system that was developed to quantify direct observations of children's eating behavior and physical activity. Data are coded simultaneously on 10 different dimensions, including aspects of the physical environment (location, persons present, availability of food items), the child's level of activity (e.g., reclining, standing, walking) and eating behavior (whether food is consumed), and the verbal and physical prompts and consequences that influence the child's consumption of food or activity level.

Norms. The coding system was tested on 42 children, aged 4 to 8 years, from diverse socioeconomic backgrounds. Observations were made once a week at the child's home and school, over an 8-week period.

Reliability. For interobserver agreement, the authors report median kappa coefficients from .71 to 1.0 for the different coding dimensions (with the exception of two categories that occurred infrequently during observations).

Internal validity. This was assessed by correlating several BEACHES variables with external variables (e.g., prompts for physical activity and caloric expenditure at home). Significant correlations were obtained for several pairs of variables.

Practicality. The complete coding definitions can be obtained from the authors of the BEACHES; however, a brief description of the coding dimensions is presented in McKenzie et al. (1991). Extensive training was necessary (up to 40 hours) before observers' ratings were considered reliable, which can make the system very expensive to use. One way to overcome this may be to reduce the number of categories that are used in future studies.

Comments. The coding system was tested on young children (ages 4 to 8 years) of Anglo and Hispanic origin. Future research should include children from diverse cultural and ethnic backgrounds as well as special populations (e.g., with physical and developmental disability).

Body Composition

Interest in and investigations dealing with body composition of the general population have a long history. However, body composition assessment data on children and special populations are more limited. Yet, the limited work that has been conducted with special populations has suggested that the body composition of children with special problems may indeed be different than that of the normal population (Berg & Isaksson, 1970; Berg & Olsson, 1970; Eddy, Nicholson, & Wheeler, 1965; Grogan, Ekvall, & Bozian, 1977). These results point to the need for instrument validation for children and special populations. The three major components of the body that are of interest include fat, lean body mass (LBM), and water. A variety of procedures have been developed to accurately measure these components for the purpose of assessing the total proportion of each of these components. The procedures vary in technique, methodology, and accuracy. This section reviews the methods of assessing body composition in children, including exceptional populations, with the limitations and assumptions of the methods presented.

Anthropometric Assessment

Anthropometric measurements include height and weight; diameters of the iliac crest, greater trochanter/acromioclavicular joints; circumference; and skinfold thickness (Bray, 1989). The height/weight chart is discussed only because it is so popularly used due to its convenience and simplicity; however, it is limited in its specificity and validity to detail the components of the body. The diameter and circumference measures are not very useful because they do not separate the various components of the makeup of the body.

National Health and Nutrition Examination Survey Growth Chart

Description of measure. With the National Health and Nutrition Examination Survey (Hamill et al., 1979), 20,320 individuals between 6 months and 74 years of age were examined. Among other variables, weight, height, and skinfold measures were taken. The chart in Figure 12.4 presents percentile of body weight and other variables. Body measurements between the 25th and 75th percentiles are said to represent "normal growth." Body measurements falling 15 percentage points above this range are considered to fall in the obese range. Individuals below the 25th percentile for height and weight ratio are classified as poor growth. Further, individuals below the 5th percentile are classified with Failure to Thrive (FTT).

Norms. The growth chart was developed based on a large number of individuals over a wide range of age and ethnic groups. Thus it is fairly representative of the population in general.

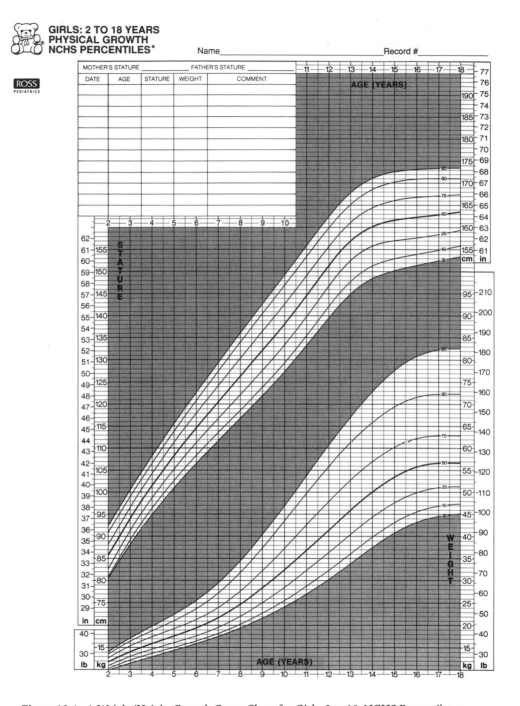

Figure 12.4. A Weight/Height Growth Curve Chart for Girls, 2 to 18, NCHS Percentiles

SOURCE: Based on "Physical Growth: National Center for Health Statistics Percentiles," by P. V. V. Hamill, T. A. Drizd, C. L. Johnson, R. B. Reed, A. F. Roche, and W. M. Moore, 1979, *American Journal of Clinical Nutrition, 32,* pp. 607-629. Data from the National Center for Health Statistics (NCHS), Hyattsville, MD. Copyright © 1979 by *American Journal of Clinical Nutrition,* American Society for Clinical Nutrition [article] and © 1982 by Ross Products Division, Abbott Laboratories [chart]. Reprinted with permission of Ross Products Division, Abbott Laboratories, Columbus, OH 43216.

Reliability. No reliability data are provided. It is easy to chart and plot the data, thus growth chart data should be highly reliable.

Validity. Although the growth chart can be reliable, its validity is somewhat questionable. The measure does not predict obesity per se. It does not show the proportion of body composition that accounts for lean mass, water, bone density, and adipose tissue. As such, incorrect conclusions may be derived without additional assessment.

Practicality. The charts can be prepared quickly, and interpretation is direct and simple, thus they are very practical for the purpose of getting a general understanding of the child's growth and developmental status in relation to age and gender-related peers. This technique is sometimes not suitable for children with physical and/or developmental disabilities (e.g., Down syndrome, cerebral palsy) because the population used in developing the normative data did not include exceptional children. Special individualized growth charts have been developed for a few of these populations (e.g., Down syndrome, Prader-Willi syndrome) (Rimmer, Kelly, & Rosentswieg, 1987).

Hydrostatic Weighing

Hydrostatic weighing (Goldman & Buskirk, 1961), also called "underwater weighing," is a technique of measuring whole-body density by the determination of whole-body volume (see Heymsfield, Allison, Heshka, & Pierson, this volume for details). Children may have a difficult time submerging under water, exhaling, and keeping movement to a minimum for the scale to settle for a correct reading to be made. Research evidenced that even adult subjects had to be trained before they could perform the maneuvers properly (Manikam, 1985). This procedure would be very impractical with physically disabled, developmentally delayed, and mentally handicapped children and adolescents without intensive behavioral preparation (Slifer, Cataldo, Babbitt, & Cataldo, 1993).

Skinfold Measurement

Measurements of the skinfold thickness of various sites of the human body have been used to measure human body composition. Skinfold calipers, which are valid if calibrated, are used for this purpose. One study (Manikam, 1985) found that comparison of various skinfold calipers (Lange, Fat-O-Meter, Slim Guide, Ross Adipometer) yielded comparable results, and the differences were not statistically significant. However, it is important to note that calipers have widely varying jaws, thus calipers that have small openings would not be practical for subjects who have very thick skinfolds (for further details, see Heymsfield et al., this volume).

Numerous predictive equations for the estimation of body density, and thus body fatness, from skinfold measurements are available. The equations range from using one skinfold site to as many as seven sites. The equations used are specific to the population (age, gender, and classification) from which the equation was derived. However, most of the equations were developed using normal adult subjects. Thus the technique is lacking validation for exceptional and pediatric populations.

Reliability. Reliability of skinfold measures with special populations (Prader-Willi syndrome, hypotonia, Down syndrome, and other metabolic and hormonal dysfunctions) is suspect. Shepherd, Roberts, Golding, Thomas, and Shepherd (1991) reported that the use of standard anthropometric measurement techniques for individuals with spina bifida was unreliable because of their lower-limb and trunk hypoplasia and paralytic musculoskeletal deformities. There is a paucity of data for these special populations (Hammer, Kraemer, Wilson, Ritter, & Dornbusch, 1991). Further research is warranted with these populations to provide greater details on the properties of their skinfold makeup, deposition, and consistency.

Validity. Because anthropometric dimensions and body fatness seem to change between the ages of 8 and 15 years (Lohman, Boileau, & Slaughter, 1989), the prediction equations developed with the adult population may not apply to children (Lohman, 1982). Further validation of skinfold prediction equations with children and special populations, in particular, is needed.

Self-Report Measures on Physical Activity

Given that it is not always feasible for someone to observe a child during all of his or her physical activities, or have sophisticated equipment to assess the quantity and quality of activity being conducted, self-report approaches would be useful if found to be reliable and valid. Some developments in this direction have taken place and are discussed below.

Rating of Perceived Exertion (RPE)

Description. The Rating of Perceived Exertion (RPE; Borg, 1962) is an associated measure between work performed and perception of stimulus intensity. The individual simply rates the perceived strenuousness of the exercise according to a Likert scale ranging from 6 to 20. The intensity level of physical performance increases as the rating increases. This scale was designed to reflect heart rate response. Adding a zero to the rating is expected to approximate the response ($6 \times 10 = 60$ beats per minute; $8 \times 10 = 80$ bpm; and so on). Individuals are trained to correlate their perception of intensity with their obtained heart rate.

Norms. There are no normative data using this measure with special or pediatric populations.

Reliability. Burke and Collins (1984) have reported a reliability of .98 using a normal adult population. There are no reliability data with children and special populations.

Validity. The validity of this test has been questionable because multiplying the perceived exertion rate by 10 does not equal the actual heart rate (Burke & Collins, 1984). Oftentimes, individuals may be reporting their emotional feelings rather than the perceived intensity of the activity itself.

Practicality. This is a very practical method for assessing the intensity of an activity. No special equipment is necessary. However, the subjectivity involved and the difficulty in training special individuals (e.g., young children, mentally handicapped individuals, individuals with Prader-Willi syndrome, Down syndrome, and so on) make it a less effective method for these populations.

Self-Report on Physical Activity (SPA)

Description of measure. The Self-Report on Physical Activity (SPA; Hastings, Darling, & Cowles, 1993) is a self-report checklist designed to assess the extent to which people take part in physical activity as well as some of the reasons they choose to take part.

Items on the checklist measure participation in sports, exercise, and physical activity and their frequency, intensity, and duration. In addition, the instrument includes four scales that measure affinity, body image, concern, and dedication. This is a new measure and it has yet to be used with nontraditional subpopulations.

Norms. Norms are not yet available.

Reliability. The testing of this instrument has produced Cronbach coefficient alphas of .86 for Affinity, .78 for Body Image, .75 for Concern, and .91 for

Dedication (Hastings et al., 1992). These data were derived using a normal adult population.

Practicality. This is a practical and useful measure. However, it requires a basic level of reading and understanding to complete the checklist.

The Fargo Activity Timesampling Survey (FATS)

Description. The Fargo Activity Timesampling Survey (FATS; Klesges et al., 1984) is an observational instrument used to assess child physical activity and related parent behaviors. The activities rated include sleeping, lying down, sitting upright, crawling, climbing, standing still, walking, and running. The categories are further divided under levels from minimal to extreme.

The children and parents are observed for 10 seconds, then the observer records parent and child behavior during the following 10-second interval. Additional information also coded is the child's physical location (e.g., bedroom, living room, kitchen, bedroom, or front or backyard). In the event that someone were to encourage or discourage activity in the child during the 10-second period, the following additional variables are recorded: agent (mother, father, sister, brother, grandmother, grandfather, relative, baby-sitter/caretaker); form of interaction (physical or verbal, encouragement or disencouragement); child behavior targeted (sleeping, lying down, sitting upright, crawling, climbing, standing still, walking, or running); and the child's response (the behaviors listed under child's behaviors targeted).

Norms. Normative data are not available at this time.

Reliability. The interobserver reliability for study one (Klesges et al., 1984; for two normal males, ages 20 and 22 months) ranged from .90 to .96. Weighted kappa ranged from .87 to .93.

The interobserver reliability for study two (Klesges et al., 1984; for seven normal males and seven normal females, ages 24 to 48 months) was reported to be above .90.

Practicality. The FATS was developed to assess child physical activity and parental influence. The instrument shows initial promise for this purpose. Its practicality is evidenced through the simplicity of the instrument and the ease with which high reliability was achieved. However, the FATS awaits further validation studies to show adequate psychometric properties; larger sample sizes across socioeconomic status (SES), diverse ethnic backgrounds, and special populations are necessary.

Assessment of Motor Activity

A number of devices that sense motion and record changes are available. These could be useful with normal children. Some of the more common ones are discussed below.

Mercury Switches

The device is worn on the body—wrist, leg, belt, and so on. A mercury switch is open when the device is tilted *less* than five degrees from the horizontal plane and closed when the device is tilted *more* than five degrees from the horizontal plane (Tyron, 1984). These devices respond only when the position change is above the threshold level. The magnitude of change is not accounted for. A number of variations of these position sensors are available (McPartland, Foster, Kupfer, & Weiss, 1976; Schulman, Suran, Stevens, & Kupst, 1979).

Reliability. The reliability of mercury switches was studied by Williamson, Calpin, DiLorenzo, Garris, and Petti (1981). They found the switches to be completely reliable and 100% accurate.

Validity. Validity studies are scarce and further work in this area is needed. Williamson and colleagues (1981) reported a lack of information on the validity of mercury switches because the number of tilts happened to be the same.

Practicality. These instruments are inexpensive to purchase, easy to operate, and simple to interpret.

Pedometers

Pedometers are devices commonly used in large movement activities such as in walking and running. The device is activated when its horizontally balanced lever is displaced. It is usually clipped on the pants at the waist.

Reliability. The pedometer may provide unreliable readings because it is subject to a number of variations in stride length/cadence. The pedometer then has to be calibrated and adjusted to intraindividual as well as interindividual movement changes for reliable information. Stunkard (1960) had subjects walk a measured mile and recorded readings of below 15% error.

Practicality. The pedometer is very inexpensive, easy to operate, and simple in data presentation. However, its interpretation of actual movement made requires user knowledge and training to adjust stride length and maintain a certain cadence. In addition, the pedometer caters to walking and/or running, limiting its application to ambulatory individuals. This instrument will not be useful with children who are nonambulatory or with paralysis of the lower extremity or amputees. This instrument is also only useful with children and individuals who are cooperative, failing which they could easily remove it, play with it, or disable it.

Nutritional Intake in the Elderly

Food intake in the elderly may be assessed by self-report, direct observation, or some combination of the two methods. All the difficulties with self-report measures of dietary intake pertain to this population, with additional issues of poor visual acuity, reading difficulties, hearing loss, and decreased memory and comprehension (Carter, McKenna, Martin, & Andresen, 1989).

A study of elderly nuns validated a 24-hour food recall measure against a videotaped record of meals actually eaten. Errors of omission occurred more frequently than errors of commission, with mixed dishes and desserts most commonly "forgotten" in the recall (Brown et al., 1990).

The accuracy of a telephone dietary recall, for which reference serving bowls and utensils were provided, was assessed in 159 elderly subjects (Dubois & Boivin, 1990) and was validated against surreptitious direct observation of the reported meal. Fat, cholesterol, and vitamin A recall contained relatively large amounts of bias. The authors noted the elderly omit fewer items from recall when they are permitted adequate time to think about what they have eaten. In addition, reading the recall back to the respondent increased recalled items by a total of 28%. No systematic differences were noted in recall of foods having a definite shape (such as bread, meat) and those requiring placement in a cup or bowl.

A shelf inventory was used in a study by Fischer, Crockett, Heller, and Skauge (1991) to assess nutrition attitudes and knowledge in a sample of almost 700 elderly living in rural areas. Foods were divided into 11 major nutritional categories and then subdivided into "encouraged" versus "discouraged" foods. Younger seniors (60-70 years old) had significantly more favorable food choices than older seniors (75-85 years old) in the categories for milk, cheese, bread, baked goods, vegetables, and legumes.

The reader is referred to Wolper et al. (this volume) for a comprehensive review of recall methodology and to reviews by Morley, Mooradian, Silver, Heber, and Alfin-Slater (1988) and Fischer and Johnson (1990) for more thorough discussions of nutritional issues in this population.

Undernutrition in the Elderly

It has been estimated that as many as 30% of apparently healthy seniors have subclinical undernutrition (Morley, Silver, Miller, & Rubinstein, 1989). Factors implicated in this process include (a) social and psychological factors, (b) diseases, (c) pharmacological agents, (d) decreased physical activity, (e) decreased basal oxygen consumption, (f) chemosensory impairment of taste and smell, and (g) altered levels of neurotransmitters and gut hormones (Schiffman & Warwick, 1988).

The true prevalence of undernutrition in the elderly is difficult to estimate. The Recommended Dietary Allowances (RDA) do not include specific values for elderly subjects, and there is a lack of consensus as to whether nutrient needs of older adults differ from those of younger adults (Hegsted, 1989; Zheng & Rosenberg, 1989). Lower median dietary intakes of some nutrients, such as vitamin C and iron, and higher prevalences of nutrient-associated clinical abnormalities have been found to be related to income (Ahmed, 1992). The National Health and Nutrition Survey (NHANES) III, currently under way, has no upper age boundary and will provide reference data including distributions for nutritional biochemistries and hematologies, growth charts, height and weight tables, population dietary intake data, and prevalence estimates for nutrition risk factors in the elderly (Kuczmarski, 1989).

The Nutrition Screening Initiative

Description of measure. The Nutrition Screening Initiative (Millen Posner, Jette, Smith, & Miller, 1993) was developed by the American Academy of Family Physicians, the American Dietetic Association, and the National Council on the Aging, Inc., as a public health campaign to aid clinicians in the assessment of nutritional problems in the elderly. It consists of a self-assessment protocol to help patients identify aspects of personal eating habits and lifestyle associated with nutritional risk. A mnemonic device (DETER-MINE) is provided for basic education on nutritional risk factors and indicators and reminders about the warning signs of poor nutritional health.[1] The clinician is provided with graded screens to help identify nutritional problems and aid in referral to the proper provider for treatment.

Norms. The instrument was administered to a stratified random sample of Medicare beneficiaries aged 70 years or older in the six New England states.

Reliability: Internal consistency. Data have not been reported.

Test-retest reliability. Data have not been reported.

Construct validity. Regression analysis was used to derive item weights that would predict poor nutrient intakes and low perceived health status. A score of 6 or more points defined persons at high nutritional risk, based on the estimated intake of five marker nutrients (protein, vitamin A, vitamin C, thiamine, and calcium) using an intake of less than 75% of the RDA as a criterion of dietary inadequacy. The second criterion was perceived health, rated on a 5-point Likert-type scale from "excellent" to "poor." The cutoff score of 6 identifies between 36% and 46% of older persons who may be at increased nutritional risk due to inadequate intake or to fair or poor perceived health.

Readability. The NSI has an appropriate reading level for its intended audience.

Practicality. The NSI appears to be a practical and useful tool for practitioners involved with the elderly. The combination of patient and provider screens is appealing, providing a graduated assessment and referral approach. The graphic style (large, bold typeface) accommodates the visual deficits experienced by many older subjects. The manual also contains the Geriatric Depression Scale and the Folstein Mini-Mental State Examination (discussed later in this chapter).

Comments. A manual for the NSI can be obtained from the Nutrition Screening Initiative in Washington, DC (see note 1 for the full address). The authors caution that the NSI is not intended as a diagnostic device but claim it is a valid and reliable measure of potential nutritional risk (White et al., 1992). Millen Posner et al. (1993) see a priority for future research being validation studies, especially among minority populations.

The Nutritional Risk Index

Description of measure. The Nutritional Risk Index (Wolinsky et al., 1990) is a 16-item questionnaire that was initially developed by building on and modifying items from the NHANES I protocol (McDowell et al., 1982). Research has shown that a score of 7 or higher is associated with a considerably greater risk of having poor nutritional status, poor health status in general, and greater use of health services.

Norms. A sample of community-dwelling elderly age 65 or older living in St. Louis, Missouri, were interviewed face-to-face at baseline and were reinterviewed by telephone at approximately 3- to 4-month and 12-month intervals.

   A second study of clinical validity used a sample of 377 male outpatients aged 55 or older. The protocol included face-to-face interviews, anthropometric procedures, hematologic assays, a 3-day food intake record, and a medical chart review.

A third clinical study was then conducted with 424 community-dwelling elderly aged 65 or greater living in Houston, Texas.

Reliability: Internal consistency. Cronbach's coefficient alpha at baseline was .603. The attrition rate in the first sample was approximately 40%. Coefficient alphas of .544 and .515 were obtained at the second and third administrations, respectively.

Test-retest reliability. Test-retest reliability was computed by correlating the NRI scores across the three waves. The resulting coefficients ranged between .65 and .71.

Construct validity. Exploratory factor analysis confirmed the theoretical five-factor structure, accounting for 47.9% of the variance in the 16 items. The NRI was added into standard regression models used to forecast the elderly's use of health services to calculate concurrent predictive validity. The NRI was found to be predictive of use of health services, and its predictive ability was not jointly shared with the standard measures of health status or other background characteristics.

In the second clinical study, the NRI was found to be significantly related to body-mass index and total energy intake (in kcals). The high-risk group was significantly more likely to be very thin, to be taking prescription drugs that could increase risk, and to have laboratory values associated with poor health.

In the third study, the clinical validity of the NRI was supported in comparison with anthropometric assessments, laboratory values, and 3-day food records using a shortened version of the instrument (13 of 16 items).

Readability. The NRI is designed for telephone administration and has an oral comprehension level acceptable for its target population.

Practicality. Objectives in the development of the NRI were that it be brief, suitable for telephone surveys, easily scored, and easily interpretable. It seems to have met these objectives.

Comments. The psychometric properties of this scale are reasonably sound. Five dimensions of nutritional risk, including mechanics of food intake, prescribed dietary restrictions, morbid conditions affecting food intake, discomfort associated with outcomes of food intake, and significant changes in dietary habits are assessed. Despite relatively low reliability coefficients, internal consistency and test-retest reliability of the NRI support efforts to refine this index. Use of the NRI as a screening device may help identify appropriate candidates for more detailed diagnostic testing.

Further development of this scale would include evaluating the NRI with both younger and institutionalized populations. The sensitivity of the NRI in detecting changes in nutritional risk has not been established. The authors suggest a randomized, longitudinal clinical trial in which persons with "at-risk" NRI scores either receive or do not receive further nutritional evaluation so as to establish the cost-effectiveness of the NRI as a screening device.

Unintentional Weight Loss

Low body weight and rapid unintentional weight loss are highly predictive of mortality and morbidity in the elderly population (Fischer & Johnson, 1990). Early signs of protein/calorie malnutrition present as changes in mental status, such as apathy, irritability, and decreased ability to concentrate as well as anorexia. Muscle wasting, edema, dehydration, and poor wound healing may represent either vitamin or mineral deficiencies (Kamel, 1990). The majority of cases of unintentional weight loss are probably accounted for by physical disease, and vitamin deficiencies may be subclinical until the stress of an illness. Dementia and depression may result in severe nutritional deficiencies (Fischer & Johnson, 1990). In addition, functional disabilities can affect the capacity of many elderly persons to obtain, prepare, and consume adequate food to maintain weight (Campbell, Spears, Brown, Busby, & Borrie, 1990). Poor dentition, resulting from tooth loss and/or poorly fitting dentures, is also a major contributor to eating problems in the elderly, as approximately 50% of Americans over the age of 65 have lost all their teeth (Olsen-Noll & Bosworth, 1989).

Eating Disorders in the Elderly

Anorexia

Anorexia, or loss of appetite, is a common occurrence in the elderly. Table 12.2 lists the major causes of anorexia and weight loss in the elderly (Olsen-Noll & Bosworth, 1989). The anorexia commonly associated with aging is characterized by little, if any, disturbance in body image or fear of obesity (Morley et al., 1988) and is thus distinguishable from anorexia nervosa, which generally affects younger patients. Nonetheless, it has been suggested that anorexia nervosa and bulimia be included in the differential diagnosis of

TABLE 12.2 Common Causes of Anorexia and Weight Loss in the Elderly

GASTROINTESTINAL DISORDERS
Peptic ulcer disease
Cholelithiasis
Intestinal obstruction
Gastric reflux
Esophageal spasm
Surgical alterations
Gastric carcinoma
Delays esophageal emptying
Chronic atrophic gastritis
Oral cavity problems
Poor dentition

METABOLIC DISORDERS
Hyperthyroidism
Hypothyroidism
Uremia
Hepatic dysfunction

TOXIC OR PYREXIAL ILLNESS

CARDIOPULMONARY DISEASE
Emphysema
Cardiac failure
Chronic bronchitis

DRUG TOXICITY
Sedatives and psychotropics
Digoxin
Laxatives
Appetite suppressants
Thiazide
Diuretics
Levodopa
Narcotics
Antibiotics
Miscellaneous drugs

NEOPLASMS

NUTRITIONAL PROBLEMS
Inadequate intake
Dietary restrictions
Inability to purchase and prepare foods for a special diet
Inadequate evaluation of patient's knowledge of nutrition
Lactose intolerance

PERCEPTUAL AND SOCIAL PROBLEMS
Hypogeusia (diminished taste)
Diminished olfaction
Poor oral hygiene
Isolation because of visual or hearing impairment
Diminished socialization

BEHAVIORAL AND PSYCHIATRIC DISORDERS
Isolation
Depression and suicidal feelings
Dementia
Alcoholism
Drug abuse
Manipulative behavior
Psychotic states
Memory impairment
Anxiety

SOURCE: From "Anorexia and Weight Loss in the Elderly: Causes Range From Loose Dentures to Debilitating Illness," by C. G. Olsen-Noll and M. F. Bosworth, 1989, *Postgraduate Medicine, 85*(3), pp. 140-144. Copyright © 1989 by McGraw-Hill, Inc. Adapted with permission.

any elderly patient presenting with weight loss and/or vomiting (Hsu & Zimmer, 1988).

The prevalence of eating disorders in the elderly, as reflected in the literature, is increasing (Hsu & Zimmer, 1988). This has been attributed to younger eating disordered patients surviving to older age with active disorders and to older patients succumbing to societal pressures to achieve extreme thinness.

Eating disorders in the elderly may develop after events of personal loss, such as bereavement. Physical changes common to aging may affect the body image of older adults in a way conducive to the development of eating disorders. R. N. Butler (1963) describes a progressive self-reflection of past experiences and a resurgence of unresolved conflicts as part of the normal aging process. This "life review" either leads to integration of new solutions to earlier difficulties or defense against intrusions of such conflicts into consciousness. Disordered eating may be a way of defending against these painful issues, by giving the older person a sense of control over his or her life. As their physical condition deteriorates, some elderly patients may use food as a weapon in an attempt to regain a failing sense of control. Food refusal and spitting out food after chewing are examples of food used as a weapon against caregivers (Morley et al., 1989).

In one of the few studies of eating disorders in the elderly, Miller, Morley, Rubenstein, and Pietruszka (1991) used the EAT-26 with male veterans. The majority of subjects with subnormal midarm circumference values (MAC), a measure of undernutrition, reported exerting "self-control around food." Anorexiclike responses were more common in depressed subjects.

To date, appropriate psychological screening measures for anorexia nervosa or bulimia nervosa in this age group have not been developed, and assessment of these disorders currently relies on subjective clinical impressions or the use of instruments normed on younger populations.

Xerostomia and Oropharyngeal Dysphagia

Xerostomia, or dry mouth, affects nearly one in five older adults and is associated with significant deficiencies of fiber, potassium, vitamin B-6, iron, calcium, and zinc. Many patients suffering from xerostomia also complain of dysgeusia (bad taste) or hypogeusia (loss of taste), which may account for the noted nutritional deficiencies (Rhodus & Brown, 1990).

Oropharyngeal dysphagia refers to disordered ability to initiate swallowing or difficulty moving food or liquid from the mouth to upper esophagus and stomach. This is related to specific results of pathological conditions or illnesses (e.g., dementia, stroke, Parkinson's disease) that may occur with

TABLE 12.3 Assessment of Dysphagia Interview

The following questions can be asked of the patient and/or family members or caretakers.

1) When did impairment begin?

2) Did the impairment worsen gradually or rapidly?

3) Does the problem vary with different textures of food, such as liquid, pudding, solid food?

4) What specifically happens when the patient swallows?

5) Does the material stop somewhere along the way?

6) Does the patient cough or choke?

7) If food collects, can the patient point to the spot in the mouth or throat where food seems to collect?

SOURCE: From "Don't Choke on This: A Swallowing Assessment," by M. Rubin-Terrado and D. Linkenheld, 1991, *Geriatric Nursing,* November/December, pp. 288-291. Copyright © 1991 by Mosby-Year Book Inc. Reprinted with permission.

greater frequency in older persons. The incidence of swallowing disorders in nursing home residents ranges from 30% to 50% (Sonies, 1992).

Dysphagia can be assessed subjectively by clinical interview and objectively by radiological studies such as swallowing videofluoroscopy. Table 12.3 is an example of a clinical interview to assess dysphagia that may be conducted with the patient or the family (Rubin-Terrado & Linkenheld, 1991).

The Dysphagia Assessment Scale

Description of measure. The Dysphagia Assessment Scale was developed by Dakkak and Bennett (1992) as a subjective measure. The scale rank orders nine foods of increasing viscosity and solidity, and the patient rates his or her perceived ability to eat the foods. The maximum possible score is 45, which indicates no difficulty in swallowing.

Norms. The scale was administered to 49 patients with endoscopically documented dysphagia.

Reliability: Internal consistency. Data have not been reported.

Test-retest reliability. Data have not been reported.

Construct validity. Approximately 7 days after completing the scale, patients were served a meal containing the nine items. An observer, blind to the scale scores, gave a score for the food actually eaten, using the same numerical values as in the patient questionnaire. Partial credit was given for foods partially consumed. The two scores were not statistically different (Questionnaire = 34.9 ± 8.4 *SD;* Observation = 37.4 ± 7.6 *SD*). Regression analysis showed that patients' perception of dysphagia and their observed ability to eat had a strong linear correlation ($r = .793$, $p < .001$).

Practicality. This scale is easily administered and practical for a variety of clinical settings.

Comments. A copy of the scale is presented in Table 12.4.

Numerical guidelines that categorize severity of dysphagia would be helpful. The scale was developed in England, so certain foods might need to be substituted for culturally diverse populations. It would be of interest to administer it at repeated intervals with the same patients to see if it could be used as a staging assessment. In addition, as this scale relies on self-rating by the patient, it is not clear if it would be of use in patients with some level of mental impairment, as is common with many elderly patients in institutional settings.

Chemosensory Changes

The ability to smell deteriorates as a function both of aging and of a number of age-related neurological degenerative disorders. The flavor of food and beverages is adversely affected, which may directly affect food intake and, subsequently, nutritional status. Upper respiratory infections are a common cause of disability, and neurological diseases (e.g., Alzheimer's and Parkinson's) as well as head injury are other contributing conditions (Doty, 1989).

The University of Pennsylvania Smell Identification Test (UPSIT) is a 40-odorant test of smell function, in the form of scratch and sniff cards (Sensonics, Inc., Haddonfield, NJ). Scores yield (a) percentile rank of the patient in relation to age/sex norms and (b) functional categories of unimpaired, impaired, and profoundly impaired status.

The ability to discriminate between tastes also declines with age. Subjective assessment can be made by asking subjects to compare their present taste experiences with their memory of past experiences. An alternative assessment compares contemporaneous reports from comparison groups of older and younger subjects using standardized taste stimuli. A forced choice assessment procedure is frequently used in which a taste solution is rated against a blank, and solutions are graded in strength to permit establishment of a sensory threshold (Weiffenbach, 1989).

TABLE 12.4 Dysphagia Scale

The patient is asked to rate his or her ability to eat the following foods.

Food	Point Value
Water, 200 ml	1
Milk, 100 ml	2
Custard,[a] 40 g (1/2 oz.)	3
Jelly,[b] 70 g (2 1/2 oz.)	4
Scrambled egg, one	5
Baked fish, 40 g ($\frac{1}{2}$ oz.)	6
White bread, one slice	7
Apple, one	8
Steak, 40 g ($\frac{1}{2}$ oz.)	9
Total	45

SOURCE: From "A New Dysphagia Score With Objective Validation," by M. Dakkak and J. R. Bennett, 1992, *Journal of Clinical Gastroenterology, 14*(2), pp. 99-100. Copyright © 1992 by Raven Press. Reprinted with permission.
a. Pudding.
b. Gelatin dessert.

Dysgeusia

Dysgeusia, or an unpleasant taste in the mouth, may be related to oral medications, nose drops, postnasal drip, stomach reflux, or inflamed oral tissues. Dysgeusias that can be rinsed away may be confined to the mouth. A dysgeusia that increases after treating the mouth with a local anesthetic may be of central origin, and the patient should be referred to a neurologist (Weiffenbach & Bartoshuk, 1992).

Table 12.5 gives an example of clinical interview questions to help differentiate between taste and olfactory loss (Weiffenbach & Bartoshuk, 1992). Chemosensory loss can be very stressful to the patient. Psychotherapy may be an appropriate referral "not because the chemosensory dysfunction is imaginary, but because the patient may need help in dealing with bizarre and distressing symptoms arising from a poorly understood, evidently untreatable, and likely progressive condition" (Weiffenbach & Bartoshuk, 1992, p. 552).

Dementia

Alzheimer's disease is a dementia associated with a progressive increase in eating and feeding problems, often accompanied by weight loss. Problems range from chewing and swallowing problems to food refusal and forgetting to eat (Bucht & Sandman, 1990).

TABLE 12.5 Assessment of Taste Versus Olfactory Loss

The following information may be obtained during a clinical interview.

Can the patient taste:

(1) Salt crystals

(2) Sugar crystals

(3) Sourness of vinegar or lemon juice

(4) Bitterness of medicines

(5) Dark chocolate

(6) Strong coffee

If patient answers, "Yes, but I can't taste anything else," patient likely has olfactory rather than taste loss. Patients reporting they can taste these substances, but that taste is weak, are likely to demonstrate true taste loss.

SOURCE: Adapted from "Taste and Smell," by J. M. Weiffenbach and L. M. Bartoshuk, 1992, *Clinics in Geriatric Medicine*, 8(3) [Special issue: "Oral and Dental Problems in the Elderly," Bruce J. Baum, Special Ed.], p. 551. Reprinted with permission.

The Folstein Mini-Mental State Examination (Folstein, Folstein, & McHugh, 1975) is a useful instrument in screening for the presence of dementia. A score of less than 26 is considered significant and may be associated with poor nutritional status. A copy of the screen is included in the Nutrition Screening Initiative manual (see previous discussion).

Depression

Depression occurs in both free-living (Blazer & Williams, 1980) and institutionalized elderly (Hyer & Blazer, 1982) and may contribute to reduced food intake and compromised nutritional status. Data from the NHANES I study found that older people (greater than or equal to 55 years) who were depressed lost more weight than those who were not depressed (DiPietro, Anda, Williamson, & Stunkard, 1992).

The Geriatric Depression Scale (GDS) is a 30-question dichotomous scale, which has been shown to be a reliable and valid measure of geriatric depression with a high degree of internal consistency (Yesavage et al., 1983). A score of 11 or higher indicates possible depression. A copy of the screen is in the Nutrition Screening Initiative manual (see previous discussion).

Overnutrition in the Elderly

Comorbidity

Overnutrition in the elderly has been associated with diabetes (M. I. Harris, 1990), ischemic heart disease (Morisaki, Kawano, Watanabe, Saito, & Yoshida, 1992), hypertension (Feskens, Bowles, & Kromhout, 1992), and osteoarthritis (White-O'Connor, Sobal, & Muncie, 1989).

There is currently little information about the independent effect of obesity on survival in subjects over the age of 70. The inverse relationship of body weight to mortality in aged men may be due to preexisting morbid conditions (Kinney & Caldwell, 1990). There is evidence that the elderly show only mildly negative attitudes toward obesity. This might be related to greater tolerance of personal differences and a decreased emphasis on slimness as a measure of personal worth as people age (M. B. Harris & Furukawa, 1986).

Anthropometry and Body Composition in the Elderly

Anthropometry

The nutritional status of elderly persons, regarding both under- and overnutrition, can be assessed by direct measures such as anthropometric measurements, biochemical analyses of blood and urine, clinical evaluation as well as assessment of indirect measures of such socioeconomic and environmental factors as mobility, income, social network, and alcohol or drug abuse (Ahmed, 1992). The most significant change in body composition over time is the decrease in lean body mass, which may compromise resistance to physiological insults such as disease and injury. In addition, as lean tissue decreases, so does the basal energy requirement, which can affect food intake, energy expenditure, and nutritional status. Bone density also decreases, putting some elderly persons at increased risk of osteoporosis (Chernoff, 1990).

Desirable Body Weight for the Elderly

One of the easiest measures to obtain and also one of the most important assessments for this population is regular monitoring of body weight. There is, however, a lack of consensus as to values for desirable weight for height in elderly persons. Horwath (1991) has argued that a case can be made for widening the BMI range considered acceptable for older persons, provided they are not affected with obesity-related medical conditions such as hypertension

TABLE 12.6 Comparison of the Weight-for-Height Tables From Actuarial Data: Non-Age Corrected Metropolitan Life Insurance Company and Age-Specific Gerontology Research Center Recommendations

| Height (feet and inches) | Metropolitan 1983 Weights[a] (25-59 yr) | | Gerontology Research Center[a] (age-specific weight range for men and women) | | | | |
	Men	Women	20-29 Years	30-39 Years	40-49 Years	50-59 Years	60-69 Years
4 10		100-131	84-111	92-119	99-127	107-135	115-142
4 11		101-134	87-115	95-123	103-131	111-139	119-147
5 0		103-137	90-119	98-127	106-135	114-143	123-152
5 1	123-145	105-140	93-123	101-131	110-140	118-148	127-157
5 2	125-148	108-144	96-127	105-136	113-144	122-153	131-163
5 3	127-151	111-148	99-131	108-140	117-149	126-158	135-168
5 4	129-155	114-152	102-135	112-145	121-154	130-163	140-173
5 5	131-159	117-156	106-140	115-149	125-159	134-168	144-179
5 6	133-163	120-160	109-144	119-154	129-164	138-174	148-184
5 7	135-167	123-164	112-148	122-159	133-169	143-179	153-190
5 8	137-171	126-167	116-153	126-163	137-174	147-184	158-196
5 9	139-175	129-170	119-157	130-168	141-179	151-190	162-201
5 10	141-179	132-173	122-162	134-173	145-184	156-195	167-207
5 11	144-183	135-176	126-167	137-178	149-190	160-201	172-213
6 0	147-187		129-171	141-183	153-195	165-207	177-219
6 1	150-192		133-176	145-188	157-200	169-213	182-225
6 2	153-197		137-181	149-194	162-206	174-219	187-232
6 3	157-202		141-186	153-199	166-212	179-225	192-238
6 4			144-191	157-205	171-218	184-231	197-244

SOURCE: From Mortality and Obesity: The Rationale for Age-Specific Height-Weight Tables," by R. Andres, 1985, in *Principles of Geriatric Medicine* (R. Andres, E. L. Bierman, & W. R. Hazzard, Eds.), pp. 311-318, New York: McGraw-Hill. Copyright © 1985 by McGraw-Hill, Inc. Reprinted with permission.
a. Values in this table are for height without shoes and weight without shoes.

and diabetes. Despite liberalized weight ranges in the 1983 insurance industry tables, Andres (1985) argues that weights are specified that are both higher than primary insurance data would justify for young adults and lower than the data would suggest for older adults. Age-specific height-weight tables have been proposed as an alternative; an example is presented in Table 12.6 (Andres, 1985).

Anthropometric Assessment of the Elderly

Recommended anthropometric nutritional assessments of an ambulatory elderly person include (a) height, (b) weight, (c), midarm circumference (MAC), (d) triceps and subscapular skinfold (Subsc SF) thicknesses, and (e) calf circumference (Calf C). In the nonambulatory person, recumbent knee height replaces standing height. MAC and skinfolds provide measures of subcutaneous adipose tissue on arm and trunk. MAC combined with triceps skinfold can provide a computation for cross-sectional area of muscle in the upper arm. Calf circumference is an indicator of general loss of muscle in response to diminished physical activity.

Chumlea (1991) offers the following considerations to enhance accuracy of measurement:

1. Person should be able to stand upright, without assistance, bare heels close together, legs straight, arms at sides, shoulders relaxed, and wearing minimal clothing. It is more important that person stand erect than that all body parts contact wall.

2. When stature cannot be measured due to spinal curvature, recumbent knee height (Knee H) should be used.

3. Recumbent measures should be taken from the left side, as this is the side from which the reference data were collected.

The reader is referred to the *Anthropometric Standardization Reference Manual* (Lohman, Roche, & Martorell, 1988), Chumlea, Roche, and Mukhergee (1987), and Mitchell and Chernoff (1991) for full reference tables and figures.

When weight cannot be obtained because of infirmity, it can be estimated from the anthropometric measures mentioned above by the following equations:

$$\text{Body weight for men} = (.098 \times \text{Calf C}) + (1.16 \times \text{Knee H}) + (1.72 \times \text{MAC}) + (0.37 \times \text{Subsc SF}) - 81.69$$

$$\text{Body weight for women} = (1.27 \times \text{Calf C}) + (0.87 \times \text{Knee H}) + (0.98 \times \text{MAC}) + (0.4 \times \text{Subsc SF}) - 62.35$$

The above equations estimate the weight of a subject within plus or minus 8.96 kg or 7.60 kg, respectively (95% probability; Chumlea, Guo, Roche, & Steinbaugh, 1988).

Body Composition

Representative body composition data are not available for the elderly. This is due in part to equipment that is not easily accessible to older subjects (e.g., underwater weighing) and the lack of appropriate referential norms. Underwater weighing may have an error rate as high as 10% to 15% because of poor performance of elderly subjects (Chumlea, Baumgartner, & Vellas, 1991). Unfortunately, age-related changes in structure of aging tissue, caused by deteriorating limb and abdominal muscle structure or tone, can alter the relation of skinfold thickness measurements (which are more readily obtainable) to other measures of body composition, as well as complicate the nutritional interpretation of such measures (Chumlea et al., 1991). A compartmental model (see Heymsfield et al., this volume) can account for the differing densities of fat-free mass and is proposed to improve estimated body composition in the elderly. Although appropriate reference norms for body water in subjects over 65 years of age do not as yet exist, some studies suggest total body water decreases with old age (Chumlea et al., 1991; Schoeller, 1989).

Assessment of Physical Activity in the Elderly

Many elderly persons maintain a sedentary life despite increasing the frequency of other health-related activities (Herbert & Teague, 1988-1989). Myers and Gonda (1986) suggest that nonparticipation in physical activities may be related to factors ranging from entrenched patterns of inactivity to myths and fears about the safety and suitability of exercise.

Assessment of physical activity in the elderly has been hampered by the lack of appropriate instruments. Direct assessment techniques (e.g., movement counters and heart rate monitors) are costly, and self-report techniques (exercise diaries) require considerable effort by both respondents and investigators to ensure accuracy.

Physical Activity Scale for the Elderly (PASE)

Description of measure. To create the Physical Activity Scale for the Elderly (PASE; Washburn, Smith, Jette, & Janney, 1993), a list of physical activity categories and specific items within each category of particular relevance to older people was generated from the existing literature on questionnaire assessment.

Norms. An initial form of the PASE was pilot tested in a small sample of community-dwelling residents. The PASE was modified and retested in field trials of samples drawn from a target area of 23 western Massachusetts cities and towns. Half the sample received home visits first and then completed the PASE by either mail or telephone. The procedure was reversed for the other half of the sample ($n = 277$ for home visit and PASE; $n = 119$ for PASE only).

Home visits included (a) standardized blood pressure measurements, (b) height and weight, (c) grip strength, (d) static balance of dominant leg, (e) isometric knee extensor strength, and (f) health status as assessed by the Sickness Impact Profile (SIP), which measures impact of disease on daily activities and behaviors in 12 functional areas (Bergner et al., 1976). Physical activity was monitored directly for 3 days via a Caltrac Personal Activity Computer (Hermokinetics, Inc., Madison, WI). Subjects also maintained an hourly physical activity diary for time spent in eight activity categories ranging from complete rest to heavy sport and recreation. Daily expenditures were calculated as multiples of METS (metabolic equivalents). Subjects then made a global rating of their level of physical activity across the 3 days, using a 5-point Likert scale ranging from "not active at all" to "extremely active."

A criterion measure of physical activity was created via principal components analysis using Caltrac counts, METS totals, and the global assessment. Optimal item weights for the PASE were derived by regressing these component scores on responses to the questionnaire. Total PASE scores were computed as the product of hours per day over 7 days spent in each activity and the respective weights of the activities, which was then summed over all activities.

Reliability: Internal consistency. Internal consistency as measured by Cronbach's coefficient alpha was .69.

Test-retest reliability. The test-retest reliability (measures were repeated 3-7 weeks after baseline) coefficient was .75 (95% $CI = .69 - .80$; $n = 254$). Mail PASE, $r = .84$; Telephone PASE, $r = .68$.

Construct validity. PASE validity was established by correlating it with the measures taken during the home visit. PASE was positively correlated with the SIP, grip strength, static balance, and leg strength but not associated with BMI or blood pressure.

Readability. The PASE has an appropriate reading level for its intended population; however, the mail version of the PASE produced an average of 17.8 points higher response than the telephone version. The authors speculate that subjects completing the mail version probably reported some activities twice (e.g., walking was reported in response to a specific question and again in response to a more general question about light/moderate recreational activity). Therefore the telephone PASE is recommended. Additional instructions have been added to the mail version, but this version has not yet been field tested.

Practicality. The PASE can be completed in approximately 5 minutes and has been developed using psychometrically based techniques.

Comments. The PASE would be a practical measure for a study using telephone contact for data collection. It remains to be seen if the mail version of the PASE will provide reliable estimates of activities. An administration package for the PASE can be purchased from the authors, which includes questionnaires and a scoring manual.[2]

Assessment in Non-Western Populations

Dietary Intake

Accurate assessment of dietary practices in culturally diverse populations is frequently compromised by a lack of culturally sensitive instruments. Literacy, language, communal consumption practices, and societal attitudes to direct questioning all affect the quality of nutritional data collected in these settings (Cassidy, 1994). In addition, bilingual interviewers may not be bicultural, which may potentiate coding biases as a result of incorrect assumptions about what is being reported (Loria, Arroyo, & Briefel, 1994).

Anorexia and Bulimia Nervosa

At present, there is limited knowledge of attitudes toward weight and food in the nondominant cultures in our society (Thomas & Szmukler, 1985). Westernization may influence eating pathology through dissatisfaction with body shape. Anorexic and bulimic eating disorders, as well as body image dissatisfaction, have been documented in many non-Western societies (Davis & Yager, 1992; Dolan, Lacey, & Evans, 1990; Hsu, 1987; Matsuura, Fujimura, Nozawa, Iida, & Hirayam, 1992; Mumford, Whitehouse, & Choudry, 1992; Nasser, 1988) as well as among North American black, Hispanic, and Native Americans (Emmons, 1992; Rosen et al., 1988; Warheit, Langer, Zimmerman, & Biafora, 1993). Prevalence may still be underestimated, as internalized racial/ethnic stereotypes may preclude practitioners from conducting a full assessment (Root, 1990).

It has been suggested that exposure to Western values is linked to increasing concern over body weight, resulting in documentable eating disorders

(Lachenmeyer & Muni-Brandner, 1988). Booth, Lewis, and Blair (1990) refer to the "shape chauvinism" of an affluent society as a factor in creating eating disorders.

Translation of Existing Instruments to Assess Eating Disorders

The greatest obstacle to assessment remains the lack of standardized instruments that have been validated on populations outside North America and Western Europe. The translation of existing instruments into other languages must be approached with caution. Cousins et al. (1992) describe a translation process that involves a professional translation into the target language, followed by a back translation to the source language by separate translators. Discrepancies in meaning or style can then be resolved. Choudry and Mumford (1992) discuss the three criteria for a valid translation, which are linguistic equivalence, conceptual equivalence, and scale equivalence. In their study in Pakistan, having translated the EAT into Urdu, it was discovered the terms *binge* and *dieting behavior* do not exist in that language. In the cultural context of rural Pakistan, some of the EAT items were found to be clearly invalid. King and Bhugra (1989) translated the EAT into local languages for a study in Northern India. However, pattern analyses of individual questions on the EAT suggested that several questions were "clearly vulnerable to misinterpretation for social and religious reasons" (p. 957).

Sohlberg (1988) attempted a cross-cultural validation of the EDI using a Swedish translation, which was not back-translated. Although Swedish samples of patients and ex-patients were highly similar to the Canadian norms for the EDI, both controls and recovered patients reported higher levels of perfectionism than Canadian norms. It is not possible to determine whether this difference is attributable to culture, language, or some combination of the two.

Chun et al. (1992) administered a translated version of the EDI to freshmen medical college students in China. Only 1.1%-1.3% of the college population met domestic, *DSM III,* or *DSM III-R* criteria for bulimia, despite 78% of women and 43% of men reporting fear of being fat. Clinical bulimia may be affected by the relative unavailability of binge foods in this population. Similarly, Lee, Hsu, and Wing (1992) feel bulimic disorders may be rare in Hong Kong because obesity is relatively rare among the indigenous population and dieting behavior is uncommon.

Nasser (1986a) administered an Arabic version of the EAT to Arab undergraduate women studying in England. The test had a positive predictive value of 55%, sensitivity of 100%, and specificity of 89%. Using the same instrument with a sample of students living in Cairo, Nasser found no cases of either anorexia or bulimia identified (Nasser, 1986b), supporting the theory that acculturation contributes to the development of eating disorders.

The lack of appropriately normed instruments is not only a problem in non-Western cultures. In a transcultural comparison using the EAT in East and West Berlin, prior to the reunification of the cities, Neumarker, Dudeck, Vollrath, Neumarker, and Steinhausen (1992) found lower scores in comparison with North American samples. Deficient discriminant validity was evidenced by extremely low scores of East Berlin patients with anorexia nervosa.

In summary, there are as yet no culture-free, psychometrically sound, and valid eating disorder assessment instruments in existence. Careful translation procedures are essential if existing instruments are to be used, and cross-validation with the original normative samples is important to ensure reliability.

Obesity, Cultural Assimilation, and Body Size

Obesity is a relatively common condition in many minority populations (Aluli, 1991; Broussard et al., 1991; Pawson, Martorell, & Mendoza, 1991). In the United States, the prevalence rate of overweight in blacks is almost double that of whites (U.S. Department of Health and Human Services, 1988).

In many non-Western cultures, a large body symbolizes beauty and material and spiritual well-being, and body weight may be positively associated with an increasing standard of living. Among the Annang people of Nigeria, if the parents are able to afford the expense, young girls are put into a "fattening room" prior to marriage, where they gain an immense amount of weight in a very short time (Brink, 1989). The weight gain is considered a measure of the girl's worth, and she is paraded seminude through the village in celebration of her new girth. In Hong Kong, greeting someone with the statement, "You have put on weight," is still regarded as a compliment (Lee et al., 1992). Thinness is associated with ill health and bad luck as opposed to the Western associations of self-discipline, attractiveness, or economic well-being.

Cultural food preferences and usual dietary practices may discourage weight loss. Ethnicity was found to be the major factor influencing food intake among Mexican Americans when compared with non-Hispanic whites (Bartholomew, Young, Martin, & Hazuda, 1990). Mexican Americans of varying social economic status have been noted as being aware of "prevailing cultural attitudes" but nonetheless harboring "residual skepticism about the desirability of being lean" (Stern, Pugh, Parten Gaskill, & Hazuda, 1982, p. 925).

Kumanyika, Obarzanek, Stevens, Hebert, and Whelton (1991) have commented:

> To the extent that blacks ascribe to the general societal dissatisfaction with being overweight but do not succeed in losing weight, a relatively tolerant social climate for obesity may weaken the motivation for repeated weight loss attempts and permit self-acceptance as an overweight person. (p. 1635S)

Heavier body weight has been shown to be more acceptable to black versus white high school-age girls (Desmond, Price, Hallinan, & Smith, 1989).

Assessment of Physical Activity in Minority Populations

Physical activity in minority populations has generally been measured by modified versions of standard physical activity assessment instruments such as the Stanford 7-day recall (Sallis et al., 1985). The reader is referred to Shelton and Klesges (this volume) for reviews of standard measures. The same caveats pertain to translation of physical activity instruments as to assessment instruments for eating disorders (see above).

Gender and Sexual Orientation

Approximately 5% to 10% of patients with anorexia are male (Barry & Lipmann, 1990). Bulimia in men may be underdiagnosed due to clinical descriptions that have focused on young women (Schneider & Agras, 1987).

To date, there have been no instruments specifically developed to assess eating disorders in nonheterosexual populations. The male subculture of homosexuality has traditionally emphasized an appearance that may make its members more vulnerable to body dissatisfaction and disordered eating (Silberstein, Mishkind, Striegel-Moore, Timko, & Rodin, 1989; Yager, Kurtzman, Landsverk, & Weismeier, 1988), although these values may be shifting as low body weight becomes associated with HIV status. Bulimia nervosa in men is also associated with homosexual or bisexual preferences, and male heterosexuals may be relatively protected, presumably via less cultural pressure for thinness (Schneider & Agras, 1987). Homosexual women have been shown to desire significantly heavier body weights, be less concerned with weight and appearance, and exhibit less drive for thinness as well as a higher degree of body satisfaction in comparison with heterosexual women (Herzog, Newman, Yeh, & Warshaw, 1992). Brand, Rothblum, and Solomon (1992) found heterosexual women and gay men were most preoccupied with their own weight, followed by lesbian women, and finally heterosexual men.

Conclusions

The list of "special populations" highlighted in this chapter is, by no means, exhaustive. The selection was driven primarily by the existing literature as well as by clinical concerns. There is a need for development of culturally sensitive assessment techniques for all the minority populations discussed in this chapter. The limited normative data currently available necessitate cautious interpretation of results when many existing instruments are used. Translation remains a valid option for some measures, providing the process is carefully performed with the above suggested checks for accuracy and meaning.

Society is placing increased emphasis on health and wellness. Special populations are an integral part of the fabric of society and therefore must be included in any comprehensive examination of behavior. Technological advances have increased survival rates among both medically compromised and aging members of society. Population-specific research is vital to ensure that appropriate services are developed to benefit the individuals in these groups. It is time to put the horse in front of the cart, where it belongs.

Cassidy (1994) titled her article on culturally sensitive food-habit research, "Walk a Mile in My Shoes," taken from a popular song. This serves as a reminder that, to understand the Other in research, one must try to become subjectively immersed in the culture of interest, as well as objectively observant. We hope our chapter has raised as many questions as it has answered and that it will serve to promote further study of these essential members of society.

Notes

1. The Nutritional Screening Manual for Professionals Caring for Older Americans as well as the "Determine Your Nutritional Health Checklist" can be ordered from the Nutrition Screening Initiative, 2626 Pennsylvania Avenue, N.W., Suite 301, Washington, DC 20037. Telephone: (202) 625-1662. The Initiative's Partners and Technical Review Committee have also prepared a series of reports that review existing literature on nutrition and aging, identify the major risk factors associated with poor nutritional status, suggest major and minor indicators of poor nutritional status, and explain the Initiative's approach to nutritional screening. Full copies and executive summaries of these reference documents are also available from the Nutrition Screening Initiative.

2. The PASE can be obtained from the New England Research Institute, Inc., Watertown, MA 02172, for approximately $40.00. This includes the original article describing the development and validation of the PASE, 50 copies of the PASE, and an administration and scoring manual. Correspondence should be directed to Kevin W. Smith, M.A.

References

Ahmed, F. E. (1992). Effect of nutrition on the health of the elderly. *Journal of the American Dietetic Association, 92*, 1102-1107.

Aluli, N. E. (1991). Prevalence of obesity in a native Hawaiian population. *American Journal of Clinical Nutrition, 53*, 1556S-1560S.

Andres, R. (1985). Mortality and obesity: The rationale for age-specific height-weight tables. In R. Andres, E. L. Bierman, & W. R. Hazzard (Eds.), *Principles of geriatric medicine* (pp. 311-318). New York: McGraw-Hill.

Archer, L. A. (1991). *The revised Children's Eating Behavior Inventory.* Unpublished manuscript.

Archer, L. A., Rosenbaum, P. L., & Streiner, D. L. (1991). The Children's Eating Behavior Inventory: Reliability and validity results. *Journal of Pediatric Psychology, 16*, 629-642.

Babbitt, R. L., & Hoch, T. A. (1992, May 24-27). *Behavioral assessment of pediatric feeding disorders.* Paper presented at the conference for the International Society for Infant Studies, Miami, FL.

Babbitt, R. L., Hoch, T. A., & Coe, D. A. (1994). Behavioral feeding disorders. In D. N. Tuchman & R. S. Walter (Eds.), *Disorders of feeding and swallowing in infants and children* (pp. 77-95). San Diego, CA: Singular Publishing.

Babbitt, R. L., Hoch, T. A., Coe, D. A., Cataldo, M. F., Kelly, K. J., Stackhouse, C., & Perman, J. A. (1994). Behavioral assessment and treatment of pediatric feeding disorders. *Journal of Developmental and Behavioral Pediatrics, 15*, 248-291.

Baranowski, T., Dworkin, R., Henski, J. C., et al. (1986). The accuracy of children's self-reports of diet: Family health project. *Journal of the American Dietetic Association, 86*, 1381-1385.

Barry, A., & Lipmann, S. B. (1990). Anorexia nervosa in males. *Postgraduate Medicine, 87*(8), 161-166.

Bartholomew, A. M., Young, E. A., Martin, H. W., & Hazuda, H. P. (1990). Food frequency intakes and sociodemographic factors of elderly Mexican Americans and non-Hispanic whites. *Journal of the American Dietetic Association, 90*, 1693-1696.

Berg, K., & Isaksson, B. (1970). Body composition and nutrition of school children with cerebral palsy. *Acta Paediatrica Scandinavica, 204*(Suppl. 204), 41-51.

Berg, K., & Olsson, T. (1970). Energy expenditure of school children with cerebral palsy as determined from indirect calorimetry. *Acta Paediatrica Scandinavica, 204*(Suppl. 204), 71-80.

Bergner, M., Bobbitt, R. A., & Kressel, S., et al. (1976). The Sickness Impact Profile: Conceptual formulation and methodology for the development of a health status measure. *International Journal of Health Services, 6*, 393-415.

Blazer, O., & Williams, C. D. (1980). Epidemiology of dysphoria and depression in an elderly population. *American Journal of Psychiatry, 137*, 439-444.

Booth, D. A., Lewis, V. J., & Blair, A. J. (1990). Dietary restraint and binge eating: Pseudo-quantitative anthropology for a medicalised problem habit? *Appetite, 14*, 116-119.

Borg, G. V. (1962). *Physical performance and perceived exertion.* Lund, Sweden: Gleerup.

Brand, P. A., Rothblum, E. D., & Solomon, L. J. (1992). A comparison of lesbians, gay men, and heterosexuals on weight and restrained eating. *International Journal of Eating Disorders, 11,* 253-259.

Bray, G. A. (1989, July). Obesity: Basic considerations and clinical approaches. *Disease-a-Month,* pp. 460-525.

Brink, P. J. (1989). The fattening room among the Annang of Nigeria. *Medical Anthropology, 12,* 131-143.

Broussard, B. A., Johnson, A., Himes, J. H., Story, M., Fichtner, R., Hauck, F., Bachman-Carter, K., Hayes, J., Frohlich, K., Gray, N., Valway, S., & Gohdes, D. (1991). Prevalence of obesity in American Indians and Alaska natives. *American Journal of Clinical Nutrition, 53,* 1535S-1542S.

Brown, J. E., Tharp, T. M., Dahlberg-Luby, E. M., et al. (1990). Videotape dietary assessment: Validity, reliability, and comparison of results with 24-hour dietary recalls from elderly women in a retirement home. *Journal of the American Dietetic Association, 90,* 1675-1679.

Bucht, G., & Sandman, P. O. (1990). Nutritional aspects of dementia, especially Alzheimer's disease. *Age and Ageing, 19*(4), S32-S36.

Burke, E. J., & Collins, M. L. (1984). Using perceived exertion for the prescription of exercise in health adults. In R. C. Cantu (Ed.), *Clinical sports medicine* (pp. 93-114). Lexington, MA: Collamore.

Burkhart, J. E., Fox, R. A., & Rotatori, A. F. (1988). Obesity in the developmentally disabled. In D. C. Russo & J. H. Kededsy (Eds.), *Behavioral medicine with the developmentally disabled* (pp. 239-263). New York: Plenum.

Butler, M. G. (1990). Prader-Willi syndrome: Current understanding of cause and diagnosis. *American Journal of Medical Genetics, 35,* 319-332.

Butler, R. N. (1963). The life review: An interpretation of the reminiscences of the elderly. *Psychiatry, 26,* 65-72.

Campbell, A. J., Spears, G. F. S., Brown, J. S., Busby, W. J., & Borrie, M. J. (1990). Anthropometric measurements as predictors of mortality in a community population aged 70 years and over. *Age and Ageing, 19,* 131-135.

Carter, W. B., McKenna, M., Martin, M. L., & Andresen, E. M. (1989). Health education: Special issues for older adults. *Patient Education and Counseling, 13,* 117-131.

Carter, R. L., Sharbaug, C. O., & Stapell, C. A. (1981). Reliability and validity of the 24-hour recall: Analysis of data from a pediatric population. *Journal of the American Dietetic Association, 79,* 542-549.

Cassidy, C. M. (1994). Walk a mile in my shoes: Culturally sensitive food-habit research. *American Journal of Clinical Research, 59*(Suppl.), 190S-197S.

Chad, K., Jobling, A., & Frail, H. (1990). Metabolic rate: A factor in developing obesity in children with Down syndrome? *American Journal on Mental Retardation, 95,* 228-235.

Chernoff, R. (1990). Physiologic aging and nutritional status. *Nutrition in Clinical Practice, 5*(8), 8-13.

Choudry, I. Y., & Mumford, D. B. (1992). A pilot study of eating disorders in Mirpur (Pakistan) using an Urdu version of the Eating Attitudes Test. *International Journal of Eating Disorders, 11,* 243-251.

Chumlea, W. C. (1991). Anthropometric assessment of nutritional status in the elderly. In J. H. Himes (Ed.), *Anthropometric assessment of nutritional status* (pp. 399-415). New York: Wiley-Liss.

Chumlea, W. C., Baumgartner, R. N., & Vellas, B. P. (1991). Anthropometry and body composition in the perspective of nutritional status in the elderly. *Nutrition, 7,* 57-60.

Chumlea, W. C., & Cronk, C. E. (1981). Overweight among children with Trisomy 21. *Journal of Mental Deficiency Research, 25*, 275-280.

Chumlea, W. C., Guo, S., Roche, A. F., & Steinbaugh, M. L. (1988). Prediction of body weight for the nonambulatory elderly. *Journal of the American Dietetic Association, 88*, 564-588.

Chumlea, W. C., Roche, A. F., & Mukhergee, D. (1987). *Nutritional assessment in the elderly through anthropometry* (2nd ed.). Columbus, OH: Ross Laboratories.

Chun, Z. F., Mitchell, J. E., & Li, K., et al. (1992). The prevalence of anorexia nervosa and bulimia nervosa among the freshman medical college students in China. *International Journal of Eating Disorders, 12*, 209-214.

Cloud, H. H. (1987). Nutrition assessment of the individual with developmental disabilities. *Topics in Clinical Nutrition, 2*, 53-62.

Cousins, J. H., Rubovits, D. S., Dunn, J. K., Reeves, R. S., Ramirez, A. G., & Foreyt, J. P. (1992). Family versus individually oriented intervention for weight loss in Mexican American women. *Public Health Reports, 107*(5), 549-555.

Dakkak, M., & Bennett, J. R. (1992). A new dysphagia score with objective validation. *Journal of Clinical Gastroenterology, 14*(2), 99-100.

Davis, C., & Yager, J. (1992). Transcultural aspects of eating disorders: A critical literature review. *Culture, Medicine and Psychiatry, 16*, 377-394.

Desmond, S. M., Price, J. H., Hallinan, C., & Smith, D. (1989). Black and white adolescents' perceptions of their weight. *Journal of School Health, 59*(8), 353-358.

DiPietro, L., Anda, R. F., Williamson, D. F., & Stunkard, A. J. (1992). Depressive symptoms and weight change in a national cohort of adults. *International Journal of Obesity, 16*(10), 745-753.

Dolan, B. M., Lacey, J. H., & Evans, C. (1990). Eating behavior and attitudes to weight and shape in British women from three ethnic groups. *British Journal of Psychiatry, 157*, 523-528.

Doty, R. L. (1989). Influence of age and age-related diseases on olfactory function. *Annals of the New York Academy of Sciences, 561*, 76-85.

Dubois, S., & Boivin, J. F. (1990). Accuracy of telephone dietary recalls in elderly subjects. *Journal of the American Dietetic Association, 90*(12), 1680-1687.

Eck, L. H., Klesges, R. C., & Hanson, C. L. (1989). Recall of a child's intake from one meal: Are parents accurate? *Journal of the American Dietetic Association, 89*, 784-788.

Eddy, T. P., Nicholson, A. L., & Wheeler, E. F. (1965). Energy expenditures and dietary intakes in cerebral palsy. *Developmental Medicine and Child Neurology, 7*, 377.

Ekvall, S. (Ed.). (1993). *Pediatric nutrition in chronic diseases and developmental disorders.* New York: Oxford University Press.

Emmons, L. (1992). Dieting and purging behavior in black and white high school students. *Journal of the American Dietetic Association, 92*, 306-312.

Feskens, E. J., Bowles, C. H., & Kromhout, D. (1992). A longitudinal study on glucose tolerance and other cardiovascular risk factors: Association within an elderly population. *Journal of Clinical Epidemiology, 45*(3), 293-300.

Fischer, C. A., Crockett, S. J., Heller, K. E., & Skauge, L. H. (1991). Nutrition knowledge, attitudes, and practices of older and younger elderly in rural areas. *Journal of the American Dietetic Association, 91*(10), 1398-1401.

Fischer, J., & Johnson, M. A. (1990). Low body weight and weight loss in the aged. *Journal of the American Dietetic Association, 90*(12), 1697-1706.

Folstein, M. F., Folstein, S. E., & McHugh, P. R. (1975). Mini-Mental State: A practical guide for grading the cognitive state of patient for the clinician. *Journal of Psychiatric Research, 12*, 189-198.

Frank, G. C. (1985). Nutrient profile on personal computers: A comparison of DINE with mainframe computers. *Health Education, 16*, 16-19.

Frank, G. C. (1991). Taking a bite out of eating behavior: Food records and food recalls of children. *Journal of School Health, 61*, 198-200.

Frank, G. C., Berenson, G. S., Schilling, P. E., & Moore, M. C. (1977). Adapting the 24-hour dietary recall for epidemiologic studies of school children. *Journal of the American Dietetic Association, 71*, 26-31.

Frank, G. C., Hollatz, A., & Webber, L. S. (1984). Effect of interviewer recording practices on nutrient intake: Bogalusa heart study. *Journal of the American Dietetic Association, 84*, 1432-1439.

Garner, D. M., Olmsted, M. P., Bohr, Y., & Garfinkel, P. E. (1982). The Eating Attitudes Test: Psychometric features and clinical correlates. *Psychological Medicine, 12*, 871-878.

Goldman, R. F., & Buskirk, E. R. (1961). Body volume measurement by underwater weighing: Description of a method. In J. Brozek & A. Henschel (Eds.), *Techniques for measuring body composition* (pp. 78-89). Washington, DC: National Research Council.

Greenswag, L. R. (1987). Adults with Prader Willi syndrome: A review of 232 cases. *Developmental Medicine and Child Neurology, 29*, 145-152.

Greenswag, L. R., & Alexander, R. C. (Eds.). (1988). *Management of Prader Willi syndrome.* New York: Springer-Verlag.

Grogan, C., Ekvall, S., & Bozian, R. (1977). The effect of physical activity and nutrient intake on the body composition of myelomeningocele patients as determined by K^{40}, urinary creatinine, and anthropometric measurements. *Federation Proceedings, 36*, 1165.

Hamill, P. V. V., Drizd, T. A., Johnson, C. L., Reed, R. B., Roche, A. F., & Moore, W. M. (1979). Physical growth: National Center for Health Statistics percentiles. *American Journal of Clinical Nutrition, 32*, 607-629.

Hammer, L. D., Kraemer, H. C., Wilson, D. M., Ritter, P. L., & Dornbusch, S. M. (1991). Standardized percentile curves of body-mass index for children and adolescents. *American Journal of Disease in Children, 145*, 259-263.

Harris, M. B., & Furukawa, C. (1986). Attitudes toward obesity in an elderly sample. *Journal of Obesity and Weight Regulation, 5*(1), 5-16.

Harris, M. I. (1990). Epidemiology of diabetes mellitus among the elderly in the United States. *Clinics in Geriatric Medicine, 6*(4), 703-719.

Hastings, P., Darling, M., & Cowles, M. (1993, August). *Further validation of a report on physical activity.* Poster session presented at the annual meeting of the American Psychological Association, Toronto, Ontario, Canada.

Hegsted, D. M. (1989). Recommended dietary intakes of elderly subjects. *American Journal of Clinical Nutrition, 50*(Suppl. 5), 1190-1194.

Herbert, L., & Teague, M. L. (1988-1989). Exercise adherence and older adults: A theoretical perspective. *Activities, Adaptation and Aging, 13*(1-2), 91-905.

Hersen, M., & Bellack, A. (Eds.). (1988). *Dictionary of behavioral assessment techniques.* New York: Pergamon.

Herzog, D. B., Newman, K. L., Yeh, C. J., & Warshaw, M. (1992). Body image satisfaction in homosexual and heterosexual women. *International Journal of Eating Disorders, 11*(4), 391-396.

Holm, V., Cassidy, S. B., Butler, M. G., Hanchett, J. M., Greenswag, L. R., Whitman, B. Y., & Greenberg, F. (1993). Prader-Willi syndrome: Consensus diagnostic criteria. *Pediatrics, 91*, 398-402.

Horwath, C. C. (1991). Nutrition goals for older adults: A review. *The Gerontologist, 31*(6), 811-821.

Hsu, L. K. (1987). Are the eating disorders becoming more common in blacks? *International Journal of Eating Disorders, 6*(1), 113-124.

Hsu, L. K. G., & Zimmer, B. (1988). Eating disorders in old age. *International Journal of Eating Disorders, 7*(1), 133-138.

Hyer, L., & Blazer, D. G. (1982). Depression in long-term care facilities. In D. G. Blazer (Ed.), *Depression in late life* (pp. 268-295). St. Louis: Mosby.

Iwata, B. A., Riordan, M. M., Wohl, M. K., & Finney, J. W. (1982). Pediatric feeding disorders: Behavioral analysis and treatment. In P. J. Accardo (Ed.), *Failure to thrive in infancy and childhood* (pp. 297-329). Baltimore: University Park Press.

Jeffrey, D. B., Lemnitzer, N. B., Hickey, J. S., Hess, M. S., McLellarn, R. W., & Stroud, J. M. (1980). The development of a behavioral eating test and its relationship to a self-report food attitude scale in young children. *Behavioral Assessment, 2,* 87-89.

Kalisz, K., & Ekvall, S. (1984). A nutritional interview for clients with developmental disorder. *Mental Retardation, 22,* 279-288.

Kamel, P. L. (1990). Nutritional assessment and requirements. *Dysphagia, 4,* 189-195.

Karvetti, R. L., & Knuts, L. R. (1981). Agreement between dietary interviews: Nutrient intake measured by dietary history and 24-hour recalls and seven-day recalls. *Journal of the American Dietetic Association, 79,* 654-660.

Kazdin, A. E. (1982). *Single-case research designs: Methods for clinical and applied settings.* New York: Oxford University Press.

King, M. B., & Bhugra, D. (1989). Eating disorders: Lessons from a cross-cultural study. *Psychological Medicine, 19,* 955-958.

Kinney, E. L., & Caldwell, J. W. (1990). The relationship between body weight and mortality in men aged 75 years and older. *Southern Medical Journal, 83*(11), 1256-1258.

Klesges, R. C., Coates, T. J., Brown, G., Sturgeon-Tillisch, J., Moldenhauer-Klesges, L. M., Holzer, B., Woolfrey, J., & Vollmer, J. (1983). Parent influences on children's eating behavior and relative weight. *Journal of Applied Behavior Analysis, 16,* 373-374.

Klesges, R. C., Coates, T. J., Moldenhauer, L. M., Holzer, B., Gustavon, X., & Barnes, J. (1984). The FATS: An observational system for assessing physical activity in children and associated parent behaviour. *Behavioural Assessment, 6,* 333-345.

Klesges, R. C., Klesges, L. M., & Coates, T. J. (1988). Observational system for assessing mealtime behaviors in children and associated parent behavior. In M. Hersen & A. S. Bellack (Eds.), *Dictionary of behavioral assessment techniques* (pp. 317-318). New York: Pergamon.

Krantzler, N. J., Mullen, B. J., Comstock, E. M., Holden, C. A., Schutz, H. G., Grivetti, L. E., & Meiselman, H. L. (1982). Methods of food intake assessment: An annotated bibliography. *Journal of Nutrition Education, 14,* 108-116.

Kuczmarski, R. J. (1989). Need for body composition information in elderly subjects. *American Journal of Clinical Nutrition, 50,* 1150-1157.

Kumanyika, S., Obarzanek, E., Stevens, V. J., Hebert, P. R., & Whelton, P. K. (1991). Weight-loss experience of black and white participants in NHLBI-sponsored clinical trials. *American Journal of Clinical Nutrition, 53,* 1631S-1638S.

Lachenmeyer, J. R., & Muni-Brandner, P. (1988). Eating disorders in a nonclinical adolescent population: Implications for treatment. *Adolescence, 23*(90), 303-312.

Ledbetter, D. H., Riccardi, V. M., Airhart, S. D., Strobel, R. J., Keenan, B. S., & Crawford, J. D. (1981). Deletion of chromosome 15 as a cause of the Prader-Willi syndrome. *New England Journal of Medicine, 304,* 325-329.

Lee, S., Hsu, G., & Wing, Y. K. (1992). Bulimia nervosa in Hong Kong Chinese patients. *British Journal of Psychiatry, 161,* 545-551.

Lohman, T. G. (1982). Measurement of body composition in children. *Journal of Physical Education and Recreation, 53*, 67-70.

Lohman, T. G., Boileau, R. A., & Slaughter, M. H. (1989). Body composition in children and youth. In R. A. Boileau (Ed.), *Advances in pediatric sport sciences* (Vol. 1, pp. 29-57). Champaign, IL: Human Kinetics.

Lohman, T. G., Roche, A. F., & Martorell, R. (Eds.). (1988). *Anthropometric standardization reference manual.* Champaign, IL: Human Kinetics.

Loria, C., Arroyo, R. D., & Briefel, R. (1994). Cultural biases influencing dietary interviews with Mexican Americans: The HANES experience. *American Journal of Clinical Nutrition, 59* (1-S), 2915.

Luiselli, J. K. (1989). Behavioral assessment and treatment of pediatric feeding disorders in developmental disabilities. In M. Hersen, R. M. Eisler, & P. M. Miller (Eds.), *Progress in behavior modification* (Vol. 24, pp. 91-131). Newbury Park, CA: Sage.

Maloney, M. J., McGuire, J. B., & Daniels, S. R. (1988). Reliability testing of a children's version of the Eating Attitudes Test. *Journal of the American Academy of Child and Adolescent Psychiatry, 5*, 541-543.

Manikam, R. (1985). *Validation of selected skinfold calipers and prediction equations in measuring body composition among college aged male and female nonathletic population.* Unpublished master's thesis, Northern Illinois University, DeKalb, IL.

Matsuura, K., Fujimura, M., Nozawa, Y., Iida, Y., & Hirayam, M. (1992). The body shape preferences of Japanese female students. *International Journal of Obesity, 16*, 87-93.

McCarran, M. S., & Andrasik, F. (1990). Behavioral weight-loss for multi-handicapped adults: Assessing caretaker involvement and measures of behavior change. *Addictive Behaviors, 15*, 13-20.

McDowell, A., Engel, A., Massey, J. T., et al. (1982). Plan and operation of the Second National Health and Nutrition Examination Survey, 1976-80. In *Vital and Health Statistics, 1*(19) (DHHS Publication No. [PHS] 82-1321). Washington, DC: National Center for Health Statistics.

McKenzie, T. L., Sallis, J. F., Nader, P. R., Patterson, T. L., Elder, J. P., Berry, C. C., Rupp, J. W., Atkins, C. J., Buono, M. J., & Nelson, J. A. (1991). BEACHES: An observational system for assessing children's eating and physical activity behaviors and associated events. *Journal of Applied Behavior Analysis, 24*, 141-151.

McPartland, R. J., Foster, F. G., Kupfer, D. J., & Weiss, B. L. (1976). Activity sensors for use in psychiatric evaluation. *Transactions on Biomedical Engineering, 23*, 175-177.

Millen Posner, B., Jette, A. M., Smith, K. W., & Miller, D. R. (1993). Nutrition and health risks in the elderly: The Nutrition Screening Initiative. *American Journal of Public Health, 83*, 972-978.

Miller, D. K., Morley, J. E., Rubenstein, L. Z., & Pietruszka, F. M. (1991). Abnormal eating attitudes and body image in older undernourished individuals. *Journal of the American Geriatrics Society, 39*, 462-466.

Mita, K., Akataki, K., Itoh, K., Ono, Y., Ishida, N., & Oki, T. (1993). Assessment of obesity of children with spina bifida. *Developmental Medicine and Child Neurology, 35*, 305-311.

Mitchell, C. O., & Chernoff, R. (1991). Nutritional assessment of the elderly. In R. Charnoff (Ed.), *Geriatric nutrition: The health professional's handbook* (pp. 363-396). Aspen/Gaithersburg, MD: Aspen.

Monturo, C. A. (1990). Enteral access device selection. *Nutrition in Clinical Practice, 5*, 207-213.

Morisaki, N., Kawano, M., Watanabe, S., Saito, Y., & Yoshida, S. (1992). Role of obesity in ischemic heart disease in elderly diabetic patients. *Gerontology, 38*(3), 167-173.

Morley, J. E., Mooradian, A. D., Silver, A. J., Heber, D., & Alfin-Slater, R. B. (1988). Nutrition in the elderly. *Annals of Internal Medicine, 109*, 890-903.

Morley, J. E., Silver, A. J., Miller, D. K., & Rubinstein, L. Z. (1989). The anorexia of the elderly. *Annals of the New York Academy of Sciences, 575*, 50-59.

Mullins, J. B., & Vogl-Maier, B. (1987). Weight management of youth with Prader-Willi syndrome. *International Journal of Eating Disorders, 6*, 419-425.

Mumford, D. B., Whitehouse, A. M., & Choudry, I. Y. (1992). Survey of eating disorders in English-medium schools in Lahore, Pakistan. *International Journal of Eating Disorders, 11*(2), 173-184.

Myers, A. M., & Gonda, G. (1986). Research on physical activity in the elderly: Practical implications for program planning. *Canadian Journal on Aging, 5*(3), 175-187.

Nasser, M. (1986a). The validity of the Eating Attitudes Test in a non-Western population. *Acta Psychiatrica Scandinavica, 73*, 109-110.

Nasser, M. (1986b). Comparative study of the prevalence of abnormal eating attitudes among Arab female students of both London and Cairo Universities. *Psychological Medicine, 16*, 621-625.

Nasser, M. (1988). Culture and weight consciousness. *Journal of Psychosomatic Research, 32*(6), 573-577.

Neumarker, U., Dudeck, U., Vollrath, M., Neumarker, K. J., & Steinhausen, H. C. (1992). Eating attitudes among adolescent anorexia nervosa patients and normal subjects in former West and East Berlin: A transcultural comparison. *International Journal of Eating Disorders, 12*(3), 281-289.

Olsen-Noll, C. G., & Bosworth, M. F. (1989). Anorexia and weight loss in the elderly: Causes range from loose dentures to debilitating illness. *Postgraduate Medicine, 85*(3), 140-144.

Palmer, S., & Horn, S. (1978). Feeding problems in children. In S. Palmer & S. Ekvall (Eds.), *Pediatric nutrition in developmental disorders* (pp. 107-129). Springfield, IL: Charles C Thomas.

Pawson, I. G., Martorell, R., & Mendoza, F. E. (1991). Prevalence of overweight and obesity in US Hispanic populations. *American Journal of Clinical Nutrition, 53*, 1522S-1528S.

Rhodus, N. L., & Brown, J. (1990). The association of xerostomia and inadequate intake in older adults. *Journal of the American Dietetic Association, 90*(12), 1688-1692.

Rimmer, J. H., Braddock, D., & Fujiura, G. (1993). Prevalence of obesity in adults with mental retardation: Implications for health promotion and disease prevention. *Mental Retardation, 31*, 105-110.

Rimmer, J. H., Kelly, L. E., & Rosentswieg, J. (1987). Accuracy of anthropometric equations for estimating body composition of mentally retarded adults. *American Journal of Mental Deficiency, 91*, 626-632.

Root, M. P. P. (1990). Disordered eating in women of color. *Sex Roles, 22*(7-8), 525-536.

Rosen, L. W., Shafer, C. L., Dummer, G. M., Cross, L. K., Deuman, G. W., & Malmberg, S. R. (1988). Prevalence of pathogenic weight-control behaviors among Native American women and girls. *International Journal of Eating Disorders, 7*(6), 807-811.

Rubin-Terrado, M., & Linkenheld, D. (1991, November-December). Don't choke on this: A swallowing assessment. *Geriatric Nursing*, pp. 288-291.

Sallis, J. F., Haskell, W. L., Wood, P. D., Fortmann, S. P., Rogers, T., Blair, S. W., & Paffenberger, R. S., Jr. (1985). Physical activity assessment in the five-city project. *American Journal of Epidemiology, 121*, 91-106.

Saris, W. H. M. (1986). Habitual physical activity in children: Methodology and findings in health and disease. *Medicine and Science in Sports and Exercise, 18*, 253-263.

Schiffman, S. S., & Warwick, Z. S. (1988). Flavor enhancement of foods for the elderly can reverse anorexia. *Neurobiology of Aging, 9,* 24-26.

Schneider, J. A., & Agras, W. S. (1987). Bulimia in males: A matched comparison with females. *International Journal of Eating Disorders, 6*(2), 235-242.

Schoeller, D. A. (1989). Changes in total body water with age. *American Journal of Clinical Nutrition, 50,* 1176-1181.

Schulman, J. L., Suran, B. G., Stevens, T. M., & Kupst, M. J. (1979). Instructions, feedback, and reinforcement in reducing activity levels in the classroom. *Journal of Applied Behavior Analysis, 12,* 441-447.

Shepherd, K., Roberts, D., Golding, S., Thomas, B. J., & Shepherd, R. W. (1991). Body composition in myelomeningocele. *American Journal of Clinical Nutrition, 53,* 1-6.

Silberstein, L. R., Mishkind, M. E., Striegel-Moore, R. H., Timko, C., & Rodin, J. (1989). Men and their bodies: A comparison of homosexual and heterosexual men. *Psychosomatic Medicine, 57,* 337-346.

Sisson, L. A., & Van Hasselt, V. B. (1989). Feeding disorders. In J. K. Luiselli (Ed.), *Behavioral medicine and developmental disabilities* (pp. 45-73). New York: Springer-Verlag.

Slifer, K., Cataldo, M., Babbitt, R., & Cataldo, M. (1993). Behavioral consultation in hospital settings. In J. Zinns, T. Kratochwill, & S. Elliott (Eds.), *Handbook of consultation services for children: Applications in educational and clinical services* (pp. 291-304). San Francisco: Jossey-Bass.

Sohlberg, C. N. S. (1988). Eating disorder inventory in Sweden: Description, cross-cultural comparison, and clinical utility. *Acta Psychiatrica Scandinavia, 78,* 567-575.

Sonies, B. C. (1992). Oropharyngeal dysphagia in the elderly. *Clinics in Geriatric Medicine, 8*(3), 569-577.

Sovner, R., & Hurley, A. D. (1986). Drug profiles II: Mesoridazine and thioridazine. *Psychiatric Aspects of Mental Retardation Reviews, 5,* 27-37.

Sovner, R., & Hurley, A. D. (1988). Drug profiles III: Heterocyclic antidepressants. *Psychiatric Aspects of Mental Retardation Reviews, 7,* 1-5.

Stern, M. P., Pugh, J. A., Parten Gaskill, S., & Hazuda, H. P. (1982). Knowledge, attitudes, and behavior related to obesity and dieting in Mexican Americans and Anglos: The San Antonio Heart Study. *American Journal of Epidemiology, 115*(6), 917-928.

Stone, E. J., Perry, C. L., & Luepker, R. V. (1989). Synthesis of cardiovascular behavioral research for youth health promotion. *Health Education Quarterly, 16,* 155-169.

Stunkard, A. (1960). A method of studying physical activity in man. *American Journal of Clinical Nutrition, 8,* 595-601.

Suzuki, M., Saitoh, S., Tasaki, Y., Shimomura, Y., Makishima, R., & Hosoya, N. (1991). Nutritional status and daily physical activity of handicapped students in Tokyo metropolitan schools for deaf, blind, mentally retarded, and physically handicapped individuals. *American Journal of Clinical Nutrition, 54,* 1101-1111.

Thomas, J. P., & Szmukler, G. I. (1985). Anorexia nervosa in patients of Afro-Caribbean extraction. *British Journal of Psychiatry, 146,* 653-656.

Thommessen, M., Heiberg, A., & Kase, B. F. (1992). Feeding problems in children with congenital heart disease: The impact on energy intake and growth outcome. *European Journal of Clinical Nutrition, 46,* 456-464.

Thommessen, M., Kase, B. F., Riis, G., & Heiberg, A. (1991). The impact of feeding problems on growth and energy intake in children with cerebral palsy. *European Journal of Clinical Health, 45,* 479-487.

Todd, K. S., Hudes, M., & Calloway, D. H. (1983). Food intake measurement: Problems and approaches. *American Journal of Clinical Nutrition, 37,* 139.

Torisky, D., Torisky, C., Kaplan, S., & Speicher, C. (1992). The NAC Pilot Project: A model for nutritional screening and intervention for developmentally disabled children with behavior disorders. *Journal of Orthomolecular Medicine, 8*, 1-14.

Tyron, W. W. (1984). Principles and methods of mechanically measuring motor activity. *Behavioural Assessment, 6*, 129-139.

U.S. Department of Health and Human Services. (1988). *The surgeon's general report on nutrition and health* (DHHS Publication No. PHS 88-50210). Washington, DC: Government Printing Office.

Van Horn, L., Gernhofer, N., Moag-Stahlberg, A., et al. (1990). Dietary assessment in children using electronic methods: Telephones and tape recorders. *Journal of the American Dietetic Association, 62*, 409-415.

Vogel, S. (1986). Oral motor and feeding problems in the tube fed infant: Suggested treatment strategies for the occupational therapist. In F. S. Cromwell (Ed.), *Occupational therapy for people with eating dysfunction* (pp. 63-79). New York: Haworth.

Warheit, G. J., Langer, L. M., Zimmerman, R. S., & Biafora, F. A. (1993). Prevalence of bulimic behaviors and bulimia among a sample of the general population. *American Journal of Epidemiology, 137*, 569-576.

Washburn, R. A., Smith, K. W., Jette, A. M., & Janney, C. A. (1993). The Physical Activity Scale for the Elderly (PASE): Development and validation. *Journal of Clinical Epidemiology, 46*(2), 153-162.

Weiffenbach, J. M. (1989). Assessment of chemosensory functioning in aging: Subjective and objective procedures. *Annals of the New York Academy of Sciences, 561*, 56-64.

Weiffenbach, J. M., & Bartoshuk, L. M. (1992). Taste and smell. *Clinics in Geriatric Medicine, 8*(3), 543-555.

White, J. V., Dwyer, J. T., Posner, B. M., Ham, R. J., Lipschitz, D. A., & Wellman, N. S. (1992). Nutrition Screening Initiative: Development and implementation of the public awareness checklist and screening tools. *Journal of the American Dietetic Association, 92*(2), 163-167.

White-O'Connor, B., Sobal, J., & Muncie, H. L. (1989). Dietary habits, weight history and vitamin supplement use in elderly osteoarthritic patients. *Journal of the American Dietetic Association, 89*(3), 378-382.

Williamson, D. F., Calpin, J. P., DiLorenzo, T. M., Garris, R. P., & Petti, T. A. (1981). Treating hyperactivity with dexedrine and activity feedback. *Behavior Modification, 5*, 399-416.

Wolinsky, F. D., Coe, R. M., McIntosh, W. A., Kubena, K. S., Prendergast, J. M., Chavez, M. N., Miller, D. K., Romeis, J. C., & Landmann, W. A. (1990). Progress in the development of a nutritional risk index. *Journal of Nutrition, 120*, 1549-1553.

Yager, J., Kurtzman, F., Landsverk, J., & Weismeier, E. (1988). Behaviors and attitudes related to eating disorders in homosexual male college students. *American Journal of Psychiatry, 145*, 495-497.

Yesavage, J. A., Brink, T. L., Rose, T. L., Lum, O., Huang, V., Adey, M., & Leirer, V. O. (1983). Development and validation of a geriatric depression screening scale: A preliminary report. *Journal of Psychiatric Research, 17*, 37-49.

Zheng, J. J., & Rosenberg, I. H. (1989). What is the nutritional status of the elderly? *Geriatrics, 44*(6), 57-58, 60, 63-64.

Appendix 12-A

Children's Eating Behavior Inventory (CEBI)

DIRECTIONS FOR FILLING OUT THE CHILDREN'S EATING BEHAVIOR INVENTORY (CEBI)

A. Please fill out the CEBI for the child you bring to the clinic.

B. Please answer *ALL* of the questions even if some do not seem to apply to your child or are hard to answer.

C. For EACH question you will need to do TWO things:

    1. Rate how often the behavior happens—circle ONE

1	2	3	4	5
NEVER	SELDOM	SOMETIMES	OFTEN	ALWAYS

    2. Tell whether the behavior is a problem for you—circle ONE   YES NO

HERE'S AN EXAMPLE: TRY IT!

    1. My child tries new foods. How often does this happen?

1	2	3	4	5
NEVER	SELDOM	SOMETIMES	OFTEN	ALWAYS

    2. Is this a problem for you?   YES NO

<u>CEBI</u>

Child's Name: _____ _____ Sex: ___ Male ___ Female
             (first)   (last)

Child's Birthday: _____ / _____ / _____
             Month   Day   Year

Today's Date: _____ / _____ / _____
             Month   Day   Year

This form completed by: ___ Mother ___ Father

                    ___ Other (Please specify): _____

486

HOW OFTEN DOES THIS HAPPEN?

1	2	3	4	5
NEVER	SELDOM	SOMETIMES	OFTEN	ALWAYS

Is this a problem
for you?

1. My child chews food as expected for his/her age _____   YES NO
2. My child enjoys eating _____   YES NO
3. My child asks for food which he/she shouldn't have _____   YES NO
4. My child feeds him/herself as expected for his/her age _____   YES NO
5. My child gags at mealtimes _____   YES NO
6. I feel confident my child eats enough _____   YES NO
7. My child vomits at mealtime _____   YES NO
8. My child takes food between meals without asking _____   YES NO
9. My child chokes at mealtimes _____   YES NO
10. My child makes food for him/herself when not allowed _____   YES NO
11. I get upset when my child doesn't eat _____   YES NO
12. At home my child eats food he/she shouldn't have _____   YES NO
13. My child uses cutlery as expected for his/her age _____   YES NO
14. At friends' homes my child eats food he/she shouldn't eat _____   YES NO
15. My child asks for food between meals _____   YES NO

IF YOU ARE A SINGLE PARENT SKIP TO NUMBER 19.
16. My child's behavior at meals upsets my spouse _____   YES NO
17. My child interrupts conversations with my spouse at meals _____   YES NO
18. I get upset with my spouse at meals _____   YES NO

IF YOU HAVE ONLY ONE CHILD SKIP NUMBER 19.
19. My child's behavior at meals upsets our other children _____   YES NO

PLEASE CHECK TO SEE THAT YOU HAVE ANSWERED *ALL* THE ITEMS.
HAVE YOU CIRCLED YES OR NO FOR EACH ITEM?

Please list any problems that were not listed above: _____

SOURCE: From *The Revised Children's Eating Behavior Inventory,* by L. A. Archer, 1991, unpublished manuscript. Copyright © 1991 by L. A. Archer. Reprinted with permission. For further information contact: Lynda Archer, Ph.D., 1 Young Street, Hamilton, Ontario, Canada L8N 1T8.

Appendix 12-B

Children's Version of the
Eating Attitudes Test (26)
(Garner et al., 1982)

Instructions: Please place an X under the word which best applies to the statements below.

Sample item: I like to eat vegetables.

Always   Very Often   Often   Sometimes   Rarely   Never

1.   I am scared about being overweight.

2.   I stay away from eating when I am hungry.

3.   I think about food a lot of the time.

4.   I have gone on eating binges where I feel that I might not be able to stop.

5.   I cut my food into small pieces.

6.   I am aware of the energy (calorie) content in foods that I eat.

7.   I try to stay away from foods such as breads, potatoes, and rice.

8.   I feel that others would like me to eat more.

9.   I vomit after I have eaten.

10.   I feel very guilty after eating.

11.   I think a lot about wanting to be thinner.

12.   I think about burning up energy (calories) when I exercise.

13.   Other people think I am too thin.

14.   I think a lot about having fat on my body.

15.   I take longer than others to eat my meals.

16.   I stay away from foods with sugar in them.

17.   I eat diet foods.

18. I think that food controls my life.

19. I can show self-control around food.

20. I feel that others pressure me to eat.

21. I give too much time and thought to food.

22. I feel uncomfortable after eating sweets.

23. I have been dieting.

24. I like my stomach to be empty.

25. I enjoy trying new rich foods.

26. I have the urge to vomit after eating.

SOURCE: From "Reliability Testing of a Children's Version of the Eating Attitudes Test," by M. J. Maloney, J. B. McGuire, and S. R. Daniels, 1988, *Journal of the American Academy of Child and Adolescent Psychiatry, 27*, pp. 542-543. Copyright © 1988 by the American Academy of Child and Adolescent Psychiatry. Reprinted with permission.

Appendix 12-C

BEACHES Dimensions and Description of Coding Categories

Categories	Description
1.0 Environment 1 alone 2 mother 3 father 4 sibling(s) 5 peer(s) 6 teacher 7 other adult(s) 8 food available 9 views TV	Describes pertinent environment conditions present during the interval. In addition to indicating who is present, codes are entered if food is accessible to the child (i.e., visible, attainable, and within 3 ft of the child) and whether or not the child watches television.
2.0 Physical location 1 inside home 2 outside home 3 outside general 4 playground/play space 5 inside school 6 cafeteria 7 outside school 8 school play space	Describes the location of the child at the end of the interval.
3.0 Activity level 1 lying down 2 sitting 3 standing 4 walking 5 very active	Provides an estimate of the intensity of the child's physical activity. Codes 1 to 4 (lying down, sitting, standing, walking) describe the body position of the child and Code 5 (very active) describes when the child is expending more energy than he or she would during ordinary walking. For example, Code 5 (very active) would be used to indicate the child is wrestling with a peer (even though he is lying on his back) or pedaling a moving tricycle or stationary bike (even though sitting).

Categories	Description
4.0 Eating behavior 1 ingests no food 2 ingests food	Describes whether or not the child ingests food during the interval.
5.0 Interactor 1 alone 2 mother 3 father 4 sibling(s) 5 peer(s) 6 teacher 7 other adult(s)	Describes persons that participate with the child in a physical or verbal exchange that is related to physical activity or eating.
6.0 Antecedents 1 none during interval 2 prompts to increase 3 prompts to decrease 4 provides imitative model 5 child request	Describes antecedent stimuli that are related to increasing or decreasing the child's eating or physical activity. Included are (a) physical (e.g., offerings) and verbal (e.g., "Eat your spinach.") prompts, (b) imitative prompts (i.e., the interactor behaves in a manner to influence the child to engage in similar physical activity or eating behavior), and (c) child requests.
7.0 Prompted event 1 not applicable 2 high-intensity activity 3 low-intensity activity 4 food	Describes the eating or physical activity behavior that was prompted. Low-intensity activities include those within physical activity Levels 1, 2, and 3, and high-intensity activities include those within Levels 4 and 5. However, prompts related to locomotor activities (e.g., walking, running, hopping, skipping, galloping, chasing, fleeing, dodging, and crawling), as well as manipulative (e.g., throwing, catching, kicking, punting, dribbling, volleying, and striking) and nonmanipulative activities (e.g., balancing, rolling, twisting, hanging, jumping) that involve gross motor movement are coded as high-intensity activities.
8.0 Child response 1 none during interval 2 complies 3 refuses	Describes the child's response to the prompt. The child may comply, refuse, or not respond during the interval.

Categories	Description

9.0 Consequences
    1 none during interval
    2 reinforce/positive
      feedback
    3 punish/negative
      feedback
	Describes the physical and verbal consequential stimuli that are associated with increased or decreased eating and physical activity. Identified reinforcers or punishers may be contingent on the behavior during the interval or are stated that they will be contingent on compliance or refusal (e.g., "Finish your lunch or you won't get your Popsicle for dinner.").

10.0 Events receiving
      consequences
    1 not applicable
    2 high-intensity activity
    3 low-intensity activity
    4 food
    5 child request
	Describes the type of eating or physical activity behavior that received consequences

SOURCE: From "BEACHES: An Observational System for Assessing Children's Eating and Physical Activity Behaviors and Associated Events," by T. L. McKenzie, J. F. Sallis, P. R. Nader, T. L. Patterson, J. P. Elder, C. C. Berry, J. W. Rupp, C. J. Atkins, M. J. Buono, and J. A. Nelson, 1991, *Journal of Applied Behavior Analysis, 24*, pp. 144-145. Copyright © 1991 by *Journal of Applied Behavior Analysis*. Reprinted with permission.

13

Identification of Psychological Problems of Patients With Eating and Weight-Related Disorders in General Medical Settings

ANNE W. RILEY

I t is very likely that most individuals with eating and weight-related problems have been seen multiple times by a primary care physician or nurse practitioner prior to receiving a formal diagnosis of their eating disorder or weight problem. Consequently, routine medical visits are an important arena for the early identification and treatment of anorexia nervosa and bulimia nervosa as well as weight problems such as obesity and underweight. Moreover, primary care providers need to ascertain the presence of significant psychological dysfunction and emotional problems among individuals with appetite or weight disturbance because such problems are likely to interfere

493

with medical recommendations. Such patients require recognition and on-going management by medical providers who can ensure that they receive treatment for their psychological disorder as well as for the nutritional and weight consequences of their eating behavior. It is probable that the variable outcome of the treatment of eating disorders and weight problems is related to the presence, type, and severity of emotional and personality problems and whether they are identified and effectively treated.

The purpose of this chapter is to outline procedures for assessing co-occurring psychological problems that affect treatment outcome for medical patients who may have an eating or weight-related problem. The intended audience is general medical providers: internists, pediatricians, family physicians, gynecologists, and nurse practitioners. It is certainly also relevant for medical specialists such as those in gastroenterology and endocrinology, to whom these patients are frequently referred. Given the reluctance of some individuals with eating and weight-related disorders to acknowledge their problems, even to themselves, the medical provider is in a key position to identify and help the patient address such problems. Patient acknowledgment of a manageable weight problem will be fostered by a medical assessment that communicates concern, a willingness to understand the patient's viewpoint, and helpfulness. The assessment must be comprehensive, going beyond the presenting problem. The techniques required to conduct this type of patient interview and interaction are not routinely taught in medical school, despite recommendations for such training (Lipkin, Quill, & Napodano, 1984). Consequently, this approach may be somewhat alien to general medical practitioners although excellent models are available for teaching it (Gorden, 1987; Lipkin et al., 1984; Novack, Dube, & Goldstein, 1992; Smith & Hoppe, 1991).

Any clinical assessment should be undertaken only if it will potentially improve treatment outcome. Effective assessment involves the patient in treatment planning, provides direction for a tailored approach to treatment, and establishes the baseline by which treatment can later be evaluated. Two modes of assessment will be addressed: the clinical interview and brief questionnaires. The emphasis is on the clinical interview as it optimally obtains information, communicates provider concern, provides reassurance, and sets the stage for collaborative treatment planning with the patient (Lipkin et al., 1984; Smith & Hoppe, 1991).

Psychological Problems in General Medicine

Patients seen in medical settings rarely identify the reason for their visit as a psychological or psychosocial problem. Nonetheless, in a national epidemiologic study, 21.7% of adults using medical services met strict criteria for a mental disorder diagnosis (Kessler et al., 1987), based on the *Diagnostic and Statistical Manual of Mental Disorders III* (*DSM-III*; American Psychiatric Association, 1980/1987). An even higher proportion of medical patients have significant psychosocial concerns, with the result that the primary care system is now well accepted as an integral part of the "*de facto* mental health system" (Regier, Goldberg, & Taube, 1978). Nonetheless, mental disorders, including anorexia nervosa and bulimia, are very poorly recognized by physicians, even as a differential diagnosis (Kessler, Cleary, & Burke, 1985; Shapiro et al., 1985).

Individuals with weight or eating-related disorders who are seen in medical settings are most likely to present for routine care, acute illness, unspecified vague complaints, or because of irregular menses, gastrointestinal problems, and symptoms of electrolyte imbalance such as extreme tiredness and cardiac arrhythmias. When patients do directly acknowledge their psychosocial problems, providers are much more likely to identify and attempt to manage them (Dulcan et al., 1989). However, individuals with eating disorders are even less likely than other patients to present their problems in terms of their psychological needs. Restrictive anorexics typically deny their disorder and need for treatment, whereas bulimics tend to be embarrassed and secretive about their bingeing and purging behavior (Foreyt & McGavin, 1988). Further reducing the likelihood of accurate identification, general medical providers typically avoid addressing psychological problems, although such failure has been shown to negatively affect medical treatment and to result in poorer medical and social functioning outcomes (Ormel et al., 1990).

Co-Occurrence of Eating Disorders and Psychological Disorders in General Medical Settings

Individuals with all but the most severe eating and weight disorders are particularly likely to be seen only by general medical providers and to have an even higher rate of emotional or behavioral disorders such as depression and obsessive and compulsive behaviors than the rest of the population (Hendren, 1983; Johnson & Connors, 1987; Walker & Shaw, 1988). Among medical outpatients generally, the prevalence of diagnosable mental disorders is roughly 20% (Kessler et al., 1987), with depression being one of the most common and disabling (Wells et al., 1989). Depression is significantly more common among those with eating disorders and is especially pronounced in bulimia (Russell, 1988).

Although depressive disorders can be life threatening, they are most commonly acute and responsive to pharmacological treatment. Recently, antidepressant medication has been shown to be fairly effective in reducing the depressive symptomatology of bulimics and in reducing bulimic episodes (Strober & Katz, 1988). Anxiety and obsessive-compulsive behavior, while also causing dysphoria, may be chronically associated with an eating disturbance (Walker & Shaw, 1988). Obsessions with one's weight and body appearance, compulsive and rigid patterns of eating, and urges that cannot be resisted are common and can be discerned in a careful medical interview. Such behaviors are aspects of obsessive-compulsive personality and, a more severe disorder, obsessive-compulsive disorder (OCD), both of which are characterized by a pervasive pattern of perfectionism and inflexibility. This rigidity may interfere with task completion and be associated with a restricted expression of affect, indecisiveness, and overconscientiousness (American Psychiatric Association, 1980/1987). Although the presence of behaviors that reflect compulsive urges and the presence of distress that is based on distorted thinking are important to identify, patients may deny that compulsive eating and dieting or distress about personal failures are problematic. Nonetheless, a mental health evaluation is indicated if such a patient has a significant weight problem. A referral that provides access to a psychiatrist may be important, as several medications now seem promising for the treatment of obsessive-compulsive disorder, and medication may be indicated for patients with other mental disorders. Initiation of psychotropic medication for such individuals by a general medical provider without psychiatric consultation is rarely indicated, primarily because general medical providers routinely prescribe dosages that are too low to be effective (Lenert, Markowitz, & Blaschke, 1993).

Even in the absence of a disorder, cognitive distortions and unreasonable belief systems may form the basis for much pathological eating-related behavior. Particularly common is dichotomous thinking in which the world is viewed in terms of extremes; if one is not perfect, then one must be a total failure. This sets the stage for seeing oneself as good only if one is thin and stringently dieting (Johnson & Connors, 1987). This type of rigid and distorted thinking is very difficult to change and again may indicate the need for collaborative treatment with a mental health professional. A final consideration is that multiple psychosocial concerns such as poor self-image, social skills deficits, and emotional distress are associated with eating disorders and weight problems (Garner & Garfinkel, 1981; Johnson & Berndt, 1983). Even individuals whose obesity or thinness is secondary to organic disorders experience significant alterations in their self-perceptions and social interactions.

Reviews of the Clinical Interview Assessment and Instruments

This section addresses the role of the family, describes the interview process with specific indications for patients with eating disorders, and reviews two questionnaires that are highly regarded for screening for psychopathology in general medical settings. Finally, an approach for interpreting a clinically positive result on a screening questionnaire for psychopathology is suggested so as to correctly ascertain which patients require a recommendation for psychological assessment.

Family Involvement in the Assessment Process

Although the patient-centered interview is the critical clinical skill and forms the basis for optimal patient care (Lipkin et al., 1984; Smith & Hoppe, 1991), the assessment and treatment of eating disorders cannot be limited to the patient her- or himself (Johnson, 1985). Because anorexia nervosa begins in early adolescence and bulimia has its onset in late adolescence (Foreyt & McGavin, 1988), and because virtually all eating patterns are exhibited at home, treatment of these individuals must be understood in the context of the family. The family should be involved to the greatest reasonable extent, to inform and support the management decisions that the provider and patient decide to implement. Parents should be interviewed separately as well as together with the adolescent (Feldman, Rosser, & McGrath, 1987), and the adult patient's family members should be involved in a similar manner. However, even phone consultation can be useful. Helping the family recognize that they are not to blame for the problem, but that they must work together to help solve it, is the fundamental objective of the initial interview. Guidance and education can subsequently be useful. Parents not only should be encouraged to urge their teen to eat well-balanced meals at regular times, they should also arrange the family schedule and meal content so that this will occur. Food purchases and availability should be discussed and an arrangement agreed on by all family members. When parents are very distressed about the eating problem or even a weight problem, it may be reasonable to suggest that the parents seek help from a nutritionist or a mental health specialist to discuss ways of helping their child.

This chapter does not offer explicit methods for assessing family functioning, for two reasons. First, there is little evidence that the available questionnaires can provide meaningful information to guide treatment planning for the range of patients' families. Second, although some instruments are widely used in research, such as the Family Environment Scale (FES; Moos & Moos, 1986), FACES III (Olsen, Portner, & Lavee, 1985), and the Family Assessment Device (Epstein, Baldwin, & Bishop, 1983), they have been normed on limited samples of middle-class white families. Investigations with sociodemographically diverse groups of families indicate that the most popular instrument, the FES, has a different factor structure and is less reliable in nontraditional and nonwhite families than it was in the normative sample (Boake & Salmon, 1983; Munet-Vilaro & Egan, 1990; Tolson & Wilson, 1990).

Serious family dysfunction can be discerned through the medical interviews; however, it will not be treated by the general medical practitioner. If the provider begins to suspect that the family is either unwittingly or purposefully subverting the treatment process, the involvement of a mental health specialist is important. If a family is unwilling to accept such a referral, the patient may have to be treated as an independent adult and collaboration with a mental health specialist may be indicated.

The Patient-Centered Interview

The sine qua non of clinical assessment is that the information collected, whether by interview, questionnaire, or laboratory test, must make a contribution to treatment planning and outcomes. The interviewing format outlined here reflects the patient-centered interview and treatment curriculum recommended by the Society for Research and Education in Primary Care Internal Medicine (Lipkin, 1987). The specific approaches suggested are based on a training curriculum developed and shown to be effective in identifying and reducing patients' psychological distress (Roter & Hall, 1992). There are several reasons for the preeminence of this type of interview. Most basically, it involves a strategy for identifying and discussing all of a patient's concerns—a provider approach that has been shown to facilitate problem improvement and result in increased patient satisfaction (Bensing, 1991; Francis, Korsch, & Morris, 1969; Starfield et al., 1979). As is true for many health problems, the successful treatment of an eating disorder requires patient-motivated behavior change. The presence of distress, distorted thinking, and psychopathology will impair the patient's ability to institute and maintain the behavior changes necessary for improvement. The patient-centered interview provides a mechanism for developing an atmosphere of mutual participation in determining the diagnosis, treatment plan, and co-occurring problems that may influence treatment success, and potential need for mental health collaboration.

Assessment in the Medical Interview

The initial moments of the visit are critical to structuring the provider-patient encounter (Gorden, 1987; Johnson & Connors, 1987). Patients typically do not expect physicians to be receptive to their emotional and/or social problems so it is up to the physician to explicitly convey to the patient the kind of information that is desirable and suitable for discussion during the visit. This can be communicated with framing statements (e.g., "It sometimes helps me in caring for a patient if I know what their home or work situation is and whether any things are bothering them"). Patients learn that life problems are related to effective health care, and this sets the stage for the physician to ask sensitive questions. The importance of setting the agenda with most adolescents and for patients with anorexia or bulimia cannot be overstated, as these are patients who tend to be quite noncommittal or suspicious in response to probing questions. As the majority of these patients are girls or women, the female pronoun will be used in the following section.

The underlying strategy for the interview is to allow the patient to tell her own story of her symptoms and life context (Lipkin et al., 1984; Roter & Hall, 1992). Once the patient hears that the interview will include psychosocial and other life problems, the information gathering begins with eliciting the full spectrum of patient concerns. Because medical complaints are often a patient's "entry ticket" to the medical visit, it is up to the provider to get the full range of concerns identified before attempting to explore any one in depth. The legitimacy of nonmedical problems can be communicated by simple confirming statements (e.g., "It is natural that a young woman would want to be attractive," and "I would be surprised if someone being given your diagnosis did not get angry and frightened").

Optimally, the home situation can also be discussed in the initial visit, although it and other concerns may need to be attended to in the follow-up visit, which should be within a week. It is critical to identify the patient's perception of the sources of distress and support available to her. This information can be obtained by exploring the eating problem in the patient's life context, a process that is best accomplished with open-ended questions and probes that provide patients with the opportunity to explain the situation in their own words. Such questions as "What stresses are you under right now?" and "How are your patterns of sleeping and eating affected when you are under stress at home or work?" can be helpful in identifying sources of and responses to stress that are often associated with eating disorders.

Once the concerns are communicated and noted by the provider, it is important to identify the patient's expectations for the visit, treatment, and treatment outcomes with straightforward questions such as this one: "How did you hope I might help you today?" Although it is not necessary to respond immediately to the stated expectations, it is necessary for the provider to explain how he or she would like the interview to proceed, to explain that the assessment will be explained to the patient, and that a treatment plan will be developed together. The patient may have what appear to be unrealistic expectations about treatment. These should be probed rather than dismissed as they may indicate poor understanding of the problems or distorted thinking. The provider uses the patient's goals for the visit as a way of introducing the medical history and physical examination. The behavior of the patient can be more illustrative than verbal responses and the medical examination provides a good opportunity for observing behavior. This can be as simple as asking the patient to weigh herself on the scale. Serious resistance or opposition to this request is an obvious indication of distress regarding body weight. Asking the patient how her weight compares with that of other women her age and height can also identify unrealistic ideals about body weight.

Once the medical assessment is complete, the provider can return to the patient's concerns. The provider may also share his or her concerns about the consequences of the eating or weight problem. For example, significant weight loss may result in such consequences as dental damage, facial hair growth, or the need for hospitalization.

After the spectrum of psychosocial and physical concerns is identified, an explicit process of prioritization should take place. The patient may be asked to order the problems so that the most pressing can be addressed in the visit. Such an activity will help in assessing the patient's ability to comprehend the urgency of problems such as malnutrition or esophagitis. Even if the physician sets the priorities, the patient should confirm that the problems are being addressed in the appropriate order.

At this point, a negotiation process has begun. The provider's explanation of how his or her assessment is consistent with and/or differs from the patient's should be explicit because the nature of the problem dictates the treatment. Treatment approaches should be outlined in a context that acknowledges the patient's concerns and/or desires, such as to develop or maintain an attractive self-image. Eliciting the patient's ideas about how to ensure that the treatment plan is consistently implemented, how to involve the family, and how to monitor success will increase her involvement and commitment.

The result of this initial interview process may make it clear that the patient has a clinical eating disorder, which is itself a mental disorder and may have significant coexisting psychopathology. Patients, including those with the most serious disorders, are often opposed to referrals for a psychological or psychiatric assessment. The family can often facilitate such a recommendation by reassuring the patient that they support the referral and would not think she is "crazy" if she sees a mental health professional. Nonacceptance of referral may mean that a patient with serious mental health needs remains the responsibility of the medical practitioner alone. In this case, a long-term agenda or contract should be established that sets goals for improvement that the patient must achieve to remain solely in medical care. Referrals to other medical specialists should be approached cautiously as they may serve to reinforce the patient's position that all problems are solely of a somatic nature.

Psychosocial Screening

Two in-depth interviews may be useful for providers in medical practices that treat a large proportion of adolescent and young adult women. Both may guide interviewing of patients who are strongly suspected of having an eating or weight disorder. Johnson (1985) has developed a comprehensive, standardized interview—the Diagnostic Survey for Eating Disorders—so that it is a "collaborative inquiry" into the eating problem. It is reported to be more productive and better accepted by patients than a traditional clinical interview in part because this systematic approach communicates that the provider is well versed in the issues related to eating disorders (Johnson & Connors, 1987). It is printed in its entirety in the book by Johnson and Connors (1987). The Eating Disorder Examination (EDE), discussed at length in the chapter by Williamson, Anderson, Jackman, and Jackson (this volume), may also be helpful to the medical practitioner in developing treatment plans.

Self-report questionnaires can also be used to identify whether it is probable that a patient has an emotional disorder. To be effective, such instruments must be relatively brief, be written in simple language, and accurately identify the majority of individuals with the symptoms/disorder. They can be used prior to the appointment, while the patient is in the waiting room. Scoring can be done by office staff, although the provider should review all the responses. In general, it is inappropriate to refer *all* patients who score above the cutoff score on these questionnaires for further psychological evaluation. Rather, the screening questionnaires should be used as one piece of information in the decision to make a referral. With most medical patients, a provider can be reasonably certain that those who *do not score* in the abnormal range (usually above a certain score) do *not* have psychological problems that require treatment and thus may be managed solely in the medical setting. Patients who do score in the abnormal range should be evaluated through the clinical interview to clarify their need for psychological assessment and potentially for mental health treatment.

No questionnaire with adequate sensitivity and specificity has been developed to screen for obsessive-compulsive behaviors in general clinical settings (Berg, 1989). Nonetheless, the characteristics assessed by instruments used in psychiatric settings such as the Maudsley Obsessive Compulsive Inventory (Hodgson & Rachman, 1977) can help guide the medical provider's interview. Symptoms such as "feeling like you have to do certain things even though you know you don't really have to," "needing to keep checking on things," "worry about being clean, hating dirt," and "having a bad conscience, even though you haven't done anything other people think is bad" may be endorsed by some patients. Of critical importance is whether the symptoms keep the individual from meaningful activities or cause time to be wasted. Often, distress is associated with obsessions and compulsions and a great deal of time is spent resisting the urges. The distress can be assessed in detail from questionnaires, although the best known instrument, the Yale-Brown Obsessive Compulsive Scale (Y-BOCS; Goodman, Price, Rasmussen, Mazure, Fleischman, et al., 1989; Goodman, Price, Rasmussen, Mazure,

Delgado, et al., 1989), has been validated for use only with patients already diagnosed with OCD.

The two instruments that will be described to assist in the clinical decision process were chosen on the basis of their reliability, validity, ease of interpretation, acceptability, and utility in the medical setting. They are (a) the General Health Questionnaire (GHQ-28) and (b) the Beck Depression Inventory (BDI).

A great number of other instruments exist to describe the presence of emotional and behavioral problems; they are less desirable in the medical setting because they are too long, difficult to score or to interpret, and the vast majority have not been tested against a "truth standard" such as a structured psychiatric interview.

Overview of the Screening Instruments

General Health Questionnaire

Variable. The General Health Questionnaire (GHQ) (Goldberg & Hillier, 1979; Goldberg & Williams, 1988) was developed to identify mental health problems that are associated with impaired work and family functioning among adults living in the community. A problem is noted only if there has been a break in normal functioning, so the questionnaire identifies acute rather than chronic problems (Goldberg, 1972). Personality characteristics that may be associated with eating disorders such as obsessive or compulsive traits would be identified only if they are associated with distress. Of the several abbreviated versions, the GHQ-28 provides the best sensitivity and specificity in detecting mental disorders diagnosed using a structured psychiatric interview in samples of general medical patients (Goldberg & Hillier, 1979). The GHQ-28 has four robust factors: somatic symptoms, anxiety and insomnia, social dysfunction, and severe depression. As with all screening instruments, it does not allow one to make specific psychiatric diagnosis.

Description. This self-administered 28-item questionnaire has four response categories that allow summative scoring, but a simpler "present-absent" scoring method in which either symptomatic response is scored as a "1" (0-0-1-1) was shown to be equal or superior to the Likert scoring method (Goldberg & Hillier, 1979).

Scores can be interpreted as indicating the severity of psychological disturbance on a continuum. The score expresses the probability that the patient has a psychiatric disorder. A cut-point of 4 is recommended. Individuals with a score of 5 or higher are said to screen positive for psychiatric disorder and have at least a 50% probability of having a psychiatric disorder (Goldberg & Hillier, 1979). Higher scores are associated with higher probabilities of disorder as well as more severe disorders. As with most screening instruments, this instrument falsely identifies a sizable portion of patients as positive for psychiatric disorder but rarely misses those who truly have a psychiatric disorder (few false negatives). An example of this is found in the original work on the GHQ (Goldberg & Blackwell, 1970). In a sample of medical patients, 102 were identified as emotionally disturbed on the GHQ. Of these, 13 (13%) were found to be not disturbed by a psychiatrist administering the Clinical Interview Schedule. In contrast to the 13% rate of false positive cases, only 2% of the medical patients who were normal on the GHQ were found to have psychiatric disorder.

Reliability: Internal consistency. In a study, the internal consistency of the GHQ-60 was found to be .95 using a split-half reliability technique. These results were interpolated to shorter versions, indicating adequate internal reliability for even the GHQ-12, which had an alpha coefficient of .83 (Goldberg, 1972). The correlations of the subscales of the GHQ-28 with one another range from .33 to .61, with five of the six correlations above .44. The subscale to total score correlations range from .69 to .79 (Goldberg & Hillier, 1979).

Test-retest reliability. Test-retest reliability of the GHQ-60 after 6 months was .90 ($N = 20$) when the stability of the patient's condition was confirmed by repeating a standard psychiatric examination (Goldberg, 1972).

Convergent and discriminant validity. The validity of the GHQ-28 has been tested around the industrialized world. It is usually compared with an error-free, "truth standard" structured psychiatric interview such as the Clinical Interview Schedule (CIS; Goldberg & Blackwell, 1970) or the Present State Examination (PSE; Wing, Cooper, & Sartorius, 1974). Convergent validity is obtained by calculating sensitivity—the probability that the screening instrument identifies all individuals determined to have a disorder by the structured interview. A form of discriminant validity is obtained by calculating specificity—the probability that those without the disorder are correctly identified. In 12 studies, the median sensitivity of the GHQ-28 was 0.86 and the specificity was 0.82. The higher sensitivity indicates that the GHQ-28 is more likely to accurately identify those with a disorder than to accurately indicate that those without disorder are actually free of disorder. This is consistent with the purpose of screening instruments because the premium is placed on not missing individuals who need care.

It is worth noting that, among patients with severe physical illness, scores may be elevated by their physical symptoms. In such patients, setting a higher threshold score may be indicated to reduce the possibility of falsely identifying these individuals as having psychiatric disorder (Bridges & Goldberg, 1986). On the other hand, there is no way to measure socially desirable or "faking good" responses. The possibility that anorexic and bulimic patients may deny their distress should always be considered.

Location. The original scale is in Goldberg and Hillier (1979). The current manual for all versions of the GHQ is titled *User's Guide to the General Health Questionnaire* (Goldberg & Williams, 1988). The full GHQ-28 is reproduced in Appendix 13-A.

Results and comments. The GHQ is probably the best instrument for screening for psychological distress associated with acute problems in the medical setting. It is in widespread use for clinical screening and research purposes and has been documented to be reliable and valid on numerous clinical samples in many different countries.

Beck Depression Inventory

Variable. The Beck Depression Inventory, Revised (BDI) (Beck, Rush, Shaw, & Emery, 1979) was developed to measure symptoms of depression as operationally defined by the following attributes: a specific alteration in mood, a negative self-concept associated with self-reproaches and self-blame, regressive and self-punitive wishes, vegetative changes, and change in activity level (Beck et al., 1979).

Description. The BDI may be used with adolescents as young as 13 and with adults. It contains 21 items, each with four self-evaluative statements rated in severity. This format may encourage more precise responding than Likert scales of "how much" a person feels a certain way, especially among those who are not particularly self-aware. A high school reading level is required. It takes 5-10 minutes to complete.

The scoring is a simple sum of the values, from 0 to 3, associated with each endorsed response. The range of possible scores is 0 to 63. Beck suggests the following guidelines for BDI cutoff scores in samples of patients diagnosed as having an affective disorder: no or minimal depression is < 10; mild to moderate depression is 10-18; moderate to severe depression is 19-29; and severe depression is 30-63 (Beck, Steer, & Garbin, 1988). Individuals in the general population who score above a cutoff score of 16 are considered at risk for having a depressive disorder. Further assessment with a medical and/or a mental health provider is required for those scoring in the abnormal range before one should entertain a diagnosis of depression.

Sample. A recent review of 25 years of evidence related to the psychometric characteristics of the BDI is the basis for the data presented below on the internal consistency reliability, stability, and validity of the BDI (Beck et al., 1988). The results from a recent study of adolescents (12-19 years old) in a psychiatric outpatient setting are also included, although no individuals with apparent eating disorders were in the study sample (Ambrosini, Metz, Bianchi, Rabinovich, & Undie, 1991). In this investigation, 122 adolescents were given a structured psychiatric interview, the K-SADS IIIR. Those receiving a diagnosis of major depressive disorder were readministered the same structured psychiatric assessment 2 weeks later. Prior to the administration of each psychiatric interview, the teens completed the BDI.

Reliability: Internal consistency. The mean coefficient alpha from 15 nonpsychiatric samples is .81; the range was from .73 to .92. Across nine psychiatric samples, the mean coefficient alpha was .86 (Beck et al., 1988).

In the study of adolescents (Ambrosini et al., 1991), the internal consistency of the BDI was good, ranging from .79 to .91 in various patient groups. Similar results were obtained in a sample of secondary school students and adolescent psychiatric inpatients, with internal consistency estimates of .86 and .90, respectively (Barrera & Garrison-Jones, 1988).

Test-retest reliability. The reproducibility or stability of the BDI is generally accepted to be quite good, naturally better in nonpsychiatric populations than in psychiatric patients. To address the potential for patients to change in their depression levels over time, Beck (1967) administered the BDI twice at an interval of 4 weeks to 38 patients on whom clinical judgments were obtained regarding the stability of their depressive symptoms. Changes in the BDI paralleled changes in clinician ratings, indicating a consistent relationship between the clinicians' and patients' reports (Beck, 1967). Subsequent studies in a traditional test-retest design using various time intervals from hours to several weeks indicate that the range of Pearson product-moment correlations is from .60 to .83 for nonpsychiatric subjects, and is somewhat lower for psychiatric patients, who would be expected to change over time. The test-retest reliability on a sample of 61 adolescents over a 2-week interval was .86, and was highest (.87) for those who continued to have a major depressive disorder and lowest (.74) for those who were recovering or were not depressed at either time (Ambrosini et al., 1991).

Convergent validity. Validity of the BDI with respect to other measures of depression is high. The mean correlation with clinical assessments of nonpsychiatric subjects is .60 and the mean correlations with three well-researched self-report measures of depression—the HRSD, Zung, and MMPI-D—are .73, .71, and .60, respectively. The BDI's correlation with these measures in psychiatric samples is consistently larger. Using the Child Assessment Schedule (Hodges, Klein, Fitch, McKnew, & Cytryn, 1981) as the criterion for major depressive disorder in a sample of adolescent psychiatric inpatients, a BDI score of ≥ 11 had a sensitivity of 81.5%, specificity of 52.6%, and positive predictive power of 71.3% (Barrera & Garrison-Jones, 1988). This indicates that using a relatively low cutoff score of 11 serves to identify the majority of teens with depression but incorrectly identifies almost half of those without depression as being in the clinical range (over 11). Raising the cutoff score would reduce the false-positive rate but would have lowered the sensitivity and positive predictive power, so that more teens with depression would have been missed.

Discriminant validity. The ability of the BDI to discriminate between normals, medical patients, and depressed individuals is well established (Beck et al., 1988). It is not recommended for use in discriminating between depression and other mental disorders but, rather, to determine if significant symptoms are present that may contribute to a lack of motivation or follow-through on the part of the patient with weight or eating-related problems.

Location. Test materials and manual are available for purchase through the Psychological Corporation (800-228-0752), 555 Academic Court, San Antonio, TX 78204.

Results and comments. The BDI is likely to be the best screening instrument for depression available for use in the medical setting. It is narrowly focused and thus not able to screen for other types of disorder. Endorsed symptoms may reflect anxiety, which is often a component of depression but may exist independently.

Individuals with eating disorders are likely to score higher than average on the BDI. The mean score for a sample of bulimics was 15.4 (Williamson, Kelley, Davis, Ruggiero, & Blouin, 1985) and for anorexics, 28.6 (Garfinkel et al., 1983). Their high scores may reflect the prevalence of depressive symptoms in these patients but may also reflect endorsement of two appetite/weight items, two items on fatigue/sleep, and an item on interest in sex. There are no other somatic symptom items in the BDI that might reflect medical rather than depressive symptoms. The BDI responses of patients who score above 16 should be reviewed to ascertain whether critical depressive items are endorsed, and these patients should be carefully interviewed regarding their hopes for the future and potential thoughts about ending their lives. Use of the BDI provides a logical way for the medical practitioner to introduce the discussion of emotional distress and can be the basis for a recommendation for a mental health referral.

Although the BDI rarely overlooks those with significant depression, it is possible. The lack of subtle content and the consistent order of the items, from least to most severe, make this instrument susceptible to a defensive response set, which is a concern in assessment of anorexics and others who deny their symptomatology (Dahlstrom, Brooks, & Peterson, 1990).

The following two representative items from the BDI indicate the general content of depressive symptoms, which include items related to guilt, irritation, decision making, thoughts of killing oneself, and energy levels as well as symptoms associated with changes in eating, weight, and sexual interest.

1. 0 I do not feel like a failure.

   1 I feel I have failed more than the average person.

   2 As I look back on my life, all I can see is a lot of failures.

   3 I feel I am a complete failure as a person.

2. 0 I don't feel I look any worse than I used to.

   1 I am worried that I am looking old or unattractive.

   2 I feel that there are permanent changes in my appearance that make me look unattractive.

   3 I believe that I look ugly.

SOURCE: From the Beck Depression Inventory. Copyright © 1987 by Aaron T. Beck. Reproduced by permission of Publisher, The Psychological Corporation. All rights reserved.

Integrating the Results of Questionnaire Screening for Mental Disorder

The primary caveat involved in the use of questionnaires to screen for psychopathology in the medical visit is that the information should be incorporated into the patient's treatment. Not infrequently, patient-completed questionnaires are placed in charts but never interpreted or discussed with the patient.

Three principles for using screening results are critical: Communicate with the patient about her or his responses within a reasonable time frame; interpret clinically abnormal results very cautiously; and explore abnormal results through further interviewing before making a referral to a mental health provider.

The basis for interpreting the results involves inspection of the endorsed items on the questionnaire, sharing concerns about the high score or specific endorsed items with the patient, and further probing the nature of the endorsed problems. The techniques for the medical interview discussed above can be employed to elicit information and to foster a sense of collaborative inquiry. This approach is likely to increase the probability that a patient will accept a recommendation for a mental health referral, if needed.

Although an abnormal score on a screening instrument does not unequivocally indicate the presence of a mental disorder, the higher the score on the GHQ and the BDI, the more likely it is that the patient has a psychiatric disorder associated with high levels of distress. Both the GHQ and the BDI have several items related to suicidal ideation and other severe signs of depression and hopelessness. Endorsement of such items is not rare in an adolescent or young adult population, with approximately 20% to 25% of community samples endorsing such items at some level and approximately 9% of high school students reporting at least one previous suicide attempt (Harkavy-Friedman, Asnis, Boeck, & DiFiore, 1987). Nonetheless, the indication of suicidal thoughts in the medical setting must be taken very seriously and may be adequate reason for ensuring that the parents or other family members become involved and that a mental health evaluation is immediately completed.

In summary, the patient-centered clinical interview forms the basis for diagnosing eating disorders as well as identifying potential emotional distress and problematic personality characteristics. The GHQ and the BDI offer structured formats for obtaining information about specific psychological symptoms and distress that can guide the medical provider in further assessing the presence and potential impact of mental health problems. Their use is appropriate only when high scores can be interpreted in a subsequent clinical interview. In combination, the screening questionnaire and medical interview are the basis for the assessment, treatment planning, and management of patients with potential eating and weight-related disorders in general medical settings.

References

Ambrosini, P. J., Metz, C., Bianchi, M. D., Rabinovich, H., & Undie, A. (1991). Concurrent validity and psychometric properties of the Beck Depression Inventory in outpatient adolescents. *Journal of the American Academy of Child and Adolescent Psychiatry, 30*, 51-57.

American Psychiatric Association. (1980). *Diagnostic and statistical manual of mental disorders* (3rd ed., revised 1987). Washington, DC: Author.

Barrera, M., & Garrison-Jones, C. V. (1988). Properties of the Beck Depression Inventory as a screening instrument for adolescent depression. *Journal of Youth and Adolescence, 15,* 165-171.

Beck, A. T. (1967). *Depression: Causes and treatment.* Philadelphia: University of Pennsylvania Press.

Beck, A. T. (1987). *Beck Depression Inventory.* San Antonio, TX: The Psychological Corporation.

Beck, A. T., Rush, A. J., Shaw, B. F., & Emery, G. (1979). *Cognitive therapy for depression.* New York: Guilford.

Beck, A. T., Steer, R. A., & Garbin, M. G. (1988). Psychometric properties of the Beck Depression Inventory: Twenty-five years of evaluation. *Clinical Psychology Review, 8,* 77-100.

Bensing, J. (1991). *Doctor-patient communication and the quality of care.* The Hague, the Netherlands: CIP GegevensKoninklijke, Bibliotheek.

Berg, C. Z. (1989). Behavioral assessment techniques for childhood obsessive-compulsive disorder. In J. L. Rapoport (Ed.), *Obsessive-compulsive disorders in children and adolescents.* Washington, DC: American Psychiatric Press.

Boake, C., & Salmon, P. G. (1983). Demographic correlates and factor structure of the Family Environment Scale. *Journal of Clinical Psychology, 39,* 95-100.

Bridges, K. W., & Goldberg, D. P. (1986). The validation of the GHQ-28 and the use of the MMSE in neurological inpatients. *British Journal of Psychiatry, 148,* 548-555.

Dahlstrom, W. G., Brooks, J. D., & Peterson, C. D. (1990). The Beck Depression Inventory: Item order and the impact of response sets. *Journal of Personality Assessment, 55,* 224-233.

Dulcan, M. K., Costello, E. J., Costello, A. J., Edelbrock, C., Brent, D., & Janiszewski, S. (1989). The pediatrician as gatekeeper to mental health care for children: Do parents' concerns open the gate? *Journal of the American Academy of Child and Adolescent Psychiatry, 29,* 453-458.

Epstein, N. B., Baldwin, L. M., & Bishop, D. S. (1983). The McMaster Family Assessment Device. *Journal of Marital and Family Therapy, 9,* 171-180.

Feldman, W., Rosser, W., & McGrath, P. (1987). *Primary medical care of children and adolescents.* New York: Oxford University Press.

Foreyt, J. P., & McGavin, J. K. (1988). Anorexia nervosa and bulimia. In E. J. Mash & L. G. Terdal (Eds.), *Behavioral assessment of childhood disorders* (2nd ed.). New York: Guilford.

Francis, V., Korsch, B. M., & Morris, J. J. (1969). Gaps in doctor-patient communication: Patients' response to medical advice. *New England Journal of Medicine, 280,* 535-540.

Garfinkel, P. E., Garner, M., Rose, J., Darby, P. L., Brandes, J. S., O'Hanlon, K., & Walsh, N. (1983). A comparison of characteristics in the families of patients with anorexia and normal controls. *Psychological Medicine, 13,* 821-828.

Garner, D. M., & Garfinkel, P. E. (1981). Body image in anorexia nervosa: Measurement, theory and clinical implications. *International Journal of Psychiatry in Medicine, 11,* 263-284.

Goldberg, D. P. (1972). *The detection of psychiatric illness by questionnaire* (GHQ-28; Maudsley Monograph No. 21). Oxford, U.K.: Oxford University Press.

Goldberg, D. P., & Blackwell, B. (1970). Psychiatric illness in a suburban general practice: A detailed study using a new method of case identification. *British Medical Journal, 2,* 439-443.

Goldberg, D. P., & Hillier, V. F. (1979). A scaled version of the General Health Questionnaire. *Psychological Medicine, 9,* 139-145.

Goldberg, D. P., & Williams, P. (1988). *A user's guide to the General Health Questionnaire.* Windsor, England: NFER-Nelson.

Goodman, W. K., Price, L. H., Rasmussen, S. A., Mazure, C., Delgado, P., Heninger, G. R., & Charney, D. S. (1989). The Yale-Brown Obsessive Compulsive Scale: II. Validity. *Archives of General Psychiatry, 46,* 1012-1016.

Goodman, W. K., Price, L. H., Rasmussen, S. A., Mazure, C., Fleischmann, R. L., Hill, C. L., Heninger, G. R., & Charney, D. S. (1989). The Yale-Brown Obsessive Compulsive Scale: I. Development, use, and reliability. *Archives of General Psychiatry, 46,* 1006-1011.

Gorden, R. L. (1987). *Interviewing: Strategy, techniques and tactics.* Chicago: Dorsey.

Harkavy-Friedman, J., Asnis, G., Boeck, M., & DiFiore, J. (1987). Prevalence of specific suicidal behaviors in a high school sample. *American Journal of Psychiatry, 144,* 1203-1206.

Hendren, R. L. (1983). Depression in anorexia nervosa. *Journal of the American Academy of Child Psychiatry, 22,* 59-62.

Hodges, K., Klein, J., Fitch, P., McKnew, D., & Cytryn, L. (1981). The Child Assessment Schedule. *Catalog of Selected Documents in Psychology, 11,* 56.

Hodgson, R., & Rachman, S. (1977). Obsessive compulsive complaints. *Behavior Research and Therapy, 15,* 389-395.

Johnson, C. (1985). Initial consultation for patients with bulimia and anorexia nervosa. In D. M. Garner & P. E. Garfinkel (Eds.), *Handbook of psychotherapy for anorexia nervosa and bulimia.* New York: Guilford.

Johnson, C. L., & Berndt, D. (1983). A preliminary investigation of bulimia and life adjustment. *American Journal of Psychiatry, 140,* 774-777.

Johnson, C., & Connors, M. E. (1987). *The etiology and treatment of bulimia nervosa.* New York: Basic Books.

Kessler, L. G., Burns, B. J., Shapiro, S., Tischler, G. L., George, L. K., Hough, R. L., Bodison, D., & Miller, R. H. (1987). Psychiatric diagnoses of medical service users: Evidence from the epidemiologic catchment area program. *American Journal of Public Health, 77,* 18-24.

Kessler, L. G., Cleary, P. D., & Burke, J. D. (1985). Psychiatric disorders in primary care: Results of a follow-up study. *Archives of General Psychiatry, 42,* 583-587.

Lenert, L., Markowitz, D. R., & Blaschke, T. F. (1993). *Primum non nocere?* Valuing of the risk of drug toxicity in therapeutic decision making. *Clinical Pharmacology & Therapeutics, 53,* 285-291.

Lipkin, M., Jr. (1987). The medical interview and related skills. In W. T. Branch (Ed.), *Office practice of medicine* (pp. 1287-1306). Philadelphia, PA: Saunders.

Lipkin, M., Quill, T. E., & Napodano, R. J. (1984). The medical interview: A core curriculum for residencies in internal medicine. *Annals of Internal Medicine, 100,* 277-284.

Moos, R. H., & Moos, B. S. (1986). *Family Environment Scale Manual* (2nd ed.). Palo Alto, CA: Consulting Psychologists Press.

Munet-Vilaro, F., & Egan, M. (1990). Reliability issues of the Family Environment Scale for cross-cultural research. *Nursing Research, 39,* 244-247.

Novack, D. H., Dube, C., & Goldstein, M. G. (1992). Teaching medical interviewing: A basic course on interviewing and the physician-patient relationship. *Archives of Internal Medicine, 152,* 1814-1820.

Olsen, D. H., Portner, J., & Lavee, Y. (1985). *FACES III manual.* Unpublished manual. (Available from D. H. Olson, Family Social Science, University of Minnesota, 290 McNeal Hall, St. Paul, MN 55108)

Ormel, J., van den Brink, W., Koeter, M. W. J., Giel, R., van der Meer, K., van de Willige, G., & Wilmink, F. W. (1990). Recognition, management and outcome of psychological disorders in primary care: A naturalistic follow-up study. *Psychological Medicine, 20,* 909-923.

Regier, D., Goldberg, I., & Taube, C. (1978). The *de facto* U.S. mental health services system: A public health perspective. *Archives of General Psychiatry, 35,* 685-693.

Roter, D. L., & Hall, J. A. (1992). *Doctors talking with patients/patients talking with doctors: Improving communication in medical visits.* Westport, CT: Greenwood.

Russell, G. F. M. (1988). The diagnostic formulation of bulimia nervosa. In D. M. Garner & P. E. Garfinkel (Eds.), *Diagnostic issues in anorexia nervosa and bulimia nervosa.* New York: Brunner/Mazel.

Shapiro, S., German, P. S., Skinner, E. A., VonKorff, M., Turner, R. W., Klein, L. E., Tetelbaum, M. L., Kramer, M., Burke, J. D., & Burns, B. J. (1985). An experiment to change detection and management of mental morbidity in primary care. *Medical Care, 25,* 327-339.

Smith, R. C., & Hoppe, R. B. (1991). The patient's story: Integrating the patient- and physician-centered approaches to interviewing. *Annals of Internal Medicine, 115,* 470-477.

Starfield, B., Steinwachs, D., Morris, I., Bause, G., Siebert, S., & Westin, C. (1979). Patient-provider agreement about problems. *Journal of the American Medical Association, 242,* 344-346.

Strober, M., & Katz, J. L. (1988). Depression in the eating disorders: A review and analysis of descriptive, family, and biological findings. In D. M. Garner & P. E. Garfinkel (Eds.), *Diagnostic issues in anorexia nervosa and bulimia nervosa.* New York: Brunner/Mazel.

Tolson, T. F. J., & Wilson, M. N. (1990). The impact of two- and three-generational black family structure on perceived family climate. *Child Development, 61,* 416-428.

Walker, C. E., & Shaw, W. (1988). Assessment of eating and elimination disorders. In P. Karoly (Ed.), *Handbook of child health assessment.* New York: Wiley.

Wells, K. B., Stewart, A., Hays, R. D., Burnam, M. A., Rogers, W., Daniels, M., Berry, S., Greenfield, S., & Ware, J. (1989). The functioning and well-being of depressed patients: Results from the Medical Outcomes Study. *Journal of the American Medical Association, 262,* 914-919.

Williamson, D. A., Kelley, M. L., Davis, C. J., Ruggiero, L., & Blouin, D. (1985). Psychopathology of eating disorders: A controlled comparison of bulimia, obese, and normal subjects. *Journal of Consulting and Clinical Psychology, 53,* 161-166.

Wing, J. K., Cooper, J. E., & Sartorius, N. (1974). *The measurement and classification of psychiatric symptoms.* Cambridge: Cambridge University Press.

Appendix 13-A

General Health Questionnaire (GHQ-28)

Please read this carefully:

We would like to know if you have had any medical complaints, and how your health has been in general, *over the past few weeks.* Please answer *ALL* the questions on the following pages simply by underlining the answer which you think most nearly applies ·to you. Remember that we want to know about present and recent complaints, not those that you had in the past.

HAVE YOU RECENTLY:

A1	been feeling perfectly well and in good health?	Better than usual	Same as usual	Worse than usual	Much worse than usual
A2	been feeling in need of some medicine to pick you up?	Not at all	No more than usual	Rather more than usual	Much more than usual
A3	been feeling run-down and out of sorts?	Not at all	No more than usual	Rather more than usual	Much more than usual
A4	felt that you are ill?	Not at all	No more than usual	Rather more than usual	Much more than usual
A5	been getting any pains in your head?	Not at all	No more than usual	Rather more than usual	Much more than usual
A6	been getting a feeling of tightness or pressure in your head?	Not at all	No more than usual	Rather more than usual	Much more than usual
A7	been having hot or cold spells?	Not at all	No more than usual	Rather more than usual	Much more than usual

512

HAVE YOU RECENTLY:

B1	lost much sleep over worry?	Not at all	No more than usual	Rather more than usual	Much more than usual
B2	had difficulty in staying asleep?	Not at all	No more than usual	Rather more than usual	Much more than usual
B3	felt constantly under strain?	Not at all	No more than usual	Rather more than usual	Much more than usual
B4	been getting edgy and bad-tempered?	Not at all	No more than usual	Rather more than usual	Much more than usual
B5	been getting scared or panicky for no good reason?	Not at all	No more than usual	Rather more than usual	Much more than usual
B6	found every-thing getting on top of you?	Not at all	No more than usual	Rather more than usual	Much more than usual
B7	been feeling nervous and uptight all the time?	Not at all	No more than usual	Rather more than usual	Much more than usual

C1	been managing to keep yourself busy and occupied?	More so than usual	Same as usual	Rather less than usual	Much less than usual
C2	been taking longer over the things you do?	Quicker than usual	Same as usual	Longer than usual	Much longer than usual
C3	felt on the whole you were doing things well?	Better than usual	About the same	Less well than usual	Much less well
C4	been satisfied with the way you've carried out your task?	More satisfied	About the same as usual	Less satisfied than usual	Much less satisfied
C5	felt that you are playing a useful part in things?	More so than usual	Same as usual	Rather less than usual	Much less than usual

HAVE YOU RECENTLY:

C6	felt capable of making decisions about things?	More so than usual	Same as usual	Less so than usual	Much less capable
C7	been able to enjoy your normal day-to-day activities?	More so than usual	Same as usual	Less so than usual	Much less than usual
D1	been thinking of yourself as a worthless person?	Not at all	No more than usual	Rather more than usual	Much more than usual
D2	felt that life is entirely hopeless?	Not at all	No more than usual	Rather more than usual	Much more than usual
D3	felt that life isn't worth living?	Not at all	No more than usual	Rather more than usual	Much more than usual
D4	thought of the possibility that you might do away with yourself?	Definitely not	I don't think so	Has crossed my mind	Definitely have
D5	found at times you couldn't do anything because your nerves were too bad?	Not at all	No more than usual	Rather more than usual	Much more than usual
D6	found yourself wishing you were dead and away from it all?	Not at all	No more than usual	Rather more than usual	Much more than usual
D7	found that the idea of taking your own life kept coming into your mind?	Definitely not	I don't think so	Has crossed my mind	Definitely has

Subscales designation:

A	-	Somatic Symptoms	C -	Social Dysfunction
B	-	Anxiety and Insomnia	D -	Severe Depression

SOURCE: From *The Detection of Psychiatric Illness by Questionnaire* (GHQ-28; Maudsley Monograph No. 21), by D. P. Goldberg, 1972, Oxford, U.K.: Oxford University Press. Reprinted by permission of Oxford University Press.

14

Assessment of Human Body Composition

STEVEN B. HEYMSFIELD

DAVID B. ALLISON

STANLEY HESHKA

RICHARD N. PIERSON JR.

B ody composition represents the net results of metabolic processes and the structural contribution of ingested nutrients and is closely related to an organism's biochemical, metabolic, and mechanical function. The study of human body composition is thus central to the evaluation of patients with obesity and eating disorders.

AUTHORS' NOTE: This work was supported in part by National Institutes of Health Grants DKY2618 and DK26687. Dr. Allison was supported by an American Diabetes Association Career Development Award. We are grateful to Anne Cartwright, Milissa Kezis, and Elizabeth M. Kucera for their help in the preparation of this manuscript and to Michael I. Goran for his helpful commentaries on an earlier draft.

The study of body composition can be divided into three areas: (a) the five-level model and associated rules, (b) methodology, and (c) biology (Wang, Pierson, & Heymsfield, 1992). This chapter will focus on one of these areas: body composition methodology. Specifically, our emphasis is on estimates of body fatness. An overview is first provided of the five-level model of body composition as it relates to measures of fatness. We then provide a simple description of general concepts related to techniques for estimating body composition. Finally, we offer detailed descriptions of the major relevant body composition methods organized by the five-level model. Within the tissue level, we also describe the measurement of adipose tissue distribution.

Five-Level Model

The human body can be divided into multiple components. These components can be organized into five levels of increasing complexity (Figure 14.1) (Wang, Pierson, et al., 1992). Each level and its associated components are distinct.

The atomic level consists of 11 main elements that constitute over 99% of body weight. Six elements—oxygen, hydrogen, carbon, nitrogen, calcium, and phosphorus—contribute to greater than 99% of body weight in healthy adults. Atomic-level measurements are important because of their close relationship to chemical components; the six elements can be used in simultaneous equations to calculate all of the major groups of chemical constituents that are found in vivo (Heymsfield et al., 1991).

The molecular level consists of six major components: lipids, most of which are triglycerides or "fat"; protein; water; glycogen; bone mineral; and nonosseus or cell minerals. Most body composition research is presently based on methods designed to evaluate molecular-level components.

Several models of the molecular level are used in body composition research. The most important of these is the two-compartment model in which body weight is equal to the sum of fat and fat-free body mass (FFM; Forbes, 1987; Heymsfield & Waki, 1991). The FFM compartment in this model is the sum of protein, water, glycogen, and mineral. This is the classic model used to evaluate total body fat and it will be described in greater detail in the methodology section.

The cell level of body composition has three main components: cell mass, extracellular fluids, and extracellular solids. The extracellular solids are mainly bone mineral and connective tissue proteins. Cell components are difficult to quantify in vivo, and instead investigators estimate either total intracellular fluid or body cell mass. Both of these components represent the total fat-free portion of cell mass (Moore et al., 1963). Although the cell level is

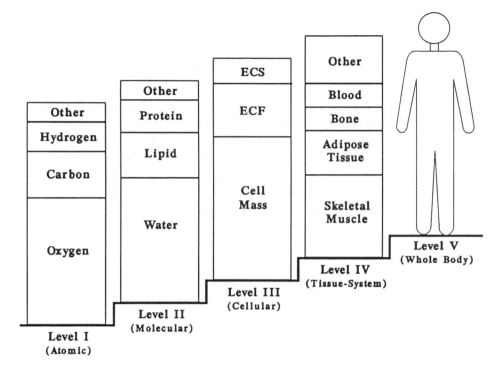

Figure 14.1. The Five-Level Model of Body Composition
SOURCE: From "The Five Level Model: A New Approach to Organizing Body Composition Research," by J. Wang, R. N. Pierson Jr., and S. B. Heymsfield, 1992, *American Journal of Clinical Nutrition, 56,* pp. 19-28. Reprinted with permission.

important in the study of energy metabolism and physiology, the lack of practical methods in this area limits clinical application. Specifically, there are no noninvasive methods of estimating fat-cell mass in vivo. Estimates of total fat-cell mass can be made by combining adipose tissue biopsy techniques and body composition measurements.

The tissue-system level of body composition represents the major organs and tissues such as skeletal muscle, bone, visceral organs, and adipose tissue. Imaging methods, such as computerized axial tomography and magnetic resonance imaging, are capable of estimating all major components at this level (Heymsfield, 1987; Sjöström, 1991). Adipose tissue, the major representation of fatness at the tissue-system level, can be evaluated using imaging methods in both the subcutaneous and the visceral components.

The whole-body level includes characteristics such as weight, stature, body density, resistance, skinfold thicknesses, and circumferences. Most clinical methods for estimating fatness and fat distribution, including weight-stature indices, anthropometric techniques, and bioimpedance analysis, are at the whole-body level of body composition.

Although each of the five levels is distinct, connections exist between components at the same level or at different body composition levels. For example, fatness is represented by total body carbon, fat, fat-cell mass, adipose tissue, and skinfold thickness at levels I to V, respectively. Some components maintain a very stable relationship with each other between different subjects. This stable relationship is important in estimating the mass of some components. For example, 85% of adipose tissue in most subjects is fat; that is, fat/adipose tissue = 0.85. These stable relations between components and their associated ratios are important in body composition methodology.

Methods of Estimating Fatness

General Concepts

There are no direct methods of evaluating components such as total body fat in vivo. All body composition methods are indirect and are based on measurement of various properties such as body density or the gamma-ray decay of certain isotopes (Heymsfield & Wang, in press; Wang, Pierson, et al., 1992). All methods can be organized into two categories as defined by the relation:

$$\text{property} \xrightarrow{A} \text{component 1} \xrightarrow{B} \text{component 2}$$

About one half of the 30 or more major components can be estimated directly from a measured property (Heymsfield & Wang, in press). This is shown as sequence A in the above relations. Property-based methods include calculation of fat and FFM from physical properties of the body such as body density (Heymsfield & Waki, 1991) and electrical resistance (Lohman, 1992), physical properties of naturally occurring isotopes such as ^{40}K (Forbes, 1987), or the physical properties of administered isotopes such as tritium (Forbes, 1987; Pace & Rathbun, 1945). Property-based methods are the foundation of body composition methodology and all components are ultimately estimated from measured properties.

The remaining body composition components can be estimated using component-based methods as shown in sequence B above. With component-based methods, a known component is used to derive an unknown component. The known component must be derived first using a property-based method (i.e., sequence A).

Both property- and component-based methods employ mathematical functions to relate the "known" property or component to the unknown component. The mathematical functions can be one of two general types.

The first involves a regression equation developed on a sample of subjects in whom the known component's mass is measured using a reference technique. The equation's validity is then usually checked by cross-validation in a new group of subjects. This type of mathematical function is used in estimating fat and FFM from skinfold measurements, bioimpedance analysis, and other widely used methods that will be described in later sections. An example is the prediction of total body protein from total body water using a regression equation based on experimental studies (Cohn et al., 1983). Total body protein and water are both subordinate components within the larger FFM component and the two components are highly correlated with each other.

The second type of mathematical function involves a biological or physiological "model." The model typically takes the form of a ratio or proportion. An example of the ratio approach is the estimation of FFM from total body water (TBW) by assuming that the ratio of TBW/FFM is 0.73. The relation between water and FFM (i.e., TBW/FFM = 0.73) was derived originally in human cadavers (Brozek, Grande, Anderson, & Keys, 1963) and animals (Pace & Rathbun, 1945) and then later validated in living humans (Lohman, 1992). From this relation we can calculate FFM as $1.37 \times$ TBW. An important consideration is that "constant" proportions and ratios are not actually constants but represent averages that normally vary in health, and will vary more or even systematically change in disease. This variability in body composition models must be quantified if the ratios are to be meaningfully used.

A component of interest can thus be estimated using either a property- or a component-based method. Two types of mathematical function are also employed, one formulated using regression analysis and the other developed using well-known biological/physiological relationships.

Specific Methods

We next describe specific body composition assessment methods at each of the five levels. Before proceeding further, we wish to introduce three tables that are central to the remainder of the chapter. The values in Tables 14.1 and 14.2 have been culled from the literature on body composition assessment with corresponding sources listed in Table 14.3. The coefficients in Table 14.1 are indicators of temporal (i.e., test-retest) reliability. The first column in Table 14.1 lists within-person coefficients of variation (CVs). In this case, the CV is defined as the ratio of the within-person standard deviation to the mean. For reasons outlined elsewhere (Allison, 1993), we consider the CV an inferior index of measurement reliability when compared with correlation-based metrics such as the intraclass correlations. However, we include it here because so many body composition investigators report their measurement reliabilities as CVs. Because the numerator of the CV represents within-

TABLE 14.1 Reliability Coefficients for Selected Body Fat Measurement Methods

Method	r_{xx}	CV
Total body electrical conductivity		
	.97 (8)	4% (8)
	.97 (18)	1% (37)
	.99 (39)	7% (46)
	.98 (44)	
	.99 (45)	
Body mass index		
	> .99 (unpublished)	≤1% (12)
	> .99 (34)	
Skinfolds		
	.91 (3)	6% (8)
	.96 (8)	4% (10)
	.93 (18)	3% (49)
	.98 (20)	
	.81 to .95 (34—for individual skinfolds)	
	.98 (49)	
Bioimpedance analysis		
	.96 (3)	6% (8)
	.96 (8)	1% (47) (within 1 day)
	.93 (18)	2% (47) (over 1 week)
	.96 (20)	2% to 5% (56)
		2% (55)
Dual energy X-ray absorptiometry/dual photon absorptiometry		
	.97 (16)	1% (2)
	.99 (8)	1% (9)
		3% (9)
		1% (8)
		4% (17)
		3% (17)
		6% (21)
		2% (23)
		2% (29)
		< 1% (33)
Underwater weighing		
	.95 (6)	1% (8)
	.97 (8)	5% (10)
	.97 (20)	4% (49)
Isotope dilution		
	.97 (8)	2% (8)
	.996 (29)	2% (23)
	.95 (18)	2% (28)
		1% (30)
		2% (31)
		1% (32)
		2% (59)
Total body potassium		
	.33 (8)	7% (8)
	.96 (28)	4% (23)
		3% (30)

TABLE 14.1 (Continued)

Method		r_{xx}	CV
			3% (32)
			3% (58)
In vivo neutron activation			
		.99 (22)	1% to 3% (22)
			3% (25)
			3% (26)
			3% (27)
			2% (59)
Ultrasound	triceps	.98 (50)	
	midthigh	.94 (50)	
	suprailiac	.90 (50)	
	paraspinal	.82 (50)	
	sacral	.94 (50)	
	epigastral	.96 (50)	
	triceps	.88 (54)	
	biceps	.99 (54)	
	subscapula	.92 (54)	
	suprailiac	.97 (54)	
	abdomen	.93 (54)	
	calf	.96 (54)	
	thigh	.89 (54)	

person variation (which, over short periods of time, is mostly measurement error), smaller CVs indicate greater reliability. The second column contains the more traditional correlational reliability estimates, either Pearson product-moment or intraclass coefficients. The numbers in parentheses next to the coefficients indicate the reference number for the corresponding source in Table 14.3. Table 14.2 contains "validity" coefficients, that is, correlations among different methods of measuring fat. Again, the numbers in parentheses next to the coefficients indicate the reference number for the corresponding source in Table 14.3.

Atomic Level

Neutron Activation Analysis and Whole-Body Counting

Theory and background. A group of methods referred to as neutron activation analysis can quantify the major elements in vivo: O, C, H, N, Ca, P, Na, and Cl. After activation by insertion of a neutron into the nucleus, each element has specific decay patterns that include a gamma photon of characteristic energy, which is released following activation of the subject using a

TABLE 14.2 Validity Coefficients for Selected Methods of Measuring Body Fat In Vivo

	TOBEC	BMI	SKIN-FOLDS	BIA	DEXA/DPA	UWW	TBW	TBK
BMI	.54 (46) .45 (48) .93 (52)							
SKINFOLD	.81 (8) .59 (8) .77 (48)	.76 (11) .70 (43) .80 (62) .80 (46) .49 (48) .80 (51) .49 (53) .64 (53)						
BIA	.74 (8) .63 (8) .72 (48)	.63 (48)	.60 (1) .74 (8) .61 (8) .51 (14) .89 (16) .81 (48)					
DEXA	.83 (8) .64 (8) .79 (48)	.57 (48)	.89 (16) .55 (24) .80 (48) .87 (10)	.77 (1) .98 (3) .83 (8) .74 (8) .49 (14) .88 (48)				
UWW	.84 (8) .62 (8) .98 (35) .89 (38) .95 (38) .95 (39) .95 (40) .96 (41) .97 (41) .98 (42) .90 (45) .75 (48)	.60 (5) .82 (5) .71 (11) .70 (5) .75 (20) .94 (36) .54 (48) .71 (50) .89 (62)	.81 (1) .65 (8) .77 (8) .92 (10) .90 (15) .90 (20) .77 (48)	.58 (1) .98 (7) .72 (8) .77 (8) .72 (20) .81 (48) .83 (56) .96 (57)	.86 (1) .76 (6) .66 (6) .82 (8) .78 (8) .87 (10) .92 (15) .86 (15) .97 (21) .84 (48)			
TBW	.72 (8) .56 (8) .94 (35) .98 (37) .99 (37) .83 (38) .81 (40) .81 (42)	.43 (48) .80 (55) .93 (52) .99 (52)	.74 (8) .65 (8) .73 (14) .55 (48)	.70 (8) .68 (8) .59 (14) .56 (48)	.70 (8) .81 (8) .81 (14) .83 (33) .65 (48)	.72 (8) .73 (8) .71 (19) .63 (48)		

TABLE 14.2 (Continued)

	TOBEC	BMI	SKIN-FOLDS	BIA	DEXA/DPA	UWW	TBW	TBK
TBW	.95 (42)							
	.96 (44)							
	.87 (46)							
	.52 (48)							
TBK	.68 (8)		.65 (8)	.67 (8)	.74 (8)	.73 (8)	.71 (8)	
	.51 (8)		.68 (8)	.68 (8)	.76 (8)	.76 (8)	.79 (8)	
	.88 (39)		.53 (14)	.33 (14)	.63 (14)	.78 (19)	.69 (14)	
	.90 (44)				.91 (21)		.83 (46)	
	.86 (46)				.87 (33)			
IVNA			.80 (13)	.79 (13)	.92 (13)	.86 (13)	.97 (13)	.92 (13)
			.78 (14)	.63 (14)	.82 (14)	.90 (58)	.97 (14)	.68 (14)
					.94 (33)			
					.98 (58)			

neutron source. *Activation* refers to the unstable higher energy state created as neutrons interact with the elements that compose living tissues. Naturally occurring ^{40}K, which constitutes 0.0118% of total body K, can be estimated by whole-body counting. Total body K can then be estimated from ^{40}K.

Several multicompartment methods can be used to estimate fat from atomic-level components. The most recent of these methods uses 11 measured and calculated elements to derive six chemical components, including fat, in vivo (Heymsfield et al., 1991). A reduced version of this approach employs estimates of total body C, N, and Ca to estimate total body fat (Kehayias, Heymsfield, LoMonte, Wang, & Pierson, 1991). These high-technology methods are used primarily for research purposes and have the advantage of requiring minimal assumptions in deriving tissue components from elemental measurements.

A more widely used and classic method for determining fat and FFM is the whole-body ^{40}K counting technique. In this approach, whole-body counting is first used to estimate ^{40}K. A ratio-based approach, as described earlier, is then used to calculate total body K as $^{40}K/0.011$.

The estimated TBK can then be used to calculate body cell mass (BCM), fat, and FFM using ratio-based techniques. That is,

$$\text{BCM or FFM (in kg)} = \text{TBK (mmols)} \times \text{Ratio} \qquad [1]$$

Here the ratio for estimating BCM and FFM are 0.0083 and 0.011, respectively. The calculation of BCM makes two assumptions: (a) that the intracel-

TABLE 14.3 Sources of Reliability and Validity Coefficients

Study	Study Number	Mean Age	N	% Male/ % Female	Mean BMI
Johansson et al. (1993)	1	37±10.2	23	100%M	NA
Venkataraman and Ahluwalia (1992)	2	1.46±.12 days	28	NA	NA
Svendsen et al. (1991)	3	75y	46	50%/50%	25.0±3.4M 25.9±4.3F
Smalley et al. (1990)	4	34.6±12y	363	41%/59%	%BF 24±9.1
Wang et al. (1989)	5	49.3±15.9y	286	35%/65%	25.3±3.3M 23±3.4F
Khaled et al. (1988)	6	24.9±3.1y	56	69%/31%	21.7±3.7
Pierson et al. (1991)	7	19-94	389[a]	40%/60%	21.2-25.7
Mazess et al. (1990)	8	NA	12	50%/50%	NA
Mazess et al. (1984)	9	23-61y	18	22%/88%	8.3-45.7
Revicki and Isreal (1986)	10	20-70y	474	100%M	38.3
Smalley et al. (1990)	11	34.6±12	36	41%/59%	%BF 24±9.1
Wang et al. (n.d.)	12	43-77y	65	43%/34%	24-32
Wang, Kotler, et al. (1992)	13	41±10y	18	100%M	20±2
Clark et al. (1993)	14[b]	39.1±14	35	100%M	24.8±2.9
Webster and Bar (1993)	15	12-18y	54	100%F	BF 10%-31%
Russell-Aulet et al. (1991)	16	45±17y	81	51%/49%	23±3
Van Itallie et al. (1985)	17	(review article)			
Ward et al. (1975)	18	NA	259	86%/14%	NA
A. S. Jackson et al. (1988)	19	28-45y	68	35%/65%	20-28
Haarbo et al. (1991)	20	23-41y	25	40%/60%	NA
Beddoe et al. (1984)	21	19-59y	64	51%/49%	NA
Albu et al. (1992)	22	48±3	10	100%F	43±1
Rammohan and Aplasca (1992)	23	52-70y	56	50%/50%	22-32
Vartsky et al. (1979)	24	(review article)			
Mernagh et al. (1977)	25	(review article)			
Kyere et al. (1982)	26	NA	6	83%/16%	%BF 3.84-14.5
Wang et al. (1973)	27	27-69	10	60%/40%	NA
Tzen and Wu (1989)	28	33-45y	7	71%/29%	NA
Cohn et al. (1984)	29[b]	20-79y	137	50%/50%	NA
Schoeller et al. (1980)	30	NA	10	70%/30%	NA
Ellis et al. (1982)	31	20-80y	211	52%/48%	NA
Heymsfield and Wang (in press)	32	60.1±21.1	13	38%/62%	22.6±1.6
Marks et al. (1989)	33	38-54y	229	41%/59%	NA
Van Itallie et al. (1986)	34	(review article)			
Garrow and Webster (1985)	35	16-64	128	18%/81%	27.2%-34.7%

TABLE 14.3 (Continued)

Study	Study Number	Mean Age	N	% Male/ % Female	Mean BMI
Cochran et al. (1988)	36	23-58	20	50%/50%	NA
Van Loan (1990)	37	11-19y	50	66%/34%	21±2.9
Horswill et al. (1989)	38	29.2±1.8y	12	58%/42%	NA
Van Loan, Belko, et al. (1987)	39	29.4±4.0y	12	100%F	%BF 37.7+ 3.3%
Van Loan, Segal, et al. (1987)	40	18-35y	157	NA	%BF 13.8-30
Van Loan and Koehler (1990)	41	35-90y	114	NA	%BF 24.5-46.3
Garn et al. (1986)	42	5-60y	4454	NA	
Van Loan and Mayclin (1987)	43	18-35y	40	50%/50%	%BF 14.46 M %BF 24.42 F
Presta, Segal, et al. (1983)	44	20-53y	32	50%/50%	23.8±6 F 26.5±6.6 M
Presta, Wang, et al. (1983)	45	25-63y	19	21%/79%	14.4-51
Kushner and Schoeller (1986)	46	28.6-53.7	58	NA	20.8-35.6
Fattante et al. (n.d.)	47	48.93y	133	38%/61%	NA
Lohman (1992)	48	(review article)			
Bellisari et al. (in press)	49	18-62y	35	49%/51%	26.0±4.2 M 25.0±5.3 F
Michielutte et al. (1984)	50	5-12y	1668	50%/50%	NA
Hergenroeder et al. (1991)	51	11-25y	1656	56%/44%	NA
Minten et al. (1991)	52	65-79y	515	51%/49%	25.5±2.9 M 27.1±4.3 F
Volz and Ostrove (1984)	53	18-26	66	100%F	%BF 22.8±4.54
Lukaski and Johnson (1985)	54	28.8±7.1	37	100%M	%BF 20.2±7.6
Rising et al. (1991)	55	30±8	156	58%/42%	%BF 34±9
Eckerson et al. (1992a)	56	22±3	68	100%M	%BF 9.1±2.2
Heymsfield, Lichtman, et al. (1990)	57	58±20	31	58%/42%	23.4±2.6
Heymsfield et al. (1989)	58	NA	13	38%/62%	NA
Eckerson et al. (1992a)	59	23±5	35	100%M	%BF 9.6±2.3
A. S. Jackson et al. (1988)	60	31±11	331	100%F	%BF 24±7
Abdel-Malek et al. (1985)	61	6-51	458	52%/48%	NA
Heymsfield, Wang, Funfar, et al. (1990)	62	NA	4	NA	NA

a. The reliability data from this article are based on only 5 of the 389 subjects.
b. These include data from the introduction.

lular K is 150 mmol/L and (b) that 25% of cell mass is intracellular solids. The ratio used for calculation of FFM is based on the early observation in cadavers that FFM contained 68 mmol K per kg (Forbes, 1987). More recently, the K/FM ratio has been revised downward and was also shown to be sex and age dependent (Pierson, Lin, & Phillips, 1974).

Reliability. Table 14.1 provides information on the reliability of TBK measurements. As can be seen in Table 14.1, with one exception, the reliability of ^{40}K counting is generally quite high.

Validity. Table 14.2 provides information on the convergent validity of TBK fat determinations. As can be seen, the validity can best be described as "modest," with intermethod correlations generally falling between .60 and .80. Thus, compared with other "high-tech" methods, the validity of TBK for measuring body fat is weak.

Moderators. Multicomponent methods of estimating fat that are based on elements such as carbon and nitrogen are generally valid across gender, age, and various ethnic groupings. This is because the measured elements are used to calculate chemical components, and the proportions of these chemical components as specific elements are extremely stable. For example, nitrogen averages 16% of protein in humans and many animal species regardless of age or gender (Cohn et al., 1980; Heymsfield & Wang, in press). Fat estimates derived using multicomponent methods, such as those based on neutron activation analysis, do include more measurement error.

Fat estimates based on TBK assume that the ratio of potassium to FFM is known and stable (Forbes, 1987). Unlike chemical linkages, however, the ratio of potassium to FFM varies with age and other factors, including disease (Forbes, 1987). Fat estimates using the TBK method are therefore valid only in subjects who are weight stable and free of serious underlying diseases. Diuretic treatment also tends to deplete potassium stores and alter the ratio of TBK to FFM (Heymsfield & Wang, in press).

Risk. Neutron activation systems expose patients to ionizing radiation. The exposure varies greatly between systems (Dilmanian et al., 1990), a few examples of which are prompt-gamma for total body nitrogen and hydrogen, 50 mrem; inelastic neutron scattering for total body carbon, 15 mrem; and delayed-gamma for total body calcium, sodium, and chlorine, 550 mrem. Pregnant women and healthy young children are not studied with these methods due to the radiation exposure. Serial studies in the same patient with neutron activation analyzers must also be carefully considered.

Whole-body counting for potassium is without hazard. Some whole-body counters have a small chamber and require long counting times, and an occasional "claustrophobic" patient cannot be studied.

Practical issues. The cost of whole-body counting and neutron activation analysis prohibits the widespread use of these methods. Costs vary between $100,000 for basic instruments to several million dollars for state-of-the art facilities. Most current facilities are therefore dedicated almost entirely to research. Whole-body counters for potassium can be found in a number of medical centers throughout the world, while neutron activation systems are far more limited in their availability.

Molecular Level

TBW and bone mineral can both be determined by property-based methods at the molecular level. The measured properties involve physical characteristics of labeled water and the attenuation of X-rays by various tissues, respectively. Both TBW and bone mineral components can be used to estimate fat and FFM.

Total Body Water

Theory and background. Because fat mass has little to no water but lean mass has much more water, body fatness can be calculated from knowledge of TBW. Dilution volumes of TBW can be estimated from the properties of three available isotopic tracers of water: ^3H_2O, D_2O, and $H_2^{18}O$. Tritium dilution volume can be estimated using a small oral or intravenous dose (.19 Bq) of ^3H_2O (Heymsfield, Lichtman, et al., 1990). Tritium can be quantified from the .018 mev beta ray decay of ^3H_2O in a scintillation counter. At our research center, the isotope is injected into a peripheral vein. Blood and urine samples are then collected at 3 hours postinjection of isotope. Tritium counts in blood at baseline and in blood and urine at $t = 3$ hours are then used to estimate the tritium dilution volume if the exact amount of label is known in the dose.

Once tritium dilution volume is known, TBW can be calculated using a component-based ratio technique. Tritium overestimates TBW because the labeled hydrogen exchanges with hydrogen atoms in other organic molecules. The exact ratio TBW/^3H_2O is unknown but probably ranges between 0.94 and 0.97. At our research center, we use the ratio 0.95 to calculate TBW as (Heymsfield, Lichtman, et al., 1990):

$$TBW \text{ (kg)} = {}^3H_2O \text{ (1)} \times 0.95 \times 0.9934 \qquad [2]$$

Here 0.9934 is the density of water at 37 degrees Celsius.

Deuterium and oxygen-18 labeled water are stable isotopes and thus non-radioactive. As with tritium, dilution volumes are estimated over several hours following an oral or intravenous dose of isotope. Methods are available for analyzing isotope in saliva (Schoeller, 1992) or in urine, thus eliminating the need for a venipuncture. Deuterium in biological samples can be analyzed using infrared spectroscopy or isotope ratio mass spectroscopy (Schoeller, 1992). The estimated ratios TBW/D_2O and TBW/$H_2{}^{18}O$ are 0.97 and 0.99, respectively (Schoeller, 1992). These ratios allow calculation of TBW from dilution volumes as in equation 2.

Once TBW is known, FFM can be calculated as

$$FFM = TBW/0.732 = 1.37 \times TBW \qquad [3]$$

which assumes that the ratio of TBW/FFM is constant at 0.732. Fat is calculated in the TBW method as body weight-FFM. There are at least three sources of variation in this ratio: measurement error, normal physiological variation, and pathological physiological variation. Hydration varies with such normal physiological states as the menstrual cycle and fasting-feeding cycle and disease states often result in fluid gain or loss with a resulting unpredictable change in hydration. The total body water method is thus not a very reliable approach to estimating fat in disease states but is a good direct measure of total body water.

Reliability. Isotope dilution methods yield extremely reliable estimates of body fat, as indicated by Table 14.1, with test-retest coefficients well above .90 in all cases.

Validity. The validity of isotope dilution methods is generally good (see Table 14.2) with convergent validity coefficients averaging around .70 to .80.[1]

Moderators. Total body water is all within the FFM component and the ratio of TBW to FFM is reasonably constant in nonobese healthy adults. Small changes in hydration (in the range of 2%) occur under normal circumstances (e.g., with the menstrual cycle). Physiological variability may increase with aging (Baumgartner, Rhyne, Garry, & Heymsfield, in press). Under- or overhydration is commonplace in diseased patients. Subjects in whom fat estimates are derived using total body water should therefore be selected carefully to exclude those individuals with abnormal hydration.

A small error might be introduced into the TBW method of estimating fat by assuming a constant ratio of isotope dilution volume to total body water space. The ratios of deuterium, tritium, and oxygen-18 dilution volumes to TBW vary slightly under physiological conditions (Goran, Poehlman, Nair, & Danforth, 1992, 1993).

Risk. Both deuterium and oxygen labeled water are stable isotopic compounds and are thus not radioactive. Both isotopes can be used in children and pregnant women. Tritium is radioactive and thus exposes the subject to a small amount of ionizing radiation. The radiation exposure is small, comparable to a chest X-ray. However, stable isotopes of water make possible the measurement of TBW in children and pregnant women with complete safety.

Practical issues. With respect to tritiated water, a scintillation counter is available in most hospitals and tritium is a very inexpensive isotope. Deuterium is also inexpensive but its analysis is more involved. Infrared analyzers are simple to operate but cost several thousand dollars to purchase, although many hospitals already own them. Vacuum distillation of specimens is required for deuterium or ^{18}O measurements, a specialized procedure requiring about 2 hours of technologist time, making these tests considerably effortful. Commercial laboratories also can analyze deuterium. Accurate measurement of oxygen-18 labeled water requires specialized mass spectroscopy procedures. $H_2{}^{18}O$ is costly ($\approx$ \$200 for an adult) and relatively difficult to acquire in large quantities.

Dual Energy X-Ray Absorptiometry

Theory and background. Dual energy X-ray absorptiometry (DEXA), an advance over dual photon absorptiometry (DPA), is a recently developed technique that relies on the differential X-ray attenuation of tissues to provide estimates of bone mineral and fat (Heymsfield, Wang, Aulet, et al., 1990; Heymsfield, Wang, Funfar, et al., 1990; Mazess, Barden, Bisek, & Hansen, 1990; Mazess, Peppler, & Gibbons, 1984). Although DEXA systems are costly, body composition estimates provided by this method are quite accurate, result in minimal radiation exposure ($<$ 1 mrem), and require only about 30 minutes for completion (Mazess et al., 1990).

DEXA systems emit X-rays at two different energies. As the X-rays pass through tissues, they are attenuated in relation to the specific tissue's mass attenuation coefficient. Calcium and phosphorous in bone mineral have high mass attenuation and are thus readily separated from surrounding soft tissues using various computer algorithms (Heymsfield, Wang, Aulet, et al., 1990; Mazess et al., 1984, 1990). The soft tissues also differ in their attenuation of X-rays due to variation in elemental composition. These soft tissue differences in X-ray attenuation at the two energies allow further resolution of soft tissues into fat and fat-free soft tissue (largely muscle).

Most DEXA systems now allow for whole-body or regional estimates of fat, fat-free soft tissue, and bone mineral mass and density (Mazess et al., 1990). Because the fat-free portion of the extremities can be quantified with DEXA, this allows approximate derivation of appendicular skeletal muscle mass (Heymsfield, Smith, et al., 1990). About 75% of total skeletal muscle is in the appendages. Regional fat estimates (e.g., limbs, trunk) are also possible with DEXA systems.

Reliability. The reliability of DEXA and DPA are generally excellent, as is clearly evident in Table 14.1.

Validity. There are now many validation studies that compare DEXA estimates with those derived by other research methods. DEXA fat estimates compare favorably with fat estimates from neutron activation analysis, underwater weighing (UWW), and TBW. In our experience, DEXA yields the most valid estimates among the readily available techniques; that is, it consistently correlates quite highly with alternative methods of estimating adiposity (see Table 14.2). In principal components analyses of correlation matrices of adiposity measurements, DEXA consistently has the highest factor pattern loading of all the measurement techniques (Fattante et al., n.d.).

Moderators. Although DEXA is usually promoted as a method of estimating fat that is independent of confounding factors often observed with other techniques, caution should be used before accepting DEXA as the "gold standard" (Roubenoff, Kehayias, Dawson-Hughes, & Heymsfield, 1993). DEXA estimates are highly "thickness dependent," with systematic errors appearing in fat estimates as the subject's transverse diameter grows larger (Roubenoff et al., 1993). Software corrections have been provided by equipment manufacturers to compensate for this error. Other less well studied factors, such as hydration, may also influence DEXA fat estimates and represent an active area of research. On the whole, the DEXA approach is indeed emerging as the most accurate of the various available techniques for estimating the fat component.

Risk. The radiation exposure for DEXA is low (< 1 mrem) and some research centers are now using DEXA to study fat in children. The low radiation exposure of DEXA allows for repeated studies in adults and makes it possible to study children (radiation exposure in children is about $\frac{1}{30}$ of a chest X-ray), although, as with all ionizing radiation procedures, benefits should be weighed carefully against risks.

Practical issues. The cost of DEXA systems ranges between $70,000 and $100,000. A small room, large enough for a bed and desk, is needed to house a DEXA system. In some states, a licensed X-ray technician is required by law to operate a DEXA system.

Ultrasound

Theory and background. Ultrasonic equipment was used to detect underwater movement of submarines beginning with World War II. Similar technology, with major refinements, can now be used to measure body composition components in humans with relative safety. No adverse consequences are recognized for relatively brief periods of ultrasound exposure. Systems applying the ultrasound concept are used widely throughout the medical care field. These include abdominal and fetal ultrasonography, echocardiography, and ultrasonic methods of assessing bone mineral density.

Ultrasound systems used in body composition research fall into two general categories, A mode and B mode. The A mode systems were developed first and are relatively simple. An ultrasound signal is transmitted from the system's probe. Signals reflected off various structures return as echoes to the system's probe. Tissue interfaces can be identified, and the thickness of adipose tissue, muscle, and other structures can be identified.

With the more recent B mode systems, a two-dimensional image of the scanned area is produced in which tissue interfaces are identified as bright lines. Most clinical ultrasound systems operate using the more versatile and informative B mode at frequencies between 3 and 5 MHz.

Reliability. Ultrasound measurements using A mode systems are generally unreliable (Chumlea & Roche, 1986). Problems exist in identifying tissue interfaces and in ensuring that the ultrasound beam is directed perpendicular to the skin surface.

Most investigators studying body composition with ultrasound use B mode systems. The main measurements are of subcutaneous adipose tissue thickness. Sites vary in reproducibility, mainly because some tissue interfaces are easier to identify than others. For example, Bellisari, Roche, and Siervogel (in press) reported reliability coefficients ranging from .82 for the paraspinal region to .98 for triceps. Volz and Ostrove (1984) reported coefficients ranging from .87 to .99 (see Table 14.1).

Validity. Once the various thickness measurements are made, absolute values for specific sites can be compared between individuals or prediction equations can be used to estimate total body fat. Not much information is available on ultrasound normative values or on the validity of the various prediction equations.

There appears to be no clear advantage of ultrasound measurements over those made by skinfolds in normal weight adults, although there is not total agreement on this point (Bellisari et al., in press; Weiss & Clark, 1987). Some suggestion exists that ultrasound measurements may have advantages in very obese or lean individuals in whom skinfold measurements may be unreliable (Bellisari et al., in press).

A few reports have appeared providing validity information on ultrasound fatness measurements but data are still scarce. Fanelli and Kuczmarski (1984) reported that, among 124 young white men, the validity of ultrasonographically determined adiposity was roughly equivalent to that of skinfolds. Ultrasonographically determined adiposity correlated between .76 and .80 with adiposity determined by hydrodensitometry (Fanelli & Kuczmarski, 1984). Extremely similar results were obtained by Volz and Ostrove (1984). Czinner and Varady (1992) provided some validity information in children.

Moderators. Edema fluid in subcutaneous compartments would increase ultrasound depth even without a change in adipose tissue mass.

Risk. Ultrasound exposure for brief time periods has no known risk.

Practical issues. Equipment for B mode scanning is relatively expensive. Lower cost systems begin at about $15,000. New systems are extremely compact. Easy transport to field studies is possible.

Cellular Level

There are no methods of assessing fat cell mass at the cellular level of body composition.

Tissue-System Level

Imaging Techniques

Theory and background. Adipose tissue and skeletal muscle mass can be quantified for specific regions of the body using imaging methods. The difference between body weight and adipose tissue is adipose-tissue-free mass.

Two types of body cross-section imaging methods are widely available: computerized axial tomography (CT) and magnetic resonance imaging (MRI). These methods are expensive, involve radiation in the case of CT, and are usually reserved for research studies. Both methods produce high-resolution cross-sectional tissue images from signals resulting from exposure of the subject to an X-ray source (CT) or electromagnetic field (MRI). Cross-sectional images provide areas of any selected organs and tissues. The area measurement can be used alone or combined with other images to construct total body volumes from multiple cross-sectional images. Volumes can be converted to weight from known tissue densities.

In addition to providing total adipose tissue, CT and MRI are capable of separating adipose tissue into subcutaneous, visceral, and intraorgan components. Adipose tissue in bone marrow cannot be accurately quantified by single photon CT, although dual photon CT can distinguish marrow fat.

Reliability. There are relatively few data available on the reliability and validity of CT and MRI for estimating adiposity; hence they were not included in Tables 14.1 and 14.2. However, some data do exist. McNeill et al. (1991) performed repeated assessments of fatness on animal tissue samples and obtained an intraindividual coefficient of variation of 2.6% for MRI.

Validity. Fowler et al. (1991; see also McNeill et al., 1991) conducted a small study (14 women) of MRI and five other techniques for assessing adiposity (including hydrodensitometry). In this sample, MRI appeared to yield the most valid estimates of fatness. Moreover, reducing the number of MRI scans per person from 17 to 4 did not significantly worsen the estimation. Although more data are obviously needed, imaging techniques, if affordable and tolerable, promise to be accurate and versatile. Imaging techniques are often used for assessment of body fat distribution, in which their validity is excellent (e.g., de Ridder et al., 1992).

Moderators and related issues. One problem with both CT and MRI is that whole-body scans are time consuming and costly. The more usual approach is to collect regional data and to assume that the regional estimate is representative of the patient as a whole. Another problem is that artifacts can be introduced into the scan by foreign objects such as hip prostheses or metallic surgical clips in the case of CT. Beam hardening is another CT phenomenon that often occurs in the path of osseous structures and creates difficulties in interpreting tissue composition in certain bony regions. Artifacts are also present in MRI images due to motion because of long scan times. For example, bowel motion due to peristalsis blurs the margins between visceral adipose tissue and bowel, making analysis difficult.

Risk. CT requires relatively high radiation exposure, and thus scanning is usually reserved for men and for postmenopausal women. Apart from psychological discomfort associated with the confined space, MRI has no known risks. The occasional "claustrophobic" patient may require sedation prior to scanning.

Practical issues. Both CT and MRI are costly tests, ranging from several hundred to over $1,000 depending on the study type and scanning method. Our experience is that, although scanners are readily available, elective studies such as for body composition are often scheduled at inconvenient times. As mentioned, some patients cannot tolerate the confined space of CT and MRI scanners, and therefore cannot be studied. These are enormously powerful research tools, but their application to low-budget and large-scale epidemiological studies is limited.

Adipose Tissue Distribution

Theory and background. As early as 1902, medical science provided hints that not only the total amount of adipose tissue but also the anatomical distribution of adipose tissue was a risk factor for early mortality. Grant (1902) stated that among men there is greater risk for mortality when abdominal girth exceeds chest girth at full inspiration. However, anthropological evidence suggests that this association may have been suspected by people long before the twentieth century (Tarui, Tokunaga, Fujioka, & Matsuzawa, 1991).

In-depth scientific study of adipose tissue distribution, its causes, and its effects on health and longevity began with Jean Vague in 1947 and has become a major area of discovery under such luminaries as Bjorntorp, Kissebah, and Pi-Sunyer. Given the importance of body fat distribution, sound measurement of this construct is crucial. However, as we shall see, this is easier said than done.

The importance of adipose tissue distribution lies in its relationship to biochemical changes (e.g., serum lipids), blood pressure, morbidity, and mortality (Seidell, Bakx, De Boer, Deurenberg, & Hautvast, 1985; Seidell, Deurenberg, & Hautvast, 1987). Most studies suggest that the increased risk of obesity is related to mesenteric and portal depots of adipose tissue. Subcutaneous adipose tissue, particularly around the hips and buttocks, appears not to markedly increase health risks. The aim of measurement techniques is to estimate the amount of mesenteric and portal adipose tissue. Methods, in decreasing accuracy, are as follows:

- *Cadaver analysis.* The information here is limited. Cadaver dissection indicates that about one third of intra-abdominal adipose tissue is retroperitoneal and not related to the increased risk of obesity (Rossner et al., 1990). The main use of cadaver studies is to validate other methods that can be used to study patients in vivo.

- *Computerized axial tomography (CT).* CT produces sharply delineated images of visceral adipose tissue in its various components. Multiple slice CT can accurately map the volumes of mesenteric and portal adipose tissue based on comparison with limited cadaver studies. Usually five or six cross-sectional images of the abdomen are made, although some studies suggest that a single slice at L3-L4 correlates well with total visceral adipose tissue.

- *Magnetic resonance imaging (MRI).* Cross-sectional images of the abdomen can also be made using MRI. Unfortunately, MRI scans require long data collection intervals and during this time there may be gastrointestinal movement. This movement obscures visceral fat boundaries. The result is that MRI is not as reliable as CT for estimating visceral adipose tissue deposits.

- *Dual energy X-ray absorptiometry (DEXA).* As noted in an earlier section, DEXA can give abdominal fat estimates. Fat cannot, however, be separated into subcutaneous and visceral components by DEXA. Some investigators (Svendsen, Hassager, Begmann, & Christiansen, 1993) suggest combining DEXA measurements with skinfolds, circumferences, or ultrasound measurements to separate DEXA-total abdominal fat into subcutaneous and visceral components.

- *Ultrasound.* Ultrasonography can be used to estimate linear dimensions in vivo. Some workers (Armellini et al., 1990) advocate the use of ultrasound to estimate intra-abdominal depth, which correlates highly with visceral adipose tissue measured by CT. Ultrasound has not progressed to a clinically useful technique because measurements remain unreliable.

- *Anthropometric measurements.* Skinfold measurements have long been used to quantify adipose tissue distribution. Such indices as the centrality index (subscapular/triceps skinfolds) have been in use for many years. The most widely used anthropometric technique is the waist to hip circumference ratio. This ratio correlates only reasonably well with visceral adipose tissue (van der Kooy & Seidell, 1993), but many studies show a relationship between the waist to hip ratio and various outcome measures such as stroke or myocardial infarction rates (Seidell et al., 1987).

Another anthropometric measurement is the sagittal diameter. As originally conceived, this measurement is made directly on a CT scan cross-sectional image. Sagittal diameter correlates reasonably well (*r*'s ranging from

.46 to .96; van der Kooy & Seidell, 1993) with visceral adipose tissue as measured by CT (Sjöström, 1993). The sagittal diameter is measured as the height from examination tabletop to abdominal peak at the level of the iliac crest as the patient lies supine (Sjöström, 1993).

Reliability. The hierarchy of techniques for measuring visceral adipose tissue, in descending order of accuracy, as noted by van der Kooy and Seidell (1993), is (a) cadaver analysis; (b) multislice computerized tomography (CT) or (less precise) multislice magnetic resonance imaging (MRI); (c) single-slice CT or MRI; (d) dual energy X-ray absorptiometry (DEXA) or dual photon absorptiometry (DPA); (e) ultrasound; (f) anthropometry (abdominal diameters, circumferences, and skinfold thicknesses); and (g) eyeball examination of subjects. For the reasons mentioned here, CT multiscan technique is considered the most accurate approach and the various anthropometric methods least accurate. The coefficient of variation for abdominal CT scans ranges from about .6% to 1.4% and the correlation of a single scan with total intra-abdominal adipose tissue area is about .95 (van der Kooy & Seidell, 1993).

Moderators. An important moderator in the measurement of adipose tissue distribution is race. Both black men and black women have consistently been shown to have more upper body fat distributions than white men and women when measured with anthropometry (Zillikens & Conway, 1990). However, it has been shown that these anthropometric indices do not correlate with risk factors in blacks as strongly as they do in whites (Dowling & Pi-Sunyer, 1993). Recently, Susan Yanovsky and colleagues showed that anthropometric markers of body fat distribution are less correlated with visceral fat by CT in blacks compared with whites (S. Yanovsky, personal communication, March 1994).

Risk. The risks of the various procedures are described in earlier sections. Multislice CT scan delivers a substantial radiation dose, although this is low for a single slice. MRI has no radiation, and DEXA radiation exposure is minimal. No risks are known for any of the anthropometric measurements.

Whole-Body Level

There are widely used methods for estimating fatness at the whole-body level: weight-stature indices, bioimpedance analysis (BIA), total body electrical conductivity (TOBEC), hydrodensitometry, and anthropometry.

Weight-Stature Indices

Theory and background. The use of weight-stature indices goes back at least to the early 1800s when the Belgian mathematician Lambert-Adolf-Jacques Quetelet analyzed census data to determine influences on mortality and began his studies of anthropometry (Bell, 1945). If all humans were the same height, weight alone would be a good clinical measure of fatness. However, variation in stature dictates that adjustment must be made in body weight to establish relative fatness in different individuals. The aim of weight-stature indices is to provide estimates of body mass that are independent of stature. Virtually all of these indices have one of two general forms:

(a) W_a/W_r or

(b) W_a/S^K

where W_a is actual weight, W_r is some reference (i.e., "ideal") weight for height, S is stature, and K is a constant. Form 2 is increasingly used and preferred to Form 1 because it is not dependent on agreeing on any particular set of reference weights and, under certain not too restrictive assumptions, can be shown to be a more general case of 1 (Benn, 1971).

Although the optimal value for K may vary slightly with such factors as gender, age, and ethnicity (Abdel-Malek, Mukherjee, & Roche, 1985; Cole, 1991; Micozzi, Albanes, Jones, & Chumlea, 1986), several studies have shown that K = 2 is usually the best choice (Cole, 1991; Lopez & Masse, 1992). K could in principle be derived anew on each investigator's sample (Abdel-Malek et al., 1985; Lee, Kolonel, & Hinds, 1981). However, Colliver, Frank, and Frank (1983) found that six of the more common indices all yielded highly similar relative rankings with pairwise correlations averaging .96. In a factor analysis of these indices, a single factor accounted for 97% of the variance in the original observations. This suggests that the choice among common weight-stature indices is a matter of little statistical concern.[2]

The most widely used weight-stature index is Quetelet's body-mass index (BMI),

$$BMI = W_a/S^2$$

where stature (S) is measured in meters and weight (W_a) is measured in kilograms. This index seems to be appropriate for use in both children and adults (Cole, 1991) although, in cross-sectional studies employing a wide age range, it should be corrected for age.

Both protein-energy malnutrition and obesity can be classified according to BMI categories. BMI is widely used in clinical populations because it is inexpensive to acquire body weight and height measurements, there are no risks involved, and calculation is simple.

Reliability. The measurement of height and weight is so simple that, given reasonable instruments, reliability coefficients approach 1.0. In our laboratory (unpublished data), even across two ordinary bathroom scales, we have found correlations between weights above .99. This suggests that these inexpensive instruments can be used to measure weight in field settings *as long as they are calibrated against a proper scale in advance.*

Validity. For most groups, BMI correlates well with other measures of fatness (r^2 typically ranging from .5 to .8; see Table 14.2). However, it taps both lean and fat mass and therefore has weak discriminant validity.

Moderators. We (Gomez, Allison, & Heymsfield, 1993) found that race (black or white) does not moderate the relationship between BMI and percentage fat as determined by DEXA. However, age is an important moderator of the BMI-fatness relationship. At equal BMIs, older adults are fatter than younger adults (Cronk & Roche, 1982). Moreover, there is some evidence that BMI is less strongly related to fatness in older versus younger adults (Micozzi & Harris, 1990). Finally, it is important to realize that BMI changes in a *markedly* nonlinear fashion with age in children (Siervogel, Roche, Guo, Mukherjee, & Chumlea, 1991), suggesting that age-standardized BMIs are probably best when studying children.

Risk. There is none.

Practical issues. One major practical issue concerns the validity of self-reported height and weight. Clearly, for collection of data in scientific inquiry, it is more desirable to actually measure body composition than to ask people to report their body composition. However, for many clinical evaluations and epidemiological studies, one may take advantage of the fact that most people know their approximate height and weight. Thus it is reasonable to ask how well self-reported height and weight can substitute for their measured counterparts.

In this regard, two issues must be considered: error and bias. *Error* refers to random error, and *bias* refers to systematic bias. The extent to which error and bias are important depends on the context of the study. If the main goal of the study entails the estimation of levels of relative weight, then minimizing bias is crucial. For example, if the major purpose of a study were to estimate the proportion of a population who have BMI above 28, then any systematic bias would bias the outcome of the study.

In contrast, if the main purpose of a study is to examine how some anthropometric indicator correlates with some other variable, then bias is unimportant because correlation coefficients are invariant under linear transformations. However, random error (i.e., unreliability) will systematically bias (i.e., attenuate) correlations.

Weight

Bias. Two excellent reviews have been published that bear on the accuracy of self-reported weight (Bowman & DeLucia, 1992; Cameron & Evers, 1990). Both reviews indicate that clear biases exist among all groups studied and that the most common bias is that of underreporting. In addition, the biases differ somewhat systematically between males and females. On average, males underestimate their weight by approximately 1.37 pounds. On average, females underestimate their weight between 1.29 and 3.86 pounds (Bowman & DeLucia, 1992). Obviously, this average degree of underreporting is fairly trivial for both males and females. However, some subgroups may underreport to a greater degree. For example, Bowman and DeLucia (1992) report that among clinical weight loss subjects the average degree of underreporting was 5.17 pounds.

The degree of bias is a function of actual weight. For women, the heavier the woman, the greater the degree of underreporting. For men, those above average weight tend to underreport and those below average weight tend to overreport. Thus, in general, self-reports tend to underestimate the prevalence of obesity (i.e., their sensitivity is low and their specificity is high). The sensitivity of obesity diagnosis based on self-reported height and weight ranges from approximately 60% to 91% (Neito-Garcia, Bush, & Keyl, 1990). Nieto-Garcia et al. offer a helpful table of the sensitivity of self-reported height and weight broken down by age, gender, education, race, and marital status.

Error. The crucial question here is what is the correlation between self-reported weight and measured weight? The greater the correlation, the less the error. Table 14.4 lists results from studies that have correlated self-reported weight, height, or BMI with their measured counterparts. In all but two cases, the correlation exceeds .90 for adults. For children, there are fewer data on self-report validity and greater caution is warranted.

In addition, several studies have also shown that adults can report on the weights of other people in their household with a fair degree of validity (e.g., J. Jackson, Strauss, Lee, & Hunter, 1990; Perry & Learnard, 1963; Wing, Epstein, & Neff, 1980). Must, Willett, and Dietz (1993) demonstrated that, although some useful information can be gleaned, remote recall of childhood BMIs are not highly correlated ($r \leq .75$) with actual childhood BMIs. Finally, evidence suggests that, while interview and questionnaire reports of weight are quite valid, estimates obtained from records of drivers' licenses are prone to substantially greater error and bias (Greenway & Bray, 1975) and should probably not be used as a primary source of information.

Height

Bias. Drawing on the studies listed in Table 14.4, a general conclusion can be made. Like weight, there are systematic but small biases in the reporting of height. Here people tend to *overreport* their height and the difference is slightly greater for males.

Error. As can be seen in Table 14.4, there is little random error in self-reported estimates of height for adults. On the other hand, children are poor reporters of their own heights, perhaps due, in part, to their relatively rapid changes in height with growth.

Bioimpedance Analysis

Theory and background. Bioimpedance analysis (BIA) is a safe, rapid, inexpensive, and practical method of evaluating fat, fat-free body mass, and total body water. Surface electrodes are applied to the skin surface of the subject's extremities. An alternating electrical current of known frequency is then passed through the distal electrodes and a lowering in current is detected by the proximal electrodes. The reduction in current, or total body impedance, is related to the complex interaction between a number of factors. These factors include distance between electrodes, volume and composition of conducting tissues, anatomical/geometric factors, and frequency of applied electrical current. Adipose tissue is a poor conductor, and lean tissues, particularly fluid compartments, are good conductors of the electrical signal. The result is that a good inverse correlation is observed between impedance (actually impedance is composed of two components, a large resistance term and a much smaller reactance term—resistance is used rather than impedance in most studies) and total body water and fat-free body mass, and high positive correlations between resistance and total body fat. Although there

TABLE 14.4 Correlations Between Self-Reported and Measured Weight, Height, and BMI

	Study	Height	Weight	BMI[a]
ADULTS	Males			
	Alverez-Torices et al. (1993)	.92	.97	.94
	Kuskowska-Wolk et al. (1991)	.92	.93	.93
	Lass et al. (1982).	.99	.99	
	Mueller et al. (1985)	.91	.94	
	Pirie et al. (1981)	.93	.92	
	Rowland (1990)	.94	.97	
	Stewart (1982)	.94	.98	
	Stunkard and Albaum (1981)			
	age < 40		.95	
	age ≥ 40		.96	
	Tell et al. (1987)		.94	
	Females			
	Alverez-Torices et al. (1993)	.83	.93	.88
	Cash et al. (1989)		.94	
	Coates et al. (1978)	.95	.96	
	Hall (1972)		.91	
	Heaney and Ryan (1988)	.94		
	Koslowsky et al. (1994)		.95	
	Kuskowska-Wolk et al. (1991)	.89	.94	.93
	Lass et al. (1982)	.96	.89	
	Mueller et al. (1985)	.91	.94	
	Paganni-Hill and Ross (1982)	.87	.89	
	Pirie et al. (1981)	.94	.94	
	Rowland (1990)	.89	.98	
	Stewart (1982)	.93	.98	
	Stunkard and Albaum (1981)			
	age < 40		.97	
	age ≥ 40		.91	
	Tell et al. (1987)		.98	
	Both sexes			
	Alverez-Torices et al. (1993)	.93	.96	.91
	Charney et al. (1976)		.96	
	Epstein et al. (1991)[b]		.90	
	Murphy et al. (1985)		.95	
	Norvell and Boaz (1986)		.91[c]	
	Perry and Learnard (1963)		.98	
	Stewart et al. (1987)	.96	.98	.94
	Stunkard and Albaum (1981)		.99	
	Wing et al. (1979)			
	Study I	.92	.98	.90
	Study II	.98	.98	.94
ADOLESCENTS	Males			
	Davis and Gergen (1994)	.86	.95	
	Females			
	Davis and Gergen (1994)	.86	.93	
CHILDREN	Boys			
	Shannon et al. (1991)	.74	.90	
	Girls			
	Shannon et al. (1991)	.62	.84	

a. Or other index of relative weight (e.g., percentage of ideal body weight); b. Includes some children; c. Averaged from four different coefficients reported.

are small measurement errors between instruments, most of the higher quality BIA systems give similar and highly reproducible estimates of resistance.

Most BIA systems are preprogrammed with body composition equations. Although these equations vary, most require age, weight, and stature in addition to estimates of impedance or resistance. Some equations also include gender and levels of fatness. Kushner, Schoeller, Fjeld, and Danforth (1992) have shown that, across age and sex, the following equation currently appears to be the best for estimating TBW:

$$TBW = 0.04 + 0.59 \ (cm^2/resistance) + 0.065(kg) \qquad [4]$$

Equation 4 can be substituted into equation 3 to solve for FFM and ultimately fatness.

Reliability. The reliability of BIA is consistently quite high with test-retest *r*'s between .93 and .96 and within-person CVs between 1% and 6%.

Validity. Most studies suggest that BIA improves the prediction of total body fat and water compared with body weight, height, or anthropometry used either alone or in combination (Kushner et al., 1992). The literature in this area is controversial, however, and new studies are rapidly appearing.

Although BIA is, for these reasons, often thought of as a "second-class" method, the data supporting its validity (in populations for which equations have been derived) are actually quite favorable. Inspection of Table 14.2 indicates that convergent validity coefficients for BIA average around .70 to .80. Thus BIA performs quite well, especially considering its modest cost and ease of implementation. Some (e.g., Mazess, 1991) have pointed out that some of this "validity" derives from the fact that height and weight are used by the BIA machines in providing fat estimates and therefore the validity of resistance per se is somewhat lower than that of BIA estimates. This is true, but for purely estimation purposes it is irrelevant. The point is that it is effective.

The following is a summary of observations related to BIA: Prediction of deuterium dilution space, which is about 4% larger than total body water, is reliable in obese subjects both before and after long-term (several months') weight loss. However, there is currently a lack of agreement about whether BIA has the sensitivity to reliably quantify small changes in body composition (Adami et al., 1993; Fulco, Hoyt, Baker-Fulco, Gonzalez, & Cymerman, 1992; Kushner et al., 1990; Vazquez & Janosky, 1991). Equations may also be inaccurate in specific populations—ethnic or racial groups—such as the Pima Indians (Rising et al., 1991). Locally developed BIA equations may thus be needed for specific ethnic groups or obese subjects.

Moderators. Bioimpedance measurements are influenced by many factors so that it is imperative that patients are maximally stable prior to study. For example, changes in body fluid volumes and electrolyte status influence conductivity and thus BIA body composition estimates. Severe edema or fluid fluxes of lesser magnitude, such as occur with the menstrual cycle, alter BIA body composition estimates (Gleichauf & Roe, 1989). Finally, patients with amputations cannot be studied using conventional BIA protocols unless specific equations are developed, although serial measurements in the same subject should be interpretable.

Risk. Bioimpedance analysis is a safe procedure and can be used regardless of age.

Practical issues. Most BIA systems are very convenient and some are even handheld simple devices. More complex systems include computers, involve use of multiple frequencies, and provide printouts of results. The cost of BIA systems ranges from about $1,000 to $5,000. The BIA procedure is rapid (about 2 minutes) and is well tolerated by most subjects.

Total Body Electrical Conductivity

Theory and background. Similar in concept to BIA, total body electrical conductivity (TOBEC) systems rely on the concept that lean tissue is a better conductor of electrical energy than fat. The TOBEC system consists of a large coil driven by a 2.5 Hz radio frequency current and a computer that processes the various signals and provides a summary of the subject's body composition.

The procedure begins by having the subject rest on a platform bed that moves in and out of the coil when the system is activated. A current is induced in the subject's body in proportion to the mass of conductive tissues and ion-containing fluids. The difference between the impedance of the empty coil and the impedance of the coil when it contains the subject is proportional to the total conductivity of the body (Horswill et al., 1989). The conductivity is then proportional to lean or fat-free body mass. Calibrations for TOBEC are usually done using reference methods for estimating total body water (e.g., dilution of tritiated water), fat, and fat-free body mass (e.g., underwater weighing) in appropriately selected subject groups. Once calibrated, TOBEC can provide estimates of fat, fat-free body mass, and total body water.

Reliability. Table 14.1 indicates that the reliability of TOBEC is excellent with test-retest coefficients averaging approximately .98.

Validity. As can be seen in Table 14.2, TOBEC typically yields convergent validity coefficients between .75 and .95.

As with other clinical methods, short-term or small changes in body composition measured over several days or weeks cannot be reliably measured in individual patients with TOBEC. Large changes in body weight over long periods of time, particularly in groups rather than individual patients, can be reliably evaluated using TOBEC. For example, Van Loan, Belko, Mayclin, and Barbieri (1987) studied body composition in 12 overweight (120%-130% ideal body weight) women who lost an average of 6.6 kg over 6 weeks using combinations of diet and exercise to create an energy deficit. The investigators found good correlations between changes in total body water, fat, and fat-free body mass detected by TOBEC and reference methods such as deuterium and underwater weighing. However, some systematic differences were observed between TOBEC and the reference methods. The investigators concluded that, with future refinements in software, TOBEC has the potential to reliably measure changes in total body water, fat, and composition of fat-free body mass during weight loss.

Moderators. Change in the water content of fat-free tissues could potentially alter TOBEC estimates of body composition. However, in one study, Cochran et al. (1988) found that altering extracellular fluid volume did not affect the accuracy of TOBEC-derived estimates of fat-free body mass in an experimental model using baby pigs. Additional studies are needed to determine if and to what extent TOBEC estimates are influenced by hydration.

Risk. TOBEC is a safe procedure and can be used in people of all ages.

Practical issues. TOBEC is rapid (1 minute per study), requires minimal technical skill in making the measurement, and patient cooperation is not needed to the same extent as in such techniques as underwater weighing. The limitations of TOBEC are its relatively high initial cost, lack of portability, and the need to calibrate it against other clinical methods such as hydrodensitometry or DEXA.

Hydrodensitometry

Underwater body weight, measured by hydrodensitometry, is used with weight in air to estimate an individual's body density (Db). An individual's Db can then be used to calculate fat and FFM.

Modern hydrodensitometry systems consist of a large heated tank of water and a scale. The subject exhales maximally, submerges, and body weight is then recorded to the scale. This provides an estimate of weight underwater at a water temperature of about 36 degrees Celsius. The subject's body weight is then measured outside the tank. Most research laboratories also measure residual lung volume either during or following the underwater weighing procedure. This allows for correction of body density for residual lung volume. The compiled results are used to calculate body volume and Db.

Body density can then be used to calculate the proportion of body weight as fat and FFM. The assumptions of this calculation are that (a) the density of fat is constant at 0.90 g/ml and (b) FFM is a homogeneous compartment with constant density 1.10 g/ml. Given these two assumptions, the fraction of body weight as fat and FFM can be calculated as (W. B. Siri, 1956; W. E. Siri, 1961):

$$\text{Fat} = [(4.95/\text{Db}) - 4.50] \, (\text{Wt}) \quad\quad [5]$$

and

$$\text{FFM} = \text{BW} - \text{fat}. \quad\quad [6]$$

Other equations for estimating fat from Db are used, and results are similar to those of equation 5.

Reliability. Under some circumstances (e.g., with the very young or very old), the reliability of UWW is suspect. This often relates to an inability of the subject to fully comply with the required procedure. However, Table 14.1 shows that reliability coefficients are generally well above .90.

Validity. As can be seen in Table 14.2, concurrent validity coefficients for hydrodensitometry or underwater weighing (UWW) are virtually always above .70 and usually above .80 when correlated with the better criteria methods.

Moderators. There are several sources of error in the hydrodensitometry method. First, the two-compartment model assumes constant densities for fat and FFM. This assumption is generally accepted for fat, given that triglyceride in all species approximates a density of 0.90 g/ml. In contrast, FFM is composed of several major chemical components such as water, protein, glycogen, and various minerals. These components differ in density from each other, and thus small relative changes in the chemical composition of FFM may change the density of FFM from the assumed value of 1.10 g/ml. Aging, ethnicity, and gender may all be associated with relative differences in FFM composition and density. The result is that errors in fat estimates may occur when using equation 5 in subjects whose density of FFM is not 1.100 g/ml.

Another source of error is in the measurement of body density. First, subject participation is required and not all individuals are capable of remaining submerged for the time required to optimally measure underwater weight. The tendency is for poor subject participation to be associated with a lower than actual underwater weight and a low body density. Fat estimates would thus be biased upward if performance during the underwater weighing were poor. Failure to exhale fully, and thus trapping air in respiratory passages, contributes to the falsely low body density. This seems to be especially problematic for older adults (Allison, Heshka, Pierson, & Heymsfield, 1992) among whom the random error variance is greater for UWW.

Risk and practical issues. The hydrodensitometry method is safe and relatively inexpensive once the basic equipment is in place (< $20,000 for the needed equipment).

Anthropometry

Theory and background. Anthropometry has a rich history in the measure of man and woman. One of the most active anthropometry laboratories in history was run by Francis Galton, one of the founding fathers of biometry. During the late 1800s, Galton collected what appear to be highly accurate data on the anthropometric characteristics of approximately 17,000 individuals (Johnson et al., 1985).

Anthropometric measurements include skinfold thicknesses and circumferences and are generally simple, safe, and easy to carry out. The equipment required is inexpensive and measurements can be made in the field or at the bedside.

Anthropometric measurements can be used to estimate total body fat, regional fat, and fat distribution. Total body fat can be inferred from a single skinfold measurement, but more typically skinfold measurements are combined to predict total body fat. The usual approach is to develop a fat prediction equation from skinfolds using a better technique, such as hydrodensitometry, as a reference for fat estimates. At birth, most fat is subcutaneous, so that skinfold measurements provide an excellent index of total body fat. With advancing age, the proportion of fat in visceral sites gradually increases and skinfold measurements are less tightly linked to total fat.

The widely used Durnin and Womersley (1974) method of estimating fat and FFM proceeds as follows: First, one must find the patient's age and weight (in kilograms). Second, skinfolds of biceps, triceps, subscapular, and suprailiac are summed and one takes the logarithm of this sum. Call this value X. Then body density (Db) is calculated using one of the age- and sex-specific equations listed here from Heymsfield (1984). For men 17 to 19 years of age, D = 1.1620 − 0.0630X; 20 to 29 years of age, D = 1.1631 − 0.0632X; 30 to 39 years of age, D = 1.1422 − 0.0544X; 40 to 49 years of age, D = 1.1620 − 0.0700X; and 50+ years of age, D = 1.1715 − 0.0779. For women 17 to 19 years of age, D = 1.1549 − 0.0678X; 20 to 29 years of age, D = 1.1599 − 0.0717; 30 to 39 years of age, D = 1.1423 − 0.0732X; 40 to 49 years of age, D = 1.1333 − 0.0612X; and 50+ years of age, D = 1.1339 − 0.0645X. Fat and fat-free mass can be calculated using previously discussed equations 5 and 6. Some anthropometric methods (e.g., Steinkamp, Cohen, Siri, Sargent, & Walsh, 1965) for estimating total body fat also include circumferential measurements, either alone or in combination with skinfolds, although, at present, these techniques are not widely used.

Reliability. The reliability of fat estimates based on skinfolds is not quite as high as the reliability of some other estimates because error variance due to the human observer probably plays a greater role. Nevertheless, as Table 14.1 indicates, the reliability is still quite good with r's generally above .90.

Validity. Skinfolds measure only subcutaneous adipose tissue and therefore might be expected to have somewhat lower validities as measures of total adiposity. Table 14.2 supports this expectation. We see that the correlations are respectable (generally between .65 and .80) but somewhat lower than for the higher-tech measures of total adiposity such as hydrodensitometry and DEXA.

Moderators. Chumlea, Roche, and Rogers (1984) have shown that the interobserver reliability of anthropometric measurements is lower among the elderly and varies by sex.

Risk. Other than occasional embarrassment when a "modest" subject is handled by a technician, anthropometry has no risk.

Practical issues. Representative anthropometric measurement sites and techniques for optimizing precision are presented in Lohman, Roche, and Martorell (1988). A high-quality skinfold caliper and inelastic measuring tape are required for optimum data collection. The skinfold caliper should apply a constant pressure throughout its measuring range and a calibration block should be used at periodic intervals to confirm the instrument's accuracy.

Infrared Interactance

Theory and background. Infrared interactance or near infrared spectrophotometry was originally used to evaluate the composition of meat and grains (Gemperline & Webber, 1989; Lanza, 1983). Systems were subsequently developed that could be used to study the composition of human tissues. The underlying concept is that the proportion of infrared energy absorbed is directly related to the composition of tissue through which the energy passes (Gemperline & Webber, 1989).

Reliability. An important step in assessing infrared interactance systems is to distinguish between earlier research-grade instruments and the newer, compact, portable, commercially available systems. The former were large complex instruments that could measure tissue characteristics very accurately (Lanza, 1983). Their development has not been pursued. The commercial systems are less complex, and their reliability is questionable. Fuller et al. (1991) reported within-subject CVs of 5% to 6% for site-specific infrared interactance readings. The commercially available systems use regional infrared measurements, similar to a skinfold measurement, and combine these results into a prediction equation that typically includes body weight, stature, and other demographic characteristics.

Validity. McLean and Skinner (1992) compared percentage fat estimates by infrared interactance to those by underwater weighing in healthy males ($r = .8$) and females ($r = .63$); superior results were found for skinfold-derived fat than for infrared-derived fat. Elia, Parkinson, and Diaz (1990) carried out a similar study and found that infrared interactance estimates of fat underestimated fatness as adiposity increased. They concluded that infrared interactance provides no advantage in measuring fatness over other simple clinical methods such as skinfold techniques. Eaton, Israel, O'Brien, Hortobagyi, and McCammon (1993) also compared infrared interactance with other methods in young white women. While group means were similar between fat derived by underwater weighing and infrared interactance, correlations were extremely poor ($n = 77$, $r = .47$); other methods of estimating fat, such as skinfolds, were superior to infrared interactance. Although at least one study has found very good estimation of fatness with infrared interactance (Conway,

Norris, & Bodwell, 1984), most other studies (e.g., Elia et al., 1990; Heyward et al., 1992; Hortobagyi, Israel, Houmard, McCammon, & O'Brien, 1992; Hortobagyi, Israel, Houmard, O'Brien, et al., 1992) have also shown that infrared interactance is, at best, a fair estimator of subcutaneous fatness and generally has little or no advantage over skinfolds. Thus, at this point, we are reluctant to recommend the use of infrared interactance for measuring adiposity if alternatives are available.

Moderators. Equations used in infrared interactance systems are based on comparison with a reference method such as underwater weighing. The nature of these prediction equations is that they tend to be population specific. However, Hortobagyi, Israel, Houmard, O'Brien, et al. (1992) showed that, at least among athletes, there was no evidence of differential validity of infrared interactance for blacks versus whites. Franssila-Kallunki (1992) reported that infrared interactance had some advantages over BIA in not showing reduced validity among the obese, but contrary findings were obtained in a larger study by Quatrochi et al. (1992), who found that infrared interactance had greater validity among younger and leaner women than among older and fatter women. Quatrochi et al.'s observation of reduced validity among the obese was confirmed by Elia et al. (1990) and Parenti et al. (1990). Another concern is the validity of the method in patients with edema or skin problems, but there is little literature on the subject.

Risk. There are no known risks of the procedure when carried out using commercially available instruments.

Practical issues. Systems are simple, safe, and portable. Commercially available systems range in price from approximately $100 to $5,000.

Conclusion

In conclusion, the investigator measuring fatness has at least two things to assess: total adiposity and body fat distribution. Methods range from the very inexpensive (but reasonably valid) self-reported height and weight to the very expensive and much more valid techniques like DEXA, IVNA, and MRI. In choosing their method, investigators must balance a host of issues including precision, bias, expense, and safety.

Notes

1. The correlations with TOBEC tend to be higher because TOBEC is essentially a way of estimating total body water and TOBEC machines have generally been calibrated against TBW estimates by isotope dilution.

2. However, using least squares methods to derive ways of residualizing weight for height in a given sample is valuable and at least as effective as any "prefabricated" BMI (Lee, Kolonel, & Hinds, 1982).

References

Abdel-Malek, A. K., Mukherjee, D., & Roche, A. F. (1985). A method of constructing an index of obesity. *Human Biology, 57,* 415-430.

Adami, G. F., Marinari, G., Gandolfo, P., Cocchi, F., Friedman, D., & Scopinaro, N. (1993). The use of bioelectrical impedance analysis for monitoring body composition changes during nutritional support. *Surgery Today: The Japanese Journal of Surgery, 23,* 867-870.

Albu, J., Smolowitz, J., Lichtman, S., Heymsfield, S. B., Wang, J., Pierson, R. N., Jr., & Pi-Sunyer, F. X. (1992). Composition of weight loss in severely obese women: A new look at old methods. *Metabolism, 41,* 1068-1074.

Allison, D. B. (1993). Limitations of the coefficient of variation as an index of reliability. *Nutrition, 9,* 559-561.

Allison, D. B., Heshka, S., Pierson, R. N., Jr., & Heymsfield, S. B. (1992, April). *Differential validity of body fat measurements across the age span.* Paper presented at the Federation of American Societies of Experimental Biology, Anaheim, CA.

Alverez-Torices, J. C., Franch-Nadal, J., Alverez-Guisasola, F., Hernandez-Mejia, R., & Cueto-Espinar, A. (1993). Self-reported height and weight and prevalence of obesity: Study in a Spanish population. *International Journal of Obesity, 17,* 663-667.

Armellini, F., Zamboni, M., Rigo, L., Todesco, T., Bergamo-Andreis, I. A., Procacci, C., & Bosello, O. (1990). The contribution of sonography to the measurement of intraabdominal fat. *Journal of Clinical Ultrasonography, 18,* 563-567.

Baumgartner, R. N., Heymsfield, S. B., Roche, A. F., & Bernardino, M. (1988). Abdominal composition quantified by computed tomography. *American Journal of Clinical Nutrition, 48,* 936-945.

Baumgartner, R. N., Rhyne, R. L., Garry, P. J., & Heymsfield, S. B. (in press). Imaging techniques and anatomical body composition in aging. *Journal of Nutrition.*

Baumgartner, R. N., Stauber, P. M., McHugh, D., Wayne, S., Garry, P. J., & Heymsfield, S. B. (in press). Body composition in the elderly using multicompartmental methods. In S. Yasumura, J. E. Harrison, K. G. McNeill, A. D. Woodhead, & F. A. Dilmanian (Eds.), *In vivo body composition studies.* New York: Plenum.

Beddoe, A. H., Streat, S. J., & Hill, G. L. (1984). Evaluation of in vivo prompt gamma neutron activation facility for body composition studies in critically ill intensive care patients: Results on 41 normals. *Metabolism, 33,* 270-280.

Bell, E. T. (1945). *The development of mathematics.* New York: McGraw-Hill.

Bellisari, A., Roche, A. F., & Siervogel, R. M. (in press). Reliability of B-mode ultrasonic measurements of subcutaneous adipose tissue and intra-abdominal depth: Comparisons with skinfold thickness. *International Journal of Obesity.*

Benn, R. T. (1971). Some mathematical properties of weight-for-height indices used as measures of adiposity. *British Journal of Preventive and Social Medicine, 25,* 42-50.

Bowman, R. L., & DeLucia, J. L. (1992). Accuracy of self-reported weight: A meta-analysis. *Behavior Therapy, 23,* 637-655.

Brozek, J., Grande, F., Anderson, T., & Keys, A. (1963). Densitometric analysis of body composition: Revision of some assumptions. *Annals of New York Academy of Sciences, 110,* 113-140.

Cameron, R., & Evers, S. E. (1990). Self-report issues in obesity and weight management: State of the art and future directions. *Behavioral Assessment, 12,* 91-106.

Cash, T. F., Counts, B., Hangen, J., & Huffine, C. E. (1989). How much do you weigh? Determinants of validity of self-reported body weight. *Perceptual and Motor Skills, 69,* 248-250.

Charney, E., Goodman, H. C., McBride, M., Lyon, B., & Pratt, R. (1976). Childhood antecedents of adult obesity. *New England Journal of Medicine, 295,* 6-9.

Chumlea, W. C., & Roche, A. F. (1986). Ultrasonic and skinfold caliper measures of subcutaneous adipose tissue thickness in elderly men and women. *American Journal of Physical Anthropology, 71,* 351-357.

Chumlea, W. C., Roche, A. F., & Rogers, E. (1984). Replicability for anthropometry in the elderly. *Human Biology, 56,* 329-337.

Clark, R. R., Kuta, J. M., & Sullivan, J. C. (1993). Prediction of percent body fat in adult males using dual energy X-ray absorptiometry, skinfolds, and hydrostatic weighing. *Medicine and Science in Sports and Exercise, 25,* 528-535.

Coates, T. J., Jeffery, R. W., & Wing, R. R. (1978). The relationship between persons' relative body weights and the quality and quantity of food stored in their homes. *Addictive Behaviors, 3,* 179-184.

Cochran, W. J., Wong, W. W., Fiorotto, M. L., Sheng, H. P., Klein, P. D., & Klish, W. J. (1988). Total body water estimated by measuring total body electrical conductivity. *American Journal of Clinical Nutrition, 48,* 946-950.

Cohn, S. H., Brennan, B. L., Yasumura, S., Vartsky, D., Vaswani, A. N., & Ellis, K. J. (1983). Evaluation of body composition and nitrogen content of renal patients on chronic dialysis as determined by total body neutron activation. *American Journal of Clinical Nutrition, 38,* 52-58.

Cohn, S. H., Vartsky, D., Yasumura, S., Sawitsky, A., Zanzi, I., Vaswani, A., & Ellis, K. (1980). Compartmental body composition based on total body nitrogen, potassium, and calcium. *American Journal of Physiology, 239,* E524-E530.

Cohn, S. H., Vaswani, A. N., Yasumura, S., Yuen, K., & Ellis, K. J. (1984). Improved models for determination of body fat by in vivo neutron activation. *American Journal of Clinical Nutrition, 40,* 255-259.

Cole, T. J. (1991). Weight-stature indices to measure underweight, overweight, and obesity. In J. Himes (Ed.), *Anthropometric assessment of nutritional status* (pp. 83-111). New York: Wiley.

Colliver, J. A., Frank, S., & Frank, A. (1983). Similarity of obesity indices in clinical studies of obese adults: A factor analytic study. *American Journal of Clinical Nutrition, 38,* 640-647.

Conway, J. M., Norris, K. H., & Bodwell, C. E. (1984). A new approach for the estimation of body composition: Infrared interactance. *American Journal of Clinical Nutrition, 40,* 1123-1130.

Cronk, C. E., & Roche, A. F. (1982). Race- and sex-specific reference data for triceps and subscapular skinfolds and weight/stature^2. *American Journal of Clinical Nutrition, 35,* 347-354.

Czinner, A., & Varady, M. (1992). Quantitative determination of fatty tissue on body surface in obese children by ultrasound method. *Pädiatrie und Pädologie, 27,* 7-10.

Davis, H., & Gergen, P. J. (1994). The weights and heights of Mexican-American adolescents: The accuracy of self-reports. *American Journal of Public Health, 84,* 459-462.

de Ridder, C. M., de Boer, R. W., Seidell, J. C., Nieuwebhoff, C. M., Jeneson, J. A. L., Bakker, C. J. G., Zonderland, M. L., & Erich, W. B. M. (1992). Body fat distribution in pubertal girls quantified by magnetic resonance imaging. *International Journal of Obesity, 16,* 443-449.

Dilmanian, F. A., Weber, D. A., Yasumura, S., Kamen, Y., Lidofsky, L., Heymsfield, S. B., Pierson, R. N., Jr., Wang, J., Kahayias, J. J., & Ellis, K. J. (1990). Performance of the BNL delayed- and prompt-gamma neutron activation systems. In S. Yasumura, J. E. Harrison, K. G. McNeill, A. D. Woodhead, & F. A. Dilmanian (Eds.), *In vivo body composition studies: Recent advances* (pp. 309-315). New York: Plenum.

Dowling, H. J., & Pi-Sunyer, F. X. (1993). Race-dependent health risks of upper body obesity. *Diabetes, 42,* 537-543.

Durnin, J. V. G. A., & Womersley, J. (1974). Body fat assessed from total body density and its estimation from skinfold thickness: Measurements on 481 men and women aged 16 to 72 years. *British Journal of Nutrition, 32,* 77-97.

Eaton, A. W., Israel, R. G., O'Brien, K. F., Hortobagyi, T., & McCammon, M. R. (1993). Comparison of four methods to assess body composition in women. *European Journal of Clinical Nutrition, 47,* 353-360.

Eckerson, J. M., Housh, T. J., & Johnson, G. O. (1992a). Validity of bioelectrical impedance equations for estimating fat-free weight in lean males. *Medicine and Science in Sports and Exercise, 24,* 1298-1302.

Eckerson, J. M., Housh, T. J., & Johnson, G. O. (1992b). The validity of visual estimations of percent body fat in lean males. *Medicine and Science in Sports and Exercise, 24,* 615-618.

Elia, M., Parkinson, S. A., & Diaz, E. (1990). Evaluation of near infra-red interactance as a method for predicting body composition. *European Journal of Clinical Nutrition, 44,* 113-121.

Ellis, K. J., Yasumura, S., Vartsky, D., & Cohn, S. H. (1982). Total body nitrogen in health and disease: Effects of age, weight, height, and sex. *Journal of Laboratory and Clinical Medicine, 99,* 917-926.

Epstein, L. H., McCurley, J., & Murdock, R. C. (1991). Estimation of percent overweight within families. *Addictive Behaviors, 16,* 369-375.

Fanelli, M. T., & Kuczmarski, R. J. (1984). Ultrasound as an approach to assessing body composition. *American Journal of Clinical Nutrition, 39,* 703-709.

Fattante, A., Allison, D. B., Hoy, M. K., & Heymsfield, S. B. (n.d.). *A comparison of methods for assessing adiposity among the obese.* Manuscript in preparation.

Forbes, G. B. (1987). *Human body composition: Growth, aging, nutrition, and activity.* New York: Springer-Verlag.

Fowler, P. A., Fuller, M. F., Glasbey, C. A., Foster, M. A., Cameron, G. G., McNeill, G., & Maughan, R. J. (1991). Total and subcutaneous adipose tissue in women: The measurement of distribution and accurate prediction of quantity by using magnetic resonance imaging. *American Journal of Clinical Nutrition, 54,* 18-25.

Franssila-Kallunki, A. (1992). Comparison of near-infrared light spectroscopy, bioelectrical impedance and tritiated water techniques for the measurement of fat-free mass in humans. *Scandinavian Journal of Clinical & Laboratory Investigation, 52,* 879-885.

Fulco, C. S., Hoyt, R. W., Baker-Fulco, C. J., Gonzalez, J., & Cymerman, A. (1992). Use of bioelectrical impedance to assess body composition changes at high altitude. *Journal of Applied Physiology, 72,* 2181-2187.

Fuller, N. J., Jebb, S. A., Goldberg, G. R., Pullicino, E., Adams, C., Cole, T. J., & Elia, M. (1991). Inter-observer variability in the measurement of body composition. *European Journal of Clinical Nutrition, 45,* 43-49.

Garn, S. M., Leonard, W. R., & Hawthorne, V. M. (1986). Three limitations of the body mass index. *American Journal of Clinical Nutrition, 44,* 996-997.

Garrow, J. S., & Webster, J. (1985). Quetelet's index (W/H^2) as a measure of fatness. *International Journal of Obesity, 9,* 147-153.

Gemperline, P. J., & Webber, L. D. (1989). Raw material testing using soft independent modeling of class analogy analysis of near-infrared reflectance spectra. *Analytical Chemistry, 61,* 138-144.

Gleichauf, C. N., & Roe, D. A. (1989). The menstrual cycle's effect on the reliability of bioimpedance measurements for assessing body composition. *American Journal of Clinical Nutrition, 50,* 903-907.

Gomez, J. E., Allison, D. B., & Heymsfield, S. B. (1993). Is BMI a differentially valid indicator of fatness in blacks and whites? *Obesity Research, 1*(Suppl. 2), 112S.

Goran, M. I., Poehlman, E. T., Nair, K. S., & Danforth, E. (1992). Effect of gender, body composition, and equilibration time on the H$_2$-to-^{18}O dilution space ratio. *American Journal of Physiology, 263,* E1119-E1124.

Goran, M. I., Poehlman, E. T., Nair, K. S., & Danforth, E. (1993). Deuterium exchange in humans: Effect of gender, body composition, and age. *Basic Life Sciences, 60,* 79-81.

Grant, F. S. (1902). Overweights in whom the abdominal girth is greater than the chest girth than the chest at full inspiration. *Proceedings of the Association of Life Insurance Medical Directors of America, 5,* 323-327.

Greenway, F. L., & Bray, G. A. (1975). Fat women are liars. *Obesity and Bariatric Medicine, 4,* 143-144.

Haarbo, J., Gotfredsen, A., Hassager, C., & Christiansen, C. (1991). Validation of body composition by dual energy X-ray absorptiometry. *Clinical Physiology, 11,* 331-341.

Hall, S. M. (1972). Self-control and therapist control in the behavioral treatment of overweight women. *Behaviour Research and Therapy, 10,* 59-68.

Heaney, R. P., & Ryan, R. (1988). Relation between measured and recalled body height. *New England Journal of Medicine, 319,* 795-796.

Hergenroeder, A. C., Wong, W. W., Fiorotto, M. L., Smith, E. O., & Klish, W. J. (1991). Total body water and fat free mass in ballet dancers: Comparing isotope dilution and TOBEC. *Medicine and Science in Sports and Exercise, 23,* 534-541.

Heymsfield, S. B. (1984). Anthropometric assessment. In R. A. Wright & S. B. Heymsfield (Eds.), *Nutritional assessment of the hospitalized patient* (pp. 27-82). Boston: Blackwell Scientific.

Heymsfield, S. B. (1987). Human body composition: Analysis by computerized axial tomography and nuclear magnetic resonance. In *AIN Symposium Proceedings* (pp. 92-96). Bethesda, MD: American Institute of Nutrition.

Heymsfield, S. B., Lichtman, S., Baumgartner, R. N., Wang, J., Kamen, Y., Aliprantis, A., & Pierson, R. N., Jr. (1990). Body composition of humans: Comparison of two improved four-compartment models that differ in expense, technical complexity, and radiation exposure. *American Journal of Clinical Nutrition, 52,* 52-58.

Heymsfield, S. B., Smith, R., Aulet, M., Bensen, B., Lichtman, S., Wang, J., & Pierson, R. N., Jr. (1990). Appendicular skeletal muscle mass: Measurement by dual photon absorptiometry. *American Journal of Clinical Nutrition, 52,* 214-218.

Heymsfield, S. B., & Waki, M. (1991). Body composition in humans: Advances in the development of multicompartment chemical models. *Nutrition Review, 49,* 97-108.

Heymsfield, S. B., Waki, M., Kehayias, J., Lichtman, S., Dilmanian, F. A., Kamen, Y., Wang, J., Waki, M., & Pierson, R. N., Jr. (1991). Chemical and elemental analysis of human in vivo using improved body composition models. *American Journal of Physiology, 261,* E190-E198.

Heymsfield, S. B., & Wang, Z. M. (in press). *The future of body composition research.* Cambridge: Cambridge University Press.

Heymsfield, S. B., Wang, J., Aulet, M., Kehayias, J., Lichtman, S., Kamen, Y., Dilmanian, F. A., Lindsay, R., & Pierson, R. N., Jr. (1990). Dual photon absorptiometry: Validation of mineral and fat measurements. In S. Yasumura, J. E. Harrison, K. G. McNeill, A. D. Woodhead, & F. A. Dilmanian (Eds.), *Advances in in vivo body composition studies: Recent advances* (pp. 327-337). New York: Plenum.

Heymsfield, S. B., Wang, J., Funfar, J., Kehayias, J. J., & Pierson, R. N., Jr. (1990). Dual-photon absorptiometry: Comparison of bone mineral and soft tissue mass measurement in vivo with established methods. *American Journal of Clinical Nutrition, 49,* 1283-1289.

Heymsfield, S. B., Wang, J., Lichtman, S., Kamen, Y., Kehayias, J., & Pierson, R. N., Jr. (1989). Body composition in elderly subjects: A critical appraisal of clinical methodology. *American Journal of Clinical Nutrition, 50,* 1167-1175.

Heyward, V. H., Cook, K. L., Hicks, V. L., Jenkins, K. A., Quatrochi, J. A., & Wilson, W. L. (1992). Predictive accuracy of three field methods for estimating relative body fatness of nonobese and obese women. *International Journal of Sport Nutrition, 2,* 75-86.

Horswill, C. A., Geesman, R., Boileau, R. A., Williams, B. T., Layman, D. K., & Massey, B. H. (1989). Total-body electrical conductivity (TOBEC): Relationship to estimates of muscle mass, fat-free weight, and lean body mass. *American Journal of Clinical Nutrition, 49,* 593-598.

Hortobagyi, T., Israel, R. G., Houmard, J. A., McCammon, M. R., & O'Brien, K. F. (1992). Comparisons of body composition assessment by hydrodensitometry, skinfolds, and multiple site near-infrared spectrophotometry. *European Journal of Clinical Nutrition, 46,* 205-211.

Hortobagyi, T., Israel, R. G., Houmard, J. A., O'Brien, K. F., Johns, R. A., & Wells, J. M. (1992). Comparison of four methods to assess body composition in black and white athletes. *International Journal of Sport Nutrition, 2,* 60-74.

Jackson, A. S., Pollock, M. I., Graves, J. E., & Mahar, M. T. (1988). Reliability and validity of bioelectrical impedance in determining body composition. *Journal of Applied Physiology, 64,* 529-534.

Jackson, J., Strauss, C. C., Lee, A. A., & Hunter, K. (1990). Parents' accuracy in estimating child weight status. *Addictive Behaviors, 15,* 65-68.

Johansson, A. G., Forslund, A., Sjödin, A., Mallmin, H., Hambraeus, L., & Ljunghall, S. (1993). Determination of body composition: A comparison of dual-energy x-ray absorptiometry and hydrodensitometry. *American Journal of Clinical Nutrition, 57,* 323-326.

Johnson, R. C., McClearn, G. E., Yuen, S., Nagoshi, C. T., Ahearn, F. M., & Cole, R. E. (1985). Galton's data a century later. *American Psychologist, 40,* 875-892.

Kehayias, J. J., Heymsfield, S. B., LoMonte, A. F., Wang, J., & Pierson, R. N., Jr. (1991). In vivo determination of body fat by measuring total body carbon. *American Journal of Clinical Nutrition, 53,* 1339-1344.

Khaled, M. A., McCutcheon, M. J., Reddy, S., Pearman, P. L., Hunter, G. R., & Weinsier, R. L. (1988). Electrical impedance in assessing human body composition: The BIA method. *American Journal of Clinical Nutrition, 47,* 789-792.

Koslowsky, M., Sceinberg, Z., Bleich, A., Mark, M., Aptar, A., Danon, Y., & Solomon, Z. (1994). Predicting actual weight from self-report data. *Educational and Psychological Measurement, 54,* 168-173.

Kushner, R. F., Kunigk, A., Alspaugh, M., Andronis, P. T., Leitch, C. A., & Schoeller, D. A. (1990). Validation of bioelectrical-impedance analysis as a measurement of change in body composition in obesity. *American Journal of Clinical Nutrition, 52,* 219-223.

Kushner, R. F., & Schoeller, D. A. (1986). Estimation of total body water by bioelectrical impedance analysis. *American Journal of Clinical Nutrition, 44,* 417-424.

Kushner, R. F., Schoeller, D. A., Fjeld, C. R., & Danforth, L. (1992). Is the impedance index (ht^2/R) significant in predicting total body water? *American Journal of Clinical Nutrition, 56,* 835-839.

Kuskowska-Wolk, A., Bergstrom, R., & Bostrom, G. (1991). Relationship between questionnaire data and medical records of height, weight, and body mass index. *International Journal of Obesity, 16,* 1-9.

Kyere, K., Oldroyd, B., Oxby, C. B., Burkinshaw, L., Ellis, R. E., & Hill, G. L. (1982). The feasibility of measuring total body carbon by counting neutron inelastic scatter gamma rays. *Physiology, Medicine, & Behavior, 27,* 805-817.

Lanza, E. (1983). Determination of moisture, protein, fat, and calories in raw pork and beef by near infrared spectroscopy. *Journal of Food Science, 48,* 471-474.

Lass, N. J., Andes, S. F., McNair, C. D., Cline, A. L., & Pecora, M. C. (1982). Correlational study of subjects' self-reported and measured heights and weights. *Perceptual and Motor Skills, 54,* 102.

Lee, J., Kolonel, L. N., & Hinds, M. W. (1981). Relative merits of the weight-corrected-for-height indices. *American Journal of Clinical Nutrition, 34,* 2521-2529.

Lee, J., Kolonel, L. N., & Hinds, M. W. (1982). The use of an inappropriate weight-height derived index of obesity can produce misleading results. *International Journal of Obesity, 6,* 233-239.

Lohman, T. G. (1992). *Advances in body composition assessment.* Champaign, IL: Human Kinetics.

Lohman, T. G., Roche, A. F., & Martorell, R. (Eds.). (1988). *Anthropometric standardization reference manual.* Champaign, IL: Human Kinetics.

Lopez, L. M., & Masse, B. (1992). Comparison of body mass indexes and cutoff points for estimating the prevalence of overweight in Hispanic women. *Journal of the American Dietetic Association, 92,* 1343-1347.

Lukaski, H., & Johnson, P. E. (1985). A simple, inexpensive method for determining total body water using a tracer dose of D20 and infrared absorption of biological fluids. *American Journal of Clinical Nutrition, 41,* 363.

Marks, G. C., Habicht, J. P., & Mueller, W. H. (1989). Reliability, dependability, and imprecision of anthropometric measurements: The second National Health and Nutrition Examination Survey 1976-1980. *American Journal of Epidemiology, 130,* 578-587.

Mazess, R. B. (1991). Bioelectrical impedance: Does resistance contribute to composition measurement. *Clinical Physics and Physiological Measurement, 12,* 93-94.

Mazess, R. B., Barden, H. S., Bisek, J. P., & Hansen, J. (1990). Dual-energy x-ray absorptiometry for total-body and regional bone-mineral and soft-tissue comparison. *American Journal of Clinical Nutrition, 51,* 1106-1112.

Mazess, R. B., Peppler, W. W., & Gibbons, M. (1984). Total body composition by dual-photon (^{153}Gd) absorptiometry. *American Journal of Clinical Nutrition, 40,* 834-839.

McLean, K. P., & Skinner, J. S. (1992). Validity of Futrex-5000 for body composition determination. *Medicine and Science in Sports and Exercise, 24,* 253-258.

McNeill, G., Fowler, P. A., Maughan, R. J., McGaw, B. A., Fuller, M. F., Gvozdanovic, D., & Gvozdanovic, S. (1991). Body fat in lean and overweight women estimated by six methods. *British Journal of Nutrition, 65,* 95-103.

Mernagh, J. R., Harrison, J. E., & McNeill, K. G. (1977). In vivo determination of nitrogen using Pu-Be sources. *Physiology, Medicine, & Biology, 22,* 831-835.

Michielutte, R., Diseker, R. A., Corbitt, W. T., Schey, H. M., & Ureda, J. R. (1984). The relationship between weight-height indices and the triceps skinfold measure among children age 5 to 12. *American Journal of Public Health, 74,* 604-606.

Micozzi, M. S., Albanes, D., Jones, D. Y., & Chumlea, W. C. (1986). Correlations of body mass indices with weight, stature, and body composition in men and women in NHANES I and II. *American Journal of Clinical Nutrition, 44,* 725-731.

Micozzi, M. S., & Harris, T. M. (1990). Age variations in the relation of body mass indices to estimates of body fat and muscle mass. *American Journal of Physical Anthropology, 81,* 375-379.

Minten, V. K. A. M., Löwik, M. R. H., Deurenberg, P., & Kok, F. J. (1991). Inconsistent associations among anthropometric measurements in elderly Dutch men and women. *Journal of the American Dietetic Association, 91,* 1408-1412.

Moore, F. D., Oleson, K. H., McMurray, J. D., Parker, H. V., Ball, M. R., & Boyden, C. M. (1963). *The body cell mass and its supporting environment.* Philadelphia: Saunders.

Mueller, W. H., Joos, S. K., & Schull, W. J. (1985). Alternative measurements of obesity: Accuracy of body silhouettes and reported weights and heights in a Mexican American sample. *International Journal of Obesity, 9,* 193-200.

Murphy, J. K., Bruce, B. K., & Williamson, D. A. (1985). A comparison of measured and self-reported weights in a 4-year follow-up of spouse involvement in obesity treatment. *Behavior Therapy, 16,* 524-530.

Must, A., Willett, W. C., & Dietz, W. H. (1993). Remote recall of childhood height, weight, and body build by elderly subjects. *American Journal of Epidemiology, 138,* 56-64.

Nieto-Garcia, F. J., Bush, T. L., & Keyl, P. M. (1990). Body mass definitions of obesity: Sensitivity and specificity using self-reported weight and height. *Epidemiology, 1,* 146-152.

Norvell, N., & Boaz, T. L. (1986). Accuracy of self-reported weights in morbidly obese patients undergoing gastric reduction surgery. *Bulletin of the Society of Psychologists in Addictive Behaviors, 5,* 19-22.

Pace, N., & Rathbun, E. N. (1945). Studies on body composition: III. The body water and chemically combined nitrogen content in relation to fat content. *Journal of Biological Chemistry, 158,* 685-691.

Paganni-Hill, A., & Ross, R. K. (1982). Reliability of recall of drug usage and other health-related information. *American Journal of Epidemiology, 116,* 114-122.

Parenti, M., Di Bartolo, P., Babini, A. C., Sorrenti, G., Saretta, B., Ceccetto, M. E., Luchi, A., Gatto, M. R., & Melchionda, N. (1990). Comparison of three methods for the rapid determination of body composition. *Minerva Endocrinologia, 15,* 207-214.

Perry, L., & Learnard, B. (1963). Letter to the editor. *Journal of the American Medical Association, 183,* 807-808.

Pierson, R. N., Jr., Lin, D. H. Y., & Phillips, R. A. (1974). Total-body potassium in health: Effects of age, sex, height, and fat. *American Journal of Physiology, 226,* 206-121.

Pierson, R. N., Jr., Wang, J., Heymsfield, S. B., Russell-Aulet, M., Mazariegos, M., Tierney, M., Smith, R., Thornton, J. C., Kehayias, J., Weber, D. A., & Dilmanian, F. A. (1991). Measuring body fat: Calibrating the rulers: Intermethod comparisons of 389 normal Caucasian subjects. *American Journal of Physiology, 261,* E103-E108.

Pirie, P., Jacobs, D., Jeffery, R., & Hannan, P. (1981). Distortion in self-reported height and weight. *Journal of the American Dietetic Association, 78,* 601-606.

Presta, E., Segal, K. R., Gutin, B., Harrison, G. G., & Van Itallie, T. B. (1983). Comparison in man of total body electrical conductivity and lean body mass derived from body density: Validation of new body composition method. *Metabolism, 32,* 524-527.

Presta, E., Wang, J., Harrison, G., Björntorp, P., Harker, W. H., & Van Itallie, T. B. (1983). Measurement of total body electrical conductivity: A new method for estimation of body composition. *American Journal of Clinical Nutrition, 37,* 735-739.

Quatrochi, J. A., Hicks, V. L., Heyward, V. H., Colville, B. C., Cook, K. L., Jenkins, K. A., & Wilson, W. L. (1992). Relationship of optical density and skinfold measurements: Effects of age and level of body fatness. *Research Quarterly for Exercise and Sport, 63,* 402-409.

Rammohan, M., & Aplasca, E. C. (1992). Caliper method vs bioelectrical impedance analysis for determining body fat in patients undergoing chronic dialysis and in healthy individuals. *Journal of the American Dietetic Association, 92,* 1395-1397.

Revicki, D. A., & Isreal, R. G. (1986). Relationship between body mass indices and measures of body adiposity. *American Journal of Public Health, 76,* 992-994.

Rising, R., Swinburn, B., Larson, K., & Ravussin, E. (1991). Body composition in Pima Indians: Validation of bioelectrical resistance. *American Journal of Clinical Nutrition, 53,* 594-598.

Rossner, S., Bo, W. J., Hiltbrandt, E., Hinson, W., Karstaedt, N., Santago, P., Sobol, W. T., & Crouse, J. R. (1990). Adipose tissue determinations in cadavers: A comparison between cross-sectional planimetry and computed tomography. *International Journal of Obesity, 14,* 893-902.

Roubenoff, R., Kehayias, J. J., Dawson-Hughes, B., & Heymsfield, S. B. (1993). Use of dual-energy x-ray absorptiometry in body-composition studies: Not yet a "gold standard." *American Journal of Clinical Nutrition, 58,* 589-591.

Rowland, M. L. (1990). Self-reported weight and height. *American Journal of Clinical Nutrition, 52,* 1125-1133.

Russell-Aulet, M., Wang, J., Thornton, J., & Pierson, R. N. (1991). Comparison of dual-photon absorptiometry systems for total-body bone and soft tissue measurements: Dual-energy x-rays versus gadolinium 153. *Journal of Bone and Mineral Research, 6,* 411-415.

Schoeller, D. (1992). Isotope dilution methods. In P. Björntorp & B. N. Brodoff (Eds.), *Obesity* (pp. 80-88). New York: Lippincott.

Schoeller, D. A., van Santen, E., Peterson, D. W., Diets, W., Jaspan, J., & Klein, P. D. (1980). Total body water measurement in humans with ^{18}O and ^{2}H labeled water. *American Journal of Clinical Nutrition, 33,* 2686-2693.

Seidell, J. C., Bakx, J. C., De Boer, E., Deurenberg, P., & Hautvast, J. G. A. J. (1985). Fat distribution of overweight persons in relation to morbidity and subjective health. *International Journal of Obesity, 9,* 363-374.

Seidell, J. C., Deurenberg, P., & Hautvast, J. G. A. J. (1987). Obesity and fat distribution in relation to health: Current insights and recommendations. *World Review of Nutrition and Dietetics, 50,* 57-91.

Shannon, B., Smiciklas-Wright, H., & Wang, M. Q. (1991). Inaccuracies in self-reported weights and heights of a sample of sixth-grade children. *Journal of the American Dietetic Association, 91,* 675-678.

Sheng, H. P., & Huggins, R. A. (1979). A review of body composition studies with emphasis on total body water and fat. *American Journal of Clinical Nutrition, 32,* 630-647.

Siervogel, R. M., Roche, A. F., Guo, S., Mukherjee, D., & Chumlea, W. C. (1991). Patterns of change in weight/stature^2 from 2 to 18 years: Findings from long-term serial data for children in the Fels longitudinal growth study. *International Journal of Obesity, 15,* 479-485.

Siri, W. B. (1956). *Body composition from fluid spaces and density: Analysis of methods* (Radiation Laboratory, Report #3349). Berkeley: University of California.

Siri, W. E. (1961). Body composition from fluid spaces and density: Analysis of methods. In J. Brozek & A. Henschel (Eds.), *Techniques for measuring body composition* (pp. 223-244). Washington, DC: National Academy of Science.

Sjöström, L. (1991). A computer-tomography based multicompartment body composition technique and anthropometric predictions of lean body mass, total and subcutaneous adipose tissue. *International Journal of Obesity, 15,* 19-30.

Sjöström, L. (1993). Impacts of body weight, body composition, and adipose tissue distribution on morbidity and mortality. In A. J. Stunkard & T. A. Wadden (Eds.), *Obesity: Theory and therapy* (pp. 13-41). New York: Raven.

Smalley, K. J., Knerr, A. N., Kendrick, Z. V., Colliver, J. A., & Owen, O. E. (1990). Reassessment of body mass indices. *American Journal of Clinical Nutrition, 52,* 405-408.

Steinkamp, R. C., Cohen, N. L., Siri, S. W. E., Sargent, T. W., & Walsh, H. E. (1965). Measures of body fat and related factors in normal adults: I. Introduction and methodology. *Journal of Chronic Diseases, 18,* 1279-1289.

Stewart, A. L. (1982). The reliability and validity of self-reported weight and height. *Journal of Chronic Diseases, 35,* 295-309.

Stewart, A. W., Jackson, R. T., Ford, M. A., & Beaglehole, R. (1987). Underestimation of relative weight by use of self-reported height and weight. *American Journal of Epidemiology, 125,* 122 126.

Stunkard, A. J., & Albaum, J. M. (1981). The accuracy of self-reported weights. *American Journal of Clinical Nutrition, 34,* 1593-1599.

Svendsen, O. L., Hassager, C., Begmann, I., & Christiansen, C. (1993). Measurement of abdominal and intra-abdominal fat in postmenopausal women by dual energy X-ray absorptiometry and anthropometry: Comparison with computerized tomography. *International Journal of Obesity, 17,* 45-51.

Tarui, S., Tokunaga, K., Fujioka, S., & Matsuzawa, Y. (1991). Visceral fat obesity: Anthropological and pathophysiological aspects. *International Journal of Obesity, 15*(Suppl. 2), 1-8.

Tell, G. S., Jeffery, R. W., Kramer, F. M., & Snell, M. K. (1987). Can self-reported body weight be used to evaluate long-term follow-up of a weight-loss program. *Journal of the American Dietetic Association, 87,* 1198-1201.

Tzen, K. Y., & Wu, C. (1989). Quality assurance and precision of dual photon absorptiometry in bone mineral measurement. *Chinese Medical Journal, 43,* 1-8.

Vague, J. (1947). La Différenciation, sexuelle, facteur déterminant des formes de l'obésité. *Presse Médicale, 55,* 339-340.

van der Kooy, K., & Seidell, J. C. (1993). Techniques for the measurement of visceral fat: A practical guide. *International Journal of Obesity, 17,* 187-196.

Van Itallie, T. B., Segal, K. R., & Funk, R. C. (1986). Total body electrical conductivity: A rapidly measured index of lean body mass. In N. G. Morgan (Ed.), *Human body composition and fat distribution* (Report No. 8, pp. 113-127). Wageningen, Holland: European Nutrition.

Van Itallie, T. B., Segal, K. R., Yang, M. U., & Funk, R. C. (1985). Clinical assessment of body fat content in adults: Potential role of electrical impedance methods. In A. F. Roche (Ed.), *Body-composition assessment in youth and adults: Reports of the Sixth Ross Conference on Medical Research* (pp. 5-8). Columbus, OH: Ross Laboratories.

Van Loan, M. D. (1990). Assessment of fat-free mass in teenagers: Use of TOBEC methodology. *American Journal of Clinical Nutrition, 52,* 586-590.

Van Loan, M., Belko, A. Z., Mayclin, P. L., & Barbieri, T. F. (1987). Use of total-body electrical conductivity for monitoring body composition changes during weight reduction. *American Journal of Clinical Nutrition, 46,* 5-8.

Van Loan, M. D., & Koehler, L. S. (1990). Use of total-body electrical conductivity for the assessment of body composition in middle-aged and elderly individuals. *American Journal of Clinical Nutrition, 51,* 548-552.

Van Loan, M., & Mayclin, P. (1987). A new TOBEC instrument and procedure for the assessment of body composition: Use of Fourier coefficients to predict lean body mass and total water. *American Journal of Clinical Nutrition, 45,* 131-137.

Van Loan, M. D., Segal, K. R., Bracco, E. F., Mayclin, P., & Van Itallie, T. B. (1987). TOBEC methodology for body composition assessment: A cross-validation study. *American Journal of Clinical Nutrition, 46,* 9-12.

Vartsky, D., Ellis, K. J., & Cohn, S. H. (1979). In vivo measurement of body nitrogen by analysis of prompt gammas from neutron capture. *Journal of Nuclear Medicine, 20,* 1158-1165.

Vazquez, J. A., & Janosky, J. E. (1991). Validity of bioelectrical-impedance analysis in measuring changes in lean body mass during weight reduction. *American Journal of Clinical Nutrition, 54,* 970-975.

Venkataraman, P. S., & Ahluwalia, B. W. (1992). Total bone mineral content and body composition by x-ray densitometry in newborns. *Pediatrics, 90,* 767-770.

Volz, P. A., & Ostrove, S. M. (1984). Evaluation of a portable ultrasonoscope in assessing the body composition of college-age women. *Medicine and Science in Sports and Exercise, 16,* 97-102.

Wang, J., Dilmanian, F. A., Thornton, J., Russell, M., Burastero, S., Mazariegos, M., Heymsfield, S. B., & Pierson, R. N. (n.d.). *In vivo neutron activation analysis for body fat: Comparisons by seven methods.* Unpublished manuscript.

Wang, J., Heymsfield, S. B., Aulet, M., Thornton, J. C., & Pierson, R. N., Jr. (1989). Body fat from body density: Underwater weighing vs. dual photon absorptiometry. *American Journal of Physiology, 256,* E829-E834.

Wang, J., Kotler, D. P., Russell, M., Burastero, S., Mazariegos, M., Thornton, J., Dilmanian, F. A., & Pierson, R. N., Jr. (1992). Body-fat measurement in patients with acquired immunodeficiency syndrome: Which method should be used? *American Journal of Clinical Nutrition, 56,* 963-967.

Wang, J., Pierson, R. N., Jr., & Heymsfield, S. B. (1992). The five level model: A new approach to organizing body composition research. *American Journal of Clinical Nutrition, 56,* 19-28.

Wang, J., Pierson, R. N., Jr., & Kelly, W. G. (1973). A rapid method for the determination of deuterium oxide in urine: Application to the measurement of total body water. *Journal of Laboratory and Clinical Medicine, 82,* 170-178.

Ward, G. M., Krzywicki, H. J., Rahman, D. P., Quaas, R. L., Nelson, R. A., & Consolazio, C. F. (1975). Relationship of anthropometric measurements to body fat as determined by densitometry, potassium-40, and body water. *American Journal of Clinical Nutrition, 28,* 162-169.

Webster, B. L., & Barr, S. I. (1993). Body composition analysis of female adolescent athletes: Comparing six regression equations. *Medicine and Science in Sports and Exercise, 25,* 648-653.

Weiss, L. W., & Clark, F. C. (1987). Three protocols for measuring subcutaneous fat thickness on the upper extremities. *European Journal of Applied Physiology, 56,* 217-221.

Wing, R., Epstein, L., & Neff, D. (1980). Accuracy of parents' reports of height and weight. *Journal of Behavioral Assessment, 2,* 105-110.

Wing, R. R., Epstein, L. H., Ossip, D. J., & LaPorte, R. E. (1979). Reliability and validity of self-reported and observers' estimates of relative weight. *Addictive Behaviors, 4,* 133-140.

Wright, R. A., & Heymsfield, S. B. (Eds.). (1984). *Nutritional assessment of the hospitalized patient.* Boston: Blackwell Scientific.

Zillikens, M. C., & Conway, J. M. (1990). Anthropometry in blacks: Applicability of generalized skinfold equations and differences in fat patterning between blacks and whites. *American Journal of Clinical Nutrition, 52,* 45-51.

15

The Big Picture

W. STEWART AGRAS

Not so long ago, there was but one eating disorder, anorexia nervosa, which together with obesity—the latter disorder being seen by some as an eating disorder, and by others, perhaps the majority, as a disorder of energy balance—set the stage for the areas of assessment covered in this volume. These assessments have been expanded in their range since the surge in the number of patients with bulimia nervosa presenting in our clinics in the late 1970s (Garner, Olmsted, & Garfinkel, 1985) and the more recent interest in binge eating disorder (McCann, Rossiter, King, & Agras, 1991; Spitzer et al., 1991). Both anorexia nervosa and obesity necessitated the assessment of weight, caloric intake, and activity levels as well as the medical and psychological complications and comorbidity associated with these disorders. The basic assessments of adiposity, food intake, and activity nicely illustrate some of the complexities associated with the assessment of eating and weight-related problems.

Are We Measuring What We Think We Are?

The Case of Obesity

As Kraemer and her colleagues point out (Kraemer, Berkowitz, & Hammer, 1990), it is not easy to define obesity, let alone measure it. These researchers argue that obesity should be defined as the excess of body fat over and above that required to maintain normal functioning. As it is virtually impossible to measure total body fat in any reasonably cost-effective manner, all the current measures of obesity are indirect; that is, we are not measuring what we say we are! Several additional definitions, often confused with the term *obesity,* are suggested by these authors. The antithesis of obesity, *emaciation,* reflects a deficit of body fat sufficient to impair the health of an individual; *adiposity* is defined as total body fat; and *leanness* is the optimal range of body fat needed to maintain health—note that this will differ in males and females to different extents depending on age. *Fat, thin,* and *ideal* are descriptive terms reflecting ranges of adiposity determined not by medical standards but by societal standards of desirability that vary widely from place to place and from time to time. Hence an individual may be regarded as fat in one culture but as ideal in another. Similarly, if a population, such as that in the United States over the last half century, demonstrates weight gains at given heights, then an individual who does not change in total body fat over the same 50 years would be regarded as becoming less fat against the shifting societal standards, that is, a cohort effect. Thus it is important to characterize individuals by birthplace, birth date, race, age, height, social class, and so on. Rarely are such fine characterizations used when assessing obesity.

Kraemer et al. (1990) further point out that any indirect measure— whether laboratory based, such as radiography or total body potassium, or some form of ponderal index such as Body Mass Index (BMI) (W (kg)/ H^2(m)), or a body shape assessment such as the ratio of abdominal to hip girth—reflects some or all of the following components: excess fat, essential fat, bone, water, lean tissue, and the errors of measurement of each of these components. Two measures of obesity may correlate well because they share the same characteristic, but one that is not related to the measurement of excess body fat.

How then are we to choose an indirect measure of obesity? *First,* the measure should be convenient. For most purposes, a measure such as underwater weighing fails to meet this criterion because many individuals, particularly the obese, will not tolerate the procedure, although the method may be useful in highly motivated populations, such as participants interested in fitness. *Second,* the measure should be reliable. Here, measures of height and weight may be more useful than skinfold measures, which are inherently less reliable because they are more difficult to obtain. *Third,* the measure should be valid. (Unfortunately, because there is no exact measure of excess fat, it is difficult to assess the measurement validity of any indirect measure of obesity.) *Fourth,* the measure should have clinical validity. Here, the ability of the chosen measure to predict morbidity and mortality rates consequent on the diagnosis of obesity is the critical feature.

Based on these criteria, Kraemer et al. (1990) consider the best indirect measure of obesity to be BMI, noting that such a measure is convenient and minimizes measurement error (if the assessment is done correctly—that is, if weight is assessed using a balance beam scale with the subject wearing a gown of known weight and if height is assessed with the subject not wearing shoes). In addition, BMI has been found to predict both morbidity and mortality rates (Bray, 1986). The extremes of the BMI range will contain errors and there will be subjects who are "obese" by measures of BMI who are not, and vice versa. Given these problems with even the most desirable measure of "obesity," research reports should not refer to such a measure as one of obesity but, instead, by the term *BMI,* or whatever measure is in fact used.

Food Intake

Assessment of food intake is equally problematic, although in this case it is not the definition of caloric or macronutrient intake that is the problem but the difficulty of measurement, whether by dietary recall; self-monitoring; food frequency recall; the use of a commissary, that is, providing meals with sufficient food choices and having subjects return all uneaten foods; or assessment within the laboratory. Each of these methods has its pros and cons in terms of validity and ease of use. Again, however, researchers tend to report their data as caloric, macronutrient, or micronutrient intake rather than as reported intake, or self-monitored intake, over a finite period of time. In each case, what is measured as food intake is an approximation of what occurs in everyday life, over months and the changing seasons.

Even more complex is the assessment of caloric intake in particular eating episodes. Let us examine, for example, the assessment of caloric intake in the bulimic, and more specifically within a binge eating episode. The form and content of binge eating episodes have been studied in two ways: in the natural environment by means of self-monitoring and in the laboratory. The majority of these studies have been confined to patients diagnosed as having bulimia nervosa rather than those with binge eating disorder. Despite reports by bulimic patients that their binges were typically very large, often greater than 5,000 kcal (Johnson, Stuckey, Lewis, & Schwartz, 1982), self-monitoring studies of patients with bulimia nervosa revealed a different picture. The first of these studies found that reported binge eating episodes averaged 1,459 calories (range 45-5,138 kcal) compared with 321 calories (range 10-1,652 kcal) in non-binge eating episodes (Rosen, Leitenberg, Fisher, & Khazam, 1986). The reported caloric intake of 65% of binge episodes fell within the range of the nonbinge episodes. The patients also reported eating more desserts and snacks and less fruits and vegetables in their binge eating episodes as compared with nonbinge episodes. Subsequent self-monitoring studies at different centers have essentially confirmed Rosen et al.'s (1986) findings with a mean reported intake during binge episodes varying between 1,173 and 2,623 kcal, and with marked variation in caloric intake both within and between individuals (Jansen, Van den Hout, & Grieze, in press; Rossiter & Agras, 1990; Woell, Fichter, Pirke, & Wolfram, 1989). All of the self-monitoring studies allowed the patient to self-define binge eating episodes, requiring loss of control over eating as the marker for a binge. These studies suggest that many binges are relatively small, but larger on average than nonbinge episodes. No differences in macronutrient content between binges and nonbinges, as distinct from differences in food type, were found in these studies.

Laboratory studies of binge eating have revealed a different picture. The average binge is larger than in the self-monitoring studies, varying from a mean of 2,963 kcal to 7,774 kcal, with a range of 83 to 25,755 kcal for binge episodes (Kaye, Gwirtsman, George, Weiss, & Jimerson, 1985; Kissileff, Walsh, Kral, & Cassidy, 1986; Mitchell & Laine, 1985; Walsh, Kissileff, Cassidy, & Dantzie, 1989; Yanovski et al., 1992). The differences between laboratory and field studies may be due in part to differences in sample selection given that many of the participants in laboratory studies were inpatients representing more severe cases of eating disorder, for the most part bulimia nervosa. It is also likely that self-monitoring underestimates the caloric content of binges because of deficiencies in recording. Additionally, in the laboratory, subjects are instructed either to eat normally or to eat as much as they like. It is possible that, within the laboratory with freely available binge food, patients are able to eat more than in their natural environment where foods are often limited by their immediate availability, hence providing a natural ending to the binge episode. Finally, and perhaps most important, the definition of an episode of binge eating is different in laboratory than in field studies. In the laboratory, instructions to binge eat are given and the response is regarded as a binge eating episode, whereas in the natural environment binges are self-defined using loss of control over eating as the marker for a binge. An overall interpretation of the differences between laboratory and field studies is that laboratory studies may overestimate caloric consumption during binge episodes and that field studies may underestimate such consumption.

One recent study approached the problem of assessing food intake in binge eaters in a different manner (Weltzin, Hsu, Police, & Kaye, 1991), simply describing 24-hour food intake in terms of caloric consumption and macronutrients in a sample of patients with bulimia nervosa and matched normal controls, without using the term *binge eating*. They found that just over 40% of the bulimic women overate as compared with the control group (7,773 ± 4,525 versus 1,845 ± 649 kcal), whereas just under 40% consumed a normal range of calories, with the remainder consuming fewer calories than the control group (709 ± 268). The majority of the bulimic's meals were within the normal range of caloric intake, similar to the findings from self-monitoring studies. In addition, the percentage of fat, but not carbohydrates, increased with increasing meal size. Once more, this study emphasizes the remarkable variation in food intake in patients with bulimia nervosa, a finding shared by all the studies of food intake in bulimia nervosa, whether laboratory or self-monitoring. It should be noted that this study did not assess eating in the natural environment but only in a laboratory environment in which food was obtained via dispensers, and then only for a 24-hour period. Nonetheless, this study is important in pointing the way toward a descriptive view of feeding in the bulimic using the term *eating episode* and describing deviations from normal feeding patterns. The study seems to demonstrate that patients with bulimia nervosa have a wider range of caloric intake than a group of normals, taking in both more calories and fewer calories than the non-eating disordered group. This reminds us that we are dealing with a disordered feeding pattern marked by both restriction and overeating. Further descriptive studies of this sort with an extended range of measures, including affect and cognitions concerning food, might lead us to characterize more exactly the disordered eating patterns of these patients.

Overall, however, we must conclude that in assessing caloric intake we may not be measuring what we think we are, and what we are most interested in, namely, food intake in the natural environment over a relatively long period of time. It may not be possible to do this, but we must be clear in our own minds, and in our research reports, about the limitations of measurement.

Physical Activity

The assessment of activity levels poses similar problems to the assessment of obesity and food intake. Similar to food intake, physical activity is of interest because it is a potentially modifiable behavior. What we are most interested in is total activity in the natural environment over a long enough period to be representative of activity levels. Such a period is probably longer than 24 hours, perhaps as long as a week because activity will differ according to day of week. In addition, activity levels vary according to season; hence a comprehensive sampling of activity levels would need to reflect the major seasonal changes. Once again, there is no gold standard against which to evaluate the accuracy of assessing activity levels, although several methods of assessment have demonstrated correlations with BMI as well as with blood pressure and

HDL cholesterol, thus demonstrating at least concurrent validity (Berkowitz, Agras, Korner, Kraemer, & Zeanah, 1985; Griffiths & Payne, 1976; Klesges, Malott, Boschee, & Weber, 1986; Sallis, Patterson, Buono, & Nader, 1988). Each of the three broad choices in assessing activity, by self-report, by transducer, or by direct observation, demonstrates advantages and disadvantages, and none of them measures exactly what we want to measure. Self-report carries with it the problem of inaccurate recording or poor recall, although long periods of time can be assessed relatively easily. Transducers can provide moderately long assessment, but only of a somewhat limited activity, such as either arm or leg movements, or of body acceleration. Direct observation, although appealing, particularly because it allows recording of type of activity, can only provide relatively short interval assessment (e.g., 90 minutes or so) in somewhat limited circumstances, even though it would appear to be the most face valid method (McKenzie et al., 1991). Once again, it is important, but frequently neglected, to qualify assessment of activity by the exact measure used and to discuss the limitations of such measures. Much of the disagreement in the literature concerning the relationships between activity levels, obesity, and other features of medical interest are no doubt due to differences in the type of assessment used.

How Can We Cope With These Difficulties?

Despite these problems, precise reporting of the measures used in a particular study and careful acknowledgment of the limitations of such measures should go a long way toward solving the measurement dilemmas outlined above. Moreover, for most areas of assessment, there are a number of measures available. By using more than one measure of a particular construct, the degree of convergent validity can be assessed. If there is agreement, then we may be reassured that we are measuring something accurately, although the alternate hypothesis that the two measures are assessing a common but not central aspect of the construct must always be considered. If there is disagreement, then the reasons for this state of affairs should be sought in further experimental work. This may illuminate the reasons for the differences between two measures of the same thing and may also lead the way to more exact measurement in the future.

Assessment in the Clinical Setting

Clinicians, including myself, are often hesitant to use structured assessment methods in the care of their patients, feeling that the relatively free-flowing clinical interview provides sufficient information regarding the disorder, and changes in the principal behaviors characterizing the disorder, and that the addition of other assessment methods is not worth the time and cost involved. This view may be misguided, and our assessments and therapeutic results might be improved by the judicious use of certain structured methods. These questions require testing in controlled studies comparing unstructured and structured approaches to diagnosis and assessment in their effects on therapeutic outcome. Only then can the cost-benefit equation be firmly established. There are three aspects to assessment in the clinical setting: initial diagnosis, assessment of ongoing critical behaviors during the course of treatment, and assessment of outcome. Table 15.1 presents some measures that might be incorporated into the clinic for the assessment and treatment of each of the eating disorders at each of these three levels (medical evaluation of each of the disorders is not considered here). The choice of these measures is dictated by ease of assessment, interpretation of the results, and usefulness in treating the patient. Clearly there are marked similarities among the different disorders for each level of assessment, although the emphasis differs somewhat among the disorders.

Diagnostic Assessment

In the case of obesity, one of the most important aspects of assessment is the discovery of associated eating disorders, particularly binge eating disorder and more rarely bulimia nervosa. It is now apparent that the combination of overweight with binge eating disorder necessitates a different approach to treatment than for the uncomplicated case of obesity. In particular it appears necessary to treat the binge eating and its emotional accompaniments, and treatments based on those successful in bulimia nervosa appear to be effective in this regard (McCann & Agras, 1990; Smith, Marcus, & Kaye, 1992; Telch, Agras, Rossiter, Wilfley, & Kenardy, 1990; Wilfley et al., 1993). It may not be reasonable, however, to use time-consuming interview methods to ascertain the presence or absence of an accompanying eating disorder. Here the use of one or another eating disorder questionnaire filled out by the patient prior to the initial interview may be helpful. Such questionnaires may be focused on binge eating (Spitzer et al., 1992) or, like the Eating Disorders Questionnaire adapted from the Eating Disorder Examination (EDE), more broadly on various aspects of eating behavior (Cooper, Cooper, & Fairburn, 1989).

Although one or another of the above questionnaires may be used in conjunction with an unstructured interview for the remaining disorders, the clinician should consider using the Eating Disorder Examination (EDE), a structured interview designed to be used by a clinician (Cooper & Fairburn,

TABLE 15.1 Initial Assessment, Follow-Up Measures, and Outcome Measures in the Clinical Setting for Obesity, Anorexia Nervosa, Bulimia Nervosa, and Binge Eating Disorder

Disorder	Initial Assessment	Follow-Up Measures	Outcome Measures
Obesity	Eating Disorders Questionnaires	Self-monitoring of food intake, exercise, and so on	Weight/height
			Quality of life*
	SCID*	Weight	
Anorexia nervosa	Eating Disorder Examination (EDE)	Self-monitoring of food intake, binge eating, and purging	Weight/height
	Eating Disorders Quest		Comorbid psycho-pathology
	SCID and SCID-II	Weight	Quality of life*
Bulimia nervosa	Eating Disorder Examination (EDE)	Self-monitoring of food intake, binge eating, and purging	Weight/height
	Eating Disorders Quest		Binge/purge frequency
	SCID and SCID-II		Dietary restraint Quality of life*
Binge eating disorder	Eating Disorder Examination (EDE)	Self-monitoring of food intake, binge eating	Weight/height
	Eating Disorders Quest		Binge frequency
	SCID and SCID-II		Comorbid psycho-pathology
			Quality of life*

NOTE: Measures marked with an asterisk are optional.

1987; Cooper et al., 1989; Wilson & Smith, 1989). This interview provides a detailed inquiry into the nature of the eating disorder and a wide range of associated behaviors. In addition, the latest version provides *DSM-III-R* diagnoses of anorexia nervosa and bulimia nervosa and can easily be adapted for the proposed diagnosis of binge eating disorder, that is, meeting criteria for bulimia nervosa without purging behavior. It is primarily a measure of eating behavior in the past 4 weeks although the diagnostic items address the past 3 months. Five subscales can be derived from the interview, namely, overeating, restraint, eating concern, shape concern, and weight concern. The interview elicits detailed information on the pattern of eating, vegetarianism, restraint including avoidance of eating, setting caloric limits and dietary rules, preoccupation with food or calories, and so on, providing a detailed clinical picture of the patient's eating behavior. The interview takes about 1 hour to administer and might easily form an integral part of the clinical assessment of eating disordered patients, although, given the aversion of clinicians to the use of structured interviews, it is regarded as optional.

Because the psychopathology associated with obesity appears to be related to the presence of binge eating and not to weight per se (Telch & Agras, 1994; Yanovski, Nelson, Dubbert, & Spitzer, 1993), it is probably sufficient for the clinician to use an unstructured screening interview for obesity uncomplicated by binge eating disorder. However, for the remaining eating disorders, including obesity accompanied by binge eating disorder, the clinician should consider using interviews such as the SCID and the SCID-II to diagnose associated psychopathology that will have to be taken into account in the treatment of such patients. Finally, the measures used in the treatment of these patients and the principal outcome measures should also form part of the initial assessment of these patients.

Follow-Up Measures

Self-monitoring forms the core follow-up measure for each of the disorders under consideration, although the focus of self-monitoring differs among the disorders. The purpose of self-monitoring in the clinic is to provide information concerning the progress of the patient in changing key behaviors, to provide data for use in continued therapy, and to provide feedback to the patient concerning progress in behavior change. In obesity, the focus is mainly on compliance with prescribed dietary changes and with exercise prescriptions. At present there is no easy way to assess caloric intake, percentage fat intake, and other macronutrients of interest from these records, although the use of specially designed programs for handheld computers may bring this information easily to hand in the near future (Burnett, 1989). In anorexia nervosa, the focus of self-monitoring is mainly on food intake, ensuring the adequacy of three meals or more each day. Binge eating and purging will need to be monitored in the bulimic anorexic. In bulimia nervosa, the focus is on monitoring binge eating and purging behaviors, and on meal composition, so that three or more adequate meals are eventually consumed each day. For binge eating disorder, the focus is mainly on the monitoring of binge eating and the consumption of three adequate meals each day. However, if weight loss is also a desirable goal, as it will be for a large number of these obese individuals, then compliance with an exercise prescription and the quality of food intake are also emphasized.

Outcome Measures

In the clinical setting, the simpler outcome measure is better to save time and expense. The assessment of weight and height is important for all the disorders, particularly so for obesity, anorexia nervosa, and binge eating disorder, where weight is a principal outcome measure. In the case of bulimia nervosa, it may be counterproductive to routinely assess weight, because such measures may intensify the patient's concerns about body shape. The waist/hip ratio is regarded as optional for obesity and binge eating disorder. However, this measure is a risk factor for cardiovascular disease, and decreases in the measure may reflect decreased risk, which, in turn, may motivate the patient. Finally, for each of these disorders, an examination of changes in the quality of life may be important, as discussed in Chapter 2 of this volume.

Assessment in the Research Setting

Choosing instruments for research requires an evaluation of parameters different than those used to choose assessments for use in the clinic. As an initial consideration, the type of research may dictate the choice of one measure over another. For example, because of the large numbers of participants involved in epidemiological research, such studies must use simpler measures than those used in more intensive explorations, such as in the laboratory. Clinical outcome studies fall between these two extremes, being able, with the smaller number of subjects, to afford more detailed assessment but not usually of the intensity used in the laboratory. These constraints must be balanced against the measurement ideal, which is to come as close as possible to measuring the construct of interest using a reliable, valid, and accurate method. As we have seen, even for some of the basic measures integral to the assessment of eating disorders, it may be almost impossible to measure the variables of interest in a face valid way.

The way in which assessment might vary between different types of studies and the limitations of those measures are indicated in Table 15.2. Although it is possible to get closer to the variable of interest in the more intensive laboratory setting, or by using laboratory methods in the natural environment, in each case the assessment falls short of the ideal.

It may also be important to reconceptualize some of the "fuzzy" variables to alter our assessment approach. Take, for example, the term *binge eating*. We have already seen that this may be self-defined by the patient, defined by the investigators' instructions, or defined by eating a large amount of food. Although some of these definitions overlap, they are by no means equivalent; a binge defined one way may not be a binge defined in another. What we seem to have done is to take a fuzzy clinical/lay term and change it into a variable to be assessed without reducing the fuzziness. Might it not be better to start over with an examination of eating episodes, as suggested earlier in this chapter?

Such episodes might be characterized by time of day, length, interepisode duration, caloric intake, nutrient intake, eating rate, and associated psycho-

TABLE 15.2 Types of Measures Used in Different Types of Studies Compared With the
Actual Behavior Being Assessed

Measure	Epidemiological	Clinical Outcome	Laboratory	Actual Behavior
Binge/purge behaviors	Questionnaire	Interview such as EDE Self-monitoring	Direct observation	Private behaviors not possible to assess
Caloric intake	Questionnaire	Self-monitoring	Direct observation (time limited)	Food intake over months
Obesity	Self-reported height/weight Direct measure	Direct measure height/weight Skinfold thickness	Direct measures Underwater weight Impedance measure	Impossible to assess amount of excess fat
Activity	Questionnaire	Questionnaire, self-monitoring, transducer	Direct observation (in natural environment)	Activity over seasons

logical variables of interest, such as level of self-control and mood, over time. Self-defined and observer-defined binge definitions might then be applied to these episodes to begin to determine the relationship between such definitions and descriptors of the eating episodes. Only then might the remarkable variation in eating behavior in patients with the same diagnosis begin to make sense.

Guiding Assessment Through Models of Disorders

All assessment is guided by some form of model of the disorder under investigation although the model used may not be made explicit, nor may it be thoroughly conceptualized by the investigator. If we do not define our models explicitly, we will never be able to modify them based on new findings. Figure 15.1 describes a simple (mostly psychosocial) model of bulimia nervosa and binge eating disorder, although almost every box could be expanded further. Although family and twin studies have concentrated on diagnostic entities such as bulimia nervosa (Kendler et al., 1991; Strober, Lampert, Morrell, Burroughs, & Jacobs, 1990), it appears that there may be genetic influences leading to the appearance of the first step in the disorder, namely, disordered eating. Such genetic factors are likely to be influenced by family interactions concerning eating, although the nature of such interactions is unknown at present. Similarly, it has been hypothesized that the shift in societal attitudes toward women's weight and shape—that is, a thinner figure, which has become desirable as the norm during the past 20 years or so—has influenced the dietary habits of women and seems to have been

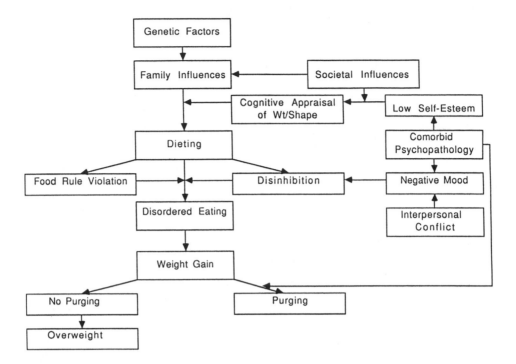

Figure 15.1. A Model of Some of the Factors Felt to Influence the Development and Maintenance of Bulimia Nervosa and Binge Eating Disorder, Exemplifying the Many Levels of Assessment That May Be Relevant to Studies of These Eating Disorders

associated with an increase in the frequency of bulimia nervosa, at least as observed in our clinics (Garner et al., 1985). These interactions presumably affect individuals' expectations regarding their shape and weight. It can be hypothesized that, if a mismatch between expectation and actual weight and/or body shape occurs, then the individual is more likely to diet, and the greater the mismatch, the more likely that dieting will be severe and will be maintained. Factors influencing the mismatch may be low self-esteem and perhaps the influence of comorbid psychopathology, such as affective disorders, anxiety disorders, and personality disorders, which have been shown to be more frequent in both the bulimic and the binge eating disorder patient than in control groups. Moreover, it now appears that this psychopathology is associated with the disordered eating behavior and not with overweight (Telch & Agras, 1994; Yanovski et al., 1993). Dietary restraint is then hypothesized to lead to disinhibition (experienced as loss of control) and to binge eating. It is likely that comorbid psychopathology also affects the degree of disinhibition.

There are, however, another set of factors that appear to affect disordered eating patterns, namely, mood changes (Arnow, Kenardy, & Agras, 1992; Bruce & Agras, 1992). Such alterations in mood, noted by many patients to occur before a binge, appear most likely to be engendered by interpersonal difficulties. Binge eating may also, at least temporarily, reduce negative mood, hence reinforcing such eating as a faulty coping mechanism for interpersonal difficulties. An excessive consumption of calories is then likely to lead to weight gain, dealt with by purging in the case of bulimia nervosa, and resulting in continued weight gain in the case of binge eating disorder. The factors guiding persons into one or another of these modes are not known at present although one might speculate that the mismatch between expectations concerning weight and shape and the reality may be greater in those who purge. Those who become obese are prone to develop one or more health complications from the disorder and are likely to eventually suffer from both physical and social disability, affecting quality of life.

Such a model can be used both to generate hypotheses concerning etiology, maintenance, and treatment and to select areas of assessment for particular types of studies. For example, within a laboratory study, the focus would be on the assessment of factors immediately controlling eating behavior as well as the eating behavior itself. Such factors include mood, self-esteem, perceptions of weight and shape, dietary restraint, hunger, fullness, disinhibition, self-control, food rule violations, and so on. Many of these variables may shift during the course of a laboratory meal, hence frequent sampling may be necessary.

On the other hand, for a treatment outcome study, rather different measures would be used. First, there would be measures of the target behaviors. For bulimia nervosa, these would include primary measures, namely, frequency of binge eating and purging, and secondary measures, namely, dietary behavior such as restraint, attitudes toward weight and shape, actual weight, measures of comorbid psychopathology, measures of mood, self-esteem, and interpersonal behaviors. In addition, consideration should be given to the assessment of food intake using self-monitoring or other methods.

In the case of binge eating disorder, the primary measures would include binge eating and weight, because obesity is a concern in the management of these patients. There is some indication that episodes of binge eating may be more poorly recalled by patients with binge eating disorder than by patients with bulimia nervosa (Rossiter, Agras, Telch, & Bruce, 1992). This may be because an episode of purging more clearly demarcates these episodes in the patient with bulimia nervosa and perhaps allows for easier recall of such episodes. For this reason, it may be preferable to assess the number of binge days in a given period rather than the number of binge episodes. An additional problem regarding sequential measurement before, during, and after treatment is apparent for such individuals, namely, that patients may alter their definition of a binge during the course of treatment. In other words, there may be an interaction between treatment and an outcome measure. Such a change may be more accurately defined within a structured clinical interview such as the EDE or by a modified self-monitoring process that assesses quantity of food consumed as well as degree of control over eating for each episode considered a binge. Secondary measures would be similar to those described for bulimia nervosa, except that assessment of disability and some indices of physical health—such as blood pressure, cholesterol levels, and waist/hip ratio—might be added.

A different set of measures would be indicated if the interest in a treatment study included measures that may predict outcome. Here the focus is on measures collected pretreatment. These might include family history of overweight or eating disorder, time of onset of weight or binge eating problems, severity of binge eating and/or purging, dietary restraint, disinhibition, comorbid psychopathology—particularly personality disorder, assessment of mood, self-esteem, and attitudes toward weight and shape. For each of these different types of study, the relationship between the secondary or predictive measures, determined by factor analysis, is important in selecting the final variables to analyze, removing as far as possible variables that are highly correlated with one another.

Some Possible Futures

Progress in assessment methods tends to be slower than in other areas. Although there is a veritable cornucopia of instruments available to measure one aspect or another of the eating disorders, as detailed in this volume, much less effort is directed toward validation of the measures. This deficiency can only be overcome by more and better instrument development and validation research. Such research needs to be fostered and better supported by funding agencies. This need is fairly urgent given the advent of newer technologies that present better ways of administering standard measures, which will give rise to a new set of measures, and no doubt a new set of problems.

Computer Technology

A wide array of standard psychological measures are now available in computerized format, and it is relatively easy to develop such formats for new measures (Burnett, 1989). Computerized administration of psychological measures has the advantage over paper-and-pencil methods in that responses are directly recorded into a database, hence removing data entry errors, and can be automatically scored immediately following the assessment. Such scores either can be obtained in hard copy displayed in various forms useful to the clinician, researcher, and patient or can be moved as a data file to a data set for further analysis. The evident disadvantage of such a method of administration would appear to be the need for a computer-literate population of subjects. It seems, however, that with a simple teaching program the vast majority of participants can use a computer-administered assessment with ease. Such interactive programs have, however, been successfully used in studies involving less well educated groups such as low-income women (Suitor & Gardner, 1992). Simple computer routines can offer participants a chance to review each response after it is made and to alter the response if it has been made incorrectly, and can also ensure that the participant answers every question, ensuring complete data collection with the minimum of effort from the clinician or researcher. Such methods offer the clinician a cost-effective way to collect clinically relevant data that can be displayed in various useful formats. For the researcher, such methods are free of missing data and relatively free of erroneous responses, and the data can be downloaded into a database.

The rapid development of the handheld computer offers even greater advantages for assessment. For example, rather than using self-monitoring to record dietary intake, binge eating, purging, and so on, a handheld computer can be used. Such a computer can store many food items in memory and, with a rapid search function, allow the subject to easily identify and enter such items, each entry being prompted for the appropriate amount consumed. Moreover, the time of entry is automatically recorded, allowing the investigator to determine the relationship of entries to actual time of eating. The handheld computer can calculate caloric intake and major nutrient intake for any time interval. Additionally, data from such a program, which could also record activity levels, can be downloaded to a database for further analysis.

Handheld computers can also be used for fine-grained analysis of the relationship of events to one another, such as the relationship of mood changes to food intake or panic attacks. Branching programs or menus can be used to assess different external or internal events at various times of day and in relationship to the behavior of interest. The computer can prompt individuals, using an alarm feature, to answer questions at predetermined times, either at fixed intervals or on a random interval schedule. An example from the study of panic disorder (Kenardy, Fried, Kraemer, & Taylor, 1992) may exemplify the usefulness of this instrumentation. Twenty female patients with panic disorder were studied intensively to examine the psychological precursors of panic attacks. They were given a handheld computer, which was used to assess psychological symptoms each hour during the waking day for a week. The computer prompted each subject at set intervals. Questions such as

"How anxious do you feel?" appeared with a 24-point visual analog scale on screen. Other questions appeared in a "yes/no" format. Subjects were also asked to report the time of onset and offset of panic attacks. The data from this study provided much useful information on the psychological precursors of panic as well as on self-reported moods of various types over the waking hours, revealing clear circadian patterns both for anxiety and for panic attacks. In addition, panic attacks were preceded by patient ratings of a significantly higher likelihood that panic would occur. Clearly such a microanalysis might easily be applied to the study of eating behavior and the eating disorders.

The advent of computerized therapy, administered by means of handheld computers, also offers opportunities to unobtrusively assess adherence to the therapeutic regimen in a more quantitative way than is possible with other methods. In one study, various aspects of use of a computerized treatment for obesity were related to outcome (Burnett, Taylor, & Agras, 1992). Of interest, various aspects of program use, such as total days of use, daily frequency of viewing goal-related feedback, and frequency of self-reports, all stored by the computer, were more highly related to weight loss than were reported caloric intake or exercise. Although computerized therapies may or may not be as effective as therapist-delivered treatments, such therapy applications may allow a finer grained analysis of adherence and its relationship to outcome than other methods.

Other Technologies

Just as handheld computers may cast a light on essentially private behaviors, so other technologies such as the video camera used in a home setting might provide information on actual feeding behavior. The miniaturization of such equipment now allows it to be more easily used in the home environment and may allow us to study behavior more effectively in such environments. Similarly, technologies, such as the use of doubly labeled water in assessing energy expenditure, allow estimation of energy expenditure in the natural environment in a relatively unobtrusive manner (Schoeller & Fjeld, 1991). Although such technologies have their own limitations, overall they are bringing us closer to assessing ongoing behavior in the person's own environment, a most important step toward the development of a valid measurement technology.

Conclusion

Even a casual reader of this excellent volume will be somewhat overwhelmed by the variety of measures described for the various eating disorders and weight-related problems. Most, if not all, readers will encounter new measures that will prove useful to them in their clinical work or in their research. Moreover, guidance as to the reliability and validity of these measures is provided if such information exists, and a thoughtful discussion of the derivation of the measure and its general utility is often to be found. Clearly we have come a long way in the development of assessment methodology.

The task ahead may, however, be more difficult, namely, to devise measures that more exactly assess what we wish to measure. In particular, there is a need to move on from paper-and-pencil measures to the assessment of behavior in the natural environment. To the extent that we use measures that fall short of this ideal, we may draw incorrect conclusions about the disorders that we are studying, or the treatment of such disorders, based on faulty feedback from instruments with unknown errors of measurement. The development of such naturalistic measures will be neither easy nor inexpensive. That, however, is what I see as the next challenge in the area of assessment methodology.

References

Agras, W. S. (1987). *Eating disorders: Management of obesity, bulimia, and anorexia nervosa.* New York: Pergamon.

Arnow, B., Kenardy, J., & Agras, W. S. (1992). Binge eating among the obese: A descriptive study. *Journal of Behavioral Medicine, 15,* 155-170.

Berkowitz, R. I., Agras, W. S., Korner, A. F., Kraemer, H. C., & Zeanah, C. H. (1985). Physical activity and adiposity: A longitudinal study from birth to childhood. *Journal of Pediatrics, 106,* 734-738.

Bray, G. A. (1986). Effects of obesity on health and happiness. In K. D. Brownell & J. P. Foreyt (Eds.), *Handbook of eating disorders: Physiology, psychology, and treatment of obesity, anorexia, and bulimia* (pp. 3-44). New York: Basic Books.

Bruce, B., & Agras, W. S. (1992). Binge eating in females: A population based investigation. *International Journal of Eating Disorders, 12,* 365-372.

Burnett, K. F. (1989). Computers for assessment and intervention in psychiatry and psychology. *Current Opinion in Psychiatry, 2,* 780-786.

Burnett, K. F., Taylor, C. B., & Agras, W. S. (1992). Ambulatory computer-assisted behavior therapy for obesity: An empirical model for examining behavioral correlates of treatment outcome. *Computers in Human Behavior, 8,* 239-248.

Cooper, Z., Cooper, P. J., & Fairburn, C. G. (1989). The validity of the Eating Disorder Examination and its subscales. *British Journal of Psychiatry, 154,* 807-812.

Cooper, Z., & Fairburn, C. G. (1987). The Eating Disorder Examination: A semi-structured interview for the assessment of the specific psychopathology of eating disorders. *International Journal of Eating Disorders, 6,* 1-8.

Garner, D. M., Olmsted, M. P., & Garfinkel, P. E. (1985). Similarities among bulimic groups selected by weight and weight history. *Journal of Psychiatric Research, 19,* 129-134.

Griffiths, M., & Payne, P. R. (1976). Energy expenditure in small children of obese and nonobese parents. *Nature, 260,* 698-700.

Jansen, A., Van den Hout, M., & Grieze, E. (in press). Clinical and non-clinical binges. *Behaviour Research and Therapy*.

Johnson, W. G., Stuckey, M. K., Lewis, L. D., & Schwartz, D. M. (1982). Bulimia: A descriptive survey of 316 cases. *International Journal of Eating Disorders, 2*, 3-16.

Kaye, W. H., Gwirtsman, H. E., George, D. T., Weiss, S. R., & Jimerson, G. T. (1985). Relationship of mood alterations to bingeing behavior in bulimia. *British Journal of Psychiatry, 148*, 479-485.

Kenardy, J., Fried, L., Kraemer, H. C., & Taylor, C. B. (1992). Psychological precursors of panic attacks. *British Journal of Psychiatry, 160*, 668-673.

Kendler, K. S., MacLean, C., Neale, M., Kessler, R., Heath, A., & Eaves, L. (1991). The genetic epidemiology of bulimia nervosa. *American Journal of Psychiatry, 148*, 1627-1637.

Klesges, R. C., Malott, J. M., Boschee, P. E., & Weber, J. (1986). The effects of parental influences on children's food intake, physical activity and relative weight. *International Journal of Eating Disorders, 5*, 335-346.

Kissileff, H. R., Walsh, B. T., Kral, J. G., & Cassidy, S. M. (1986). Laboratory studies of eating behavior in women with bulimia. *Physiology & Behavior, 38*, 563-570.

Kraemer, H. C., Berkowitz, R. I., & Hammer, D. L. (1990). Methodologic difficulties in studies of obesity: I. Measurement issues. *Annals of Behavioral Medicine, 12*, 112-118.

McCann, U. D., & Agras, W. S. (1990). Successful treatment of nonpurging bulimia nervosa with desipramine: A double-blind, placebo-controlled study. *American Journal of Psychiatry, 147*, 1509-1513.

McCann, U. D., Rossiter, E. M., King, R. J., & Agras, W. S. (1991). Nonpurging bulimia nervosa: A distinct subtype of bulimia nervosa. *International Journal of Eating Disorders, 10*, 679-688.

McKenzie, T. I., Sallis, J. F., Nader, P. R., Patterson, T. L., Elder, J. P., Berry, C. C., Rupp, J. W., Atkins, C. J., Buono, M. J., & Nelson, J. A. (1991). BEACHES: An observational system for assessing children's eating and physical activity behaviors and associated events. *Journal of Applied Behavior Analysis, 24*, 141-152.

Mitchell, J. E., & Laine, D. C. (1985). Monitored binge-eating behavior in patients with bulimia. *International Journal of Eating Disorders, 4*, 177-183.

Rosen, J. C., Leitenberg, H., Fisher, C., & Khazam, C. (1986). Binge-eating episodes in bulimia nervosa: The amount and type of food consumed. *International Journal of Eating Disorders, 5*, 255-267.

Rossiter, E. M., & Agras, W. S. (1990). An empirical test of the DSM-III-R definition of binge. *International Journal of Eating Disorders, 9*, 513-518.

Rossiter, E. M., Agras, W. S., Telch, C. F., & Bruce, B. (1992). The eating patterns of non-purging bulimic subjects. *International Journal of Eating Disorders, 11*, 111-120.

Sallis, J. F., Patterson, T. L., Buono, M. J., & Nader, P. R. (1988). Relation of cardiovascular fitness and physical activity to cardiovascular disease risk factors in children and adults. *American Journal of Epidemiology, 127*, 933-941.

Schoeller, D. E., & Fjeld, C. R. (1991). Human energy metabolism: What have we learned from the doubly labeled water method? *Annual Review of Nutrition, 11*, 355-373.

Smith, D. E., Marcus, M. D., & Kaye, W. (1992). Cognitive-behavioral treatment of obese binge eaters. *International Journal of Eating Disorders, 12*, 257-262.

Spitzer, R. L., Devlin, M. J., Walsh, B. T., Hasin, D., Wing, R., et al. (1991). Binge eating disorder: To be or not to be in DSM-IV. *International Journal of Eating Disorders, 10*, 627-630.

Spitzer, R. L., Devlin, M., Walsh, B. T., Hasin, D., Wing, R., Marcus, M., Stunkard, A., Wadden, T., Yanovski, S., Agras, S., Mitchell, J., & Nonas, C. (1992). Binge eating disorder: A multisite field trial of the diagnostic criteria. *International Journal of Eating Disorders, 11,* 191-203.

Strober, M., Lampert, C., Morrell, W., Burroughs, J., & Jacobs, C. (1990). A controlled family study of anorexia nervosa: Evidence of familial aggregation and lack of shared transmission with affective disorders. *International Journal of Eating Disorders, 9,* 239-254.

Suitor, C. W., & Gardner, J. D. (1992). Development of an interactive, self-administered computerized food frequency questionnaire for use with low-income women. *Journal of Nutrition Education, 24,* 82-85.

Telch, C. F., & Agras, W. S. (1994). Binge eating, obesity, and psychopathology: Are they related? *International Journal of Eating Disorders, 15,* 53-61.

Telch, C. F., Agras, W. S., Rossiter, E. M., Wilfley, D., & Kenardy, J. (1990). Group cognitive-behavioral treatment for the nonpurging bulimic: An initial evaluation. *Journal of Consulting and Clinical Psychology, 58,* 629-635.

Walsh, B. T., Kissileff, H. R., Cassidy, S. M., & Dantzie, S. (1989). Eating behavior of women with bulimia. *Archives of General Psychiatry, 46,* 54-58.

Weltzin, T. E., Hsu, L. K. G., Police, C., & Kaye, W. H. (1991). Feeding patterns in bulimia nervosa. *Biological Psychiatry, 30,* 1093-1110.

Wilfley, D. E., Agras, W. S., Telch, C. F., Rossiter, E. M., Schneider, J. A., Cole, A. G., Sifford, L., & Raeburn, S. D. (1993). Group cognitive-behavioral therapy and group interpersonal therapy for the nonpurging bulimic: A controlled comparison. *Journal of Consulting and Clinical Psychology, 161,* 296-305.

Wilson, G. T., & Smith, D. (1989). Assessment of bulimia nervosa: An evaluation of the Eating Disorder Examination. *International Journal of Eating Disorders, 8,* 173-179.

Woell, C., Fichter, M. M., Pirke, K. M., & Wolfram, G. (1989). Eating behavior of patients with bulimia nervosa. *International Journal of Eating Disorders, 8,* 557-568.

Yanovski, S. Z., Leet, M., Yanovski, J. A., Flood, M., Gold, P. W., Kissileff, H. R., & Walsh, B. T. (1992). Food selection and intake of obese women with binge eating disorder. *American Journal of Clinical Nutrition, 56*(6), 975-980.

Yanovski, S. Z., Nelson, J. E., Dubbert, B. K., & Spitzer, R. L. (1993). Association of binge eating disorder and psychiatric comorbidity in obese subjects. *American Journal of Psychiatry, 150,* 1472-1479.

Author Index

Skre, I., 322
Slade, P. D., 124, 130, 132, 134, 358, 359, 360
Slaughter, M. H., 452
Slawson, D., 219, 228
Slifer, K., 451
Small, A., 12, 15
Small, A. C., 7
Smalley, K. J., 524
Smead, V. S., 177
Smiciklas-Wright, H., 541
Smith, D., 135, 319, 320, 322, 353, 475, 568
Smith, D. E., 567
Smith, E. L., 243
Smith, E. O., 525
Smith, I. D., 34
Smith, J. E., 12, 13, 14
Smith, K., 87
Smith, K. W., 457, 458, 470
Smith, M., 317, 361, 362, 363, 381
Smith, M. C., 161, 312, 317, 357, 361
Smith, N. J., 82
Smith, O. W., 37
Smith, P. C., 36, 37, 38, 39, 49
Smith, R., 524, 530
Smith, R. C., 494, 497
Smith, S. A., 91
Smith, S. D., 108
Smolowitz, J., 524
Smucker, R., 224
Snell, J. L., 251
Snell, M. K., 541
Snitzer, L., 45, 46
Snow, M. G., 389, 405, 406
Snow, R. C. K., 186
Snyder, D. K., 46
Snyder, F. F., 96
Sobal, J., 467
Sobell, J., 225, 226, 227, 228
Sobol, A. M., 32, 41, 46
Sobol, W. T., 535
Sohlberg, C. N. S., 473
Solomon, L. J., 475
Solomon, Z., 541
Solyom, L., 133
Somerfield, M., 33
Sonies, B. C., 463
Sörbom, D., 168, 390, 401
Sorensen, T., 340
Sorenson, A. W., 243

Sorenson, T., 121, 122
Sorlie, P., 214
Sorrenti, G., 549
Sovner, R., 434
Sowers-Hoag, K., 43
Spana, R. E., 131, 132
Spanier, G. B., 44, 45, 46
Spears, G. F. S., 460
Spector, I. P., 45
Speicher, C., 436
Speizer, F. E., 222, 227, 228
Spencer, C. P., 159
Spilker, B., 33
Spitzer, R., 16
Spitzer, R. L., 16, 303, 314, 315, 317, 321, 322,
    323, 340, 346, 561, 567, 569, 572
Srebnik, D., 126, 129, 130, 135, 138
Staats, S., 39, 40, 41, 72
Stackhouse, C., 437, 445
Staffieri, J. R., 83, 98-99
Stahl, M. J., 36
Stampfer, M. J., 222, 227, 228
Stancer, H. C., 133
Stanton, A. L., 266, 268, 294
Stanton, G. C., 34, 36
Stapell, C. A., 441
Starfield, B., 498
Starr, A. M., 40, 41
Staveren, W. A., 173, 174
Steel, R. P., 38, 39
Steer, R. A., 504, 505, 506
Stefan, L., 187
Steger, J. C., 48
Steiger, H., 16
Stein, A. D., 253
Stein, D. M., 155
Stein, R. F., 35, 91
Steinbaugh, M. L., 469
Steinhausen, H. C., 474
Steinkamp, R. C., 547
Steinwachs, D., 498
Stelzer, C. M., 96
Stephens, M. A. P., 27
Stern, M. P., 95, 474
Stetson, B., 245, 246, 248, 255
Stevens, T. M., 455
Stevens, V. J., 475
Stevenson, J. F., 396
Stewart, A., 495

Subject Index

About the Contributors

W. Stewart Agras obtained his M.D. from University College, London, in 1955 and completed his residency and Fellowship in Psychiatry at McGill University in 1961. He served on the faculty of the University of Vermont College of Medicine (1961-1969) and was then appointed Professor and Chairman of the Department of Psychiatry at the University of Mississippi Medical Center. Since 1973 he has been Professor of Psychiatry at Stanford University School of Medicine. His research interests have been in the investigation of behavior change in areas such as compliance, essential hypertension, and other cardiovascular risk factors as well as the eating and anxiety disorders. In 1974 he began one of the first programs in behavioral medicine in the United States, which continues today at Stanford University. He has been Editor of the *Journal of Applied Behavior Analysis* and the *Annals of Behavioral Medicine*. In addition he has been President of the Association for the Advancement of Behavior Therapy (AABT) and was the first President of the Society for Behavioral Medicine. He has also spent 2 years at the Center for Advanced Study of the Behavioral Sciences and in addition was codirector of one of the summer programs for promising young faculty at the Center.

Vincent C. Alfonso earned his doctorate from the Clinical/School Psychology Program at Hofstra University in 1990. In addition, he works as a staff psychologist at the Crossroads School for Child Development. He is on the faculty of the School Psychology Program at the Fordham University Graduate School of Education. His research interests include the measurement of subjective well-being and life satisfaction, psychoeducational assessment, and primary prevention. He and David B. Allison are the authors of the Extended Satisfaction With Life Scale (ESWLS). He is also the President of the School Division of the New York State Psychological Association.

David B. Allison received his Ph.D. in clinical psychology from Hofstra University in 1990, after which he completed a postdoctoral fellowship at the Johns Hopkins University School of Medicine. He recently completed a second postdoctoral fellowship at the National Institute of Health-funded Obesity Research Center (ORC) at St. Luke's/Roosevelt Hospital and Columbia University College of Physicians and Surgeons. He is currently Associate Research Scientist at the ORC. His areas of interest include human obesity and measurement, research design, and data analysis. Within the area of human obesity, he primarily focuses on etiology and sequelae. He has been supported by an American Diabetes Association Career Development Award and is currently supported by a First Award from the National Institute of Diabetes Digestive and Kidney Diseases for the study of the genetic causes of between- and within-population variation in obesity. He has won several awards including the American Society for Clinical Nutrition's 1992 Post-Doctoral Fellow Award.

Drew A. Anderson, M.A., is a clinical psychology graduate student at Louisiana State University. His research has focused on the development of assessment methods for eating problems.

Roberta L. Babbitt is Assistant Professor of Psychiatry and Behavioral Sciences at the Johns Hopkins University School of Medicine. She is the Director of the Pediatric Feeding Disorders Program and Outpatient Behavioral Pediatrics Clinic in the Department of Behavioral Psychology at the Kennedy Krieger Institute. She received her Ph.D. in applied behavior analysis and research from Columbia University. She has published a number of journal articles and book chapters on the assessment and treatment of pediatric feeding disorders and compliance with medical regimens. Her areas of research and practice include pediatric feeding disorders, obesity, behavioral pediatrics, preparation for medical procedures, pain management, parent and staff training, and behavioral oncology.

Lynn Edlen-Nezin received her master's degree at Ferkauf Graduate School of Psychology/Albert Einstein College of Medicine, Yeshiva University, New York, and is a doctoral candidate in health psychology. Her thesis is based on data from a long-term prospective study of voluntary weight loss in elderly women, funded by the National Heart, Lung and Blood Institute, and is concerned with a biopsychosocial profile of the optimal candidate for weight reduction in this age group. She is a research consultant in the Department of Epidemiology and Social Medicine and is currently involved in the development of a computer-guided weight management intervention. Her publications include articles on dietary management of diabetes and coronary heart disease. She is certified in fitness instruction by the American College of Sports Medicine and has an extensive background in the field of physical exercise. She is the former director of employee fitness for the Rockefeller University, as well as training director of the Sports Training Institute, in New York City.

Myles S. Faith is a graduate student in clinical and school psychology at Hofstra University and is a staff therapist at the Institute for Rational Emotive Therapy. His research interests include body image, emotional eating, and obesity-related issues.

Bernard S. Gorman received his Ph.D. (1971) in personality and social psychology from the City University of New York and completed postdoctoral studies in psychotherapy at the Institute for Rational Emotive Therapy. Over the years, he has had a constant interest in developing and applying multivariate statistical techniques. He has written numerous articles and presented many convention papers in the areas of personality assessment, multivariate analysis, and relationships between cognition and affect. He coauthored the textbook *Developmental Psychology* (1980) with Theron Alexander and Paul Roodin and coedited the research monograph *The Personal Experience of Time* (1977) with Alden Wessman. He is the author of several instructional computer packages. He is Professor of Psychology and State University of New York Faculty Exchange Scholar at Nassau Community College/SUNY, where he teaches courses in clinical and developmental psychology. He also holds an adjunct professorship in Hofstra University's Graduate Psychology Programs, where he teaches courses in multivariate statistical analysis, computer applications in psychology, and psychometrics. He combines his interests in measurement research, clinical issues, and teaching at Queens Children's Psychiatric Center, where he is a psychologist in the Quality Assurance and Program Evaluation Department. He is currently Vice-President of the Metropolitan New York Chapter of the American Statistical Association.

Stanley Heshka earned his M.Sc. and Ph.D. degrees in social psychology from Columbia University, New York. He is currently Research Associate at the Obesity Research Center in New York. He has written more than 50 publications in the areas of obesity and psychology.

Steven B. Heymsfield is Professor of Medicine at Columbia University College of Physicians and Surgeons. He is also Deputy Director of the Obesity Research Center at St. Luke's-Roosevelt Hospital in New York and a visiting scientist at Rockefeller University. He is currently president-elect of the American Society of Parenteral and Enteral Nutrition. Trained in internal medicine at Mount Sinai School of Medicine and Emory University School of Medicine, his early clinical and research areas included causes and treatment of malnutrition in hospitalized patients. He developed and then investigated specialized feeding methods for hospitalized patients. An outgrowth of this work was his longstanding interest in nutritional assessment and the study of human body composition. His recent research includes clinical and metabolic aspects of obesity. He is author of more than 200 publications, is on the editorial boards of several nutrition journals, and has won several awards for his research.

Lori P. Jackman, M.A., is a clinical psychology intern at the University of California, Davis. Her research interests are eating disorders in female athletes and cognitive conceptualizations of psychopathology.

Sheryl R. Jackson, Ph.D., is Assistant Professor of Psychiatry and Behavioral Neurobiology at the University of Alabama at Birmingham Medical Center. Her current research interests are anxiety disorders and impulse control disorders.

Robert C. Klesges is Professor at the Center for Applied Psychological Research, Memphis State University, and codirector of the Prevention Center at the University of Tennessee, Memphis. He is author of more than 100 articles and chapters, many focusing on the effects of smoking on body weight and the relation of physical activity to body weight.

John E. Kurtz, Ph.D., is NIH Research Fellow, Rehabilitation Institute of Michigan, Detroit, MI.

Katharine Loeb is currently a doctoral candidate in clinical psychology at Rutgers University. Previously, she worked in research and assessment at the Eating Disorders Unit of the New York State Psychiatric Institute at Columbia Presbyterian Medical Center. She has had extensive training in the administration of the Eating Disorder Examination and the Structured Clinical Interview for the *DSM-III-R* and has been named an adviser to the eating disorders section of the *DSM-IV.* In addition, she has conducted a study comparing interview and self-report measures in assessing the diagnostic features of bulimia nervosa.

Ramasamy Manikam, Ph.D., is currently the Assistant Director of the Outpatient Behavioral Pediatrics and Feeding Clinic in the Department of Behavioral Psychology at the Kennedy Krieger Institute. He is also an Instructor in Psychiatry and Behavioral Sciences at the Johns Hopkins University School of Medicine. He attained his doctoral degree in clinical psychology at Louisiana State University. He has extensive experience in the field of exercise science. His master's thesis was on validation of skinfold calipers using hydrostatic weighing as the criterion measure. He has been a consultant for health clubs and director of faculty fitness programs. He currently consults for Prader-Willi individuals in a group home, and in his clinic provides services for children and adolescents who are obese due to multiple etiologies.

Leslie C. Morey, Ph.D., is Director of Clinical Training and Associate Professor in the Department of Psychology at Vanderbilt University, Nashville, TN. He taught previously at the Yale University School of Medicine and at the University of Tulsa. He has written more than 75 articles, books, and chapters on the assessment of personality and psychopathology, and he is the author of the Personality Assessment Inventory, a widely used clinical assessment instrument.

Clodagh M. Murphy received her M.S. degree in severe handicapping conditions from Johns Hopkins University. She is currently a medical student at the University of Dundee, Scotland. She completed a predoctoral internship in behavioral pediatrics and developmental disabilities at the Kennedy Krieger Institute and the Johns Hopkins University School of Medicine. Her publications are in the area of obesity in the developmentally disabled, autism, and other developmental disability syndromes. Research interests include Prader-Willi syndrome, pervasive developmental disorders, and self-injurious behavior.

Richard N. Pierson Jr. established a Body Composition Research Unit in 1967 in the Department of Medicine at St. Luke's/Roosevelt Hospital Center. During a career of 28 years as Director of Nuclear Medicine, his research addressed two areas. The first was the angiographic principles underlying nuclear cardiology. The second was the use of radiotracers in studying the metabolism of the body compartments. He has been appointed Director of the Bioengineering Institute at Columbia University and chapter President of the Society of Nuclear Medicine. He has been President of the New York County Medical Society and the New York County Health Services Review Organization and Vice-Chair of the Board of Directors of Empire Blue Cross/ Blue Shield. He has served as Speaker of the American Medical Peer Review Association, as founding President of its research arm, the American Medical Review Research Center, as President of the Alliance for Continuing Medical Education, and as a member of the House of Delegates of the American Medical Association, representing first the Medical Society of the State of New York, and subsequently the Society of Nuclear Medicine. He will serve as codirector of the new Center for Research in Clinical Nutrition in the New York area.

Kathleen M. Pike, Ph.D., is currently Chief Psychologist on the Eating Disorders Unit at New York Psychiatric Institute and Assistant Professor of Clinical Psychology at Columbia Presbyterian Medical Center. She earned her Ph.D. in clinical psychology from Yale University in 1989 and completed her clinical internship at Beth Israel Medical Center in New York City. She was appointed Visiting Research Scientist at Yale University before joining the staff of Columbia Presbyterian Medical Center. For the past 10 years, she has been an active member of both the American Psychological Association and the Bush Center for Child Development and Social Policy. In addition, she has a private practice in New York City.

James O. Prochaska, Ph.D., is Director of the Cancer Prevention Research Consortium and of the Self Change Laboratory and is Professor in the Department of Psychology at the University of Rhode Island. He received his Ph.D. in clinical psychology in 1969 at Wayne State University. He has published more than 100 papers on behavior change for health promotion and disease prevention and on the eclectic approach to psychotherapy. He is the originator of the transtheoretical model of change and author of *Systems of Psychotherapy* and *The Transtheoretical Approach: Crossing the Traditional Boundaries of Therapy.*

Anne W. Riley, B.S.N., Ph.D., is Assistant Professor in the Department of Health Policy and Management in the School of Hygiene and Public Health at the Johns Hopkins University and holds a joint appointment in the Department of Psychiatry and Behavioral Sciences in the School of Medicine. She received her Ph.D. (1986) in clinical psychology from Virginia Polytechnic Institute and State University and her B.S. in nursing science (1969) from Old Dominion University. Her current research is in the areas of child and adolescent health status measurement, detection and management of children's emotional and behavioral problems by medical providers, help seeking and health services use by children and adolescents, especially those with mental health problems, and the epidemiology of mental disorders among youths.

Joseph S. Rossi, Ph.D., is Director of Research at the Cancer Prevention Research Center and Associate Professor in the Department of Psychology, the University of Rhode Island. He received his Ph.D. at the University of Rhode Island in 1984 in experimental psychology. He has published more than 60 scientific papers and contributed more than 100 presentations at national and international scientific conferences. He is principal investigator or co-principal investigator on several funded research projects, including *BEACH-Based Interventions for Skin Cancer Prevention, Educational Intervention Research for Skin Cancer Prevention and Control, Accelerating the Process of Change for Cancer Prevention, Cancer Prevention via School and Home Channels, Accelerating Progress Toward Smoking Cessation in Pregnant Women, Reaching Black Women for Dietary Intervention to Reduce Breast Cancer Risk, Cervical Cancer Prevention in Low-SES Teens, Exercise Expert System for Cardiovascular Disease Prevention, Models of Change for Women's Contraceptive Behavior, Increasing Physical Activity at the Workplace,* and *Self-Help Models and Interventions for Smoking Cessation.* He has been active in the development of the transtheoretical model for more than 10 years for a wide range of health behaviors. He also specializes in research methodology and statistics, including statistical power, meta-analysis, multivariate statistics, structural equation modeling, psychometric measurement and scale development, and expert computer systems.

Susan R. Rossi, Ph.D., R.N., is an NIH Postdoctoral Research Fellow at the Cancer Prevention Research Center, the University of Rhode Island. She did her undergraduate work in Nursing at Duke University and received an M.S.N. in 1982 and her Ph.D. in nursing in 1993 at the University of Rhode Island. She is co-principal or co-investigator on several funded research projects, including *Accelerating the Process of Change for Cancer Prevention, Extension of the Transtheoretical Model of Behavior Change to Dietary Fat Reduction, Longitudinal Study of Self-Change in Dietary Fat Reduction,* and *Reaching Black Women for Dietary Intervention to Reduce Breast Cancer Risk.* She has published a number of articles and presented numerous papers at national and international conferences on dietary fat behavior change. She has been active in the adaptation of the transtheoretical model to the areas of diet and weight control. Her substantive research interests include dietary and other health behavior change, health promotion, cancer prevention, special populations, and allergy and environmental exposure. Her methodological interests include instrument development and multivariate and structural equation modeling techniques for data analysis.

David G. Schlundt, Ph.D., is Assistant Professor of Psychology and Assistant Professor of Medicine at Vanderbilt University in Nashville, TN. He earned an M.A. in clinical psychology from the University of Wisconsin in 1979 and a Ph.D. in clinical psychology from Indiana University in 1982. His research has focused on the interface between nutrition and behavior. His interests include the assessment of eating behavior; assessment of body image; the influence of environmental, emotional, and cognitive variables on eating behavior; and the development and evaluation of clinical interventions. He has worked with eating behavior in eating disorders, hypertension, obesity, and diabetes. Dr. Schlundt has coauthored a book on eating disorders and has published more than 80 scientific papers.

Mary Lee Shelton, M.S., is a clinical psychology intern at the University of Alabama at Birmingham. For the past 5 years, she has been a graduate student at the University of Memphis, specializing in the areas of behavioral medicine, pediatric psychology, and clinical dietetics. She has held supervisory positions on grant-supported study teams investigating childhood obesity, smoking cessation, body composition, and metabolism. In the past few years, she has focused her work primarily on the prevention of cardiovascular risk factors in children and the prevention of stress fractures in college athletes. She has published scientific articles in these areas and plans to continue working with these groups of individuals.

Jane A. Summers is currently the director of a mental health service for adults with developmental handicaps at Chedoke-McMaster Hospitals in Hamilton, Ontario, Canada. She received her Ph.D. in school psychology from the University of Toronto in 1991. She previously held a faculty appointment in the Department of Psychiatry and Behavioral Sciences at the Johns Hopkins University School of Medicine and served as Director of Outpatient Services for the Department of Behavioral Psychology at the Kennedy Krieger Institute in Baltimore, Maryland. Her research interests include mental health problems in persons with developmental disabilities, autism and pervasive developmental disorders, and developmental disability syndromes.

J. Kevin Thompson, Ph.D., is Associate Professor of Psychology, Department of Psychology, University of South Florida, Tampa. He received his Ph.D. from the Department of Psychology, University of Georgia, in 1982 and has been at the University of South Florida since 1985. His research interests include eating disorders, body image, and psychotherapy integration. His current research involves a variety of topics in the area of body image, including etiological factors (especially in the areas of developmental forces and sociocultural pressures), assessment issues, development of cognitive processing models of body image disturbance, and the effects of silicone breast explantation on body image and psychological functioning. He is on the editorial board of the *International Journal of Eating Disorders* and is an ad hoc reviewer for numerous journals. He has published three other chapters in the area of body image and wrote *Body Image Disturbance* in 1990. He is currently editing *Body Image, Eating Disturbance, and Obesity: An Integrative Guide for Assessment and Treatment* (forthcoming from American Psychological Association Books).

Wayne F. Velicer, Ph.D., is codirector of the Cancer Prevention Research Consortium and Professor, Department of Psychology, at the University of Rhode Island. He received his Ph.D. in quantitative psychology in 1972 at Purdue University. He has published more than 100 papers on a wide variety of topics including research methods, multivariate statistics, expert system technology, measure development, and the development of the transtheoretical model of change for health promotion and disease prevention.

B. Timothy Walsh is Professor of Clinical Psychiatry at the College of Physicians and Surgeons at Columbia University and Director of the Eating Disorders Research Unit at New York State Psychiatric Institute. He earned his medical degree from Harvard Medical School in 1972 and completed his internship at Dartmouth Medical School. He went on to complete his residency in psychiatry at the Albert Einstein College of Medicine in New York, where he became chief resident in 1977. He sits on the editorial boards of the *International Journal of Eating Disorders* and *Obesity Research* and was chair of the Eating Disorders Work Group of the American Psychiatric Association's *DSM-IV* Task Force. For the past 15 years, he has conducted investigations of eating disorders and depression, including their origins and their psychological and pharmacological treatment.

Donald A. Williamson, Ph.D., is Professor of Psychology at Louisiana State University and Director of its Psychological Services Center. He is Chief of Psychology at Pennington Biomedical Research Center and Program Director for the Eating Disorders Program of Our Lady of the Lake Hospital, Baton Rouge, Louisiana. His primary research area is eating disorders and obesity. He has published more than 100 articles on topics related to health psychology and eating problems. His research has focused on the development of assessment methods for eating problems.

Carla Wolper, M.S., is Nutritionist and Research Coordinator at the Weight Control Unit, Obesity Research Center, St. Luke's/Roosevelt Hospital, a teaching hospital of Columbia University College of Physicians and Surgeons in New York City. She has been at St. Luke's since 1990 and is an adjunct faculty member in Nutrition at Hunter College in New York City. She is a member of the Nutrition Professionals Section of the American Heart Association, New York City Affiliate.

Harold E. Yuker is Mervyn Schloss Distinguished Professor of Psychology and Director of the Center for the Study of Attitudes Toward Persons With Disabilities at Hofstra University. He has been at Hofstra since 1948 and has held several research and administrative posts in addition to his teaching. As Director of the Center for the Study of Higher Education from 1965 to 1975, he did research related to teaching and faculty members and published several research studies as well as two monographs on the subject of faculty workload. From 1976 to 1982, he took time out from research and writing to serve as Provost of the university. After leaving that position, he established the Center for the Study of Attitudes Toward Persons With Disabilities at Hofstra. For more than 40 years he has been engaged in research dealing with attitudes toward disabilities and disabled persons. He and his colleagues developed the ATDP (Attitudes Toward Disabled Persons) Scale, which is the most used measure of its kind. His research has resulted in the publication of many articles, several research monographs, and an edited book, *Attitudes Toward Persons With Disabilities* (1988). He is a Fellow of the Division of Rehabilitation Psychology of the American Psychological Association and in 1991 received the Roger Barker Distinguished Research Award from them.